21st Century Security and CPTED

Designing for Critical Infrastructure Protection and Crime Prevention

Randall I. Atlas

CRC Press
Taylor & Francis Group
Boca Raton London New York

CRC Press is an imprint of the
Taylor & Francis Group, an **informa** business

Auerbach Publications
Taylor & Francis Group
6000 Broken Sound Parkway NW, Suite 300
Boca Raton, FL 33487-2742

© 2008 by Taylor & Francis Group, LLC
Auerbach is an imprint of Taylor & Francis Group, an Informa business

No claim to original U.S. Government works
Printed in the United States of America on acid-free paper
10 9 8 7 6 5 4 3 2 1

International Standard Book Number-13: 978-1-4200-6807-8 (Hardcover)

Library of Congress Cataloging-in-Publication Data

21st century security and CPTED : designing for critical infrastructure protection and crime
    prevention / editor Randall I. Atlas.
        p. cm.
    Includes bibliographical references and index.
    ISBN 978-1-4200-6807-8 (hardback : alk. paper) 1. Crime prevention and architectural design. 2.
    Crime prevention. 3. Security systems. I. Atlas, Randall I. II. Title: 21st century security and crime
    prevention and architectural design. III. Title: Twenty-first century security and CPTED.

HV7431.A125 2008
364.4'9--dc22   2008008310

Visit the Taylor & Francis Web site at
http://www.taylorandfrancis.com

and the Auerbach Web site at
http://www.auerbach-publications.com

Contents

PART I   Background and Theory

Chapter 1

Chapter 2

Chapter 3

Chapter 4

Chapter 5

Chapter 6

Chapter 7

Chapter 8

Chapter 9

PART II   Protecting The Built Environment

PART III   Applications of CPTED in the Built Environment

PART IV   *How Do You Know You Are Making A Difference?*

Chapter 31

Randy Atlas and Gregory Saville

Chapter 32

Foreword

My name is Randy Atlas, the author and editor of this book. I am both an architect and a criminologist. This does not make me a "criminal architect," but rather an architect with a different point of view. Using the reasoning skills I was taught as a criminologist combined with the creative design skills of an architect, I understand the value of problem seeking before problem solving. The current tendency is to throw money shamelessly at security equipment as a problem solving measure. The real solutions will evolve from thorough understanding of the problems. How often has our built environment contributed to the attraction of criminal or terrorist activity? This book is intended to be the follow-up of previous books on Crime Prevention Through Environmental Design (CPTED), defensible space, and building security. It is especially oriented to students of architecture, design, urban planning, security, and criminal justice.

The number one criticism I hear when I conduct CPTED trainings around the United States is "why don't the architects know about CPTED and how to design secure buildings?" The answer is quite straightforward. Most architects are unfamiliar with CPTED and security design because they were never taught CPTED in their college educations. It is not something that usually comes up in continuing education. While CPTED is based in common sense, the specific skills are something that most architects are just not made aware of or taught. Criminal justice and security students have read about it, but most likely have not taken a course to learn it. Most of the practitioners of CPTED are police officers. They are aware of CPTED, and most law enforcement agencies have crime prevention units. CPTED is mentioned in most basic law enforcement training classes. However, having police trained in CPTED is not enough to have the built environment changed.

I have been known in the conference circuit as the voice of cynicism and sarcasm. This is because I don't believe that the direction and efforts of the Department of Homeland Security and local law enforcement have been properly focused on the real threats. Most of the information presented to the architectural and engineering community after 9/11 has been about progressive structural failure collapse, flying glass, and 100-foot setbacks. These are legitimate considerations when you are designing an embassy, but do not really apply to a strip shopping center, a middle school, or an apartment complex.

As a result, the architects dismiss the value of designing security into the architecture and infrastructure because it does not relate to them. In fact, at an American Institute of Architects (AIA)-sponsored workshop in Albuquerque in 2000 on homeland security, I spoke to a room of 500 architects and asked how many of them were actually designing high-security buildings that might use the information that was presented. About a half-dozen raised their hands, and they were mostly from firms around the loop of Washington D.C., who are wired for embassies or high security military applications. The other 99 percent of the architects raised their hands when I asked if they were designing schools, multi-family residential housing, hospitals, or retail and shopping facilities. Very few architectural firms will ever have the opportunity to design a State Department building or maximum-security prison.

The focus of most funding by the Department of Homeland Security is the protection of our infrastructure using security technology, such as CCTV, access control and perimeter protection, and technology that can smell weapons or identify terrorists by facial features. One government publication suggested that the primary security aspect of designing safe schools was placing cameras throughout the schools and grounds. CCTV does not prevent any crime or acts of terror in a school. In fact, it is well known that the kids will act out in front of the cameras just to get a rise out of the teachers. Can we not see that homeland security is about crime prevention and making our built environment safe from acts of crime, workplace violence, and acts of terror?

What are you pretending not to know: that a burglar looks for an opportunity to break in? That a robber looks for an asset to steal or take by force? That a rapist looks to induce fear and hurts his victim? That an angry fired employee is going to get payback for having his job security and career torpedoed? Or some religious zealot, who insists on imposing his belief system on us, trespasses in a building to survey the best ways to break in and plant a bomb or sabotage the infrastructure system?

It does not take a rocket scientist to understand that the human characteristics of greed, revenge, and jealousy provide the basis of cultivating the skills and abilities to create fear and panic in our cities and buildings. This book is about creating safe cities, safe work environments, and safe places to live and play. The fire codes have had protection of assets and prevention of fire as their primary concern for over 150 years, but law enforcement has been unable to make any real inroads to crime prevention as a prime directive. Reactionary crime response has been the primary focus of resources and manpower, not proactive event prevention.

This book examines the architectural surety from the perspective of risk analysis and premises liability. The risk analysis process looks at the value of the assets criticality and the replacement value of protecting the assets. Risk managers in the private sector corporate world typically have offices close to the CEO or president. However, in law enforcement the crime prevention or CPTED officer is usually located in the building basement, like the Maytag repairman waiting for the phone to ring. The crime prevention officers are not viewed as valuable or critical to the mission of the police department. Until crime prevention is seen as an equal to fire prevention there will be no significant gain. Can you imagine a fire department being downsized because there were not any fires this year? Imagine saying "sorry firefighters, you did too good of a job this year, so we are going to have to downsize your department and cut back on the trucks and dogs." No, the fire departments are viewed and measured as successful by preventing the costly and usually avoidable mistakes of fire. The regulations, codes, plan review, inspections, equipment, etc. are all part of the cost of doing business, because they have to.

This book discusses the competing needs framed by the American culture of openness and access versus the need for protection from threats to security and safety. The real issue is what level of inconvenience will be tolerated by the imposition of security before people just avoid the activity or space. Current examples of this dilemma are the hassles of flying, or the hassles of going into a courthouse. If a restaurant line is too long, people will bail out and just go somewhere else. How do architecture and technology keep the flow of goods and services into our buildings, yet have accountability for the integrity of legitimate mail, vendors, staff, and visitors? As new residential communities, shopping centers, and government centers are planned and built, there need to be guidelines and standards to draw upon as reference points similar to National Fire Protection Association (NFPA) Life Safety Code or Americans with Disabilities Act Accessibility Guidelines (ADAAG). This book examines the next generation of design based on emerging security and safety concerns, processes, and materials that can meet expectations of owners and building tenants.

I have asked for contributions from members of what I affectionately call the CPTED mafia, who have in their own individual rights been published in CPTED or are the master trainers along with me. Their perspectives will help give additional balance to a growing field of the merging of security and architecture and the evolution of CPTED into the 21st century.

Maximum value is gained by your full participation. Enjoy the challenge of looking at the built environment from a different point of view.

Acknowledgments

This book has been a long time in coming. I took an Insight Transformational Growth seminar in leadership training back in the 1990s, and one of the goals established for me was to write a book. While I have written and published hundreds of articles and a few chapters in books by other people, I resisted writing a book about my own experiences and expertise. After the events of September 11, 2001 it became obvious to me that there was little information available for design professionals and law enforcement on security design and CPTED that was relevant in the age of terrorism and infrastructure protection, and what was available was either dated or mostly about security electronics and military defense, not about the process of accomplishing a functional integrated security system and crime prevention.

I invited some of the brightest and most knowledgeable persons in the field today to make contributions to this book, as I feel that collaborative efforts are more enlightened than solo attempts. Over the course of my career many people have inspired and motivated me, but none were more supportive than my parents. I spent twelve years in college, acquiring four degrees in architecture, criminal justice, and criminology, and that could not have happened without the support and backing of my parents Fred and Janet Atlas. The person responsible for steering me into the unusual and unique field of blending of architecture with security was my uncle Rocky Pomerance, who was Chief of Police for Miami Beach. Rocky gave me a copy of Oscar Newman's *Defensible Space* just before I attended college. I understood then how I would combine my interests in architecture, criminal justice, and criminology.

I would like to thank Gregory Saville and Trish Warren for editing the book and believing in me when I was ready to give up on this arduous project. Their efforts were tireless and are appreciated.

Gregory Saville wrote several chapters in the book, including Chapter 7, on second generation CPTED and Chapter 13 on ATRiM for infrastructure protection. We co-wrote Chapter 29, "Measuring Success," and Chapter 31, "Implementing CPTED." Gerry Cleveland, an internationally renowned youth prevention expert, was also co-developer of second generation CPTED, and his writings with Greg Saville are included in Chapter 7.

Severin Sorensen, CPP is an accomplished CPTED expert and trainer, and we had the pleasure of working together on many CPTED trainings for U.S. Housing and Urban Development. Severin and his associate, John Hayes, wrote Chapter 6 on theory and concepts of CPTED drawing from the CPED curriculum they authored for U.S. HUD in 1998.

W. Douglas Fitzgerald contributed his extensive security systems and electronics experience in Chapter 5, "The Interface between Architects and Engineers."

Rich Grassie assisted in writing and preparation of the materials in Chapters 11 and 12, dealing with risk, threat, vulnerability assessment and defining your assets. I have served with Rich on the American Society of Industrial Security, Security Architecture and Engineering Council for many years.

Tony DiGregorio is a pioneer in the field of infrastructure protection and blast resistance. Tony contributed his expertise to Chapter 10, on terrorism and infrastructure and Chapter 15, "Designing for Explosive Resistance."

Richard Schneider reviewed and contributed to Chapter 18, on creating safe and secure schools. Dick was the lead researcher in the development of the Florida Safe Schools Design Guidelines update conducted in 2003. Those guidelines serve as a model for architects and administrators.

Michael S. Scott generously contributed his expertise for Chapter 19 on robbery at automated teller machines, the research for which was conducted for the U.S. Department of Justice Office of Community Oriented Policing Services, Problem Oriented Guides for Police Services.

Crime against convenience stores and gas stations has been a very high priority on the CPTED research and study. While I was teaching a CPTED class at Florida Atlantic University School of Architecture, one of my students, Stavros Moforis, ran a gas station. His personal knowledge of running this type of building was helpful, and he contributed to Chapter 25, "Designing Safe Gas Stations and Convenience Stores."

Editor

Randall (Randy) I. Atlas, Ph.D., AIA, CPP is president of Counter Terror Design, Inc. and vice president of Atlas Safety & Security Design, Inc., in Miami, Florida. Dr. Atlas is a nationally recognized speaker, trainer, and writer on Crime Prevention Through Environmental Design and has worked in these capacities for the National Crime Prevention Institute, the American Institute of Architects, and the American Society of Industrial Security (ASIS). Atlas is a Certified Protection Professional (CPP) with ASIS and is a member of the Security Architecture and Engineering Council. He is a technical assistance consultant to the U.S. Department of Housing and has conducted numerous CPTED and infrastructure security audits throughout the United States. Dr. Atlas has contributed to the *Protection of Assets* manual, and *Access Control & Security Systems*, *Security Technology & Design*, and *Security Management* magazines. He serves on the National Fire Protection Association 730 Committee on Premises Security and contributed to *NFPA 730: Guide for Premises Security* (NFPA, 2006,Quincy, MA), and has served on the ASIS committee, developing security guidelines. Dr. Atlas serves on the American Society of Testing Materials (ASTM) F33 Committee on Corrections and Detention Facilities, and the ES4 Committee on Homeland Security. Atlas serves as an expert witness on many premises security cases and as an architectural consultant on large justice architecture projects. Dr. Atlas earned his doctorate in criminology from Florida State University, a masters of architecture from the University of Illinois, and has bachelor degrees in architecture and criminal justice from the University of Florida and the University of South Florida, respectively.

Contributors

Douglas Fitzgerald, CPP, CFE, CHS-III has over 27 years experience in physical and electronic security and countermeasures design. He has been involved in all aspects of assessments, design, development of construction documents, and reliability testing. He constantly shares his expertise and methodologies with others in a wide variety of educational venues and courses. He is currently the chairman of the American Society for Industrial Security's (ASIS) Security Architecture and Engineering Council and has also served on the Threat Advisory Systems Guideline Committee and was involved in the development of the Physical Security Professional (PSP) examination. His extensive background in anti-terrorism and counter-terrorism for government and corporate facilities around the world provides him with an understanding of security issues on a global level. He is a sought-after lecturer on terrorism, black-hat exercises, vulnerability assessments, countermeasures design, operational policies, and procedures and training. Doug is a Certified Protection Professional, a board Certified Fraud Examiner, and is certified in homeland security level 3.

Richard Grassie, CPP is president of TECHMARK Security Integration, Inc., a Boston firm providing security design and technology integration services. Grassie has served as a security consultant to Fortune 500 companies as well as institutional and governmental clients around the world. His career has spanned over 36 years of progressively responsible positions in the military and private sector. He has extensive experience in proactive risk management, security systems design, and security program integration for multi-facility campus security systems. Grassie is a past chairman of the ASIS Security and Architecture and Engineering Council, is a Certified Protection Professional (CPP), has written numerous articles, conducts training seminars on security for private and public sectors, and contributed writings to *Security Planning and Design: A guide for Architects and Design Professionals* (AIA National; John Wiley & Sons).

Gregory Saville is an urban planner and is director of Alternation, an international consulting firm specializing in safe growth and community development. He is one of the founders of the International CPTED Association. He has delivered CPTED design programming and training around the world, including at the Sydney 2000 Olympics, the Japan Urban Research Safety Institute, the Royal Canadian Mounted Police, and the U.S. Department of Justice. He is adjunct professor with the University of New Haven's national security program and the University of Calgary's Faculty of Environmental Design.

Severin L. Sorensen, CPP, M.Phil. is a subject matter expert on CPTED and Situational Crime Prevention. Sorensen is president and CEO of Sikyur.com, a leading security advisor to Chief Security Officers (CSOs). Mr. Sorensen is the former chairman (2006–2007) of the Physical Security Council of ASIS International, representing the largest organization for security professionals worldwide with more than 35,000 members (www.asisonline.org). Mr. Sorensen routinely advises thought leaders in the security industry on emerging trends in security, advanced video surveillance, outdoor perimeter protection technologies, and Crime Prevention Through Environmental Design (CPTED). He is a security advisor to the U.S. Department of Homeland Security (DHS) on Physical Security Emerging Trends in Technology. From 1994 to 2005, Sorensen was president and CEO of Sparta Consulting Corporation (www.spartasolutions.net), a company he founded that performed security consulting, security systems integration, and remote video monitoring solutions. Mr. Sorensen was Program Manager of HUD's CPTED initiative from 1994 to 2002. He earned the Certified Protection Professional (CPP) certification, and is a former member and faculty trainer of the International Association of Professional Security Consultants. Mr. Sorensen earned the M.Phil. Degree in Economics (international political economy) from King's College, Cambridge University, England (1988), and B.S. degrees with honors in economics and political science at the University of Utah (1986).

Michael S. Scott is the director of the Center for Problem-Oriented Policing, Inc. and is clinical assistant professor at the University of Wisconsin-Madison Law School. He developed training programs in problem-oriented policing at the Police Executive Research Forum (PERF) and is a judge for the Herman Goldstein Award for Excellence in Problem-Oriented Policing. He was the 1996 recipient of PERF's Gary P. Hayes Award for innovation and leadership in policing. He was formerly chief of police in Lauderhill, Florida, served in various civilian administrative positions in the St. Louis Metropolitan, Fort Pierce, Florida, and New York City police departments; and was a police officer in the Madison, Wisconsin police department.

Richard H. Schneider, PhD, AICP is professor of urban and regional planning and research foundation professor at the University of Florida's College of Design, Construction and Planning. His research and teaching focus on crime prevention planning and design. A consultant to numerous law enforcement and planning agencies, he is co-author of Florida's *Safe School Design Guidelines* (2003). He is principal investigator for U.S. Department of Justice-funded GIS crime mapping projects and is a consultant to the United Nations. Dr. Schneider is co-author of the UN-HABITAT's *Global Report on Human Settlements 2007*, which focuses on threats to human security including crime and violence. His books *Crime Prevention and the Built Environment* (Routledge 2007) and *Planning for Crime Prevention: An International Perspective* (Routledge 2002), co-authored with Professor Ted Kitchen, are among the first comprehensive texts on the United States and United Kingdom literature in this field. He is a charter member of the American Planning Association and a member of the American Institute of Certified Planners.

Part I

Background and Theory

1 What, Me Worry?*

Alfred E. Newman was the poster boy for *Mad* magazine, and his motto was, "What, me worry?" After all, what is all the fuss about these days with crime, workplace violence, security, and terrorism? Are these the end of days? Are newspaper headlines and TV reporting mostly for sensationalism or are the perceived threats real? Crimes such as vandalism, terrorism, burglary, shoplifting, employee theft, assault, and espionage endanger lives and threaten the built environment. Despite this, security and safety as a design consideration have often been inadequately addressed and poorly funded. However, in some jurisdictions in North America and Europe, authorities require security and safety plan reviews as part of the building permit process in the same way they require life safety and fire prevention reviews.

Architectural and urban designs that take into account safety from crime, and security against criminal damage or terrorism is what I simply term here as "security" design. I am not ignoring other definitions of "security" or other forms of crime prevention. I am merely focusing on that specific element of security and crime prevention that relates to the physical opportunity for victimization, damage, and harm. From that perspective, security design is more than bars on windows, a security guard booth, a camera, or a barrier wall. Security design involves the systematic integration of design, technology, and operation for the protection of three critical assets—people, information, and property. Protection of these assets is a concern in all types of buildings and all forms of urban property. To the architect, these are considerations that need attention throughout the design and construction process from programming, schematic design, design development, preparation of construction documents, bidding, and through to the final construction.

To the urban design professional (landscape architects, civil engineers, architects, urban planners), or any creator of public and private spaces (developers, builders, community groups, municipal governments), the most efficient, least expensive way to provide security is during the earliest phases of development. For a planner or developer, this means the earliest conceptual stages. For an architect, it means the design process. Architects, or any other urban designers, can be called upon to address security and crime concerns. They must be able to determine security requirements, be familiar with security technology, and understand the architectural implications of security needs.

The process of designing security into architecture is known as **Crime Prevention Through Environmental Design** (CPTED). It involves designing the built environment to reduce the opportunity for, and fear of, crime and disorder. This approach to security design recognizes the intended use of space in a building and is different from traditional security practice, which focuses on denying access to a crime target with barrier techniques such as locks, alarms, fences, and gates. CPTED takes advantage of opportunities for natural access control, surveillance, and territorial reinforcement. If the design process includes CPTED, it is possible for natural and normal uses of the environment to meet the same security goals as physical and technical protection methods. That is one of the goals of this book.

* Portions of the text in this chapter consist of articles and other content previously written by the author including possible portions found in the following ASIS International publication *Protection of Assets (POA) Manual,* ASIS International (various contributors), ASIS International, ©2004. We offer special thanks to ASIS International for permission to reproduce common content in this work.

THE NEW REALITY

The urban designer must now integrate and combine security concepts, architectural elements, and security technologies into a balanced holistic solution. This can best happen by obtaining a grasp of fundamental security design concepts, principles, and strategies. Urban designers and others concerned with such matters such as security and facility managers, or law enforcement need to focus on building-related security and safety vulnerabilities and risks.

Since the events of 9/11, the security and urban design fields face new challenges to design, redesign, retrofit and renovate, and operate buildings to ensure the health, safety, and welfare of occupants, visitors, and the public. How can we create more awareness in design professionals, especially architects, of the issues and alternatives for safety and security in their work?

This book examines emerging design trends based on security and safety concerns, processes, and materials. The trends you will read about meet new and expanding expectations of building owners and tenants, government agencies, and private companies. This book addresses these new realities in building security and occupant safety in a number of ways, including critical infrastructure, commercial, government, private, and public buildings for both new design and retrofit. This book explores current and future safeguards from security threats for structures and the people who work and visit our built environment. It includes the role of building codes, premises security negligence, laws, and regulations.

Today, there is a rapidly expanding supply of security technology products. Clearly, security is on the minds and budgets of a growing number of property owners, facility managers, and building supervisors. The demand for more secure facilities, coupled with computerized technology, is making access control and intrusion detection into a science of its own. Security needs for a building must be determined early, as part of the project programming and definition process. Burglary, industrial espionage, shoplifting, riots, vandalism, assault, rape, murder, and employee theft are crimes that imperil lives and drive up the cost of doing business. As crime concerns increases more each year, architects are being called upon to address security problems by incorporating security into the design and construction in all building types. That has led to this book.

There are dire consequences for failing to update our design and planning expertise. In buildings, for example, designing without security in mind can lead to lawsuits, injuries, the need for additional security personnel, and expensive retrofitting with protection equipment. Furthermore, if not properly planned for and installed, that equipment can distort important building design functions, add to security personnel costs, and result in exposed unsightly alarm systems or blocked doors and windows.

It is primarily the client's responsibility to define the potential threats to people, property, and information, and to determine the level and cost of the protection that will be provided. The client may need a security specialist to clearly define the scope of security requirements in the programming phase. This book also will help clients understand the new kinds of security requirements they need to seek in a changed world.

Once the client and security professional identify the security concerns, the security system is designed to implement those objectives. With the proliferation of security devices, along with rapid advances in system technology, security planning requires specialists with a working knowledge of these technologies. Yet, architects also must have a basic understanding of the principles of application and operation of security technology as well as an appreciation of the basic tenets of effective security programming. Any building must meet specific functional criteria, and it is from function that the design evolves. A building must permit efficient job performance, meet the needs of the user, and protect the user from safety hazards and criminal acts that affect the production and service delivery of the building's users.

Architects worry about the fortress mentality (see Figure 1.1 and Figure 1.2) of security professionals while security professionals are concerned about the architect's failure to include security elements in the design of the building from the ground up. The conflict is not over whether to include

FIGURE 1.1   Fortress architecture or architorture?

FIGURE 1.2   Carryover of fortress design to today's buildings seems out of place.

security equipment in the building design. Rather the conflict lies between a building's openness, on one hand, and control of access and restrictions of activities, on the other.

Securing a building that was not originally planned to be secure is expensive. Architects have to sacrifice much more of a building's openness in retrofitting for security than they would if the facility had been designed for security from the outset. A lack of forethought during the design of the facility can mean costs for protection personnel and operating expenses far greater than they need to be. This is particularly evident in many of today's buildings, where modern design and materials result in facilities that are especially vulnerable.

All of these factors point to an obvious conclusion: Urban designers and architects can make the greatest contribution to meeting a project's security objectives. In particular, architects generally make the basic design decisions about circulation, access, building materials, fenestration, and many other features that can support or thwart overall security aims. The most reliable and proven approach to accomplish the goal of combining security with design decisions is commonly known as the environmental design model called CPTED (pronounced sep-ted)—Crime Prevention Through Environmental Design. This book presents modern applications of CPTED, what is now termed first generation CPTED, for addressing today's demand for secure design. It will later present a chapter on the emerging field of second generation CPTED and how that perspective expands the model.

The environmental design approach to security recognizes the space's designated or redesignated use, which defines a security or CPTED solution compatible for that use. Good security design enhances the effective use of the space and at the same time prevents crime. The emphasis in CPTED falls on the design and use of space, a practice that deviates from the traditional target-hardening approach to crime prevention. Traditional target hardening focuses predominantly on denying access to a crime target through physical or artificial barrier techniques such as locks, alarms, fences, and gates. The traditional approach tends to overlook opportunities for natural access control and surveillance. It can also make environments sterile, unsightly, and unfriendly. Often, natural and normal uses of the environment can avoid fortressing while still accomplishing the effects of mechanical hardening and surveillance.

DEFINING ROLES

ROLE OF THE CLIENT

To define precisely the vulnerabilities and threats to People, Information, and Property (PIP); to assess the level and cost of protection, and the coverage that will be provided; to develop the definition of security needs and provide the architect with a pragmatic description of protection requirements; to define who and what needs protection; to define the assets and the importance of each asset worth protecting.

ROLE OF THE RESIDENT, EMPLOYEE, OR OCCUPANT

The perspective of people who actually work and live in a particular place is among the most important. They may not actually be the paying client or the security professional on staff, but their view is critical. After all, they will be the ones most often using the space in the future. Their perspective can be surveyed by the security manager/consultant. They also can be brought into the process during the architectural programming, for example, during collaborative design focus group sessions called design charrettes. There are many different strategies to canvass the perspective of the users of a place. Their view is critical however, if only to determine their unique perspective of security vulnerabilities.

ROLE OF THE SECURITY MANAGER/CONSULTANT

To help the client describe and elaborate the protection requirements and the level of protection required in each area; to help the client assess the threats, security needs, and crime vulnerabilities; to help with the planning of access control, security zoning, target hardening, and surveillance systems; to define the basic security concepts with operational procedures and security manpower allocation; and define the types, location, and tasks of security personnel.

How does the security professional use the services of the architects to the highest potential? The renovation, addition, or new construction of your place of business may require the security professional and the owner to interface with the design professional in new and challenging ways. The security professional may be an employee of the business and responsible for many sectors of security and safety within that business. The architect or design professional will need many types of information from the owner/client and security professional to develop the architectural program and design an efficient and secure building. The person who can provide critical information to the architect about security needs and procedures is typically the security director. If there is no security director, then a trained security professional should be hired to provide that knowledge and assistance to the company and architect.

ROLE OF THE ARCHITECT

To incorporate the security program information into effective space and circulation planning; to provide clear sightlines for surveillance, and planned access controls at entrances and exits; to design for the appropriate location of sensitive or restricted areas; to design for the planned placement of security personnel; to provide architecture that uses design elements to closely coordinate security technology and personnel.

The architect can play a vital role in designing effective natural access control, surveillance, and territorial reinforcement strategies. Security design poses three challenges for architects:

- **Determining requirements.** Security needs must be determined early in the project's programming and problem definition stage. The design team should analyze the designated purpose of how the space or building will be used. The designated purpose will be clear when designers examine the cultural, legal, and physical definitions of what the prescribed, desired, and acceptable behaviors are for that space. The space can then be designed to support the desired behaviors and the intended function of the space. The design team should inquire about existing policies and practices, so that this information will be integrated in the programming process.
- **Knowing the technology.** Rapid advances in the technology of security systems makes keeping up to date a challenge. Many projects today, even routine ones, may involve security system specialists as part of the team. As with other areas of specialization, architects must have a basic understanding of security principles. Design professionals must be in a position to evaluate and implement technical security specialists and security equipment manufacturers.
- **Understanding architectural implications.** Designs must integrate the complicated and sometimes conflicting goals of security and life-safety issues as well as other project requirements. Space, function, and people must be planned to support the security objectives of detection, delay, and response to unwanted or criminal situations, as well as the prevention of those situations in the first place.

These roles and challenges outline the new shape of urban design and architecture in the 21st century. At times, the roles will be clearly laid out, at others they will be informal. But it is important that there is some understanding of how each group relates to the other in order to program safe and secure urban design and architecture (see Figure 1.3).

FIGURE 1.3 Designing a secure future in the built environment.

FIGURE 1.4 Designing for the next generation.

This represents the focus of this book: the exploration of current and future safeguards from security threats and how to employ CPTED for natural and normal uses of the environment to meet security goals. It also describes the ways in which architects and designers are being called on more than ever before to address security problems. By uncovering modern applications of CPTED for both designer and clients, you will see how to tackle today's demand for secure design in a changed world (see Figure 1.4).

The next chapter describes how to get started.

2 Getting Started*

DON'T BE PARANOID!

"So what are you afraid of?" "What's the worst that can happen?" "Don't be so paranoid!"

You have probably heard one or more of these types of statements from people in your family or work environment. You may have asked yourself these questions. The answers are sometimes intuitive, and sometimes they are a result of thorough investigation. There is a methodology to ascertain the level of **threat** and **risk**, but first we must understand what these terms mean. Once we understand the threats and risks, then we can design the appropriate level of CPTED and security strategy to counter them.

Achieving the correct level of protection against site-based threats can be very expensive, and is highly dependent on the nature of the protected assets and the threat against which they require protection. Determining what is required is a matter of identifying the perceived risks. If the designer is to assist in providing protection in the design of the site, an assessment of the security requirements must be accomplished, preferably before the design begins, but certainly no later than the beginning of the architectural programming phase. This assessment is the responsibility of the owner; however, it is incumbent on the designer to ensure that the nature of the security requirements is determined before the design begins. Failing to make a definitive plan at the outset will certainly result in design changes, delays, and cost increases to the owner, and to the architect if the owner "discovers" the security needs later in the design process.

The site assessment should answer four questions:

1. What are the **assets** (persons, places, information, property) that require security protection?
2. What are the criminal or other **threats** (street crime, workplace violence, terrorism, sabotage) against which the assets must be protected?
3. What are the **vulnerabilities** of the assets to the threats (for example, if workplace violence is a threat, can uncontrolled persons enter private workspace unchallenged)?
4. What are the **countermeasures** (for example, does the design channel visitors through controlled site access portals) required to mitigate the threat?

The result of the assessment will be a set of recommended countermeasures that may be priced and presented to the owner in a priority order so selections may be made from those recommendations that are prudent and cost effective. In the case of the government standards, or industry guidelines, the assessment results in the assignment of a defined Level of Protection (LOP) with specified countermeasures. When the LOP is defined, the specified countermeasures are priced and again the owner may select appropriate measures depending on a prudent level of protection and the cost effectiveness of the measure. (AIA, 2004)

* Portions of the text in this chapter consist of articles and other content previously written by the author including possible portions found in the following ASIS International publication *Protection of Assets (POA) Manual*, ASIS International (various contributors), ASIS International, ©2004. We offer special thanks to ASIS International for permission to reproduce common content in this work.

Additional details for threat and risk assessment are included in later chapters. For the time being, it is important to appreciate the basics of security design and the elements that go into making a place safer.

DESIGNING FOR SECURITY IS A PROCESS

Before the security system design begins, a sequence of evaluations needs to be conducted in order to create the security master plan. These steps are outlined here:

Asset Definition. What are the vital assets—people, information, or property? What are the most important assets? What are the secondary assets? What level of protection is needed for each area?

Threat Definition. What are the threats to each asset? Who and what are you protecting? Could threats be vandalism, espionage, burglary, theft, assault, sabotage, or robbery? How would threats be accomplished? When? Why? By whom? Where? What kind of attack might be used to hit the target? Are the threats highly probable, possible, or unlikely?

Vulnerability Analysis. Are the threats real or perceived? Compare the costs for the protection of each asset group with the cost of potential loss. Compare different kinds of security measures possible for protection of the assets.

WHAT IS BEING PROTECTED

One of the first steps in the threat and vulnerability analysis is to identify the assets to be protected. All assets can be sorted into the following categories:

People, **I**nformation, and **P**roperty.

People—People are among the most important assets needing protection (Figure 2.1). The people needing protection may be employees, visitors, patrons, service providers, and executive VIPs. The asset of humans is protection from assault, kidnapping, murder, robbery, and terrorism. Failure to protect invited and uninvited guests on a property can be grounds for premises liability litigation.

FIGURE 2.1   People who live, work, and play in our built environment need to be considered and protected.

FIGURE 2.2 The data must be safe and secure for the continuity of business. (Photo courtesy of www. iStockphoto.com.)

Information—Information is an asset that needs protection (Figure 2.2). Almost all businesses have vital information that could potentially cripple or destroy an operation. Computer records, blueprints, financial information, proprietary secrets, personnel records, and accounting systems are the backbone of any business. Information protection is a critical element of a security plan. Knowing who has the information, where it is, when it is accessible, and how it could be compromised are critical issues for which there must be appropriate design.

Property—Property is an asset that needs protection. Property can refer to cars on a parking lot, airplanes in a hanger, or office supplies in a closet. The threat analysis will help identify which property assets are to be protected (Figure 2.3). The architect can then use the security requirements identified into the design of the building, and incorporate them into the entire building process.

In order to provide information in a format that the architect can work with effectively, the security professional should identify the vital corporate assets that need protection (Figure 2.4).

FIGURE 2.3 The assets of the workplace are the materials and stock.

FIGURE 2.4   People are an irreplaceable asset. (Photo courtesy of www.iStockphoto.com.)

NEEDS ASSESSMENT

With any of the three assets, there are some critical need assessment questions. These include:

Who are the users? (visitors, staff, service crews)
What can the users do in the building? (tasks, recreation, work)
Why are the particular users there? (official business, guests)
When do the users arrive and leave? (time, shift, patterns)
Where can users enter the building? (horizontal, vertical transportation patterns)
How can the users get there? (access methods, pedestrian and vehicular circulation)

The security professional will need to be clear on the implications of each answer to these questions. More advanced models, such as the ATRiM risk assessment computer model, are described in later chapters. For example, ATRiM's CPTED risk assessment functions are automated onto handheld PDA computers and comprise part of a much larger training program. However, at minimum, a risk assessment process should be prepared for the architect. The security professional should ask the same six key questions to all respondents, from the vice president of a company to the janitorial cleaning service. Answers to these questions will help the security professional determine the *security implications* and the *design implications*.

Taking the example of the janitorial service, the *security implications* might be:

1. Control of after-hour access
2. Verification of cleaning employee status
3. Security manpower to sign in and supervise entry and exit
4. Key control

These security concerns could then translate into *design implications*, such as:

1. A sign-in desk for the service trades
2. Design of access control system to allow staff to control entry and log in movement
3. Placement of garbage dumpsters
4. Location of service elevator
5. Location of service doors
6. Alarm systems for offices and control room tie-in and deactivation.

These are just a small sample of issues and concerns that an urban designer, such as an architect, should collect from the security professional. The architectural program or problem-seeking stage should incorporate the information developed from answering these six questions. Later, this information will be passed on to the problem solution stage of architecture: the schematic drawings, design development drawings, and construction documents.

"3-D"—THE BASIS OF SECURITY DESIGN

The crime prevention through environmental design approach recognizes the building environments' designated or redesignated use. The emphasis of security design falls on the design and use of space, a practice that is different from traditional target hardening. Traditional target hardening, or fortressing, focuses predominately on denying access to a crime target through physical or artificial barrier techniques such as locks, alarms, fences, and gates. The traditional approach tends to overlook opportunities for natural access control and surveillance. As mentioned in Chapter 1, sometimes the natural and normal uses of the environment can accomplish the same effects of mechanical hardening and surveillance.

Environmental security design or CPTED is based on three functions of human space:

Designation—What is the purpose or intended use of the space?
Definition—How is the space defined? What are the social, cultural, legal, and psychological ways in which the space is defined?
Design—Is the space defined to support the prescribed or intended behaviors?

SUMMARY

The built environment is not a result of unconscious decisions but, rather, a collaboration of many persons making hundreds of decisions. Keep records of the decision-making process so that further on down the road, if events happen, there is a record of who, why, and how decisions were made. This chapter is the start of demonstrating that the security design process is applicable to all buildings (see Figure 2.5). The architect should design for security in the planning and design stages, or the owner will pay for it later at a much greater cost. The health, safety, and welfare of building users depend on good security planning and design.

FIGURE 2.5 Protecting the property and the architecture is critical to the mission of Homeland Security. (Photo courtesy of www.iStockphoto.com.)

As one can easily see, a great deal of thought and money goes into making a building secure. However, an architect cannot change human nature, and a certain amount of criminal and terror acts will be perpetrated in spite of the best-laid plans.

Security systems come in many varieties, but crime is not monolithic. Furthermore, it is ironic that the sort of crime that most people fear is not that which occurs most frequently. Stranger to stranger crimes—assault, murder, rape, and robbery—are less common than white-collar crime. Most criminals don't tote a gun. The terrorism of the 21st century will probably be suicide bombings, chemical and biological attacks, industrial espionage, identification theft, computer pilfering, and destruction of records. Can an architect play a part in preventing white-collar crime? He or she can certainly create an environment of safety, which fosters a sense of responsibility among employees. It may also be possible to design limited and controlled access for easy accountability. In such an atmosphere, combined with competent managerial practices, the employees are less likely to accept behavior that is unethical, disruptive, or that may threaten their own company and community.

CPTED and Defensible Space Design have generally been practiced without the benefit of a systematic process or assessment as dictated in the scientific method. Most practitioners are in the law enforcement arena, and have gained their CPTED expertise by attending one or several trainings. The police officer CPTED practitioner is seldom given the time, resources, or expertise to conduct pre (before) and post (after) evaluations of crime hot spots requiring improvements. The universal solution has been to conduct a "quick and dirty" study of a troubled neighborhood or housing project requiring attention as a result of crimes, illegal drugs, or gang-related activity. The typical practitioner develops recommendations without the benefit of gathering all of the relevant information; without the benefit of power or authority to implement recommendations; without the power to make design or management decisions that curtail, limit, or eliminate the problems; and without the ability or resources to evaluate or measure the success or failure of the recommendations. Each new site or crime project invoked reinventing the process again without any standard code or protocol (Figure 2.6).

The CPTED practitioner often goes to a potential crime site with their CPTED toolbox of "experience." Like a magician empowered to pull a rabbit from a hat, the CPTED practitioner often must pull the divergent forces of architecture, operational/management practices, governmental bureaucracy, and vested interests together in a collaborative process. Each new situation requires creative problem solving. Alhough there is no universally agreed standard of care that applies to architectural security in both the public and private sectors, there are standards that exist in the public sector for federal buildings, and there is the precedent set by premises security negligence case law that provides a standard of reasonableness. The needs of the many outweigh the needs of

FIGURE 2.6 Do you believe in the magic of CPTED? Often the CPTED practitioner pulls the rabbit out of the hat by having to develop solutions without the benefit of a consistent methodology or scientific method.

the few, or the one. The common good, the highest good, is met by designing our buildings with security and safety with the same vigor as fire codes, and accessibility codes.

Finally, environmental design can never eliminate crime completely because it does not attack root causes, unless it begins to evolve into the second-generation CPTED practices described later in this book. Architectural security design may only be responsible for shifting the places where crime occurs. Yet, environmental control does go a long way toward making people feel more positive about their work environment, not to mention justifying the cost effectiveness of including building security in the design and construction process.

REFERENCES

Atlas, R. (2002) The sustainability of CPTED: Less magic more science! *The CPTED Journal* 1(1) 3–14.
Atlas, R. (2006) Architect as nexus: Cost effective security begins with design. *ArchiTech,* 30–34.
Crowe, T. (2000) *Crime Prevention through Environmental Design: Applications of Architectural Design and Space Management Concepts,* 2nd ed. Oxford: Butterworth-Heinemann.
Demkin, J. (Ed.) (2004). *Security Planning and Design: A Guide for Architects and Building Design Professionals.* American Institute of Architects. Hoboken, NJ: John Wiley & Sons.

3 The Challenge of Architecture in a Free Society[*]

Form follows function.

That was a familiar tenet of 20th-century architecture, originally expressed by the Bauhaus school of design and popularized in America by the architect Louis Sullivan and his student Frank Lloyd Wright. Yet most architecture has focused on form rather than function. It is as if the structure itself, harmony with the site, and integrity of the materials have become the function. Less emphasis has been placed on the activities taking place inside the building. As a whole, the profession continues to be dominated by the view that architecture is a matter of aesthetics (Figure 3.1), and that form only follows form (Wikipedia, Nov. 2006).

> The intrinsic significance of our craft lies in the philosophical fact that we deal in nothing. We create emptiness through which certain physical bodies are to move—we shall designate these physical bodies for convenience as humans. By emptiness I mean what is commonly known as rooms. Thus, it is only the crass layman who thinks that we put up stonewalls. We do nothing of the kind, we put up emptiness. (Ayn Rand, *The Fountainhead,* 1943)

Architecture, by definition, is built for people. Architecture is the enclosure in which people live their lives. The behavior of people within the architecture demonstrates the dynamically moving social fabric of the human race (Heimsath, 1977). Any building must meet specific functional criteria, and from the function the design evolves. A building must permit efficient job performance, meet the needs of the user, and protect the user from safety hazards and criminal acts that affect the production of goods and service.

> An architect uses steel, glass, and concrete, produced by others, but the materials remain just so much steel, glass, and concrete until he touches them. What he does with them is individual product and his individual property. (Rand, 1943)

Architects worry about the fortress mentality of security professionals, whereas security professionals are concerned about the architects' failure to include security elements into the design of the building from the ground up. The conflict is not over whether to include security equipment in the building design but, rather, the conflict lies between a building's openness, on the one hand, and control of access to it, on the other.

It is always bad news when it becomes necessary to secure a building that was not originally planned to be secure. It is also very expensive. Architects have to sacrifice much more of a building's openness in retrofitting for security than they would if the facility had been designed for security from the outset. Making matters worse, protection, personnel, and operating expenses are greater

[*] Portions of the text in this chapter consist of articles and other publications previously written by the author including possible portions found in the following Wiley publications: *Architectural Graphics Standards, 10th Edition*, Ramsey/Hoke, The American Institute of Architects, John Wiley & Sons, ISBN: 0471348163, ©2000. *Security Planning and Design: A Guide for Architects and Building Design Professionals,* Demkin, The American Institute of Architects, John Wiley & Sons, ISBN: 0471271567, ©2004. We offer special thanks to the American Institute of Architects and John Wiley & Sons for permission to reproduce common content in this work.

FIGURE 3.1   Form or function in modern architecture? (Photo courtesy of iStockphoto.com.)

than they need to be because of a lack of forethought during the design of the facility. This condition is particularly evident in many of today's buildings (Figure 3.2), where modern design and materials can result in facilities that are especially vulnerable.

Oscar Newman's (1972) concept of "defensible space" focused on the vulnerability of urban housing architecture to crime because of poor design and lack of territorial responsibility by residents. Research has shown that criminals do not move about randomly through their environment looking for a target (Repetto, 1974) but use a spatial search process to try to find victims or targets that match their perceptual generalizations. When a match occurs, crime is likely to occur. One of the first steps in deciding to commit a crime is using cues from the environment to help select a path toward a victim or target.

Canadian criminologists Patricia and Paul Brantingham (1991) write that altering the conditions that provide the opportunities for criminal behavior can curb crime. Great financial resources are required to change existing buildings and neighborhoods to reduce environmental crime cues. Once a building enters the construction phase, it is generally too expensive to make changes to the structural system. When a building is occupied, it is even more difficult and expensive to make security improvements. The result is that security measures must adapt to the existing physical conditions, which limit their effectiveness. Many modern buildings, for example, use glass and free-flowing interiors extensively (Figure 3.3). Even though the world seems to have become less secure

FIGURE 3.2 Modernism and post-modernism generations of architecture show us the form of our built environment. (Photo courtesy of iStockphoto.com.)

and more prone to crime and terrorism, many buildings fail to incorporate any CPTED or security features to compensate for this vulnerability. For a building to be made truly secure, security considerations must be in the architectural drawings from the very beginning.

FIGURE 3.3 Glass exteriors reflect our vanity and our vulnerability? (Photo courtesy of iStockphoto. com.)

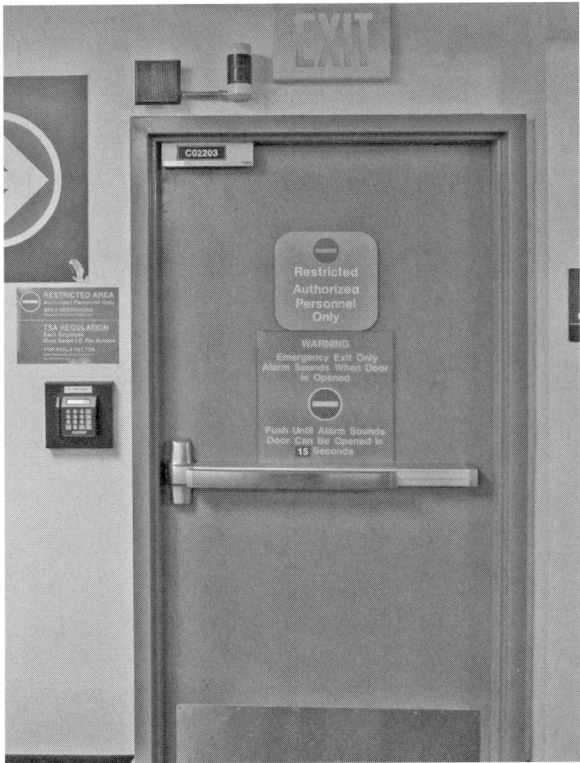

FIGURE 3.4 An example of integrated security technology and signage to make a doorway restricted.

THREE KEYS IN BUILDING DESIGN

Architects often view security requirements as obtrusive and distracting from the appearance of their buildings. Although security detection devices can be made and installed unobtrusively, many security requirements such as desks and consoles need to keep a high profile. This creates the security zoning needed to prevent the opportunity for access by unwanted parties.

If security has not been designed into the building from the start, security must rely on technological systems such as closed-circuit television (CCTV). When CCTV is installed without a compatible physical design, the CCTV observers cannot distinguish ordinary behavior from deviant behavior and thus respond to the appropriate emergency quickly.

In facilities that were not planned with security in mind, the number and variety of people coming and going frequently overwhelm receptionists and electronic entrance controls. Often the design of parking lots, entrances, and lobbies did not anticipate the control requirements (Figure 3.4). One example is the open service counter, such as cashier, pharmacy, and payroll counters. Whether alarmed or not, these generally are not designed to be secure. They practically encourage robbery attempts.

Inappropriate parking and pedestrian traffic patterns invite extraneous persons and congestion in critical or hazardous areas such as loading docks, mechanical areas, and inventory, production, and assembly areas, thereby encouraging accidents, theft, vandalism, and assault. Electronic window and door detectors installed after the fact may be compromised through plasterboard walls or suspended ceilings.

In today's climate of security litigation, the consequences of failing to secure a building are great to the owner and the designer of the building. Security litigation is increasing at a tremendous pace. Attorneys and expert witnesses are closely viewing lighting, parking lots, landscaping,

FIGURE 3.5 Fortress — overprotecting us from acts of crime and terror.

security hardware, and visibility. Juries are keen to hear how the owner and architect failed to consider the foreseeability of crime in the building design.

Architects and designers can make the greatest contribution to meeting a project's security objectives because they make the basic design decisions about circulation, access, building materials, fenestration, and many other features that can support or thwart overall security aims (Figure 3.5).

For the building process to come to life, there are three key players. The first is the architect, who designs the building for the owner. Second is the owner who commissions the building and typically manages it after the building is finished. The third role is that of regulatory government (local, state, or federal). The architect, operating for the owner, works within the constraints of regulatory government as expressed through deed restrictions, zoning laws, health, fire, and building codes. Thus, the built environment is a reflection of the needs of the owner, as defined by the owner; yet it also is a product of the regulatory guidelines of the government agencies protecting health and safety, and the experience and insight of the architect, as demonstrated through the design. If change is to occur within the building process, it is going to occur within the existing roles of these three players.

The architect's job is to use the security requirements identified by the security professional into programmatic directives. The design team uses the program to start the design of the building. The architectural program is one of the most important phases in the whole building process. The program establishes the scope of work, the parameters, and initial budgeting for the building.

Owners will ask that architects design what is economically sound, socially useful, and aesthetically pleasing. Regulatory agencies will control, through a series of prohibitions or incentives, the physical health and safety aspects of a building. Architects will design within the accepted standards of care of the profession and the aspirations of the community as a whole, as the architectural professionals perceive them. If positive change is going to occur in the building process, it could occur by a dramatic change in society's needs, or a shift in economics that will make certain building forms more or less feasible (for example, the change in U.S. federal architecture after the Oklahoma City bombing and subsequent GSA General Services Administration Security Design Standards). These shifts would influence owners in establishing their needs. Change can occur by legislation (i.e., CPTED Codes, Ordinance, Resolutions), or by influencing the architects who are active, ongoing participants in building after building.

How architects design is a product of the theory they use in design and the procedure society has established for producing buildings. Because theory can be changed or influenced without major disruption, the issue of procedure is addressed first. (Heimsath, 1977)

The current design procedure is well illustrated by the standard contract document produced by The American Institute of Architects (AIA). Although the document is basically sound, it exemplifies two major weaknesses in the design process (Heimsath, 1977, p. 26): the lack of requiring both a programming phase and a feedback or Post Occupancy Evaluation (POE) phase also called Facility Performance Evaluations (FPE) (Zimring, 2006). The omission of these phases, in turn, points to the physical bias of architecture, giving little direct attention to the needs of inhabitants as dynamic beings moving in time and space. Sadly, although true in the 1970s, it is mostly like that today. There has been some increased awareness in programming and postoccupancy evaluations on building designs, but mostly in large public sector projects, city halls, courthouses, hospitals, and so on. It has been my experience that in private sector, the client is usually unwilling to pay for the prearchitectural programming and postoccupancy evaluations. As a representative typical example, the Office of Financial Management (OFM, July 2006) states in its "Guidelines for Determining Architect/Engineer Fees for Public Works Projects" that the basic fee breakdown is based on the phases of Schematic Design, Design Development, Construction Document, Bidding, Construction, and the Final Project Costs. Programming and POEs are not even mentioned in the basic A/E services. Because these two important evaluation steps are not part of basic A/E services they often are ignored and overlooked in most design jobs. Programming and postoccupancy evaluations are considered extra services that most clients are unwilling to pay for, and thus we lose the opportunity to evaluate our buildings on what is working and not working well so that we don't make the same mistakes.

So it is evident that security needs should be discussed initially during the programming phase of design. It is the client's responsibility to define precisely the potential threats to people, information, and property and to determine the level and cost of the protection that will be provided. Many owners, clients, and developers may only have a casual awareness of security and of what they need to protect. They may not have the knowledge and experience to develop adequate strategies or security plans (Figure 3.6).

THE ARCHITECTURAL PROGRAM

The architectural program is like the menu to a restaurant, defining what you are going to serve, who are you going to serve, and how much are you going to charge. This is the point at which you can make a difference with security. From this point forward, security considerations will always require changes in drawing, and additional time and money. That is why programming for security is important. Security needs must be determined early. Defining what is needed usually involves a combination of common sense and methodical investigation. The client may need a security specialist to develop the protection requirement of this phase. Many architects help clients locate a qualified security specialist for their building type and security needs.

Programming is presented in AIA documents as the responsibility of the client: "The Owner shall provide full information, including a complete program, regarding their requirements for the project." The architect is required to confirm such a program in preparing schematic designs, but

FIGURE 3.6 Does the design reflect what is happening inside? (Photo courtesy of iStockphoto.com.)

the word "confirm" hardly suggests a major role in developing a database for alternatives that might include not building at all. The architect, if requested specifically by the owner, may undertake additional programming steps. Payment for such services is listed as an additional service, under Article 1.3. It has been my experience that architects typically, receive minimal compensation for the programming phase that produces the behavioral data. Once the commission is secure, the programming phase is often done hastily, and with minimal effort because it is not a directly billable expense as part of the basic architectural engineering services. If the architectural program and behavioral data is not introduced in the beginning of the job, the design professional cannot be as effective in directing the design, and for the basic and irrevocable decisions that will be made subsequently, without considering behavior of the intended users. (Heimsath, 1977; Kumlin, 1995; AIA 1990, 2003; Preiser, 1993; WBDG, 2006).

Second, there is no scientific feedback phase in the current design process. The scientific method in the social sciences uses a methodology to test hypothesis by examining the cause-and-effect relationship. The decision-making and response stages of architecture are lacking a feedback process to understand the cause and effect of the design decisions on the building users and the surrounding community. There is no required feedback process built into the architectural design process. There is not even a widespread understanding by the architectural community as to the important role feedback or POEs might play. For example, it is common that design award juries are not instructed to question the end users of the buildings of the architecture firm. Design awards are given when the buildings are just opened or first occupied (Figure 3.7). There are even unbuilt design awards to the buildings that never were constructed.

Architects interviewed for new jobs are asked to make verbal and visual presentations. When a panel for a potential job conducts interviews of architects, it often occurs in one sitting, ostensibly to compare their abilities. Seldom are the buildings, which architects design, considered in terms of their social success. The architect's past projects are demonstrated with slide shows or PowerPoint computer presentations to showoff their physical characteristics. The buildings are seldom visited to find out how well they actually work. From a crime and safety perspective, this is a potential disaster waiting. It is impossible to improve without learning how to improve. The risk assessments described in this book emerge from the scientific literature on what works, what doesn't, and how to improve building designs.

In fact, back in 1986 Cooper, Marcus, and Sarkissian stated that "architects usually are forced to fall back on their own experience and their perceptions of the future tenants' needs. There is,

FIGURE 3.7 "It is better to look good than to feel good. You know, you look marvelous!" Billy Crystal, *Saturday Night Live*, 1993. Our buildings might look good, but they often don't feel good (sick building syndrome, mold, crime, accidents, bad circulation patterns, etc.). (Photo courtesy of iStockphoto.com.)

however, an alternative . . . post occupancy evaluations provide useful information about what works and what fails from the residents' perspectives (Cooper Marcus, and Sarkissian, 1986, p. 1).

Building clients and design professionals are not the only ones concerned about security during the design process. Many jurisdictions require a security review by the police as part of the building-permit approval process, much the same as with fire safety requirements. Inspectors evaluate the plans for obvious spots where assaults, muggings, break-ins, and other crimes of opportunity may exist. Many jurisdictions have security ordinances that require certain lighting level, as well as secure door and window designs and hardware. New and evolving security guidelines and standards by the National Fire Protection Association (NFPA 730, Guide for Premises Security, and NFPA 731, Standard for the Installation of Electronic Security Systems, 2006; Uniform Building Code Security Guidelines, 1997; GSA Security Standards, 1995; ISC Security standards for GSA leased spaces, 2004), serve as a basis for minimum standards and direction for security and design professionals.

If security is treated as one of the many design requirements, then the implementation and costs for such measures will be no more a burden to the project owners than fire safety features or landscaping requirements. The basic premise of Crime Prevention Through Environmental Design (CPTED) is that proper design and effective use of the built environment can lead to a reduction in the incidents of crime and fear of crime, thereby increasing the quality of life. The environmental design approach to security recognizes the space's designated or redesignated use, which defines a security or CPTED solution compatible with that use. Good security design enhances the effective use of the space at the same time prevents crime and potential acts of terror.

CPTED EMERGES ON THE SCENE

The emphasis in CPTED design falls on the design and use of space, a practice that deviates from the traditional target-hardening approach to crime prevention. Traditional target hardening focuses predominantly on denying access to a crime target through physical or artificial barrier techniques such as locks, alarms, fences, and gates. The traditional approach tends to overlook opportunities for natural access control and surveillance. Sometimes the natural and normal uses of the environment can accomplish the effects of mechanical hardening and surveillance. These conclusions evolved from the many applications of CPTED and Defensible Space from its inception.

FIGURE 3.8   Housing in San Juan; fear is the message. Living behind fences and barred windows.

Defensible Space and CPTED were evolving at the same time in the early 1970s. Many social scientists, criminologists, and architects criticized the Defensible Space findings and research in public housing work for being architecturally deterministic (Figure 3.8). Oscar Newman responded to this criticism by stating:

> From reviewing the literature that has emerged from the CPTED movement—a spin off of Defensible Space—I am surprised by how poorly the Defensible Space concept is understood and how often it is misused. I had always thought of my ideas as comparatively simple and down to earth. And, when explaining them, I have tried to avoid mystery and mumbo jumbo. Yet, a whole cult has sprung up around these misgivings, with its own pseudo-language, misbegotten concepts, and rituals. After reading the literature and examining the projects that have been built in the name of CPTED and Defensible Space, I am troubled by my failure to communicate my ideas clearly. (Newman, 1996. p. 6)

Many sociologists, while acknowledging the problem of a dysfunctional community, cannot see the connection of social disorder to architecture. On a small scale, architecture may influence a particular building or particular rooms on a particular group of people. But when architecture is conceived as a building process affecting the culture of a society, then the decision to locate low-income minorities in high densities without significant social programs is of critical influence on subsequent behavior. For example, the placement and size of the infamous Cabrini Green Housing (Chicago Housing Authority) was determined as a design decision, not as a social decision. The owner and architect set the social organization in motion by deciding on the building, the location, the density, and the configuration (Heimsath, 1977, p. 14).

The subsequent housing disasters at Cabrini Green in Chicago, the Pruitt Igoo Housing in St. Louis, and dozens of other projects around the United States finally woke the sleeping bureaucratic giant, U.S. Housing Urban Development (HUD). Current HOPE VI projects are using low-rise townhouse plans that incorporate Defensible Space/CPTED strategies and New Urbanism/Traditional Neighborhood Design principles. The primary emphasis should be on revitalizing the residents of public housing, not just the residences of public housing (HOPE VI Developments, 1999, p. 3). Current public housing developments need to be meeting the goals of providing a clean, functional, and safe living environment, as well as providing the resident an opportunity for self-sufficiency. Besides good architecture, there is a triad of other needs for the residents to succeed:

FIGURE 3.9 Designing safe environments needs to include high-risk areas like parking. (Photo courtesy of iStockphoto.com.)

- Job training (so people are employable)
- Day care (so people are available to attend both job training and their new jobs), and
- A foundation of education, especially for adolescents.

CPTED has an established process to evaluate the linkages between the built environment and criminal behavior, yet CPTED as an "environmental design science" has failed because of the lack of systematic testing and evaluation of projects, the lack of a systematic risk assessment process, and the lack of standardization (Figure 3.9).

For many years, the CPTED practitioner has reinvented the process for each project. CPTED practitioners must start to read new books and articles on environmental research, and learn how to do it. In 1996, the situation moved in a positive direction with the formation of the International CPTED Association (ICA), a semiprofessional organization aimed at advancing the quality of CPTED practice through certification, education, and information conferences. Since then, the ICA has slowly instituted a CPTED certification process that demands, among other things, experience in assessing risk and utilizing best practices in CPTED (http://www.cpted.net).

The utilization of the scientific method and using a risk-assessment model is what the future and long-term goals should be for the successful implementation of CPTED into the architecture. It is time for the future of CPTED and security architecture to "GET SMART:"

- **S**pecific goals of what crimes are to be reduced and experience outcome

- **M**easurable and replicable goals and results in the form of POEs (Post Occupancy Evaluations)
- **A**chievable goals and results by clearly defined action steps
- **R**ealistic goals that are well grounded and have a scientific basis
- **T**imed goals for a logical sequence, and ordering of action steps

The application of CPTED in the architecture process can never entirely eliminate crime because it does not attack the root causes: money, power, and class struggles. Architectural security design may only move crime to other, more vulnerable, areas. It remains easier to remodel a building than to create jobs for teenagers. Design can provide an environment conducive for legitimate human law abiding activity, but it cannot create such control if the social fabric of the community is fragmented. The inclusion of security and life safety functions into the architecture adds greatly to the potential for a safer and more cost-effective work and living environment.

The field of fire prevention and life safety has successfully moved beyond the fear and panic, to understanding the science of what causes fires and how the architecture can prevent them. By understanding and improving the scientific method of CPTED we can prevent the fear and opportunity for a great deal of crime and improve the quality of life. Chapter 4 will reveal how CPTED works to accomplish that.

REFERENCES

AIA (1990) American Institute of Architects. *Handbook of Professional Practice.* Washington, DC.

AIA (2003) American Institute of Architects. *Handbook of Professional Practice.* Washington, DC.

Atlas, R. (2006) Designing for security. *The Construction Specifier.* April, 83–92.

Atlas, R. (2006) Architect as nexus: Cost effective security begins with design. *ArchiTech* May–June, 30–34.

Atlas, R. (2004) Security design concepts. *Security Planning and Design: A Guide for Architecture and Building Design Professionals.* American Institute of Architects, Washington, DC: Wiley.

Atlas, R. (2004) Defensible space: An architectural retrospective. *Master Builder.* Sept/Oct 1(1).

Atlas, R. (2003) Loss prevention returns to its roots with CPTED. *Plant Safety & Maintenance.* April.

Atlas, R. (2000) Design considerations: Setting standards in security architecture. *Door and Hardware.* June.

Atlas, R. (1999) Secure facility design, environmental design that prevents crime! *The Construction Specifier.* April.

Atlas, R. (1998) Designing against crime: The case for CPTED training for architects. *Florida Architect.* Summer.

Barrow, J. (1991) *Theories of Everything.* Oxford University Press.

Brantingham, P.L. and Brantingham, P.J. (1991) *Environmental Criminology.* Beverly Hills: Sage.

Cisneros, H. (1996) *Defensible Space: Deterring Crime and Building Community.* Washington, DC. U.S. Department of Housing and Urban Development.

Cooper-Marcus, C. and Sarkissian, W. (1986) *Housing as if People Mattered: Site Guidelines for Medium-Density Family Housing.* Berkeley: University of California Press.

Crowe, T. (2000) *Crime Prevention through Environmental Design: Applications of Architectural Design and Space Management Concepts,* 2nd ed., Butterworth-Heinemann, Oxford.

Heimsath, C. (1999) *Behavioral Architecture: Toward an Accountable Design Process.* New York: McGraw Hill. 1977 HOPE VI Developments, Issue 35, April. p. 3.

ISC Interagency Security Committee. (2004) Security Standards for Leased Spaces. September.

OFM. (2006) Guidelines for Determining Architect/Engineer Fees for Public Works Building Projects. Office of Financial Management. State of Washington. July. www.ofm.wa.gov/budget/instructions/capinst/appendixb.pdf.

Kuhn, T. (1962) *The Structure of Scientific Revolutions.* University of Chicago Press.

Kumlin, R. (1995) *Architectural Programming: Creative Techniques for Design Professionals.* New York: McGraw-Hill.

Life Safety Code 101. (1988) National Fire Protection Association. pp. 100–101x.

Newman, O. (1972) *Defensible Space: Crime Prevention through Urban Design.* New York: Macmillan.

Newman, O. (1992) *Improving the Viability of Two Dayton Communities: Five Oaks and Dunbar Manor.* Great Neck, NY: The Institute of Community Design.

Newman, O. (1996) Creating Defensible Space. Washington DC: U.S. HUD. April.

Preiser, W. (1993) *Professional Practice in Facility Programming*. New York: Van Nostrand Reinhold.

Rand, A. (1943) *The Fountainhead*. New York: Bobbs-Merrill.

Repetto, T. (1974) *Residential Crime*. Cambridge, MA: Ballinger.

Saville, G. and Wright, D. (1998) *A CPTED Design and Planning Guide for Planning and Development Professionals*. Ottawa: Canada Mortgage and Housing Corporation and the Royal Canadian Mounted Police, pp. 33–47.

U.S. General Services Administration. (2004) Protective design and Security Implementation Guidelines.

U.S. General Services Administration, U.S. Department of Justice. (1995) Vulnerability Assessment of Federal Facilities, June.

Wilson, E.B. (1952) *An Introduction to Scientific Research*. McGraw-Hill.

Wekerle, G. and Whitzman, C. (1995) *Safe Cities: Guidelines for Planning, Design, and Management*. New York: Van Nostrand Reinhold.

Whole Building Design Guide. E. Cherry, J. Petronis (Eds.). *Architectural Programming*. 2006.

Wikipedia. (2006) www.wikipedia.org/wiki/form_follows_function, Nov.

Zimring, C. (2006) *Facility Performance Evaluation. Whole Building Design Guide*.

4 Introduction to Planning of a Building

Security needs for a building must be determined early, as part of the project programming and definition process. Burglary, industrial espionage, shoplifting, riots, vandalism, assault, rape, murder, and employee theft are crimes that imperil lives and drive up the cost of doing business. As crime increases, incorporating security into the design and construction in all building types is critical for crime prevention.

Designing without security in mind can lead to lawsuits, injuries, and expensive retrofitting with protection equipment, as well as to the need for additional security personnel. If not properly planned for and installed, that equipment can distort important building design functions, add to security personnel costs, and result in exposed unsightly alarm systems or blocked doors and windows.

THE ARCHITECTURAL PLANNING PROCESS

Any building must meet specific functional criteria, and from the function the design evolves. A building must permit efficient job performance, meet the needs of the user, and protect the user from safety hazards and criminal acts that affect the production and service delivery of the building's users.

Securing a building that was not originally planned to be secure is expensive. Architects have to sacrifice much more of a building's openness in retrofitting for security than they would if the facility had been designed for security from the outset. Protection personnel and operating expenses are greater than they need to be because of a lack of forethought during the design of the facility. This condition is particularly evident in many of today's buildings, where modern design and materials have resulted in facilities that are especially vulnerable.

To understand how a building is designed will shed insight into the architectural process (see Figure 4.1 and Table 4.1). The following steps illustrate a traditional building construction process:

- Programming—Information supposedly provided by the owner to the architect on why, what, and for whom the building is planned.
- Schematic Design—The architect processes the programming information and develops bubble diagrams reflecting circulation patterns and proximity relationships. The diagrams evolve into single line drawings of the floor plan, site plan, and elevations, as the beginnings of engineering considerations.
- Design Development—The architect has presented his or her ideas to the client and made design corrections. The drawings become more sophisticated, include more engineering considerations such as structural, mechanical, electrical, ventilation, and site planning. Drawings are put into a larger scale; usually 1/4 inch equals one foot.
- Construction Documents (or working drawings)—These are the final drawings prepared for construction purposes. All technical data are presented in the drawings and are accompanied by technical written specifications.
- Bids for construction and selection of contractor—The architectural drawings and specifications are put out to bid for qualified contractors who will provide the service at the lowest price.

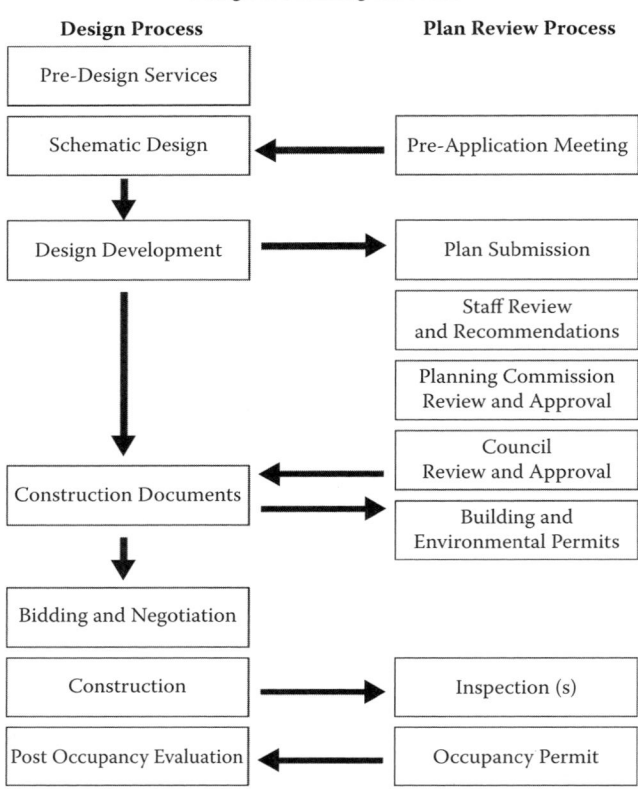

FIGURE 4.1   The design and planning process.

It should be evident that the stage to initially bring up security needs is in the programming phase of the design process. It is primarily the client's responsibility to define precisely the potential threats to people, information, and property and to determine the level and cost of the protection that will be provided. Many owners, clients, and developers may only have a casual awareness of security and of what they need to protect; they may not have the knowledge and experience to develop adequate strategies or security plans.

That is why architectural programming for security is very important. Security needs must be determined early. Defining what is needed usually involves a combination of common sense and methodical investigation (Figure 4.2).

The architect's job is to convert the security requirements identified by the security professional into programmatic directives. The design team uses the program to start the design of the building. The architectural program is one of the most important phases in the whole building process. The program establishes the scope of work, the parameters, and initial budgeting for the building.

Security design also involves the effort to integrate the efforts of community citizens and law enforcement officers to prevent crime through the design and use of the built environment. Design professionals can use three basic strategies for crime prevention through environmental design: natural **access control**, natural **surveillance**, and natural **territorial reinforcement**. Each of these strategies can be implemented through organized methods: manpower, (police, security guards, receptionists); mechanical methods (technology products, alarms, CCTV, gadgets); and natural methods (site planning, design, landscaping, signage).

Access control is a design concept directed at reducing the opportunity and accessibility for crime. Organized methods of access control include security guard forces. Mechanical strategies

TABLE 4.1
Programming Process

Integrating Security and CPTED into Buildings Process Increments and Tasks*	Primary Participants				
	Client	Architect	Consultant	Contractor	User
Predesign					
Verify project scope, goals, and objectives	x	x			
Identify client's values and expectations	x	x			
Confirm budgets and schedules		x			
Identify anticipated expertise for security (identify consultants)	x	x			
Verify security team structure and procedures		x	x		
Develop security work plan		x	x		
Gather security-related information and data			x		
Perform asset analysis			x		
Perform threat analysis			x		
Perform vulnerability analysis			x		
Perform risk analysis			x		
Identify potential security measures			x		
Define and prioritize cost/benefits for measures		x	x		
Report findings (either separately or in programming report)		x	x		
Identify functional security design criteria	x	x	x		
Design					
Apply security concepts in programming/schematic design		x			
Evaluate security design aspects against other design aspects	x				
Apply security concepts in design development		x			
Evaluate security design aspects against other design aspects	x				
Prepare cost estimates for security measures		x			
Design documents reviewed by security consultant		x	x		
Construction Documentation					
Integrate security measures into working drawings		x			
Select and specify security components and systems		x			
Verify costs of security elements against budget		x			
Construction documents reviewed by security consultant		x	x		
Construction					
Communicate security objectives to contractor or designer-builder	x	x			
Install security elements, components, and systems				x	
Inspect installation for quality, workmanship, etc.		x	x	x	
Operation					
Test performance of building security features and systems				x	
Instruct users on security features and operation		x	x		
Prepare security operation plans and procedures			x		x
Prepare emergency operation plans and procedures			x		x

TABLE 4.1 (CONTINUED)
Programming Process

	Primary Participants				
Integrating Security and CPTED into Buildings Process Increments and Tasks*	Client	Architect	Consultant	Contractor	User
Conduct periodic drills and tests					x
Update plans and procedures on periodic basis					x

* Specific tasks vary depending on project type and scope; the sequence of tasks is not necessarily sequential; the roles of participants vary depending on security expertise of architect and client; project delivery method will affect roles and sequence of events.

Source: *Security Planning and Design: A Guide for Architects and Building Design Professionals*, The American Institute for Architects, Joseph A. Demkin (Editor); ©2004, John Wiley & Sons. Reprinted with permission of John Wiley & Sons.

include target hardening such as locks and card key systems. Windows may have protective glazing that withstands blows without breaking. Doors and window hardware may have special material and mountings that make them difficult to tamper with or remove. Walls, floors, or doors may be specially reinforced in high security areas with materials that are difficult to penetrate. Natural methods of access control make use of spatial definition and circulation patterns. An example of natural design is the use of security zoning. By dividing space into zones of differing security levels, such as unrestricted, controlled, and restricted, sensitive areas can be more effectively protected. The focus of access control strategies is to deny access to a crime target and create in offenders, a perception of risk and detection, delay, and response.

Effective access control is often the key to many security threats (Figure 4.3). Access control might be strongly considered in these areas:

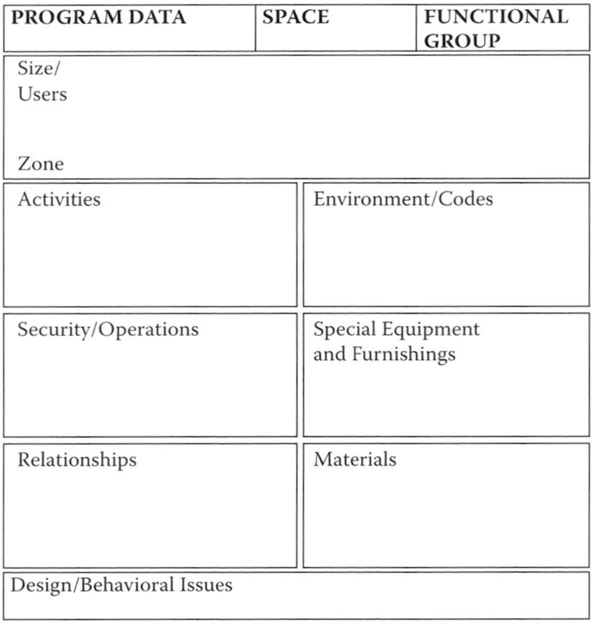

PROGRAM DATA	SPACE	FUNCTIONAL GROUP
Size/ Users Zone		
Activities	Environment/Codes	
Security/Operations	Special Equipment and Furnishings	
Relationships	Materials	
Design/Behavioral Issues		

FIGURE 4.2 Program data collection chart.

FIGURE 4.3 Security layering and territorial boundaries are like a pair of protective arms around a property.

- All entrances and exits to the site and building
- Internal access points in restricted or controlled areas
- Environmental and building features used to gain access (trees, ledges, skylights, balconies, windows, tunnels)
- Security screening devices (guard stations, surveillance, identification equipment)

Surveillance strategies are design concepts directed at keeping intruders under observation. Organized surveillance strategies include police and guard patrols. Lighting and CCTV are mechanical strategies for surveillance, and natural strategies include windows, low landscaping, and raised entrances.

Territorial strategies suggest that physical design can create or extend the sphere of territorial influence so that users develop a sense of proprietorship. This sense of territorial influence (Figure 4.4) can alert potential offenders that they don't belong there, that they are at risk of being seen and identified, and that their behavior will not be tolerated or go unreported. Natural access control and surveillance contribute to a sense of territoriality, boosting security by encouraging users to protect their turf. Organized territorial strategies typically include neighborhood crime watches,

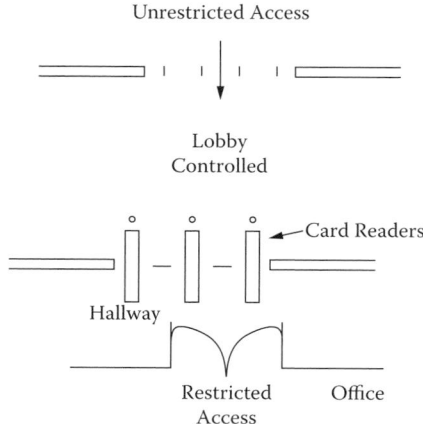

FIGURE 4.4 The diagram shows a funnel effect that has people going though the wide opening and then getting narrower and narrower as they move from unrestricted to controlled and then restricted zones.

receptionists, guard stations; mechanical strategies can be perimeter sensing systems; natural territorial strategies include fences, walls, and landscaping.

LAYERS OF SECURITY: SITE, BUILDING, INTERIOR, AND POINT

Whenever possible, **security planning should begin during the site selection process**. The greatest opportunity for achieving a secure operation begins with locating a site that meets architectural requirements and also provides for security advantages. The security analysis in site planning should begin with an assessment of conditions on-site and off-site, taking into account topography, vegetation, adjacent land uses, circulation patterns, neighborhood crime patterns, police patrol patterns, sight lines, areas for concealment, location of utilities, and existing and proposed lighting. Other key factors for site security planning are off-site pedestrian circulation, vehicular circulation, access points for service vehicles and personnel, employee access and circulation, and visitor access and circulation (Figure 4.3).

The **site analysis** represents the first level of security defense planning, which considers the site perimeters and grounds of the facility. Site design measures can include walls, heavy plantings, fences, berms, ditches, lighting, natural topographic separations, or a combination of such elements. Several factors to consider at this stage are:

- What is the physical makeup of the site and how does it influence security?
- What are the land uses surrounding the site?
- What is the type and frequency of criminal activity in the area?

A site that has high security risks may not be automatically disqualified just because of crime if the location is desirable. The owner may choose the site but acknowledge the security threats and vulnerabilities, and address them properly through design, technology, manpower, and security management.

The second level of security defense planning is the **perimeter or exterior of the building**. The building shell and its openings represent, after the site perimeter and grounds, the crucial second line of defense against intrusion and forced entry. The area being protected should be thought of as having four sides as well as a top and bottom. The principal points of entry to be considered are the windows, doors, skylights, storm sewers, roof, floor, and fire escapes.

Doors and windows are by nature among the weakest links of a building and inherently provide poor resistance to penetration. Attention must be paid to the doorframe, latches, locks, hinges, and panic hardware, the surrounding wall and the door leaf. Window considerations for secure design include the type of glazing material, the window frame, the window hardware, and the size of the opening.

The building shell itself is a security consideration, for the type of construction will determine the level of security. Most stud walls and metal deck roof assemblies can be compromised with hand tools in less than two minutes. Concrete block walls, which are not reinforced, can be broken quickly with a sledgehammer or a car can drive through them. In South Florida, cars driving through the front of the stores broke into Service Merchandise stores and Sports Authority stores. The architect's challenge and the security consultant's task, is to provide security that is attractive and unobtrusive, while providing balanced and effective deterrence to unauthorized access.

The third level of security that the architect should design for is **internal space protection** and **specific internal point security**. Sensitive areas within a facility may warrant special protection with security technology, manpower, and restricted design circulation. The level of protection may be based on zones, with access to the zones limited to persons with the required level of security clearance.

Proper application of the zoning or security-layering concept depends on the control of employees, visitors, vendors, and others. The idea is to allow them to reach their destinations but prevent them from entering areas where they have no business. Controlling access to each department of a building, where appropriate, screens out undesirable visitors, reduces congestion, and helps employees identify and challenge unauthorized persons (Figure 4.5).

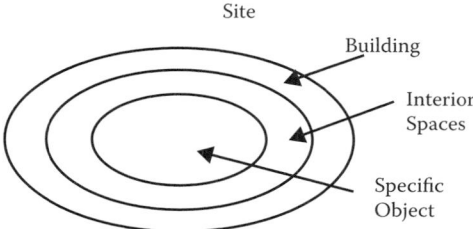

FIGURE 4.5 Security zones.

The zoning design goals are accomplished through the use of the following types of zones: unrestricted zones, controlled zones, and restricted zones. Some areas of a facility should be completely unrestricted to persons entering the area during the hours of designated use. The design of unrestricted zones should encourage persons to conduct their business and leave the facility without entering controlled or restricted zones. Unrestricted zones might include lobbies, reception areas, snack bars, certain personnel and administrative offices, and public meeting rooms.

Controlled zone movement requires a valid purpose for entry. Once admitted to a controlled area, persons may travel from one department to another without severe restriction. Controlled zones might include administrative offices, staff dining rooms, security offices, office working areas, and loading docks.

Restricted zones are sensitive areas that are limited to staff assigned to departments within those particular areas. Sections within restricted zones frequently require additional access control. Functions and departments located in restricted zones may include vaults, sensitive records, chemicals and drugs, food preparation, mechanical areas, telephone equipment, electrical equipment, control rooms, laboratories, laundry, sterile supply, special equipment, and sensitive work areas.

The security-zoning concept, or onion layers approach, is being used effectively in the designs of hospitals, jails, courthouses, laboratories, and industrial plants. Once circulation patterns are successfully resolved through security zoning, physical security systems (mechanical CPTED solutions) can be considered.

Security professionals that have studied environmental security design know that the first level of security planning starts with securing the site perimeter and grounds. There are many means available for securing the grounds against trespassing. The most common ways include walls, chain link fences, moats, and other barriers. One way to deter trespassers is to use landscaping.

Landscaping can establish one of the most important action steps against trespassing by establishing a property line. Marking the property boundary is the first step because it actually deters some people who might otherwise walk in and engage in criminal or unauthorized activity.

There is a dilemma when it comes to establishing privacy versus security in project developments. The balance can be difficult and varies from application to application. A low hedge or fence establishes a boundary psychologically and physically says which is public and which is private property. A picket fence establishes an edge without obscuring the view or limiting surveillance. If trees are added above the fence, there can be a sense of enclosure but still have the ability to see into the property between the fence and tree canopy.

Block or brick walls offer protection to hiding the thief as well as securing the property owner. Bare walls also invite graffiti. Walls supplemented with landscaping can provide protection and a more effective barrier. Thorny bougainvillea, Carissa, wild lime, or rather toothy brushes planted in combination with a wall can combine the best of resources. Individual plants can discourage trespassers when strategically placed.

CPTED security design process can be applied on a macro to micro level. The three levels are site security design, building perimeter, and inner building space or point protection. Electronic intrusion detection, perimeter protection, and access control techniques must be elements in a total security system and design approach. Each technique has distinct technological and operational characteristics, and environmental reactions, along with differing requirements for installation and maintenance. In order to determine which security technology is the most cost-effective and appropriate, the following questions should be answered by the owner, architect, and competent security consultant:

1. *What will the system be used for?* For example, is the system designed to prevent escape or intrusion; for high or low security profile security; provide for an interior or exterior system; what are the methods of responding to alarms; and how long of a delay from criminal entry is desired? To justify the use of an electronic access control system the client will need to know what areas and equipment are to be protected, but also what the potential loss or damages will cost. Each security situation is unique; there are no package solutions.

2. *What are the operational aspects of a security system that is required, and what is their priority?* The type of alarm system needs to be defined, as well as the allowable false alarm rate tolerance. Inquiry is made on the proposed transmission system from sensors to alarms, for example, radio waves, hard-wired, dedicated circuits multiplex systems? What is the backup system in power and hardware? How are the alarms assessed for effectiveness, for example, with CCTV, lights, horns, bells, or printed records? Does the system have tamper alarms, self-tests, or lightning protection? Each security system requires calls for careful forethought on the implementation and operation.

3. *What are the environmental impacts that affect the security system?* Examples of such conditions are weather, water surfaces, wildlife, vegetation, and corrosive condition of acid rain or salt. Information is needed on topographic conditions of the site, are there any man-made impacts such as structure, traffic patterns, industry controls?

CONCLUSION

Security and CPTED needs to be included in the earliest stages of the planning and design process. The consequences are usually dire if security is an afterthought: people get hurt or loose their lives, buildings and property are damaged, and the costs in human toll and in retrofit are high. Why have the design communities been so resistant to include security and CPTED into the many layers of projects? Primarily cost and inconvenience. Post 9/11, the costs and inconvenience are no longer valid arguments. Resistance is futile, and to pretend that protecting the site, the building or interior assets, or that there will not be serious consequences for not doing so is naive. The exciting aspect of designing safe buildings and infrastructure is that it serves the health, safety, and welfare of the building occupants, its property, and strengthens the sense of community.

REFERENCES

Atlas, R. (2006) Architect as nexus: Cost effective security begins with design. *ArchiTech,* 30–34.
Atlas, R. (2006) Designing for security. *The Construction Specifier,* 83–92.
Atlas, R. (2004) Security design concepts. *Security Planning and Design: A Guide for Architecture and Building Design Professionals.* Washington, DC: American Institute of Architects, Wiley.
Atlas, R. (1998) Designing against crime: The case for CPTED training for architects. *Florida Architect,.*
Atlas, R. (1998) Designing for crime and terrorism: CPTED training is essential, *Security Design and Technology.*
Atlas, R. (1993) Programming architectural security in facilities. In W. Preiser (Ed.), *Professional Practice in Facility Programming.* New York: Van Nostrand.
Atlas, R. (1992) Successful security. *Buildings: Facilities Construction & Management.*
Crowe, T. (2000) *Crime Prevention through Environmental Design: Applications of Architectural Design and Space Management Concepts,* 2nd ed. Oxford: Butterworth-Heinemann.

Crowe, T. (1991) *Crime Prevention through Environmental Design: Applications of Architectural Design and Space Management Concepts.* Boston, MA: Butterworth-Heinemann.

Demkin, J. (Ed.). (2004) *Security Planning and Design: A Guide for Architects and Building Design Professionals.* Washington, DC: American Institute of Architects.

5 The Interface between Architects and Engineers

Douglas Fitzgerald and Randy Atlas

To design safe infrastructure, it is crucial to understand the relationship between architects and engineers and how the security designer needs to interface with them.

Most of the time, architects and engineers develop construction documents and coordinate their efforts without a security designer as part of their team. This is not uncommon, as we find that the electrical engineer, and not an electronics specialist, generally designs fire alarms and building automation systems. However, with the onset of advanced technologies and the associated complexities, fire safety and security systems have become disciplines unto themselves. The design profession used to be of the mind set that security was much like the telephone company, in that you construct the building and then request that the security contractor come and install their equipment. Today's facilities require far more planning and design. Architecture is a complex and creative discipline that requires specific skills, years of education, and a long track record of project experience to master. Architects, engineers, and security professionals must all communicate with each other and coordinate their specific requirements, but they do not need to do each other's jobs. Clearly we must appreciate what each one has to offer to the design process.

INVOLVING OTHERS IN DESIGN

The architectural process has a lot to offer the security designer, but first the architect needs to fully understand the process and phases of integrating security into built environment. The security consultant can get confused with architectural references to phases, percentages, schematic design, design development, and construction documents and specifications. If we place ourselves in the position of being head of the security department, then picture the discussions within the client's organization taking place around the water cooler with the Chief Financial Officer asking if the security department should be involved in the planning of the new building or renovation. Much to your surprise, you are invited to attend next week's architectural presentation design meeting. At this meeting the architect has plastered the walls with schematic design drawings and color renderings of their newest creation. As you look over the plans for spaces or features identified as "security," you are beginning to get that sinking feeling. The entrance lobby looks way too small for your screening equipment, there is no security command center, the generator and fuel tank are placed against the side of the building, and from your perspective the issues go on and on. This process is repeated nationwide day after day in hundreds of buildings.

Because the architecture firm never considered the multiple sites of the client, they have only concerned themselves with the current project being renovated. However, as is true with most locations, each possible site has attributes that may help or hinder our security plan. The correct approach is to determine positive and negative aspects of each site attribute or characteristic and then associate an overall cost with your security plan.

For instance, one site may be adjacent to a river that provides a natural barrier against vehicular intrusion, while another site has absolutely no defined perimeter from its neighbors and is accessible on all sides. Because the proposed facility is concerned with this type of threat, the countermeasure cost on the first site is minimal, whereas at the second site the client will need to make a significant investment in aesthetically pleasing barriers. Sometimes the process leads to logical solutions and sometimes it does not; however, the development of a security program does avoid last-minute and costly surprises to the project. Developing the security program is where one-on-one meetings with the architect can provide the most effective communication of needs and systems information. The architect and/or engineers also may have concepts that they have used on other sites that may be relevant or applicable for this new job.

The greatest challenge is to keep the planning and design process from getting too far ahead of the security director or consultant. Depending on the contract the architect/engineer has with the client, each change order that results will incur additional cost to the job. If the client intends to sign off on each of the design and security drawings, it is important to make sure that the security director/consultant is part of that process so that the changes, recommendations, or alterations are incorporated before the client's acceptance.

INTEGRATED DESIGN

If a functional security system design is not carefully planned and programmed, the security features in a building can become nonfunctional and very expensive hardware. In the past, the security systems did not "talk" to each other as in what is referred to as "integrated." It was understood that the security guard who was monitoring the security equipment knew that door number 8 is associated with intercom station number 3, and was viewed by camera number 19. In the past, the closed circuit television system had a wall of monitors, which usually provided more heat for the room than actual security for the facility. The monitoring equipment was piled up on top of each other, with little concern for ergonomic design. The security equipment was designed and placed as an afterthought. How do we avoid making these same mistakes again?

We should go back to the architectural process, specifically the programming phase. If function really does drive form, then the security consultant and systems designer must consider the mission of the space and users in the finest detail. If the architectural program accounts for the space and functionality of each item that requires square footage in the facility, then security needs must be considered with the same foresight as electrical equipment, lighting systems, fire safety systems, accessibility equipment, and acoustical treatment.

DESIGNING THE COMMAND CENTER

The security designer should start with the envisioned security command center and then inventory and determine space requirements for each of the items needed. Although a command center serves as an office space, there are a few unique pieces of equipment that are beyond typical office furniture. One example would be the security filing cabinets, which should be a UL (Underwriters Laboratory) class 5 type, and weigh in excess of 400 pounds each. One cabinet in the room does not constitute a problem, but a wall of cabinets creates a dead load that may be a structural consideration of which the architect and structural engineer must be aware. Another example would be parcel/package x-ray screening equipment, which requires electrical power. The special considerations of the scanners are not the electrical load, as much as the placement of the scanner. The scanners are often large and bulky and are usually placed in the center of the room. The same is true with the security command center consoles, which require power and communications infrastructure, for present-day requirements, but also future technological upgrades and growth. The command center also may have the need for raised computer room type flooring.

In most control centers, the operator needs to have writing tablets in front of them, reference materials, operations manuals, task lights, drinking cups, and so on. Each item needs to be placed in or stored in properly sized drawers. The designer also should consider the ergonomic issues of

FIGURE 5.1   An example of an ergonomically incorrect design, with monitors too small and too far away to be effective.

the operators in that some will be left-handed and some right-handed. They may need to design a console for left-handed use, or design them to be flexible enough to let the operator move the items such as telephones and radio microphones to their most efficient position.

The main equipment to be monitored in a control center needs careful consideration regarding placement and sizes (see Figure 5.1). With the onset of flat-screen monitors, there is more usable space on the walls, but the operators must readily and easily interpret the data being presented on these screens. In a hospital control room I visited, there were eight video camera images displayed on a 17" monitor, resulting in useless images, referred to in the industry as "squint-a-vision."

Ideally, the console operator should be able to monitor all of the equipment with minimal head movement, and without straining their neck (see Figure 5.2). Most of the consoles that are designed

FIGURE 5.2   This control room is located in a parking garage and is remotely watching 64 cameras. Staff was nowhere to be found.

FIGURE 5.3   This control room is out of control. Human factors was not a design consideration here.

today tend to have more fully integrated electronic security systems but also have a lot of ancillary equipment such as elevator control systems, fire alarm control systems, building automation control systems, computer-aided dispatch systems, radio base stations, and video monitors.

Experience has shown architects and security consultants that in order to avoid making design mistakes in control center design (see Figure 5.3), it is recommended to create scaled cardboard mockups of each piece of equipment, place them on an appropriately sized tabletop and watch different operators place them in the order they prefer. Mockups are exercises that sometimes produce one preferred layout, or one layout per operator, and may require some compromise. Mockups also demonstrate to the clients that for the frequency of operation, some equipment does not always need to be located on the console. However, this must be approached with caution when the frequency of use is associated with emergency operations or crisis management and removing it from the readily accessible position would cause adverse effects.

In the design of a control center, the systems designer can account for all the equipment being properly distributed, and should determine the number of consoles that will be required (see Figure 5.4). The security designer can then focus on the other items in the control center such as printers, fax machines, file cabinets, key cabinet, breathing apparatus cabinets, shredders, and storage cabinets. After accounting for these items, the design team can go back to the mockup model space and place the scaled cardboard equipment mockups around on the empty floor. If the control room is to have a teller type window for document/key exchange, this is the optimum time to consider on which wall it should be placed. It is also important to consider the perspective of the individual approaching the outside of the teller window and what they will see inside the room. The designer may determine if the client wants to obscure some of the vision line. The consultant also should

FIGURE 5.4   This control panel is well planned and has favorable human factor operational considerations.

review how the occupants will enter the room and whether or not the command center will require an entry vestibule or sally-port.

All too often, the signage indicating where the command center is located is not clear. Accessibility of the control center is another important policy decision, whether the command center is reachable by the public or not. If the command center is a self-functioning space (see Figure 5.5) there may need to be a small kitchenette and restroom. Some command center designs prefer that the electronic security equipment room be adjacent to the command center, with its entry requiring that staff enter the security vestibule/sally-port but not enter the command center itself for security control reasons.

The design requirements for a command center might read as follows:

The security command center shall consist of 500 square feet and be equipped with a 4-inch raised floor to facilitate infrastructure cabling. Entry into the command center shall be through a security vestibule/sally-port with attack resistive doors rated for 45 minutes. The interior of the vestibule will be equipped with a teller window and document pass tray ballistically rated against high power handguns.

FIGURE 5.5   Technology can only take us so far. People problems and security can be aided by integrated security design, but not solved.

The vestibule/sally-port shall as a minimum consist of 60 square feet. The security vestibule shall have a separate door entering the security electronics equipment room. The security equipment room shall consist of 160 square feet. Adjacent to and accessible from the security command center shall be a unisex bathroom of 40 square feet and a wet kitchenette area with sink, microwave, coffee station and refrigerator. The command center, vestibule/sally-port and equipment room walls shall be constructed of CMU walls with vertical and horizontal rebar reinforcement. The command center shall have positive air pressurization from all adjacencies and have a separate HVAC system with dedicated fresh air makeup and individual temperature controls for the command center and equipment room.

Our security design criteria may be somewhat different and resemble the following:

- Two fully functional consoles and one supervisory console in a triangular configuration with three 52" wall-mounted plasma displays
- Each console will consist of these components:
- One security management and control computer with 17" flat-screen display
- One elevator monitoring and control computer with 17" flat-screen display
- One 17" flat-screen CCTV display
- One operator's telephone console with busy lamp field
- One base station radio with desktop microphone
- One task light
- One Standard Operating Procedures manual (SOP) in 3" binder
- One Emergency Operating Procedures manual (EOM) in 4" binder
- Three 3" reference manuals
- One intercommunications handset/headset with network selector switch
- Two 4" drawers
- One 2" drawer
- One adjustable/articulating keyboard tray
- Two class 5 security containers
- Two printer stands with printers
- One fax machine
- Two Scott SCBA cabinets (Recessed wall mount)
- One key control cabinet (Surface wall mount with 120VAC uninterruptible power)

Most often, the architects and engineers will need the security consultant to provide them with cut-sheets from the equipment manufacturer so they can obtain dimensional, power, and mounting requirements. The systems designer should remember that dimensions may vary with manufacturers and that they may need to specify some components without substitution, or be willing to accept the difference, which could affect other trades and equipment.

DESIGNING THE SAFE LOBBY

The next major security systems design issue is the entrance lobby. In our example, the client's new facility has only one main lobby and the client desires to screen visitors and packages coming into our facility. Our first consideration is the number of people that enter through the entrance at approximately 8:00 a.m. and 12:45 p.m., two of our busiest time periods. Upon review of the lobby design the designer may also note an egress peak at 12:02 p.m. and 5:10 p.m. The Security Director has obtained management approval to use optical turnstiles for employees. After looking at the architect's schematic design drawings the security consultant may note a number of difficult issues. First, the designer will need to plan for enough space to permit everyone inside and away from adverse weather prior to gaining full facility access (see Figure 5.6).

FIGURE 5.6 A lobby that was retrofitted with security screening equipment. Now the lobby is cluttered and does not have proper cuing space during busy peak times.

FIGURE 5.7 Optical Turnstiles used in a large office building.

When the security consultant and design team review the existing lobby layout and use, it is important to conduct personnel counts sorted by the categories of staff, visitors, and service deliveries based on short time intervals. This data will then be converted into through-put rates that will define the number of entry lanes needed. In the case of facilities that permit staff to enter without being screened through x-ray package inspection and/or weapons detection the through-put rate of optical turnstiles with access readers is greater than standard weapons/explosives screening (see Figure 5.7). If the agreed-on level of security for the client is only screening visitors, then we may only have one lane for security screening and multiple lanes for access control. This will vary with each facility and the required level of protection and detection. In our example, the facility data indicated that the client has a need for three optical turnstile lanes that are bidirectional and include one screening lane.

FIGURE 5.8 Turnstiles and lobby design permit good screening.

Because the proposed new facility will require utilization of a visitor management system to track and issue visitor badges, the security department will need to establish a badging area adjacent to the screening area. The security designer will want to utilize the same process used in the command center design, to functionally layout and appropriately size out the badging office or kiosk. Whether the badging office is located before or after the screening point becomes a separate issue for discussion with the client. If the client permits individuals with briefcases and packages to be waiting in the lobby prior to screening, this could prove to be a dangerous practice. If the security department requires visitors and staff to be screened first, then security staff must control the visitors while waiting to be badged or awaiting visitor escorts. The screening management decisions will affect the architecture and lobby design, but rapidly screening items entering the facility is still a very important policy and procedure (see Figure 5.8).

When the lobby layout is finalized, then the systems designer can now select the types of turnstiles used (see Figure 5.9 and Figure 5.10), along with the metal detection archways or portals and the scanning/inspection equipment. Most security designers want to keep clear lines of separation between ingress and egress paths of travel to avoid objects and contraband from being passed between persons incoming and outgoing. Aesthetics play an important role in the lobby design and screening lanes. In most cases when users enter buildings they are looking at x-ray machines with monitors placed on top of the equipment, lots of ugly cables, an occasional coffee cup and lots of plastic bins that were never in the architect's vision of the main entrance. Hopefully the architect received his or her project portfolio photo before someone showed up with the eyesore of security screening equipment.

One of the many values of communicating closely with the architectural staff is the ability to design the millwork around the security equipment, utilizing similar materials to those used in the lobby (see Figure 5.11). This coordination greatly improves visual aspects of the equipment and can result in replacing the costly stainless steel cabinets that would be out of place in the context of the proposed architecture (see Figure 5.12).

For example, once the client and security director decide on the type of turnstile, then the systems designer can discuss placements and finishes of the turnstiles with the architect and/or interior designer, including them in the selection and specification process. The electrical engineer must also be consulted to ensure that power and signal conduits are stubbed-up and correctly routed. At this juncture, the design team may want to create a scaled mockup of the space and test it operationally

FIGURE 5.9 An example of access control screening with clear glass or plastic panels. The path is wide enough to allow a person in a wheelchair to pass.

prior to final design documentation. A successful and functional security control room or command center can only be accomplished with closely orchestrated communication and coordination with all of the affected disciplines, each of which may have something to contribute to the process. Most will have something to include in their construction documents.

DESIGNING LOADING DOCKS

Another area of vulnerability and security concerns is the loading dock area. The security consultant and design team are faced with a completely new set of challenges. Each facility vulnerability assessment and threat analysis must determine the amount of risk the client is willing to accept. If

FIGURE 5.10 This hands-free access control has clear panels that prevent persons from piggybacking behind an employee.

FIGURE 5.11   The lobby screening at a federal courthouse has package and person screening built into the architecture.

the concern for security, safety, and business continuity merits inspecting items entering the facility, then the security director is faced with whether or not to screen items arriving on the loading dock. The key questions in securing the loading docks include:

• Does the client want to inspect everything that is brought in by visitors?
• Does the client want to inspect everything that is delivered?
• Does the client want to inspect items carried by staff members?

In the example of a courthouse, the answer is "yes" to all three questions, but in most corporations, security screening comes down to a yes only for the loading dock and visitors areas.

In the example of screening visitors, security staff will usually select x-ray inspection equipment with a tunnel opening of approximately 24" wide by 18" high much like those we see utilized by the Transportation Security Administration (TSA) in airports. However, for loading docks, this

FIGURE 5.12   Revolving doors are great tools to permit controlled entrance and prevent piggybacking, but they are not friendly to wheelchairs and subsequently a glass swinging door is also provided to allow accessible entrance to persons with disabilities.

FIGURE 5.13 Technology is rapidly changing in package screening to allow for the changing threats of contraband.

may prove to be too small. Each organization will have different needs based on the materials that they receive. In some cases the conveyance belt needs to be at floor level to avoid having to lift the items up to the belt level. Before the layout of a dock area, the security consultant must analyze the frequency and quantity of items being delivered each day of the week to the building under design or renovation. The risk assessment also can reveal some needed operational changes, such as when the client accepts deliveries. If the client's loading dock only receives small items, then the client might be best served by selecting the identical screening equipment proposed for the lobby (see Figure 5.13). Parallel equipment also can serve as a backup should the lobby equipment fail, and replacement would only require that the client swap out the machines. If the client's need is greater, then it is time to consider equipment that has a larger tunnel opening, typically 38" wide by 38" high. This is also a time to start discussions with the architect about screening alternatives, because most machines conveyer belts are still 12" above finished floor level. The system designer may want to request that the architect depress the floor level at the machines location so that they can keep the conveyer belt level with the floor.

The security consultant needs to coordinate with the electrical engineer to provide the source of power. When creating slab depressions or millwork around equipment, remember that replacement equipment in the future may not consist of the same dimensions. Therefore, allow a little extra space and utilize filler panels to make up the difference. The systems designer should also coordinate with the persons responsible for this area regarding all standard and emergency operations requirements to ensure an efficient and safe working environment.

Designing a control or command center with today's threats also should take into consideration challenges such as vehicular attacks, chemical/biological threats, and blast protection. In the areas of blast protection and chemical/biological mitigation and protection, the design will probably require

FIGURE 5.14   This convenience store added camera after camera. There are six cameras in this picture. Can you find all of them?

consulting engineers who are specifically educated in these areas. Chemical/biological protective designers are specialized and usually have ties to the biomedical field or industrial engineering field specifically working with hazardous materials. Many mechanical engineering firms have worked in the areas of HEPA and ULPA air filtration. Great leaps are being made by manufacturers in the areas of real-time monitoring for detection and early warning of chemical and biological threats; however, this is also producing unacceptable levels of nuisance and false positive alarms.

The USACE Protective Design Center (PDC) in Omaha, Nebraska, has published many design guidelines related to Force Protection and Antiterrorism ensuring facility survival through maintaining adequate setbacks and sound engineering practices. These publications are now approved for limited distribution and have two general support manuals. The Interagency Security Committee has released the ISC Security Design Criteria for new Federal Office Buildings and Major Modernization Projects available for official use only. These references and standards are constantly being revised and updated and it is paramount to clarify the version or release that will be utilized for your project and are discussed in much greater detail in a later chapter.

After addressing the exterior components of the security system, the security consultant can now focus on control and detection devices throughout the building (see Figure 5.14). Usually this is accomplished through user group or departmental design sessions to locate the equipment on the most recent floor plans. As simple as this fixture placement review seems, this also requires a lot of coordination with other disciplines. For instance, it is very easy to locate a wedge or dome CCTV camera housing in the center of a hallway ceiling on the plans; the hard part is making sure that there is not a fire protection sprinkler head or exit sign or structural beam right in front of the camera's field of view.

The security consultant and contractors must be able to understand the dropped ceiling plan of the architects or interior designers to spot conflicts. The same is true with locating door control devices. Understanding the code requirements and coordinating with the architect and hardware consultant is both difficult and time consuming, but it ensures that keying schedules, finish schedules, and operating parameters for the system integration are correct. In order to have the equipment layout complete, enlarged details of our command center, screening areas, loading dock and any other areas are developed along with system riser diagrams indicating the interconnection and interrelation of all of the security devices. Equipment schedules will be developed for each device

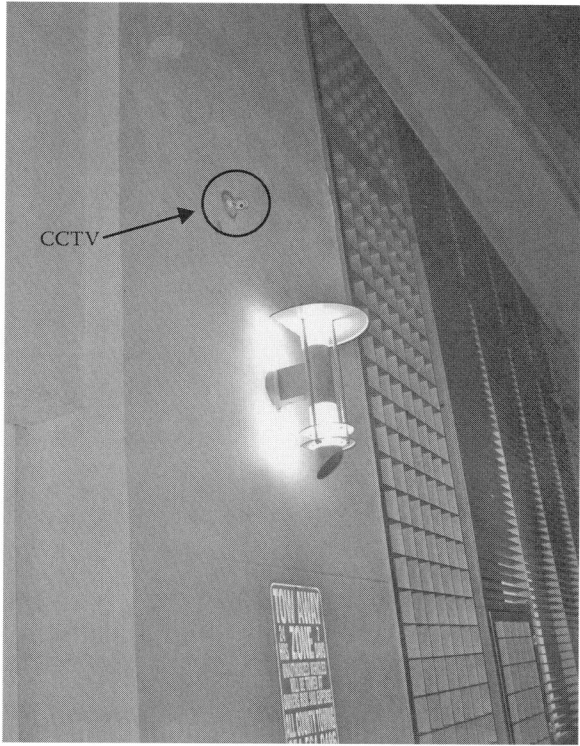

FIGURE 5.15   The current generation of CCTV cameras are so small that they are almost invisible within the context of the architecture.

indicating types, color, manufacturer, operational sequences, and installation details indicating the requirements for constructability.

A WELL THOUGHT-OUT SECURITY SYSTEM

Once the drawings are complete, the systems designer develops the written specifications. Specifications are either technical or performance based. The security designers need to make sure that if they specify a piece of equipment, they also specify required programming or integration that goes along with it (see Figure 5.15). The contractor may only be obligated to bring the equipment to site, set it in place, and turn it on. It may not be his responsibility to verify that the equipment works with all the other equipment and systems.

SUMMARY

A successful project is like listening to an orchestra play; as long as everyone is playing the same piece of music and keeping time, it's enjoyable. But if each musician is playing a different score and refuses to follow the conductor, the audience will be in for a long evening of painful and uncoordinated noise. Security system design has evolved to a point where it requires its own specialists, including electronics experts. The electrical engineer is not typically trained in the areas of security and system design. This is similar to the example of dentists who no longer clean teeth; they have oral hygienists do that, and do a better job of it. The same can be said for security systems design. By having an electronics specialist do the design and specifications and coordinate with the others from the very beginning of the design process, the architect and design team will easily be able to integrate the security consultant's fixtures and furnishings. Using the CPTED methodology to determine the appropriate mechanical response to the infrastructure needs assures the client of getting a well thought-out functional security system that can respond to the threat, risk, and vulnerability analysis.

REFERENCES

FEMA 426 Reference Manual to Mitigate Potential Terrorists Attacks Against Buildingsh, 2003.
FEMA 427 Primer for Design of Commercial Buildings to Mitigate Terrorist Attacks, 2003.
FEMA E155 Building Design for Homeland Security, 2004.
Vulnerability Assessment of Federal Facilities. U.S. Department of Justice. June 28, 1995.
GSA Security Criteria. General Services Administration, Chapter 8, PBS-PQ-100.1, 2001.
Interagency Security Committee (ISC) Security Design Criteria for New Federal Office Buildings and modernization Projects. September 29, 2004.
Unified Facilities Criteria (UFC) DoD Minimum Antiterrorism Standards for Buildings. October 8, 2003.
Unified Facilities Criteria (UFC) DoD Minimum Antiterrorism Standoff Distances for Buildings. October 8, 2003.

6 Understanding CPTED and Situational Crime Prevention***

Severin Sorensen, John G. Hayes, and Randy Atlas

Crime Prevention Through Environmental Design (CPTED) is an environmental criminology theory based on the proposition that the appropriate design and application of the built and surrounding environment can improve the quality of life by deterring crime and reducing the fear of crime. Security and crime prevention practitioners should have a thorough understanding of CPTED theory, concepts, and applications in order to work more effectively with local crime prevention officers, security professionals, building design authorities, architects and design professionals, and others when designing new or renovating existing buildings.

This chapter is intended to provide the reader with the basic information required to understand and apply the theory and concepts of CPTED. We do not expect to make the reader an instant expert on crime; few people have a clear understanding about the true nature of crime and criminal behavior. However, CPTED is based on common sense and a heightened sense of awareness of how people are using a given space for legitimate and illegitimate criminal purposes.

IN THE BEGINNING

For centuries, historians and researchers have studied the relationship between the environment and behavior. CPTED draws from a multidisciplinary base of knowledge to create its own theoretical framework including the fields of architecture, urban design and planning, landscape architecture, sociology, psychology, anthropology, geography, human ecology, criminology and criminal justice.

The first widely published studies of crime and the environment were done by a group of University of Chicago sociologists (Park, Burgess, Shaw, and McKay). The researchers viewed the social disorganization or lack of community control found in specific inner-city districts as generating high crime rates, which decreased in concentric circles away from the central business district. In making this case, the University of Chicago sociologists rejected the tenets of early criminological theory that had focused on the characteristics of individuals as causal agents in crime.

After the early works of Burgess, Park, Shaw, and McKay, urban planner Jane Jacobs (1961) developed the "eyes on the street" theory. Using personal observation and anecdote, Jacobs suggested that residential crime could be reduced by orienting buildings toward the street, clearly distinguishing public and private domains and placing outdoor spaces in proximity to intensively used

* The authors wish to thank Ellen Walsh, Marina Myhre, and Ronald Clarke, who contributed to the Sorensen et al. (1998) Development of CPTED curriculum for the U.S. Department of Urban Development, which material was used as a resource in the development of this chapter.

** Portions of the text in this chapter consist of articles and other publications previously written by the author including possible portions found in the following Wiley publications: Architectural Graphics Standards, 10th Edition, Ramsey/ Hoke, The American Institute of Architects, John Wiley & Sons, ISBN: 0471348163, ©2000; Security Planning and Design: A Guide for Architects and Building Design Professionals, Demkin, The American Institute of Architects, John Wiley & Sons, ISBN: 0471271567, ©2004. We offer special thanks to the American Institute of Architects and John Wiley & Sons for permission to reproduce common content in this work.

areas. Jacobs's book *The Death and Life of American Cities* gave police and planners the awareness of the value of "eyes on the street" as a crime prevention tool.

CONTEMPORARY CRIMINOLOGICAL THINKING ON CRIME, CRIMINALS, AND POTENTIAL TARGETS

The term "crime prevention through environmental design" first appeared in a 1971 book by criminologist and sociologist C. Ray Jeffrey. Inspired by Jacobs's work (1961), Jeffrey (1971) challenged the old guard of criminology theory to take an interdisciplinary approach to crime prevention. In this work, Jeffrey analyzed the causation of crime from an interdisciplinary approach, drawing from criminal law, sociology, psychology, administration of justice, criminology, penology, and other fields. He also drew from relatively new fields at that time—including systems analysis, decision theory, environmentalism, behaviorism, and several models of crime control.

Although different crimes are affected in different ways by the environment in which they occur, almost every type of "street crime," crimes against persons or property, is influenced in some way by physical design, layout, or by situational factors such as the presence of a victim or target, the lack of guardianship, and the lack of surveillance opportunities. Theories of crime, such as environmental criminology, focus specifically on analyzing the environmental factors that provide opportunities for crime to occur. For this reason, most theories of crime can also be classified as "crime opportunity" theories. Environmental criminology, rational choice, situational crime prevention, routine activity, opportunity model, geography of crime, and hot spots of crime are all examples of criminological theories that explain factors that provide criminal opportunities (Sorensen, 1998).

Studies conducted in the 1970s–1990s (primarily by the National Institute of Justice in the United States) demonstrated that certain environments tended to encourage informal social gatherings and contacts, crime, and raised the fear of crime. These environments include poorly lighted areas, high-rise buildings with inappropriate tenant mix, apartment buildings with large numbers of units that shared one primary entrance, and very heavily trafficked streets. Conversely, researchers found that the presence of community centers and well maintained public parks, and so on, increased social interaction, natural surveillance and other informal social controls, thus reducing both crime and the fear of crime.

According to the ***rational choice*** theory approach, criminal behavior occurs when an offender decides to risk breaking the law after considering personal factors (the need for money, cheap thrills, entertainment, revenge) and situational factors (potential police response, availability of target, lighting, surveillance, access to target, skill and tools needed to commit the crime). Before committing a crime, most criminals (excluding drug-stupid impulse crimes, acts of terrorism, and psychopathic criminals) will evaluate the risks of apprehension, the seriousness of expected punishment, the potential value of gain from the crime, and how pressing is the need for immediate criminal gain.

The decision to commit a specific type of crime is thus a matter of personal decision making based on an evaluation of numerous variables and the information that is available for the decision making process. Burglary studies have shown that burglars forgo a break-in if they perceive that the home is too great a security challenge, that the value or rewards of the goods to be taken are not worth the effort, and the target might be protected by guards, police, capable guardians (grandmothers, doormen, front desk staff, secretaries and receptionists, housekeepers, large dogs). The evidence suggests (Siegal, 1999, p. 104) that the decision to commit crime, regardless of substance, is structured by the choice of:

1. Where the crime occurs
2. The characteristics of the target, and
3. The means and techniques available for the completion of the crime.

In addition to crime prevention theory, security professionals should also understand contemporary criminological views on how criminals pick their targets and how criminal choice is influenced by the *perception of vulnerability* that the target projects.

TARGET SELECTION

Studies of professional and occasional criminals have suggested that they choose their targets with a rational decision making process. Criminals take note of potential targets every day: keys left in cars, open or unlocked residential or commercial establishments, untended homes while on vacation, etc. Studies of burglary (Repetto, 1974; Scarr, 1973) indicate that houses located at the end of cul-de-sacs, surrounded by trees, make very tempting targets. Some research indicates that street criminals use public transportation or walk so it is more likely they will gravitate to the center of a city, particularly areas more familiar to them that also provide potential targets in easily accessible and open areas.

The environment shapes the factors, or cues that contribute to development of criminal opportunities, and to the formation of specific patterns of opportunities (Brantingham, 1991, 1993). Once the patterns of opportunities are created, patterns of crime soon follow. The crime prevention specialist analyzes those opportunities, patterns of opportunities, and patterns of crime to devise and implement appropriate situational and crime specific prevention measures.

The Brantinghams' research hypothesized that criminal choices are influenced by the **perception** of target availability and vulnerability. The Brantinghams posited that individual criminal events must be understood as confluences of offenders, victims, criminal targets, and laws in specific settings at particular times and places. Criminals often choose certain neighborhoods for crimes because they are familiar and well traveled, because they appear more open and vulnerable, and because they offer more potential escape routes. Thus, the more suitable and accessible the target, the more likely the crime will occur.

POTENTIAL OFFENDERS' PERSPECTIVE

Research has shown that the features of the physical environment can influence the opportunity for crime to occur. The physical surroundings clearly influence the potential offenders' perceptions and evaluation of a potential crime site. Part of this evaluation also includes determining the availability and visibility of natural guardians (residents, passers-by, dogs, etc.) at or in close proximity of the site under consideration. Offenders, when deciding whether or not to commit a crime in a location, generally do so after considering the following questions (NIJ Study, 1996), *assuming* a **rational offender** perspective:

- How easy will it be to enter the area?
- How visible, attractive, or vulnerable do the targets appear?
- What are the chances of being seen?
- If seen, will the people in the area do something about it?
- Is there a quick, direct route for leaving the site after the crime is committed?

Thus, the physical features of a site may influence the choices of potential offenders by altering the chances of detection and by reshaping the public verses private space in question. If a potential criminal feels the chances of detection are low, or if a criminal is fairly certain that they will be able to exit without being identified or apprehended, the likelihood of crime increases. In effect, if a location lacks a *natural or capable guardian,* it becomes a more likely target for crime.

CONCEPT OF CAPABLE GUARDIAN

Routine activity theory suggests that the presence of **capable guardians** may deter crime. Criminals will generally avoid targets or victims who are perceived to be armed, capable of resistance, or potentially dangerous. Criminals will generally stay away from areas they feel are aggressively patrolled by police, security guards, by nosy neighbors, or live-in family members like grandparents. Likewise, criminals avoid passive barriers such as alarm systems, fences, locks, barking dogs, or related physical barriers.

This avoidance is intuitively logical to the experienced law enforcement or security practitioner. Criminals will look for the easiest path rather than expose themselves to greater risk, unless they perceive the risk is justified enough to override their perception. The concept of natural surveillance and capable guardians are very powerful tools for reducing the *perceived and actual vulnerability* a site poses to a potential criminal. CPTED strategies employ the concept of capable guardians within the **organizational** (people) classifications of strategies.

CRIMINAL CHOICE

Criminals or potential criminals are conditioned by personal factors (Pezzin, 1995) that may lead them to choose crime. Research also shows that criminals are more likely to desist from crime if they believe:

- Future earnings from criminal activities will be low
- Other attractive but legal income-generating opportunities are available

Agnew (1995) believes people more likely to choose a life of crime over conformity to socially acceptable behavior demonstrate the following personality traits:

- They lack typical social constraints and perceive freedom of movement, even in areas and spaces where they are uninvited or unwelcome
- They have less self-control and do not fear criminal punishment
- They are typically facing a serious personal problem that they feel forces them to choose risky behavior (similar to the classic white collar criminal)

At any given time, there are individuals who are capable of criminal behavior, and will take advantage of vulnerable targets, whether they are people, buildings or other facilities, and that the perception of vulnerability drives the criminal choice, in terms of which actual target they attack.

CPTED AS DEFENSIBLE SPACE

Oscar Newman published his study of CPTED in residential areas (1971, 1973) and how the architecture contributes to victimization by criminals in his work *Defensible Space, Crime Prevention through Urban Design*. In this work, Newman explored the concepts of human territoriality, natural surveillance, and the modification of existing structures to effectively reduce crime. Newman argued that physical construction of residential environment could elicit from residents a behavior that contributes in a major way towards insuring their security. The form of buildings and their groupings enable inhabitants to undertake a significant self-policing function. The primary function of defensible space is to release latent attitudes in the tenants, which allow them to assume behavior necessary to the protection of their rights and property. Defensible space is a surrogate term for the range of mechanisms, real and symbolic barriers, strongly defined areas of influence, and improved opportunities for surveillance that combine to bring the environment under the control of its residents. Newman's work became the foundation for what we know today as Crime Prevention through Environmental Design (CPTED).

Oscar Newman (1971, 1973) coined the term "Defensible Space" as he studied the relationship between particular design features and crime that occurred in public housing developments in New York. The four components of Newman's study were:

- Defining perceived zones of territorial influence
- Providing surveillance opportunities for residents and their guests
- Placing residential structures (public areas and entries) close to safe areas
- Designing sites and buildings so those occupants are not perceived and stigmatized as vulnerable

Those sites and buildings that were perceived as most vulnerable and isolated had similar characteristics:

- Unassigned open spaces that were unprotected, uncared for, and provide opportunities for residents and outsiders to engage in illegitimate activities
- An unlimited number of opportunities to penetrate the site with uncontrolled access—the multitude of entry points provided offenders with easy entry and numerous escape routes
- The lack of territoriality and boundary definition that discouraged the legitimate residents from claiming space and taking control of the site—residents were often unable to recognize strangers from legitimate users
- Lack of opportunities for natural surveillance and supervision
- Design conflicts between the incompatible uses and users—incompatible activities are located next to one another

Defensible space is divided into four levels of territoriality: *Public*, *Semipublic*, *Semiprivate*, and *Private*. *Public* areas are typically the least defensible. A car driving on a public street would not automatically arouse suspicion. If the street were a cu-de-sac, however, this is a *semipublic* area. If there were only five homes in the circle, the driver would be expected to stop at one of the five homes or leave. *Semiprivate* areas might include sidewalks or common areas around residential areas. Although most people may not confront a stranger in a common area, they are likely to call the police if the person does not appear to belong there. *Private* areas are different in rental communities than in single-family home neighborhoods. In a typical apartment complex, the private area may not begin until you actually enter into the unit. This is especially true if several units share a common balcony or stairways. In a single-family home neighborhood, owners may consider their front yard to be a private, or defensible space (see Figure 6.1).

There are many ways to establish defensible space. By planting low-growing hedges or bushes, the property manager can show a defined property line. By posting signs and stating ground rules such as "No Trespassing" or "No Soliciting," the owner has established the area as defensible space and removed the excuse for noncompliance or criminal behavior.

Newman used his theory to modify housing developments by implementing some of the most basic elements of CPTED design: high fences, designated paths, architectural treatment to distinguish private, semiprivate, semipublic, and public spaces, and improved lighting. Defensible space design should link territoriality and surveillance by creating designs where the observer feels the area under surveillance is under their sphere of influence, and part of their responsibility to actively prevent crime. The environment of the building should be designed so that the observer can recognize or identify the victim or target as part of their property and the observer has a vested interest to intervene and prevent the crime from occurring. Increased legitimate traffic of people and vehicles are positive experiences that are characteristic of a safe place. People who live, work, and play in an area will tend to feel a certain ownership and responsibility, and will try to protect an area (see Figure 6.2). Proximity to areas with high volume of legitimate usage encourages the same sense of territoriality, responsibility, and effective surveillance.

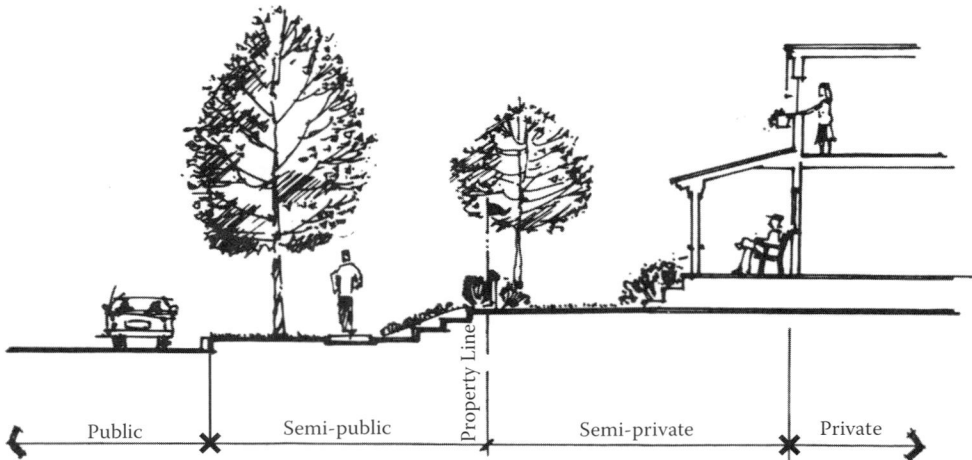

FIGURE 6.1 Section showing the territorial layering from street to the residence, public to private space. (Reprinted with permission and courtesy of the City of Vancouver Planning Department, Vancouver, BC, Canada.)

Newman's work came under criticism for methodological weakness, and academicians viewed his work as architecturally deterministic (Atlas, 1983). Architecture does not force people to engage in certain behaviors, but the environment and social controls can exert a strong influence on how people respond to their spaces. Not everyone in a slum is a criminal, and not everyone in an upper-class gated community is an outstanding citizen. Part of the problem of the Defensible Space theory was the assumption that the illegitimate users or criminals could be easily identified by the legitimate residents, but the reality was that the residents were often unwilling or unable to determine who belonged on the property, because of the high turnover in residents, and the additional challenge that many of the criminals were often residents, or their neighbors' children (Merry, 1981). Subsequent CPTED demonstration projects in the 1970s by the Westinghouse Corporation were generally unsuccessful as they attempted to extend the defensible space concept to school, commercial, residential, and transportation environments where territorial behavior is much less natural than in the multifamily residential context.

FIGURE 6.2 Defensible space used in residential townhouses on a Riverwalk in Chicago.

As the defensible space theory and CPTED swept the nation's law enforcement (Cisneros, 1996) and architectural communities, the National Crime Prevention Institute (NCPI) was established as a Division of the School of Police Administration at the University of Louisville in 1971. By 2006, the NCPI had trained over 40,000 police officers, criminal justice planners, local government officials, private security representatives, and individuals representing numerous other organizations. Today, law enforcement directed crime prevention programs exist at every level of government in the United States and Canada, largely modeled after the approach developed and institutionalized by police in Great Britain. Many believe the work of the NCPI, now reorganized as the Institute of Public Security and Community Safety, and related organizations have significantly reduced crime in North America and raised awareness to crime prevention by the public-at-large by basing their training on the principles and practices of Defensible Space and CPTED.

BASIC CRIME PREVENTION ASSUMPTIONS

The need for CPTED in the design and planning process is based on the belief that crime and loss prevention are inherent to human functions and activities, not just something that police or security people do. What we do right or wrong with our human and physical resources produces a lasting legacy. Once the building concrete, brick, mortar, and glass is set, it becomes infinitely more difficult and expensive to make structural changes that would allow security to be designed into the building and site.

CPTED is a specialized field of study focusing on:

1. *Physical environments* such as a building park office space, apartment, and so on. The physical environment can be manipulated to produce behavioral effects that will reduce the fear and incidence of certain types of criminal acts.
2. *Behavior of people* in relationship to their physical environment. Some locations seem to create, promote, or allow criminal activity, incivilities or unruly behavior, whereas other environments elicit compliant and law-abiding conduct.
3. *Redesigning or using existing space more effectively* to encourage desirable behaviors and discourage crime and related undesirable conduct. It is through the insight and framework of CPTED, which serves to develop and ensure a better-designed and used environment. CPTED practice suggests that crime and loss are by-products of human functions that are not working properly.

Since the 1970s, CPTED has been attributed to the concept that the proper design and effective use of the built environment can lead to a reduction in the fear and incidence of crime (predatory stranger-to-stranger type), as well as an improvement of the quality of life (Crowe, 1991, with expansion of basic CPTED definition by Atlas, 1991).

Tim Crowe (1991) refined the ideas of Oscar Newman, and with his experience in the Westinghouse CPTED project from the 1970s, he established a system to categorize CPTED solutions. Crowe organized this multidisciplinary CPTED methodology (see Figure 6.3) to match the function of the crime area, similar to Newman's layering of space from private to public spaces.

FIGURE 6.3 CPTED interrelationships.

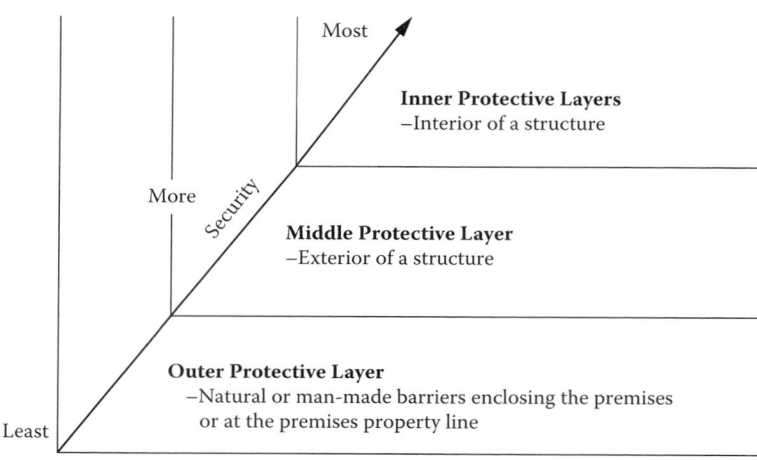

FIGURE 6.4   Security zoning.

Crowe suggested that CPTED involves the design of physical space in the context of the needs of the legitimate users of the space, the normal and expected (or intended) use of the space and the predictable behavior of both the legitimate users and offenders. In this regard, the proper function must not only match a space that can support it, but the design must assure that the intended behavior has the opportunity to function well and support the control of behavior.

In general, Crowe (1991) suggests that there are three basic ***classifications*** to crime prevention through environmental design measures:

1. ***Mechanical measures***—also referred to as target hardening, this approach emphasizes hardware and technology systems such as, locks, and security screens, windows, fencing and gating, key control systems, access control systems, closed circuit television (CCTV), and similar physical barriers. Mechanical measures must not be relied on solely to create a secure environment but, rather, be used in context with people and design strategies.
2. ***Organizational or Human Measures***—focus on teaching individuals and vested groups steps they can take to protect themselves, or the space they occupy, at home or work. Organizational methods of CPTED include block watches, neighborhood watch, security patrols, police officer patrols, concierge stations, designated or capable guardians, and other strategies using people as the basis of security with the ability to observe, report, and intervene.
3. *Natural Measures*—Designing space to ensure the overall environment works more effectively for the intended users, while at the same time deterring crime. Natural methods of CPTED use good space planning and architecture to reduce user and use conflicts by planning compatible circulation patterns. An example of natural design is the use of **security zoning**. By dividing space into zones of differing security levels (see Figure 6.4), such as unrestricted, controlled, and restricted, sensitive areas can be more effectively protected. The focus of access control strategies is to deny access to a crime target and create in offenders, a perception of risk and detection, delay, and response.

Within these three CPTED classifications, there are several key concepts that allow CPTED to be implemented according to Crowe: Natural Access Control, Natural Surveillance, and Territoriality.

Natural Access Control

This is intended to deny access to crime targets and to create a perception of risks to offenders. Natural methods of access control make use of spatial definition and circulation patterns. Access control is a design concept directed at reducing the ease of opportunity for crime. Because many criminals look for an easy escape, limiting area access is an effective way to deter criminal activity. Access control includes creating a sense of turf, but it focuses on entry and exit points into buildings, parks, parking lots, and neighborhoods. Closing some entryways and opening others in strategic locations is one way of doing this. Access control can be demonstrated by having one way into and out of a location, with devices such as a security post or the use of mechanical gates. Others who use "alternative methods" to enter an area look suspicious, stand out, risk detection and identification which increase the risk of apprehension. It is important to assess how the intended users are entering the property, so CPTED practitioners will often look at mobility paths, footprints in the dirt and gravel, and wear patterns in the grassy areas.

MECHANICAL ACCESS CONTROL

This includes the use of security gates, which have proven very effective at reducing auto thefts, burglaries, and drive-by shootings. Most perpetrators of these crimes do not want to exit the way they entered, as it gives witnesses the opportunity to record license plates and get better suspect information. Sometimes simply locking one door, opening another, and notifying residents of the change can accomplish access control. In libraries and shopping mall stores, patrons are channeled past an attendant who can observe all those who enter and exit. Sometimes these places are equipped with electronic point-of-sales screening devices, but often by merely having the access point controlled can be enough. Another example may be to try to deter burglars from entering lower story windows by choices made in planting a row of dense, thorny bushes near the windows in addition to locking devices and possibly an alarm system based on the risks associated with that particular facility.

Employing barriers such as doors, fences, shrubbery, and other man-made and natural obstacles can limit access to a building, or other defined space. Windows may have protective glazing that withstands blows without breaking. Door and window hardware may have special material and mountings which make them hard to remove or tamper resistant. Walls, floors, or doors may be specially reinforced in high security areas with materials that are difficult to penetrate (see Figure 6.5). To keep trespassers from climbing over walls for instance, property management could plant a hearty cactus in the area where it will be highly visible. The use of dirt berms or large rocks can also keep unwanted visitors from entering private property with a vehicle.

Oscar Newman felt that apartments should channel residents through one or two common entrances, so that they get to know each other and so that access is controlled. That way, intruders can more easily be identified. The same concept applies to residential neighborhoods where gates and street closing can similarly achieve control goals.

ORGANIZED ACCESS CONTROL

This entails the use of patrol or courtesy personnel to control who enters the property. Distribution of parking permits affixed to registered vehicles will identify which vehicles belong to the residents and which ones are not. Enforcement of visitor parking and towing abandoned vehicles from lots and streets improves the image and milieu of being an environment not supporting criminal activity.

NATURAL SURVEILLANCE

This consists of increasing visibility within and around a facility by encouraging its legitimate occupants and casual observers (police, others) to increase the observation, detection, and reporting of trespassers or misconduct. Surveillance strategies are directed at keeping intruders under observation and undesirable behavior under control. Placing eyes on the street from the windows and balconies of the neighborhood was an idea that Jane Jacobs discovered during her work in New York's Greenwich Village (Jacobs, 1961). Placing legitimate eyes, or capable guardians, on the street can help to make a place unattractive to offenders; thus, preventing the street from becoming

FIGURE 6.5 Hurricane-rated laminated glass provides a security barrier to burglary attempts as well, as this example of an attempted break-in at a county office building demonstrates. The exterior layer of glass broke from the attack, but the interlayer held the glass laminates together and deterred repeated attacks. The glass is intended to stop a 2 × 4 piece of wood from penetrating at 110 mph.

a preference for them to commit crime. This can be accomplished by the proper placement of windows, adequate lighting, and removing obstructions to enhance sightlines, including softening "hard corners" to increase visibility and standoff distance.

Surveillance is the ability to look into an area, and the ability to look back out. It can be formal or informal. Things that inhibit surveillance are overgrown trees and shrubs, structural elements, block walls and poor lighting. Natural surveillance is when good visual connection and observation is naturally occurring. As people are moving around an area, they will be able to observe what is going on around them, provided the area is open and well lit. Other ways to achieve natural surveillance include careful landscaping and planting design, and placing high-risk targets in plain view of nearby residents, such as expensive cameras or display items near a sales clerk.

Organized surveillance includes security patrols and other people or capable guardians who are organized to watch a targeted area. Although this is the most effective deterrent to crime, it is also the least cost effective. Whereas it may be necessary to employ security patrols or off-duty police, once the patrols are discontinued, there is generally nothing left to show for your investment. By far, the most preferable method of surveillance is natural surveillance through good design.

When surveillance cannot be achieved through natural means, sometimes using mechanical or electronic means, such as using close circuit television can be used. Mechanical surveillance

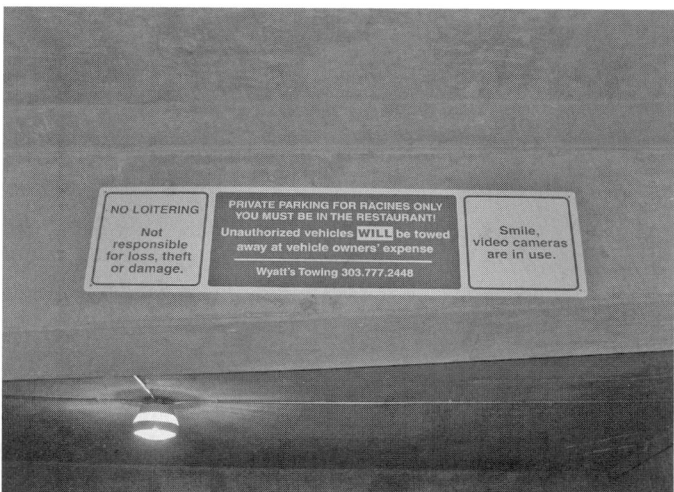

FIGURE 6.6 Signage in a parking garage advising users they are being videotaped.

employs the use of cameras, mirrors, and other equipment that allows an individual to monitor an area remotely. Once the equipment is purchased, maintenance of these devices is a long-term renewed cost in addition to the organized cost of supervision. The design of CCTV surveillance systems is an important contributor to their efficacy. Some systems record only the continuous flow of time, while others are alarmed by an event or motion. Modern systems might use other sensors tied to the surveillance system. Regardless, effective remote monitoring requires that you answer the questions of who is watching the camera monitors, and how are they responding when there is an incident? How will the CCTV systems be maintained? CCTV is best utilized for extraordinary behavior, not ordinary behavior that is often overlooked (see Figure 6.6). New technologies are allowing critical incidents to be observed, recorded digitally, and activate an appropriate response by police, guards, or management.

Any architectural design that enhances the chance that a potential offender will be, or might be, seen is a positive measure for surveillance. Often, it is not just the fact that the offender might be seen that matters. It is that the offender "thinks" or perceives they will be seen and identified that can help deter the opportunity for crime.

Natural Territorial Reinforcement/Boundary Definition

This is about establishing a sense of ownership by property owners or building occupants to increase vigilance in identifying trespassers and sending the message that a would-be-offender will be identified and challenged. Territorial reinforcement strategies involve creating or extending the sphere of influence of legitimate users so that users develop a sense of proprietorship. This sense of territorial influence can alert potential offenders that they don't belong there, that they are at risk of being seen and identified, and that their behavior will not be tolerated or go unreported.

Natural access control and surveillance contribute to a sense of *territoriality*, boosting security by encouraging users to protect their turf. Organized *territorial* strategies typically include people efforts like neighborhood crime watches, receptionists, and guard stations. Mechanical *territorial* strategies can be perimeter-sensing fence systems, interior motion sensors. Natural *territorial* strategies include use of fences, walls, and landscaping such as berms.

One example of territoriality strategy would be the use of small edging shrubbery along a sidewalk in an apartment intended for clearly marking the territory of individual apartments and potentially discouraging trespasser from cutting through the area. In addition, the theory holds that people will definitely pay more attention to and defend a particular space or territory from trespass

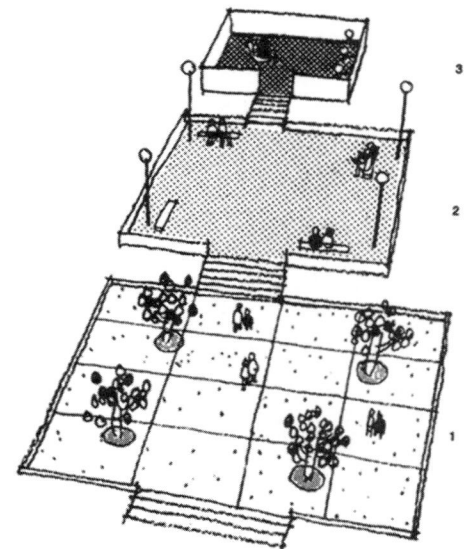

FIGURE 6.7   Hierarchy of space from public plazas to private space of residences.

if they feel a form of "psychological ownership" in the area. Thus, it is possible, through real or symbolic boundary definition that the legitimate residents are responsible for a property, and it is likely that they will tend to defend this property from incursion.

Defining who uses a territory or a place is a major aspect of reducing opportunities for crime. The goal is to turn a particular area over to legitimate users of that environment so that they will be more likely to adopt ownership over that defined place. This will make it less likely that people who do not belong in the space will be at risk to commit criminal or nuisance behavior at a high-risk location. The CPTED concept of Territoriality is similar to Oscar Newman's Defensible Space, the reassigning of physical areas so local people can be responsible for, and control, their own public environment. Although this does not automatically oust criminals, it can render them less effective.

Territoriality can be accomplished by using a hierarchy of space as defined in the Defensible Space theory, such as subdividing public spaces into semi-public and semi-private spaces (see Figure 6.7). For example, a Starbuck's coffee shop (see Figure 6.8), which places chairs and tables onto the sidewalk directly in front of their store,

FIGURE 6.8   Starbuck's store adds defensible space to this apartment building.

FIGURE 6.9   Territoriality example with symbolic barriers (fencing), porches, and level changes to channel persons around and into the main entrance of the property.

tends to reassign this public space as part of Starbuck's territory. This can help deter loiterers from hanging in front of the store.

Similarly, symbolic property makers in the front yard of residential homes or apartment buildings, such as short fences, hedges and plantings (see Figure 6.9), pavement stones, and front yard lighting, can demarcate the front area as belonging to residents of the building. This can make residents feel safer when entering or exiting their building; it can contribute to fewer burglaries, and it can reduce the opportunity for other crimes there.

Good territoriality demonstrates a sense of "ownership," alerting potential offenders that they don't belong there and they will be seen and reported, because undesirable behavior will not be tolerated (see Figure 6.10).

Crowe acknowledged that crime prevention though environmental design solutions should be integrated with the function of the buildings, or at least the location where they are being implemented. In the CPTED approach, a design is proper if it recognizes the designated use of the space; defines the crime problem incidental to, and the solution compatible with the designated use; and incorporates the appropriate crime prevention strategy that enhances the effective use of the space.

EXPANSION OF BASIC CPTED

In addition to the three basic classifications mentioned earlier, current CPTED practitioners and security planners also consider the following concepts.

MANAGEMENT AND MAINTENANCE

In order for spaces to look well cared for and crime free, they must be maintained to the standard of care that would be appropriate for that building type or use. The "Broken Window" theory (Wilson, 1982) suggests that an abandoned building or car can remain unmolested indefinitely, but once the first window is broken the building or car is quickly vandalized. Maintenance and the care of a building and its physical elements such as lighting, paint, signage, fencing, walkways, and repair of broken items is critical for advertising to the criminal element that someone cares and is responsible for the upkeep. Management of properties is essential to ensure maintenance is kept

FIGURE 6.10 Security layering and boundary definition in a private home.

up to the standards of care. If a rental property is well maintained (see Figure 6.11), it shows that management, or the owner, cares for and will defend the property against crime and incivilities, in order to keep the value of the property as high as possible. A property that is not maintained may indicate that the management is not concerned about the property, and might overlook or ignore criminal activity.

Property management can be the building owners, or assigned to outside contract or property managers. Some residential multifamily housing have live-in resident managers. A manager who lives on the property will get to know the problems both inside and outside intimately. Management policy and procedures create the impetus: to hire security patrols, have electricity bills paid on time so the lights will turn on, hire the trash removal company to pick up garbage from dumpsters, and pay a gardener to mow the grass and trim the overgrown landscaping. Management is a critical step in crime prevention because they have the ability for screening of tenants, the wording and enforcement of lease agreements that include a zero tolerance drug and crime policy, the hiring of staff, and the repair of broken items.

Crime often congregates in areas where there are dilapidated and abandoned buildings, in places where litter and graffiti are rampant, and where the area looks as though no one cares. Furthermore, if the property has several city code infractions, a property manager may lose the ability to deal effectively with criminal activity. For example, a manager attempting to evict a troublesome tenant might find that person who is facing eviction may threaten to report the infractions to the city if the manager proceeds with the eviction process. In this case the manager may be forced to look the other way. If the property had been maintained in a clean fashion there would be nothing to hold

FIGURE 6.11   Maintenance is critical for setting a standard of care of expected behaviors and intolerance for litter and vandalism.

against management. More important, the property would be more likely to attract legitimate users in the first place.

Management and maintenance go hand in hand. A property can be an award winning design, but if no one is there to make sure that the property is maintained, bills get paid, residents/tenants get screened, illegally parked cars get towed, bad tenants evicted, and the lights get turned on, then the property will quickly fall into disrepair and start attracting criminal behavior.

LEGITIMATE ACTIVITY SUPPORT

This involves the appropriate use of building functional spaces, such as recreational facilities and common areas. Activity support fills the area with legitimate users so that any abusers will leave. It may be difficult to believe that filling an area with legitimate users will cause the deviant user or abusers to leave, but the opposite is also true. If you fill an area with deviant users, the legitimate users will withdraw. To promote activity support utilizes the common areas effectively. By incorporating seating areas, picnic areas, porches, and other amenities into open areas the legitimate users will participate in the normal day-to-day functions and maintain ownership of the property. A crime prevention program will only be effective if the residents engage in the defined, designated, and designed (*3-D Concept*) legitimate activities that were intended by the architecture and function of the space or building. Drug and criminal activity thrive in undesignated spaces because the residents and management do not claim the space, nor provide legitimate activities to undermine or replace the criminal activities.

Examples of user and use conflicts are placing senior centers near taverns and pubs, or next to elementary schools. Placing a school near an industrial complex, and having adult video stores and pawnshops near day care facilities are also incompatible land uses. The solution to some of these problems is not only mixed use but also the careful consideration of compatible land uses that minimize potential conflicts between user groups. At the level of urban planning, zoning regulations are typically the tool that creates compatible land use.

FIGURE 6.12 Park benches in park can attract legitimate and illegitimate activity. Because the bench was designed without intermediate railings, it facilitated homeless users making the bench their bedroom.

The CPTED practitioner will ask the questions if a land feature or physical structure is not being used as it was intended. Does the intended design fit the designated use, and if not, what is causing the problem? Who are the intended users? Why are the legitimate users not using an area? Why are the criminals frequenting an area? Why is it inviting to the undesirable users? What will discourage them?

Activity support means that in urban parks you might schedule community barbecues and sports activities to reinforce legitimate uses of the park (see Figure 6.12). This can be the case with gazebos in the neighborhood parks, which can be places where drugs are sold. Scheduling legitimate activities in the gazebo can prevent this unwanted drug or gang behavior from happening.

Activity generators are land uses or urban features that create plenty of local activity. They are neither positive nor negative, but they can generate opportunities for crime if they are poorly planned or operated. For example, telephone booths and automatic bank machines are often included in strip malls. Depending on where they are placed, and when they are used, these activity generators can cause problems (see Figure 6.13). Drug dealers might use the phones for drug sales; the ATM may be the site of robberies. Farmers markets are set up on weekends in otherwise deserted downtowns or industrial areas that draw many legitimate users and business enterprises.

Activity generators are considered large scale since they do not operate in isolation of the surrounding land uses (see Figure 6.14). It is insufficient to place housing to encourage activities in a commercial area, if the housing is isolated into small pockets, without local amenities, and lack sufficient services. People will not place their eyes on the commercial street if they have no reason to look outside. By contrast, some kinds of activities such as hot dog or flower vendors can provide legitimate uses and surveillance in certain areas, such as, parking lots of football stadiums, thereby placing more eyes into the parking lot to deter theft from cars or witness assaults on patrons.

DISPLACEMENT

Displacement was cited as one of the biggest problems with CPTED initially. Simply moving crime from one place to another offers no real solution to neighborhood problems. However, in the past decade research has shown that displacement is not as damaging as previously thought (Saville,

FIGURE 6.13 Illegitimate users attracted to unsupervised area.

2004). In fact, five different forms of displacement have been discovered and any one of them can be either positive or negative, depending on how they are used.

The five forms of displacement are:

1. Place Displacement: a problem is moved from one place to another.
2. Time Displacement: a problem is moved from one time to another.
3. Target Displacement: the offender changes the target, while keeping the time and place the same, such as robbing drug dealers versus robbing seniors out for a walk.
4. Method Displacement: the offender changes the method by which the problem is caused, such as displacing gun robberies to strong-arm robberies.
5. Offense Displacement: an offense changes from one type (robbery) or another (burglary).

FIGURE 6.14 Positive activity generators, Main Street, USA.

An example of positive displacement would be displacing teens out of a schoolyard where vandalism is occurring, over to a nearby recreation center where programs are established for them and the kids are supervised. If displacement is controlled, it can be the CPTED practitioner's best tool.

The displacement of crime serves as a powerful crime prevention tool because it disrupts the flow and location of the criminal business enterprise. Patrons buying drugs know to go to certain people at certain locations. Signals, cues, and signs are used to advertise that drugs or criminal activity are available. With the continual shifting of drugs and crime, they are never able to root long enough to take over an area. Thus, crime displacement is an effective tool to disrupt the availability of crime activity by moving it to the next house, the next neighborhood, the next city. The continual movement weakens the sustainability of the criminal behavior.

AVOIDING CONFLICTING USER GROUPS AND INCOMPATIBLE LAND USES

Separating land uses is one of the most common urban planning principles used today. This is useful for environmental reasons, but it can have some negative public safety impacts. For example, although placing light warehousing in isolated industrial parks is useful to keep residential land uses more livable, it leaves the warehouses vulnerable to unobserved nighttime burglaries. Therefore, target hardening security and patrols become necessary.

Additionally, it is difficult to create a sense of community when people use a neighborhood for only one single thing. For this reason, some modern planning practices have returned to the concept of the mixed-use neighborhood, as Jacobs recommends with the eyes on the street. It is also a component of a current urban planning philosophy called New Urbanism (Plater and Zyberk, 2000; Calthorpe, 1993).

By gaining an understanding of the key concepts of natural access control, natural surveillance, territorial reinforcement, management and maintenance functions, legitimate activity support, displacement, and avoiding conflict of uses, it is possible to put theory into action and use CPTED to address community disorder, workplace violence, street crime, or acts of terrorism. It is the application of these concepts that differentiates CPTED from other traditional target hardening and fortressing techniques. CPTED does this by exploring opportunities, or by allowing the many CPTED concepts into initial consideration of the space configuration and circulation patterns of the building or site. In many instances the use of target hardening without consideration for the built environment has created a fortress effect leaving residents and legitimate users of a place to feel unsafe and isolated. The target hardening approach by itself is usually not architecturally aesthetically pleasing, and often results in opposition by architects and others involved in site and design planning matters.

BEYOND THE 3-D CONCEPT

The CPTED approach recognizes the building environments' designated or redesignated use. This is a practice that is different from the traditional target hardening approach to crime prevention. Traditional target hardening, or fortressing, focuses predominately on denying access to a crime target through physical or artificial barrier techniques such as locks, alarms, fences, and gates. The traditional approach tends to overlook opportunities for natural access control and surveillance. Sometimes the natural and normal uses of the environment can accomplish the same effects of mechanical hardening and surveillance. CPTED involves the design of physical space, the normal and expected use of that space and the predictable behavior of the appropriate users of the area as well as potential offenders of that space. Environmental security design or CPTED is based on three primary functions of human space:

Designation—What is the purpose or intention of the space?

Definition—How is the space defined? What are the social, cultural, legal, and psychological ways the space is defined?

Design—Is the space defined to support the prescribed or intended behaviors?

The following questions provide an evaluation of the purpose of the space definition in terms of management and identity, and its design as it relates to the desired function and behavior management, sometimes referred to as the ***three D's*** (Crowe, 1991, 2000), but expanded here to include other aspects as well (Atlas, 1996):

3-Ds Plus

Designation

- What is the designated purpose of this space?
- For what purpose was it originally intended?
- How well does the space support its current use or its intended use?
- Is there a conflict? If so, how and where?

Definition

- How is the space defined?
- Is the ownership of the space clear?
- Where are the boarders of the space?
- Are there social or cultural definitions that affect how the space is being, or will be used?
- Are the legal/administrative rules clearly established in policy and effectively enforced?
- Are signs present indicating the proper use of the space or defining limits of access?
- Are there any conflicts or confusion between purpose and definition of the space?

Design

- How well does the physical design support the intended function?
- How well does the physical design support the desired or accepted behaviors?
- Does the physical design conflict with or impede the productive use of the space or proper functioning of the intended human activity?
- Is there any confusion or conflict in which physical design is intended to control or modify behaviors?

In addition to the CPTED classic 3 Ds, there are other "Ds" that take us beyond the basics. The other "Ds" may apply:

Deterrence

- Does the presence of security personnel deter illegitimate activity and promote intended behavior?
- Does the physical design and layout permit good surveillance and control of access to and from the property?
- Does the presence of intended behavior deter or discourage illegal or illegitimate activities?

Detect

- Is there the ability to control entry onto the property or building?
- Is there an assessment process of when an intrusion is legitimate or illegitimate?

- Is the detection of intrusions accomplished by the physical design, mechanical technology systems, or operational manpower?
- Is there communication of an intrusion to some person or agency responsible for responding?

Delay

- Are there passive barriers?
- Are there active barriers?
- Are there guards or designated responders?
- How much delay time is needed for the property to detect and respond?

Response

- What are the role and the post orders of the responder guard?
- What equipment is needed to support a complete response?
- What are the tactics used to respond quickly and clearly?
- What training is given to respond to the appropriate level of threat?

Report

- What is the communications network to document intrusions or call for further assistance?
- What is the written protocol for incident reports?
- How is the documentation organized and stored?
- Is the information in sufficient detail and clear?

Discriminate

- Is there training for staff to discriminate or distinguish legitimate from illegitimate users or threats?
- Is the equipment sufficiently sensitive to distinguish false from real threats?

Neutralize

- Has the threat been sufficiently deterred?
- Has the system been reset and tested to prevent complacency or false alarms?
- Have the criminals, attackers, or threats been controlled, law enforcement contacted, and the scene resecured?
- In the event of fire, smoke, or flood—has the threat been neutralized and damage assessed, and the scene secured to prevent contamination or pilferage?

All of these steps must be addressed for a comprehensive approach to provide security and prevent crime. If a conflict or unanswered question is revealed after using the questions above to assess a physical space, then that indicates a modification should take place. A vulnerable area could be an indication that the space is poorly defined or not properly designated to support or control the intended function, thus increasing the likelihood that crime or the fear of crime may develop. Thus, the challenge is to develop an Automatic Teller Machine (ATM) location in a shopping mall location to ensure it is not only functional but also maximizes the personal safety of legitimate users.

Once these questions have been answered the space is assessed according to how well it supports *natural access control, natural surveillance,* and *territoriality.* These questions are intended to ensure that there are no conflicts between the intended space activity and expected behaviors. For example, if an access control system is difficult to use or experiences frequent outages, employees will often prop doors open to make their routine travel more convenient. In addition to choosing a poor access control system, the original designers also failed to educate users on the importance of maintaining the integrity of the security system.

CPTED'S INFLUENCE ON SITUATIONAL CRIME PREVENTION

Situational crime prevention was developed in the late 1970s and early 1980s in Great Britain. Although it was influenced by Jeffrey's work in CPTED and Newman's work in Defensible Space, new research only contributed to the expansion of situational crime prevention, not to its initial inception. CPTED and the Defensible Space theory were more focused on the design of buildings and places, whereas situational crime prevention sought out to reduce crime opportunities in all behavioral contexts.

Situational prevention is comprised of opportunity-reducing measures that are directed at very specific forms of crime. It is involved in the management, design, or manipulation of the immediate environment in as systematic and permanent way as possible so to increase the effort and risks of crime and reduce the rewards as perceived by a wide range of offenders.

Research caused a shift in the focus of practical crime control policy from attention on the offender and his or her personality or background, to the general influences of the surrounding environment that contribute to criminal behavior by creating opportunities that may not otherwise exist. Clarke (1992) contributed to practical situational crime prevention by developing crime prevention techniques that can generally be applied to almost any situation (see Table 6.1).

Situational Crime Prevention has been successfully applied in multifamily residential low-income housing. However, experienced security practitioners can readily apply these techniques to commercial, industrial, and governmental facilities. Situational crime prevention utilizes *rational choice*

TABLE 6.1
Techniques of Situational Crime Prevention

Increase the effort	Increase the risks	Reduce the rewards	Reduce provocations	Remove excuses
1. Target harden • Steering column locks and immobilizers • Anti-robbery screens • Tamper-proof packaging	6. Extend guardianship • Take routine precautions: go out in group at night, leave signs of occupancy, carry phone • "Cocoon" neighborhood watch	11. Conceal targets • Off-street parking • Gender-neutral phone directories • Unmarked bullion trucks	16. Reduced frustrations and stress • Efficient queues and polite service • Expanded seating • Soothing music/ muted lights	21. Set rules • Rental agreements • Harassment codes • Hotel registration
2. Control access to facilities • Entry phones • Electronic card access • Baggage screening	7. Assist natural surveillance • Improved street lighting • Defensible space design • Support whistleblowers	12. Remove targets • Removable car radio • Women's refuges • Pre-paid phone cards for pay phones	17. Avoid disputes • Separate enclosures for rival soccer fans • Reduce crowding in pubs • Fixed cab fares	22. Post instructions • "No parking" • "Private property" • "Extinguish campfires"
3. Screen exits • Ticket needed for exit • Export documents • Electronic merchandise tags	8. Reduce anonymity • Taxi driver IDs • "How's my driving?" decals • School uniforms	13. Identify property • Property marking • Vehicle licensing and parts marking • Cattle branding	18. Reduce emotional arousal • Controls on violent pornography • Enforce good behavior on soccer field • Prohibit racial slurs	23. Alert conscience • Roadside speed display boards • Signatures for customs declarations • "Shoplifting is stealing"
4. Deflect offenders • Street closures • Separate bathrooms for women • Disperse pubs	9. Utilize place managers • CCTV for double-deck buses • Two clerks for convenience stores • Reward vigilance	14. Disrupt markets • Monitor pawn shops • Controls on classified ads • License street vendors	19. Neutralize peer pressure • "Idiots drink and drive" • "It's OK to say no" • Disperse troublemakers at school	24. Assist compliance • Easy library check-out • Public lavatories • Litter bins
5. Control tools/weapons • "Smart" guns • Disabling stolen cell phones • Restrict spray paint sales to juveniles	10. Strengthen formal surveillance • Red light cameras • Burglar alarms • Security guards	15. Deny benefits • Ink merchandise tags • Graffiti cleaning • Speed humps	20. Discourage imitation • Rapid repair of vandalism • V-chips in TVs • Censor details of modus operandi	25. Control drugs and alcohol • Breathalyzers in pubs • Server intervention • Alcohol-free events

Source: CPTED Matrix table reprinted courtesy of Ron V. Clarke.

theory as its theoretical framework, and follows a methodology that analyzes the opportunities for a specific crime to occur in a particular situation, and prescribes solutions targeted at removing those criminal opportunities. Rational choice theory is based on a model of behavior that the offender weighs the costs, risks, and rewards of committing a specific crime at a particular time and place.

Situational crime prevention measures are effective because they are practical, cost effective, and permanent alterations to the physical environment that are designed to fit specific types of crimes. Situational crime prevention uses five approaches:

- Increasing the effort needed to commit crime
- Increasing the risks associated with crime
- Reducing the rewards of crime
- Reduce provocations
- Removing the excuses for illegal behavior by inducing shame or guilt

Increasing the effort for crime is accomplished by the strategies of:

1. Target hardening measures—which increases the effort by creating physical barriers such as locks, screens, steel doors, fences, and shatterproof glass.
2. Access control measures increase the effort by limiting access to the vulnerable areas.
3. Removing or deflecting offenders increases the effort by displacing offenders outside the target area.
4. Controlling the facilitators of crime (limiting access to the tools and devices that criminals use or need to commit a crime, that is, removing access to cans of spray paint, collect call only public telephones, shopping carts, towing abandoned cars, weapon screening policies, etc.).

Increasing the perceived risks associated with crime, so there is increased risk of the criminal being identified and/or caught in the act, is accomplished with the following strategies:

1. Entry and exit screening increases risk by monitoring who enters an area and what and who is leaving the property.
2. Formal surveillance by CCTV and security guards.
3. Surveillance by employees, concierge, parking attendants, security guard stations.
4. Natural surveillance with window placement, external lighting, limiting blind spots, cutting hedges.

Reducing anticipated rewards is accomplished with strategies of:

1. Target removal eliminates the incentive for crime. A no-cash policy removes the threat of robbery, other target removal strategies include direct deposit checks, removable car radios, cashless transactions.
2. Identifying the property of value. Identifying stolen property makes it more difficult for criminals to sell and easier to return to the owner.
3. Reducing temptation (examples such as gender neutral listing, rapid repair of vandalism and graffiti).
4. Denying the benefits of gain (plantings on potential graffiti walls, ink explosion kits in bank money bags, computer PINs for credit cards and car radios, rendering them useless if stolen or tampered with).

Reducing provocations is accomplished with strategies that:

1. Reduce frustrations and stress with muted lighting and soothing music.
2. Avoiding disputes by having fixed rates or fares, or separating rival soccer or football fans.
3. Reduce emotional arousal by not tolerating racial slurs, enforcing civilities, limited access to pornography.
4. Neutralize peer pressure with anti-drug and anti-drinking programs to counter "coolness."
5. Discourage imitation by rapid repair of vandalism and not publicizing incidents.

Removing the excuses of noncompliant behavior is accomplished through:

1. Rule and boundary setting. This refers to the rules and regulations that all organizations need to impose on their employees' bad conduct. Making rules explicitly removes the ambiguity that permits legitimate persons to commit offenses and excuse their crimes with claims of ignorance or misunderstanding.
2. Stimulating conscience. Policies that openly declare against shoplifting, speeding, smoking, drug use, littering, and so on.
3. Controlling Inhibitors. Examples include drug-free zones, weapon-free policy, drinking age laws, V-chip for video stations, age restriction to pornography sites.
4. Facilitating compliance. If the desired behavior or outcome is made easier than the illegal or illegitimate behavior, most people will choose to comply. Examples include designated trash sites to stop illegal dumping, or public bathrooms to prevent inappropriate bathroom activities, convenient trash bins for litter.

CPTED and other crime prevention approaches, such as situational crime prevention, rely on the assumption that crime sites or offensible spaces can be improved and transformed from a crime generator to a powerful crime prevention tool. From a routine activity and environmental criminology perspective, certain situations or environments may curb, constrain, or limit criminal opportunities. Thus, although certain conditions create criminal opportunities of particular environments, likewise certain environments can prevent crimes from occurring.

APPLICATIONS OF SITUATIONAL CPTED

Applying CPTED requires a knowledge and understanding of basic crime prevention theory and practice. There are a number of operating assumptions for crime prevention officers that are relevant to security personnel and others engaged in loss and crime prevention planning and implementation, which are also relevant to CPTED:

- Potential victims and those responsible for their safety must be assisted to take informed actions to reduce their vulnerability to crime
- The actions potential victims can take to prevent crime are limited by the control they can exert over their environment
- Focus must be given to the environment of the potential victim rather than that of the potential criminal
- Crime prevention is a practical verses a moralistic approach to reducing criminal motivation by reducing the opportunities to commit crime
- Punishment and rehabilitation capabilities of courts and prisons, police apprehension, and so on, can increase the risk perceived by criminals and have a significant, but secondary, role in criminal opportunity reduction

- Law enforcement agencies have a primary role in the reduction of crime by providing crime prevention education, guidance, and information to the public, institutions, and other community organizations
- Crime prevention can be both a cause and effect of efforts to revitalize urban and rural communities
- Crime prevention knowledge is continually developing and is interdisciplinary in nature; thus, there must be a continual analysis of successful practices and emerging technologies and the sharing of this information among practitioners

Crime prevention strategies must remain flexible and creative to be effective. Success in one situation does not necessarily mean that success can be transferred to another similar set of circumstances without proper consideration to cultural, environmental, and other factors.

Crime Prevention through Environmental Design (CPTED), and an associated program called Situational Crime Prevention, works! Here are two examples.

Fort Lauderdale, Florida

From 1987 to 1990, the City of Fort Lauderdale, led by Sgt. Gene Farmer, enacted a strict code enforcement policy to remove crime facilitators and to set boundaries against unlawful activities. The city modified its codes in the following manner to allow for more effective enforcement and to reduce crime opportunity. Codes were modified to authorize the police to arrest for misdemeanor or municipal ordinance violations. State laws and county ordinances were incorporated into the municipal ordinance reducing confusion over prevailing laws and rules. Buildings or other properties deemed to be "unsafe structures" were to be demolished. Property owners were held responsible for activities occurring on their properties (e.g., the city mailed letters to those property owners where drugs were sold).

To enforce the codes, a five-person code team composed of a police officer, a building code inspector, a fire code inspector, a tax collector, and an architect/design professional completed the following tasks during a four-year period:

- Inspected more than 1,712 dwelling units
- Investigated more than 4,500 complaints
- Cited more than 25,000 code violations
- Secured more than 400 units
- Demolished 110 crack houses
- Generated more than $500,000 in fines collected between 1987 and 1990

These measures led to the following improvements:

- 56% decrease in drug offenses
- 34% decrease in homicides
- 23% decrease in police workload

Specific targeted CPTED measures focused on troubled settings resulted in significant improvement for the city in terms of reduction of crime and increases in quality of life.

Cincinnati, Ohio

The Cincinnati Metropolitan Housing Authority implemented two crime prevention measures, which could prove useful for any metropolitan public location. These simple measures were designed to remove inducements for crime and reduce the rewards of crime. To remove inducements for crime, the Cincinnati Metropolitan Housing Authority (CMHA) purchased additional garbage cans to be distributed throughout their properties, and purchased "garbage vacuums" to drive through its housing developments, and vacuum litter much faster than it could be collected by hand. Adding trash cans encouraged their use; quick cleanup with the commercial vacuums reinforced the Housing Authority goal of a clean site. Removing the litter also reduced or eliminated the hiding places for drug stashes, and reduced the stigma of poor appearance.

The CMHA rapid graffiti removal policy reduced the rewards of crime by minimizing the amount of time that graffiti was visible. Gangs often use graffiti as a territorial marker or as a road sign for drug markets. If graffiti is removed as soon as it is discovered, its benefits decrease. Graffiti removal also eliminates the opportunity for rival gangs to leave their graffiti correspondence to each other.

SUMMARY

Situational crime prevention consists of a set of opportunity reducing measures directed at the potential offender: increase the effort, increase the risks, reduce the rewards, reduce the provocations, and remove the excuses for criminal behavior. CPTED differs slightly, with its focus on altering the physical environment to reduce criminal opportunities. The major difference between these two crime prevention methods is the scope and depth of devising and applying crime prevention measures. Situational crime prevention falls within the theoretical framework of criminal opportunity theories, such as rational choice, routine activities, and environmental criminology.

CPTED draws on the multidisciplinary theoretical background from the social and physical sciences that serve as the basis for CPTED's environmental alterations. Newman's work in defensible space and Crowe's first generation work in CPTED have paved the way for the next generation of CPTED that incorporates elements of behavioral psychology and sociology of human behavior with the architectural modifications needed to make a safe environment.

Although Situational Crime Prevention and CPTED differ in terms of their theoretical base, they can be used together and even compliment each other. CPTED and Situational Crime prevention are valuable tools for security directors and law enforcement, especially POP (Problem Oriented Policing) the SARA Model, and Community Oriented Policing.

Police officers, security directors, and design professionals typically want standards, guidelines, and directives to tell them what to do in different environments in order to respond to the threats for security. It is important to remember that before a standard is made, the theory and practice must withstand vigorous research and the test of time to prove its worthiness. There is value in understanding the "why" of crime, not just responding to each new threat after the fact. CPTED and Situational Crime Prevention are interdisciplinary and holistic theoretical-based approaches to understanding the basis for criminal and terrorism behavior. The root of the problem can never be solved unless we thoroughly understand the subtleties of the relationship between environment and behavior.

It is important to distinguish that CPTED is not always enough to stop crime (Sorenson, 1999). If CPTED measures are employed alone, they can sometimes create more problems than they solve in the community, neighborhood, or project in which they are implemented. Certain CPTED or security measures may create or exacerbate tension between groups in the community because certain people or groups may not feel they are benefiting from the correct crime prevention measures. Secondly, persistent or motivated offenders or youth may dedicate time and unlimited energy to figuring out how to overcome the CPTED measures resulting in corrections that end up being fortress-like target hardening. Finally, CPTED measures do not address the social and economic problems of the community, neighborhood, society, or building project. The solution is to integrate a CPTED program with additional initiatives, and collaborate building processes to make the community or neighborhood whole.

REFERENCES

AICrime 17 June 2003, N0.3. ISSN 1448–1383 Australian Institute of Criminology. www.aic.gov.
au/publications/crm.

Atlas, R. (1983) Architectural determinism. Dissertation, Florida State University.

Atlas, R. (1991) The other side of CPTED. *Security Management.*

Atlas, R. (1996) Beyond the 3-D Concept: Protection of Assets Manual. Santa Monica, CA: Merritt.

Agnew, R. (1995) Determinism, indeterminism, and crime: An empirical exploration, *Criminology* 33,
83–109.

Brantingham, P. and Brantingham, P. (1991) *Environmental Criminology*. Beverly Hills, CA: Sage.

Brantingham, P. and Brantingham, P. (1993) Environment routine and situation: Toward a pattern of crime. In
R. Clarke (Ed.) *Routine Activity and Rational Choice: Advances in Criminological Theory, Vol. 5*. New
Brunswick, NJ: Transaction Publishers.

Calthorpe, P. (1993) *The Next American Metropolis*. Princeton, NJ: Princeton Architectural Press.

Cisneros, H. (1996) *Defensible Space: Deterring Crime and Building Community*. Washington, DC. U.S.
Department of Housing and Urban Development.

Clarke, R. V. (1983) Situational crime prevention: Its theoretical basis and practical scope. In M. Tonry and N.
Morris (Eds.), *Crime and Justice: An Annual Review of Research*. Chicago: University of Chicago Press.

Clarke, R. V. (1992) *Situational Crime Prevention: Successful Case Studies*. Albany, NY: Harrow and
Heston.

Jacobs, J. (1961) *The Death and Life of Great American Cities*. New York: Vintage Press.

www.crimereduction.gov.uk/learningzone/scptechniques.htm.

Sorensen, S. L., Hayes, J. G., Walsh, E. W., and Myhre, M., *Crime Prevention through Environmental Design*,
Washington, DC: U.S. Department of Housing and Urban Development, 1997; revised 1999; curriculum
prepared for Public Housing; www.SIKYUR.com/seeSecuritytoolbox for CPTED Manual and Briefs.

7 Second-Generation CPTED
The Rise and Fall of Opportunity Theory

Gregory Saville and Gerard Cleveland

This chapter introduces a modern variant on the CPTED theme explored elsewhere in this book—Second-Generation CPTED. We ignore the facts of unsafe neighborhoods in our efforts to make them safer. We send in the police, take out the offenders, and tinker at the edges by modifying physical conditions that create opportunities for crime.

The ingredients for safe and healthy neighborhoods are not a mystery. One only need consider functioning, vibrant, and low crime communities. They have similar characteristics. They have a full range of citizen participation (Checkoway and Finn, 1992; Saville and Clear, 2000). They have community dialogue and partnerships (Barton, 1993; National Institute of Justice, 1996) and they have a full measure of, and programs for, social cohesiveness (Brower, 1996; Schorr, 1997). They have a distinct local culture and a diverse population with ample opportunities for positive interactions (Langdon, 1994; Aberley, 1994; Adams and Goldbard, 2001). They also have a capacity to provide opportunities for residents to work together to reduce opportunities and motives for crime (Wekerle and Whitzman, 1995; Gilligan, 2001). These are the facts that characterize a safe neighborhood.

These are the factors that the emerging field of Second-Generation CPTED seeks to cultivate while building, or rebuilding, our urban areas. They hearken back to the original values espoused by Jane Jacobs in her book *Death and Life of Great American Cities* (1961)—a work often cited as a founding document of CPTED.

Dysfunctional and disordered neighborhoods are places of violence and disorder. They contain significant crime hotspots, and risks for victimization are high (Skogan, 1990; Spellman, 1992). They are places of low social cohesion and high fear; for example: places where school absenteeism is rampant, where residents infrequently speak to neighbors, or where people are too afraid to go outside at night (Markowitz et al., 2001; Gibson et al., 2002). Such places foster opportunities for crime and when crime happens, there is no local capacity to respond in an effective fashion (Baba, 1989; Foster, 1995). There are few opportunities for positive and respectful social interactions between people and groups within the community (Green et al., 1998; Saville and Clear, 2000).

In our efforts to make places safer, we draw on the traditional criminal justice systems, such as the police or the courts. They, in turn, use enhanced patrol, enforcement, or sentencing strategies, methods that are predicated on traditional theories of crime—deterring crime through the threat of arrest and sanction.

Beyond enforcement, there are motive reduction programs and opportunity reduction programs. There are many examples of social prevention programs that attempt to reduce the root causes—the motives—for crime. Literacy training and job creation are two examples. Unfortunately motive prevention programs too frequently are applied in a generic fashion as though one size fits all.

One of the most persistent crime opportunity theories arguably is CPTED (Jeffery, 1971; Newman, 1972). CPTED training across the world teaches practitioners such as police officers and architects how to use lighting, landscaping, and urban design to enhance the territoriality of vulnerable locations, making it difficult for offenders to commit crime with impunity. In truth, as we have seen earlier in this book, many studies on the long-term effectiveness of all these approaches are mixed (Sherman, 1997). There is no single strategy that works best. The problem of crime is complex and, when it comes to preventing it, one size does not fit all.

Consider the award winning projects submitted over the past decade to the Herman Goldstein Problem Oriented Policing Award program. Summarizing a hundred projects over a decade, Scott reports that there are on average five different kinds of strategies in successful projects, and at least half of those include CPTED and social/educational programs. In short, when neighborhood problems have actually been reduced or eliminated, the most effective answer included both motive reduction and opportunity reduction (Scott, 2001). At the street level of preventing crime, it is not a case of either/or that solves our crime problems.

A singular or narrow approach stands in stark contrast to current crime prevention policy. In Canada, for example, the National Crime Prevention Council employs a motive reduction program called Crime Prevention through Social Development. Strategies include education, literacy enhancement, and parenting programs, among others. These are classic motive reduction strategies and they are reminiscent of Second-Generation CPTED—except for one fact. They tend to ignore the importance of opportunity reduction. Few, if any, of the projects they fund incorporate the proven crime prevention strategies of First-Generation CPTED. Some call this the logic of throwing the baby out with the bathwater.

Motive preventers claim CPTED ignores the "root causes" of crime and may end up simply displacing crime problems to other places. Opportunity preventers counter that "root causes" are not unimportant but that ameliorating long-standing social inequities is difficult, if not impossible. In fact, when we shift from the abstract theoretical debates of the criminologists and policy makers and move to the specific place where crime actually occurs, distinctions between motive and opportunity vanish. It is the reality of prevention at the level of the street, based upon years of hands-on prevention experience, which led to the creation of Second-Generation CPTED.

FIRST-GENERATION CPTED

The principles and history of traditional CPTED are fairly well known and they are discussed in other parts of this book. There is no need to review them here other than to say that, ever since Jacobs outlined the basis for territorial control and eyes on the street (Jacobs, 1961) very little has changed with CPTED theory in the past 30 years.

Territoriality is the foundation for all First-Generation CPTED strategies. Access control modifies entranceways and exits so that legitimate users of a space can control access into buildings and neighborhoods. Natural surveillance suggests the same, except it employs sightlines, lighting, landscaping, and design to place eyes on that street. Symbolic signage, hierarchy of space, improving management and maintenance are also strategies to enhance territorial control in a particular area. They help legitimate users take ownership of areas and impinge on the ability of offenders to offend with impunity without notice or fear of capture. They are all opportunity reduction strategies. The definition of CPTED is all about "reducing the opportunity and fear of crime." (Crowe, 2000)

CPTED TNG (THE NEXT GENERATION: BOLDLY GOING WHERE NO CPTED HAS GONE BEFORE)

In 1998, Saville and Cleveland created Second-Generation CPTED. It expands the theory of First-Generation CPTED by moving beyond the design-affects-crime debate to include social factors. It is beyond the activity support strategy suggested by Newman and Crowe in First-Generation CPTED era. Second-Generation CPTED seizes on Jane Jacobs's (1961) original formulation that a sense of neighborliness and community are at the core of safe streets (Colquhoun, 2004). It incorporates a wide range of social crime prevention strategies in a holistic way, but it does so in specific situations in local places.

Previous social prevention programs took aim at crime through job creation and economic revitalization. Second-Generation CPTED does not discount such ideas, but many of those are large-scale, long-term strategies. Instead, Second-Generation CPTED focuses on the specific social and cultural dynamics existing in each individual neighborhood.

Second-Generation CPTED employs four new strategies—the four Cs:

1. Social Cohesion
2. Connectivity
3. Community Culture
4. Threshold Capacity

Where First-Generation CPTED aims to enhance territorial control and defensible space, Second-Generation CPTED extends that concept by acknowledging that people are not likely to have strong territorial feelings unless they develop a sense of shared standards for positive behavior and neighborliness. They must actually care about the people and place where they work, play, and live, and they cannot limit that caring just to their shared public places. Prevention must expand into the private areas of community life if it is to become truly holistic. Only when prevention expands to encompass the four "Cs" can it truly be recognized as a holistic strategy. Only then can sustainable safety emerge from those shared standards of behavior that bring people together for a common purpose.

Consequently, Second-Generation CPTED reduces crime motives by dealing with the cultural, social, and emotional needs of people at the specific locales where crime is or may be most acute.

SOCIAL COHESION

Just as *territoriality* is the core of First-Generation CPTED, *social cohesion* is the core of Second-Generation CPTED. To encourage a safe community, it employs a wide range of strategies. These range from emotional intelligence (Goleman, 1995; Salovey, 1990), to the literacy of conflict training, such as showing how to have respectful disagreements without resorting to violence (Cleveland and Saville, 2003).

Cohesion strategies enhance relationships between residents. Neighborhood Watch may create a network of watchers, but it does not teach problem solving or conflict resolution to those who live in the neighborhood. That is the same reason why the First-Generation CPTED strategy called *activity support* rarely creates long-term social cohesion.

A few of the characteristics that define social cohesion include:

• Participation in local events and organizations
• Presence of self-directed community problem-solving
• Extent to which conflicts are positively resolved within the community, e.g. restorative justice programs (Zellerer, 2002)
• Prevalence of friendship networks within the community
• Extensive positive relations between friendship networks

We divide social cohesion into two components: *Social Glue* and *Positive Esteem*.

Social Glue involves strategies that bring members of the community together to take responsibility for their street, block, organization, or town. For example neighbors may plan social events or learn new methods to deal with crime risks, such as First-Generation CPTED.

One social glue strategy that we use is problem-based learning (PBL). This educational technique has its roots in adult education where facilitators support stakeholders to develop their own hands-on training seminars. They learn prevention principles by crafting actual solutions to real problems in their own neighborhoods, all the while creating links between each other. The links that the learners subsequently forge using PBL have the value of including the very people who have influence to make positive changes.

In the mid-1990s, Saville and Atlas applied this method in Reno, Nevada during traditional CPTED training. The participants identified their own neighborhood problems to which they applied their new CPTED skills. Through this process they learned the city did not have a long-term CPTED planning policy and so they created one. It was approved by the City Council and today members of that original group conduct ongoing CPTED training and participate in regular CPTED reviews for development proposals. We had similar success when we brought the method known as the Safety Audit to the Church Street pedestrian mall in Burlington, Vermont. As a result of their ongoing work and the findings of their safety audit, residents and business people created new physical and management strategies to enhance territoriality and defensible space at the mall. Burlington now has one of the most vibrant, and safest, pedestrian malls in the country.

Positive Esteem relates to the characteristics that individuals within the neighborhood need for cohesion to occur. Primary among these personal characteristics are conflict resolution and self-confidence skills. When community participants are deficient at resolving conflicts they frequently retreat into their own homes. This can cause social alienation and isolation. If they resolve conflicts in negative ways, such as physical altercations, this leads to violence.

Another self-esteem strategy for cohesion includes emotional intelligence training. *Emotional intelligence* (Salovey and Mayer, 1990; Goleman, 1995) provides methods to enhance individual competencies in self-awareness and conflict resolution. As part of a larger effort to expand police training to encompass CPTED and community problem solving, Saville and Cleveland have been funded by the U.S. Department of Justice COPS Office to create a new National police instructor development-training program. This program focuses on the development of Emotional Intelligence training skills for police officers from rookies who will work in troubled neighborhoods, to chiefs of police (http://www.pspbl.com).

CONNECTIVITY

Connectivity means the neighborhood has positive relations and influence with external agencies, such as government funding sources. For the CPTED practitioner who employs Second-Generation CPTED, this means teaching grant-writing skills, establishing linked Web communities, and fostering neighborhood empowerment teams for participatory planning.

Although internal cohesiveness is an important factor detracting from crime motives, it is also critical that the neighborhood does not operate in isolation (Barton and Silverman, 1994). There are important lessons for problem solving from other neighborhoods. There must be a mechanism to connect and communicate with media outlets to publish success or solicit public support. This means that every organization or neighborhood needs connectivity outside itself. Practitioners should teach participants how to make connections with other groups with similar problems and to forge political links with various levels of government.

Some characteristics of connectivity include:

- Existence of networks with outside agencies, for example, shared Web sites
- Grant-writers or access to grant-writing services
- Formal activities with outside groups, organizations, or neighborhoods
- Adequate transport facilities (ride-sharing, bicycle paths, public transit) linking to outside areas

COMMUNITY CULTURE

CPTED practitioners sometimes forget what is significant about Jacobs's "eyes on the street" is not the sightlines or the streets, but the eyes. We don't need neighborhoods of watchers; we need a sense of community where people care about who they are watching. Community culture brings people together in a common purpose. This is how local residents begin to share a sense of place and why they bother to exert territorial control in the first place (Adams and Goldbard, 2001).

A few of the characteristics that define culture within a community include:

- Presence and effectiveness of gender and minority equality strategies
- Gender-based programs, for example, violence against women
- Extent of social and cultural diversity within a neighborhood
- Prevalence of special places, festivals, and events
- Extent of community traditions and cultural activities, for example, art fairs, sports role models
- A unique sense of pride or distinctiveness based on the attributes or characteristics of the residents, occupants, or users of the space involved

For example, Westville is a neighborhood just outside the central core of New Haven, Connecticut. Surrounded by high crime hotspots, the neighborhood is constantly at risk of increasing crime. However, for years community organizers encourage local artists to run art festivals and street fairs (www.westvillect.org).

Working together in 2003, they obtained a historic preservation designation, thereby protecting the neighborhood from impending roadway expansion and the deterioration of walkable streets. Businesses now organize to clean up streets. A walkable and safe street can contribute to a sense of community and help people enjoy the public realm in positive ways. Art festivals and street fairs are cultural events that bring people together in common purpose. These efforts not only help prevent crime but they also have the added benefit of developing a shared sense of purpose and belonging within the culture of community that arises from those efforts.

DeKeseredy reminds us that a major shortfall within CPTED is that it ignores the violence occurring beyond the public street, for example domestic violence against women in public housing projects (DeKeseredy et al., 2004). "Ninety percent of more than 1.27 million U.S. public housing households are headed by women . . . and that exploratory research shows that many of them are frequently and severely abused by male intimates and acquaintances" (DeKeseredy et al., 2004, p. 28). No crime prevention strategy can be considered holistic if it ignores such a large portion of the crime problem. He suggests that Second-Generation CPTED can address this shortfall by moving beyond gender-neutral CPTED initiatives. We agree and add we must also move beyond minority-neutral CPTED initiatives.

An example of cultural strategies includes what social planner Wendy Sarkissian calls "Stories in a Park" (Sarkissian et al., 2003). The project, in the disadvantaged suburb of Eagleby in the Gold Coast of Australia, ran from March to June 2000. Crime statistics for the park did not indicate a high crime rate, possibly because the area had a negative stigma and residents did not report crime. However, the stigma attached to the park led to high fears and a lack of participation in neighborhood affairs. Residents described the park as poorly lit, abandoned, and attracting antisocial behavior.

Sarkissian shows how celebration, animation, and storytelling were brought to the community to enhance the place making of Eagleby Park. Celebration involved encouraging residents, students, and the unemployed in creating a festival in the park. Animation involved bringing a local artist to work with children in the park for three weeks, creating community art for the park, and conducting day and night activities thereby animating the park in the minds of residents.

Storytelling was one of the most innovative cultural strategies. It included getting local children to write negative stories about their perceptions of the park, and then placing these stories into a papier-mâché eagle to burn them during a public celebration. "In Eagleby, we argued that the stories people tell about their communities, the myths of a people and a place, determine how people interact, perceive, and use public space. We reasoned that for people to undertake more incidental physical activity in their neighborhood, they need supportive environments and, at a symbolic or archetypal level, the environment of stories is just as fundamental as the environment of physical amenity" (Sarkissian, 2003, p. 37–38).

Not only did the fear of crime decline in the park, but also a process of ongoing renewal began in the community. Upgrading the park and other public places became a feature of community life. Residents report in evaluations that community pride has improved and people within the neighborhood were themselves capable of running additional sessions to maintain momentum. Furthermore, economic activity also expanded with the creation of the Flying Eagle Facilitators, a facilitation group in the neighborhood that was a direct antecedent to the project.

THRESHOLD CAPACITY

Second-Generation CPTED seizes on the concept of social ecology. Although First-Generation CPTED works to minimize crime opportunities through design, Second-Generation CPTED establishes balanced land uses and social stabilizers. Stabilizers include safe congregation areas or events for young people while minimizing destabilizing activities that tip an area into crime, such as illegal pawn shops and abandoned buildings.

The concept of the *tipping point* is another threshold idea (Saville, 1996; Saville and Wong, 1994). The movement toward "community imbalance," colloquially described as "tipping," refers to the capacity of any given activity or space to properly support the intended use. Too many abandoned homes in a neighborhood have been shown to act as a magnet for certain types of crime (Spellman, 1993). Too many bars in a small area can generate an exorbitant number of bar related problems such as assaults, drunk driving, and disorder incidents (Saville and Wong, 1994).

Some characteristics of capacity include:

- Human-scale, land use density, and maximum diversity
- Balance of social stabilizers, for example, community gardens, street entertainment, street food vendors for downtown lunches
- Minimal congestion versus maximum intensity of use
- Plentiful access to social and economic resources
- Crime generators below critical threshold, for example, number of abandoned homes per neighborhood, number of bars in an area.

REVITALIZING A TORONTO HOUSING PROJECT

One of the first full-scale efforts to combine Second with First Generation CPTED, as well as security, was in the San Romanoway apartments in a lower income community in north Toronto. The community has a long tradition of crime and respondents to a victimization survey portrayed a community in crisis. Drug abuse, violent crimes, youth delinquency, and fear levels were all significantly higher than other communities across the country (Rigakos, 2002). In fact, although police had spent considerable resources responding to crime in this community, over one in ten continued to be burglarized; almost 10% continued to be victims of violent crime (Rigakos, 2002).

A Toronto parapolice company headed by Ross McLeod provided security services in the San Romanoway Project. In 2000, the property owners were convinced to institute prevention and community-building strategies in a report called the San Romanoway Foundation Document written by McLeod, Saville, and Cleveland. Between 2000 and 2001, they began preliminary work to outline this collaborative action research agenda. It marked the first time in Canada that such a comprehensive Second-Generation CPTED strategy was implemented on such a large scale.

Team members began to research the social ecology of the San Romanoway by creating a neighborhood profile. The first step was a series of site visits to the property to speak to residents, managers, and security officers, and also to conduct a CPTED review. This included a photo survey of the exterior and interior portions of the site. It also included collecting management records and security reports about the property.

San Romanoway comprises high-rise apartments with 4,000 residents living in over 800 units on the corner of Jane Street and Finch Avenue. The site includes a recreation center with a swimming pool, though the pool had been inoperable for some time. In a later survey, over 80 percent of the residents described themselves as recent immigrants, and one in five relied on social support or welfare (Rigakos, 2002).

The three 20-story tower blocks are designed in a bleak, modernist style with brick and cement exteriors. Most units have a single balcony. There were no gardens or landscaped areas on site except for an area of grass berms obstructing sightlines at the southwest corner.

It was obvious to onlookers that there were many problems with the maintenance on site. The grounds were littered, access lights were inoperable, and there were abandoned vehicles in the underground parking lots. The post boxes within the building were located in an alcove creating an entrapment area and elevators were in a state of disrepair. Many locations along walkways were unlit and in other locations lights were broken. These observations reinforced the serious problem with image and poor territoriality on site.

The San Romanoway Foundation Document outlined a series of steps for further action, including an extensive social survey of residents, as well as conducting a series of meetings with residents. It also identified First and Second Generation CPTED strategies, and enhanced security provisions.

The preliminary recommendations included First-Generation CPTED strategies, such as improving the lighting, installing boarder fencing to reinforce access control, and improving the on site maintenance to enhance image. Additional recommendations also included Second-Generation strategies such as regular meetings to build local cohesion between residents, activities on site such as community gardens, and others.

The survey results indicated over 20 percent relied on welfare or government disability payments to survive, and one in four was unemployed. Over 30 percent indicated they immigrated to Canada within the past 5 years. This has implications for building social cohesion on site since different cultures have various methods of socializing. Different groups tended to cluster in different buildings on site, indicating that community building would need strategies particular to the site and common to everyone.

The foundation document confirmed that access control or natural surveillance strategies, in and of themselves, will have little effect on an environment where residents may not know who is trespassing, and may be too fearful to take action. Maintenance and better lighting are also unlikely to create an environment where residents will take over territorial control of their neighborhood. Territoriality must include community building and involvement of residents in order to be effective.

The project team was convinced there were security, physical, and social strategies to bring people together that might have lasting impacts. This would require a stronger sense of social cohesion and community culture, especially if residents were to begin to feel a stronger sense of territoriality and ownership over their own affairs in the neighborhood.

The property owners were reluctant to spend their own resources to implement some of the security or First-Generation CPTED changes. Boundary access control fencing and modifications to landscaping were very expensive. However, the tennis court and nearby area fencing was improved. No further extension of the fencing took place and lighting was also not improved because of a reluctance to spend funds. However, funds from an outside agency were obtained to build a community garden and also construct a safe playground area for children. This reinforced the importance of connectivity during project work. It also led new project mangers to focus exclusively onto Second-Generation CPTED.

Even with the exclusive focus on Second-Generation CPTED there was improvement. For example, because connectivity infers that a neighborhood should encourage connections with external agencies, outreach efforts targeted outside funding agencies. Local politicians were brought into the project and appeared during media photo opportunities. Eventually over $500,000 grant funds were directed to San Romanoway, mostly for Second-Generation CPTED initiatives.

These initiatives include social cohesion programs such as an anger management program, youth mentoring, and computer classes in a new computer room. Additionally, they funded a full-time teacher and social worker to help students expelled from school. Community cultural programs include a Tamil cultural dance group, tennis clubs, and a homework club.

Today, residents themselves work together and participate in a non-profit organization called the San Romanoway Revitalization Association to coordinate activities on site. A recent follow-up study found there has been a 23 percent decrease in violent crimes since the Second-Generation CPTED strategies began in 2002, including a 30 percent drop in robberies, sexual assaults, and assaults by strangers. There also has been a 21 percent decline in burglaries (http://pamorama. cqrleton.ca/2006-12/69.htm).

It became clear to the original team members that, had there been funding for the full range of security and traditional CPTED programs, there is no doubt the eventual impact would have been even more significant. That approach is now called the Safe Growth Model of neighborhood revitalization (http://www.cip-icu.ca/2007conference/presentations%20for%conference/ESOI_SafeGrowth Planning.pdf). Based on prevention research, and experience in this project, we confirmed that there is no single approach that works best. A complete Safe Growth Model with First- and Second-Generation CPTED strategies, and security provisions, has the best chance of ensuring sustainable, long-term community safety. San Romanoway was the first step in a new model of prevention.

SOCIAL COHESION IN ACTION: ENGAGING ABORIGINAL YOUTH IN WESTERN AUSTRALIA

Another project where Second-Generation CPTED strategies had impact is a recent aboriginal education program in Western Australia. This program focuses on the social cohesion component of Second-Generation CPTED; however, in this case, it is titled *Capacity Building*. This is because the focus is on the personal capacities of individuals within the community. The objective is to reduce absenteeism by truant students, as well as enhance the overall involvement in community problem solving.

As we suggested earlier, there is little point in creating safe physical environments in First-Generation CPTED if those who live in those environments choose not to participate in community life. This is particularly the case with young people and the schools they attend. It is not surprising we associate a large majority of social disorder and crime problems with disaffected young people who drop out of school. They find academic activities too boring and quite disconnected to their own lives. Therefore, engaging young people is a crucial component of any community-building strategy, especially where truancy and absenteeism are rampant. Building social cohesion through community involvement of disaffected participants—especially disaffected young people—obviously represents a major test of any program's viability. In Western Australia, in 2002 when this program began, Aboriginal employees became the focus. The goal was to develop a particular set of skills. For years, Aboriginal employees had tried to develop community participation to support local schools, but they were failing because they lacked the required conflict resolution, emotional intelligence, and project management skills.

Aboriginal employees intuitively knew that the cultural disconnect between Aboriginal and mainstream Australian societies had a great deal to answer for, but they themselves, as employees of the system, were unsure of how they could bridge that divide. They also knew their children had the right to expect the same access to opportunity as other Australians, but because of their own discomfort with challenging a system that had failed them, these educators and other Aboriginal community members were often spectators in this debate rather than full participants. Much of that passivity and detachment has changed since this program began across the state in 2002.

ABSENTEEISM: A SYMPTOM OF COMMUNITY BREAKDOWN

Within the education sphere, a high level of absenteeism served as a significant indicator of the difficulty that Aboriginal families faced. Aboriginal students, on average, missed almost one day of school each week. This translates to missing over a year of schooling by the end of primary school and over 2 years by the end of secondary school (MCEETYA-2001). The failure of Aboriginal students to engage with the schooling process is a significant factor in limiting the access to opportunity that many in the Aboriginal community faced. The causes of such high levels of absenteeism were both varied and complex and no easy solution existed to remedy the problem. To reduce the problem however, the individual competencies—personal capacities—of Aboriginal students, parents and educational staff had to be developed before any improvements were likely to occur. In other words, there is little sense in building state of the art schools if no one wants to attend and the curricula has little relevance to the learners.

The program helped to identify, develop, and empower three groups involved in the schooling process, which included Aboriginal support staff, parents of Aboriginal students and Aboriginal students from years 6 to 12. Generally, Aboriginal community members, including parents, education employees and students themselves had not had the opportunity to fully develop their own leadership potential and use it in ways that they determined to be beneficial in support of community improvements. Consequently, this program developed personal and local school strategies to improve student attendance, evaluate personal competencies known as emotional intelligence, developed a greater repertoire of communication skills, and taught participants how to design, manage, and present the results of a local improvement project.

The key outcome of the program was to ask Aboriginal support staff to focus on local solutions to poor student attendance and other forms of disengagement from the education system.

To be effective leaders, Aboriginal classroom assistants and other Aboriginal community support members needed to have their communication, conflict resolution, self-awareness, emotional intelligence skills, and knowledge enhanced, nurtured, and developed through a series of workshops. The focus of most of these workshops was a combination of personal development exercises and technical skills acquisition.

PROBLEM-BASED LEARNING

In addition to the learning sessions, the participants undertook problem-based learning (PBL) projects that they implemented in their schools, families, or communities. The PBL projects reflected real life community needs and attempted to resolve issues or problems of importance to participants or other Aboriginal community members.

To ensure responsiveness to participant's needs and interests, all facilitators were required to prepare work that was specifically relevant to their areas of expertise. There is little sense offering drug information strategies and crime reduction workshops if education workers have a focus that lies elsewhere. In most instances, the projects by the participants and the involved agencies included:

- Education outcomes in Western Australia (how they relate to Aboriginal Australians)
- Emotional and Multiple Intelligence Awareness
- Goal setting
- Conflict and situational control
- Assertiveness
- Literacy
- Substance abuse
- Problem-based learning

Preliminary Outcomes: The Kimberly Region

Project personnel collected initial evaluation data for one project area, the Kimberly region. Preliminary results are encouraging. Between 2004 and 2005, there was improvement in 21 of 27 schools, in both primary and secondary grades.

According to Ms. Judy McGinn, District Attendance Coordinator for the Kimberley region, we should be careful when drawing absolute conclusions from any data that relies on individual staff to input attendance figures. She indicates that when we disaggregate the data to individuals, we see a trend that the more involved a student feels with the school and community, the more likely he would be to attend and participate. However, cultural movements of Aboriginal people make attendance-keeping difficult. Aboriginal people are frequently transitory. As families, they attend cultural events, land council meetings, and sadly, funerals for family members. Often these events are inclusive of the entire family. Therefore, when Aboriginal people in the north travel to far-away towns, they remove their children from school.

In spite of the difficulties, Ms. McGinn reports that the Aboriginal staff—as well as the students they taught—were significantly impacted by the Capacity Building in a variety of ways. For example, there was more motivation to participate and achieve when those in the community were trained and valued rather than given the *fly in-fly out* treatment by the non-Indigenous. The ripple effect from the adults to the children was evident across the region (personal communication, November 2007).

The most significant aspect has been the qualitative feedback from Aboriginal employees who describe the training as an essential tool to help them function effectively in the non-Indigenous school system.

We also know that preliminary results suggest the reversal of a long-term serious trend toward lack of involvement by Aboriginal students in their own learning. Aboriginal staff describes being more inclined to take leadership roles and engage with students and staff more readily. In addition, they are now more receptive to managing and developing school and community projects. To use the terminology of one participant, "We are no longer sitting in the back seat of education at our school. We are driving the bus."

There is still a need for more data to assess the ongoing impact on attendance, suspensions, and student participation. In addition, there is need to monitor the overall cohesion, social conditions, and crime patterns within the community as the program proceeds. At this point, it has been necessary to expand efforts to include First-Generation CPTED improvements at the schools and communities.

One lesson stands out for any project aimed at community involvement—our focus must be on employees who are permanent members of the community. In this instance the project avoided a focus on teacher training for the reason that often the teachers are non- residents who only remain in the remote communities for a year or two. The key to ensure success is to provide leadership training for those within the community who have local knowledge and connections to local Aboriginal culture.

SUMMARY

If you begin to employ Second-Generation CPTED strategies and teach the essentials of the four Cs, you arm yourself and your community against violence, social conflict, and emotional detachment. For those persons and professionals interested and involved in making engaging and sustaining community involvement, we believe there is no better way than to incorporate the concepts of Second-Generation CPTED to the basics of First-Generation CPTED. Developing and sustaining a sense of community and involvement by the legitimate users of the built environment is the best insurance against social detachment, crime inflation, and occupant apathy.

REFERENCES

Aberley, D. (1994) *Futures by Design: The Practice of Ecological Planning.* Gabriola Island, BC: New Society Publishers.

Adams, D. and A. Goldbard (2001) *Creative Community: The Art of Cultural Development.* New York: Rockefeller Foundation.

Baba, Y. and Austin, D. M. (1989) Neighborhood environmental satisfaction, victimization, and social participation as determinants of perceived neighborhood safety. *Environment and Behavior* 21, 763–780.

Barton, S. (1993) *Austin's Concept for Community Policing: Achieving Self-Reliant Neighborhoods through Community Policing.* Washington, DC: National Institute of Justice.

Barton, S. E. and Silverman, C. (1994) *Common Interest Communities: Private Governments and the Public Interest.* Berkeley: University of California: Institute of Government Studies Press.

Checkoway, B. and Finn, J. (1992) *Young People as Community Builders.* Ann Arbor: Center for the Study of Youth Policy, University of Michigan.

Cleveland, G. and Saville, G. (2003) An Introduction to 2nd Generation CPTED: Part 1. *CPTED Perspectives* 6(2), 4–8.

Cleveland, G. and Saville, G. (1998) 2nd Generation CPTED: An Antidote to the Social Y2K Virus of Urban Design. Paper presented at the 3rd Annual International CPTED Conference, Washington, DC, December.

Colquhoun, I. (2004) *Design Out Crime: Creating Safe and Sustainable Communities.* Oxford, England: Elsevier Architectural Press.

Crowe, T. Crime Prevention Through Environmental Design, 2nd ed. Burlington, MA: Elsevier (2000).

DeKeseredy, W. S., Shahid, A., Renzetti, C., and Schwartz, M. D. (2004) Reducing private violence against women in public housing: Can second-generation CPTED make a difference? *The CPTED Journal* 3(1), 27–37.

Eedle, P. (2002) Al Queda takes the fight for "hearts and minds" to the web, *Jane's Intelligence Review,* August: 22–26.

ELES. (2001) Critical Infrastructure Protection Plan. Emergency Law Enforcement Services Sector, Washington, DC: February.

Foster, J. (1995) Informal social control and community crime prevention. *British Journal of Criminology* 35(4), 563–583.

General Accounting Office. (2003) *Critical Infrastructure Protection: Efforts of the Financial Services Sector to Address Cyber Threats.* Washington, DC: United States General Accounting Office.

Gibson, C. L., Zhao, J., Lovrich, N. P., and Gaffney, M. J. (2002) Social integration, individual perceptions of collective efficacy, and fear of crime in three cities. *Justice Quarterly* 19(3), 537–564.

Gilligan, J. (2001) *Preventing Violence.* New York: Thames and Hudson.

Goldfarb, M. (2003) *Protecting first responders: A reference guide for police executives on biological, chemical, and radiological threats.* June 2003 discussion draft, Police Executive Research Forum.

Goleman, D. (1995) *Emotional Intelligence.* New York: Bantam.

Green, D. P., Strolovitch, D. Z., and Wong, J. S. (1998) Defended neighborhoods, integration, and racially motivated crime. *American Journal of Sociology* 104(2), 372–403.

Jacobs, J. (1960) *The Death and Life of Great American Cities.* New York: Vintage Books.

Jeffery, C. R. (1971) *Crime Prevention through Environmental Design.* Beverly Hills, CA: Sage.

Langdon, P. (1994) *A Better Place to Live.* Amherst: The University of Massachusetts Press.

La Vigne, N. G. and Wartell, J. (Eds.). (2000) *Crime mapping case studies: Successes in the field.* Vol 2. Washington, DC: Police Executive Research Forum.

Levan, V. (2004) Second-generation CPTED at work: Building community culture bridges in Parisian Belleville. *The CPTED Journal* 3(1), 3–14.

McEwety, A. (2001) Exploring Pathways for Indigenous Students. Taskforce on Indigenous Education, unpublished discussion paper. Perth, Australia. June. 13, 14.

Markowitz, F.E., Bellair, P. E., Liska, A. E., and Liu, J. (2001) Extending social disorganization theory: Modeling the relationships between cohesion, disorder, and fear. *Criminology* 39, 293–320.

National Institute of Justice (1996) *Communities Mobilizing Against Crime: Making Partnerships Work.* Washington, DC: U.S. Department of Justice, National Institute of Justice.

Newman, O. (1972) *Defensible Space: Crime Prevention through Urban Design.* New York: Macmillan.

Rigakos, G., Sealy, D., and Tandan, A. (2002) *The San Romanoway Community Crime Survey: Base-Line Data.* Ottawa: Carleton University.

Salovey, P. and Mayer, J. (1990) Emotional intelligence. *Imagination, Cognition, and Personality* 9(3), 185–211.

Sarkissian, W. (2003) Stories in a park. Second-generation CPTED in practice: Reducing crime and stigma through community storytelling. *The CPTED Journal* 2(1), 34–45.

Saville, G. and Cleveland, G. (2003a) An Introduction to 2nd Generation CPTED: Part 2. *CPTED Perspectives* 6(1), 7–9.

Saville, G. and McLeod, R. (2003) The Past, Present and Future of Parapolicing. Paper presented at In Search of Security: An International Conference on Policing and Security, Law Reform Commission of Canada, Montreal, Quebec, February 19–22.

Saville, G. and Clear, T. (2000) Community renaissance with community justice. *The Neighborworks Journal* 18(2), 19–24.

Saville, G. and Wright, D. (1998) Putting Neighbours Back in the Neighborhood: Strategies for Safety, Urban Design, and Cohousing. Paper presented at the 1998 Biennial Meeting of the Western Association of Sociology and Anthropology, Vancouver, British Columbia, Canada.

Saville, G. (1996) Searching for a neighborhood's crime threshold. *Subject to Debate*, 10(10): 1–6. Washington, DC: Police Executive Research Forum publication.

Saville, G. and Wong, P. (1994) Exceeding the Crime Threshold: The Carrying Capacity of Neighbourhoods. Paper presented at the 53rd Annual Meeting of the American Society of Criminology, Miami, Florida.

Schorr, L. B. (1997) *Common Purpose: Strengthening Families and Neighborhoods to Rebuild America*. New York: Anchor.

Scott, M. S. (2000) Problem-Oriented Policing: Reflections on the First 20 Years. Washington, DC: U.S. Department of Justice, Office of Community Oriented Policing Services.

Sherman, L., et al. (1997) *Preventing Crime, What Works, What Doesn't, What's Promising*. Washington, DC: U.S. Department of Justice, National Institute of Justice. Available at: http://www.preventingcrime.org/report/index.htm.

Skogan, W. G. (1990). *Disorder and Decline: Crime and the Spiral of Decline in American Neighborhoods*. New York: Free Press.

Spelman, W. (1993). Abandoned buildings: Magnets for crime? *Journal of Criminal Justice* 21,481–495.

U.S. Department of Justice. (2000) *Responding to terrorist victims: Oklahoma City and beyond*. Washington, DC: Office for victims of Crime, U.S. Department of Justice.

Wekerke, G. R. and Whitzman, C. (1995) *Safe Cities: Guidelines for Planning, Design, and Management*. New York: Van Nostrand.

Zellerer, E. and Cannon, J. (2002) Restorative justice, reparation and the Southside Project. In D. Karp and T. Clear (Eds.), *What Is Community Justice?* Thousand Oaks, CA: Sage, pp.89–107.

8 Premises Liability
Design against Security Negligence Lawsuits

Criminologists have studied the causation of criminal behavior for the last three hundred years, and have usually associated crime with urban centers. However, the flight from the cities to suburbia over the last three decades has created lucrative magnets of crime in the suburbs such as, office parks, apartment complexes, industrial sites, or multiunit residential properties. The courts are finding the owners liable for criminal acts that occur on their property.

Owners and property managers, as well as the security directors working for them, have some obligations and responsibilities in the prevention of premises liability litigation. The most important steps a security manager can undertake to prevent premises liability are:

1. Identify the level of criminal activity in the site and the neighborhood. The evaluation should include a three-year history, with periodic annual reviews. The radius of area for review will vary from site to site but typically averages about a half-mile radius. Consult a security expert for a site-specific recommendation for your property. Crime maps (see Figure 8.1) can be generated using GIS (Geographical Information Systems), to develop the hot spots, or comparative analysis can be done using a variety of factors and crime and victim statistics as is used with the CAP Risk Analysis (see Figure 8.2).
2. Conduct a security survey or audit that identifies the assets to be protected, the threats, vulnerabilities, and recommendations for security improvement. The survey should be submitted in a written report form, and used as the basis for a plan of action. The recommendations should be prioritized and ranked based on risk and threats and the value of the asset being protected.
3. Provide a total security delivery system. Security is more than the guard gate, perimeter fence, wall construction, closed circuit television, security patrol, or detection technology. A security delivery system is the functionally integrated approach for the protection of people, information, and property using access control, surveillance, operational or management strategies.
4. Do as you say, say as you do! If you start a security program, complete it. The installation of CCTV with no one watching the monitors, or having broken equipment, or not having trained staff to respond to emergencies, creates a false sense or "illusion of security." The illusion can be very damaging in court.

In order to determine the level of preparedness, or adequacy, of your facility the following questions should be answered:

- Do you maintain good relations with the local police agency and are you able to obtain copies of crime reports of events happening on your property?
- Do you maintain active membership associations that have strong national standards (such as ASIS [American Society of Industrial Security], BOMA [Building Office Managers Association], or IREM [Institute of Real Estate Managers])?

WEDNESDAY   JUNE 25, 2003

New police unit to target hot spots

Responding to an increase in gang-related homicides, the Chicago Police Department on Tuesday announced a plan that targets gang hot spots to reduce violent crime in the city. There have been 272 homicides in Chicago thus far this year, five more than during the same period last year.

HOMICIDES BY DISTRICT
Jan. 1–June 24

POLICE DIST.	2002	2003
1. Central	3	0
2. Wentworth	12	6
3. Grand Crossing	15	17
4. S. Chicago	19	17
5. Calumet	13	19
6. Gresham	16	10
7. Englewood	26	22
8. Chicago Lawn	10	12
9. Deering	16	21
10. Marquette	15	24
11. Harrison	28	28
12. Monroe	12	6
13. Wood	3	7
14. Shakespeare	11	14
15. Austin	14	13
16. Jefferson Pk.	1	1
17. Albany Pk.	2	6
18. E. Chicago	8	7
19. Belmont	3	5
20. Foster	5	6
21. Prairie	4	3
22. Morgan Park	5	9
23. Town Hall	4	1
24. Rogers Park	4	3
25. Grand Central	18	15
TOTAL	**267**	**272**

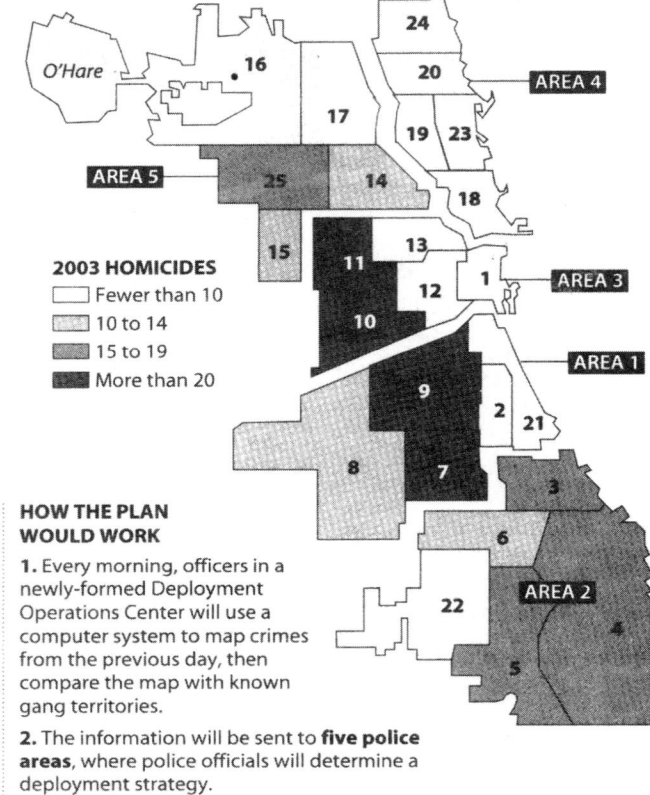

2003 HOMICIDES
- ☐ Fewer than 10
- 10 to 14
- 15 to 19
- More than 20

HOW THE PLAN WOULD WORK

1. Every morning, officers in a newly-formed Deployment Operations Center will use a computer system to map crimes from the previous day, then compare the map with known gang territories.

2. The information will be sent to **five police areas**, where police officials will determine a deployment strategy.

3. Ten teams of 10 officers, known as the Targeted Response Unit, will be deployed to specific locations in the city each day.

Source: Chicago Police Department

FIGURE 8.1   Chicago Hot Spots. (*Chicago Tribune* graphic.)

- Have you established policy and procedures for notifying tenants or residents of the development of security and crime problems, and have you identified to whom observations should be reported?
- Do you record and log all incidents and keep them on file for that jurisdiction's statue of limitation of negligence?
- Do you have a clearly stated mission of security, job description, shift description, and essential functions outlined?
- Are you able to provide or ensure that sufficient training is given to security and nonsecurity staff on the proper practices of security at that site?
- Do you review, update, and document all policies and procedures at least annually?
- Do you ensure that all employees are issued their own copy of Policy and Procedures and sign off that they reviewed them?

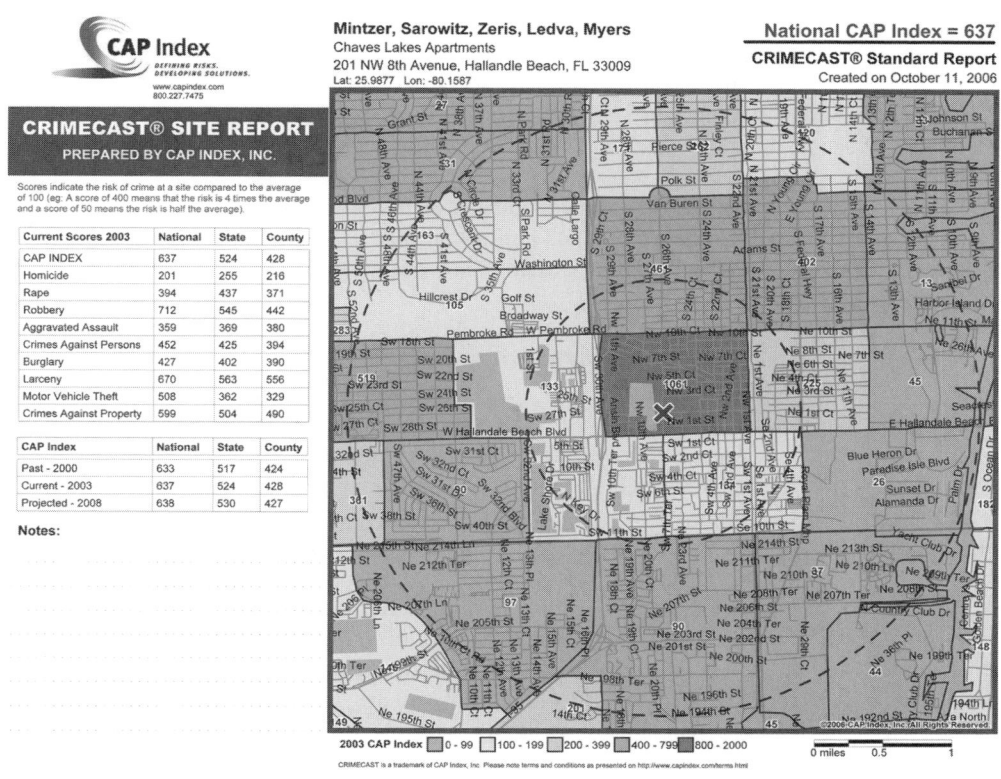

FIGURE 8.2 Cap risk analysis for an apartment building where an incident took place. The CAP risk number for this building and immediate block was 637, meaning that this site has 6.3 times the national average of risk of crime. (Image reprinted courtesy of CAP Index, Inc. www.capindex.com.)

- Can you ensure that all locks and locking devices are of sufficient quality and quantity to protect tenants from an unauthorized entry?
- Have locking devices on doors and windows been inspected at least annually, and reviewed on each tenant entry or user turnover?
- Have intercom, security alarm, fire safety, and CCTV systems been periodically tested, inspected, and documented at least annually?
- Is there even and consistent lighting levels in all exterior parking areas, walkways, and entries, which meet industry standards of the Illumination Engineering Society of North America or local building codes?
- Does the entire perimeter fencing stay maintained and in good condition without breeches?
- Do residential units have door viewers provided for all main entries?
- Are vacant building spaces and units kept secured at all times to prevent unwanted criminal activity?
- Are all keys properly and continuously controlled for their distribution? Is the inventory of keys kept in a secure location? Is there a key control P&P (policy and procedure) that is followed?
- Is foliage around the grounds and building perimeter trimmed to eliminate hiding spaces and allow exterior lighting penetration?
- Are all roof, basement, and utility and mechanical space doors secured to prevent unlawful entry?
- Are security bars, grill, or screens designed to allow fire egress in the event of an emergency?
- Are the buildings designed to screen persons and visitors who do not belong on the property?

- Are all utilities, power supplies, telephones, air conditioners, generators, and gas containers placed in as secure a manner as possible?
- Do all advertising and marketing materials accurately and adequately represent the level and type of security at the site?
- Do rental agents, managers, or staff misrepresent the level of security or history of crime at the site?
- Are disclaimers used in lease agreements and contracts, and are warnings posted in common areas, such as, pools, parking areas, and mail areas, alerting residents of potential risks?
- Are all tenants and residents kept informed of any changes in security and criminal events that require warning?
- Are all employees thoroughly screened, tested, and their backgrounds checked prior to employment?

These questions will be the first ones asked by a security expert in the event of a personal injury or premises liability litigation. How many can you answer affirmatively? And for every question that you answer "no," there will be a dollar amount associated with it that could be assessed as damages by the courts.

Examples of security negligence cases I have worked on include: a man is robbed in an apartment lobby left unguarded in the afternoon; a woman is attacked in a parking lot of a design showroom; a faulty door allows a rapist to enter an apartment building and rape a tenant; a faulty stairway design allows for a serious injury to an elderly visitor at a condominium; a hotel room balcony facing an open atrium is wide enough to allow a child to slip through and fall ten stories; an inmate hangs himself from an air return grill over the toilet that is not properly secured; a secretary walks through a sliding glass door in an office that had no window markings on it; an entry rug in a bank buckles when the doorjamb hits the edge of the carpet and trips an elderly client; and a child is accidentally shot in an apartment walkway by a stray bullet from a drug deal gone bad. These are just a few examples of the cases that are being litigated under premises liability case law.

According to a study published in 1984 by Professor Lawrence Sherman, a criminology professor, the number of major awards reported nationwide each year in security liability cases increased 3,000% between 1965 and 1982; simultaneously, the average dollar amount awarded in those cases increased by 5,000% (Johnson, *New York Times,* 17 March 1985). Moreover, the study suggests that almost half of the major awards are from four states: New York, New Jersey, Florida, and the District of Columbia. Security negligence lawsuits are one of the fastest growing civil torts in the United States currently.

The trends and patterns of premises liability case law has been studied extensively by Liability Consultants Inc. (Bates, 1993, 1999, 2004). The highlights of their 1993 research found that:

- Rape and sexual assault were the most common incidents leading to a claim of inadequate security;
- Multi-unit residential properties and hotels/motels were the two most often sued defendants;
- Apartment units, parking areas, and hotel rooms were the most common places for assaults to occur;
- The average settlement (between 1983 and 1992) over a half a million dollars and the average verdict was $3.35 million.

The highlights of Liability Consultants conducted an update in 1999 and then again in 2004 and their key findings were:

- Assault and battery accounts for more inadequate security lawsuits compared to rape and sexual assault from the earlier study. Assaults and battery accounted for 37% of lawsuits, with sexual assault 21% and robbery 12%, and wrongful death 12%.

- Parking lots are the leading location where crimes committed on a property led to a lawsuit. Retail stores are second and apartment buildings are now third.
- Multi-unit residential properties are the type of business most often sued, as it was in the earlier study. Commercial industries followed by restaurants and bars are most often sued.
- The amount for settlements and verdicts was between $250,000 and $500,000. The awards are more equitable and there are fewer high verdicts than in prior years.

To protect yourself, your property, or your client against potential lawsuits, a security/safety expert should be employed to look for vulnerabilities in the building and conduct a risk analysis. The security expert can be used to reduce the foreseeability and liability of crimes and accidents. The expert can check your city's codes for specifications and fire-safety regulations. The expert can serve in a crime preventative role, and a critical role in litigation prevention.

Rape, robbery, burglary, thefts, and safety concerns are addressed in the risk analysis and security audit. The audit gives the owner direction of the challenges that need addressing and what is a reasonable standard of care. The risk analysis also serves to put the owner on notice as to defects in the building or staff. However, if the owner can show that reasonable steps were made to correct defects, they have greatly enhanced their defensibility in a case.

A key issue in security and safety liability cases is the "foreseeability" of a crime or accident at a given location. If several tenants have been robbed or attacked in a parking lot or building lobby, further criminal incidents can be considered foreseeable, and thus preventable. Legal liability increases dramatically if no action is made to correct the defect.

The expert in security and safety can provide a risk analysis or security threat analysis to assess the vulnerability, foreseeability, and precedent of crime or accident incidents. The landlord, building management, and/or owner have certain duties that have been established in court decisions. These duties include:

1. Reasonable care;
2. Contractual duty based on implied warranty of habitability; and
3. The landlord, like an innkeeper, must exercise ***reasonable care*** to protect a guest or invited party from third party actions, that is, the duty of care.

In reviewing cases from around the United States the courts have examined many different facts and issues and now operate under the doctrine of the "*totality of circumstances.*" Therefore, all factors are taken under consideration, not just if there had been similar crime of the subject property before the present action. The following criteria seemed to be most frequent that lead to premises liability litigation:

1. Prior crime on the premises; that is, foreseeability, constructive and actual notice.
2. Prior crime in the neighborhood, or being in a "high-crime area," thus having increased awareness that the environment around the target was at greater risk.
3. If similar building complexes in the area have a "standard of care" better than the subject property, and took reasonable measures, and were aware or experienced precedent, then their action establishes your property's "standard of care."
4. Does physical maintenance and upkeep of existing conditions in the building meet industry standards? Were the conditions in the building up to the standard of care? Items might include the working order of lights, doors, locks, fences, closed circuit television, and intercoms.
5. The adequacy of the security delivery system to detect, delay, or deter criminals. Foreseeability and adequacy are the overall measure by which security legal cases are usually judged.
6. The availability and performance of security personnel are key factors to be considered. Verify employee screening, training, policy and procedures, response time, and qualifications.

7. Is there active or constructive notice of prior crimes or any defective condition to management or tenants? Did the landlord have notice of prior criminal incidents or defective conditions? Did the landlord have notice of a broken door, faulty stairway, burned out light, or past crimes?

8. The lack of warnings to the tenants for dangerous conditions. Were the tenants warned of an activity, so as to be put on notice and take care, that is, posting caution for slippery conditions, or ask for escort to their car and was denied, a rape on the property and residents not told, car thefts and owners not told to lock their cars?

9. Look for violations of statutes, codes, or regulations. A breach of a building code or ordinance provides strong support for negligence and liability.

10. Deceased measures of safety and security below a prior level of reliance, and expectations. Were services cut back because of finances or management changes and the tenants not notified of the cutback or change in services?

The security/safety/design professional can provide a vital part in determining and establishing these ten conditions. Whether the expert is operating in a preventative, non-litigation situation, or working as an expert witness for the defense or plaintiff, these key issues must be addressed to determine the reasonable or "standard of care," foreseeability, criminal precedent, premises liability, preventability, and the most appropriate response for correction of crime on the property.

Many crime and accident sites have architectural or environmental contributory factors that may or may not be attributable to the landlord. Architecture impacts the safety and security of a building in many different features including: stairs and ramp design, handrails, interior and exterior lighting, floor materials, parking lot design, blind spots, appliances, doors, windows, and access control systems, building circulation patterns, and elevators. The choice of fixtures, furnishings, and finishes are architectural decisions that are often made in a vacuum without consultation with the owner/client or the security director or consultant.

The result of the lack of communication between the design professional and the security professional is that the environment has features that create or promote the potential for crime or accidents to occur. Many of the design defects or poor planning decisions could be avoided with application of CPTED practices. The overall design of the building, even without specific security devices, is part of any security plan. Design features with particular significance for security include clear sight lines of vulnerable areas, appropriate lighting levels, the placement of the building on the site, physical barriers such as fences, walls, landscaping, doors and windows, and hardware.

The security/safety expert can assist the attorney in litigation by looking at the scene of a crime or accident and determining what the variables were that led to the cause of the incident. A risk analysis of a property might include some of the following questions:

- Could persons be struck by any item?
- Could persons be blinded by change in lighting or surprised by floor surfaces changes?
- Are there any potholes or trenches not covered or marked that someone could fall into?
- Does the design make provisions for avoiding excessive demands on persons with respect to their height, build, ability to reach, ability to balance, their walking gait, strength or grip?
- Is the risk of injury increased for persons wearing long sleeves, loose clothes, walking barefoot, high heels, or neckties?
- Is there sufficient lighting for surveillance of exterior grounds and interior common spaces?
- Are there guards or assigned persons to patrol the grounds or challenge the entry of strangers?
- Are windows on the ground floor secured?
- Are doors sturdy, with secure hinges and deadbolt locks?

- Are lobbies and elevators equipped with mirrors in their corners to allow visibility and assist in robbery and rape prevention?
- Are fire escape doors locked from the outside to prevent unauthorized entry?
- Are employees screened and provided with written security rules, regulations, and policies?
- Are there hiding spots and dead-end corridors that act as entrapment areas?
- Are there sufficient staging areas for people in lobby areas so not to create a conflict of space and users?
- Are there opportunities for natural surveillance by building users to courtyards, and parking lots, and foyers?

These questions are intended to determine if the conditions that lead to the incident could have been preventable or foreseeable. In some cases, the conditions on the premises at the time of the incident, such as poor lighting, inadequate supervision by security personnel, faulty locks, or improper maintenance of fences, may make the crime foreseeable. The goal is to have the property meet the "standard of care." The standard of care is most often defined by the customs and practices commonly followed within an industry or building type. The standard may be further elaborated by national codes (Americans With Disabilities Act Accessibility Guidelines, NFPA 101 Life Safety Code), state and local ordinances, building codes, industry standards (OSHA), industry guidelines (NFPA 730 Premises Security Guidelines 2006), publications and journals, and practices unique to a particular geographic area (all of the motels in a several-mile radius near the interstate have secure after-hour cash passthroughs and locked lobbies). The strongest standards are those that the defendants impose on themselves in their policy and procedures manuals and in the business practices that management and employees follow. If businesses do not follow their own precedent or practices indicative of their industry, the stage is set for persons to be injured or killed, and subsequent litigation.

SUMMARY

Most security professionals and lawyers say the best way to determine the "adequacy," and at the same time protect the building owners from lawsuits is through inspection of the premises by an independent nonvested consultant. From a legal viewpoint, independent inspections, such as a threat analysis, can be used in court to support the building management's security decisions in the event of a lawsuit (Johnson, *New York Times,* 1985).

The security or alarm expert is liable for his or her recommendations, to the extent of the proficiency and completeness of the package or solutions he or she recommends. A security company might offer an inspection for free, but the hook is the pressure to purchase a proprietary system or guard service at a substantial cost. There is no free lunch. The cost incurred for the expert now gets you a qualified opinion before litigation, or the owner can pay for the expert to defend him later in court.

The best prevention of litigation is proactive involvement by a security expert before a problem exists. But will the client pay for it? They will if the cost benefit analysis shows the value of such proactive action. The expert can also assist if litigation is imminent by assessing the vulnerabilities or defensibility of the site or building. In summary, experts can be used many ways to prevent or reduce the liabilities of premises liability. Security professionals can save clients money by addressing the total security needs and reducing early obsolescence. Owners may be reluctant to pay for security design and planning, because they are often too focused on the short-term bottom line. But the real bottom line is that everyone loses when security is an afterthought.

Architects should prepare themselves for the increasing demand for security design in all types of architecture. An educated client is their best consumer. Clients must realize that security is as important as energy conservation, fire prevention, and accessibility compliance. How much security is enough? It is sufficient when a balance is reached between the level and type of risk and the cost of minimizing those risks. The costs are always there, either by investing in security proactively, or paying in court costs and litigation in premises security negligence. The choice is yours; choose wisely.

REFERENCES

Atlas, R. (1990) Pay me now or pay me later. *Security Management*, 42–45.

Atlas, R. (2005) The security audit and premises liability. *Spotlight on Security for Real Estate Managers*, 2nd ed. Chicago, IL: IREM.

Atlas, R. (2006) Reducing premises liability. *Police Forum*.

Bates, N. (1993) *Major Developments in Premises Liability*. Sudbury, MA: Liability Consultants.

Bates, N. (1999) *Major Developments in Premises Security Liability II, 1999 Study*. Sudbury, MA: Liability Consultants.

Bates, N. (2004) *Major Developments in Premises Security Liability III, Study*. Sudbury, MA: Liability Consultants.

CAP Risk Analysis, CAP Index Inc. Exton, PA. http://www.capindex.com

Chicago Tribune (2003) Police Target Hot Spots. 25 June.

Johnson, K. (1985) Protecting the building from liability claims. *New York Times*, 17 March.

Sherman, L. W., Gartin, P. R., and Buerger, M. E. (1989) Hot spots of predatory crime: Routine activities and the criminology of place. *Criminology* 27, 27–55.

Sherman, L. W. and Sherman, E. R. (1983) Crime liability: A new business burden. *Los Angeles Times*, 13 January.

Sherman, L. W. and Klein, J. (1984) *Major Lawsuits over Crime and Security: Trends and Patterns, 1958–82*. Institute of Criminal Justice and Criminology, University of Maryland.

The Miami Herald (2006) Violent crime in U.S. on Upswing. 1–2A.

9 Offensible Space

CRIMINALS, CPTED, AND THE EMERGENCE OF TERRORISM

This chapter examines how the criminal community has successfully altered their environment to obstruct police and the law-abiding community efforts by using "Offensible Space" strategies. It is not only a matter for crime. This is a matter of new importance considering the emerging threat of terrorism. If criminals employ offensible space to their advantage, so, too, can terrorists. The chapter sets the stage for the chapters that follow regarding terror risk assessments around critical infrastructures and the emerging role of CPTED in the new threat environment.

The typical law-abiding community perceives the role of police to protect their persons and property. In reality, the police role consists of very limited, overextended manpower, with diminished resources to combat the drug and criminal business enterprise. Now they add antiterrorism programs to their job description. There has been a concerted effort in law enforcement over the past few decades to shift focus on crime prevention with community oriented policing and problem solving, rather than simply "after the fact" strategies to apprehend criminals and solve crime retroactively (Peak and Glensor, 2004).

Accompanying this law enforcement shift to community policing and problem solving, violent crime rates have declined since 1994, reaching the lowest level ever recorded in 2004. After declining for many years, property crime rates stabilized after 2002. According to the Federal Bureau of Investigation's Uniform Crime Reports, the violent crime rate decreased two percent from 2003 to 2004. From 1995 to 2004 the rate fell 32%. The property crime rate decreased 2% from 2003 to 2004. From 1995 to 2004, the rate fell 23% (Bureau of Justice Statistics, 2006).

Both those trends are changing. "Violent street crime did not go away on September 11," said Jim Pasco, executive director of the Fraternal Order of Police, the nations largest police union (*Miami Herald,* 2006, p. 2A). The first half of 2006 showed an overall increase of violent crime of 3.7%, and robberies increased almost 10%, murders are up 1.4%, and aggravated assaults increased 1.2%. The increases, which were felt in regions across the country, follow an overall jump of 2.4% for violent offenses in all of 2005. In 2005, violent crime posted its largest overall increase since 1991. The FBI said the number of reported robberies was up in cities of all sizes, with the largest increase being almost 13% in cities with populations of 10,000 to 24,999. Robberies and murders in large metropolitan areas increased 8.4%. Experts said the crime upsurge reflected an increase in gang violence. Federal aid to state and local police has declined from $2.5 billion in 2001 in the Clinton Administration, to $890 million in 2006 in the Bush administration (*Miami Herald,* 2006, p. 2A).

Despite a long-term declining trend in crime, the most recent data is showing some dramatic increases and overall trends for increased violence and crime. Those trends are expected to continue through 2010. As a criminologist, my observation of urban behavior in my travels and expert witness testimony has supported that the public does not feel safer, and acts accordingly. Average working folks are afraid. School children and teachers are scared. Elderly persons are scared. Decreasing funding to law enforcement that was used to hire more officers, and support community oriented policing, has dried up. Crime prevention programs, which have always suckled the last drops of police department funding on a good day, is left to fend for themselves.

Communities have been providing increased resources for crime reduction through the hiring of more police, building more prisons, increasing the community awareness, and in some communities around the country, implementing security and crime prevention codes and ordinances.

However, the crime problems facing urban America will not be answered through an increased police force or firepower (Jacobs, 1961; Newman, 1973, Atlas, 2004).

DEFENSIBLE SPACE

In 1969, Oscar Newman coined the expression "Defensible Space" as a surrogate term for a range of mechanisms, real and symbolic barriers, strongly defined areas of influence, and improved opportunities for surveillance, that combine to bring the environment under the control of its residents (Newman, 1973, p. 8). But what if its residents are the criminals?

Newman suggests that design would return productive use of public areas in housing environments beyond the doors of individual apartments back to the users. Hallways, lobbies, grounds, and surrounding streets have usually been considered beyond the control of the building inhabitants.

Oscar Newman's effort in developing Defensible Space concepts for urban dwellers' security led to a shift in law enforcement to include crime prevention instead of merely crime apprehension. The theory of Defensible Space started development in the CPTED arena in 1973 with a research project by the Westinghouse Corporation funded by LEAA (Law Enforcement Assistance Administration, U.S. Department of Justice) to test CPTED in commercial, residential single family developments, and school environments (Westinghouse, 1973). The emphasis of this crime prevention movement was to return control of the built environment to law abiding users.

In order to implement Defensible Space concepts, it is necessary to have consensus, group cohesion, or cooperation among the residents, owners, and managers of the specific environment. This is a point often missed by target hardening and security strategies. It is a point recently reintroduced into CPTED by the emerging field of Second Generation CPTED, which provides specific strategies for strengthening the social capital in a community.

Financial resources are also needed for implementation of security measures. Financial resources may be used to make physical design improvements, hire manpower to provide additional security, and improve the technology and communication network systems to facilitate reporting and surveillance of incidents. In order to implement CPTED into the built environment, there must also be power. Power is the political muscle to get things done and have someone empowered to make the decisions to get things done, such as a city manager, a property manager, home owner associations, and private business owners.

It has been my observation and personal experience that Defensible Space and CPTED strategies have generally not been successfully implemented in most low-income urban public housing environments. Because of the lack of resources, or commitment, public low-income housing continues to be threatened by crime (see Figure 9.1), gang activity, and illegal drug enterprise. The

FIGURE 9.1   Abandoned apartments are taken over by drug users and spotters, and also used as meth labs.

majority of places where Defensible Space and CPTED have been used successfully are in middle-class and high-income privately operated housing environments, and commercial environments.

Middle- and high-income private housing can effectively use defensible space concepts because they have the resources and consensus to implement change. Private apartment buildings or housing subdivisions charge a maintenance fee to all renters and owners. This fee pays for security patrols, CCTV, doormen, perimeter walls and fencing, outdoor and perimeter lighting, access control systems, and so on. Consensus is reached unanimously, since all owners are required to pay the maintenance fee if they choose to live there. So although middle- and upper-income citizens get enhanced security and protection, lower-income residents are still victimized disproportionately.

OFFENSIBLE SPACE

Another major group of users who have successfully used the principles of Defensible Space and CPTED are drug dealers and criminals. Drug dens and criminal hotspots have mastered the CPTED principles for the illicit purpose of creating a safe place, or "*Offensible Space*" to conduct crime. Criminals have access to the two key requirements for successful implementation of Offensible Space: resources and consensus. Drug dealers and criminals have access to large amounts of money illegally earned to make the necessary physical and operational changes for security (see Figure 9.2). Consensus is achieved through total control of the environment with power of intimidation and the willingness to back up their intentions. Thus, criminals use Defensible Space and environmental design strategies in enhancing their security and obstruct justice. That is "Offensible Space."

Although it is early in the evolution of this idea in North America, we can easily see how terrorists use this same strategy to terrorize with impunity. So in addition to preventing crime, this is also why CPTED makes sense as a harm minimization and prevention strategy for anti-terrorism around critical infrastructures. The chapters that follow show how this is the case.

THE EMERGENCE OF AN IDEA

Newman (1973, p. 9) stated that four elements of physical design both individually and in concert, contribute to the creation of secure environments (for the law-abiding user):

FIGURE 9.2 An apartment complex trashed by drug dealers who burrow through the walls to escape police.

1. The territorial definition of space in developments reflecting the area of influence of the inhabitants. This works by subdividing the residential environment into zones toward which adjacent residents easily adopt proprietary attitudes.
2. The positioning of apartment windows to allow residents to naturally survey the exterior and interior public areas of their living environment.
3. The adaptation of the building form and idiom that avoid stigma of peculiarity that allows others to perceive the vulnerability and isolation of the inhabitants.
4. The enhancement of safety by locating residential developments in functionally sympathetic urban areas immediately adjacent to activities that do not provide continued threat.

Territorial behavior involves personalization of or marking of a place or object and communication that it is "owned" by a person or group. Defensive responses may sometimes occur when territorial boundaries are violated (Altman, 1975, p. 107). Furthermore, territories form a continuum defined by duration of occupancy and psychological centrality. Public territories such as bus seats or city sidewalks are least central and enduring, whereas primary territories such as homes, are most central and enduring (see Figure 9.3). In between are secondary territories, such as neighborhoods, which are also characterized by shared ownership among members of a group (Altman and Chemers, 1980).

Brown and Altman (1981) proposed that territorial marking intentions by owners, and responses to territorial violations vary along a similar continuum. Primary territories serve as extensions of the owner's sense of identity; thus, the markers include important (see Figure 9.4), personally meaningful symbols reflecting the owner's personal style and decorative tastes (e.g., nameplates, art objects, flower gardens).

Public territories are less central to the owner's self-concept. Accordingly, the markers show less variety and include less meaningful objects representing the owner's explicit claims to space (e.g., no trespassing signs). Violations of primary territories provoke strong reactions (e.g., physical retaliation, legal sanctions) while violations of public territories provoke weak reactions (e.g., verbal retaliation, territory abandonment). Therefore, personal markers, such as nameplates, may imply greater attachment to, and defense of, a territory. They may also deter territorial intrusions as effectively as more traditional defensive markers such as no trespassing signs (Brown and Altman, 1981).

Newman's observations of crime in public housing projects, found high-crime rates when a public territory, one where individuals can act without fear of censure by residents, immediately

FIGURE 9.3 The backyards are walled in to hide drug and gang activities, demarking the alley as territory for the criminals.

FIGURE 9.4 The litter serves as a marker or environmental cue that drug activity is near and that the legitimate users don't care. The litter also serves as a place to hide the drug stash.

surrounded the poorly marked primary territory of the home (see Figure 9.5). Conversely, Newman found low crime rates when a semipublic area provided a protective buffer zone between totally private areas. The semipublic areas, such as playgrounds, corridors, and plazas are areas over which residents share feelings of ownership and control. The resident's proprietary feelings are believed to translate into upkeep and personalization of the area, neighborhood cohesiveness, and censure of unacceptable behavior in the neighborhood.

Such observations led Newman to promote the use of Defensible Space urban designs that allow residents to survey their territory and that allow clear articulation of the boundaries between public and private regions. This is how the urban designer and architect can help support the residents' "latent territoriality and sense of community" and allow them control over their neighborhoods. Prospective criminals who detect an atmosphere of mutual neighborly concern are presumably discouraged from initiating and/or completing crimes (Newman, 1972, p. 13).

FIGURE 9.5 Even though the apartment building was designed as a courtyard for good visibility and an access gate system, the property is under the control of the criminals and gang members.

FIGURE 9.6   Real barriers keep this drug safe from police intervention.

Defensible Space employs territorial indicators such as symbolic barriers, real or actual barriers, tracers, detectability, and social climate (see Figure 9.6). Symbolic barriers are physical qualities, which communicate the territorial concern and person identity of the owners (Newman, 1972). In a residential setting the landscaping, hedges, welcome mats, and the color of the house all serve as marking or personalization indicating territoriality. Such markers may communicate the territorial concerns of specific families or of entire blocks.

Previous research has related certain types of such markers to rapid territorial defenses (Edney, 1972), to feelings of territorial security control (Pollack and Patterson, 1980). Actual barriers are aspects of a security system such as locks, fences (see Figure 9.7), alarms, and guards that may impede access (Newman, 1972). Tracers are cues that inform violators of probable presence or absence of residents, neighbors, or authorities. Detectability is a factor that includes various aspects of visual or auditory accessibility. Examples include positioning of houses, trees and plantings, motion-activated light sensors, squeaky gates, or barking dogs. Detectability is important since the owners' territorial concern may not lead to effective defense unless residents can easily survey their territory. Residents' visual contact with neighbors also may promote shared territorial concern and defense for the street, and some studies have demonstrated lower crime rates for more visually accessible targets (Mawby, 1977; Odekunle, 1979; Waller and Okihiro, 1978). Social climate refers to the behavioral evidence of individual or shared concern for and defense of an area. An example

FIGURE 9.7   Fencing deflects the drug sellers to the street from this elderly apartment building.

FIGURE 9.8   The front yard fencing is much larger than it needs to be. Is it for keeping people in or keeping people out?

would include a resident's challenge to the approach of strangers or to the occurrence of deviant behavior near the home (Brown and Altman, 1983) (see Figure 9.8).

Defensible Space as Newman had envisioned it was to be evolved in a social/spatial hierarchy from private to semiprivate to semipublic to public level. In the collective human habitat, the hierarchy was to extend from the personal space of the apartment to the open street. The variables used in creating Defensible Space and CPTED are now being used for creating Offensible Space for criminals. Criminals are using access control, surveillance, and territorial strategies to obstruct law enforcement and ensure the security of their illegal businesses.

Since 1970, there have been numerous studies and attempted applications (Westinghouse, 1975) of CPTED and Defensible Space but have met with only limited short-term success. By the end of the 1970s, Defensible Space and CPTED fell into relative obscurity. These concepts have fallen on hard times as a result of the lack of resources to make the operational changes and physical changes needed, and lacked the consensus by the users, or persons with power.

The law-abiding community generally lacks the control over the built environment and the long-term commitment to cope with the slowness of change. For example, as budget cutbacks became inevitable during the Reagan administration in the late 1980s, the Federal Department of Housing and Urban Development (HUD) was not in a position to implement the costly and staff intensive changes needed to reduce criminal opportunity in public housing. HUD has made a considerable effort in the 1990s and early 21st century to incorporate New Urbanism and safe neighborhood design concepts in new communities.

TURNING DEFENSIBLE SPACE BACKWARDS

It has been the middle- and upper-income private housing environments that have been able to take measures to provide security for the building users. Those environments successfully implement Defensible Space features that:

1. *Spot criminals*—identify persons or strangers who do not belong in the specific environment.
2. *Watching others*—surveillance to keep an eye on children, neighbors, property, or unusual behavior that require notification.

3. *Reporting problems to the police*—residents and staff being trained to look for outsiders or criminals, and having the ability to watch the property with surveillance techniques can quickly respond to an incident with police and private security.
4. *Provide a communication network*—private security guards can use walkie-talkies, or telephones to call for police assistance or intervention. Residents can phone security staff with a potential problem or activate an alarm system that is monitored by the building or authorities.
5. *Make physical and mechanical improvements to the environment to reduce the opportunity for crime*, such as security grilling on windows, solid core doors, alarm systems, attack dogs, dead bolt locks, and so on.

Of course, none of these strategies say much about who actually lives in the place. It is assumed that legitimate, law-abiding citizens live there. But that is often not the case, or the situation may change as new groups move into and out of neighborhoods. Conversely, criminals, and potential terrorists, are protected in such fortresses. They use Defensible Space features to create their own Offensible Space. Some examples include:

1. *Lookouts to spot police or outsiders*—Kids on bicycles act as lookouts for police or outsiders, and shout codes to the criminal.
2. *Access control*—The spotters and door guards keep a watchful eye on those approaching the area and quickly make a determination of who is a legitimate drug buyer/user or criminal cohort. Once cleared, the person is allowed entry to the house.
3. Instead of reporting crime to the police, *the criminals use police scanners and walkie-talkies and cell phones to report any potential violation of their offensible space* for swift action.
4. *A communication network is established* using an intricate set of codes for the spotters on bikes to notify the dealer for discarding any evidence and fleeing the scene.
5. *Mechanical improvements in building security*—the use of solid doors, locks, window bars, attack dogs, rattlesnakes, booby-traps, and so on to slow down police entry and prevent the ripoff of drugs by other drug dealers.

CRIMINALS TAKE OVER

Atlas (2002) conducted a study to measure Offensible Space features at 50 police-known crime sites in South Florida. Data was gathered from personal observation in rides with police cars and personal cars. The negative use of access control, surveillance, and territoriality features in Offensible Spaces sites were consistently observed in the different sites studied.

The Atlas study observed access control features that demonstrated:

1. People screening by criminals to determine who would qualify to gain entry into the crime site to buy drugs, and so on.
2. Often windows were boarded, or had iron bars or security devices (see Figure 9.9).
3. Deadbolts, peepholes, and security gates were used to screen people to determine who had access to the crime site.

FIGURE 9.9   The vantage point of a corner location.

FIGURE 9.10   The stairwell portholes of the building shown here were used as a lookout tower for the drug dealers, who could see police coming for miles.

Surveillance control strategies used at the crime sites revealed:

1. Extensive use of spotters, often in the form of juveniles who cannot be convicted or receive any substantial legal sanction for aiding the dealer. The spotters provide an informal audio-visual surveillance network and alarm system that is very effective. The spotters may earn hundreds of dollars per day by shouting warning codes when police or outsiders approach.
2. Use of peepholes through heavily reinforced doors to screen visitors.
3. Often spotters are placed on roofs or upper floors of the apartment building to serve as lookouts with a better vantage point (see Figure 9.10). Typically, upon the spotting of police everyone disappears. The spotters would most commonly watch outsiders from benches and yard areas (open areas of common turf), and balconies (see Figure 9.11).
4. The most common location for an Offensible Space is an apartment or building on the corner. The buildings are usually linear and do not allow a direct view of doors from the street. The corner vantage point allows better surveillance on who is approaching the building (see Figure 9.12).

FIGURE 9.11   A spotter watching me carefully.

FIGURE 9.12   Spotter looking out corner window with the advantage of location.

5. None of the crime sites had a lighted entrance and most of the crime sites had no working exterior lights at all.

Crime magnet sites used territorial features to solidify the criminal's sphere of influence. Territorial features observed:

1. Tight clustering of buildings at right angles to a major traffic corridor.
2. There is usually little or no landscaping.
3. There is usually no separation between the public street and the front entrance of the crime site, such as a yard, landscaping, trees, fences, etc.
4. There are usually signs of vandalism, graffiti, and litter. Often there is obvious building code and/or life safety violations (see Figure 9.13, Figure 9.14, and Figure 9.15).
5. Most crime magnets are on corner locations of a building in the middle of a block, allowing many avenues for escape and observation.

FIGURE 9.13   Cars were vandalized in high-crime, high-risk areas.

FIGURE 9.14   Chopped up cars were often used to store drugs in.

FIGURE 9.15   Trash in a building alcove attracts more garbage and rats.

There appears to be a pattern of Offensible Space utilized at the high crime sites. Offensible Space tactics use access control, surveillance, and territoriality features to create an impenetrable environment able to resist police entry or competitive raiding (see Figure 9.16 and Figure 9.17). Newman (1973, p. 12) suggests that architecture can create or prevent crime. I disagreed with this architecturally deterministic view (Atlas, 1982) and suggested that architecture's role in behavior is very subtle and difficult to measure. In some places, certain kinds of space and spatial layout favor the clandestine activities of criminals, especially considering the type of people who might gravitate to these spaces. If these criminal sites were located in middle- or upper-class neighborhoods would there still be crime, or would the surrounding influence drive away the criminal element?

Jane Jacobs (1961) suggested citizens should take control of the streets with increased involvement and participation. Instead, in many communities, criminals have been taking claim of the streets and semipublic areas as part of the sphere of their Offensible Space. Sidewalks and streets adjoining the main drug/crime site quickly became part of the turf of the criminal. Fences, walls, barricades are commonly established to create a series of barriers for police or law abiding citizens.

The employees of the drug dealer or criminal gang make the sense of proprietorship or territoriality real. These employees act as lookouts, enforcers, and distributing agents. If a person is not at the Offensible Space site doing business they are made to feel very uncomfortable quickly, and experience a sense of danger and risk for personal safety.

FIGURE 9.16   Fencing was used to deter police as much as other criminals.

FIGURE 9.17   A pit bull at the entrance was the drug dealer's front door alarm system.

A series of behavioral and environmental cues are given to the non-criminal that makes the statement that you have entered unto an Offensible Space zone (see Figure 9.18 and Figure 9.19). Offensible Space is the reverse mirror image of Defensible Space with bad intentions. The combination of muscle enforcers at the access points, the dilapidated condition of the surrounding area, the homogeneity of racial/ethnic mix, the openness of the dealing, and the level of related violence, makes a statement of clear and present danger to anyone who does not belong in that area or is not doing business with the dealer (see Figure 9.18).

FIGURE 9.18   Signage tells the story of risk.

FIGURE 9.19 Signage and fencing serve as a double-edged barrier.

FIGURE 9.20 Fencing protecting a drug dealer's yard.

The implications are that the majority of law-abiding citizens cannot afford "Defensible Space" tactics, nor do they have the power or consensus to implement the strategies uniformly. Where they have tried to react, they have had limited success. For example, over the last thirty years one crime prevention strategy has been the citizen crime watch. Neighborhood watches are formed, reactively, to an initial series of criminal events. But once the crime is displaced geographically, the community energy and participation of citizens often fades.

CPTED features are relatively successful in more wealthy residences since owners subsidize them. The owners can implement a building perimeter, a doorman for the screening of visitors, exterior lighting, private security guards walking and driving patrol, parking access control, alarm systems, communications networking with building users and security staff. Unfortunately, the great majority of Americans cannot afford the high rent or maintenance fees to pay for Defensible Space advantages.

The general public does not have the money, energy, or muscle to back up the commitment for keeping criminals away. The law-abiding community often cannot achieve consensus to put up walls, change street design, hire more police, obtain better lighting, or erect guardhouses or barricades. On the other hand, criminals can successfully use Offensible Space tactics in their criminal environments because they have the resources (see Figure 9.20), the power, and the ability to make the changes they desire. Criminals have substantially more control over their working and living environment than the average law-abiding citizen.

PREVENTING OFFENSIBLE SPACE

The solution to Offensible Space lies in a comprehensive multi-level approach of crime prevention through environmental design. Jeffery (1971) proposes primary, secondary, and tertiary prevention strategies. Crime must be attacked at the roots and causes, not just the symptoms. One of the steps to reduce Offensible Space sites is to identify them, notify the owner of criminal activity if appropriate, and then confiscate or tear down the property using nuisance and abatement ordinances as the legal vehicle. Police are using the Racketeer Influenced and Corrupt Organizations (RICO) Act to confiscate properties and other forfeiture laws to put the criminals out of business.

There are policies and strategies that can reduce the opportunity for Offensible Space to gain such control over the vulnerable areas in your town. Most communities have sufficient laws on the books now to control this problem if resources were spent enforcing:

1. Building code and zoning regulations, especially as they relate to litter, safety violations, signage, parking, lighting, and so on.
2. Establish nuisance and abatement ordinances that establish legal and physical procedures for responding to forfeiture of defaulted properties, condemnation, and razing of abandoned structures used as crack dens.
3. Implement CPTED awareness in the building review and law enforcement process to design security into new buildings and renovations.
4. Increase awareness and emphasis on law enforcement patrol patterns to crime prevention rather than just criminal apprehension.
5. Create an enforcement component of police and building department inspectors to fine and arrest property owners for litter, and knowingly permitting criminal transactions on the property.
6. Establish and nurture crime- and block-watch programs for residences, businesses, and school zones.
7. Increase pedestrian traffic where appropriate with legitimate users, and use street closures to define neighborhoods and reduce illegitimate vehicular traffic.
8. Provide life skill education to all ages of school children on how to cope successfully with life's challenges and reduce the need to escape the pain of living with drugs or alcohol. Some of these strategies are employed in the Toronto and Western Australia case studies described in Chapter 7 under the Second Generation CPTED title "capacity building."

Crimes are committed because they are easy to commit. A person sees an easy opportunity and so commits a crime, regardless of the legality or consequences. Increasing the effort needed to commit a crime eliminates casual criminals.

Target hardening is one method of increasing the effort using techniques such as: improving locks to be dead bolts; upgrading window screens; using break resistant glazing; increased use of fencing; magnetic locking doors. Another technique is access control, which includes installing barriers, designing paths, walkways, and roads, so that unwanted and unauthorized users are prevented from entering vulnerable areas. Barriers may include limiting entrance to specific individuals, places or times; security vestibules, parking lot barriers, entry phones, visitor check-in booths, guard stations, vehicle control systems, biometric screening for access control. Some ways of reducing Offensible Space include:

- Controlling access to a facility by pedestrian and vehicular movement patterns.
- Divide interior and exterior spaces into small, easily identified areas that are associated within a specific group of individuals or users.
- Have detection devices easily visible to increase the perceived risk to the offender and by posting signs advertising the use of such devices.
- Minimizing the number of entrances to the interior of a building, with the function of the remaining entrances clearly identified. Entrances should be secured when not in use.
- Provide keyed access to vulnerable areas such as laundry rooms, storage areas, elevators, bathrooms.
- Control parking lot access by means of gates, badges, and security passes.
- Emergency stairs and exits should be restricted in their intended use by equipping them with alarm panic bars with time egress delays and no exterior door handles.
- Install barriers on vulnerable openings such as ground floor windows, exterior fire stairs, roof openings, and skylights. Fence off problem areas to prevent unauthorized access and funnel movement along desired paths.
- Provide lockable security areas for items, which are stored in low surveillance areas, or items that are easily portable.
- Control access for servicing and deliveries.

- Screening devices should be used when appropriate, to allow legitimate building users and guests. Employee screening should be separate for use of badges or IDs.
- Formal surveillance by use of security personnel and hardware such as CCTV and intrusion detection systems.
- Informal surveillance by use of the facility employees uses the existing resources of doormen, concierge, maintenance workers, and secretaries to increase site surveillance and crime reporting.
- Improving natural surveillance by careful architectural placement of windows, doors, lighting, and controlled landscaping and plantings.
- Interior lighting enhances opportunities for casual or formal surveillance in spaces visible through doors and windows. Lighting should be even, without deep shadows, and fixtures should be vandal-proof.
- Interior blind spots, such as alcoves, and dead end corridors create vulnerable entrapment areas and should be eliminated when possible.

Reducing the rewards of crime makes illegal activity less worthwhile or nonproductive to commit. This includes techniques that make targets of crime less valuable to the offender, or which remove crime targets that have value to the criminal. To reduce the rewards of crime, the design professional can remove the high-risk target from the premises or the architectural program (so as to not design that high-risk area as part of the scope of work), identifying or tagging property assets, removing the inducements for crime, and rule the boundary setting. Removing the inducements of crime include removing those targets before they can become an easy opportunity such as:

- Vacant lots, apartments, offices, and spaces should be used or given to legitimate users to protect against vandalism and damage.
- Exterior walls should be painted with graffiti resistant epoxy and/or landscaped with creeping vines to prevent the wall from acting as a mural for graffiti taggers.

Clearly stating the ground rules against crime and establishing standard procedures to punish those who violate the rules with consequences can accomplish removing the excuses for criminal behavior. Clearly defined regulations and signage prevents offenders from excusing their crimes with claims of ignorance or misunderstanding.

CPTED AND TERRORISM

Can CPTED prevent acts of terrorism and reduce Offensible Space? Very possibly! CPTED emphasizes problem seeking before rushing into problem solving. CPTED starts with a threat and vulnerability analysis to determine the weakness and potential for attack. Attack from criminal behavior, or attack from terrorist activity only reflect a change in the level and types of threats. The process and challenges are the same. CPTED and Defensible Space planning are a planning process, as compared to fortressing or target hardening. When designing against crime or terrorism the security consultant must resist the rush for quick answers. What the CPTED process does is ask the questions about (1) access control; (2) natural surveillance; (3) territorial reinforcement; (4) maintenance; and (5) management strategies can (a) increase the effort to commit crime or terrorism, (b) increase the risks associated with crime or terrorism, (c) reduce the rewards associated with crime or terrorism, and (d) remove the excuses why people do not comply with the rules and exhibit inappropriate behavior. The CPTED process provides the direction to solve the challenges of crime and terrorism with organizational (people), mechanical (technology and hardware), and natural design (architecture and circulation flow) methods.

SUMMARY

Offensible Space is a byproduct of society's inability to uniformly apply crime prevention and law enforcement in the community. Offensible Space is a result of the community's and government's disorganization and lack of citizen and political consensus. Offensible Space is the result of criminals and terrorists being organized, motivated, and well financed to create a crime environment that is resistant to outside intrusion or detection. Until the law-abiding community achieves a higher level of organization, consensus, and commits adequate resources to fight the criminal community, Offensible Space sites will be growing and posing a clear and present danger to society.

As one can easily see, a lot of thought and money goes into making a building secure. However, an architect cannot change human nature, and many criminal acts will be perpetrated in spite of the best-laid plans. Accept that our built environment cannot be defended against every potential threat. No building security system could have prevented the act of terrorism of 11 September 2001, or the bombing of our embassies, or courthouses. But there are many action steps that could have been taken in between the conception of the plan and the implementation that could have reduced the opportunity for successful implementation of their plans.

Security systems come in many varieties, but crime is not monolithic. Furthermore, it is ironic that the type of crime that most people fear is not the type that occurs most frequently. Stranger to stranger crimes (assault, murder, rape, and robbery) are less common than white-collar crime. Most criminals don't tote a gun. The terrorism of the 21st century will probably not be bombings, but rather industrial espionage, computer pilfering, and destruction of records, biological, and chemical terrorism. The greatest threat to us on a day-to-day basis is from workplace violence and street crime. Designing against the threats of crime and workplace violence is going to greatly reduce the likelihood of acts of terrorism. It is all about controlling access and basic CPTED principles. Even terrorists have to access our buildings and assets.

Urban design is one of the least used pieces of the security puzzle to make our public and private buildings safe and secure. CPTED and Defensible Space planning create the environment for better security by allowing natural surveillance and unobstructed visibility, controlling access to persons who belong on the property, preventing unauthorized access of persons onto the property, integrating the security technology into functional design and architecture, allowing the legitimate building users to be your capable guardians for legitimate activity and deterrence of criminal activity. If we choose to surrender control of our buildings and facilities to the criminals, drug dealers, and terrorists, they will use the tools of CPTED and Offensible Space against us, more effectively, than we can protect against the people with bad intentions.

With the growing threat to our country from drugs, crime, and the lack of uniform response, the United States has become very vulnerable to another group of organized criminals: terrorists. Even after the attack on 9/11, security and crime prevention has only resulted in a minimal substantial change in most building environments. Many of the office buildings and government centers that had added post-9/11 security measures and guards have reverted back to minimal security, because of the expense and perceived lack of threat. The only place where security has really changed substantially to date is in courthouses and airports. The chapters that follow describe how to improve this situation.

REFERENCES

Altman, I. (1975) *Environment and Social Behavior: Privacy, Personal Space, Territory, and Crowding,* Monterey, CA: Brooks/Cole.

Altman, I. and Chemers, M. M. (1980) *Culture and Environment.* Monterey, CA: Brooks/Cole.

Atlas, R. (1979) Police's Role in Crime Prevention. Paper presented to the American Society of Criminology.

Atlas, R. (1982) Prison Violence: Architectural Determinism. Doctoral dissertation, Florida State University.

Atlas, R. (1989) Just when you thought it was safe. *Professional Safety Magazine,* American Society of Safety Engineers, 28–33.

Atlas, R. (1990 Offensible Space Crime Environment Study. Unpublished study, University of Miami.

Atlas, R. (1991) Offensible Space: The other side of CPTED. *Security Management Magazine.*

Atlas, R. (2002) Sunrise Boulevard Streetscape CPTED Analysis. Broward County, Florida.

Atlas, R. (2004) Defensible space: An architectural retrospective. *Master Builder* 1(1).

Atlas, R. (2003) How are criminals using CPTED—Offensible Space. *Security Management*, 146–148.

Atlas, S. (1988) Just when you thought it was safe to go back in the . . . building!" *Security Management*, 64–73.

Atlas, S. (1994) Environmental barriers to crime. *Ergonomics in Design*, 9–16.

Architectural Record. (2001) October, 24–26.

Bureau of Justice Statistics. (1990) *Victimization Levels and Rates, Preliminary 1989.* Washington, DC: U.S. Department of Justice.

Brown, B., and Altman, I. (1983) Territoriality, defensible space and residential burglary: An environmental analysis. *Journal of Environmental Psychology 3,* 203–220.

Brown, B. B. and Altman, I. (1981) Territoriality and residential crime: A conceptual framework. In P. J. Brantingham and P. L. Brantingham (Eds.), *Urban Crime and Environmental Criminology.* Beverly Hills, CA: Sage.

Crowe, T. (2000) *Crime Prevention through Environmental Design,* 2nd ed. Boston: Butterworth-Heinemann.

Environmental Design Technical Group News, EDRA. September 2001.

Edney, J. (1972) Property, possession, and permanence: A field study in human territoriality. *Journal of Applied Social Psychology, 2,* 272–282.

Jacobs, J. (1961) *The Death and Life of Great American Cities.* New York: Vintage Press.

Jeffery, C. R. (1971) *Crime Prevention through Environmental Design.* Beverly Hills, CA: Sage.

Mawby, R. I. (1977) Defensible space: A theoretical and empirical appraisal. *Urban Studies, 14,* 169–79.

Newman, O. (1972) *Defensible Space: Crime Prevention through Urban Design.* New York: Macmillan.

Odekunle, F. (1979) Victims of property crime in Nigeria: A preliminary investigation in Zaria. *Victimology: An International Journal, 4.*

Peak, K. and Glenson, R. (2004) *Community Policing and Problem Solving: Strategies and Practices,* 4th ed. New York: Prentice Hall.

Pollack, L. M. and Patterson, A. H. (1980). Territoriality and fear of crime in elderly and non-elderly homeowners. *Journal of Social Psychology, 11,* 119–129.

Report to the Nation on Crime and Justice. U.S. Department of Justice, Bureau of Justice Statistics. 2006.

Security Watch, (2001) *Bureau of Business Practice Newsletter,* Oct., 4

Waller, I. and Okihiro, N. (1978) *Burglary: The Victim and the Public.* Toronto: University of Toronto Press.

Westinghouse Electric Corporation (1975) *Elements of CPTED.* Arlington, VA: LEAA Grant.

Werkerle, G. and Whitzman, C. (1995) *Safe Cities: Guidelines for Planning, Design and Management.* New York: Van Nostrand.

U.S. Department of Justice·Office of Justice Programs, Bureau of Justice Statistics, Crime & Justice Electronic Data Abstracts, Key Crime & Justice Facts at a Glance Dec. 2005. Web site: http://www.ojp.usdoj.gov/bjs/

Uniform Crime Reports, Federal Bureau of Investigation. Web site: http://www.fbi.gov/ucr/2005prelim/20050penpage.htm

Part II

Protecting The Built Environment

10 Terrorism and Infrastructure Protection

Risks and Protection

Randy Atlas and Tony DiGregorio

After the terrorist attacks of September 11, 2001, the subject of security in infrastructure facilities gained interest among engineers, security professionals, and public and private entities. Drinking water facilities, waste treatment plants, electrical generation plants, natural gas pipelines, and communication networks serve thousands of communities within the country. They are the most important support for life in the built environment, bringing communities to civilized standards of life. Infrastructure is the most feasible indicator of the economic capacity of the United States and most advanced countries, at the same time is susceptible to potential threats with devastating consequences for human life and economy. Most governments view critical infrastructure as those assets, services, and systems that support the economic, political, and social life of a country whose importance is such that any entire or partial loss or compromise could:

- Cause large-scale loss of life
- Have a serious impact on the national economy
- Have other grave social consequences for the community
- Be of immediate concern to the national government

Critical infrastructure is categorized as these major sectors:

- Communications
- Emergency services
- Energy and power suppliers and distribution
- Finance
- Food and food supply
- Government and public service
- Health
- Public safety
- Transportation systems: air, water, sea, rail

The most common risks for infrastructure facilities arise from natural disasters, human mistakes, crime, sabotage, and terrorism. Infrastructure facilities design aims to protect buildings from natural disasters, reduce the possibilities of human errors, and protect working personnel from the event of an accident. Although the focus is primarily on natural disasters, sabotage or terrorist attacks also must receive design considerations. Crime Prevention Through Environmental Design (CPTED) principles bring a new perspective to critical infrastructure buildings in order to protect these facilities against potential crime, sabotage, and terrorism and natural disasters.

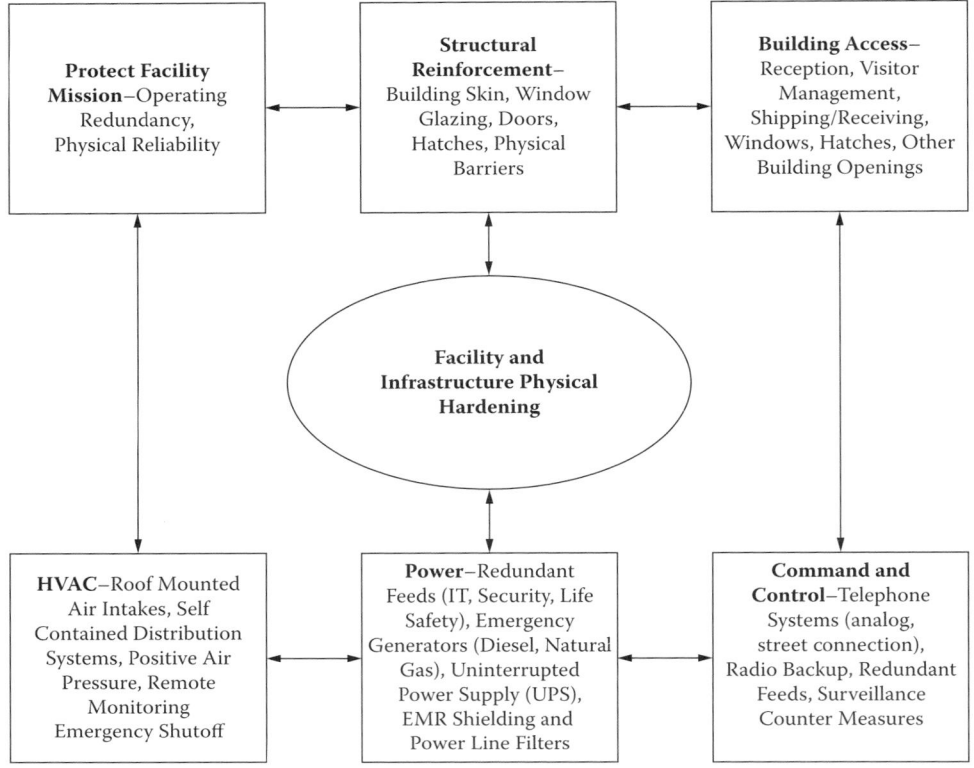

FIGURE 10.1 Facility and infrastructure security.

The CPTED risk-assessment process, described elsewhere in this book, examines how critical infrastructure facilities can be a powerful weapon in the wrong hands. The purpose of this chapter is to establish how CPTED principles support design considerations (see Figure 10.1) in order to create safer infrastructure facilities.

WATER TREATMENT AND WASTE MANAGEMENT

The most obvious example of critical infrastructure and one of the most precious assets in our environment is water. All life depends on good drinking water and waste treatment.

The water that we drink and manage can come from ground water supplies or surface water. To extract ground water from aquifers by wells, each water-supply system uses one or more wells, commonly arranged in clusters or well fields. The type of well used depends on the kind of geological conditions of the aquifer, because the way water enters the well is by drilling a hole below the well casing. Ground water extracted from wells is sent to a water treatment plant and after being treated, water is sent to a pump station, where it is pumped to an elevated storage tank. From the elevated tank, the water is sent to a water main and then to a water distribution system that supplies urban areas. Surface water may be obtained from natural or regulated lakes, or from reservoirs by pumping water to a treatment plant. According to the U.S. Department of the Interior Report 86–4122, treatment for surface water is more complex than for ground water because of the variable amounts and character of suspended and dissolved material.

Water treatment methods range from the simple process of disinfectection, through chlorination to remove biological impurities, to the complex process of water softening and desalination, to change or reduce the concentration of chemicals in the water. Even with its complexity, desalting is one of the most used processes. Filtration treatment removes suspended particles, some bacteria, color, and taste, by passing water through a permeable fabric or porous bed of material (Stein, 2000, p. 578).

Disinfection is the most important health related water treatment, because, in the primary phase it destroys microorganisms that can cause disease in humans. Then, secondary disinfection maintains a disinfectant residual in the treated water that prevents microorganism regrowth (Stein, 2000, p. 579).

PROTECTION OF WATER DISTRIBUTION AND WASTE TREATMENT PLANTS

Unprotected potable water plants can be used as a powerful weapon of sabotage and terrorism and their protection is critical. The first consideration for water infrastructure facilities protection is location. Generally water and waste treatment facilities are located in isolated places, next to rivers or lakes far from urban areas, often near to industrial complexes. These location requirements provide favorable conditions for CPTED implementation because of ample opportunities for surveillance, access control, and territoriality strategies, which can be easily applied for the detection of any illegitimate activity.

Water systems are vulnerable at multiple points. Contaminants can be introduced at sources of the water, the treatment systems of the water, distribution systems, sewage and wastewater treatment systems, and the discharge systems. The risks to water supply are public health risks from the use of contaminated water. There is also the potential for economic loss from lack of usable water. The risks to wastewater and storm water are public health and safety risks from explosion of volatile contaminants, aerosolization/vaporization of pathogens and toxic materials vented to environment, disruption of treatment process, use of contaminated sludge etc. There are also the economic risks from use of contaminated sludge inappropriately.

An example of security upgrades and security site improvements is the Austin Water Treatment Plant (see Figure 10.2).

Security upgrades for water treatment plants after 9/11 typically include a computer based plant security system utilizing security card access and monitoring cameras with all activities monitored from the Water Treatment Plant control room. The control room should be classified as the most vulnerable area once inside the plant. The process allows the operator to control filter back washing, pump start/stops, chemical dosage changes, and numerous other routine operational functions.

FIGURE 10.2 Water treatment plant entranceway.

FIGURE 10.3   George T. Lohmeyer Regional Wastewater Treatment Plant perimeter fence.

The computerized system also provides remote pumping and storage facilities controls, process alarming, data logging, and reporting functions. In addition to security functions, the computer interface provides a window to the operational process and allows the operator to control and monitor many operational processing functions.

The monitoring equipment typically will include security camera monitors, a multiplexing computer, video recorders, and alarm sensors. Once inside the plant, there should be a clearly defined hierarchy of private to public spaces. CPTED strategies emphasize a layered system that should be fundamental in this type of facility. Among other attributes desired, the plant will typically use perimeter fencing, setbacks to the primary buildings and tanks, a secured gate, intercom, access control, CCTV coverage of essential areas, lighting, and warning signage.

Special design considerations for water and wastewater facilities to achieve improved security are to plan for redundancy, flexibility, and to back up power supply. Whether the threat is a natural disaster or terrorist attack, "stuff happens" and the ability to have quick business recovery is critical.

An example of layered security in this type of facility is the George T. Lohmeyer Regional Wastewater Treatment Plant, located in the industrial area adjacent to Port Everglades, Fort Lauderdale, Florida (see Figure 10.3).

CPTED has been used in the design and site planning of this facility. The façade of the plant blends with the urban character of the street and character of the industrial buildings in the area. Site boundaries are defined by an iron picket fence. The transparency of the fence is a positive characteristic as it permits natural surveillance from a police car from the adjacent streets. The name of the building is properly identified in the sign placed at the setback area.

Access to the plant is through a well-marked and signed entrance. Along the adjacent road, a solid wall substitutes for the iron picket perimeter fence to hide the nature of the buildings inside from an outsider's view. The public has vehicular access only, controlled from the administrative building by staff using CCTV surveillance. The parking lot and administrative building are located in an open area that permits for natural surveillance and access control. Personnel use small golf carts to move throughout the plant complex. The entrance gate can be a vulnerable point and is secured only by a chain and a mortise lock. On a critical note, a large portion of the chain link fence that protects the property is covered by vegetation and tall trees, making this area difficult for surveillance and gives the idea of an unprotected area. At the same time, this fence is not properly

FIGURE 10.4 Plant setbacks from street.

lighted, even though all plant interior roads are well illuminated (see Figure 10.4, Figure 10.5, Figure 10.6, and Figure 10.7).

The George T. Lohmeyer Regional Wastewater Treatment Plant understood the need for CPTED and security elements to be designed into the facility and does prove to be a good working example of security and functionality working together.

NATIONAL INTEREST IN INFRASTRUCTURE SAFETY

There are other examples of an increased interest to create safer critical infrastructure. The Infrastructure Security Partnership (TISP) Web site (http://www.tisp.org) shows an array of activities and seminars about infrastructure safety. This organization was established as a forum for U.S. based public and private sector nonprofit organizations to collaborate on issues regarding the security of the nation's built environment, including natural and man-made disasters. TISP acts as a national asset facilitating dialogue on physical infrastructure security. TISP represents more than two million individuals and hundreds of firms involved in the planning, design, construction, and operation of the nation's critical infrastructure.

FIGURE 10.5 Plant access gate for parking and administrative office is left unlocked, undermining all of the other physical security measures.

FIGURE 10.6   Plant layout signage explains where buildings are located.

Another example is the Environmental Protection Agency Web site (http://www.epa.gov/) that state emergency response plans describe the actions that a drinking water or wastewater utility would take in response to a major event, such as natural disasters or man-made emergencies. They should address the issues raised by the utility's vulnerability assessment. Emergency Response plans, along with a Vulnerability Assessment, help water utilities to evaluate their susceptibility to potential threats, and identify corrective actions to reduce or mitigate the risk of serious consequences from vandalism, insider sabotage, or terrorist attack.

Water and wastewater facilities must comply with the Bioterrorism Act of 2002, which "requires community drinking water systems serving populations of more than 3,300 persons to conduct assessments of their vulnerabilities to terrorist attack or other intentional acts and to defend against adversarial actions that might substantially disrupt the ability of a system to provide a safe and reliable supply of drinking water."

FIGURE 10.7   Perimeter fencing around the water treatment plant defines the borders.

Water Infrastructure in Residential, Commercial, and Office Buildings

The way water is used and stored depends on the type of building. Drinkable water infrastructure in buildings becomes one of the most important assets to be protected. It is important to identify where the water is located and how the system works. Small, low buildings with moderate demand of water use an *upfeed distribution system*. Water is obtained from the street mains. Tall buildings pump water from the street main to a roof storage tank known as *downfeed distribution system*. The storage tank is controlled by building maintenance personnel only. "In most high rise buildings, 60 stories and more, an entire rooftop crowded with equipment and technical facilities is needed to serve the stories below" (Stein, 2000, p. 644).

The authors of *Mechanical and Electrical Equipment for Buildings* (Stein, 2000) explain that since the 1960s, most tall buildings have a two-story band above the structural roof that houses the necessary mechanical equipment and technical facilities. This roof area can include the following items:

- Water storage tanks
- Two-story penthouses over elevator banks
- Chimneys
- Plumbing vents
- Exhaust blowers
- Air conditioning cooling towers
- Cantilevered rolling ring to support scaffold for exterior window washing
- Perimeter track for the window washing ring
- Photovoltaic cells and/or solar collectors for DHW

Thus, roofs are a high-risk and vulnerable area of a building, and CPTED recommendations need to be taken into consideration. The equipment on most building roofs works in coordination with equipment located in basement mechanical rooms. Both are the ends of a complex grid that forms the heating, ventilation, and air conditioning (HVAC) system, and potable water system. These systems support the artificial environment of the building that directly affects people's well-being.

Clearly, with the potential that a terrorist might disperse chemical, biological, or radioactive agents throughout a building, the whole HVAC and potable water system must be protected. Ideally, a full risk-assessment protocol should be enacted on a regular basis, such as the computerized ATRiM risk-assessment model described elsewhere in this book. At a bare minimum, a few CPTED and security design considerations are:

- Access to building roofs must be limited to maintenance staff only.
- Building roofs must be treated as mechanical areas. Thus, access to roofs must be strictly controlled through keyed locks, access control, or comparable measures. Fire and life safety egress should be carefully reviewed when restricting roof access.
- Fencing or other barriers should restrict access from adjacent roofs.
- Roof doors should be monitored for opening and closing.

PROTECTING ELECTRICAL INFRASTRUCTURE

Overhead electric service is commonly used because of the low cost of this delivery of the utility. By contrast, underground electric service has a high cost but becomes more popular because of the lack of overhead physical and visual clutter, service reliability, and long life.

Power is generated at the generating stations, usually located near a source of water for cooling purposes, such as a lake or a large pond. To facilitate power transportation to bulk load centers, the voltage is transformed to higher voltage. The voltage transformation takes place at a substation outside the generation plant. The power is transmitted over a system of high voltage lines.

To feed urban areas, the high voltage is transformed to a lower level at substations. The substations are located in strategic places closer to the loads to reduce voltage for distributing the power to residential, commercial, and industrial customers (Beaty, 1998, p. 5).

At all stages of this process, security is one of the main issues to take in consideration. Every step is sensitive to be affected by unexpected natural forces, accidents, sabotage, or terrorism having consequences in human life. The level of risk depends on the repercussions on human life and ecology.

The scale of a failure in a generation plant can be more devastating than a failure in a distribution system. Security in generation plants is more strict and sophisticated. Nevertheless, malfunction in the distribution system is more common. According to Beaty, about 90% of customer outages in the United States are caused by problems with distribution system equipment. A fault in a single distribution line could affect customers in a neighborhood (see Figure 10.8). A fault in a transformer would only affect a few customers. A fault at a substation could affect a section of town and many hundreds of customers. Outages in the distribution systems occur by thousands every day, caused mainly by accidents (vehicle crash into poles), by animals (birds, snakes, squirrels), and by trees.

Generation plants are located in remote areas near a source of water to keep the machinery fresh. Despite this, the building itself needs to have design consideration such as being separated from neighbor areas by a tree buffer or sound-absorbing walls.

Like any other secured building, protection and control of the premises is based on a layered system, where the physical presence of security personnel is the first and most direct way to remind employees, visitors, or intruders that complying with procedures is not optional (Barnett and Bjornsgaard, 2000, p. 260). With a strong territoriality definition a building complex projects an image of a "highly secured place." Following the principle of territoriality, plant layout has to be designed creating a clear definition between public, semipublic, and restricted areas. Access to private areas is narrowed through a system of lobbies, waiting rooms, corridors, and locked doors.

Once inside the plant, visitor's activity, pedestrian badges, and vehicular badges have to be collected in a checkpoint area. This checkpoint has to be strategically located to be able to see any point from it.

As in water treatment plants, one of the most vulnerable areas in power generation complexes is the control center. In the control center, technical operations of the whole electric power system are coordinated. Operators have an overall picture of their system and interconnection points with other neighboring utilities through map boards, computer screens, and monitoring data. In addition, the dispatchers control any emergency-operating plan that may need to be implemented. Direct access to control rooms (see Figure 10.9) has to be restricted and preferably controlled with card key integrated access control systems. Control rooms have to be located far from public areas.

Transformers are devices that change or transform alternating current of one voltage to an alternating current of another voltage (Stein, 2000, p. 937). An electrical substation is an outdoor infrastructure in which several transformers are placed that reduce voltage from high-tension lines to the voltage needed for domestic use. Often these devices are sitting on an open piece of land next to a building, which makes them extremely vulnerable to attack (see Figure 10.10 and Figure 10.11).

There are also outdoor transformer units used on the premises of buildings. These small transformers are common, instead of the indoor transformer units, for a number of operational and practical reasons (making them difficult to remove for security reasons alone). Some of the reasons they are outside the building include:

- They do not require interior building space
- To reduce the noise problems within buildings
- They are easy to maintain and replace
- To reduce the interior heat problems
- To have an opportunity to use low-cost, long-life, oil-filled units

A Unit Substation or a Load Center Substation is an assembly that contains a primary circuit breaker, a step-down transformer, meters, controls, and secondary switchgear. The type of

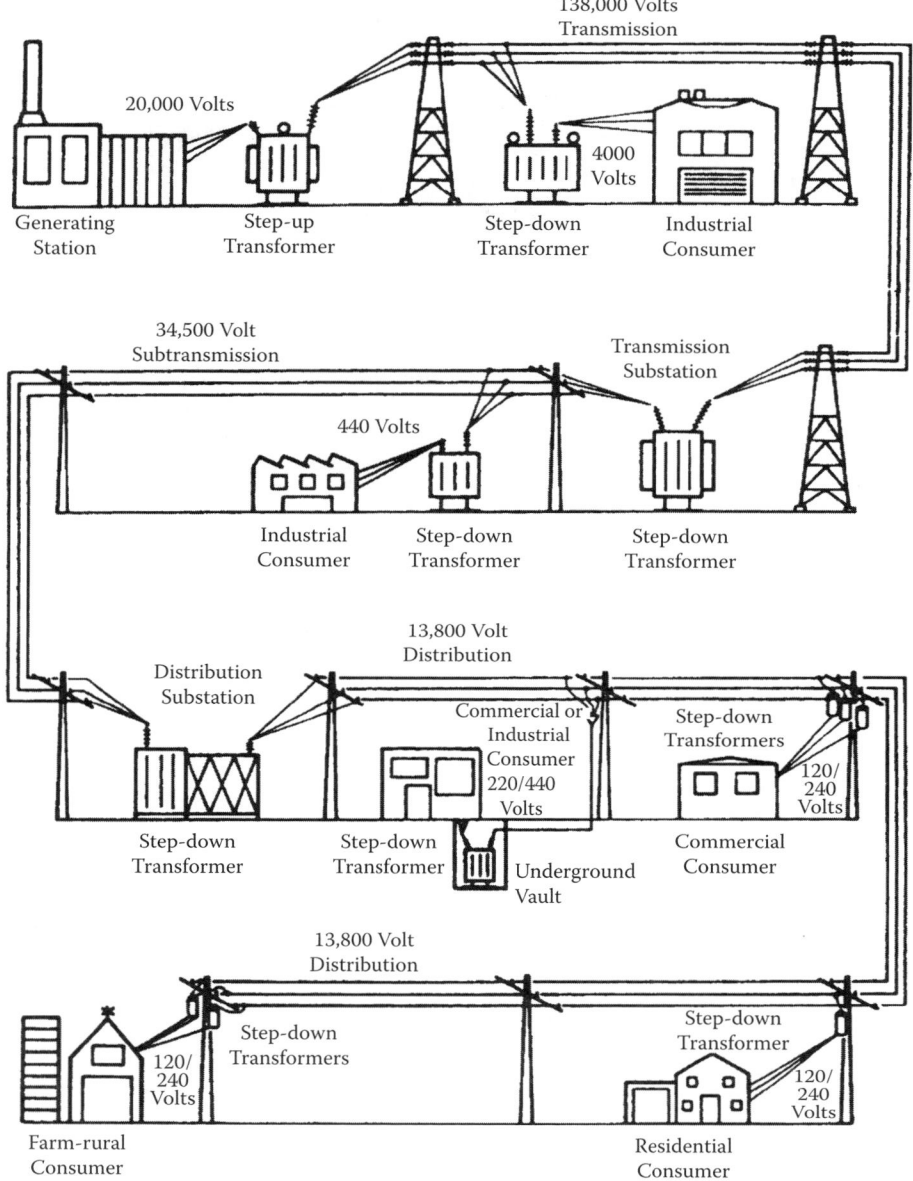

FIGURE 10.8 Underground electric service. (*Mechanical and Electrical Equipment for Buildings*, 9e; Benjamin Stein, ©2000, John Wiley & Sons. Reprinted with permission of John Wiley & Sons, Inc.)

transformer utilized governs the position on the site of a substation (Stein, 2000, p. 959). Access to this area must be restricted whenever possible.

OUTDOOR ELECTRICAL SUBSTATIONS/DESIGN CONSIDERATIONS

Electrical substations contain all the necessary equipment and devices to transform the voltage levels, monitor the status and operation of the equipment and circuits, and house protective systems such as relays, circuit breakers, switches, and so on (Beaty, 2000, p. 37). Thus, an electrical substation is an outdoor infrastructure to place several transformers that reduce voltage from high-tension

FIGURE 10.9 Control room for power distribution and transmission lines. The lines have to be secure, but so does the control room.

lines to the voltage needed for domestic use (see Figure 10.12). The amount of land required for substation placement is dependent on the number of circuits and equipment needed.

In order to make possible the implementation of the CPTED principles of access control and territoriality for electrical substations, it is important to start with the definition of physical barriers. Chain link fencing is the most often used for definition and perimeter protection. The fence line should be as straight as possible to provide easy observation and should be setback at not less than fifty feet from the substation structure.

FENCE SIGNAGE

The purpose of fencing is to act as a symbolic barrier between the public areas and the private areas. All types of fencing can be cut through and climbed over with sufficient resources and time.

FIGURE 10.10 Transformer sited remotely on grounds. The transformer should be locked and checked for tampering.

FIGURE 10.11   Transformer adjacent to building façade provides good surveillance but can also act as a hiding place and used as improvised explosive device (IED).

Fencing primarily serves as a symbolic barrier, to deter persons who would accidentally come close to the equipment (see Figure 10.13). There are a variety of fence materials that are available, and no one fence is perfect for all applications, but the primary CPTED goal is the concept of territoriality. The key aspect of territoriality is boundary definition; and fencing is what boundary definition is all about.

Fencing is the first line of defense for protecting water infrastructure, or power substations, or most commercial facilities. Fence height should be between 6 and 16 feet high with proper support and with posts placed equidistant at 10-foot intervals (see Figure 10.14). Because most infrastructure facilities will not have security surveillance personnel, the number of entrances should be kept to a minimum to keep persons entering the property and facility to a few controlled and observed points. Entrances should be locked and lighted during dark hours, with lighting provided along

FIGURE 10.12   Electrical substations must be secured from trespassing and tampering.

FIGURE 10.13 Signage for fences gives trespassers warning.

the fence line and at all entrances. The area on either side of the fence should be kept free of trees, cars, dumpsters, or any other item that can help an intruder climb over the fence.

"No Trespassing," "Private Property," and "Danger, High Voltage" signs should be securely attached to the fence fabric, and should be placed at various points along the fence line (see Figure 10.15).

DESIGN CONSIDERATIONS FOR MECHANICAL ROOMS AND SPACES

One of the most important recommendations given by the National Institute of Occupational Safety and Health (NIOSH) (2002) for buildings' physical security is that building owners and managers should be familiar with their buildings and understand what assets require protection and what characteristics about the building and its occupants make it a potential target. Having knowledge of the physical vulnerabilities allow security actions to be more efficient. Building infrastructure is one of the most valuable assets; at the same time, it is a vulnerable asset because it can become a tool for sabotage. HVAC system can become a conduit to spread chemical, biological, or radiological threats. Power disruption or outage can paralyze building performance and generate chaos.

Because of the nature of the processes involved in the production of electrical power, safety in power plants is focused more in protecting the working environment inside the plant than on

FIGURE 10.14 A high security fence for a government facility using the full menu of physical and mechanical solutions.

the grounds. Typically generation plants are located in remote areas near a source of water to keep the machinery cool and running. The service core building needs to have CPTED and security design considerations built in. One of the most important considerations in designing the external grounds is setback and separation from neighbor areas by a landscape tree-buffer, sound-absorbing walls, and perimeter fencing.

WHAT TO DO FOR PROTECTION OF CRITICAL INFRASTRUCTURE

Design considerations that should apply to infrastructure protection are extensive. They should follow a proper risk assessment as described in other parts of this book. Above all, it is important to appreciate that the security measures taken will vary from building to building. Once a proper risk assessment is concluded, the following examples of the specific strategies that might apply (FEMA 426, 2003; Atlas, 2004):

FIGURE 10.15 Fence signage warning people of the dangers.

PROTECTING INFRASTRUCTURE AGAINST CBR

WHAT NOT TO DO

In the NIOSH publication "Protection from Chemical, Biological, and Radiological Attacks" (2002, p. 166), important things *not* to do in changing the building infrastructure systems to protect a building from a CBR attack are addressed. They include:

- Do not permanently seal the outdoor air intakes. Buildings require a steady supply of outdoor air appropriate to their occupancy and function. This supply should be maintained during normal operations. Closing off the outdoor air supply vents will adversely affect the building occupants and reduce the environmental quality.
- Do not modify the HVAC system without first understanding the effects on the building systems or the occupants.
- Do not interfere with the fire protection and life safety systems. The fire suppression and smoke evacuation systems should not be altered without specific guidance from a HVAC life safety engineer.

The NIOSH publication addresses security concerns in preventing terrorist access to a targeted facility (NIOSH, pp. 17–18). Most buildings' critical infrastructure is located in the entry area, storage areas, roof, and mechanical areas. Although the security measures taken will vary from building to building, the process of analysis and developing an appropriate response is what CPTED risk assessments, the ATRiM© model, and other assessment programs are especially tailored to do effectively.

The security actions that are typically applicable to many building types include the following:

FIGURE 10.16   Air intake vents on the street level are exposed to sabotage.

1. Prevent access to outdoor air intakes (see Figure 10.16 and Figure 10.17). Outdoor air enters the building through these intakes and is distributed throughout the building by the HVAC system. Introducing CBR agents into the outdoor air intakes allows a terrorist to use the HVAC system as a means of dispersing the agent throughout the building. Securing the outside air intakes is a critical line of defense in limiting the exposure of a building to a CBR attack.

2. Relocate outdoor air intake vents. Ideally, the intake should be located on a secure roof or high sidewall. The lowest edge of an outdoor intake should be placed at the highest feasible level above the ground or above any nearby accessible level (such as adjacent retaining walls, loading docks, or handrails).

FIGURE 10.17   Air intake accessible from public walkway is extremely vulnerable.

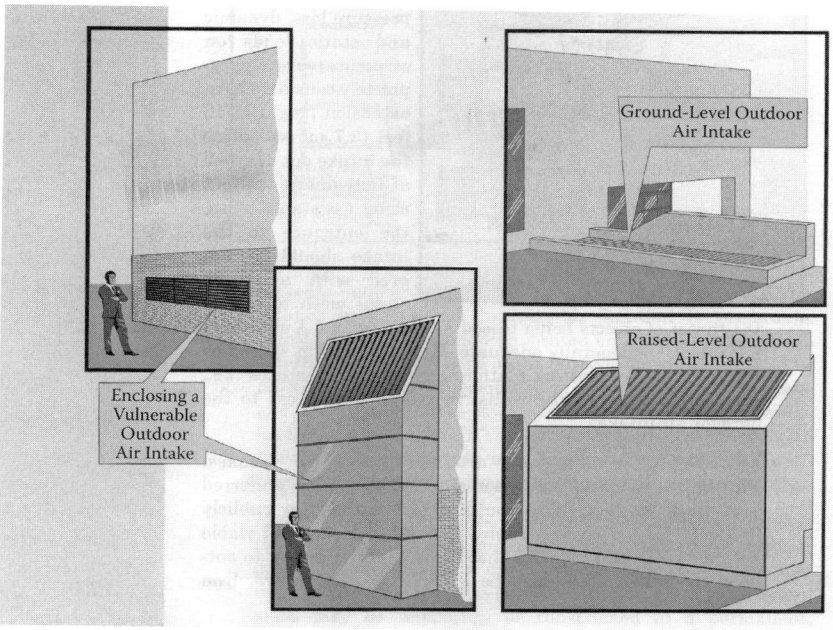

FIGURE 10.18 Vents need to be shielded. (NIOSH, 2002, p. 18.)

3. Extend outdoor air intakes. The goal is to minimize public accessibility to the vents. The higher the extension the better, as long as other design constraints are considered (dynamic and static loads on structures). An extension height of 12 feet is considered a height out of reach for individuals without some assistance. The entrance to the intake should be covered with a sloped metal mesh to reduce the threats of objects being tossed into the intake. A minimum of a forty-five-degree slope is adequate (NIOSH, 2002, p. 18).

4. Establish a security zone around the air intakes. Outdoor intakes should be physically inaccessible by the public (see Figure 10.18). Fencing should be used to create a safe buffer space to those ventilation infrastructure elements. Gates and doors should be locked to prevent trespass and access to the intakes. The buffer zones should be monitored with CCTV, security lighting, or intrusion detection devices.

5. Prevent public access to the mechanical areas. Mechanical areas may exist at one or more locations within a building. These areas provide access to the centralized mechanical systems, including water, electrical, HVAC, filters, air handling units, and exhaust systems. Locks and card access, should strictly control the access to mechanical spaces and have doors monitored into such spaces to alert security when doors are open.

6. Prevent public access to building roofs. Many chillers, vents, elevators, and HVAC units are located on the roof. Roofs with HVAC should be treated like other mechanical areas with strict access control protocols.

7. Implement security measures, such as guards, alarms, and cameras to protect vulnerable areas. Security personnel, barriers that deter loitering, intrusion detection sensors, and observation cameras that are monitored can alert designated security personnel of breaches near air intakes or other vulnerable high-risk locations.

8. Lobbies, mailrooms, loading docks, and storage areas should be physically isolated from the rest of the building. These types of spaces are the areas where bulk quantities of CBR agents might enter a building. To prevent widespread contamination the HVAC systems for these high-risk areas should be isolated and the areas maintained at a negative pressure relative to the rest of the building, but at a positive pressure relative to the outdoors. The

physical isolation of these areas (well sealed floor to roof deck walls, sealed wall penetrations) is critical to maintaining the pressure differential. Lobbies, mailrooms, and loading docks should not share a return air system or return pathway like a ceiling plenum with other areas of the building.

9. Building access from lobby areas should be limited by security checks of individuals and packages before their entry into secure areas. Lobby isolation is particularly critical in buildings where the main lobbies are open to the public. Similar checks of incoming mail should also occur before its conveyance into the secure building areas. Side entry doors that circumvent established security boundaries should be strictly controlled, alarmed, and monitored.

10. Secure return air grilles using special security screws that have unique heads and special tools for installation.

11. Restrict access to building operation systems by outside personnel. To deter tampering by outside maintenance personnel, a building staff member should escort these individuals throughout their service visit and should visually inspect their work before final acceptance of their service. Restrict access to building information. Information, drawings, specifications, and manuals of all building systems should be strictly controlled.

12. General building physical security upgrades should coincide with layered levels of security that are consistent with CPTED strategies. Controlling and restricting access will reduce the probability of the building being a target.

As highlighted in the chapters on risk assessment, CPTED, and the ATRiM model, facility security and safety is complex. NIOSH indicates that reducing a building's vulnerability to an airborne chemical, biological, or radiological attack requires a comprehensive approach. Appropriate protective measures should be based on the threat profile and a security assessment of the building, its occupants, and assets. Physical security is the first layer of defense, but other issues are also critical. CPTED suggests it is important to consider prevention and security measures using operational, mechanical, and natural methods.

Measures used for protection of assets in events of terrorism will also have a residual value in protection against human-caused hazards and weather-caused hazards. A new federal courthouse in Gulfport, Mississippi, designed to meet the GSA Federal Security standards, survived Hurricane Katrina in 2005 (see Figure 10.19 and Figure 10.20).

Buildings designed to resist terrorism also may resist burglary, hurricanes, and earthquakes. Impact resistant glazing with strengthened frames can help protect against the effects of bombs, hurricanes, or burglary. Earthquake structural strengthening of buildings may assist in deflection of impact and explosion effects of bombs. Protecting against progressive structural failure collapse will protect against bombs, earthquakes, and hurricanes. Improved fire suppression techniques will provide additional protection from the effects of bombs or arson attacks. Unprotected buildings can pay the ultimate consequences for not making the architectural and structural improvements.

In Gulfport, Mississippi, the disparity of damage from Hurricane Katrina was readily apparent from classic brick and steel construction, as compared to GSA compliant security design. These buildings are located in the same town, in close proximity, with the same environmental threats, but dramatically different outcomes. The way in which we construct our buildings will determine how our infrastructure survives in man-made or natural disasters.

SUMMARY

You have seen how Crime Prevention Through Environmental Design can be an effective risk management methodology for determining the assets, threats, risks, vulnerabilities, and appropriate protective strategies for our built environment and critical infrastructure. Regardless of what methodology private sector or public government chooses to use to conduct their assessments, it

FIGURE 10.19   Gulfport, Mississippi, federal courthouse after Hurricane Katrina, undamaged by the ferocious storm because the building was designed to meet new federal security standards.

FIGURE 10.20   Gulfport, Mississippi, church damaged by Hurricane Katrina.

is imperative to understand the limitations and benefits of a functional integrated security design system.

One urban design profession—architects—has been notoriously inattentive to the details of security and protection for mechanical systems and closets, HVAC design, and the delivery of utility services to buildings and communities. After 9/11, the impact from the tragic loss of life has grown into an expanded obligation for infrastructure protection. From that date forward, there is an obligation of design and security professionals to protect the critical infrastructure and to have business continuity planning in place. Protection of critical infrastructure demands the design field to plan for security in all aspects of the built environment.

REFERENCES

Atlas, R. (2004) Security design concepts. *Security Planning and Design: A Guide for Architecture and Building Design Professionals*. Washington, DC: American Institute of Architects, Wiley.

Atlas, R. (2004) *Safeguarding Buildings against Attacks from Terror and Crime with CPTED*. AIA 2004 National Convention Continuing Education.

Barnett, D. (2000) *Electric Power Generation. A Non Technical Guide*. Tulsa, OK: Pennwell Series.

Beaty, W. (1998) *Electric Power Distribution Systems. A Non Technical Guide*. Tulsa, OK. Pennwell Non-Technical Series.

Bioterrorism Act of 2002. http://www.fda.gov/oc/bioterrorism/bioact.html.

National Institute for Occupational Safety and Health (NIOSH), Department of Health and Human Services (2002) *Guidance to Protecting Building Environments from Airborne Chemical, Biological or Radiological Attacks*. Cincinnati, OH: Centers for Disease Control and Prevention.

National Fire Protection Association (2006) *NFPA 730 Guide for Premises Security 2006 Edition*. Quincy, MA: Author.

National Infrastructure Security Coordination Centre. Available at: http://www.niscc.gov.uk.

FEMA 426 (2003) *Reference Manual to Mitigate Potential Terrorist Attacks Against Buildings*. Risk Management Series.

Stein, B. (2000) *Mechanical and Electrical Equipment for Buildings*, 9th ed. New York: John Wiley & Sons.

The Infrastructure Security Partnership (TISP). Available at: http://www.tisp.org/tisp.cfm.

Union of Concerned Scientists. Available at: http://www.ucsusa.org/clean_energy/nuclear_safety/spent-reactor-fuel-security.html.

University of Florida. *Plant Management in Florida Waters*. Available at: http://aquat1.ifas.ufl.edu/guide/industry.html.

U.S. Department of the Interior Geological Survey (1989) *Water for Florida Cities*. Water resources investigation Report 86–4122.

U.S. Environmental Protection Agency. Available at http://www.epa.gov/ebtpages/water.html.

Whitman, D. (1997) *Geology and Water Resources of South Florida*. Miami: Florida International University.

APPENDIX

SITE SECURITY CONSIDERATIONS

- Clearly define premises perimeter.
- Have no more than two designated and monitored entrances.
- Project an image of a secured place.
- Design a layered system of security.
- Minimize concealment opportunities in landscaping and street furniture, such as hedges, bus shelters, benches, and trash receptacles.
- Establish setbacks of approximately 20 feet; all perimeter walls need to be secured and free of trees or structures that can be used to climb.
- Protect the perimeter with a wall or fencing; in some infrastructure types with double-wall system.
- Use adequate artificial lighting.
- Define main entrance or public access and define any other entries so that all public entries and exits are controlled in one point; control room for security center with CCTV circuits, access checkpoint, control personnel to access to secured rooms.
- Position all pedestrian entrances next to vehicle entrances for supervision.
- Eliminate or reduce concealment opportunities.
- Avoid opaque fencing landscaping walls that might provide hiding spaces.
- Design site circulation to minimize speeds of vehicles and eliminate direct approaches to structures.
- Incorporate vehicle barriers into site design, such as walls, fences, fountains, trees, art, and flagpoles.
- Ensure adequate site lighting.
- Locate critical offices away from uncontrolled public spaces.
- Separate delivery processing facilities from remaining buildings.
- Design for access by emergency responders and their equipment.
- Identify and provide alternate water supplies for fire suppression.
- Eliminate or control site access through utility easements, tunnels, corridors, or manholes.
- Provide a clear zone and thoroughly illuminate.
- Avoid dead end driveways and pathways.
- Provide access to and from the back of buildings.
- Use plantings and landscape design to prevent easy passage.

BUILDING AND INTERIOR ARCHITECTURE SECURITY CONSIDERATIONS

- Secure control rooms with key card system.
- Always have an emergency plan to reestablish infrastructure workability in case of an unexpected event.
- All risky areas have to be properly identified and isolated from regular worker traffic. All infrastructure facilities need to have their special safety features to provide a safety environment for workers because of the nature of the machinery used, high voltages, chemicals, biological, radiological materials. Access to waste disposals needs to be restricted and continuously supervised.
- Any visit from external personnel needs to be supervised and guided by internal personnel until work is completed.
- Install measures to protect chemicals such as ammonia and chlorine.

- Increase perimeter protection of a facility by using setbacks, landscape design, vehicle barriers, planters, bollards, and security lighting.
- Plan for additional security features in buildings housing hazardous materials.
- Upgrade security features at water holding and treatment facilities.
- Design technology systems to monitor for contamination of supplies.
- Consider the placement and security of communication systems, information backup systems, and power supply back-up systems.
- Design security features as a high priority of critical buildings such as government operations, communication centers, fuel supply centers, and emergency services.
- Consider carefully where employee and visitor entrances are located and if they are combined to minimize queuing in unprotected areas and maximizing usage of security posts.;
- Design employee and visitor screening areas into the foyers and lobbies.
- Minimize bomb device concealment opportunities such as trash receptacles, mailboxes, and planters.
- Carefully consider whether restrooms and service spaces are located in non-secure areas.
- Locate critical assets such as people, activities, and systems away from entrances, vehicle circulation and parking, and loading and maintenance areas.
- Separate and put distance between high and low risk activities.
- Separate high risk activities from publicly accessible areas.
- Separate building utilities from service docks and hardened utilities.
- Locate delivery and mail processing facilities remotely or at exterior of the building. Prevent delivery or service vehicles from driving into or under the building.
- Establish areas of safe refuge and egress paths that discharge into safe passages.
- Locate emergency stairwells and systems away from high-risk areas.
- Restrict roof access and have the door(s) monitored.
- Design the walls, doors, windows, ceilings, and floors to be burglar resistant.
- Provide fire and blast resistant separation for sprinkler, standpipes, risers, and the fire alarm system components.
- Use visually open, impact resistant laminated glass or polycarbonate for stair towers and elevators in parking facilities and garages.
- Make sure way finding and signage is clear and informative.
- Place elevators close to the main entrances, with interiors in view when the elevator doors are open.
- Design stairwells to be visible without solid walls.
- Provide interior windows and doors for visibility into hallways.

STRUCTURAL SECURITY CONSIDERATIONS

- Design exterior building skin to be blast resistant after a proper risk assessment.
- Engineer the structural elements and connections to resist blast loads and progressive structural failure.
- Install blast resistant windows and frames.
- Ensure that other openings such as vents are blast resistant.
- Enclose critical building components within hardened walls, floors, and ceilings.

MECHANICAL ENGINEERING SECURITY CONSIDERATIONS

- Locate utility and ventilation systems away from entrances, vehicle circulation and parking, and loading and maintenance areas.
- Protect utility lifelines (water, power, communications, etc.) by concealing, burying, or encasing.

- Locate air intakes on roof or as high as possible. If not elevated, secure within secured fencing or enclosure.
- Use motorized dampers to close air intakes when not operational.
- Locate roof-mounted equipment away from building perimeter.
- Ensure that stairways maintain positive pressure.
- Provide redundant utility and ventilation systems.
- Provide filtration of intake air.
- Provide secure alternate drinking water supply.

ELECTRICAL ENGINEERING SECURITY CONSIDERATIONS

- Locate utility systems and lifelines away from entrances, vehicle circulation and parking, loading, and maintenance areas.
- Implement separate emergency and normal power systems; ensure that backup power systems are periodically tested under load.
- Locate primary and backup fuel supplies away from entrances, vehicle circulation and parking, loading, and maintenance areas.
- Secure primary and backup fuel supply areas.
- Install exterior connection for emergency power.
- Install adequate site lighting.
- Maintain stairway and exit sign lighting.
- Provide redundant telephone service.
- Ensure that critical systems are not collocated in conduits, panels, or risers.
- Use closed-circuit television (CCTV) security system.

FIRE PROTECTION ENGINEERING

- Ensure compliance with building and life safety codes and standards, including installation of up-to-date fire alarm and suppressions systems.
- Locate fire protection water supply system critical components away from entrances, vehicle circulation and parking, and loading and maintenance areas.
- Identify/establish secondary fire protection water supply systems.
- Install redundant fire water pumps (e.g., one electric, one diesel) and locate them apart from each other.
- Ensure adequate, redundant sprinkler and standpipe connections.
- Install fire hydrant and water supply connections near sprinkler/standpipe connections.
- Supervise or secure standpipes, water supply control valves, and other system components.
- Implement fire detection and communication systems.
- Implement redundant off-premises fire alarm reporting.
- Locate critical documents and control systems in a secure, yet accessible place.
- Provide key box near critical entrances for secure fire access.
- Provide fire- and blast-resistant fire command center.
- Locate hazardous materials, comprehensive pre-incident and recovery plans.
- Implement guard and employee training.
- Conduct regular evacuation and security drills.
- Regularly evaluate fire protection equipment for readiness and adequacy.

GENERAL SECURITY CONSIDERATIONS

- Develop secure backup or remote takeover control center capabilities.
- Secure electrical utility closets, mechanical rooms, and telephone closets.
- Do not co-locate security system wiring with electrical and other service systems.

- Implement elevator recall capability and elevator emergency message capability.
- Implement intrusion detection systems and provide 24-hour off-site monitoring.
- Implement and monitor interior boundary penetration sensors.
- Implement color closed-circuit television (CCTV) security system with recording capability.
- Install call boxes and duress alarms.
- Install public and employee screening systems (metal detectors, x-ray machines, or search stations).

PARKING SECURITY CONSIDERATIONS

- Minimize off-site parking on adjacent streets/lots and along perimeter.
- Control all on-site parking with ID checks, security personnel, and access systems.
- Separate employee and visitor parking.
- Eliminate internal building parking.
- Ensure natural surveillance by concentrating pedestrian activity, limiting entrances/exits, and eliminating concealment opportunities.
- Use transparent/nonopaque walls whenever possible.
- Prevent pedestrian access to parking areas other than via established entrances.

11 Problem Seeking before Problem Solving
*Gauging Your Asset Base******

Although the focus of this book is on preventing criminal behavior, workplace violence, and terrorism in the built environment, the exercise of assessing risk and examining threats can have positive impacts upon safety and security in many ways. Hurricanes Katrina, Rita, and Wilma demonstrate that the lack of preparation, understanding, and resources was catastrophic in the communities and critical infrastructure affected by the wind and water damage. Faulty evacuation plans for people in low-lying areas collapsed the infrastructures of several major cities, including gas and oil industries. In South Florida, a Category One hurricane (among the weakest) knocked out 98% of the power grid for weeks. Above-ground utility poles were vulnerable to the winds and resulted in thousands of wood and concrete telephone and power poles being snapped or knocked down. Gas stations could not sell gas because they did not have electricity or backup power generators to run their pumps. Ironically, the worst fear from an act of terrorism was effectively caused by a ***known*** and ***predictable*** natural event in our country—hurricanes.

Had there been an asset analysis as part of assisting risks to show the value of proactive and preventative measures, a more effective response and protection might have been available to victims. A proper asset analysis might have significantly minimized and mitigated the impact from these disasters. Buildings would be built differently; glazing systems would be different; utilities would be delivered differently; information and data would be protected differently; gas stations would be required to have backup generators; utilities would be buried; and evacuation plans would be mandatory, water drainage and runoff protection would not be optional.

Conducting thorough asset analyses and threat assessments will help prevent, and mitigate terrorist and criminal acts. But, as you have seen earlier, they can have many other positive benefits as well.

Designing the built environment to survive the hazards of crime, workplace violence, and terrorism is not well understood by the design or law enforcement communities. There are many types of hazards that can impact the usability of a building by its legitimate users. The ability of our buildings to survive the threat and impact of criminal and terrorist attacks, let alone risks from natural causes depends on understanding the qualitative factors that evaluate the organizational requirements, recovery efforts and impacts, and loss of personnel and infrastructure (FEMA 426, 2003, p. 26).

This chapter examines different methodologies used to determine the risks, vulnerabilities, and assets to complete the security assessment, while the next chapter examines the concept of threat assessment. Asset and risk assessment is the ***problem-seeking*** part of the CPTED process.

* Portions of the text in this chapter consist of articles and other publications previously written by the author including possible portions found in the following Wiley publications: *Architectural Graphics Standards*, 10th edition, Ramsey/Hoke, The American Institute of Architects, John Wiley & Sons, ISBN: 0471348163, ©2000. *Security Planning and Design: A Guide for Architects and Building Design Professionals*, Demkin, The American Institute of Architects, John Wiley & Sons, ISBN: 0471271567, ©2004. We offer special thanks to the American Institute of Architects and John Wiley & Sons for permission to reproduce common content in this work.

** Assistance was provided by Richard Grassie in preparation of this chapter.

Problem solving properly occurs *after* the risk assessment and problem seeking, or understanding the risks, threats, and vulnerabilities is completed. The process of gathering and analyzing all of the information mentioned above becomes the elements of determining the relative levels of risk. The levels of risk determine whether the target has a high or low probability of attack, and the level of consequence. Higher risks threats may require greater security countermeasures. The security countermeasures and CPTED may be applied as part of a functional integrated security design system. The word "system" is not only intended to refer to electronics, but rather a systematic and global approach to reduce the hazards, risks, threats, and vulnerabilities to a building (the environment) and its users.

A significant step in risk assessment is defining and analyzing hazards. Although all hazards should be addressed, resource limitations usually do not allow this to happen all at one time. Risk assessment can establish priorities to address the most dangerous situations first, and later those least likely to occur and cause major problems (NIOSH, 2003, p. 2).

Risk analysis and management give us the ability to anticipate, prevent, and/or mitigate hazards and the ability to establish safe and secure environments for our homes, workplaces, and public gathering places. The assessment process will first identify the assets (the subject of this chapter), and then conduct the threat assessment (the subject of the next chapter) to identify the potential and actual threats and hazards. It will then conduct a vulnerabilities analysis, which compares the identified threats to the critical assets of a building in order to determine protection weaknesses. After the vulnerability assessment analysis is completed, the risk assessment analyzes the threat, the value of the assets, and potential vulnerabilities to determine the level of acceptable risk against the range of possible and probable threats.

Urban design professionals need to address these security challenges as an integral element of their design services. In order for the design professional to accommodate the security features into the architecture, a security needs assessment or a security director, under the direction of the owner or client, must conduct a vulnerability analysis. That is why it is necessary to examine the assets, threats, and security needs assessment as part of the *architectural programming process*. The following security assessment questions are drawn from Grassie's publication "Security Risk Analysis" (2004) and the chapter that was written for the AIA book on building security in 2004. The questions provide a basic framework for beginning the process.

WHAT ARE THE ASSETS?

Careful asset and threat assessment are important steps because they define the nature and level of protection. The security needs assessment will focus on the weaknesses and potential for attacks by identifying:

- The assets (people, information, and property)
- The types of threats from crime, and the criticality for protection (What is the mission of the building? What and who are the probable targets? How easy can the asset be replaced?)
- The modes of attack (Is the threat from outside or within? How will the perpetrator gain access to the property? Is the attack likely? What tool or weapons will they use?).

The level of vulnerability will determine:

- The level of protection needed to meet the goals of the program.
- What are the time and money constraints?
- What are the threats?
- What is the chance of occurrence of harm or loss scenarios?
- What is the perceived level of threat so far?
- What is the probability of being a victim?

Security practitioners often confuse the terms threat and risk. The distinction between threat and risk can be summed up as follows: **threat** is the **source** of harm or loss, whereas **risk** is the **probability of harm or loss** given a particular threat source and corresponding vulnerability in asset protection considering likely threat scenarios. This confusion often results in flawed designs because the designer has concentrated too many of his or her resources on countering threat sources that may be highly unlikely to a target an asset, whereas the designer should have paid more attention to both threat and risk.

Security designers must anticipate threats, identify vulnerabilities, and quantify risks. They must then anticipate the worst possible consequences and ultimately weigh the cost of any countermeasure recommendations against the perceived cost benefit or reduced potential for loss. Determination of cost-effective protective measures and their integration is the result of a structured decision making process that begins with a sound risk analysis. The analysis considers the individual and collective contribution of each protection strategy according to the comprehensive and complete system's requirements.

Today's threats can range from unsophisticated common criminals to highly sophisticated, well-armed, and trained professional career criminals, terrorist cells, or extremist groups. These threats can target and attack either an organization's physical or electronic assets, or both. Any adversary, regardless of sophistication, who targets a particular site, facility, or information asset, usually considers the potential success and fruits of the attack in relation to the risk of being detected and apprehended. The owner of the facility or assets, on the other hand, strives to decrease asset exposure with the right selection of countermeasures to ensure that asset is protected and preserved. So, risk analysis is a concept shared by those who target and those who protect assets.

The owner's attempt to protect assets begins with the process known as a requirements analysis, which is merely the front end of a risk assessment. A formal requirements analysis always begins with a consideration of assets requiring protection, and proceeds through succeeding tasks such as determining likely threat sources and scenarios, resulting vulnerabilities or weaknesses in current protection, potential risk of loss or damage to the assets. It culminates in the identification of functional requirements. These requirements or statements of protection objectives, as they are commonly known, form the basis for the eventual selection of countermeasures to provide an adequate level of protection for the identified critical assets.

The security assessment process follows a logical flow (FEMA 426, 2003, pp. 1–9):

- Assets Value
  - Identify the criticality of the assets
  - Identify the assets of people, information, and property
  - Identify the types of user groups and number in the building
- Threat Assessment
  - Identify each threat
  - Define each threat
  - Determine the threat level for each threat
- Vulnerability Analysis
  - Identify the site conditions
  - Identify the building systems and design issues
  - Evaluate the design issues against the type and level of threat
  - Determine level of protection sought for each strategy measure used against each threat
- Risk Assessment
  - What is the likelihood?
  - What is the impact of occurrence regarding loss of life, property, and business continuity?
  - Determine the relative risk for each threat against each asset
  - Select countermeasures that have the greatest benefit and value/cost for reducing the risk

There are many ways to combine these assessments. For example, the automated ATRiM software described in Chapter 13 of this book employs prevention specialists with security personnel to conduct risk assessment audits on site. However, it conducts only the Assets Value and Vulnerability Analysis components of the security assessment. There are other methods that approach the security assessment differently. Regardless of the approach, it is important to recognize that security assessments use a combination of quantitative and qualitative techniques involving efforts such as surveys, data gathering, and expert evaluation. When the risk of hostile acts is greater, risk analysis methods draw on information and data from intelligence and law enforcement bodies (Grassie, 2004).

The design of integrated security systems begins with the realization that there are certain assets at risk, as well as, operational requirements for control of personnel and facilities, which must be implemented to protect the business or organization. In the requirements analysis process described in the sections that follow, the owner or the designer considers:

- The range of assets to be protected based on their criticality to the organization (asset analysis)
- The range of events (threat assessment) potentially confronting the assets to be protected
- The relative exposure of assets given the potential threats and risks (vulnerability assessment), and
- The probability that a potential loss event will become an actual loss event (risk assessment).

Grassie (2004) indicates there are important steps in the site survey that should be considered. The following questions describe this process in more detail, beginning with the initial design basis site survey.

WHAT IS ASSET VALUE ASSESSMENT?

An asset analysis considers the following factors:

1. Identification of the assets
2. Categorizing assets
3. Physical/operational asset criticality

Site surveys and discussions with owners and ultimate users of assets provide data on specific assets requiring protection consideration. Each organization differs according to those personnel, material, and information assets they are responsible to protect. Coming up with a list of organizational assets can be a difficult, daunting task simply because people tend to differ on what is valuable, or intrinsic, within an organization.

IDENTIFYING ASSETS

The process begins with the identification of an organization's assets. When identifying assets, do not attempt to initially categorize them as critical or noncritical. Simply attempt to come up with as many asset types as can be imagined for the organization. Usually, this process results in some truly enlightening results for the participants. Most people in an organization are rarely asked to do so in relation to the organization's mission, but in an asset analysis they are specifically asked to identify those personnel, material, and information assets that are both primary and secondary to the successful accomplishment of the mission. Simply thinking through such a process can be an extremely valuable learning experience.

Identifying a building's critical assets can be accomplished in a two-step process (FEMA 426, 2003, p. 32): First define and understand the building's core functions, mission statement, and processes. Secondly, identify the building infrastructure that includes the critical components, the critical information systems and data, the life safety systems and safe refuge areas, and the security systems and features.

CATEGORIZING ASSETS

Note that asset types are identified as people, not specifically as managers or directors. They are not specific to computer or other proprietary information but are generally referred to as information assets. These distinctions are important for threat, vulnerability, and risk analysis as they help focus the security or designer's thinking in terms of all personnel and information types and in terms of issues such as asset criticality.

Assets are categorized for analysis purposes as primary (i.e., people, physical resources, information, and image, etc.) and secondary (i.e., support resources such as generator, fuel, etc.). If secondary assets are deemed critical to the primary asset, then the secondary asset must undergo the same level of protection analysis as the primary asset.

Two types of asset categories are identified in the methodology: those of primary importance to the organization such as people, information, and property central to the manufacturing or production process, for example, and those of secondary importance.

An asset can be tangible, such as tenant, facilities, equipment, activities, operations, and information, or intangible, such as processes or a company's reputation. In order to achieve the greatest risk reduction at the least cost, identifying and prioritizing a building's critical assets is a vital first step in the process to identify the best prevention measures to improve its level of protection prior to a criminal or terrorist attack. Recognizing that people are a building's greatest asset, the risk assessment process helps identify and prioritize infrastructure where people are most at risk and require protection (FEMA, 2003, pp. 1–10).

HOW TO DETERMINE ASSET CRITICALITY?

Critical assets are usually thought of as those with intrinsic or monetary value and those important to the conduct of daily operations; those indicated critical by organizational policy.

Here is a list of criteria, which may help in determining asset criticality:

- Monetary value
- Intrinsic value
- Economic value
- Operational value
- Regulatory value
- Intangible value
- Truly invaluable: personnel

We tend to separate physical/operational assets from information assets when dealing with such issues as criticality or sensitivity as shown in methodology. The **physical/operational asset criticality** is in direct proportion to its value in the organization, whereas an information asset is thought of more in terms of its sensitivity to the organization's daily operations. However, as we emerge from an industrial society to an information-based society, information assets become much more important. This is because the loss of proprietary or trade information can rarely, if ever, be effectively replaced. Conversely, the loss of physical assets central to an organization's mission usually can be replaced, albeit at a cost to the organization in terms of replacement and down time.

OPERATIONAL ASSET CRITICALITY

The most important step involves determining asset criticality, for it is that specific aspect alone which eventually determines how a particular asset will receive analysis emphasis for protection purposes. As shown in Figure 11.1, physical and operational asset criticality is based upon five factors ranging from not critical to essential.

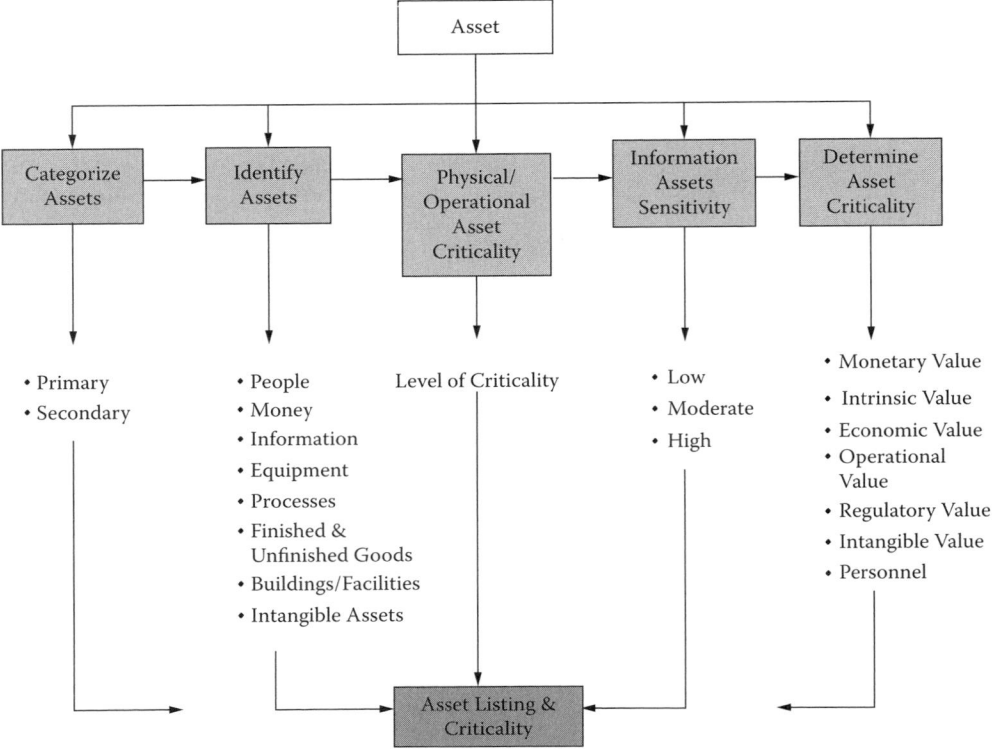

FIGURE 11.1   Chart demonstrating asset analysis.

Informational Asset Sensitivity

In contrast to operational asset criticality, information asset sensitivity is based on a different set of factors beginning with very low with a score of "1" to very high with a score of "5." Assigning scores to asset listings provides the analyst with the means to create cutoff points, such as essential to moderately critical and very high to moderate, for those assets. These scores will then be combined with the results of determinations conducted later in the risk analysis process.

WHAT KIND OF FACTORS SHOULD BE CONSIDERED?

According to the FEMA 426 (2003) publication of protecting your building against a terrorist attack (p. 1–11) should include:

- What are the building's primary services or outputs?
- What critical activities take place at the building?
- Who are the building's occupants and users?
- What inputs or services are needed from external organizations for a building's success or continuity?

A vital step to improve a building's critical assets is the process to improve its level of protection prior to a terrorist attack. Recognizing that people are a building's most critical asset, the process described throughout this step will help you to identify and prioritize those assets where people are most at risk and require protection (FEMA 452, 2005).

Layers of defense provide a traditional approach in security engineering and use concentric circles extending out from an area or site to the building or from the asset that requires protection. They are similar to the layers of skin around an onion. They can be seen as demarcation points for different security strategies. Identifying the layers of defense early in the assessment process will help you to understand better the assets that require protection and determine your mitigation options (FEMA, 2005).

First Layer of Defense involves understanding the characteristics of the surrounding area, including construction type, occupancies, and the nature and intensity of adjacent activities. It is specifically concerned with buildings, installations, and infrastructure outside the site perimeter. For urban areas, it also includes the curb lane and surrounding streets.

Second Layer of Defense refers to the space that exists between the site perimeter and the assets requiring protection. It involves the placement of buildings and forms in a particular site and understanding which natural or physical resources can provide protection. It entails the design of access points, parking, roadways, pedestrian walkways, natural barriers, security lighting, and signage. For urban areas, it refers specifically to the building yard.

Third Layer of Defense deals with the protection of the asset itself. It proposes to harden the structures and systems, incorporate effective heating, ventilation, air-conditioning (HVAC) systems and surveillance equipment, and wisely design and locate utilities and mechanical systems. Note that, of all blast mitigation measures, distance is the most effective measure because other measures vary in effectiveness and can be more costly. However, often it is not possible to provide adequate standoff distance. For example, sidewalks in many urban areas may be less than 10 meters (33 feet), while appropriate standoff may require a minimum of 25 meters (82 feet). If GSA Security Standards were applicable for a leased or owned building, they would desire up to a 100 foot setback. That's a tall order in most urban downtown settings.

In conducting an assessment of the assets, the survey team should look at the elements that make a particular building and its occupants, valuable or special. If the event is criminal in nature, the assets may be very focused and small, such as a particular person, or money in a vault, a piece of art, or data from a computer.

Acts of terrorism are often more global in nature and scale, and may have different boundaries in achieving the end goals of project destruction. In that regard, it is important to know how many people could be killed if there was catastrophic loss in a building:

- What happens to the primary building functions if there was a loss or stoppage?
- Is there critical or sensitive information that is housed within this property?
- Is there back up or redundancy of data or products of this building? How would primary building assets be replaced and what would the costs be?
- Where are the locations of key equipment, data, utilities, communications systems in the building and property?
- Are there contingency arrangements, business continuity plans in place, and training should such an event occur?

After the building assets have been identified, those assets that would cause serious disruption to operations and services should be given a value or score from very high value to very low value. This value assignment will be important in determining priorities and appropriate protection strategies.

WHAT ARE THE LAYERS OF DEFENSE?

IDENTIFYING CRITICAL ASSETS FOR THE FIRST LAYER OF DEFENSE

One of the first steps when identifying your critical assets is to understand your surrounding areas and how construction types, occupancies, functions, and activities adjacent to your asset can pose a threat or serve to protect your asset. It is essential to understand the interdependencies and distance that separate your building and off-site facilities. Off-site facilities can include (FEMA, 2005, pp. 2–10):

- Landmarks and iconic buildings
- Law enforcement, fire departments, and hospital buildings
- Federal facilities
- Embassies
- Key commercial properties
- HazMat storage areas and chemical manufacturing plants
- Transportation (roads, avenues of approach, bridges, railroads, tunnels, airports, and ports)
- Telecommunications and utility services

IDENTIFYING CRITICAL ASSETS FOR THE SECOND LAYER OF DEFENSE

To identify your critical assets, you need to understand how important they are in terms of protecting people and key operations. When determining your asset value, you may ask the following questions (FEMA, 2055, pp. 2–11):

- Are perimeter fences or other types of barrier controls in place?
- Where are the access points to the site or building?
- Are there vehicle and pedestrian access control at the perimeter of the site?
- Does the site circulation prevent high-speed approaches by vehicles?
- Is there a minimum setback distance between the building and parked vehicles?
- In dense, urban areas, does curb lane parking allow uncontrolled vehicles to park unacceptably close to a building in public rights-of-way?
- What are the existing types of vehicle antiram devices for the site or building?
- Do existing landscape measures/features (walls, fountains, berms, etc.) deflect or dissipate the blast pressure?
- Are these devices at the property boundary or at the building?

IDENTIFYING CRITICAL ASSETS FOR THE THIRD LAYER OF DEFENSE

When estimating your critical assets within the third layer of defense, you need to consider the structural and nonstructural soundness of your building, as well as the possibility of mechanical, plumbing, and electrical systems ability to continue operations after an attack. Given the evolving nature of the terrorist threat, it is hard to estimate the value of your assets. For example, because of the catastrophic consequences of progressive collapse, evaluating the structural components of your building can become a high priority. Windows that are the weakest part of a building can become a crucial issue.

Other important elements for blast design may include hardening of mechanical and electrical systems and creating appropriate redundancies. The location of air-intakes and limiting the access of the public to main systems can become critical for reducing potential damage from terrorist and other attacks. The upgrade of HVAC systems and the adoptions of efficient HEPA (high efficiency particulate air) filtering systems can become a key consideration when establishing critical assets.

When determining your critical assets for the third layer of defense, you may ask the following questions (FEMA 452, 2005, pp. 2–11):

- What is the designed or estimated protection level of the exterior walls against the postulated explosive threat?
- Is the window system design on the exterior façade balanced to mitigate the hazardous effects of flying glazing following an explosive event (glazing, frames, anchorage to supporting walls, etc.)?
- Do nonwindow openings, such as mechanical vents and exposed plenums, provide the same level of protection required for the exterior wall?
- Is the incoming water supply in a secure location? Is there a secure alternate drinking water supply?
- Are the incoming air intakes in a secure location?
- How much fuel is stored on the site or at the building and how long can this quantity support critical operations? How is it stored? How is it secured?
- Is roof access limited to authorized personnel by means of locking mechanisms?
- What are the types and levels of air filtration?
- Are there provisions for air monitors or sensors for CBR agents?

SUMMARY

In order to protect the people, information, and property of our buildings and critical infrastructure, the security professional must understand what those assets mean to the business or government entity or property owner. The rush to develop security solutions cuts short the need to ask the questions and understand what is valued and worthy of being protected, and what assets can be replaced.

The risk assessment process starts with looking at those items of value and rates and ranks them. By understanding the real and symbolic value of the assets, the threats and vulnerabilities to those assets will make better sense and become more realistic. The asset analysis is the starting point to understand the concept of "consequences" if the property owners and users do not protect the key assets.

The events of recent times, including hurricanes, fires, floods, and acts of terrorism, have demonstrated, beyond any reasonable doubt, the potency of not being prepared for the actions that will result in catastrophic loss. The security professional is the right person to do the assessment, and make sure that the information is passed on to the design professional to accommodate the needed protection and backup of those identified key assets.

REFERENCES

Grassie, R. (2004) *Reducing Risk in Buildings*. MA: Techmark.

A.I.A. American Institute of Architects (2004) *Building Security through Design: A Primer for Architects, Design Professionals, and their Clients*. J.A. Demkin, Ed. Wiley & Sons, 2004, New Jersey.

NIOSH (2003) Focus on Prevention: Conducting a Hazard Risk Assessment. Prepared by Michael J. Brinch, Jr., CMSP1 Launa G. Mallett, PhD. 2, U.S. Department of Health and Human Services, Public Health Service Centers for Disease Control and Prevention, National Institute for Occupational Safety and Health, Pittsburgh Research Laboratory, Pittsburgh, PA. July 3, p 2.

1999 State Domestic Preparedness Equipment Program, Assessment and Strategy development Tool Kit, May 1999.

FEMA 452. (2005) A How-To Guide to Mitigate Potential Terrorist Attacks against Buildings. Risk Management Series. January.

FEMA 426 (2003) Reference Manual to Mitigate Potential Terrorist Attacks against Buildings. Risk Management Series. December.

12 Assessing Threats and Risks*

To stop a terrorist or physical attack on a building is very difficult. Any building or site can be breached or destroyed with enough planning, resources, and intention. However, the more secure the building or site and the better the building is designed to withstand an attack, the better the odds the building will not be attacked, or suffer less damage if attacked. Terrorists often select targets that have some value as a target, such as an iconic commercial property, symbolic government building, or structure likely to inflict significant emotional or economic damage such as a shopping mall or major transportation hub (FEMA, 2003, pp. 1–21).

Criminals also select targets based on the reward(s) they are seeking. It may be a car to steal, a woman in a garage, access to the roof to do drugs, or a computer to steal to obtain trade secrets. In all of these cases, the harm to person and property are only part of the damage. The psychological impact on victims can be equally devastating. The catastrophic damage to a high school from vandals trashing a classroom over the weekend can be perceived just as disruptive as loss from a hostage situation, from a disgruntled employee, or a car bomb going off in front of an embassy.

It is important to understand the capabilities and intentions of possible threat sources in our built environment. This is the topic of threat assessment and this chapter outlines some of the basics.

THREAT ANALYSIS

In order to have insight into the range of threat possibilities, assistance should be sought from security professionals, law enforcement, CPTED practitioners, counterterror specialists, emergency management, local fire departments, and other agencies that would be relevant for the assets to be protected.

An analysis of the following factors should be performed to determine the nature and composition of various threat sources:

1. Identification of threats
2. Specificity of threats
3. Possible motivation(s)
4. Asset attractiveness to adversaries
5. Adversaries' possible tactics and skill level
6. Adversaries' desired results

Criminals have different motivations for committing crimes. Some criminal acts are rational, based on needs of money, goods, or services, and some are compulsive and irrational, often based on drug or alcohol addiction. Persons engaged in acts of terror seek to instill fear and publicity for their cause or political gain through their actions. Their tools may be different from the street criminal, but often their acts begin with trespassing, unauthorized entry, loitering, burglary, theft, assault, and other acts of criminal intent. Therefore it is reasonable to assume that the process of protecting a building against terrorism is also going to make the building safer against burglars or car thieves, and vice versa.

---

* Richard Grassie assisted in the preparation of materials for this chapter.

The threats to be considered include, but are not limited to:

1. Threats against people such as robbery, rape, biochemical attacks, bombs, arson, and assaults
2. Threats against property such as burglary, theft, tampering, bombs, arson, and vandalism
3. Ideological-based criminal activity such as terrorism or hate crimes, whether occurring on property or neighboring properties
4. Activities related to special events that can result in criminal acts and threats to people and property

Grassie (2004) describes the new realities in threat assessment. Some of the main points are:

1. To deal effectively with these workplace risk realities, companies must be assured that measures taken to create a safe and secure workplace are consistent with perceived and likely threats. For security assessment purposes, consider the full range of conventional and unconventional threats to the safety and security of an organization's facilities.
2. A threat is any action with the potential to afflict harm or loss in the form of death, injury, destruction, disclosure, interruption of operations, or denial of services. The hostile actions of criminals, disgruntled employees, terrorists, and others can pose a threat to buildings and their occupants.
3. Threat analysis defines the level or degree of the threats against a facility by evaluating the intent, motivation, and possible tactics of those who carry them out. The process involves gathering historical data about hostile events and evaluating which information is relevant in assessing the threats against the facility. A threat analysis addresses the following questions:
   a. What factors about the building owner or occupant invite potential hostility?
   b. How conspicuous is the building?
   c. Does it have any symbolic value?
   d. How vulnerable does the building appear?
   e. What political events may generate new hostilities?
   f. Have facilities like this been targets in the past?
4. There is a wide range of possible threats to critical infrastructures such as buildings. The ATRiM program described in the next chapter establishes a risk matrix to clarify some of those threats. Grassie provides a more general outline of sources of risks. They include the following:
   a. *Forced unauthorized entry*, violent or surreptitious, with or without tools.
   b. *Bombs* to damage or destroy building structures, which in turn can cause injuries and deaths. The blast effects of a bomb are based on its size (referred to as load) and its point of detonation (which may be outside or inside a building).
   c. *Ballistic* assaults on building occupants, often using weapons such as handguns and assault rifles. Other ballistic assaults may use mortars, missiles, vehicles, and aircraft to inflict building damage with intent of harming building occupants.
   d. *Biochemical* tactics using biologic and chemical agents to affect the health of building occupants. Such tactics include contaminating mail and freight shipments and introducing biochemical substances directly into grates, air intakes, and other building openings and through service utilities such as water systems.

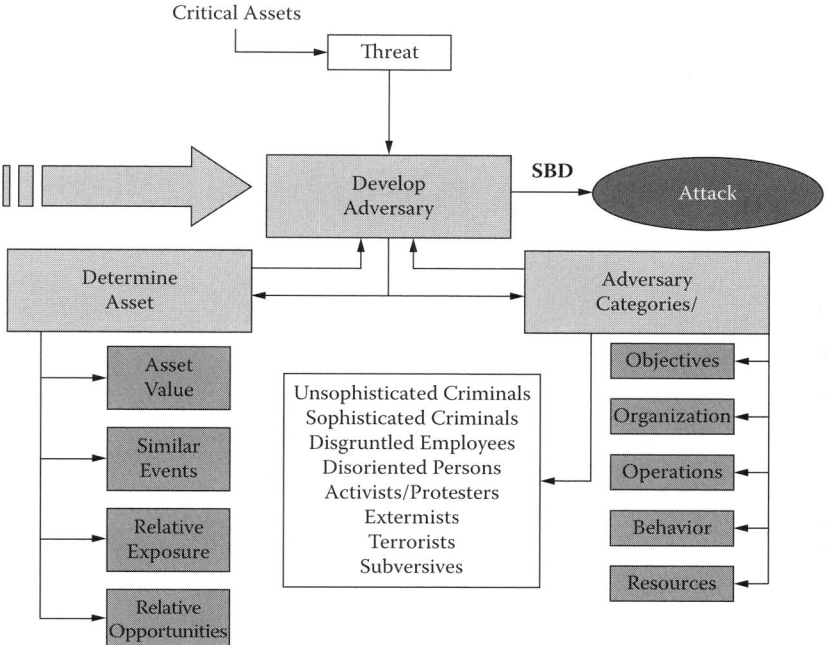

FIGURE 12.1   Threat analysis.

EVALUATING TERROR THREATS

FEMA 426 (2003) (p. 1–22) experts suggest that there are five factors to evaluate terrorist threats in your environment:

1. **Existence** of hostile persons or organizations to the assets. Who are they and are they present and near the asset?
2. **Capability** of the aggressors to carry off an attack to the prescribed asset. Is there a history of constructive or actual notice of criminal or terrorist activity in your area or building type?
3. **History** of the potential aggressors, criminals, or terrorists. Have the aggressors engaged in similar incidents recently? What tactics did they use? How did they acquire their demonstrated capabilities?
4. **Intention** addresses the issue of what does the potential aggressor hope to achieve? Is it money, glory, or fame? What is the anticipated reward for the act of crime or terror?
5. **Targeting** by the aggressor on the victim property. Has the perpetrator been conducting surveillance on the property and scoping out escape routes and determining levels of resistance or protection?

The terrorist or perpetrator will analyze the assets, like a building or intended target to determine the appropriate means of attack, type of weapon, and tactics to employ in defeating the building or critical mission, or business function (see Figure 12.1) The threat analysis should involve sufficient detail of the range of risks so that the strategies for prevention and response are thorough and complete.

VULNERABILITY ANALYSIS

A vulnerability analysis is an in-depth analysis of the building functions, systems, and site characteristics to identify the building weaknesses and need for protection. The goal is to determine proactive and preventative actions to reduce the weaknesses to the expected threats or hazards. A

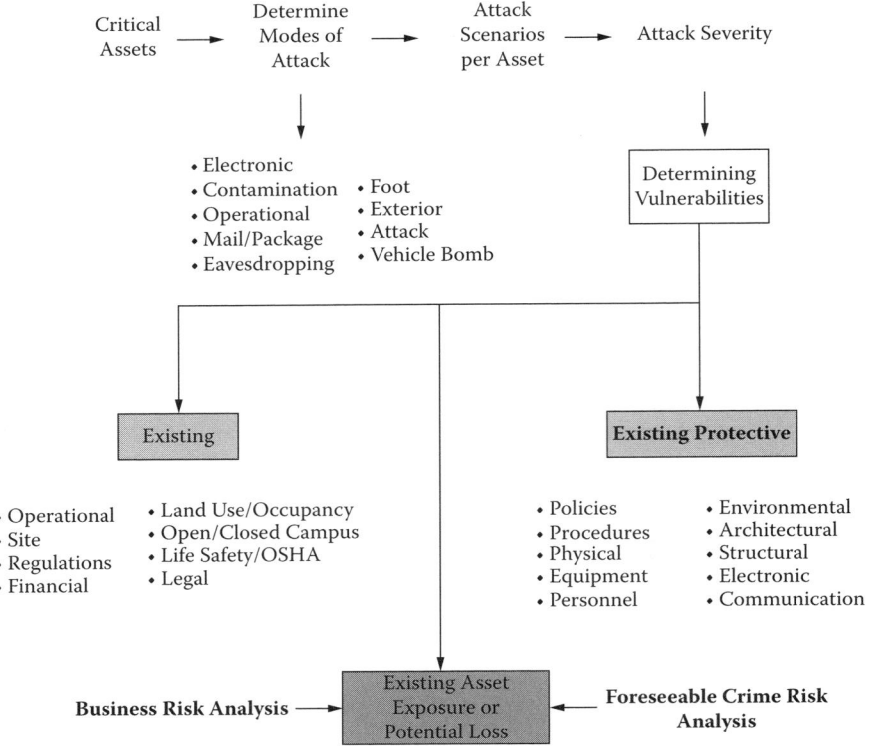

FIGURE 12.2   Determining vulnerabilities.

vulnerability analysis (see Figure 12.2) should be performed for the existing built environment, and the results and findings integrated into the design for new construction or renovation of buildings (FEMA 426, 2003, p. 1–24).

When conducting a vulnerability analysis, the following elements should be considered:

1. The environment surrounding the assets. Conduct an assessment of criminal activity in the immediate area. The assessment should identify crime patterns, trends, and frequency as well as local businesses' response
2. The occupancy and use of the building
3. The grounds (property and structures) surrounding the premises
4. The building perimeter security
5. The common areas within the building
6. The perimeter and interior security of individual areas.

Vulnerability is anything that can be taken advantage of to carry out a threat. Vulnerabilities in a building may be in its design and construction, its technological systems or its operations (e.g., security procedures and practices, or administrative and management controls). Although largely a subjective process, vulnerability analysis identifies how specific weaknesses may invite and permit the accomplishment of a threat.

Examples of site and building vulnerabilities include:

- Surrounding terrain and adjacent structures
- Site layout and elements, including perimeter and parking
- Location of and access to incoming utilities

- Degree or resistance of structure to blast
- Building circulation patterns and spatial arrangements
- Location of higher risk assets within a facility

The U.S. Department of Justice (1999) uses an objective approach in determining vulnerability for a building or site. The factors include:

- Level of visibility. What are the perceived awareness of the target's existence and the visibility of the target to the general populace, or to the terrorist in particular?
- The asset value of the target site. What is the usefulness of the site to the population, community, economy, company, or organization?
- Target value to potential threat element or aggressor. Does the target serve the ends or means of the aggressors identified in the threat assessment?
- Accessibility to the target by the aggressor. Does the aggressor have the means and abilities to gain access to the identified assets?
- Target threat of hazard. Are CBR materials present in quantities that could be hazardous if released? What are the setbacks of the buildings from potential threats?
- Site population capacity, what is the maximum number of individuals at the building or site at a given time? What is the potential loss of life in the worst-case scenario?
- Potential for collateral damage. What is the potential loss of life and property within a one-mile radius of the target site (FEMA, 2003, p. 1–32)?

As you will see with the ATRiM software in the next chapter, each critical infrastructure or building can be assessed, scored, and ranked. The ability to put an objective number on the vulnerability of a building provides the survey team the ability to quantitatively examine the proposed building and its threats and assets. There are numerous methodologies available to analyze vulnerability of buildings, sites, or specific targets and no one method is best in all cases. Whatever methodology used, a good start is looking at the whole picture of problem seeking before problem solving.

Risk Assessment

Risk is the potential for a loss of or damage to an asset. Risk is based on the likelihood or probability of the hazard occurring and the consequences of the occurrence (FEMA, 2003, p. 1–35).

It is possible to calculate risk using the results of the asset value, threat, and vulnerability described earlier. A risk assessment should be conducted and documented for existing and newly constructed premises. If a documented risk assessment does not exist, one should be conducted for existing premises. A risk assessment should be conducted if there are changes of ownership or change in the type of occupancy or mission of the building.

A risk analysis should be performed to determine if the threat should be accepted, avoided, transferred, or controlled. The identification of strategies should include prevention as well as mitigation methodologies.

A cost-benefit analysis should prioritize the prevention and mitigation strategies by assessing their feasibility, impact, and potential cost. The result of the cost-benefit analysis should be a set of recommended countermeasures. The objective of this analysis is to provide countermeasures that may be prudent and cost-effective.

The Security Program

It is possible to implement a robust security program following a full security risk assessment. This risk assessment model helps identify those hazards that would lead to situations with the greatest probability for occurring, and the greatest severity to the operation. These hazards are the first priority for future security program training, risk mitigation, and response preparation.

Prevention and mitigation strategies can include the following:

1. CPTED principles
2. Physical security devices
3. Electronic security devices
4. Security personnel
5. Administrative procedures including supervision, training, preemployment screening, documentation

To formulate a security program, it is first necessary to complete each stage of the risk assessment process. In order to assess the degree of security needed for a particular location, it is necessary to consider the following factors:

- Type of business
- Attractiveness to the criminal in terms of goods, cash, and possible confidential information
- Potential escape routes for the removal of stolen goods (these may not be the same as the entry route)
- Ease of access from either the streets, open areas, adjacent roofs, floors above and below the premises concerned if not under single occupancy, and from adjoining premises
- Degree of inherent security of the premises in relation to its construction
- Vulnerability relative to local trends in crime
- Surveillance provided either by normal public activity, routine police patrol of the area or by security patrolling of the premises or its surroundings

VULNERABILITY OF SITE AND BUILDING

In addition to this criteria, the analysis also should include consideration of types of space around the building. Each level of space will have special conditions and require assessment before amalgamating into the overall security plan:

- The peripheral space or the grounds and environment around the buildings
- The parametric space or immediate space adjacent to the building
- The volumetric space or area within the building

Risk analysis uses findings from asset, threat, and vulnerability analyses to examine the consequences of hostile actions for the building owner. The results of the risk analysis are used to determine which security measures can most effectively counteract potential damage and losses. The cost of each measure is evaluated according to how it contributes to achieving the desired level of protection. Decision makers responsible for new design or retrofit projects can then establish priorities and make informed decisions about security choices (AIA, 2004). Decisions are based on the likelihood of risk occuring and the potential impact of risk. This is demonstrated in Figure 12.3.

The risk analysis survey should cover the following areas:

- Overall site
- Architectural features
- Structural systems
- Building envelope
- Utility systems

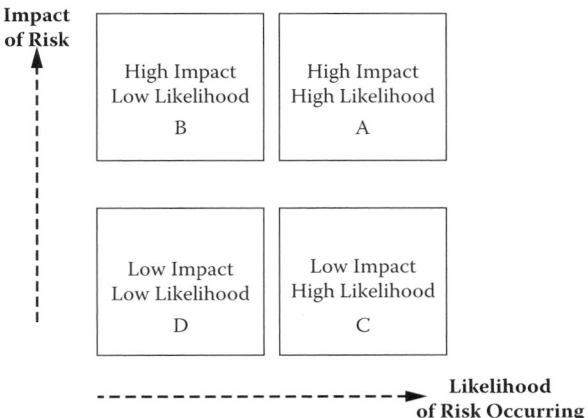

Impact of Risk

High Impact
Low Likelihood
B

High Impact
High Likelihood
A

Low Impact
Low Likelihood
D

Low Impact
High Likelihood
C

Likelihood of Risk Occurring

FIGURE 12.3   Impact of risk versus likelihood.

- Mechanical systems (HVAC)
- Plumbing (water) and gas systems
- Electrical systems
- Fire alarm systems
- Communications and information technology systems
- Equipment operations and maintenance
- Security systems
- Security master plan (FEMA, 2003, p. 1–46).

These thirteen areas cover the critical areas and systems that are present in most buildings today. In addition, Grassie (2004) provides some additional tips, listed here.

Determining Scope/Cost of Potential Loss: Risk analysis concentrates on determining the scope and potential costs of potential losses so an organization can apply risk decision criteria to either provide a specific level of protection to the asset, or seek other risk offset means.

Categorizing Loss Event Impact and Probability: The next step involves the designer categorizing each potential loss event impact and probability.

Loss Event Probability: Ranges from certain, highly probable, moderately probable, probable, and not probable in terms of its impact.

Security Response: Once these have been determined, designers must consider established organization risk management criteria such as accepting the potential for loss, avoiding it, diffusing it, offsetting it with insurance, transfer the risk, reducing the risk by movement, or acquiring a redundant asset and eliminating the risk through security countermeasures.

Determining Level of Protection: Finally, the designer is left with certain risks to assets that must be managed by means other than offsetting or transfer. This is where the designer determines the appropriate level of protection for each asset under risk, and begins to design a security program that is responsive to a specific asset protection need. At this phase, the designer categorizes assets and groups of assets in terms of level of protection criteria such as very high, high, moderate, low, and very low. This criterion then becomes the basis for determining asset protection requirements and countermeasures selection.

The outcome of the analysis can be used to target resources at the types of events that are most likely to occur and/or are most destructive (NIOSH, 2003, p. 3). Security designers must anticipate threats, identify vulnerabilities, and quantify risks. They must then anticipate the worst possible

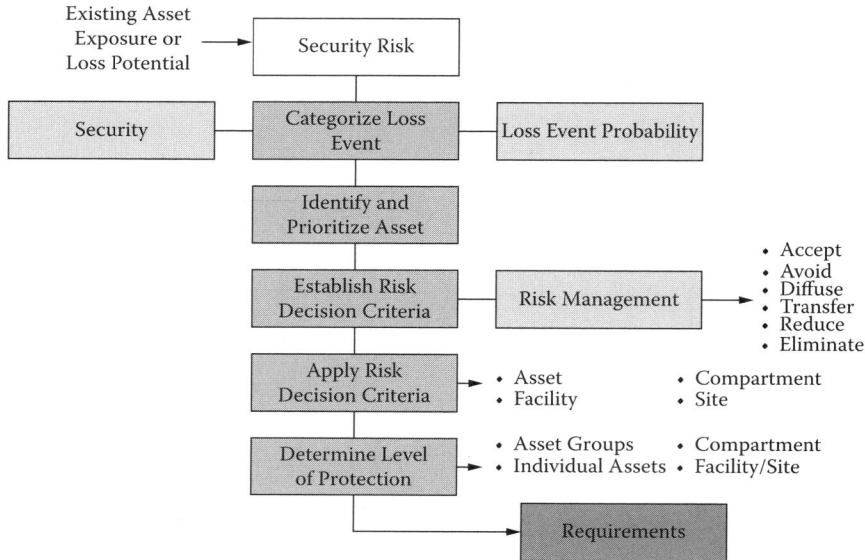

FIGURE 12.4 Understanding security risk.

consequences and ultimately weigh the cost of any countermeasure recommendations against the perceived cost benefit, or reduced potential for loss. Determination of cost-effective protective measures and their integration, is the result of a structured decision process beginning with a sound risk analysis, which considers the individual and collective contribution of each asset protection strategy according to the complete system's requirements. The design of integrated security systems begins with the realization that there are certain assets at risk as well as operational requirements for control of personnel and facilities that must be implemented to protect the business or organization (see Figure 12.4).

SUMMARY

The result of the risk assessment process will be a set of recommended countermeasures that may be priced and presented to the owner in a priority order so selections may be made of those recommendations that are prudent and cost-effective. In the case of the government standards, the assessment results in the assignment of a defined Level of Protection (LOP) with specified countermeasures. When the LOP is defined, the specified countermeasures are priced and again the owner may select appropriate measures, depending on a prudent level of protection and the cost effectiveness of the measure. The recommendations become the standard of care for that building or property. It is incumbent on the property owner to evaluate the recommendations seriously and implement as many as feasible. If the owner does not take the recommendations as a mandate for improvement, and subsequently there is an incident, the liability will fall on that owner or manager for the losses and consequences.

REFERENCES

American Institute of Architects (AIA) (2004) *Building Security Through Design: A Primer for Architects, Design Professionals, and Their Clients.* New York: Wiley & Sons.
European Prestandard (1995) Prevention of Crime, Part 3: Dwellings and Part 4: Shops and Offices.
BS EN 13541 (2001) Glass in building—Security glazing—Testing and classification of resistance against explosion pressure.

BS EN 356 (2000) Glass in building—Security glazing—Testing and classification of resistance against manual attack.

BS EN 1063 (2000) Glass in building—Security glazing—Testing and classification of resistance against bullet attack.

BSI BS 8220–1 (1996) Guide for Security of Buildings against Crime. Part 1: Dwellings.

BS 8220–2 (1996) Security of buildings against crime. Part 2: Offices and shops.

BS 8220–3 (1996) Security of buildings against crime. Part 3: Warehouses and distribution units.

EN 50130–4 on 16 August 1996.

Grassie, R. (2004) Chapter 4: Security Risk Analysis. *Reducing Risk in Buildings*. MA: Techmark.

NIOSH, (2005) National Institute for Occupational Safety and Health. Focus on Prevention: Conducting a Hazard Risk Assessment. Prepared by M. J. Brinch, Jr., and L. G. Mallett. U.S. Department of Health and Human Services.

Public Health Service Centers for Disease Control and Prevention. (2003) Pittsburgh Research Laboratory, Pittsburgh, PA, July, p.2.

State Domestic Preparedness Equipment Program, (1999) Assessment and Strategy development Tool Kit, May.

FEMA 452. (2005) A How-To Guide to Mitigate Potential Terrorist Attacks against Buildings. Risk Management Series. January.

FEMA 426. (2003) Reference Manual to Mitigate Potential Terrorist Attacks against Buildings. Risk Management Series. December.

U.S. Department of Justice. (1999) State Domestic Preparedness Equipment Program, Assessment and Strategy Development Tool Kit. Washington, DC: May.

13 The ATRiM Model for Critical Infrastructure Protection

Gregory Saville

Is it possible to prepare adequately for terror attacks? There is obvious benefit to assembling important agencies to coordinate responses during the first critical moments of an attack. Most emergency plans dedicate a significant portion of their content to responses. The sad fact of those plans is that they prepare for responding during or after the attack has already happened. By definition, the emergency response is NOT an act of prevention or mitigation of the crime and terror. In truth, there are very few critical infrastructure protection models available for antiterrorism prevention.

This chapter describes the recent development of one such model—ATRiM, the *Anti-Terror Risk Infrastructure protection Model*—a new computerized critical infrastructure protection system that combines the proven prevention strategies of CPTED and environmental security with the training and software package of modern technology. In terms of the risk-assessment process described in previous chapters, ATRiM completes the vulnerability and asset analysis portion of the security review process.

Unlike prevention of crime, prevention of terror events is relatively new. Critical infrastructure in this chapter refers to nonmilitary infrastructure. That is because military security systems, such as simulations for blast effects and chemical plume dispersion models, are rarely shared with the public. This is in spite of the fact that almost 80% of all critical infrastructures are owned and operated by public, nonmilitary sources.

Critical infrastructures present some unique vulnerability challenges such as cascading and escalating failures. Cascading occurs when attacking one target cascades to affect other similar infrastructures. Consider the case of the damaged Ohio electricity generating station that caused the entire eastern seaboard power grid to go offline a few years ago. Equally damaging is when one failed infrastructure escalates onto other different kinds of infrastructures. For example, the destruction of transportation routes, such as rail or roadway bridges, can escalate the impact on other infrastructures by preventing the delivery of fuel and emergency services.

Clearly, there is much to gain from mitigating, or preventing, attacks on critical infrastructures.

LESSONS FROM THE PAST

The theory of crime prevention has a rich legacy, but it is important not to confuse crime with terrorism. Crime emerges from a myriad of social, economic, and psychological dysfunction. Terrorism may have those dimensions, but political action and military strategy are at its core. Therefore the motives of the criminal offender and the terrorist vary considerably. Few store robbers or burglars are willing to sacrifice their own lives in the act of their crime. Most hope to escape. As we have seen in recent years, many terrorists do not.

However, some forms of crime prevention have been successful precisely because they do not focus on motive but, rather, on the specific opportunity the offender seeks to commit the crime. These strategies are described throughout this book as Crime Prevention Through Environmental

Design (CPTED) and Situational Crime Prevention. They assess the specific crime opportunity risks in the physical environment. The key to success of CPTED is specificity.

The same lessons apply to critical infrastructures. The ATRiM model seizes the lessons of analytical specificity. It helps asset mangers or property owners appreciate that not every target in a critical infrastructure is high risk. It provides a tangible strategy for prioritizing risk and enhancing the prevention at any given critical infrastructure.

Do protective measures provide complete protection against terrorism? That is unlikely. But it is likely that such measures can reduce the impact of a potential threat. Additionally, they can provide opportunities for the apprehension of terror suspects prior to the event.

A CRITICAL INFRASTRUCTURE PROTECTION PLAN

Every place with vulnerable assets should have in place a Critical Infrastructure Protection Plan in order to be prepared for major emergencies and terror attacks. The protection plan incorporates sections on threat warnings, response procedures, and assorted roles and responsibilities. These are mitigation strategies and they outline how to coordinate the response of agencies during and after a terror attack. The protection plan also incorporates preventive measures to improve asset survivability. Those are called remediation strategies.

There is a growing list of services available to enhance protection plans. They include new technologies for mapping potential terror crime targets (LaVigne and Wartell, 2000), methods for expanding partnerships for first responders, and conducting risk audits by identifying key individuals who may be involved in terrorist activities. The ATRiM significantly expands those by protecting infrastructures through the use of an advanced CPTED risk audit.

A protection plan should not be considered thorough upon the completion of a risk audit. Audits provide only one remediation strategy in an overall Critical Infrastructure Protection Plan. There are a number of stages of risk management in successful plans, and they have been presented in detail in previous chapters. It is sufficient here to list them:

1. **Asset appraisal**. This includes an inventory of the existing vulnerable targets under consideration. This appraisal is context based in that it depends on the type of potential target that terrorists might select.
2. **Threat assessment**. This deals with the likelihood and possible attack severity of a given target. It typically hinges on the ebb and flow of the current political climate. It therefore relies heavily on reliable intelligence and police data, along with competent synthesis and analysis of that data. In this chapter, we combine the asset appraisal with the threat assessment into the first step of the ATRiM model.
3. **Vulnerability analysis**. In one case this may apply to flaws in physical design and critical operations of a power plant that are vulnerable to arson or bombings. In another case it may apply to areas of a food-processing factory vulnerable to product contamination. We apply vulnerability analysis in the second and third steps of the ATRiM model.
4. **Risk assessment**. This involves a look at the severity of attack and the impact that may result. This topic is partially covered in the first step of ATRiM. Known generally as catastrophe risk modeling, the leading research is currently found in the work of insurance risk management (Woo, 2002; 1999). But because most catastrophic insurance losses came from natural disasters, in a post-9/11 world much of that modeling is now obsolete, or at least in need of significant revision.

INTRODUCTION TO THE PROBLEM

The vast majority of communities will never directly experience a terrorist event. However, it is critical that public safety officials work to prevent the possibility of such an event taking place, as well as plan should such an unlikely event occur.* (Chapman, 2002)

In contrast to this reality is the fact that, while local places may have low risks of terror attack, the complexity of global affairs and the interconnected nature of critical infrastructures makes even the most remote community vulnerable to global events. Unfortunately, antiterror services to municipalities are fairly new, and relatively sparse. That is one of the main reasons for this book.

There are some antiterror services available to law enforcement officials.** They include computer technologies for mapping potential terror targets, methods for expanding partnerships for first responders, and investigative tactics for identifying key individuals who may be involved in terrorist activities.

Furthermore, there has been considerable work on architectural features to protect against terrorist bombings (Atlas, 1995, 1996, 1998, 1999). For example, the design of the new Oklahoma City Federal Building includes structural hardening, extensive setbacks with cement bollards, and protective window glazing in order to harden the target against future attacks.***

The ATRiM model expands that work by seizing on the latest thinking in crime prevention through environmental design to protect physical infrastructure resources in a coherent and efficient manner.

A caveat is important at this point. Focusing on physical assets and property protection does not infer protection against personal victimization is unimportant. That is a topic of ongoing research (Goldfarb, 2003; IACP, 2001; U.S. Dept. of Justice, 2000). The current discussion also does not minimize the importance of cyber-terrorism as an essential aspect of critical infrastructure. There is growing literature on that topic as well (General Accounting Office, 2003; Eedle, 2002; ELES, 2001).

In addition, there is a hidden benefit from the crime prevention concept known as the diffusion of benefits. Because the ATRiM model aims to help local officials enhance the safety of key assets, it is equally likely that any attack deterred at one of these sites will most certainly save lives in and around that facility. This will indirectly benefit the community in a number of ways beyond protecting the physical asset. As pointed out in previous chapters, antiterror and crime preventive design measures may also protect against natural disasters, such as hurricanes.

CRITICAL INFRASTRUCTURE AND TERRORISM

In recent years, there has been a growing list of what is considered a critical infrastructure. ATRiM deals only with destruction, or disruption, of physical assets (Motleff et al., 2002). The assets comprise local infrastructures identified in the National Strategy for The Physical Protection of Critical Infrastructure and Key Assets published by the White House in 2003. These assets include:

1. Agriculture and food
2. Water, including dams
3. Public health
4. Emergency services
5. Defense industrial base
6. Telecommunications and information systems (computers)
7. Energy, including nuclear power plants
8. Transportation: air, sea, and rail

---

* There are a growing number of government publications on the topic. The review by Chapman et al. is an excellent overview. It is available online at http://www.cops.usdoj.gov.
** A good description of many of those resources is included in Chapman et al.
*** For more details, see the Whole Building Design Web site at http://www.wbdg.org/design/provide_security.php.

9. Banking and finance
10. Chemical industry and hazardous materials
11. Postal and shipping
12. Government facilities
13. Commercial key assets
14. National monuments and icons

Examples of terror targets that affect both property and persons include the domestic terrorism event at the Alfred R. Murrah Federal Building in Oklahoma City. Terrorists also can disrupt critical infrastructures while targeting the people who use them. This was the case of the Sarin nerve agent used by domestic terrorists in the Tokyo subway attack in 1995, or the anthrax attacks on postal stations and government offices by unknown assailants in the United States.

DO WE KNOW WHAT KIND OF ATTACKS TERRORISTS WILL USE?

There is no way to be certain. Terrorists can modify tactics as easily as targets. However, based on past experience, potential attacks have been categorized by intelligence think tanks into the following general topics:

Assassination
Armed assault
Bombings
Arson
Hijacking
Hostage-taking
Kidnapping
Product contamination
Cyberterrorism
Weapons of mass destruction (WMD)*

These categories are not exhaustive, nor are they mutually exclusive. For example, in the 9/11 attacks, terrorists combined aircraft hijacking and used planes as bombs. Obviously, it is crucial that intelligence services provide law enforcement with adequate information regarding the potential types of attacks terrorists might use so they can be incorporated into risk audits.

For the purpose of infrastructure protection only the following threats will apply:

1. Bombings (including "dirty bombs")
2. Arsons
3. Product Contamination
4. WMD (Weapons of Mass Destruction)

With the exception of cyberterrorism, the other forms of attack pertain directly to violence against persons, not property.

In addition, WMD pertain here primarily to biological or chemical weapons. Because of the overwhelming destructiveness of even low yield nuclear weapons, it is doubtful that any current form of CPTED is an appropriate strategy for prevention. However, some CPTED strategies may help in an indirect way, such as speeding up the identification of suspicious activities and items.

---

* Jane's Information Group is a military and security research think tank. This review is from their publication *Jane's Facility Security Handbook*, (Alexandria, Virginia: Jane's Information Group: June, 2000, pp. 20–29). There is no way to know all possible terrorist methods as they continually change. This list provides only an overview.

The application of these four strategies is not without precedent. There is evidence of both bombings and chemical weapons (WMD) as attack strategies. For example, since 1995 five major transportation systems have suffered terror attacks worldwide including London, Madrid, Paris, Tokyo, and the Tarragona Airport in Spain. The attack strategies were either bombings or, in the case of Tokyo, chemical weapons. Similarly, nine U.S. government facilities have been attacked since 1990 including embassies in Karachi, Calcutta, Manila, Tanzania, Nairobi, Athens, Moscow, Peru, and the Okalahoma Federal building in 1995. Bombings or grenades attacked all those facilities. Most recently in 2006, Canadian intelligence and police authorities conducted pre-emptive arrests of twenty terror suspects who were reportedly searching for suitable critical infrastructures to bomb in Canada.

Beyond the anthrax attacks following 9/11, there are others in which terrorists use WMDs domestically. This includes the 1984 Oregon Rajneeshee cult that contaminated restaurant salads bars using salmonella, and the 1990 Minnesota terror group Patriot's Council that produced Ricin poison to kill government officials.

Clearly, the threat is real and there is a need for more sophisticated risk assessment models. Additionally, selection of the ATRiM-defined attack modes is supported by the bombings, product contamination, and WMDs used thus far to target vulnerable sites.

ATRIM'S AUDIT PROCESS

CPTED principles provide the auditor with the framework for using the ATRiM model. This model is modified from other audit tools that CPTED practitioners employ, however unlike ATRiM, none of those other audit tools were created specifically for the purpose of critical infrastructure protection related to terrorist threats.

ATRiM combines both quantitative and qualitative methods for audits. Auditors assemble and train a team from those who work or manage an infrastructure. The ATRiM software employs a computerized risk assessment algorithm to analyze the audit data collected by the team during the site review.

BEYOND CHECKLISTS

There are three important lessons from the preceding discussion:

1. Strictly quantitative checklist approaches rarely capture the context of a particular environment.
2. Contemporary CPTED audit models are not designed for preventing terrorism at critical infrastructures. However, many features of those models have applicability, and those features have been adapted for the ATRiM.
3. No contemporary CPTED audit models incorporate Second-Generation CPTED, which examine the social, cultural, and managerial aspects of a critical infrastructure.

ATRiM combines various First- and Second-Generation CPTED, as well as situational prevention, concepts to produce a list of 12 specific strategies.

1. Territoriality
2. Access control
3. Surveillance
4. Image/maintenance
5. Increase the effort to commit crime
6. Increase risks to criminal
7. Reduce rewards from crime
8. Reduce factors that provoke crime

9. Social cohesion
10. Connectedness
11. Community culture
12. Capacity threshold

It is then possible to compile four categories of potential terror attacks:

1. Bombings (including "dirty bombs")
2. Arsons
3. Product contamination
4. WMD[*]

By placing the prevention strategies on one side of a chart, and the terror attack risks on another, it is possible to create a CPTED risk matrix for auditing a site. Keep in mind that each vertical column in the matrix lists eleven separate assessment categories, or cells (see Table 13.1). Within each cell, there are a range of potential assessment activities the audit team needs to complete (see Table 13.2).

DOCUMENTING DATA WITHIN EACH CELL

Each cell in the matrix is labeled, for example, A1 and B2. Each cell represents a different evaluative category, for example, A1 represents territorial factors related to arson at the particular site being audited. Cell B2 represents surveillance factors related to potential bombings at the site being audited.

To conduct a CPTED risk assessment audit of a site, auditors need to address each of the categories in the matrix and document the strengths and weaknesses of the site under audit. They document their audit onto handheld computers installed with ATRiM audit protocols, as well as with software extensions that can allow for a Geopositioning System (GPS) and 3D Computer Aided Design. For example, they can use the matrix categories to collect field notes, record details of each building, take digital photo images, or locating each comment to a particular architectural feature. These notes can then be transferred to an overall field report with recommendations for improvements.

TABLE 13.1
ATRiM Risk Assessment Matrix

	Arsons	Bombings	Product Contamination	Weapons of Mass Destruction
Territoriality	A1	B1	P1	W1
Surveillance	A2	B2	P2	W2
Access controls	A3	B3	P3	W3
Image and maintenance	A4	B4	P4	W4
Increase effort to commit crime	A5	B5	P5	W5
Increase risks of getting caught	A6	B6	P6	W6
Reduce rewards from crime	A7	B7	P7	W7
Cohesion	A8	B8	P8	W8
Neighborhood connectedness	A9	B9	P9	W9
Community culture	A10	B10	P10	W10
Capacity threshold	A11	B11	P11	W11

[*] The term *weapon of mass destruction* means any weapon or device that can cause death and harm to a significant number of people through the use of the release of radiation, biological, or chemical toxin.

TABLE 13.2

ATRiM Audit Activities for Assessing Bomb Risks

B1—Territoriality	How are vulnerable areas on site supervised or controlled by employees, and by security for the prevention of bombings?
	Are semiprivate areas used demarcated to separate the private areas from the public?
	Do areas on site provide territorial control to prevent bomb placement?
B2—Surveillance	Are there adequate perimeter, rooftop, parking lot, and passageway lighting to observe potential bomb locations?
	Are there vision barriers that will hinder or help sightlines to observe bombers before they become a risk?
	Are there good natural surveillance sightlines in public areas such as parking lots?
B3—Access controls	Are there adequate zone controls on entranceways such as passes for visitors?
	Are passes collected and recorded on exit?
	Is there a balance between security fencing, cement barriers to bomb distance specifications, and good visibility for security?
B4—Image and maintenance	Is there adequate cleaning and maintenance on site to remove flammable or combustible material for bombs?
B5—Increase effort to commit	Do features on site provide opportunities for bombings, such as window boxes or landscaping features where bombs might be concealed?
	Is there hardening of vulnerable targets on site, such as protecting electrical systems, panel boards, circuit breakers, and power relays from damage or bombings?
B6—Increase risks of getting caught	Are there security or police patrols?
	Are there identification badge controls?
	Are there electronic monitoring devices into secure areas?
B7—Reduce rewards for crime	Can vulnerable assets on site be removed or concealed?
	Are there any possible benefits to terror attack on site that can be denied?
B8—Cohesion	Is there positive interaction between security/police and capable guardians on site and do they effectively cooperate to monitor security?
	Are there security education and training programs for staff?
B9—Neighborhood connectedness	Do employees have opportunities to monitor visitors on site; do they speak to them, find out who they are?
	Are outside groups involved with the site in any positive way so they can help with security?
	Are there clear and specific protocols for cooperating with outside enforcement agencies?
B10—Community culture	How is staff morale and how does it affect participation in infrastructure protection?
B11—Capacity threshold	Do all employees, staff, or organizational members participate in infrastructure protection, or only a few?
	Can security information about potential risks be employed to create a critical mass of organizational members who are committed to infrastructure protection?

The most important factor is that each CPTED category on the side of the matrix is addressed and correlated to each risk category on the top of the matrix. That will ensure that a systematic methodology is applied throughout the infrastructure.

THE AUDIT PROCESS

In traditional CPTED assessments, a single CPTED practitioner walks around a site with a checklist in hand. This is a speedy way to collect information. Unfortunately, one auditor cannot possibly know how all the various design features work. Even with interviews it is unlikely that a single person can incorporate enough information during the audit process. The ATRiM process expands the traditional CPTED approach and supplements the review process by including these personnel in the ATRiM training sessions, and subsequent auditing process. These personnel also assist in reviewing security operating procedures, site plans, and other detailed information in and around the audit site.

PRIMARY AND SECONDARY AUDIT TEAMS

In the first phase of the audit process the auditor selects two or three members of an audit team. They are called the primary team.

All members of the primary team must possess security clearance. The lead auditor secures the data. For this reason, the ATRiM software encrypts the data for access only to key personnel.

The primary team then conducts the audit(s), and reviews security procedures, using six categories of the matrix:

- Territoriality
- Surveillance
- Access controls
- Increase effort to commit
- Increase risks of being caught
- Reduce rewards

The primary team then selects other members who may include employees from the organization, residents from the local community, and other stakeholders related to the infrastructure. This is the secondary audit team.

The secondary audit team then conducts an additional audit, along with interviews and focus groups, for the remaining categories of the matrix:

- Image and maintenance
- Cohesion
- Connectedness
- Community/organizational culture
- Capacity threshold

Each audit is based on the physical and operational context at that site. For example, in a power generating plant it is necessary to determine the natural surveillance opportunities. It may be necessary to interview staff on site to get their impressions. It will also be necessary to review strategies that increase risks to offenders, like the methods of formal surveillance, such as CCTV placement, television monitor quality, and review the security arrangements for using the equipment.

When the data is collected, it is downloaded into the analytical software where vulnerabilities are rated based on a computerized risk algorithm. The lead auditor and the primary team review the findings and prioritize a list of recommendations to minimize risks at the site. These recommendations build a set of remediation strategies that can become the first stage of a Critical Infrastructure Protection Plan.

Applying the Matrix Cells during the Audit Process

Once properly trained in the methods and the software operation, the primary audit team spends time reviewing the external and internal portions of the site. Their review is broken into four sections. An example of one section appears in Table 13.2.

These are a few sample questions the audit team answers during the assessment for Bombings (Table 13.2). The team uses their CPTED knowledge, local site familiarity, as well as daytime and nighttime audits to build a database from the matrix. They use the ATRiM software and the program leads them through the audit.

THE PLANNING PROCESS

With any Critical Infrastructure Protection Plan, there are a number of phases beyond the audit process that help enhance security. It is worth briefly describing how ATRiM fits into those phases.

Phase 1—Asset Identification and Vulnerabilities

Scanning the community for critical infrastructures and developing a priority list and time schedule for the audits.

In Phase 1, it is necessary to survey the community, or the site under consideration, for the critical infrastructure assets. Some will be well known, whereas others will not. The scanning process produces a list of vulnerable assets as a starting place.

There are also a few resources that can assist. This includes computerized geographic information systems (GIS), such as crime maps, and land use/engineering mapping resources.

Cooperation from the police and intelligence community is also necessary. Local law enforcement, state justice organizations, and federal agencies such as the FBI, all possess intelligence capabilities and can help identify the likelihood of attack at a particular critical infrastructure or the vulnerable assets at a site. They can help in the audit process and are ideal participants in the audit teams.

Once a list of infrastructure assets is compiled, it is necessary to develop a work plan by prioritizing each site and contacting the relevant stakeholders. At a minimum, primary ATRiM audit team members should include a member of the local intelligence or law enforcement community, employees, and property managers from the site, engineers or urban design specialists, maintenance personnel, and a security official from the property. An expert in CPTED to help facilitate the audit is also required.

Phase 2—The Audit

It is necessary to divide the audit team into primary and secondary audit teams. This is especially the case in highly sensitive infrastructures, such as power plants or chemical facilities, where liability and product secrecy is a factor. In these cases, the primary team members are a subset of the secondary team, however they possess security clearances at the audit site.

The timeline of audits depend entirely on the size and scope of the infrastructure. Some may last no longer than a few hours. Others will require repeat visits over a period of weeks. In venues where no protection plan exists, one advantage to conducting audits using ATRiM is that the audit results are the first step in creating a protection plan.

Phase 3—Implementation

It may take many months to implement all the recommendations, depending on the budgetary constraints facing that infrastructure. Some recommendations can be put in place immediately. The phasing of recommendations depends on the priorities of each area of vulnerability. If requested, the

ATRiM software also has the capacity to independently link to an online database with a list of suggested preventive strategies.

SUMMARY

Critical infrastructures are vulnerable only insofar as they are ignored. It may not be ultimately possible to prevent all terror attacks, but as crime prevention research has shown, headway can be made with a systematic approach to the problem.

Traditional security reviews and CPTED audits are insufficient for the type of risk created by contemporary terrorism. Because risks vary with the complexity of each vulnerable asset, audits need to be comprehensive, flexible, and based on state-of-the-art prevention research. There is no doubt that the current social and political climate giving rise to modern terrorism demands a rethinking of the safety we have taken for granted.

REFERENCES

Atkins, S., Husain, S., and Storey, A. (1991) The Influence of Street Lighting on Crime and Fear of Crime. *Crime Prevention Unit Paper* 28. London: Home Office.

Atlas, R. (1995) Oklahoma City: The blast, the repercussions, and a special report on defensible space. *Engineering News Record.*

Atlas, R. (1999) Designing against terror: Site security planning and design criteria. *Architectural Graphics Standards.*

Atlas, R. (1996) Coping with threats from bombs to break-ins. *Architectural Record.*

Atlas, R. (1998) Designing for crime and terrorism: CPTED training is essential. *Security Technology and Design.*

Atlas, R. (2004) *Safeguarding Buildings Against Attacks from Terror and Crime with CPTED.* AIA 2004 National Convention Continuing Education.

Barnet, D. (2000) *Electric Power Generation. A Non-Technical Guide.* Tulsa, OK.

Beaty, W. (1998) *Electric Power Distribution Systems. A Non-Technical Guide.* Tulsa, OK.

Bennet, R.R. and Flavin, J. M. (1994) Determinants of fear of crime: The effect of cultural setting. *Justice Quarterly.* 11:357–81.

Carroll, B. and Carroll, L. (Eds.) (2001) *Solving Crime and Disorder Problems.* Washington, DC: Police Executive Research Forum.

Chapman, R. et al. (2002) *Local Law Enforcement Responds to Terrorism: Lessons in Prevention and Preparedness. COPS Innovations.* Washington, DC: U.S. Department of Justice, Office of Community Oriented Policing. Available online at http://www.cops.usdoj.gov.

Checkoway, B. and Finn, J. (1992). *Young People as Community Builders.* Ann Arbor, MI: Center for the Study of Youth Policy, University of Michigan.

Clarke, R. V. (1980) Situational crime prevention: Theory and practice. *British Journal of Criminology,* 20, 136–147.

Clarke, R.V.G. (1992) *Situational Crime Prevention: Successful Case Studies.* New York, NY: Harrow and Heston.

Colquhoun, I. (2004) *Design Out Crime: Creating Safe and Sustainable Communities.* Oxford: Architectural Press. 2004.

Cousins, L. (1998) Ethnographic Windows on Urban Disorders, *Journal of Contemporary Ethnography,* 27(2), 278–284.

Critical Infrastructure Assurance Office, http://www.ciao.gov.

Department of Health and Human Services. (2002) *Guidance to Protecting Building Environments from Airborne Chemical, Biological or Radiological Attacks.* Centers for Disease Control and Prevention, National Institute for Occupational Safety and Health. Cincinnati, OH: NIOSH Publication.

Eedle, P. "Al Queda takes the fight for 'hearts and minds' to the web," *Jane's Intelligence Review,* August, 2002: 22–26.

ELES. Critical Infrastructure Protection Plan. Emergency Law Enforcement Services Sector, Washington, DC: February 2001.

General Accounting Office. *Critical Infrastructure Protection: Efforts of the Financial Services Sector to Address Cyber Threats.* Washington, DC: United States General Accounting Office. 2003.

Goldfarb, M. *Protecting First Responders: A Reference Guide for Police Executives on Biological, Chemical, and Radiological Threats.* June 2003 discussion draft, Police Executive Research Forum, 2003.

La Vigne, N. G., & Wartell, J. (Eds.). *Crime Mapping Case Studies: Successes in the Field (Volume 2).* Washington, DC: Police Executive Research Forum. 2000.

U.S. Department of Justice. *Responding to Terrorist Victims: Oklahoma City and Beyond.* Washington, DC: Office for Victims of Crime, U.S. Department of Justice, 2000.

Woo, G. (2002, 1 February) Quantifying Insurance Terrorism Risk. Paper presented at the National Bureau of Economic Research Meeting, Cambridge, MA.

Woo, G. (1999) *The Mathematics of Natural Catastrophes.* London: The Imperial College Press.

14 Protecting Buildings and Infrastucture with CPTED

The attacks on the World Trade Center and the Pentagon and the Oklahoma City bombing are forever etched as terrorism landmarks in our collective memory. Terrorism represents a real threat for our society and to our peace of mind. The face of terrorism is undergoing systemic changes as the level of terrorist sophistication increases with the availability of knowledge and materials with which to carry out these acts of violence. Knowledge about bombs and terror has proliferated to the point that virtually any terrorist or criminal can find the information needed to build virtually any kind of explosive device.

Timothy McVeigh, who blew up the Alfred R. Murrah Federal Building, stated in an interview shortly after his arrest that he picked that particular building because "it was more architecturally vulnerable." Who would have ever thought that a rental truck and a load of manure could be so deadly (see Figure 14.1).

What can we do to diminish the threats and losses to persons, information, and property? How do you reduce the opportunity and fear of terrorism in the built environment with Crime Prevention Through Environmental Design? This chapter will address how to reduce the threats and vulnerabilities in buildings by changing how we design and use our spaces.

LESSONS LEARNED FROM THE WORLD TRADE CENTER

People watching the horror on live TV were shocked that the World Trade Center buildings collapsed. The towers, built in 1972–1973, were 110 stories tall, and experienced progressive structural collapses similar to that caused by the 1995 explosion to the Alfred R. Murrah Federal Building in Oklahoma. The two plane crashes into the towers destroyed columns and floors on several stories, which transferred excessive loads to the remaining structural columns. Explosions and raging fire weakened the remaining columns, which were already overloaded. The original design had provided for the structural strength to withstand a Boeing 707, which was a large jet of its time but held a lower fuel capacity. The design of the towers was substantial enough to withstand the impact of a jet without toppling instantly. Even with huge gaping holes, the remaining columns were sufficiently strong to hold the structure up for over 45 minutes and allow 20,000 people to escape. The jet fuel released a much higher heat than paper or plastic burning, which might be the contents of a normal office fire. Fire suppression systems in the towers did not include foam sprinklers that

---

In Prison, McVeigh Admits to Bombing

May, 1995

From prison, Timothy McVeigh has apparently admitted to committing the Oklahoma City bombing. Two unnamed sources, who spoke on condition of anonymity, said McVeigh told them he was surprised to learn from newspapers that children had been killed in the blast, that he was unaware there was a day-care facility in the building.

According to the two people who spoke to him in prison, McVeigh also said he had targeted the federal building specifically because it housed government offices and was architecturally vulnerable, more so than other potential federal buildings.

Source: Multiple news agencies.

FIGURE 14.1 Article on Timothy McVeigh. (Excerpted from multiple news sources. Image from public records.)

could deal with the jet fuel fires. Both of the crashed jets were fully fueled for transcontinental flights, making them "flying bombs."

Fireproofed steel loses half its strength when it reaches 1,100 degrees Fahrenheit, and fails rapidly after 1,600 degrees Fahrenheit. The temperatures inside the building were estimated to be over 2000 degrees. The steel columns, weakened by fire, finally buckled, and the floors they supported dropped on top of each other in a "pancaking" action. Each falling floor overburdened the columns and floor below, causing the buildings to tear themselves down (*Architectural Record,* 2001, pp. 24–26). Designers agree that few structures short of a missile silo, no matter what their height, can endure such aggressive attacks.

Environmental design might not have been able to prevent the tragic events of 9/11, but the design of our public and private spaces does relate to safety and security through planning for: crowd behavior in high-density environments; wayfinding and design of escape routes; placement and type of building security features; design for high risk environments; and effective design of the built environment providing the building users with less stress, less confusion, and less opportunity to be a victim of a crime (*Environmental Design Technical Group News,* 2001).

THE GSA STANDARDS: ARCHITECTURAL GUIDELINES FOR FEDERAL FACILITIES

In June 1995, President Clinton mandated basic standards of security for all federal facilities. The mandate states that each Federal building shall be upgraded to the minimum-security standards recommended for its audited security level by the Department of Justice. In November 2001, President Bush signed a bill federalizing airport security screeners and antiterrorism legislation that empowers law enforcement and the military to take preventative actions.

Before the U.S. Marshall's Service conducting a vulnerability assessment in the wake of the Murrah Building bombing in 1995, there were no government-wide standards for security at federal buildings. The U.S. Marshall's Service Building Security Study developed 52 standards, primarily covering perimeter security, entry security, interior security, and security technology planning. Each federal building was rated within five levels of security based on facility size, facility population, and level of public access, with Level I being minimum security and Level V being a defense plant or nuclear facility. Most courthouses with a multi-tenant, multistory building are considered Level III and require shatter resistant glass, controlled parking, 24-hour CCTV monitoring and videotaping, x-ray weapon and package screening, and a photo identification system.

The GSA Security Standards encourages a Defensible Space/ Crime Prevention Through Environmental Design (CPTED) approach to clearly define and screen the flow of persons and vehicles through layering from public to private spaces. Edges and boundaries of the properties should clearly define the desired circulation patterns and movements. The screening and funneling of persons through screening techniques is an effort to screen legitimate users for the building from illegitimate users who might look for opportunities to commit crime, workplace violence, or acts of terrorism.

The result of one year of work by the GSA panel is a set of criteria covering four levels of protection for every aspect of security in the U.S. Marshall's report. The U.S. Marshall's report made a large number of recommendations for both operational and equipment improvements. The GSA Security Standards addresses the functional requirements and desired application of security glazing, bomb resistant design and construction, landscaping and planting designs, site lighting, natural and mechanical surveillance opportunities (good sight lines, no blind spots, window placement, and proper application of CCTV). These recommendations were further subdivided according to whether they should be implemented for various levels of security (e.g., a Level I facility might not require an entry control system, while a Level 4 facility would require electronic controls with CCTV assessment).

What follows are some of the general guidelines the architect and engineering team should address for major renovations or new construction on any federal building. Although not required, the exercise of due diligence suggests that state governments and commercial businesses also consider these standards in new construction as a comparable reference point or standard of care.

The GSA Security Standards have the following key areas that are addressed that are applicable to most comparable buildings:

1. Perimeter and Exterior Security
   - Parking area and parking controls
   - CCTV monitoring
   - Lighting to include emergency backup
   - Physical barriers
2. Entry Security
   - Intrusion detection system
   - Upgrade to current life safety standards
   - Screen mail, persons, packages
   - Entry control with CCTV and electric door strikes
   - High security locks
3. Interior Security
   - Employee ID, visitor control
   - Control access to utilities
   - Provide emergency power to critical systems
   - Evaluate location of daycare centers
4. Security Planning
   - Evaluate the locations of tenant agencies in leased buildings, and assess security needs and risk
   - Install security film on exterior windows
   - Review/establish blast standards for current relevant projects and new construction
   - Consider blast-resistant design and street setbacks for new construction of high-risk buildings (Level III or IV)

The GSA criteria takes a balanced approach to security, considering cost-effectiveness, acknowledging acceptance of some risk, and recognizing that Federal buildings should be not bunker or fortress-like, but open, accessible, attractive, and representative of the democratic spirit of the country. The guidelines suggest prudent, rather than excessive, security measures are appropriate in facilities owned by and serving the public.

In addition to these general recommendations, the GSA standards are further broken down into three different levels: external site, buildings, and internal design.

On a site level, the GSA standards recommend:

- Eliminate potential hiding places near the facility
- Provide unobstructed view around the facility
- Site or place the facility within view of other occupied facilities
- Locate assets stored on site, but outside of the facility within view of occupied rooms of the facility
- Minimize the signage or indication of assets on the property
- Provide a 100-foot minimum facility separation from the facility boundary, if possible
- Eliminate high-speed avenues of approach perpendicular to the building
- Minimize the number of vehicle access points
- Eliminate or strictly control parking beneath facilities
- Locate parking as far from the building as practical (yet address ADA spaces and proximity) and place parking within view of occupied rooms or facilities
- Illuminate building exterior or exterior sites where assets are located

- Secure access to power/heat plants, gas mains, water supplies, electrical and phone service
- Consider space for placement of hardware and servicing
- Plan for redundant wiring
- Plan for backup power
- Plan for intrusion detection devices
- Plan for site intrusion detection
- Plan for boundary penetration sensors
- Plan for motion detection systems
- Plan for access control systems
- Plan for contraband and weapons detection
- Plan for explosive detectors
- Plan for credential readers and positive personnel identification systems
- Plan for security control and information display systems

On a building level, the GSA standards recommend:

- Employ the concept of security layering
- Locate assets in spaces occupied 24 hours a day where possible
- Locate activities with large visitor populations away from protected assets where possible
- Locate protected assets in common areas where they are visible to more than one person
- Place high-risk activities, such as the mailroom, on the perimeter of the facility

On an interior security level, the GSA standards recommend:

- Employee and visitor identification systems
- Secure the utility closets and vulnerable utilities
- Develop emergency plans, policies, and procedures
- Have daycare located and protected from unauthorized access
- Screening points where applicable for weapons, pilferage, or identification
- Secured and controlled shipping and receiving areas with integrated access control, CCTV, intercoms, data logging, and report capabilities

WHAT ABOUT BUILDINGS IN THE PRIVATE SECTOR?

In the private sector, the American Society of Testing Materials (ASTM) Premise's Liability Committee was disbanded in 1997 by lobbying pressures for developing minimum-security guidelines for multitenant residential housing environments. Their effort was resurrected with the National Fire Protection Association (NFPA) several years latter. The NFPA regulates fire protection and life safety requirements and security is definitely considered part of a life safety issue. NFPA Premises Security Committee developed the 730 and 731 occupant-based security Guidelines which were passed in 2005, and are beginning to serve as industry standards. Europe has had minimum-security standards since 2000.

The ATRiM program outlined in Chapter 13 is one of the first comprehensive steps for helping facility managers, architects, and designers conduct basic, and advanced, CPTED retrofits for the purpose of antiterror protection. It does this by taking into consideration four attack modes: bombings, arsons, product contamination, as well as elementary WMD. What about using CPTED to design private buildings in the first place?

The CPTED process provides a holistic methodology to meet the challenges of crime and terrorism with three approaches: organizational methods (people—security staff, capable guardians), mechanical methods (technology—hardware, barriers, hardening), and natural design methods (architecture, design, and circulation movement flow). Property owners must determine the assets they want to protect, the level of risk they are willing to assume and how much they can afford to spend protecting their sites, facilities, employees, and other occupants (Nadel, 2004). A comprehensive building security plan integrates three elements: design, technology, and operations—each consisting of policies and procedures. These elements are most effective when used together and are appropriate to protect structures against terrorism, natural disasters, crime, and workplace violence.

For example, if one of the vulnerabilities of a threat analysis for a government building is the challenge of a truck bomb, and the goal is to distance a potential bomb from the façade of the building, then the CPTED approach would propose careful consideration of:

- Where is the parking placed?
- How does service delivery get screened and controlled?
- How do pedestrians flow into the building?
- How many entrances are there for the public, staff, and service?
- Is there one main entrance for the public?
- How much distance is the exterior path of travel from the street, pedestrian plaza, to the building facade?
- Do all four facades have setbacks from the street?
- What is the most appropriate bollard system or vehicular barrier system?
- Do bollards or planters create blind spots or sleeping places for homeless persons and street criminals?
- Does a threat exist from bicycle and motorcycle bombers, thus requiring a smaller barrier net?
- Does surveillance from the building to the street remain unobstructed?
- Do landscaping and plantings remain unobstructed?
- Do barriers hinder accessibility by persons with disabilities?
- Where do private or public security forces patrol?
- Are security patrol patterns unobstructed and verified with a guard tour system?
- Is the structure of the building designed with structural redundancy?
- Does the building become a less appealing target by layers of buffer zones that make it more difficult for an intruder to reach the intended target?
- If the building is at high risk of a bomb threat, have the structural components been designed to allow for the negative pressure effects of an explosion?
- If the building is at high risk of a bomb threat, are the window systems a balanced design to protect against the threat of broken glass using blast curtains, or blast resistant glazing materials?
- Does lighting around the property provide a uniform level of light to resist shadows or hiding places?
- Are there CCTVs in places of extraordinary activity to detect inappropriate behavior and record and monitor that activity?
- Does the building have a consistent and comprehensive weapon-screening program for the building users, staff, packages, and mail?
- Does the property use security layering to create a sense of boundary of the property (site), the building, and specific points within the building?
- Do management and maintenance practices and policies support security operations, the use of security staff, monitoring devices, weapon screening procedures for people and property, the screening of employees' backgrounds, and the physical upkeep of the premises?

It is evident that a lot of thought and money goes into making a building secure. However, neither an architect nor a security director can change human nature, and criminal acts will be perpetrated in spite of the best-laid plans. Our built environment cannot be defended against every potential threat. No building security system could have prevented the act of terrorism of 9/11, or the bombing of our embassies, or courthouses. But there are many active steps that can be taken to reduce the opportunities and fears of crime, and increase our awareness of the threats. Our goal is to design safe buildings that protect our assets of people, information, and property.

Design includes architecture, engineering, landscaping, and site planning. The first line of defense is the site perimeter. Site placement and layout is the single most important goal in planning to resist terrorism and security threats in the protection of life, property, and operations (FEMA 426, 2003, 2–6). Building placement is important relative to the ability to have access control and natural surveillance. Building orientation can have an impact on the spatial relationship to the site, its orientation relative to the sun, and its height and volume relative to the site. The placement and amount of open space is important to site security, specifically as it applies to the ability to observe the perimeter and detect intruders, vehicles, and hide contraband. Another benefit of open space is the standoff distance from the blast energy of an explosion.

Designers should understand that the impact of vehicular circulation patterns could make a facility or site more vulnerable if security implications are not carefully considered. The designer can propose a roadway system, to minimize vehicle velocity, thus using the roadway itself as a protective measure (FEMA, 2003, 426 2–11). Straight-line approaches to buildings should not be used, because these give cars and trucks the opportunity for gathering speed and momentum to crash into the building. Raised entrances, low landscaping, dirt berms, strategically placed decorative boulders, bollards, fencing and curved driveways can render vehicular attack difficult or impossible. Architectural landscape elements like raised planter beds, park benches, lamp posts, serpentine or curving roads, traffic calming devices, site lighting, and trash receptacles serving as vehicle barriers prevent a direct line of approach and a direct line of sight to the building (Feldman, 2005).

Buildings with layers of buffer zones are much less appealing targets than those without them (see Figure 14.2). Placing visitor parking in an area not directly adjacent to the building can also be a deterrent insofar as terrorist vehicles cannot be parked for detonation purposes in an effort to destroy or damage the building. Natural surveillance, or the ability to see with an unobstructed view of who is entering the property and whether it is for a legitimate use, is an important part of the safety plan. The best placement of the footprint of a freestanding building is one that has all façades set back from the street.

Beyond environmental design, other relatively low-cost precautions can be as basic as protecting vulnerable utilities by locking manholes in the street and securing areas such as electrical rooms, fan rooms, mechanical rooms, and telecommunications spaces inside the building with locks and alarms (Feldman, 2005).

Other measures include developing operational policies and procedures including the increased use of security personnel, motion sensors, cameras, and closed-circuit TV as part of a more comprehensive security plan; biometrics, proximity card readers and other forms of electronic access controls; and defenses integrated into heating, ventilation, air-conditioning (HVAC), and other systems. To counter a chemical attack, defense design experts recommend installing air intakes above grade, either on the roof or at least three or four stories above ground (Feldman, 2005).

Other built-in defenses for existing buildings could include air-detection systems and carbon filters to protect against chemical releases and high efficiency particulate air filters used in conjunction with UV3 light wands to achieve a high capture rate of spores or other biological agents. In existing buildings, where renovating the entire HVAC system is likely to be cost-prohibitive, an alternative is to put vulnerable areas such as the lobby, mailroom, and receiving dock on a separate HVAC zone. Then, if there is a release in the lobby, it is not transmitted throughout the entire building. The design also can positively pressurize the building lobby or even the whole building, in the event there is an external release, it is kept outside those areas by the pressure (Feldman, 2005).

Pressurizing a building and locking it down can protect against an external release. The goal in defending against an internal release is to isolate the contaminated area and purge it as quickly as possible. The process of protecting people and property against terrorism is much easier to implement into new buildings. In a new building the costs to isolate the lobby, the loading dock, and

Images courtesy of the National Capital Planning Commission's *National Capital Urban Design and Security Plan* 2002

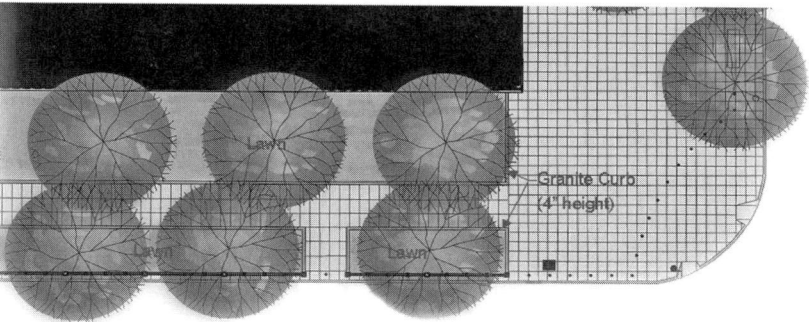

FIGURE 14.2 Street setbacks and reinforced street furniture as proposed for Washington, DC. (Reproduced courtesy of the National Capital Planning Commission (www.ncpc.gov/), Urban Design Security Plan, 2002.)

mailroom areas are minimal, and a building owner should incorporate that level of defense (Feldman, 2005).

Other defenses against terrorism include hardened floors, walls, and doors that are difficult to penetrate, tamper-resistant door and window hardware, and use of security zoning. Dividing building space into zones with varying security levels such as unrestricted, controlled, and restricted can more effectively protect sensitive areas. The focus of access control strategies is to deny access to a crime target and create in offenders, a perception of risk and detection, delay and response.

When a building progressively collapses, as in the Oklahoma City bomb blast, it falls domino-style after one or more columns fails. The total collapse took less than three seconds. In a protective design structure, one or two columns may collapse but the rest of the building remains standing, allowing some time for occupants to escape.

Understandably, the first recommendation of the Final Report of the National Construction Safety Team on the Collapses of the World Trade Center Towers (U.S. Commerce Department's National Institute of Standards and Technology) is to use protective design to avoid progressive collapse. The report is expected to lead to more cutting edge solutions and improved code requirements in cities nationwide. Occupants also can escape quicker from a collapsing building if staircases are located at the opposite ends of a building and lead to exits going directly outdoors and not into a lobby.

Based on the results of a three-year federal study of the 9/11 terrorist attack, the U.S. Commerce Department called for several major changes in the planning, construction, and operation of skyscrapers in its National Institute of Standards and Technology report, Final Report of the National Construction Safety Team on the Collapses of the World Trade Center Towers. It also selected other buildings needing changes to improve survival and prevent natural or accidental calamities from terrorist attacks. The recommendations for improved public safety in tall and high-risk buildings, intended to serve as a basis for improvements in the way buildings are designed, constructed, maintained, and used. It addresses nine distinct areas:

- Increased structural integrity
- Enhanced fire resistance of structures
- New methods for fire resistance design of structures
- Improved active fire protection
- Improved emergency response
- Improved building evacuation
- Improved procedures and practices to encourage code compliance
- Improved emergency response
- Continuing education and training of fire protection engineers, structural engineers, and architects

What issues should the architect address with the owner and security director, or consultant? Based on the security layering principles described in earlier chapters, the architect will address security concerns on a site level, building level, and interior space level.

Site Planning

- Access
- Service delivery
- Circulation patterns
- Lighting quality and quantity
- Perimeter defense

Main Lobby

- Visitor control issues
- Building fire system location
- Reception/guard kiosk design and equipment provisions
- Architectural security barrier design—turnstiles, glass enclosures, reception areas, and so on
- Retail tenant security adjacent to lobby areas
- Development of unobtrusive CCTV surveillance
- Controlling access into emergency stairwells adjacent to the main lobby
- After-hours access control into the main lobby
- Alarm monitoring of perimeter doors
- Main lobby lighting

Parking Garage

- Valet or self-parking
- Public, private, or mixed use
- Segregated parking levels
- Executive parking security

- Need for and use of CCTV surveillance system, emergency signaling system, intercom system, and guard tour system
- Lighting issues, including type of lighting and number of footcandles to be provided

Loading Docks

- Amount of vehicular traffic flow expected
- Impact, if any, on street traffic or pedestrian walkways
- Storage of package and materials
- Distribution of deliveries throughout the building
- Development of necessary CCTV surveillance and intercom systems
- Provision of remote door release controls

Emergency Stairwells

- Restricting access or allowing use by the public for interfloor traffic
- Communication provisions in stairwells
- Emergency exit alarm devices on doors
- Alarm monitoring of the stairwells
- Access control into and out of the stairwells

Miscellaneous

- Elevator bank access control and architectural design
- Communication provisions in elevator vestibules on individual floors
- Public washrooms
- Mail services
- Deliveries
- Security in mechanical areas
- Door hardware for telephone, electrical, and storage closets
- Security for fuel and water storage areas
- Roof access
- Tunnel or skyway connections to other nearby buildings
- Plaza security—issues related to landscaping, lighting, and use of unobtrusive surveillance systems
- Elevator cab communication devices

Building Tenant Security

- A comprehensive access control program to encompass elevator car access control requirements and individual floor access control measures
- Security measures for individual departments and operations that may have additional security requirements
- Executive floor security
- Receptionist workstations
- Boardroom or executive conference room access control issues
- Vestibule construction of freight elevator lobbies
- Console room design
- Secured storage areas, vaults, and safes within tenant space
- Closet space for security-related equipment
- HVAC and power requirements for security operations

Major Systems That Should Be Addressed

- Fire and life safety
- Public address
- CCTV surveillance
- Access control
- Alarm monitoring
- Radio communication
- Emergency signaling
- Intercom
- Guard tour
- Door control
- Uninterruptible power supply

The following are recommended CPTED design features that may be applicable to your building:

- Place unsafe activities in safe areas where there is natural surveillance and supervision.
- Design the exterior of a structure so it is difficult to climb.
- Minimize the number of exterior openings at or below grade.
- Protect all building openings against entry or attack.
- Provide for extra conduit for growth and changes.
- Design walls to resist penetration by intruders possibly using cars, hand tools, explosives, and so on.
- Provide sufficient space in the lobby or entry areas for verification, identification, and screening of users, i.e. sign-in desks, contraband detection equipment such as X-ray machines, and personal identification equipment.
- Provide adequate space for maintaining security equipment.
- Protect all utilities and control panels from disruption by unauthorized persons.
- Design elevators, stairways, and automated locking mechanisms not to compromise security during emergency evacuations.
- Design lighting for proper illumination in coordination with CCTV—reduce glare, increase view of field.
- Design perimeter to be well defined and supported by natural barriers such as landscaping, mechanical barriers such as walls, fences, buried sensors, motion sensors, proximity sensors, and by organizational methods such as guard patrol.
- Integrating the security technology into functional design and architecture, allowing the legitimate building users to be your capable guardians for legitimate activity and deterrence of criminal activity.

The following measures should be considered in the design of entry control points (FEMA 426, 2003, 2–38):

- Design entry roads to sites and to individual buildings so that they do not provide direct or straight line vehicular access to high-risk buildings. Route major corridors away from concentrations of high-risk buildings.
- Design access points at an angle to oncoming streets so that it is difficult for a vehicle to gain enough speed to break through the stations.
- Minimize the number of access roads and entrances into a building or site.
- Designate entry to the site for commercial, service, and delivery vehicles, preferably away from high-risk buildings whenever possible.

- Design the entry control point and guard building so that the authorization of approaching vehicles and occupants can be adequately assessed, and the safety of both gate guards and approaching vehicles can be maintained during periods of peak volume.
- Approach to the site should be designed to accommodate peak traffic demand without impending traffic flow in the surrounding road network.
- Provide pullover lanes at site entry gates to check suspect vehicles. When necessary, provide a visitor/site personnel inspection area to check vehicles prior to allowing access to a site or building.
- Design active crash barriers, such as bollards, speed bumps, vehicle barriers, as may be required to control vehicle speed and slow incoming vehicles to give entry control personnel adequate time to respond to unauthorized activities.
- Design the inspection area so that it is not visible to the public, when necessary. Place appropriate landscape plantings to accomplish screening.
- Consider current and future inspection technologies for screening vehicles.
- Provide inspection bays that can be enclosed to protect inspection equipment in the event of bad weather.
- Design inspection areas large enough to accommodate a minimum of one vehicle and a pullout lane.
- Consider providing a walkway and turnstile for pedestrians and a dedicated bicycle lane.
- If possible, provide a gatehouse for the workstations and communications equipment of the security personnel. It may also serve as a refuge area in the event of an attack.
- Provide some measure of protection against hostile activity if ID checking is required between the traffic lanes. Cameras and lighting will be important features.
- For high-security buildings, provide a final denial barrier to stop unauthorized vehicles from entering the site.
- Design the barrier system to impede both inbound and outbound vehicles. The system should include traffic control features to deter inbound vehicles from using outbound lanes for unauthorized access. Barrier devices that traverse both roadways should be included in the design. The safety features discussed above for inbound lanes should also be provided in the outbound lanes.

APPLICATION OF GSA SECURITY STANDARDS TO ALL BUILDING TYPES

Whatever the building or its use, security for antiterrorism and crime prevention criteria should be similar to fire safety, accessibility, and structural integrity. Any piece of architecture should establish a hierarchy of space that goes from open access by the public, to semipublic, to semiprivate, to private spaces. Any areas or spaces that are unassigned to a specific purpose or capable guardian should be avoided as it becomes "no-man's land" and not claimed, protected, or defended by any individual or group. Traffic patterns of pedestrians and vehicles into sites and buildings should be carefully thought out and controlled for the desired goal. The design of any building should maximize the potential for natural observation by the legitimate building users.

Target hardening is one method of increasing the effort using techniques such as: improving locks to be dead bolts; upgrading window screens; using break resistant glazing; increased use of fencing; magnetic locking doors. Another technique is access control, which includes installing barriers, designing paths, walkways, and roads so that unwanted and unauthorized users are prevented from entering vulnerable areas. Barriers may include limiting entrance to specific individuals, places or times; security vestibules, parking lot barriers, entry phones, visitor check-in booths, guard stations, vehicle control systems, bio-metric screening for access control.

SUMMARY

The goal for designers, landscape architects, and security professionals to prevent or reduce the opportunity for terror incidents, and the fear or incidence of crime, should be to think holistically, yet minimize fortress design and target hardening. Fortress minimization should be the goal, except where it may be specifically required only after thorough analysis and study. The design professional must address the issue of how architectural design features and approaches can be enhanced by security without imposing objectionable and unreasonable measures on the aesthetics and functionality of the building. As you have seen throughout this part of the book, there are a number of necessary assessments and analytical steps that accompany any security design. In short, when designing buildings with antiterrorism and crime prevention in mind, the design and security professional should:

- Conduct the need assessment and include it as part of the architectural programming process.
- Determine the level of criticality and threats to the building assets.
- Change how people use the building for legitimate authorized uses.
- Use security technology last, once the circulation patterns are clear and the architecture of form reflects the function of facility.
- Use the national standards as a starting point to establishing a standard of care, in order to improve efficiency, safety, and security, and to reduce premises liability from negligent security design and practices.

Architecture is, unfortunately, one of the least used pieces of the security puzzle to make public and private buildings safe and secure. CPTED planning creates the environment for better security by allowing natural surveillance and unobstructed visibility, controlling access to persons who belong on the property, preventing unauthorized access of persons onto the property, integrating the security technology into functional design and architecture, and allowing the legitimate building users to be your capable guardians for legitimate activity and deterrence of criminal activity. Finally, environmental design can never eliminate crime or terrorism completely because it does not attack root causes. Architectural security design may shift the places where crime or terrorism occurs, but in the process the offender must start a new target search, and is thus put at greater risk of apprehension before the event occurs. Furthermore, environmental control does go a long way toward making people feel better about their work and living environment, and that empowers people to act in a safer manor, and to design buildings in a safer, more resistant manner.

Architects and security professionals should avoid worrying about events over which they have no control: real estate markets, zoning regulations, fire department inspections, and operational policies. They should focus instead on the things over which they do have control: good CPTED design, integrated security systems, competent training and staff, and keeping a watchful eye on workplaces, living environments, and residences to see how CPTED design might fit.

REFERENCES

American Society of Industrial Security (ASIS). http://www.asisonline.org/.

ASTM F 1642 (2004) Standard test method for glazing systems subject to airboat landings. American Society of Testing Materials. West Conchohocken, PA.

Architectural Record (2001) October. 24–26.

Atlas, R. (1998) Just when you thought it was safe to go back in the building. *Security Management*, 64–73.

Atlas, R. (2004) Security design concepts. Security Planning and Design: A Guide for Architecture and Building Design Professionals. Washington DC: American Institute of Architects, Wiley.

Atlas, R. (2006) Architect as nexus: Cost effective security begins with design. ArchiTech (May–June), 30–34.

Atlas, R. (2006) Designing for Security. The Construction Specifier (April), 83–92.

Crowe, T. (2000) Crime Prevention Through Environmental Design, 2nd ed. Boston: Butterworth–Heinemann.

DiGreggario, A. Applied Research Associates, Alexandria VA.

Environmental Design Technical Group News (2001) EDRA. September.

FEMA 426 (2003) Reference Manual to Mitigate Potential Terrorists Attacks Against Buildings.

FEMA 427 (2003) Primer for Design of Commercial Buildings to Mitigate Terrorist Attacks.

FEMA E155 (2006) Building Design for Homeland Security.

Feldman, W. (2005) Developers and owners design properties to minimize loss in event of terrorist attacks. *Journal for Property Managers*. IREM Institute of Real Estate Managers. Oct.

Final Report of the National Construction Safety Team on the Collapses of the World Trade Center Towers (2005) U.S. Commerce Department, National Institute of Standards and Technology.

Final Report of the National Construction Safety Team on the Collapses of the World Trade Center Towers (2005) U.S. Commerce Department, National Institute of Standards and Technology.

GSA Security Criteria (1997) General Services Administration, October 8.

Interagency Security Committee (ISC) (2001) Security Design Criteria for New Federal Office Buildings and modernization Projects. September 29.

Miami Herald (1995) I did it, bombing suspect tells two. 5/19.

Nadel, B. (Ed.) (2004) *Building Security: Handbook for Architectural Planning and Design*, New York: McGraw-Hill.

Newman, O. (1973) *Defensible Space: Crime Prevention Through Urban Design*. New York: Macmillan.

Unified Facilities Criteria (UFC) (2002) DoD Minimum Antiterrorism Standards for Buildings. July 31.

Unified Facilities Criteria (UFC) (2002) DoD Minimum Antiterrorism Standoff Distances for Buildings. July 31.

Vulnerability Assessment of Federal Facilities. (1995) U.S. Department of Justice. June 28.

Security Watch (2001) *Bureau of Business Practice Newsletter*, Oct., 4.

Werkerle, G. and Whitzman, C. (1995) *Safe Cities: Guidelines for Planning, Design and Management*. New York: Van Nostrand.

15 Designing for Explosive Resistance

Randy Atlas and Tony DiGregorio

It is widely known today that critical infrastructure is the target of choice by terrorists. From bridges, water treatment plants, power plants, symbolic buildings, transportation hubs, and banking, critical infrastructure represents the backbone of the economy in a democratic society. With a majority of the critical infrastructure in the private sector, it is important to note that responsibility for security and protection rests with the owners of infrastructure themselves. The nudging and supervision of the federal government is necessary to make sure there is a standard of care. For example, the Maritime Transportation Security Act creates security goals for the maritime industry. Pending legislation for the Chemical Facilities Security Act would mandate security duties for the chemical industry. Water treatment facilities and nuclear power facilities have existing federal standards and regulations regarding security. The challenge with getting the private sector to develop security standards and emergency plans is that each sector operates in somewhat of a vacuum. Until a major disaster specific to a particular infrastructure prompts national regulations, such as dams breaking, bridges collapsing, or widespread food contamination, private sector infrastructure owners will be slow to make changes.

The attack on the New York World Trade Center brought to light our worst fears in a security nightmare: out of control fires, structural collapses, failure of emergency fire safety systems, failure of emergency backup power systems, and the horror of evacuation from a high rise building. Any building can suffer from an explosion as a result of a terrorist attack, or more likely a faulty water heater, or propane gas heater.

How should the security manager design their building to resist the damage from an explosion? The first and most critical step is to identify the vulnerable areas of your building and the most likely sources of the potential threats. The World Trade Center was a target for terrorism because the building represented corporate America, and one-stop shopping for maximum impact for killing persons and disrupting corporate America. The unsecured parking garage in the first attack provided the opportunity to get a bomb into the structure. The World Trade Center was designed to make money and welcome the public. Security considerations were not a primary factor in the design, and the results were catastrophic.

Since the explosive attacks on American embassies in the early 1980s, embassies are now designed with setback distance and a series of barriers between the building and the surrounding local environment. It is common to have awnings or eaves over the windows to prevent a rocket launched missile or a hand-thrown grenade to directly penetrate a window and explode in the building. The eaves serve to help deflect attacks and localize the damage to the outside of the building. Windows and glazing are designed to be blast-resistant, reducing or preventing shards of glass acting as shrapnel. Another well-known material used for break resistance as well as ballistic resistant glazing is polycarbonate. Polycarbonate plastic is used in jails and prisons because of its break-resistant qualities.

If an explosion occurs within a building, either by a bomb or propane gas explosion, the structural elements may be vulnerable to progressive structural collapse. The Beirut bombing of U.S. troops in their dorm had a high number of casualties because of the collapse of the building. The bombing of the Murrah Federal Office Building resulted in progressive structural collapse that was the principal cause of 168 deaths. If buildings are designed to withstand an earthquake in California, then a building can be designed to survive an explosion long enough to allow survivors to evacuate.

Details of building construction are very valuable to persons intent on destroying a building using explosives. It is important that blueprints and structural engineering drawings remain under strict security, and that the architects and engineers be educated in the importance of the security of the drawings. The drawings reveal which columns and walls are structural or load bearing walls. The structural frame may need to have redundancy designed into the building to compensate if a portion is compromised. Expansion joints and shear stress points, such as those designed for earthquake resistance, could provide the needed flexibility for building movement in an explosion.

Many building designs clad the structural steel components with precast panels. This is beneficial for providing some distance between the bomb effects and the structural steel. If there are areas within a building that have a propensity for explosion, such as: ammunition storage, storage of chemicals or fuels, or mechanical rooms where propane gas is used, then the use of blowout walls is desired. Blowout walls are designed to give during the explosion and let out the positive pressure from the explosion. Out of necessity, rooms requiring blowout walls must be on the perimeter of the facility. Additionally, the interior walls should be blast resistant to the design threat to prevent interior damage to the building while directing the explosive force to the exterior wall.

It is common that building designs strive for large open interior spaces. While this condition may be aesthetically appealing, the greater the distance, or spacing between the columns, the greater potential for damage in the event of collapse. Typically, a building with column spacings in excess of 30 feet will require blast engineering to assure blast resistance. A building that could be a potential target for terrorism should be designed for structural resistance to explosion. Computer-generated programs are available that look at different explosive scenarios and depict how different types of explosive devices could damage your building. The engineer then designs for a specific level of resistance as determined by your risk and threat assessment.

Careful consideration should be given to providing redundancy in life safety systems. The architect can design the smoke evacuation system, fire sprinklers, uninterrupted power supply, and the emergency lighting systems to be zoned, in the event that one part of the building is destroyed the whole building does not have systems failure. Many government buildings have been designed for resistance to car bombs with vehicular barriers and spatial separation of vehicles from buildings. Commercial buildings like the World Trade Center, since the 1993 event, have accepted explosion as a risk consideration. The parking entries and plaza were redesigned to deter or prevent unauthorized vehicles from entering those spaces. Buildings of the future will need to add new design criteria for explosion resistance, along with fire resistance and crime resistance. Understanding the vulnerabilities of a building to a potential attack will identify ways to improve your chances for survival in such a misfortune.

The design of structures to be resistant from blasts incorporates many structural engineering elements and theories that are beyond the scope of this book. The structural engineer will be considering the factors of static and dynamic loads. A blast engineer will examine explosive impact loads on the building and structure. If the building type warrants it, the structure can be designed for survivability that would delay or prevent collapse rather than allow catastrophic failure. Architects do not engage in structural design, but we do hire structural engineers to be part of the design team. Architects and security professionals do not need to know the equations and calculations, but be able to ask the questions and direct those professionals (the engineers) that do have knowledge and expertise for structural and blast resistant design.

The best preventative measures for protecting against blasts are a *four-step* layer approach. Providing a *safe zone* or *setback* is best for explosions occurring outside the structure, and screening and restricting parking and vehicle access provides a safe zone. However, the setback space will vary on the bomb size that is presented. Second, *screening of goods* onto the property and in the building will reduce the likelihood of a bomb being introduced into the building or site. However, this measure is extremely obtrusive to the conduct of normal commerce and building operations. Third, having *blast-resistant exterior shell,* with shatter-resistant windows and frames is an important factor, but is expensive and may require the structure be structurally reinforced. Just filming windows does not add real protection, as the frame and wall housing the frame must be equally reinforced. Fourth, having the *structure blast-resistant.* In theory, this sounds good, but the expense and construction impact may deter most commercial and nonmilitary facilities from this course of action. A risk assessment must guide the decision maker. Typically, blast resistant design adds 4 to 8 percent to the cost of the building shell. Computer modeling programs are now available to evaluate if a facility is at risk, and if so what areas are most vulnerable and need to be reinforced.

Designing against explosions is just one of the many threats that critical infrastructure face. One of the first issues that should be addressed when designing against explosions is whether the explosion is on the *outside or inside* of the structure. Designing to resist the explosive wave from the outside has different design objectives than dealing with an explosion placed within a building that must decompress.

In 2005, several reports were issued that addressed the lessons learned from the September 11, 2001 attacks and the collapse of the World Trade Center Towers. Some of the important lessons learned that will apply to architecture and high rises of the future are the planning of egress routes, the engineering building systems, fire proofing of structural elements, designing against progressive structural failure, placement and width of stairwells and elevators, and the use of impact-resistant materials in the building core, truss design, fire safety, sprinkler and smoke evacuation systems, power backup systems, building communication systems, and much more.

Until recently, securing our infrastructure, for example, ports, airports, factories, refineries, power plants, industrial parks, military bases, and borders, has primarily meant a gated fence around the perimeter, guards, guns, and cameras. But these strategies have proven to be inadequate and don't provide a realistic level of security and protection against today's threats. Intelligent use of CPTED design strategies can reduce manpower, and more importantly use the security resources smartly. Intelligent video motion detection, infrared night vision, chemical and biological sniffers, advanced package screening, and portal weapon and contraband screening, virtual fences, biometric controlled access control, all functionally integrated together can provide a comprehensive, yet *transparent approach* to building security and infrastructure protection.

The federal government has developed and implemented antiterrorism standards for all of its buildings that evolved from the Oklahoma City Federal Building bombing that resulted in the publication and adoption of the Vulnerability Assessment of Federal Buildings completed on June 28, 1995. In 1997 The General Services Administration published the GSA Security Design Criteria. The Interagency Security Committee (ISC) modified GSA Criteria and initially adopted the ISC Security Design Criteria in May 2001. The ISC document was adopted to ensure that security becomes an integral part of the planning, design, and construction of new federal office buildings and major modernization projects. The criteria consider security in all building systems and elements, much of which addresses the prevention or design against explosions. Since the original adoption, the ISC Security Design Criteria have been modified twice. The most current version is dated September 2004 and are under review.

The ISC Security Design Criteria serves as the current model for addressing the appropriate security design criteria for a project based upon a facility specific risk assessment and analysis of all available information on security considerations. A security master plan starts the process with careful evaluation of the building site selection, the designated level of protection, use of CPTED on building shapes, and placement of the building on the site. Site planning and landscape design elements are now set forth for issues such as vehicle access, service delivery, parking considerations and access, public road access, infrastructure connections, setbacks of the building from the public streets, and choices in planting materials and street furniture.

The building architecture is examined in the ISC Criteria for blast and terror issues in the material and methods choices for the building. Those choices include structural systems, glazing materials, location of lobbies, mailrooms, loading docks, and other vulnerable building functions. Structural engineering concerns are addressed to prevent progressive structural failure and to have the building elements resist explosive attacks. Walls, roofs, structural framing, lobbies, mailrooms, loading docks, exterior windows and glazing systems, building core elements of elevators and stairwells, all receive attention. Mechanical engineering issues must address utilities, the HVAC for ventilation and air quality issues, protection against airborne contaminants and protection of the air intake systems. Working ventilation equipment is important to evacuation of a building damaged by blast or fire. Critical mechanical spaces and utility systems should also be protected from attack.

Electrical engineering systems must meet the ISC Criteria to address the critical life safety systems of fire alarm, sprinkler systems, security, communications, lighting, and back up emergency power systems. Lessons learned from the 1993 World Trade Center attack included the placement of the entire emergency and back up systems in the basement that severely compromised evacuation when an explosion in the garage took out all of the security and life safety systems. Fire protection or life safety engineering is addressed in the ISC Criteria that consider the need for redundancy of some systems based on the lesson learned in WTC 1993 and the Murrah Building. Buildings with a high threat of terrorist attack require redundant protection of the utility systems, active fire protection, and smoke evacuation systems.

The ISC Security Criteria address electronic and physical security systems. Areas that are addressed are the control centers, building management systems, camera placement and recording, locking systems, access control, interior space protection, alarm systems, and more. Parking security is addressed on how persons are screened, access control, service delivery, and design criteria for protecting against explosions in garages.

Understanding how much damage explosions can do has been the topic of many military security books and is not the purpose of this publication. What the architect or security professional needs to know is that there are standards and criteria out there that are good frames of reference, even if you are not designing a federal building, especially since most of the critical infrastructure is private sector. Explosive devices are delivered in a variety of forms. The size of the delivery means normally dictates the size of the explosive charge. Letter bombs, package bombs range from 2 to 50 pounds TNT equivalent. Car and truck bombs range from 250 pounds to thousands of pounds of TNT equivalent. A letter bomb or small package could potentially destroy an unprotected mailroom or loading dock. A car or truck bomb can destroy a building. The importance of keeping large bombs away from buildings cannot be overemphasized.

Bombs can be delivered to a building environment through a variety of means: mail, car, person, rocket launcher, missile, hand delivered, or suicide bomber. Once the credible threats and hazards are determined, the appropriate or reasonable level of protection measures can be designed. The primary things to consider in protecting a facility from explosions are:

1. Building setback and distance from public ways
2. Perimeter protection
3. Glass and glazing systems
4. Structural hardening
5. Progressive structural collapse protection
6. Safe refuge area and evacuation routes

Setbacks have been discussed in earlier chapters and only need reminding that the distance that building skin is from the threat is critical in the level of structural hardening. It is also critical that the setback is protected with devices that prevent the entry of vehicles except at protected entryways. If an office building or courthouse only has 30 feet of protected setback from the public roadways, the structural engineering, architectural design, and CPTED responses will be much more target hardening than a building that is at protected set back of 100 feet. In downtown urban environments, there is often no choice as to what the building footprint can be due to the limitations of the sidewalk, zoning requirements for setback, and the ability to provide protection.

Perimeter protection can be accomplished with a variety of low and high profile means. Some low profile means include arroyos, ditches, and berms in the landscape site design. Vehicle barriers are often expensive, high-profile tools of preventing vehicles onto a site or into a building. Retaining walls and planters are another means of vehicle barriers and creating setbacks. Whatever physical barriers are created, it is important to remember that handicap accessibility must be maintained without compromising the needs for access control. Fencing has been dramatically improved to include cabling systems capable of stopping vehicles.

Glass and glazing systems are common tools used by architects to cover a majority of the skin of many buildings today. When the risk assessment has determined a risk from explosions, then the use of blast-resistant windows becomes an important design and structural consideration. Windows and their frames can be designed to fully resist a given level of blast load and the threat of breakage and flying debris. Laminated glass is used in most blast-resistant and hurricane resistant glazing. This type of glass is composed of a sandwich of several bonded lites of glass with a plastic interlayer or polycarbonate between them. Laminated glass may fracture, but fragments remain bonded to the interlayer and held in place if properly glazed. The glass must be anchored in the window frame with a bite engineered by a blast engineer, as compared to a normal commercial frame that only has one-quarter inch of bite for glass anchored in the frame. The frame itself must be reinforced to be part of the building structure so as not to blow out or become detached from the structure.

In 2005, Hurricanes Katrina and Wilma did damage to brand new high-rise residential condominium towers on the oceanfront that allegedly used new code-compliant glazing systems. The glass that was damaged was found to be a result of the window frames not being properly anchored into the structure. The hurricane force winds sucked the window frames out of their walls, and debris cracked the hurricane rated glass. The glass was not anchored into the frame with enough bite or metal, and was subsequently sucked out. With a balanced design, the wall should be stronger than the anchorage, the anchorage should be stronger than the frame, and the frame should be stronger than the glazing.

Structural hardening should focus on the areas that are easily impacted such as walls, roofs, floor slabs and beams, frames (steel or reinforced concrete), and the foundations. A blast engineer will determine the thickness of materials and the connections needed to handle shear and torque. The stressors on a building from an earthquake or hurricane are different than the shock waves from a blast outside or inside a building. The important thing to remember is that depending on the threat level, the blast engineer can take into consideration what the blast requirements should be and design for them. Because air blast loads rapidly decay with distance, the highest loads are at the base of the building and decay with height. When an exterior blast outside a building occurs, the blast wave will break windows, and exterior walls will blow inwards. Some structural columns may be damaged. The blast waves force the floor slabs upward disengaging them from the support systems. As the final stages of the blast wave occur, the wave surrounds the structure and creates downward pressures on the roof and outward pressures on all sides. These types of stressors are unique to blast, as compared to natural disasters. Innovative wall systems can be designed to absorb blast effects better and also reduce solar heat gain, as well as envelope heat transfer by using multiple layers, specially designed building openings, crumple zones, and special reinforcing.

When building structural elements disconnect from their connections, a failure of primary structural elements leads to a collapse of the adjoining members, which in turn leads to additional collapse. Progressive structural failure was evident in the Oklahoma City Federal Building bombing and the 9/11 World Trade Centers attack. The shape of the building can play a role in its vulnerability to damage. Intersections in buildings shaped like an L, W, or U are more likely to trap the shock wave at the vortex, which may amplify the effect of the air blast (see Figure 15.1) Large or gradual reentrant corners will have less effect than small or sharp corners or overhangs. Convex-shaped

FIGURE 15.1   Building shape impacts the ability to deflect a blast wave. (Photo courtesy of iStockphoto. com.)

buildings are preferred, rather than concave shapes for the exterior of buildings to reduce the effects of blasts.

Spatial organization plays a role in blast design. Typically, mechanical rooms are placed on the building exterior, which is good security design, to facilitate placement of large equipment but it also acts as a way of reducing the risk of explosion deep in the center of the building. The mailroom also should be considered a high-risk room and placed on the building exterior with blow out walls considered in the event of a letter bomb. It is recommended that the lobby and loading dock areas be placed on the building exterior, outside the building footprint when possible, because they are very vulnerable to attack.

The next generation of high rises and large building projects will rethink how the building core is designed and the placement of fire stairwells and safe refuge areas and routes. Lessons learned from the World Trade Center collapse included stairwells that scissor next to each other, or are placed adjacent to each other can be compromised by a fire incident or explosion and doom building users above the fire line. New facility design will be considering the placement of stairwells farther apart to provide maximum possibilities of survival in case of a catastrophic incident. Stairs may be designed wider to allow better building occupant flow. Safe refuge areas will have better fire department emergency response communications systems. Better marking and wayfinding signage of egress paths, stairs, and door markings will be provided so that occupants can easily find ways out, despite smoke or fire conditions using luminescent materials and battery or backup generators provided lighting. Smoke evacuation systems and automatic fire sprinklers will be required and, in some cases, redundant in high-rise buildings to improve public safety in our buildings and reduce the risk of failure.

Recent events in Europe and the Middle East have shown that not all bombs will be dropped, planted, or driven to a site. How do we protect our buildings from someone walking into a mall or office building lobby and blowing themselves up? The best way to reduce the opportunity for a suicide terrorist attack is to enforce a standoff clear zone in which only screened vehicles or people are allowed to enter. Security personnel should be trained to observe unusual behavior and activities and be comfortable to challenge persons engaging in scoping out behavior without a reason for being on the property. All service deliveries and couriers should be screened and identified by security staff and have set times for loading dock access. Screening of packages and service delivery should occur at a safe or remote location to be screened and then delivered securely to the facility. Security staffing should have extensive background checks and have shifts rotated regularly to avoid patterns that could compromise staff. Emergency evacuation drills and procedures must be practiced and annually updated. Automatic visual and audible systems should be used for evacuations to give pretaped messages and directions. Visitors and employees should be screened and required to present identification or have identification badges, preferably using biometric to reduce identity errors. Training and practice of drills and evacuations are essential for an automatic and intuitive response by the building occupants and the staff. The risk threat vulnerability assessment is the first and last step in reducing and identifying the potential for suicide attacks and terrorist incidents. It all comes back to the planning and research to make a good program work.

If one of the outcomes of a threat analysis for a government or high profile commercial office building is the risk of attack by a truck bomb, and the goal is to distance the bomb from the building, then the CPTED approach would propose careful consideration of the following:

- How close can the terrorist get to the building exterior?
- What streetscape and landscape elements are used to prevent car bombs?
- Where are the different types of parking placed? (Visitors, Service, VIPs, ADA)
- Can parking beneath facilities be eliminated or strictly controlled?
- Can the number of vehicular entrances be minimized to just one?
- How does service delivery get screened and accepted?
- How do pedestrians flow into the building?
- How many entrances are there for the public, staff, and service? Are they controlled?
- Is there one main entrance for the public?
- What is the distance of the exterior path of travel from the street to the building façade?
- Do all façades have setbacks from the street? Is there enough land to provide 100-foot minimum setbacks?
- What is the vehicle barrier system used? Bollards, planters, pop-ups?
- Do planters and landscaping provide opportunities for hiding contraband or bombs?
- Does the threat exist from bicycles and motorcycle bombers?
- Are exterior trash containers set back from the building as much as possible and transparent to permit easy inspection for contraband?
- Does surveillance from the building to the street remain unobstructed?
- Do the barriers hinder persons with disabilities from having a clear path of travel?
- Are security patrol patterns unobstructed and verified by a guard tour system?
- Is the building designed with structural redundancy?
- Does the building become a less appealing target because of increasing layers of security?
- Have the structural components been designed to allow the decompression effects of an explosion? (Is the building designed to sustain local damage, with the structural system as a whole remaining stable and not being damaged to a disproportionate extent?)
- Are the window systems designed in a balanced way to protect against the threat of broken glass by security filming, blast curtains, or blast resistant glazing materials?

- Are stairs wider than needed for evacuation ease? Are stairwells at opposite sides of the building?
- Are stairs and elevator shafts encased in steel and reinforced concrete?
- Are air intakes hard to access and/or at least 40 feet above the ground?
- Do subterranean parking level stairwells empty to a lobby floor before going into the upper levels of the building?
- Does lighting around the property provide a uniform level of light to reduce shadows and hiding places?
- Is there CCTV coverage in places of extraordinary activity, rather than ordinary activity to record and monitor that activity?
- Are potential hiding spaces near the facility eliminated?
- Does signage minimize the indication of assets on the site?
- Is access secure to the power plants and distribution, HVAC, gas mains, water supplies, electrical and phone closets, emergency generator, and backup fuels, rooftop equipment, communications equipment, and data lines?
- Does the building have a consistent and comprehensive weapons screening program for the building users, staff, mail, and packages?
- Does the property use concentric security layering to create an increasing sense of territoriality going from the perimeter, to the building, to interior points of the building?
- Do management and maintenance practices and policies support security operations?

DESIGNING BUILDINGS TO PROTECT AGAINST BOMBINGS AND OTHER TERROR THREATS

In urban buildings, where car and truck bombs are a threat, street furniture and site elements such as bollards and planters can be engineered to resist the velocity and speed of vehicles. For protection against flying debris—the main cause of injury in a bomb blast—designers can minimize glass at street level, reinforce windows with security film or replace glass panels with polycarbonate. Installing "blast windows" made of laminated glass that crumbles rather than shatters and a cable catch to contain any laminated glass failing to crumble is another option. The building can also be retrofitted with a cladding material more resistant to blast. Among the range of threats for many buildings is the risk of bombs. The following are some design lessons learned from the Alfred R. Murrah Courthouse bombing and the World Trade Center bombing.

APPLICATION OF SECURITY STANDARDS TO BUILDING TYPES

The process described here can apply to all forms of architecture:

Institutional architecture: police stations, courthouses, jails and prisons, post offices, schools, hospitals, airports
Commercial architecture: office buildings, shopping centers, retail stores, restaurants, and entertainment facilities
Residential architecture: Single-family homes, townhouses, low-, mid-, and high-rise multifamily residential facilities, planned urban developments, hotels, rental apartments, public housing.

  Key defensive architectural site design considerations for bomb resistance (FEMA 426, 2003) include:

- Establish a secured perimeter around the building that is as far from the building as is feasible. Setbacks of 100 feet are desired (see Figure 15.2).

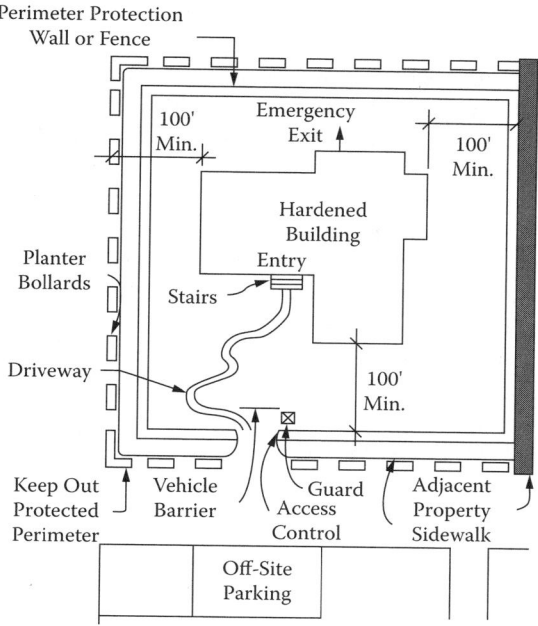

FIGURE 15.2 Secured site plan. (Ramsey, C. G. and Hoke, J. R. Jr; ©2000, Architectural Graphic Standards, 10th ed; John Wiley & Sons. Reprinted with permission of John Wiley & Sons.)

- Use poured in place reinforced concrete for all framing including slabs, all columns, and roofs. As a guide, roofs and base slabs should be at least 8 inches thick, exterior walls 12 inches thick, and columns spaced no more than 30 feet apart. A blast engineer is necessary to design structures for specific size threats.
- Use "seismic detailing" at connection points (i.e., interconnect rebar in slabs with rebar in columns and beams so framing within a building becomes an integrated whole).
- Reinforce floor slabs and roofs using a two-way reinforcing scheme (i.e., place rebar in a crisscross pattern with concrete).
- Design windows that comprise no more than 15% of the wall area between supporting columns or occupy no more than 40% of a structural bay.
- If the building is at high risk of a bomb threat, use a balanced window design to resist blast pressures.
- Install specially designed blast curtains inside windows that can catch pieces of glass, while permitting air blast pressure to pass through the curtain as part of a balanced window design.
- Design artistically pleasing concrete barriers as flower planters or works of art and position them near curbing at a distance from the building, with less than four feet of spacing between them to block vehicular passage.
- Build new buildings in a simple geometric rectangular layout to minimize the "diffraction effect" when blast waves bounce off U-shaped or L-shaped buildings causing additional damage.
- Drastically reduce or totally eliminate ornamentation on buildings that can easily breakaway causing further damage to building occupants or pedestrians at street level. All external cladding should be made of lightweight materials that will minimize damage when they become flying objects following an explosion (or hurricane!).
- What is the building footprint relative to the total land available?
- What is the building location relative to site perimeter and adjacent land uses?

- What are the access paths via foot, rail, water, air, and car, in terms of the ability to support a secure perimeter?
- What are the current and proposed infrastructure and vulnerabilities, including easements, right-of-ways, power lines, water mains, and utilities?
- Proximity to fire and police stations, hospitals, shelters, and other critical facilities that could be of value in the event of an attack?
- What kinds of natural hazards or environmental considerations exist around the site?
- What are the presence of natural physical barriers such as water features, dense vegetation, and terrain that could provide access control, and /or shielding of the site?
- Are there any topographic and climatic characteristics that could affect the performance of chemical agents and other weapons?
- What is the natural surveillance from outside boundaries onto the site? Are there vegetation and plantings in proximity of the building or site that could screen covert activity?

Site Security Design elements can include:

- Bollards/planters (see Figure 15.4)
- Curbs
- Vehicle barriers (see Figure 15.3)
- Security lighting
- Signage and ground rules
- Gates
- Eliminate high-speed avenues of approach perpendicular to the building (see Figure 15.5)
- Minimize the number of vehicle access points
- Eliminate or strictly control parking beneath facilities
- Locate parking as far from the building as practical (yet address ADA spaces and proximity) and place parking within view of occupied rooms or facilities
- Illuminate building exterior or exterior sites where assets are located
- Secure access to power/heat plants, gas mains, water supplies, electrical and phone service.

The CPTED process and security threat assessment process would look at the following high-risk targets as vulnerabilities for terrorist targets:

- Engineering and backup power/utility systems
- Mechanical, ventilation, and water treatment systems
- Communications systems including the computer facilities
- Supply and storage areas, including loading and receiving docks, warehouses, volatile substances or materials storage
- Transportation facilities that include rail, bus, train, seaports, and airports
- Human targets which can include political figures, CEOs, or casual observers to impact collateral damage such as school children or shoppers
- Government, military facilities, chemical plants, explosives, or volatile materials

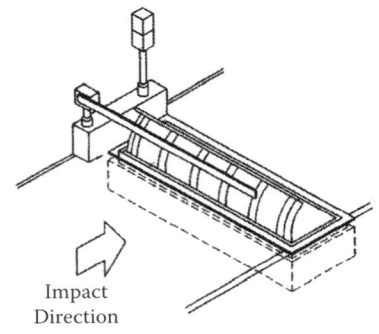

Impact Direction

FIGURE 15.3 Retractable barrier. (Ramsey, C. G. and Hoke, J. R. Jr; ©2000, *Architectural Graphic Standards*, 10th ed; John Wiley & Sons. Reprinted with permission of John Wiley & Sons.)

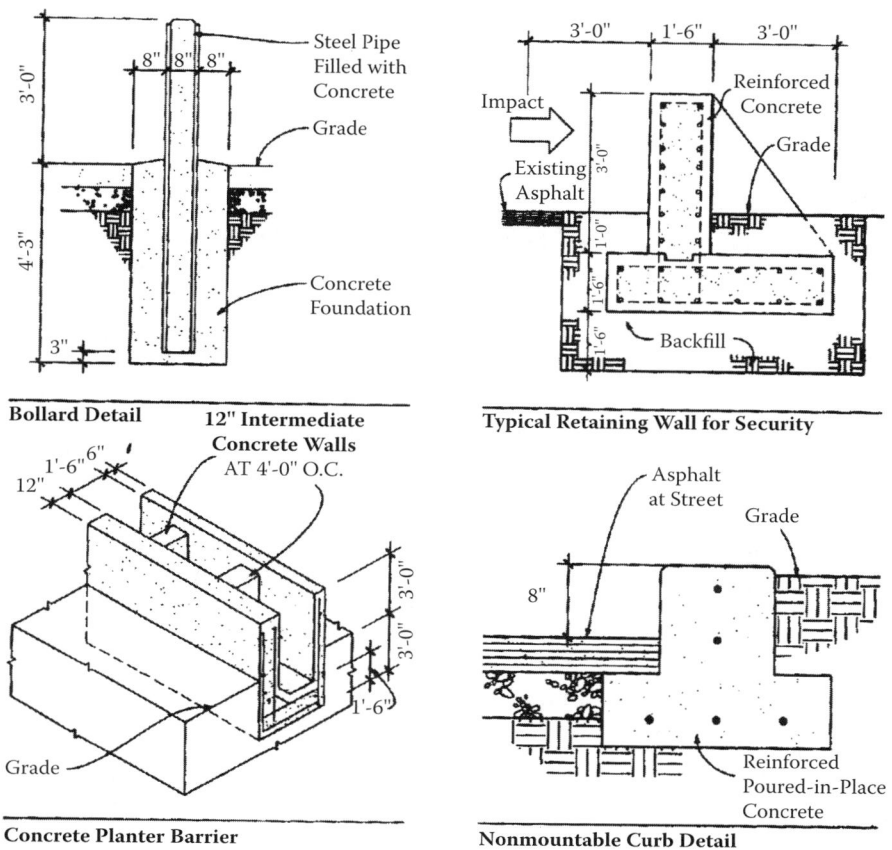

Bollard Detail

12" Intermediate Concrete Walls AT 4'-0" O.C.

Typical Retaining Wall for Security

Concrete Planter Barrier

Nonmountable Curb Detail

FIGURE 15.4 Typical bollard. (Ramsey, C. G. and Hoke, J. R. Jr; ©2000, *Architectural Graphic Standards*, 10th ed; John Wiley & Sons. Reprinted with permission of John Wiley & Sons.)

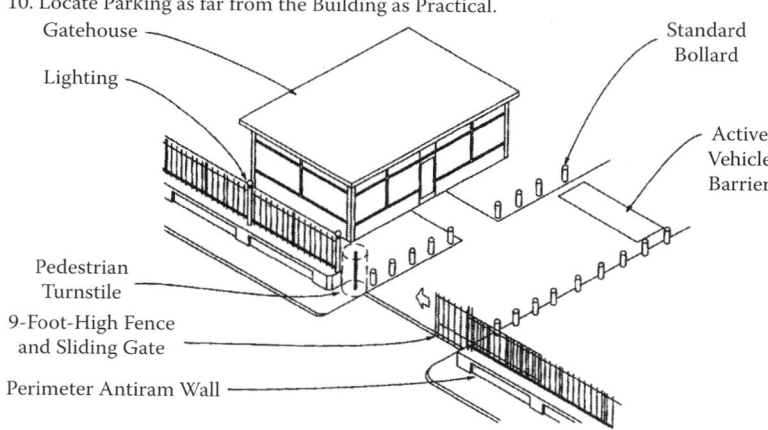

FIGURE 15.5 Sally port design for buildings. (Ramsey, C. G. and Hoke, J. R. Jr; ©2000, *Architectural Graphic Standards*, 10th ed; John Wiley & Sons. Reprinted with permission of John Wiley & Sons.)

To avoid creating a fortress-like design, owners can implement *transparent security*—security invisible to the eye. However, owners must determine when they want security to be visible, and then have the flexibility to increase security under certain circumstances—letting the public know an area is under surveillance (Nadel, 2004).

SUMMARY

Designers of critical infrastructure buildings and those structures evaluated to be high risk should now include antiterrorism and blast resistance, as some of the factors that they must address on every project. Architects and structural engineers need to become familiar with the basic principles of blast-resistant and progressive collapse resistant design.

It is possible to go beyond the obvious target hardening of structures and critical infrastructure to reduce the terrorist threat by adapting CPTED principles and practices. It is as if the updated CPTED was antiterrorism through environmental design. CPTED and transparent security practices can facilitate security access control needs and reduce the fear and opportunity from acts of terrorism. Architects, engineers, and security professionals can be educated to consider the key elements of security, structural integrity, improved emergency evacuation, screening capabilities for people and packages, good siting of the building for maximum setbacks, and designing for good natural surveillance to enhance challenging potential criminal or terrorist activities.

REFERENCES

ASTM F 1642 Glass Hazard Criteria, American Society of Testing Materials.

Atlas, R. (2000) Site security barriers. *Architectural Graphics Standards*. 10th ed. New York: John Wiley, pp. 163–164.

FEMA 426 (Dec. 2003) Reference Manual to Mitigate Potential Terrorists Attacks Against Buildings.

FEMA 427 (Dec. 2003) Primer for Design of Commercial Buildings to Mitigate Terrorist Attacks.

FEMA E155 (2006) Building Design for Homeland Security.

GSA Security Criteria (Nov. 2000). General Services Administration, Ch 8, PBS-PQ-100.1.

Interagency Security Committee (ISC) (2004) Security Design Criteria for New Federal Office Buildings and modernization Projects. 29 September.

Nadel, A.B. (2004) *Building Security: Handbook for Architectural Planning and Design*. New York: McGraw-Hill.

Unified Facilities Criteria (UFC) (2003) DoD Minimum Antiterrorism Standards for Buildings. 8 October.

Vulnerability Assessment of Federal Facilities. (1995) U.S. Department of Justice. 28 June.

16 Codes and Standards of Care for Infrastructure Protection
Or, Complaining is Pretending You Have a Choice!

In my experience, the general architectural community has never been properly educated or trained in the ways of designing for security, Defensible Space design, or CPTED practices. There are only a handful of schools of architecture in the United States that have CPTED or security as part of their curriculum (Florida Atlantic University School of Architecture, University of Florida, Virginia Tech, Rutgers University). There are no requirements for Defensible Space and CPTED awareness or knowledge to be part of the architectural licensing or testing process. Yet, every architect must learn and know fire safety regulations, evacuation paths of travel, and how to design an accessible bathroom stall.

The standardization of fire prevention, a very close cousin of crime prevention, is based on the belief (theory), practice, and principal that the people's safety is the highest law. The fundamental goals of the building and life safety codes is the preservation of human life and property from fire and other life safety hazards related to buildings and building construction through enlightened and proper design; construction and inspection of all buildings and structures; uniformity in building regulations; the development of better methods of construction based on rational analysis; and the establishment of a sound basis for the growth of a defined geographic area.

The National Fire Protection Association's Life Safety Code had its origin by an assigned committee in 1913. The committee devoted its attention to the study of notable fires involving loss of life, and in analyzing the causes of this loss of life. This work led to the preparation of standards for the construction and arrangement of exit facilities for factories, schools and other building types. In 1921, the Committee was enlarged to include representation of certain interested groups not previously participating, and work was started on further development and integration of life safety features in all classes of occupancy. The National Fire Protection Association published the first edition of the Building Exits Code in 1927. However, the Code was not in suitable form for adoption into law, as it had been drafted as a reference document containing many advisory provisions useful to designers of buildings, but not appropriate for legal use. The Committee re-edited the Code and results were incorporated into the 1956 edition and subsequently refined and updated over the years (NFPA, Life Safety Code, 1988, p. 101).

Imagine the changes in our built environment if a crime prevention committee had been developed in the early 1900s to prevent and reduce the loss of life resulting from crime and terror in our built environment! How would the architecture have changed if a Life Safety-Security Code had been established to rationally and logically determine the minimum requirements for safe and crime resistant buildings? What if specific requirements and provisions had been established for security and crime prevention through standards and codes, and adopted as law and national standards of care?

Owners will ask that architects design what is economically sound, socially useful, and aesthetically pleasing. Regulatory agencies will control, through a series of prohibitions or incentives, the physical health and safety aspects of a building. Architects will design within the accepted standards of care of the profession, and the aspirations of the community as a whole, as the architectural professionals perceive them. If positive change is going to occur in the building process, it could occur by a dramatic change in society's needs, or a shift in economics that will make certain building forms more or less feasible (for example, the change in U.S. federal architecture after the Oklahoma City bombing and subsequent GSA and ISC Security Design Standards). These shifts would influence owners in establishing their needs. Change can occur by legislation (i.e., CPTED Codes, Ordinance, Resolutions), or by influencing the architects who are active, ongoing participants in building after building.

WHY IS FIRE PREVENTION THAT DIFFERENT FROM CRIME PREVENTION?

Fire prevention and life-safety codes developed a systematic and scientific process to establish measurable and predictable criteria for buildings to prevent fires, structural failures, and other life-threatening events. Saville proposed that a documented crime prevention risk assessment process be conducted during the development of new urban designs. A crime prevention risk assessment, in conjunction with crime prevention recommendations, represents the most systematic and comprehensive method devised to date for determining the potential problems that an urban development site might experience (Saville, 1998). The implementation of a CPTED risk assessment process provides a guideline or standard of care for developers, CPTED practitioners, architects and planners, CPTED consultants, or police officers.

CPTED can be applied before or after a site is developed. It also can be applied on the basis of scale: small, medium, or large projects. The appropriate CPTED risk assessment process allows the CPTED practitioner to determine which CPTED tactics need to be applied. Based on the scale of the development or building, varying amounts of data and analysis will be required in order to make sound well-balanced decisions.

Good building security design is based on good assessment of building risks. Once the risk assessment identifies specific threats, the appropriate design standards can be used. The question is how far should security design be taken when trying to respond to all the identified risks? That point is particularly pertinent when it comes to the risk of terrorist attacks, but it also applies to the danger of crime (Jeffrey Cosiol, Building Operators Management, 2005).

In fact, the American courts have been the single most dominant force in establishing standards of care for building environments through premises security negligence litigation. The courts have established that there is a duty to provide reasonable security to building users, including third-party invitees. The court decisions throughout the United States have been ultimately more successful in making changes in how architecture is built, but it has usually been at the expense of someone's misery and usually after the fact. To have codes, standards, and proactive guidelines, there must be a willingness to take some risks and set the pace.

The federal government and private business have been looking to National codes and standards for years, but it was the Oklahoma City bombing that moved the formation of the GSA Security Standards for all federal buildings. It is not mandated to be applicable for state and local government entities or private business. There has been much resistance to formalizing standards because of the fear of lawsuits for noncompliance, as with the Americans With Disabilities Act. Private and public business had to make costly and inconvenient changes to the built environment in order to comply with the Americans With Disabilities Act Accessibility Guidelines (ADAAG). The consequences of premises security negligence and the large judgments have kept the movement for compliance in force.

Events of 9/11 changed focus of the vulnerability of architecture to acts of terror. Security is becoming a greater priority in the design, construction, operation, and management of buildings and facilities. Before the tragedy of 9/11, Security equaled Access Control + Surveillance + Response (guards, police). After 9/11, Security was enhanced to mean Access Control + Surveillance +

Response + Building Hardening + Bio/Chemical/Blast Protection. There has been an increase in the establishment of local government CPTED and security ordinances, resolutions, and guidelines.

For example, the Department of Homeland Security has proposed regulations that will go into effect in 2007 for chemical facility antiterrorism standards. The proposed regulations will require that chemical facilities fitting certain profiles complete a security risk assessment in determining their overall level of risk. High-risk facilities will then be required to conduct vulnerability assessment and submit site security plans that meet DHS performance standards. Performance standards will be designed to achieve specific outcomes, such as securing the perimeter and critical targets, controlling access, deterring theft of potentially dangerous chemicals, and preventing internal sabotage. National organizations are clamoring to develop their own security guidelines. There are no universal security codes or standards that apply to both public and private sector buildings. There are only building specific standards and guidelines that may not uniformly apply to the challenges of architects and developers.

Standards promulgated by the Department of Defense (DOD), the General Services Administration (GSA), the Federal Emergency Management Agency (FEMA), Department of Homeland Security (DHS), and professional organizations (NFPA, ASTM, UBC) provide the guidance for the design of most buildings. The Uniform Building Code (UBC) developed an appendix for their building code to establish minimum standards to make dwellings resistant to unlawful entry, and it is called the 1997 Uniform Building Security Code. The National Fire Protection Association's 2006 document, NFPA 730, Guide for Premises Security, is loosely based on the federal standards described here. Many physical security standards were developed using DOD and State Department experience with terrorism attacks over many years. These antiterrorism standards are based on classified parameters and test results from destructive research on building envelope systems, mainly glazing, skin and structural systems. Security standards also take into account everyday life and property protection policies (Cosiol, 2005).

The Standards of Care that exist today in the security world are:

- GSA Vulnerability Assessment of Federal Buildings, June 1995
- GSA Facilities Standards for Public Buildings, 2000
- ISC Security Standards for Leased Spaces (U.S. Federal Buildings) September 2004
- UFC 4–010–01 DOD Minimum Antiterror Standards 2002
- ASTM F588 Glazing, F33 locks, doors
- NFPA 730 Guide for Premises Security 2006
- NFPA 731 Standards for the installation of Electronic Premises Security Systems 2006
- 1997 Uniform Building Security Code (minimum standards to make dwellings resistant to unlawful entry, this is an appendix to Chapter 10 of the Uniform Building Code).
- NIOSH Guidance for Protecting Building Environments from Airborne Chemical, Biological, or Radiological Attacks Department of Health and Human Services Centers for Disease Control and Prevention National Institute for Occupational Safety and Health May 2002
- ASIS Risk Assessment Guidelines 2004
- IESNA RP20–98 Lighting for Parking 1998
- IESNA G 1–03 Guidelines on Security Lighting 2003

CPTED Codes and Resolutions as exemplified by the cities of

- Tempe, Arizona
- Broward County, Florida
- Sarasota, Florida
- Tampa, Florida
- Orlando, Florida
- Ann Arbor, Michigan

DOD, GSA, FEMA, NIOSH, and NFPA standards provide the basis for planning and designing security into the built environment. The federal standards can be used as guides for the design of private building security measures, but are not required. Security standards for most events, with the exception of explosive, projectile, and CBR events, are well developed and well understood, and are built on basic principles of preventing crime, or other antisocial behavior, or on established corporate security standards. The designs of most private buildings, apart from high-visibility or high-value buildings, do not typically address the risk of terrorist type attacks or bombings. Nevertheless, building owners need to have a basic knowledge of these standards, as their buildings may be adjacent to a high-risk building, or a Federal building, or be an icon target.

The current unclassified Unified Facilities Criteria (UFC) 4–010–01 DOD Minimum Antiterrorism Standards for Buildings describes levels of protection for different types of buildings without or within a controlled perimeter. These standards may apply to old and new buildings and to government facilities, whether owned or leased. The explosive load that a DOD building must withstand is based on classified standards. Federal building designers are provided with the blast loads buildings must be designed to withstand. Most DOD and federal buildings have well-established standards for access control and CCTV systems to protect against outside and inside threats. GSA facility standards for the Public Buildings Service provide standards similar to the DOD UFC, but they also provide additional architectural, structural, and mechanical-electrical-plumbing considerations for achieving the desired protection against defined threats. The newly released GSA Primer for Design of Commercial Buildings to Mitigate Terrorism Attacks is another derivative of the UFC DOD Minimum Antiterrorism Standards for Buildings (Cosiol, 2005).

In addition to standoff distances and unobstructed space, the design of new buildings must include measures to prevent progressive collapse if the building is three stories or more, as well as improved glazing to minimize hazards from glass fragments, segregated entrance areas for effective access control, and placement of critical-use spaces within interior building areas. Mechanical and electrical design standards address fresh air intake locations, emergency air distribution shutoff systems, utility routing, and redundant utilities (Cosiol, 2005).

The practicality of these standards must be determined when it comes to existing buildings in the nonmilitary built environment. Buildings in most downtown urban settings cannot be sited to meet the design standoff requirements of 50 to 150 feet. In most cases, existing high-rise buildings cannot be reinforced in a cost-effective manner to avoid structural progressive collapse brought on by an explosion. Yet there are items that can be altered easily and cheaply, such as relocating existing air intakes or installing emergency air handler shutoff systems. Glazing systems can be reinforced; blast curtains and safety film can be added to protect building occupants from flying debris from an explosion. Retrofitting a building to be resistant to terrorist attack is often an expensive and painstaking effort. But once there has been an attack somewhere, all building properties and managers are on notice to take corrective and preventative action.

The impact on security standards of care from the recent NFPA 730 Guidelines and 731 Standards for Premises Security is too early to be determined. This set of guidelines and standards could eventually have the same effect on building design as other NFPA life safety codes, with an impact on insurance rates, building designers and owner liability. High-value buildings or buildings with critical missions—such as command and control centers, special laboratories, R&D facilities, and State Department buildings—need to meet additional standards and criteria developed by the facility stakeholders when the protection of the facility is as important as the safety of the occupants regardless of the costs. The reality of building security standards, however, is that budget usually sets the ultimate standard. Most building owners agree that security issues must be addressed in concert with other building life safety standards, design, and operational objectives and must be integrated into the overall building design (Cosiol, 2005).

DIFFERENT FEDERAL STANDARDS: SIMILARITIES AND DIFFERENCES

While the UFC serves as an antiterrorism standard of care for physical security for military buildings, the Interagency Security Committee developed the ISC Security Design Criteria for New Federal Office Buildings and Major Modernization Projects on September 29, 2004. The document and standards are restricted to access by the public and only when you have a contract on a federal job or you have a security clearance will the documents become available to the architect. That being said, the ISC Security Design Criteria are modeled after the GSA Standards developed after the 1995 Murrah Courthouse attack referenced elsewhere in this book. Here is a comparison between the UFC and the ISC security standards so that the subtleties can be understood.

The ISC/GSA Security standards focus on new construction of general purpose office buildings and new or lease construction of courthouses. It also includes lease-constructed projects submitted to Congress for authorization. The standards apply to new leases (as of 29 September 2004) and existing leased buildings based on risk assessment and wherever feasible.

The UFC/DoD minimum security standards apply to all new inhabited buildings, existing inhabited buildings meeting certain high risk or threat "triggers," and inhabited leased buildings subject to security risk "triggers."

UFC standards apply to buildings that are inhabited by eleven or more people and where a person occupies more that 430 square feet. The UFC also applies if the building is a primary gathering area for 50 or more people. The ISC Standards are applicable to a tiered system of four levels.

Level I: ≤ 10 people and ≤ 2500 sf
Level II: 11 to 150 people and 2500 to 80,000 sf
Level III: 151 to 450 people and 80,000 to 150,000 sf
Level IV: ≥ 450 people and > 150,000 sf

The standoff distances of the UFC standards are 33 feet for a minimum, and a conventional construction standoff distance ranging for a small blast at 82 feet, and a projected moderate level blast at 148 feet. The ISC has a recommended setback of at least 50 feet for a small blast and 100-foot minimum setback if the risk assessment determines the risk to be from a large blast. The ISC considers that 40% of the building façade is allowed to fail catastrophically and still comply with the standards. The setback standards are based on two explosive weights, based on whether there is a controlled perimeter or not. A controlled perimeter is one at which a security search can take place, but does not necessarily need barriers.

UFC Standoff Distance for Conventional construction uses the example of an open perimeter parking around a building to use so many pounds of dynamite at a 33 ft. setback (34 psi/81 psi/msec), or X pounds of dynamite at an 82-foot setback (6 psi/30 psi/msec). With a controlled perimeter the code plans for Y pounds at an 82-foot setback (13 psi/78 psi/msec). If the building has a hardened exterior and structural reinforced type of construction, the same explosive weights will result in lesser standoff distances.

ISC Standard Standoff Distance for a Medium Protection Level recommends a standoff of 50 feet from the building exterior. The blast design for 4 psi/28 psi-msec = 100 lbs. @ 128 feet. On a High Protection Level, the recommended standoff is at 100 ft. (Design for 10 psi/89 psi-msec = 500 lbs. @ 122 feet.)

The UFC allows trash containers at the setback limits (82 ft. or 33 ft.); however, at the very least, there should be unobstructed space the first 33 feet from the building. The UFC addresses parking beneath buildings should either be eliminated, or allowed if the facility is hardened with access control. The ISC/GSA standards do not address issues such as trash containers. Unobstructed space is not covered either. Parking beneath buildings can occur in low-risk security buildings by the public if they present identification. Medium- to low-risk security buildings can provide for employee parking beneath buildings. In medium security buildings, parking beneath should only be selected government employees. In higher security buildings, parking beneath a building should only be selected government employees with a security need or clearance.

Progressive structural failure is the single greatest design consideration protecting buildings against blasts. There are structural differences between the government standards. The UFC addresses progressive collapse by requiring design features that would prevent a collapse of a three or less story building. The UFC prohibits unreinforced exterior masonry walls. Windows are to be laminated glass (at a minimum) with specific performance requirements based upon the projected blast requirements. Interior construction issues are not addressed. Exterior doors are required to open outward and provide limited hazard protection. Equipment bracing is required to brace items over 31 lbs.

The ISC/GSA security standards want progressive collapse to be prevented, but does not limit the stories height of a building to be protected. Use of unreinforced exterior masonry walls is not addressed. Windows are to be designed for specific performance requirements specified by the particular job. Interior construction requirements for a medium security facility are to harden critical elements within 25 feet of high-risk areas. Higher security level buildings should harden critical elements within 25 feet of high-risk areas. Exterior doors should be designed against forced entry. Equipment bracing is not addressed in ISC.

The codes have differences as it applies to mechanical and architectural issues (see Table 16.1). UFC requires mailrooms to be located on the building perimeter. Mailroom ventilation should be separate and dedicated air ventilation system. Air intakes should be above 3 meters. Emergency air shutoff should be provided. Stairwell pressurization is not addressed. The ISC/GSA standards address mailrooms to be away from critical components and use disposal containers. Mailroom ventilation is not addressed. Air intakes should be at a high level, and not ground level. Emergency air shutoff is not addressed. Stairwell pressurization should be at a medium and high level of pressure.

CONCLUSIONS

Many requirements are similar between the two codes. Blast requirements are similar, but there are important differences: standoff and blast loads. The applicability to leased buildings is required for Department of Defense existing buildings and addressed on a case by case basis. For ISC, the applicability is based on risk/threat assessment. ISC standards addresses physical security issues, while the UFC does not. Both codes provide for varying levels of protection, but with different goals and results in some cases.

SECURITY AND ACCESSIBILITY: NATIONAL CODES

ADA AND SECURITY

On January 26, 1992, the Americans With Disabilities Act of 1990 (ADA) and the Department of Justice's regulations became effective. The ADA is a civil rights law, but it applies to all state and

---

TABLE 16.1

Difference between the Uniform Federal Security Code and the Interagency Security Committee

Issue	UFC	ISC/GSA
Mass notification	Required for primary gathering and billeting	Not addressed
Loading dock location	Not addressed	Away from utilities
Fuel storage	Not addressed	Away from high-risk areas
Emergency fuel storage	Not addressed	Protect
Fire protection	Not addressed	Addressed
Physical security	Not addressed	Addressed (locks, BMS, CCTV, sensors, etc.)

local government entities. ADA was eventually adopted for all federal facilities overtaking the Uniform Federal Accessibility Standards (UFAS) as now the law of the land. But the ADA is not a building code. It looks, acts, and feels like a building code, but is not. The ADA developed the Accessibility Guidelines (ADAAG) to provide the architectural community guidance and clarity on how to implement the ADA. The ADA is a perfect example of how a national law was passed and put into practice that set up a uniform standard of care, similar to the fire regulations and standards of the Life Safety Code of NFPA. The ADA does impact building security and requires careful consideration of fixtures, finishes, and furnishings.

Title III of ADA applies to businesses and other organizations that operate places of *public accommodation*, such as restaurants, theaters, hotels, retail stores, doctors' and lawyers' offices, private schools, day care centers, libraries, transportation facilities, and hospitality facilities.

This law affects architecture, life safety design, and building security technology dramatically. Some of the most critical impacts on building security will be in building access, door hardware, fire egress, and system controls. Building access is interpreted by the ADA Act to mean any access point to a building or portion of building used for the purpose of entering. Access control readers into buildings will have to be within reach 15 inches to 48 inches from the ground. Instructions for card readers or controls will have to be in Braille for the visually disabled.

Door hardware, for example handles, pulls, latches, locks, and other operating devices, shall have a shape that is easy to grasp with one hand and does not require tight grasping. Lever, push type, U-shaped mechanisms are acceptable. Round knobs, thumb latches, or any device that requires squeezing is not acceptable. Door closers are required to take at least 3 seconds to move to a point of 3 inches from the latch. Automatic door closers will not open back to back faster than 3 seconds and shall require no more than 15 pounds per foot to stop the door movement. Revolving doors must have provisions to accommodate the width of a wheelchair, and if automatic must allow 3 seconds before turning to allow proper passage. Interior hinged doors shall be able to be opened with a minimum force of 5 pounds per foot. Exterior doors must be able to be opened with a minimum force of 8.5 pounds per foot, as compared to the previous force allowed of 25 pounds per foot.

All of the requirements about locks, hardware, and door systems have the impact affecting security of the building and the architectural design. While the intent of the law is to accommodate the disabled, it also may accommodate criminals taking advantage of the slow door delays and one step release to gain entry into a building undetected. Piggybacking and undetected entry are serious compromises to a building's security and other ways for compensating for this will have to be devised.

It is common for medical facilities and institutional facilities to have wide heavy metal security doors. With the new requirements, being able to open or close these doors with minimal force will require careful selection of door closers and hinges. Many criminal justice facilities have metal detector devices that will need to accommodate a handicapped person. However, wheelchairs are made of primarily metal which sets off most detectors. A security breach occurred in Miami, Florida when an inmate had smuggled cocaine and a gun from court into jail within his hollow wooden leg. New technology innovations may need to be invented, such as an all-plastic wheel chair that will allow passage by a nonambulatory person through a metal detector.

Elevators in many new high-rise buildings have security access control features as part of their operation. The ADA act calls for all buttons and controls at 42 inches, but not above 48 inches above floor level and will have visual signals to indicate when each call is registered and answered. Elevator doors will remain open for at least 3 seconds.

Countertops and table heights are another area addressed that will impact the design and security. Bank countertops have been purposely designed to be high (52 inches) to discourage robbers from easily jumping over the counter and to give employees a sight line advantage over customers. New regulations require counters to be 28 to 34 inches. Thirty-four inches is the maximum height for counters. A security control room console would have to be 28 to 34 inches, including reception desks and screening stations. It may be necessary to provide these counters on raised but accessible platforms to provide the control and sight line superiority required for functional use.

The American Disability Act has many potential effects of changing the architectural and security environments. The ADA has a three-prong effect on the ability of the disabled to function in the built environment: (1) job applications—allowing all handicapped persons to be considered for employment and equal and fair administration of job applications, including for positions in security; (2) job functions—can a qualified individual with handicaps perform the job?; and (3) physical facilities—providing access to the same facilities that the nonhandicapped employee or person enjoys, such as lunchrooms, gyms, rest areas, changes in building levels.

With regard to physical facilities, one of the areas that will be affected is that of interior alarm systems that serve as a means of fire evacuation from buildings. Alarm systems for evacuation must provide systems for the blind, deaf, and non-ambulatory. Thus, there must be visual alarms, public address systems giving directions (loudly). The announcements must exceed 15 decibels but not exceed 120 decibels for 30 seconds duration. So the new standards will provide hard-of-hearing persons assistance, and for those not hard of hearing the new requirements will probably make us hard of hearing.

Another critical area that will be affected by the ADA is in automatic teller machines (ATMs), and cash disbursement machines. ATMs at banks, supermarkets, and shopping malls, must have operating controls that comply with the control height of 15 inches to 54 inches, and have operating instructions in Braille. The tray pull mechanism must be designed in a way that does not require tight grasping (no knobs). Any work counters for filling out paperwork must be at a height of 28 to 34 inches. One security problem that emerges from this is that someone standing behind an ATM user in a wheelchair can look over the shoulder and gain access to security codes and private information. How can the privacy needs be met in context of accessible ATMs is yet to be resolved. Some kind of privacy screen is needed to prevent surreptitious viewing of the transaction.

The ADA act states that any device used to prevent the removal of shopping carts from stores shall not prevent access from the store's premises or egress to those in wheelchairs. The use of security bollards is widespread from supermarkets to the White House. Special consideration will need to be placed on design to resolve the conflict issues of handicapped access, yet prevent people from leaving a designated area with a shopping cart, or being able to drive a car though an area for a terrorist attack.

Hospitality facilities and hotels are required to have one room of each class of sleeping room or suite to be designed and constructed to comply with the ADA act. It is also required that 5% of the rooms or suites must comply with the requirements for persons with hearing impairments. All rooms will be available along an accessible route. Vending machines, paper towel containers, paper cup containers, and elevator controls will all have to be accessible from 15 inches to 48 inches from the floor.

In summary, the ADA Act has radically changed how people use the physical environment. Architects will have to comply with very strict requirements that allow the many types of disabled persons to use the buildings unobstructed and unencumbered. While making buildings more open and accessible is valuable to persons with disabilities, it poses a very serious challenge to the security professional to keep the buildings contents, users, and information under control and safe.

SUMMARY

So, what is the experience that we are looking for? A sense of security; feelings of safety; a building that is useable and accessible; a building that is open, yet controlled; a building that avoids circulation conflicts; a building that responds to the many user needs; a building that allows for changes in use and users without it becoming a prison.

Are we getting the information we need? CPTED seeks to identify undesirable features that can be avoided at the design stage by using vulnerability and threat analysis to determine anticipated weaknesses and potential for attack! The owner must communicate the security needs in order to get a responsive design . . . but are we getting the information to the architect early enough to make a positive difference?

In order to reach a physical target, such as a building, car, or person, the criminal or terrorist must travel across the property, sidewalk, front yard, foyer, or parking lot to get to the asset. If the site is defined, observed, well lit, channeled, maintained, and supervised the probabilities for crime are reduced. The prime objective of crime prevention is achieved by reducing the opportunities to commit particular crimes by increasing the risks associated with crime, increasing the effort needed to commit a crime or act of terror, reducing the rewards of the crime, and removing the excuses for inappropriate or criminal behavior.

Is there really any difference designing against terrorism or against crime? Designing for ordinary crime is going to reduce the threat for most terrorist activity. CPTED must be part of the redesign process of courthouses, office buildings, and corporate America. CPTED represents a planning process that reduces the opportunity for terrorism, because it reduces the architectural vulnerability. The real threat, however, is from street level crime and workplace violence, not terrorism. Buildings need to be designed to reduce crime with the same level of attention as fire prevention. Protecting people, information, and property must be a high priority for all buildings, not just those deemed as high risk targets for terrorism. Target hardening and fortressing may be partially necessary but does not reflect how people use public architecture. Public architecture must be designed to reduce their architectural vulnerability.

Security and CPTED codes and standards set the bar for security and design professionals to have a common criterion from which to measure. Whether the criterion is a federal standard, or a local CPTED ordinance, the design community is making the built environment less vulnerable to the threats and risks of criminals and terrorists. Security standards of care must serve the goals and mission of the built environment, not the other way around. Are we prepared to be the visionaries of the future? "Are the needs of the many greater than the needs of the few, or the one?" (Spock, *Star Trek II*).

To affect the most change in present and future architecture, the process of how architects design the built environment will need to include crime prevention, security, along with fire prevention, and accessibility. If these elements are not mandated in building codes, national standards, or municipal regulations the design and construction fields will not be compelled to include them. The crime prevention and security features will just be an expensive bonus feature, but never part of the basics as the other required features like fire prevention and accessibility requirements. The GSA, UFC, and NFPA standards serve as a model of what is needed to be done in making all architecture and infrastructure resistant to crime, workplace violence, terrorism, and natural disasters.

REFERENCES

Atlas, R. (2006) Architect as nexus: Cost effective security begins with design. *ArchiTech* (May–June), 30–34.

Atlas, R. (2004) Security design concepts. *Security Planning and Design: A Guide for Architecture and Building Design Professionals*. Washington, DC: American Institute of Architects, Wiley.

Atlas, R. (2002a) Planting and shaping security success. *Security Management*, 42–43.

Atlas, R. (2002b) Design considerations: Setting standards in security architecture. *Door and Hardware*, 23–24.

Atlas, R. (2000) The impact of ADA on security. Door and Hardware, 30–321.

Atlas, R. (1998a) Designing against crime: The case for CPTED training for architects. *Florida Architect*, 23–24.

Atlas, R. (1998b) Designing for crime and terrorism: CPTED training is essential. *Security Design and Technology*, 40–53.

Atlas, R. (1992a) Impact of ADA on security. *Protection of Assets Bulletin*. Merritt Company.

Atlas, R. (1992b) Handicap accessibility affects security. *Access Control*, 38–39

Atlas, R. (1992c) Successful security. *Buildings: Facilities Construction & Management*, 23–30.

Atlas, R. (1992d) Will ADA handicap security? *Security Management*, 37–38.

Atlas, R. (1991) Architect input among first steps in design. *Access Control*, 25–26.

Atlas, R. (1989) Designing for safety: Building code update. *Florida Architects Journal*, 14.

Atlas, R. (1986) Crime prevention through building codes. *Journal of Security Administration*, 9(2) 3–11.

Biggs, J. M. (1964) *Introduction to Structural Dynamics*. New York: McGraw-Hill.

Cosio, J. Building Operating Management: High Standards for Security. Available at: http://www.facilitiesnet.com/bom/article.asp? id=3616, 2005.

Unified Facilities Criteria (UFC) (2002) DOD Minimum Antiterrorism Standards for Buildings, Dec.

Broward County, Florida CPTED Resolution (1994).

Sarasota, Florida CPTED Resolution (1992).

Tampa, Florida CPTED Ordinance (2001).

Tempe, Arizona CPTED Ordinance (1990).

Americans With Disabilities Act Accessibility Guidelines (1994) ADAAG. U.S. Department of Justice.

Facilities Standards for the Public Buildings Service. (2000) General Services Administration. Submission Requirements Revised November 2000–PBS-P100.

Mays, G. S., and Smith, P. D. (1995) *Blast Effects on Buildings: Design of Buildings to Optimize Resistance to Blast Loading*. London: Thomas Telford.

National Research Council. (1995) *Protecting Buildings from Bomb Damage*. Washington, DC: National Academy Press.

Saville, G., and Wright, D. (1998). *A CPTED Design and Planning Guide for Planning and Development Professionals*. Ottawa: Canada Mortgage and Housing Corporation and the Royal Canadian Mounted Police.

NFPA, Life Safety Code 101, (1988) National Fire Protection Association, Quincy MA, 101.

NIOSH (2002) Guidance for Protecting Building Environments from Airborne Chemical, Biological, or Radiological Attacks, Department of Health and Human Services Centers for Disease Control and Prevention National Institute for Occupational Safety and Health, May 2002.

Air Force Engineering and Services Center (1989) Protective Construction Design Manual, ESL-TR-87-57. Prepared for Engineering and Services Laboratory, Tyndall Air Force Base, FL.

NFPA 730 (2006) Guide for Premises Security 2006 Edition, National Fire Protection Association, Quincy, MA.

NFPA 731 (2006) Standard for the Installation of Electronic Premises Security Systems 2006 Edition, National Fire Protection Association, Quincy, MA.

U.S. Department of the Army. (1986) Fundamentals of Protective Design for Conventional Weapons, TM 5-855-1. Washington, DC, Headquarters, U.S. Department of the Army.

U.S. Department of the Army. (1994) Security Engineering, TM 5–853 and Air Force AFMAN 32–1071, Volumes 1, 2, 3, and 4. Washington, DC, Departments of the Army and Air Force.

U.S. Department of the Army. (1990) Structures to Resist the Effects of Accidental Explosions, Army TM 5–1300, Navy NAVFAC P-397, AFR 88–2.Washington, DC, Departments of the Army, Navy and Air Force.

U.S. Department of Energy. A Manual for the Prediction of Blast and Fragment Loading on Structures, DOE/TIC 11268. Washington, DC, Headquarters, U.S. Department of Energy. (1992).

The Institute of Structural Engineers (1995) *The Structural Engineer's Response to Explosive Damage*. SETO: London.

Uniform Building Security Code (1997) International Conference of Building Officials. Whittier, CA.

APPENDIX A

FACILITIES SECURITY STANDARDS FOR THE PUBLIC BUILDINGS, GENERAL SERVICES ADMINISTRATION, NOV. 2000

The following pages are two examples of security standards dealing with building security, infrastructure protection, anti-terrorism, and applied CPTED principles and practices.

Chapter 2 of the Facilities Standards discusses the General Requirements for model codes and standards adopted by GSA. This section highlights regulations and standards that apply to **site design**.

Building Entrances: Building entrances shall be designed to make it impossible for cars to drive up and into the lobby. Planters can be provided as barriers; bollards are also acceptable if well integrated with the design of the building entrance. Barriers to vehicle access should be visually punctuated and as unobtrusive as possible to pedestrians. Consideration should be given to incorporating security features that allow for flexible use of the site. If addressed skillfully, planters, trees, or sculpted bollards can be employed to provide amenities while meeting vehicle barrier requirements. High blank walls should be avoided; lower walls with sitting edges are preferable, but should be designed to discourage skateboarders. GSA buildings should have one main entrance for staff, visitors, and the public. In large buildings a second entrance may be designated for employees only. Buildings may have additional doors used for egress or access to service areas. These doors should not be used as entrances. Original primary entrances at historic buildings should be retained as such. Closure of ceremonial entrances and redirecting public access to below grade and other secondary entrances for security or accessibility purposes is discouraged. Wherever possible, access for the disabled to historic buildings should be provided at, or nearby original ceremonial entrances.

Chapter 8 of the GSA Facilities Design Guidelines addresses access control and intrusion detection systems. Security must be an integral part of building and site planning, starting at the earliest phase and continuing throughout the process. A multidisciplinary team will determine the appropriate design criteria for each project, based on a facility-specific risk assessment and an analysis of all available information on security considerations, constraints, and tenant needs.

In historic buildings, to minimize loss of character, design criteria should be based on facility-specific risk assessment and strategic programming. Strategic programming includes focusing security modifications on vulnerability points and locating less vulnerable activities in the historic buildings. All security/egress issues shall be discussed with both GSA regional fire protection engineer and physical security specialists.

Zones of Protection: A zoned protection system is used, with intensifying areas of security beginning at the site perimeter and moving to the interior of the building.

Crime Prevention through Environmental Design (CPTED) techniques should be used to help prevent and mitigate crime. Good strategic thinking on CPTED issues such as site planning, perimeter definition, sight lines, lighting, etc., can reduce the need for some engineering solutions.

Capability to Increase or Decrease Security: Designs should include the ability to increase security in response to a heightened threat, as well as to reduce security if changes in risk warrant it.

Multidisciplinary Approach: Improving security is the business of everyone involved with Federal facilities including designers, builders, operations and protection personnel, employees, clients, and visitors. Professionals who can contribute to implementing the criteria in this document include architects and structural, mechanical, fire protection, security, cost, and electrical engineers. Blast engineers and glazing specialists may also be required, as well as building operations personnel and security professionals experienced in physical security design, operations, and risk assessment. Each building system and element should support risk mitigation and reduce casualties, property damage, and the loss of critical functions. Security should be considered in all decisions, from selecting architectural materials to placing trash receptacles to designing redundant electrical systems.

Site Security Requirements: Site security requirements, including perimeter buffer zones, should be developed before a site is acquired and the construction-funding request is finalized. This requirement may be used to prevent the purchase of a site that lacks necessary features, especially sufficient setback, and to help reduce the need for more costly countermeasures such as blast hardening.

Adjacent Sites: When warranted by a risk assessment, consideration should be given to acquiring adjacent sites or negotiating for control of rights-of-way. Adjacent sites can affect the security of Federal facilities.

Access Control and Electronic Security: Electronic security, including surveillance, intrusion detection, and screening, is a key element of facility protection; many aspects of electronic security and the posting of security personnel are adequately dealt with in other criteria and guideline documents. These criteria primarily address access control planning—including aspects of stair and lobby design—because access control must be considered when design concepts for a building are first conceived. While fewer options are available for modernization projects, some designs can be altered to consider future access control objectives.

Perimeter Protection Zone. Site perimeter barriers are one element of the perimeter protection zone. Perimeter barriers capable of stopping vehicles of ____ lbs., and maximum speeds of ____, shall be installed *(project-specific information to be provided by the Federal agency to the architect and engineer)*. A vehicle velocity shall be used considering the angle of incidence in conjunction with the distance between the perimeter and the point at which a vehicle would likely be able to start a run at the perimeter. A barrier shall be selected that will stop the threat vehicle. Army TM 5–853–1 and TM 5–853–2/AFMAN 32–1071, Volume 2 contain design procedures. In designing the barrier system, consider the following options:

- Using various types and designs of buffers and barriers such as walls, fences, trenches, ponds and water basins, plantings, trees, static barriers, sculpture, and street furniture;
- Designing site circulation to prevent high speed approaches by vehicles; and
- Offset vehicle entrance from the direction of approach to force a reduction in speed;
- Provide space for inspection at a location to be determined;
- Provide design features for the vehicular inspection point that stop vehicles, prevent them from leaving the vehicular inspection area, and prevent tailgating.

Site Lighting: Provide effective site lighting levels. At vehicular and pedestrian entrances, __FC (footcandles) *(project-specific information to be provided)* horizontal maintained foot-candles; and for perimeter and vehicular and pedestrian circulation areas, __FC horizontal maintained foot-candles. In most circumstances, perimeter lighting should be continuous and on both sides of the perimeter barriers, with minimal hot and cold spots and sufficient to support CCTV and other surveillance. However, for safety reasons and/or for issues related to camera technology, lower levels may be desirable. Other codes or standards may restrict site lighting levels.

Site Signage: Confusion over site circulation, parking, and entrance locations can contribute to a loss of site security. Signs should be provided off site and at entrances; there should be on-site directional, parking, and cautionary signs for visitors, employees, service vehicles, and pedestrians. Unless required by other standards, signs should generally not be provided that identify sensitive areas.

Landscaping: Landscaping design elements that are attractive and welcoming can enhance security. For example, plants can deter unwanted entry; ponds and fountains can block vehicle access; and site grading can also limit access. Avoid landscaping that permits concealment of criminals or obstructs the view of security personnel and CCTV, in accordance with accepted CPTED principles.

Chapter 8 Architecture and Interior Design of GSA Facilities Design Standards

The following security criterion does NOT apply to all projects. Follow each criterion only if instructed to by your project-specific risk assessment. Many criteria are based on the recommendations of a specific building risk assessment/threat analysis. Where the criteria include a blank or offer a choice of approaches, the recommendations from risk assessment will provide information for filling in the blank or suggesting a choice of approaches.

Planning

Office Locations: Offices of vulnerable officials should be placed or glazed so that the occupant cannot be seen from an uncontrolled public area such as a street. Whenever possible, these offices should face courtyards, internal sites, or controlled areas. If this is not possible, suitable obscuring glazing or window treatment shall be provided, including ballistic resistant glass, blast curtains, or other interior protection systems.

Mixed Occupancies: When possible, high-risk tenants should not be housed with low-risk tenants. If they are housed together, publicly accessible areas should be separated from high-risk tenants.

Public Toilets and Service Areas: Public toilets, service spaces, or access to vertical circulation systems should not be located in any non-secure areas, including the queuing area before screening at the public entrance.

Loading Docks and Shipping and Receiving Areas: Loading docks, and receiving and shipping areas should be separated by at least 50 feet in any direction from utility rooms, utility mains, and service entrances including electrical, telephone/data, fire detection/alarm systems, fire suppression water mains, cooling and heating mains, etc. Loading docks should be located so that vehicles will not be driven into or parked under the building. If this is not possible, the service shall be hardened for blast.

Retail in the Lobby: Retail and other mixed uses, which are encouraged by the Public Buildings Cooperative Use Act of 1976, create public buildings that are open and inviting. While important to the public nature of the buildings, the presence of retail and other mixed uses may present a risk to the building and its occupants and should be carefully considered on a project-specific basis during the risk assessment process. Retail and mixed uses may be accommodated through such means as separating entryways, controlling access, and hardening shared partitions, as well as through special security operational countermeasures.

Stairwells: Stairwells required for emergency egress should be located as remotely as possible from areas where blast events might occur. Wherever possible, stairs should not discharge into lobbies, parking, or loading areas.

Mailroom: The mailroom should be located away from facility main entrances, areas containing critical services, utilities, distribution systems, and important assets. In addition, the mailroom should be located at the perimeter of the building with an outside wall or window designed for pressure relief. It should have adequate space for explosive disposal containers. An area near the loading dock may be a preferred mailroom location.

Interior Construction

Lobby Doors and Partitions: Doors and walls along the line of security screening should meet requirements of UL752 Level__ *(project-specific information to be provided)*.

Critical Building Components: The following critical building components should be located no closer than __ feet in any direction to any main entrance, vehicle circulation, parking, or maintenance area *(project-specific information to be provided)*. If this is not possible, harden as appropriate:

- Emergency generator including fuel systems, day tank, fire sprinkler, and water supply;
- Normal fuel storage;
- Main switchgear;
- Telephone distribution and main switchgear;
- Fire pumps;
- Building control centers;
- UPS systems controlling critical functions;

- Main refrigeration systems if critical to building operation;
- Elevator machinery and controls;
- Shafts for stairs, elevators, and utilities; and
- Critical distribution feeders for emergency power.

Exterior Entrances: The entrance design must balance aesthetic, security, risk, and operational considerations. One strategy is to consider co-locating public and employee entrances. Entrances should be designed to avoid significant queuing. If queuing will occur within the building footprint, the area should be enclosed in blast resistant construction. If queuing is expected outside the building, a rain cover should be provided.

Equipment Space: Public and employee entrances should include space for possible future installation of access control and screening equipment. In historic buildings place security equipment in ancillary spaces where possible.

Entrance Co-Location: Combine public and employee entrances.

Garage and Vehicle Service Entrances: All garage or service area entrances for government controlled or employee permitted vehicles that are not otherwise protected by site perimeter barriers shall be protected by devices capable of arresting a vehicle of the designated threat size at the designated speed. This criterion may be lowered if the access circumstances prohibit a vehicle from reaching this speed.

Additional Features

Areas of Potential Concealment: To reduce the potential for concealment of devices before screening points, avoid installing features such as trash receptacles and mailboxes that can be used to hide devices. If mail or express boxes are used, the size of the openings should be restricted to prohibit insertion of packages.

Roof Access: Design locking systems to meet the requirements of NFPA 101 and limit roof access to authorized personnel.

New Construction

Progressive Collapse: Designs that facilitate or are vulnerable to progressive collapse must be avoided. At a minimum, all new facilities shall be designed for the loss of a column for one floor above grade at the building perimeter without progressive collapse. This design and analysis requirement for progressive collapse is not part of a blast analysis. It is intended to ensure adequate redundant load paths in the structure should damage occur for whatever reason. Designers may apply static and/or dynamic methods of analysis to meet this requirement. Ultimate load capacities may be assumed in the analyses. In recognition that a larger than design explosive (or other) event may cause a partial collapse of the structure, new facilities with a defined threat shall be designed with a reasonable probability that, if local damage occurs, the structure will not collapse or be damaged to an extent disproportionate to the original cause of the damage. In the event of an internal explosion in an uncontrolled public ground floor area, the design shall prevent progressive collapse due to the loss of one primary column, or the designer shall show that the proposed design precludes such a loss. That is, if columns are sized, reinforced, or protected so that the threat charge will not cause the column to be critically damaged, then progressive collapse calculations are not required for the internal event. For design purposes, assume there is no additional standoff from the column beyond what is permitted by the design.

Building Materials: All building materials and types acceptable under model building codes are allowed. However, special consideration should be given to materials which have inherent ductility and which are better able to respond to load reversals (i.e., cast in place reinforced concrete and steel construction). Careful detailing is required for material such as pre-stressed concrete, pre-cast concrete, and masonry to adequately respond to the design loads. The construction type selected must meet all performance criteria of the specified level of protection.

Exterior Walls: If designing for a limited load, design exterior walls for the actual pressures and impulses up to a maximum of __ psi and __psi-msec *(project-specific information to be provided)*. The designer should also ensure that the walls are capable of withstanding the dynamic reactions from the windows. Shear walls that are essential to the lateral and vertical load bearing system, and that also function as exterior walls, shall be considered primary structures. Design exterior shear walls to resist the actual blast loads predicted from the threats specified. Where exterior walls are not designed for the full design loads, special consideration shall be given to construction types that reduce the potential for injury.

If designing for a full load: Design the exterior walls to resist the actual pressures and impulses acting on the exterior wall surfaces from the threats defined for the building.

Forced Entry: Security of Swinging Door Assemblies shall comply with ASTM F 476 Grade __ *(project-specific information to be provided)*, as well as measurement of Forced Entry Resistance of Horizontal Sliding Door Assemblies ASTM F 842 Grade __ *(project-specific information to be provided)*. Design for a medium protection level (per TM 5–853) for walls would be the equivalent of 4" concrete with #5 reinforcing steel at 6" interval each way or 8" CMU with #4 reinforcing steel at 8 in. interval. TM 5–853 provides other alternatives for low, medium, and high protection.

Exterior Windows: The following terms are to be applied and identified for each project-specific risk assessment:

- No restrictions—No restrictions on this type of glazing.
- Limited protection—These windows do not require design for specific blast pressure loads. Rather, the designer is encouraged to use glazing materials and designs that minimize the potential risks. Preferred systems include: thermally tempered heat strengthened or annealed glass with a security film installed on the interior surface and attached to the frame; laminated thermally tempered, laminated heat strengthened, or laminated annealed glass; and blast curtains. Acceptable systems include thermally tempered glass; and thermally tempered, heat strengthened or annealed glass with film installed on the interior surface (edge to edge, wet glazed, or daylight installations are acceptable). Unacceptable systems include untreated monolithic annealed or heat strengthened glass and wire glass.

The minimum thickness of film that should be considered is 4 mil. In a blast environment, glazing can induce loads three or more times that of conventional loads onto the frames. This must be considered with the application of anti-shatter security film. The designer should design the window frames so that they do not fail prior to the glazing under lateral load. Likewise, the anchorage should be stronger than the window frame, and the supporting wall should be stronger than the anchorage. The design strength of a window frame and associated anchorage is related to the breaking strength of the glazing. Thermally tempered glass is roughly four times as strong as annealed, and heat strengthened glass is roughly twice as strong as annealed.

Design up to the specified load. Window systems design (glazing, frames, anchorage to supporting walls, etc.) on the exterior facade should be balanced to mitigate the hazardous effects of flying glazing following an explosive event. The walls, anchorage, and window framing should fully develop the capacity of the glazing material selected.

The designer may use a combination of methods such as government produced and sponsored computer programs (e.g., WINLAC, GLASTOP, SAFEVU, and BLASTOP/WINGUARD) coupled with test data and recognized dynamic structural analysis techniques to show that the glazing either survives the specified threats or the post damage performance of the glazing protects the occupants. When using such methods, the designer may consider a breakage probability no higher than 750 breaks per 1000 when calculating loads to frames and anchorage.

While most test data use glazing framed with a deep bite, this may not be amenable to effective glazing performance or installation. It has been demonstrated that new glazing systems with a 3/4-inch minimum bite can be engineered to meet the performance standards with the application of structural silicone. However, not much information is available on the long-term performance of glazing attached by structural silicone or with anchored security films.

Window Fenestration: The total fenestration openings are not limited; however, a maximum of 40 percent per structural bay is a preferred design goal.

Window Frames: The frame system should develop the full capacity of the chosen glazing up to 750 breaks per 1000, and provide the required level of protection without failure. This can be shown through design calculations or approved testing methods.

Anchorage: The anchorage should remain attached to the walls of the facility during an explosive event without failure. Capacity of the anchorage system can be shown through design calculations or approved tests that demonstrate that failure of the proposed anchorage will not occur and that the required performance level is provided.

Glazing alternatives are as follows:

- Preferred systems include: thermally tempered glass with a security film installed on the interior surface and attached to the frame; laminated thermally tempered, laminated heat strengthened, or laminated annealed glass; and blast curtains.
- Acceptable systems include monolithic thermally tempered glass with or without film if the pane is designed to withstand the full design.
- Unacceptable systems include untreated monolithic annealed or heat-strengthened glass, and wire glass.

In general, thicker anti-shatter security films provide higher levels of hazard mitigation than thinner films. Testing has shown that a minimum of a 7 mil. thick film, or specially manufactured 4 mil. thick film, is the minimum to provide hazard mitigation from blast. The minimum film thickness that should be considered is 4 mil. Not all windows in a public facility can reasonably be designed to resist the full forces expected from the design blast threats. As a minimum, design window systems (glazing, frames, and anchorage) to achieve the specified performance conditions for the actual blast pressure and impulse acting on the windows up to a maximum of ____ psi and ____ psi-msec. As a minimum goal, the window systems should be designed so that at least __ percent of the total glazed areas of the facility meet the specified performance conditions when subjected to the defined threats *(project-specific information to be provided by the client)*.

In some cases, it may be beneficial and economically feasible to select a glazing system that demonstrates a higher, safer performance condition. Where tests indicate that one design will perform better at significantly higher loads, that design could be given greater preference. Where peak pressures from the design explosive threats can be shown to be below 1 psi acting on the face of the building, the designer may use the reduced requirements of Exterior Walls, Limited Protection, in this section.

Additional Glazing Requirements:

- Ballistic windows, if required, shall meet the requirements of UL 752 Bullet-Resistant Glazing Level __ *(project-specific information to be provided).* Glassclad polycarbonate or laminated polycarbonate, are two types of acceptable glazing material.
- Security glazing, if required, shall meet the requirements of ASTM F1233 or UL 972, Burglary Resistant Glazing Material: This glazing should meet the minimum performance specifications, however, special consideration should be given to frames and anchorages for ballistic resistant windows and security glazing since their inherent resistance to blast may impart large reaction loads to the supporting walls.
- Resistance of Window Assemblies to Forced Entry (excluding glazing) ASTM F 588 Grade__ *(project specific information to be);* see above for glazing.
- Design for eavesdropping and electronic emanations is beyond the scope of the criteria.

Non-Window Openings: Non-window openings such as mechanical vents and exposed plenums should be designed to the level of protection required for the exterior wall. Designs should account for potential in-filling of blast over-pressures through such openings. The design of structural members and all mechanical system mountings and attachments should resist these interior fill pressures.

Interior Windows: Interior glazing should be minimized where a threat exists. The designer should avoid locating critical functions next to high-risk areas with glazing, such as lobbies, loading docks, etc.

Parking: The following criteria apply to parking inside a facility where the building superstructure is supported by the parking structure:

- The designer shall protect primary vertical load carrying members by implementing architectural or structural features that provide a minimum 6-inch standoff.
- All columns in the garage area shall be designed for an un-braced length equal to two floors, or three floors where there are two levels of parking.

For lobbies and other areas with specified threats:

- The designer shall implement architectural or structural features that deny contact with exposed primary vertical load members in these areas. A minimum standoff of at least 6 inches from these members is required.
- Primary vertical load carrying members shall be designed to resist the effects of the specified threat.

Loading Docks: The loading dock design should limit damage to adjacent areas and vent explosive force to the exterior of the building. Significant structural damage to the walls and ceiling of the loading dock is acceptable. However, the areas adjacent to the loading dock should not experience severe structural damage or collapse. The floor of the loading dock does not need to be designed for blast resistance if the area below is not occupied and contains no critical utilities.

Mailrooms and Unscreened Retail Spaces: Mailrooms where packages are received and opened for inspection, and unscreened retail spaces (see Architecture and Interior Design, Planning, Retail in the Lobby and Mailroom) shall be designed to mitigate the effects of a blast on primary vertical or lateral bracing members. Where these rooms are located in occupied areas or adjacent to critical utilities, walls, ceilings, and floors, they should be blast and fragment resistant. Significant structural damage to the walls, ceilings, and floors of the mailroom is acceptable. However, the areas adjacent to the mailroom should not experience severe damage or collapse.

Venting: The designer should consider methods to facilitate the venting of explosive forces and gases from the interior spaces to the outside of the structure. Examples of such methods include the use of blowout panels and window system designs that provide protection from blast pressure applied to the outside but that readily fail and vent if exposed to blast pressure on the inside.

Structural Engineering Considerations:

Structural and Non-Structural Elements—To address blast, the priority for upgrades should be based on the relative importance of a structural or non-structural element, in the order defined below:

- **Primary Structural Elements**—the essential parts of the building's resistance to catastrophic blast loads and progressive collapse, including columns, girders, roof beams, and the main lateral resistance system;
- **Secondary Structural Elements**—all other load bearing members, such as floor beams, slabs, etc.;

- **Primary Non-Structural Elements**—elements (including their attachments) which are essential for life safety systems or elements which can cause substantial injury if failure occurs, including ceilings or heavy suspended mechanical units; and
- **Secondary Non-Structural Elements**—all elements not covered in primary non-structural elements, such as partitions, furniture, and light fixtures.

Priority should be given to the critical elements that are essential to mitigating the extent of collapse. Designs for secondary structural elements should minimize injury and damage. Consideration should also be given to reducing damage and injury from primary as well as secondary non-structural elements.

Loads and Stresses: Where required, structures shall be designed to resist blast loads. The demands on the structure will be equal to the combined effects of dead, live, and blast loads. Blast loads or dynamic rebound may occur in directions opposed to typical gravity loads.

For purposes of designing against progressive collapse, loads shall be defined as dead load plus a realistic estimate of actual live load. The value of the live load may be as low as 25 percent of the code-prescribed live load. The design should use ultimate strengths with dynamic enhancements based on strain rates. Allowable responses are generally post elastic.

Good Engineering Practice Guidelines: The following are rules of thumb commonly used to mitigate the effects of blast on structures. Details and more complete guidance are available in the Technical Manuals listed in the New Techniques, Methods and References section. The following guidelines are not meant to be complete, but are provided to assist the designer in the initial evaluation and selection of design approaches.

For higher levels of protection from blast, cast-in-place reinforced concrete is normally the construction type of choice. Other types of construction such as properly designed and detailed steel structures are also allowed. Several material and construction types, while not disallowed by these criteria, may be undesirable and uneconomical for protection from blast. To economically provide protection from blast, inelastic or post elastic design is standard. This allows the structure to absorb the energy of the explosion through plastic deformation while achieving the objective of saving lives. To design and analyze structures for blast loads, which are highly nonlinear both spatially and temporally, it is essential that proper dynamic analysis methods be used. Static analysis methods will generally result in unachievable or uneconomical designs.

The designer should recognize that components might act in directions for which they are not designed. This is due to the engulfment of structural members by blast, the negative phase, the upward loading of elements, and dynamic rebound of members. Making steel reinforcement (positive and negative faces) symmetric in all floor slabs, roof slabs, walls, beams, and girders will address this issue. Symmetric reinforcement also increases the ultimate load capacity of the members. Lap splices should fully develop the capacity of the reinforcement. Lap splices and other discontinuities should be staggered. Ductile detailing should be used for connections, especially primary structural member connections. There should be control of deflections around certain members, such as windows, to prevent premature failure. Additional reinforcement is generally required.

Balanced design of all building structural components is desired. For example, for window systems, the frame and anchorage shall be designed to resist the full capacity of the weakest element of the system. Special shear reinforcement including ties and stirrups is generally required to allow large post-elastic behavior. The designer should carefully balance the selection of small but heavily reinforced (i.e., congested) sections with larger sections with lower levels of reinforcement.

Connections for steel construction should be ductile and develop as much moment connection as practical. Connections for cladding and exterior walls to steel frames shall develop the capacity of the wall system under blast loads. In general, single point failures that can cascade, producing wide spread catastrophic collapse, are to be avoided. A prime example is the use of transfer beams and girders that, if lost, may cause progressive collapse and are therefore highly discouraged.

Redundancy and alternative load paths are generally good in mitigating blast loads. One method of accomplishing this is to use two-way reinforcement schemes where possible.

In general, column spacing should be minimized so that reasonably sized members can be designed to resist the design loads and increase the redundancy of the system. A practical upper level for column spacing is generally 30 ft. for the levels of blast loads described herein.

In general, floor-to-floor heights should be minimized. Unless there is an overriding architectural requirement, a practical limit is generally less than or equal to 16 ft. It is recommended that the designer use fully grouted and reinforced CMU construction in cases where CMU is selected. It is essential that the designer actively coordinate structural requirements for blast with other disciplines including architectural and mechanical.

The use of one-way wall elements spanning from floor-to-floor is generally a preferred method to minimize blast loads imparted to columns. In many cases, the ductile detailing requirements for seismic design and the alternate load paths provided by progressive collapse design assist in the protection from blast. The designer must bear in mind, however, that the design approaches are at times in conflict. These conflicts must be worked out on a case-by-case basis.

Mechanical Engineering: The mechanical system should continue the operation of key life safety components following an incident. The criteria focus on locating components in less vulnerable areas, limiting access to mechanical systems, and providing a reasonable amount of redundancy.

Air System

Air Intakes. On buildings of more than four stories, locate intakes on the fourth floor or higher. On buildings of three stories or less, locate intakes on the roof or as high as practical. Locating intakes high on a wall is preferred over a roof location.

Utility Protection

Utilities and Feeders: Utility systems should be located at least 50 feet from loading docks, front entrances, and parking areas.

Incoming Utilities: Within building and property lines, incoming utility systems should be concealed and given blast protection, including burial or proper encasement wherever possible.

Smoke Control (Removal) Systems

Smoke Evacuation. In the event of a blast, the available smoke removal system may be essential to smoke removal, particularly in large, open spaces. This equipment should be located away from high-risk areas such as loading docks and garages. The system controls and power wiring to the equipment should be protected. The system should be connected to emergency power to provide smoke removal. The designer should consider having separate HVAC systems in lobbies, loading docks, and other locations where the significant risk of internal event exists. Smoke removal equipment should be provided with stand-alone local control panels that can continue to individually function in the event the control wiring is severed from the main control system.

During an interior bombing event, smoke removal and control is of paramount importance. The designer should consider the fact that if window glazing is hardened, a blast may not blow out windows, and smoke may be trapped in the building.

Electrical Engineering:

The major security functions of the electrical system are to maintain power to essential building services, especially those required for life safety and evacuation; provide lighting and surveillance to deter criminal activities; and provide emergency communication.

Service and Distribution

Distributed Emergency Power: Emergency and normal electric panels, conduits, and switchgear should be installed separately, at different locations, and as far apart as possible. Electric distribution should also run at separate locations.

Normal Fuel Storage: The main fuel storage should be located away from loading docks, entrances, and parking. Access should be restricted and protected (e.g., locks on caps and seals).

Emergency Fuel Storage: The day tank should be mounted near the generator, given the same protection as the generator and sized to store approximately __ hours of fuel *(project-specific information to be provided)*. A battery and/or UPS could serve a smaller building or leased facility.

Tertiary Power: Conduit and line can be installed outside to allow a trailer-mounted generator to connect to the building's electrical system. If tertiary power is required, other methods include generators and feeders from alternative substations.

Emergency Generator: The emergency generator should be located away from loading docks, entrances, and parking. More secure locations include the roof, protected grade level, and protected interior areas. The generator should not be located in any areas that are prone to flooding.

Utilities and Feeders: Utility systems should be located away from loading docks, entrances, and parking. Underground service is preferred. Alternatively, they can be hardened.

Power and Lighting

Site Lighting: Site lighting should be coordinated with the CCTV system.

Restrooms: Emergency power should be provided for emergency lighting in restrooms.

Communications and Security Systems

Redundant Communications: The facility could have a second telephone service to maintain communications in case of an incident. A base radio communication system with antenna should be installed in the stairwell, and portable sets distributed on floors. This is the preferred alternative.

Radio Telemetry: Distributed antennas could be located throughout the facility if required for emergency communication through wireless transmission of data.

Alarm and Information Systems: Alarm and information systems should not be collected and mounted in a single conduit, or even co-located. Circuits to various parts of the building shall be installed in at least two directions and/or risers. Low voltage signal and control copper conductors should not share conduit with high voltage power conductors. Fiber-optic conductors are generally preferred over copper.

Empty Conduits: Empty conduits and power outlets can be provided for possible future installation of security control equipment.

Fire Protection Engineering

The fire protection system inside the building should maintain life safety protection after an incident and allow for safe evacuation of the building when appropriate. While fire protection systems are designed to perform well during fires, they are not traditionally designed to survive bomb blast. The three components of the fire protection system are:

1. Active features, including sprinklers, fire alarms, smoke control, etc.;
2. Passive features, including fire resistant barriers; and
3. Operational features, including system maintenance and employee training.

Active System

Water Supply: The fire protection water system should be protected from single point failure in case of a blast event. The incoming line should be encased, buried, or located 50 ft. away from high threat areas. The interior mains should be looped and sectionalized.

Dual Fire Pumps: Electric and Diesel. To increase the reliability of the fire protection system in strategic locations, a dual pump arrangement could be considered, with one electric pump and one diesel pump. The pumps should be located apart from each other.

Egress Door Locks: All security locking arrangements on doors used for egress must comply with requirements of NFPA 101, Life Safety Code.

Electronic Security: The purpose of electronic security is to improve the reliability and effectiveness of life safety systems, security systems, and building functions. When possible, accommodations should be made for future developments in security systems.

The following criteria are only intended to stress those concepts and practices that warrant special attention to enhance public safety. Please consult design guides pertinent to your specific project for detailed information about electronic security.

Control Centers and Building Management Systems:

Operational Control Center (OCC), Fire Command Center (FCC), and Security Control Center (SCC): The SCC and OCC may be co-located. If co-located, the chain of command should be carefully pre-planned to ensure the most qualified leadership is in control for specific types of events. The security designer should provide secure information links between the SCC, OCC, and FCC.

Backup Control Center (BCC): A backup control workstation should be provided in a different location, such as a manager or engineer's office. If feasible, an off-site location should be considered. A fully redundant BCC should be installed (this is an alternative to the above).

Security for Utility Closets, Mechanical Rooms, and Telephone Closets:

Key System: Anticipate use of a key system.

Intrusion Detection: Some or all of the following basic intrusion detection devices should be provided:

- Magnetic reed switches for interior doors and openings;
- Glass break sensors for windows up to scalable heights;
- Balanced magnetic contact switch sets for all exterior doors, including overhead/roll-up doors.

Monitoring: Monitoring should be done at an off-site facility. Use an on-site monitoring center during normal business hours. Have a 24-hour on-site monitoring center.

Closed Circuit TV (CCTV): A color CCTV surveillance system with recording capability shall be provided to view and record activity at the perimeter of the building, particularly at primary entrances and exits. A mix of monochrome cameras should be considered for areas that lack adequate illumination for color cameras.

Duress Alarms or Assistance Stations: Call buttons should be provided at key public contact areas and as needed in the offices of managers and directors, in garages, and other areas that are identified as high risk locations by the project-specific risk assessment.

Parking Security

Parking restrictions help keep threats away from a building. In urban settings, however, curbside or underground parking is often necessary and/or difficult to control. Mitigating the risks associated with parking requires creative design and planning measures, including parking restrictions, perimeter buffer zones, barriers, structural hardening, and other architectural and engineering solutions.

Parking on Adjacent Streets: Parking is often permitted in curb lanes, with a sidewalk between the curb lane and the building. Where distance from the building to the nearest curb provides insufficient setback, and compensating design measures do not sufficiently protect the building from the assessed threat, parking in the curb lane shall be restricted as follows:

- Allow unrestricted parking.
- Allow government-owned and key employee parking only.
- Use the lane for standoff. Use structural features to prevent parking.

Parking on Adjacent Properties: The recommended minimum setback distance between the building and parked vehicles for this project are __ *(project-specific information to be provided).* Adjacent public parking should be directed to more distant or better-protected areas, segregated from employee parking and away from the facility.

Parking Inside the Building: Special consideration are needed if parking occurs inside a building such as:

- Public parking with ID check;
- Government vehicles and employees of the building only;
- Selected government employees only;
- Selected government employees with a need for security.

On-site Surface or Structured Parking: Adjacent surface parking shall maintain a minimum standoff of __ feet. Parking within __ feet of the building shall be restricted to authorized vehicles *(project-specific information to be provided*).

Parking Facilities:

Natural Surveillance. For all stand-alone, above ground parking facilities, maximizing visibility across, as well as into and out of the parking facility shall be a key design principle. The preferred parking facility design employs express or non-parking ramps, allowing the user to park on flat surfaces. Pedestrian paths should be planned to concentrate activity to the extent possible. For example, bringing all pedestrians through one portal rather than allowing them to disperse to numerous access points improves the ability to see and be seen by other users. Likewise, limiting vehicular entry/exits to a minimum number of locations is beneficial. Long span construction and high ceilings create an effect of openness and aid in lighting the facility. Shear walls should be avoided, especially near turning bays and pedestrian travel paths. Where shear walls are required, large holes in shear walls can help to improve visibility. Openness to the exterior should be maximized. It is also important to eliminate dead-end parking areas, as well as nooks and crannies. Landscaping should be done judiciously, not to provide hiding places. It is desirable to hold planting away from the facility to permit observation of intruders.

Stairways and Elevators:

- Stairways and elevator lobby design shall be as open as the local or state building code permits. The ideal solution is a stair and/or elevator waiting area totally open to the exterior and/or the parking areas. Designs that ensure that people using these areas can be easily seen—and can see out—should be encouraged. If a stair must be enclosed for code or weather protection purposes, glass walls will deter both personal injury attacks and various types of vandalism. Potential hiding places below stairs should be closed off; nooks and crannies should be avoided.

- Elevator cabs should have glass backs whenever possible. Elevator lobbies should be well lighted and visible to both patrons in the parking areas and the public out on the street.

Perimeter Access Control: Security screening or fencing may be provided at points of low activity to discourage anyone from entering the facility on foot, while still maintaining openness and natural surveillance. A system of fencing, grilles, doors, etc. should be designed to completely close down access to the entire facility in unattended hours, or in some cases, all hours. Any ground level pedestrian exits that open into non-secure areas should be emergency exits only and fitted with panic hardware for exiting movement only. Details of the parking access control system will be provided for the designer.

Surface Finishes and Signage: Interior walls should be painted a light color (i.e., white or light blue) to improve illumination. Signage should be clear to avoid confusion and direct users to their destination efficiently. If an escort service is available, signs should inform users.

Lighting: Lighting levels should comply with standards recommended by the Illuminations Engineering Society of North America (IESNA) Subcommittee on Off-Roadway Facilities as the lowest acceptable lighting levels for any parking facility.

Emergency Communications: Emergency intercom/duress buttons or assistance stations should be placed on structure columns, fences, other posts, and/or freestanding pedestals and brightly marked with stripping or paint visible in low light. If CCTV coverage is available, automatic activation of corresponding cameras should be provided, as well as dedicated communications with security or law enforcement stations. It is helpful to include flashing lights that can rapidly pinpoint the location of the calling station for the response force, especially in very large parking structures. It should only be possible to re-set a station that has been activated at the station with a security key. It should not be possible to re-set the station from any monitoring site. A station should be within 50 feet of reach.

CCTV: Color CCTV cameras with recording capability and pan-zoom-tilt drivers, if warranted, should be placed at entrance and exit vehicle ramps. Auto-scanning units are not recommended. Fixed-mount, fixed-lens color or monochrome cameras should be placed on at least one side of regular use and emergency exit doors connecting to the building or leading outside. In order for these cameras to capture scenes of violations, time-delayed electronic locking should be provided at doors, if permitted by governing code authorities. Without features such as time delayed unlocking or video motion detection, these cameras may be ineffective.

APPENDIX B

ANOTHER APPROACH FOR SECURITY DESIGN

The basis for many of the present-day security standards comes from the Unified Facilities Criteria (UFC) Department of Defense (DOD) Minimum Anti-terrorism Standards for Buildings UFC 4–010–01 Dec. 2002. The following section sets forth the pertinent sections of the UFC that apply to infrastructure protection and CPTED.

Philosophy: The overarching philosophy upon which this document is based is that comprehensive protection against the range of possible threats may be cost prohibitive, but that an appropriate level of protection can be provided for all Department of Defense (DOD) personnel at a reasonable cost. That level of protection is intended to lessen the risk of mass casualties resulting from terrorist attacks. Full implementation of these standards will provide some protection against all threats and will significantly reduce injuries and fatalities for the threats upon which these standards are based. The costs associated with those levels of protection are assumed to be less than the physical and intangible costs associated with incurring mass casualties. Furthermore, given what we know about terrorism, all DOD decision makers must commit to making smarter investments with our scarce resources and stop investing money in inadequate buildings that DOD personnel will have to occupy for decades, regardless of the threat environment. There are three key elements of this philosophy that influence the implementation of these standards.

Design Practices. The philosophy of these standards is to build greater resistance to terrorist attack into all inhabited buildings. That philosophy affects the general practice of designing inhabited buildings. While these standards are not based on a known threat, they are intended to provide the easiest and most economical methods to minimize injuries and fatalities in the event of a terrorist attack. The primary methods to achieve this outcome are to maximize standoff distance, to construct superstructures to avoid progressive collapse, and to reduce flying debris hazards. These and related design issues are intended to be incorporated into standard design practice in the future.

Design Strategies. There are several major design strategies that are applied throughout these standards. They do not account for all of the measures considered in these standards, but they are the most effective and economical in protecting DOD personnel from terrorist attacks. These strategies are summarized below.

Maximize Standoff Distance. The primary design strategy is to keep terrorists as far away from inhabited DOD buildings as possible. The easiest and least costly opportunity for achieving the appropriate levels of protection against terrorist threats is to incorporate sufficient standoff distance into project designs. While sufficient standoff distance is not always available to provide the minimum standoff distances required for conventional construction, maximizing the available standoff distance always results in the most cost-effective solution. Maximizing standoff distance also ensures that there is opportunity in the future to upgrade buildings to meet increased threats or to accommodate higher levels of protection.

Prevent Building Collapse. Provisions relating to preventing building collapse and building component failure are essential to effectively protecting building occupants, especially from fatalities. Designing those provisions into buildings during new construction or retrofitting during major renovations, repairs, restorations, or modifications of existing buildings is the most cost effective time to do that. In addition, structural systems that provide greater continuity and redundancy among structural components will help limit collapse in the event of severe structural damage from unpredictable terrorist acts.

Minimize Hazardous-Flying Debris. In past explosive events where there was no building collapse, a high number of injuries resulted from flying glass fragments and debris from walls, ceilings, and fixtures (non-structural features). Flying debris can be minimized through building design and avoidance of certain building materials and construction techniques. The glass used in most windows breaks at very low blast pressures, resulting in hazardous, dagger-like shards.

Minimizing those hazards through reduction in window numbers and sizes and through enhanced window construction has a major effect on limiting mass casualties. Window and door designs must treat glazing, frames, connections, and the structural components to which they are attached as an integrated system. Hazardous fragments may also include secondary debris such as those from barriers and site furnishings.

Provide Effective Building Layout. Effective design of building layout and orientation can significantly reduce opportunities for terrorists to target building occupants or injure large numbers of people.

Limit Airborne Contamination. Effective design of heating, ventilation, and air conditioning (HVAC) systems can significantly reduce the potential for chemical, biological, and radiological agents being distributed throughout buildings.

Provide Mass Notification. Providing a timely means to notify building occupants of threats and what should be done in response to those threats reduces the risk of mass casualties.

Facilitate Future Upgrades. Many of the provisions of these standards facilitate opportunities to upgrade building protective measures in the future if the threat environment changes

Controlled Perimeter. These standards assume that procedures are implemented to search for and detect explosives to limit the likelihood that a vehicle carrying quantities of explosives could penetrate a controlled perimeter undetected. It is further assumed that access control will include provisions to reject vehicles without penetrating the controlled perimeter.

Levels of Protection. The potential levels of protection are described in Table 16.1, Table 16.2, and Table 16.3. These standards provide a Low level of protection for billeting and primary gathering buildings and a Very Low level of protection for other inhabited buildings. Greater protection is provided for primary gathering buildings and billeting because of the higher concentration of personnel and the more attractive nature of the target. If the minimum standoff distances are provided, or if mitigating measures are provided to achieve an equivalent level of protection, and if the threats are no greater than those indicated in Table B.1, the risk of injuries and fatalities will be reduced. Threats higher than those envisioned in Table B.1 will increase the likelihood of injuries and fatalities regardless of the level of protection. Refer to the DOD Security Engineering Manual for detailed guidance on levels of protection and how to achieve them for a wide range of threats.

Minimum Standoff Distances. The minimum standoff distances identified in Table B.1 were developed to provide survivable structures for a wide range of conventionally constructed buildings and expeditionary/temporary structures. These buildings range from tents and wood framed buildings to reinforced concrete buildings. For a more detailed discussion of this issue, refer to the DOD Security Engineering Manual.

Conventional Construction Standoff Distance. The standoff distances in the "Conventional Construction Standoff Distance" column in Table B.1 are based on explosive safety considerations that have been developed based on years of experience and observation. Those standoff distances may be conservative for heavy construction such as reinforced concrete or reinforced masonry; however, they may be just adequate for lighter-weight construction.

Effective Standoff Distance. Because standoff distances from the "Conventional Construction Standoff Distance" column of Table B.1 may be overly conservative for some construction types, these standards allow for the adjustment of standoff distances based on the results of a structural analysis considering the applicable explosive weights in Table B.1. For new buildings, even if such an analysis suggests a standoff distance of less than those shown in the "Effective Standoff Distance" column of Table B.1, standoff distances of less than those in that column are not allowed to ensure there is a minimal standoff distance "reserved" to accommodate future upgrades that could be necessitated by emerging threats. In addition, the 10-meter (33 feet) minimum is established to ensure there is no encroachment on the unobstructed space. For existing buildings, the standoff distances in the "Effective Standoff Distance" column of Table B.1 will be provided except where doing so is not possible. In those cases, lesser standoff distances may be allowed where the required level of protection can be shown to be achieved through analysis or can be achieved through building hardening or other mitigating construction or retrofit.

Temporary and Expeditionary Construction. The standoff distances are based on blast testing conducted against TEMPER Tents, SEA Huts, General Purpose Shelters, and Small Shelter Systems. With adequate analysis those distances may be able to be reduced without requiring mitigating measures.

Exempted Building Types. For the reasons below some building types are exempted from some or all of these standards. The minimum standards should be applied to the exempted building types where possible.

SECURITY DESIGN CRITERIA

B-1   SITE PLANNING

Operational, logistic, and security requirements must be integrated into the overall design of buildings, equipment, landscaping, parking, roads, and other features. The most cost-effective solution for mitigating explosive effects on buildings is to keep explosives as far as possible from them. Standoff distance must be coupled with appropriate building hardening to provide the necessary level of protection to DOD personnel. The following standards detail minimum standoff distances that when achieved will allow for buildings to be built with minimal additional construction costs. Where these standoff distances cannot be achieved because land is unavailable, these standards allow for building hardening to mitigate the blast effects. Costs and requirements for building hardening are addressed in the DOD Security Engineering Manual.

B-1.1   STANDARD 1. MINIMUM STANDOFF DISTANCES

The minimum standoff distances apply to all new and existing (when triggered) DOD buildings covered by these standards. The minimum standoff distances are presented in Table B.1 and illustrated in Figure B.1 and Figure B.2. Where the standoff distances in the "Conventional Construction Standoff Distance" column of Table B.1 can be met, conventional construction may be used for the buildings without a specific analysis of blast effects, except as otherwise required in these standards. Where those distances are not available, an engineer experienced in blast-resistant design should analyze the building and apply building hardening as necessary to mitigate the effects of the explosives indicated in Table B.1 at the achievable standoff distance to the appropriate level of protection.

The appropriate levels of protection for each building category are shown in Table B.1, and are described in Table 16.1 and Table 16.2 and in the DOD Security Engineering Manual. For new buildings, standoff distances of less than those shown in the "Effective Standoff Distance" column in Table B.1 are not allowed. For existing buildings, the standoff distances in the "Effective Standoff Distance" column of Table B.1 will be provided except where doing so is not possible. In those cases, lesser standoff distances may be allowed where the required level of protection can be shown to be achieved through analysis or can be achieved through building hardening or other mitigating construction or retrofit.

B-1.1.1   Controlled Perimeter

Measure the standoff distance from the controlled perimeter to the closest point on the building exterior or inhabited portion of the building.

B-1.1.2   Parking and Roadways

Standoff distances for parking and roadways are based on the assumption that there is a controlled perimeter at which larger vehicle bombs will be detected and kept from entering the controlled

TABLE 16.1
Levels of Protection: New Buildings

Level of Protection	Potential Structural Damage	Potential Door and Glazing Hazards	Potential Injury
Below AT Standards	Severely damaged. Frame collapse/massive destruction. Little left standing.	Doors and windows fail and result in lethal hazards.	Majority of personnel suffer fatalities.
Very Low	Heavily damaged—onset of structural collapse: Major deformation of primary and secondary structural members, but progressive collapse is unlikely. Collapse of non-structural elements.	Glazing will break and is likely to be propelled into the building, resulting in serious glazing fragment injuries, but fragments will be reduced. Doors may be propelled into rooms, presenting serious hazards.	Majority of personnel suffer serious injuries. There are likely to be a limited number (10% to 25%) of fatalities.
Low	Damaged—unrepairable. Major deformation of non-structural elements and secondary structural members and minor deformation of primary structural members, but progressive collapse is unlikely.	Glazing will break, but fall within 1 meter of the wall or otherwise not present a significant fragment hazard. Doors may fail, but they will rebound out of their frames, presenting minimal hazards.	Majority of personnel suffer significant injuries. There may be a few (<10%) fatalities.
Medium	Damaged—repairable. Minor deformations of non-structural elements and secondary structural members and no permanent deformation in primary structural members.	Glazing will break, but will remain in the window frame. Doors will stay in frames, but will not be reusable.	Some minor injuries, but fatalities are unlikely.
High	Superficially damaged. No permanent deformation of primary and secondary structural members or non-structural elements.	Glazing will not break. Doors will be reusable.	Only superficial injuries are likely.

perimeter. Where there is a controlled perimeter, the standoff distances and explosive weight associated with parking and roadways in Table B.1 apply. If there is no controlled perimeter, assume that the larger explosive weights upon which the controlled perimeter standoff distances are based (explosive weight I from Table B.1) can access parking and roadways near buildings.

Therefore, where there is no controlled perimeter, use standoff distances from parking and roadways according to the distances and the explosive weight associated with controlled perimeters in Table B.1. Measure the standoff distance from the closest edge of parking areas and roadways to the closest point on the building exterior or inhabited portion of the building. In addition, the following apply:

B-1.1.2.1 New Inhabited Buildings
The minimum standoff for all new buildings regardless of hardening or analysis is 10 meters (33 feet) for both parking areas and roadways.

B-1.1.2.2 Existing Inhabited Buildings
Where possible, move parking and roadways away from existing buildings in accordance with the standoff distances and explosive weights in Table B.1. It is recognized, however, that moving

TABLE 16.2
Levels of Protection: Existing Buildings

Level of Protection	Potential Structural Damage	Potential Door and Glazing Hazards	Potential Injury
Below AT standards	Severely damaged. Frame collapse/massive destruction. Little left standing.	Doors and windows fail and result in lethal hazards.	Majority of personnel suffer fatalities.
Very Low	Heavily damaged—onset of structural collapse. Major deformation of primary structural members, but progressive collapse is unlikely. Collapse of secondary structural members and non-structural elements.	Glazing will break and is likely to be propelled into the building, resulting in serious glazing fragment injuries, but fragments will be reduced. Doors may be propelled into rooms, presenting serious hazards.	Majority of personnel suffer serious injuries. There are likely to be a limited number (10% to 25%) of fatalities.
Low	Damaged—unrepairable. Major deformation of secondary structural members and minor deformation of primary structural members, but progressive collapse is unlikely. Collapse of non-structural elements.	Glazing will break and is likely to be propelled into the building, but should result in survivable glazing fragment injuries. Doors may fail, but they will rebound out of their frames, presenting minimal hazards.	Majority of personnel suffer significant injuries. There may be a few (<10%) fatalities.
Medium	Damaged—repairable. Minor deformations of secondary structural members and no permanent deformation in primary structural members. Major deformation of non-structural elements.	Glazing will break, but will remain in the window frame. Doors will stay in frames, but will not be reusable.	Some minor injuries, but fatalities are unlikely.
High	Superficially damaged. No permanent deformation of primary and secondary structural members or non-structural elements.	Glazing will not break. Doors will be reusable	Only superficial injuries are likely.

existing parking areas and roadways or applying structural retrofits may be impractical; therefore, the following operational options are provided for existing inhabited buildings:

B-1.1.2.2.1 Parking Areas
Establish access control to portions of parking areas that are closer than the required standoff distance to ensure unauthorized vehicles are not allowed closer than the required standoff distance. For primary gathering buildings and billeting, if access control is provided to prevent unauthorized parking within the required standoff distance, controlled parking may be permitted as close as 10 meters (33 feet) without hardening or analysis. Controlled parking may be allowed closer if it can be shown by analysis that the required level of protection can be provided at the lesser standoff distance or if it can be provided through building hardening or other mitigating construction or retrofit.

B-1.1.2.2.2 Parking on Roadways
Eliminate parking on roadways within the required standoff distances along roads adjacent to existing buildings covered by these standards.

TABLE 16.3

Levels of Protection: Expeditionary and Temporary Structures

Level of Protection	Potential Structural Damage	Potential Injury
Below AT Standards	Severely damaged. Frame collapse/massive destruction. Little left standing.	Majority of personnel suffer fatalities.
Very Low	Heavily damaged. Major portions of the structure will collapse (over 50%). A significant percentage of secondary structural members will collapse (over 50%).	Majority of personnel suffer serious injuries. There are likely to be a limited number (10% to 25%) of fatalities.
Low	Damaged—unrepairable. Some sections of the structure may collapse or lose structural capacity (10 to 20% of structure).	Majority of personnel suffer significant injuries. There may be a few (<10%) fatalities.
Medium	Damaged—repairable. Minor to major deformations of both structural members and non-structural elements. Some secondary debris will be likely, but the structure remains intact with collapse unlikely.	Some minor injuries, but no fatalities are likely.
High	Superficially damaged. No permanent deformation of primary and secondary structural members or non-structural elements.	Only superficial injuries are likely.

B-1.1.2.2.3   Parking for Family Housing

For existing family housing with 13 or more units per building within a controlled perimeter or where there is access control to the parking area, parking within the required standoff distances may be allowed where designated parking spaces are assigned for specific residents or residences. Do not label assigned parking spaces with names or ranks of the residents. Do not encroach upon existing standoff distances where the existing standoff distances are less than the required standoff distances. For example, where the required standoff distance is 10 meters, but existing designated parking is only 8 meters (27 feet) from existing family housing, that parking may be retained, but additional parking will not be allowed closer than 8 meters (27 feet.)

B-1.1.3   Parking and Roadway Projects

Where practical, all roadway and parking area projects should comply with the standoff distances from inhabited buildings in Table B.1. Where parking or roadways that are within the standoff distances in Table B.1 from existing buildings are being constructed, expanded, or relocated, do not allow those parking areas and roadways to encroach on the existing standoff distances of any existing inhabited building. That applies even where such projects are not associated with a building renovation, modification, repair, or restoration requiring compliance with these standards.

B-1.1.4   Trash Containers

Measure the standoff distance from the nearest point of the trash container or trash container enclosure to the closest point on the building exterior or inhabited portion of the building. Where the standoff distance is not available, harden trash enclosures to mitigate the direct blast effects and secondary fragment effects of the explosive on the building if the applicable level of protection can be proven by analysis. If unauthorized personnel secure trash enclosures to preclude introduction of objects into the enclosures, they may be located closer to the building as long as they do not violate the unobstructed space provisions of Standard 3. Openings in screening materials and gaps between the ground and screens or walls making up an enclosure must not be greater than 150 mm (6 inches).

TABLE B.1
Minimum Standoff Distances and Separation for New and Existing Buildings

Location	Building Category	Applicable Level of Protection	Standoff Distance or Separation Requirements		
			Conventional Construction Standoff Distance	Effective Standoff Distance[1]	Applicable Explosive Weight[2]
Controlled Perimeter or Parking and Roadways without a Controlled Perimeter	Billeting	Low	45 m[4] (148 ft.)	25 m[4] (82 ft.)	I
	Primary Gathering Building	Low	45 m[4][5] (148 ft.)	25 m[4][5] (82 ft.)	I
	Inhabited Building	Very Low	25 m[4] (82 ft.)	10 m[4] (33 ft.)	I
Parking and Roadways within a Controlled Perimeter	Billeting	Low	25 m[4] (82 ft.)	10 m[4] (33 ft.)	II
	Primary Gathering Building	Low	25 m[4][5] (82 ft.)	10 m[4][5] (33 ft.)	II
	Inhabited Building	Very Low	10 m[4] (33 ft.)	10 m[4] (33 ft.)	II
Trash Containers	Billeting	Low	25 m (82 ft.)	10 m (33 ft.)	II
	Primary Gathering Building	Low	25 m (82 ft.)	10 m (33 ft.)	II
	Inhabited Building	Very Low	10 m (33 ft.)	10 m (33 ft.)	II
Building Separation (For new buildings only)	Billeting	Low	10 m (33 ft.)	No antiterrorism minimum	III[3]
	Primary Gathering Building	Low	10 m (33 ft.)	No antiterrorism minimum	III[3]
	Inhabited Building	Very Low	No antiterrorism minimum	No antiterrorism minimum	Not applicable

Source: Unified Facilities Criteria (UFC) Department of Defense (DOD) Minimum Anti-terrorism Standards for Buildings UFC 4–010–01 Dec. 2002.

[1] Even with analysis, standoff distances less than those in this column are not allowed for new buildings, but are allowed for existing buildings if constructed/retrofitted to provide the required level of protection at the reduced standoff distance.

[2] See UFC 4–010–10, for the specific explosive weights (kg/pounds of TNT) associated with designations—I, II, III. UFC 4–010–10 is For Official Use Only (FOUO)

[3] Explosive for building separation is an indirect fire (mortar) round.

[4] For existing buildings, see paragraph B-1.1.2.2.

[5] For existing family housing, see paragraph B-1.1.2.2.3.

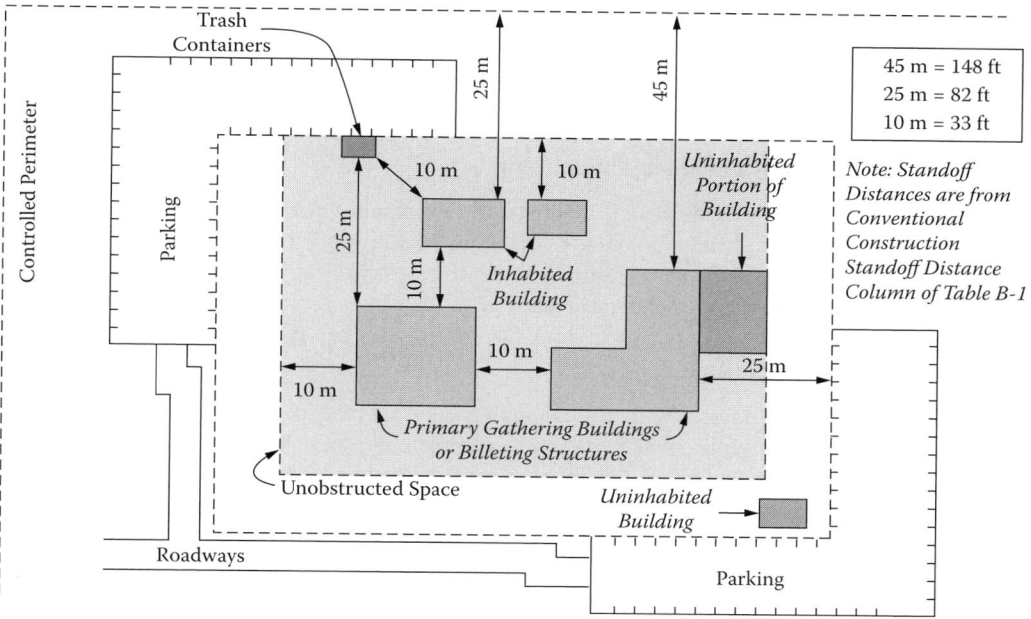

FIGURE B.1 Standoff distances and building separation—controlled perimeter. (Figures based on original image from the Unified Facilities Criteria (UFC), DoD Minimum Antiterrorism Standards for Buildings: Department of Defense, October 8, 2003.)

B-1.2 STANDARD 2. BUILDING SEPARATION

Building separation requirements apply to new buildings and are established to minimize the possibility that an attack on one building causes injuries or fatalities in adjacent buildings. The separation distance is predicated on the potential use of indirect fire weapons.

B-1.2.1 Billeting and Primary Gathering Buildings

For all new billeting and primary gathering buildings, ensure that adjacent inhabited buildings are separated by at least the distances in Table B.1. Where it is necessary to encroach on those building separations, analyze the structure and provide hardened building components as necessary to mitigate the effects of the explosive indicated in Table B.1 to the appropriate level of protection shown in Table B.1. Levels of protection are described in Table 16.1 and in the DOD Security Engineering Manual.

B-1.2.2 Other Inhabited Buildings

There are no minimum separation distances required for antiterrorism purposes for inhabited buildings other than billeting and primary gathering buildings.

B-1.3 STANDARD 3. UNOBSTRUCTED SPACE

It is assumed that aggressors will not attempt to place explosive devices in areas near buildings where these explosive devices could be visually detected by building occupants observing the area around the building. Therefore, ensure that obstructions within 10 meters (33 feet) of inhabited buildings or portions thereof do not allow for the concealment from observation of explosive devices 150 mm (6 inches) or greater in height. This does not preclude the placement of site furnishings or plantings around buildings. It only requires conditions such that any explosive devices placed in that space would be observable by building occupants. For existing buildings where the standoff distances for parking and roadways have been established at less than 10 meters (33 feet) in accordance with paragraph B-1.1.2.2, the unobstructed space may be reduced to be equivalent to that distance.

B-1.3.1   Electrical and Mechanical Equipment

The preferred location of electrical and mechanical equipment such as transformers, air-cooled condensers, and packaged chillers is outside the unobstructed space or on the roof. However this standard does not preclude placement within the unobstructed space as long the equipment provides no opportunity for concealment of explosive devices.

B-1.3.2   Equipment Enclosures

If walls or other screening devices with more than two sides are placed around electrical or mechanical equipment within the unobstructed space, enclose the equipment on all four sides and the top. Openings in screening materials and gaps between the ground and screens or walls making up an enclosure will not be greater than 150 mm (6 inches). Secure any surfaces of the enclosures that can be opened so that unauthorized personnel cannot gain access through them.

B-1.4   STANDARD 4. DRIVE-UP/DROP-OFF AREAS

Some facilities require access to areas within the required standoff distance for dropping off or picking up people or loading or unloading packages and other objects. Examples that may require drive-up/drop-off include, but are not limited to, medical facilities, exchanges and commissaries, childcare centers, and schools.

B-1.4.1   Marking

Where operational or safety considerations require drive-up or drop-off areas or drive-through lanes near buildings, ensure those areas or lanes are clearly defined and marked and that their intended use is clear to prevent parking of vehicles in those areas.

B-1.4.2   Unattended Vehicles

Do not allow unattended vehicles in drive-up or drop-off areas or drive-through lanes.

B-1.4.3   Location

Do not allow drive-through lanes or drive-up/drop-off to be located under any inhabited portion of a building.

B-1.5   STANDARD 5. ACCESS ROADS

Where access roads are necessary for the operation of a building (including those required for fire department access), ensure that access control measures are implemented to prohibit unauthorized vehicles from using access roads within the applicable standoff distances in Table B.1.

B-1.6   STANDARD 6. PARKING BENEATH BUILDINGS OR ON ROOFTOPS

Eliminate parking beneath inhabited buildings or on rooftops of inhabited buildings. Where very limited real estate makes such parking unavoidable, the following measures must be incorporated into the design for new buildings or mitigating measures must be incorporated into existing buildings to achieve an equivalent level of protection.

B-1.6.1 Access Control

Ensure that access control measures are implemented to prohibit unauthorized personnel and vehicles from entering parking areas.

B-1.6.2 Structural Elements

Ensure that the floors beneath or roofs above inhabited areas and all other adjacent supporting structural elements will not fail from the detonation in the parking area of an explosive equivalent to explosive weight II in Table B.1.

B-1.6.3 Progressive Collapse

All structural elements within and adjacent to the parking area will be subject to all progressive collapse provisions of Standard 7 except that the exterior member removal provision will also apply to interior vertical or horizontal load carrying elements. Apply those provisions based on an explosive equivalent to explosive weight II in Table B.1.

B-2 STRUCTURAL DESIGN

If the minimum standoff distances are achieved, conventional construction should minimize the risk of mass casualties from a terrorist attack. Even if those standoff distances can be achieved, however, incorporate the following additional structural issues that must be incorporated into building designs to ensure that buildings do not experience progressive collapse.

B-2.1 STANDARD 7. PROGRESSIVE COLLAPSE AVOIDANCE

Progressive collapse is considered to be significant risk for buildings of three or more stories. Basements will be considered stories if they have one or more exposed walls. For all new and existing inhabited buildings of three stories or more, design the superstructure to sustain local damage with the structural system as a whole remaining stable and not being damaged to an extent disproportionate to the original local damage. Achieve this through an arrangement of the structural elements that provides stability to the entire structural system by transferring loads from any locally damaged region to adjacent regions capable of resisting those loads without collapse. Accomplish this by providing sufficient continuity, redundancy, or energy dissipating capacity (ductility, damping, hardness, etc.), or a combination thereof, in the members and connections of the structure. For further guidance, refer to American Society of Civil Engineers Standard 7–98 and to detailed guidance in the DOD Security Engineering Manual. In addition, the measures below apply to all buildings of three or more stories.

B-2.1.1 Columns and Walls

Design all exterior vertical load-carrying columns and walls to sustain a loss of lateral support at any of the floor levels by adding one story height to the nominal unsupported length. While this standard is based on the assumption of an external threat, where parking beneath buildings is unavoidable, this provision also applies to internal vertical load carrying columns and walls.

B-2.1.2 Exterior Member Removal

Analyze the structure to ensure it can withstand removal of one primary exterior vertical or horizontal load-carrying element (i.e., a column or a beam) without progressive collapse.

B-2.1.3 Floors

Design all floors with improved capacity to withstand load reversals due to explosive effects by designing them to withstand a net uplift equal to the dead load plus one-half the live load.

B-2.2 STANDARD 8. STRUCTURAL ISOLATION

B-2.2.1 Building Additions

Design all additions to existing buildings to be structurally independent from the adjacent existing building. This will minimize the possibility that collapse of one part of the building will affect the stability of the remainder of the building. Alternatively, verify through analysis that collapse of either the addition or the existing building will not result in collapse of the remainder of the building.

B-2.2.2 Portions of Buildings

Where there are areas of buildings that do not meet the criteria for inhabited buildings, design the superstructures of those areas to be structurally independent from the inhabited area. This will minimize the possibility that collapse of the uninhabited areas of the building will affect the stability of the superstructure of the inhabited portion of the building. Alternatively, verify through analysis that collapse of uninhabited portions of the building will not result in collapse of any portion of the building covered by this standard. This standard is not mandatory for existing structures, but it should be implemented where possible.

B-2.3 STANDARD 9. BUILDING OVERHANGS

Avoid building overhangs with inhabited spaces above them where people could gain access to the area underneath the overhang. Where such overhangs must be used, incorporate the following measures into the design for new buildings. Incorporate mitigating measures into existing buildings to achieve an equivalent level of protection.

B-2.3.1 Parking and Roadway Restrictions

Ensure that there are no roadways or parking areas under overhangs.

B-2.3.2 Floors

Ensure that the floors beneath inhabited areas will not fail from the detonation underneath the overhang of an explosive equivalent to explosive weight II where there is a controlled perimeter and explosive weight I for an uncontrolled perimeter. Explosive weights I and II are identified in Table B-1.

B-2.3.3 Superstructure

The progressive collapse provisions of Standard 7, including the provision for loss of lateral support for vertical load carrying elements, will include all structural elements within and adjacent to the overhang.

B-2.4 STANDARD 10. EXTERIOR MASONRY WALLS

Masonry walls that are not reinforced are prohibited for the exterior walls of new buildings. A minimum of 0.05 percent vertical reinforcement with a maximum spacing of 1200 mm (48 in) will be provided. For existing buildings, implement mitigating measures to provide an equivalent level of protection.

B-3 ARCHITECTURAL DESIGN

Even where the minimum standoff distances are achieved, many aspects of building layout and other architectural design issues must be incorporated to improve overall protection of personnel inside buildings.

B-3.1 STANDARD 11. WINDOWS AND GLAZED DOORS

To minimize hazards from flying glass fragments, apply the provisions for glazing and window frames below for all new and existing inhabited buildings covered by these standards. Windows and frames must work as a system to ensure that their hazard mitigation is effective. These provisions apply even if the minimum standoff distances are met.

The specific requirements below will result in windows that comply with this standard for windows with visual glazing openings of 2.8 square meters (30 square feet) or less. For larger windows, refer to the DOD Security Engineering Manual. The specific requirements below will result in windows that comply with this standard for windows with visual glazing openings of 2.8 square meters (30 square feet) or less. For larger windows, refer to the DOD Security Engineering Manual.

B-3.1.1 Glazing

Use a minimum of 6-mm (1/4-in) nominal laminated glass for all exterior windows and glazed doors. The 6-mm (1/4-in) laminated glass consists of two nominal 3-mm (1/8-in) glass panes bonded together with a minimum of a 0.75-mm (0.030-inch) polyvinyl-butyral (PVB) interlayer. For insulated glass units, use 6 mm (1/4-inch) laminated glass inner pane as a minimum. For alternatives to the 6-mm (1/4-in) laminated glass that provide equivalent levels of protection, refer to the DOD Security Engineering Manual.

B-3.1.2 Window Frames

Provide frames and mullions of aluminum or steel. To ensure appropriate window responses, design frames, mullions, anchorages, and window hardware to resist a static load of 7 kilopascals (1 lb per square in) applied to the surface of the glazing. Frame and mullion deformations shall not exceed 1/60 of the unsupported member lengths. The glazing shall have a minimum frame bite of 9.5-mm (3/8-in) for structural glazed window systems and 25-mm (1-in) for window systems that are not structurally glazed. Design supporting elements and their connections based on their ultimate capacities. In addition, because the resulting dynamic loads are likely to be dissipated through multiple mechanisms, it is not necessary to account for reactions from the supporting elements in the design of the remainder of the structure. Alternatively, use frames that provide an equivalent level of performance. For existing buildings, complying with this standard may require replacement or significant modification of window frames, anchorages, and supporting elements.

B-3.1.3 Mitigation

Where the minimum standoff distances cannot be met, provide glazing and frames that will provide an equivalent level of protection to that provided by the glazing above as described in Table 16.1 and Table 16.2 for the applicable explosive weight in Table B.1.

B-3.1.4 Window Replacement Projects

Whenever window or door glazing is being replaced in existing inhabited buildings as part of a planned window or glazing replacement project, whether or not the building meets the triggers in paragraph 1–6.2, install glazing that meets all of the requirements above.

B-3.2   STANDARD 12. BUILDING ENTRANCE LAYOUT

The areas outside of installations are commonly not under the direct control of the installations. Where the main entrances to buildings face installation perimeters, people entering and exiting the buildings are vulnerable to being fired upon from vantage points outside the installations. To mitigate those vulnerabilities apply the following measures:

B-3.2.1   New Buildings

For new inhabited buildings, ensure that the main entrance to the building does not face an installation perimeter or other uncontrolled vantage points with direct lines of sight to the entrance.

B-3.2.2   Existing Buildings

For existing inhabited buildings where the main entrance faces an installation perimeter, either use a different entrance as the main entrance or screen that entrance to limit the ability of potential aggressors to target people entering and leaving the building.

B-3.3   STANDARD 13. EXTERIOR DOORS

For all new and existing buildings covered by these standards, ensure that all exterior doors into inhabited areas open outwards. By doing so, the doors will seat into the doorframes in response to an explosive blast, increasing the likelihood that the doors will not enter the buildings as hazardous debris.

B-3.4   STANDARD 14. MAILROOMS

The following measures address the location of rooms to which mail is delivered or in which mail is handled in new and existing inhabited buildings. The measures involve limiting collateral damage and injuries and facilitating future upgrades to enhance protection should they become necessary.

B-3.4.1   Location

Where a new or existing building covered by these standards must have a mailroom, locate that mailroom on the perimeter of the building. By locating the mailroom on the building perimeter there is an opportunity to modify it in the future if a mail bomb threat is identified. Where mailrooms are located in the interior of buildings, few retrofit options are available for mitigating the mail bomb threat.

B-3.4.2   Proximity

Locate mailrooms as far from heavily populated areas of the building and critical infrastructure as possible. This measure will minimize injuries and damage if a mail bomb detonates in the mailroom. Further, it will reduce the potential for wider dissemination of hazardous agents. These apply where the mailroom is not specifically designed to resist those threats.

B-3.4.3   Sealing

To limit migration into buildings of airborne chemical, biological, and radiological agents introduced into mailrooms, ensure that mailrooms are well sealed between their envelopes and other portions of the buildings in which they are located. Ensure the mailroom walls are of full height construction that fully extends and is sealed to the undersides of the roofs, to the undersides of any floors above them, or to hard ceilings (i.e. gypsum wallboard ceiling). Sealing should include visible cracks, the interface joints between walls and ceilings/roofs, and all wall and ceiling/roof penetrations. Doors will have weather stripping on all four edges. Refer to the DOD Security Engineering Manual for additional guidance.

B-3.5 STANDARD 15. ROOF ACCESS

For all new and existing inhabited buildings covered by these standards, control access to roofs to minimize the possibility of aggressors placing explosives or chemical, biological, or radiological agents there or otherwise threatening building occupants or critical infrastructure.

B-3.5.1 New Buildings

For new buildings eliminate all external roof access by providing access from internal stairways or ladders, such as in mechanical rooms.

B-3.5.2 Existing Buildings

For existing buildings, eliminate external access where possible or secure external ladders or stairways with locked cages or similar mechanisms.

B-3.6 STANDARD 16. OVERHEAD MOUNTED ARCHITECTURAL FEATURES

For all new and existing buildings covered by these standards, ensure that overhead mounted features weighing 14 kilograms (31 pounds) or more are mounted to minimize the likelihood that they will fall and injure building occupants. Mount all such systems so that they resist forces of 0.5 times the component weight in any direction and 1.5 times the component weight in the downward direction. This standard does not preclude the need to design architectural feature mountings for forces required by other criteria such as seismic standards.

B-4 ELECTRICAL AND MECHANICAL DESIGN

Electrical and mechanical design standards address limiting damage to critical infrastructure, protecting building occupants against chemical, biological, and radiological threats, and notifying building occupants of threats or hazards.

B-4.1 STANDARD 17. AIR INTAKES

Air intakes to heating, ventilation, and air conditioning (HVAC) systems that are designed to move air throughout a building that are at ground level provide an opportunity for aggressors to easily place contaminants that could be drawn into the building.

B-4.1.1 New Buildings

For all new inhabited buildings covered by this document locate all air intakes at least 3 meters (10 feet) above the ground.

B-4.1.2 Existing Buildings

The above requirement is recommended, but not mandatory, for existing inhabited buildings covered by these standards.

B-4.2 STANDARD 18. MAILROOM VENTILATION

To ensure airborne chemical, biological, and radiological agents introduced into mailrooms do not migrate into other areas of buildings in which the mailrooms are located, provide separate, dedicated air ventilation systems for mailrooms. Refer to the DOD Security Engineering Manual for additional guidance.

B-4.2.1   Other Heating and Cooling Systems

Building heating and cooling systems such as steam, hot water, chilled water, and refrigerant may serve mailrooms as long as the airflow systems for the mailrooms and other areas of the buildings in which they are located remain separate.

B-4.2.2   Dedicated Exhaust Systems

Provide dedicated exhaust systems within mailrooms to maintain slight negative air pressures with respect to the remainder of the buildings in which the mailrooms are located so that the flow of air is into and contained in the mailrooms. Though the airflow into the mailrooms will not eliminate the potential spread of contamination by personnel leaving the mailroom, it will limit the migration of airborne contaminants through openings and open doorways.

B-4.2.3   Outside Intakes and Exhausts

Provide mailroom ventilation system outside air intakes and exhausts with low leakage isolation dampers that can be closed to isolate the mailrooms.

B-4.2.4   Isolation Controls

Provide separate switches or methods of control to isolate mailrooms in the event of a suspected or actual chemical, biological, or radiological release.

B-4.3   STANDARD 19. EMERGENCY AIR DISTRIBUTION SHUTOFF

For all new and existing inhabited buildings, provide an emergency shutoff switch in the HVAC control system that can immediately shut down air distribution throughout the building except where interior pressure and airflow control would more efficiently prevent the spread of airborne contaminants and/or ensure the safety of egress pathways. Locate the switch (or switches) to be easily accessible by building occupants. Providing such a capability will allow the facility manager or building security manager to limit the distribution of airborne contaminants that may be introduced into the building.

B-4.4   STANDARD 20. UTILITY DISTRIBUTION AND INSTALLATION

Utility systems can suffer significant damage when subjected to the shock of an explosion. Some of these utilities may be critical for safely evacuating personnel from the building or their destruction could cause damage that is disproportionate to other building damage resulting from an explosion. To minimize the possibility of the above hazards, apply the following measures:

B-4.4.1   Utility Routing

For all new inhabited buildings, route critical or fragile utilities so that they are not on exterior walls or on walls shared with mailrooms. This requirement is recommended, but not mandatory, for existing buildings.

B-4.4.2 Redundant Utilities

Where redundant utilities are required in accordance with other requirements or criteria, ensure that the redundant utilities are not collocated or do not run in the same chases. This minimizes the possibility that both sets of utilities will be adversely affected by a single event.

B-4.4.3 Emergency Backup Systems

Where emergency backup systems are required in accordance with requirements or criteria, ensure that they are located away from the system components for which they provide backup.

B-4.5 STANDARD 21. EQUIPMENT BRACING

Mount all overhead utilities and other fixtures weighing 14 kilograms (31 pounds) or more to minimize the likelihood that they will fall and injure building occupants. Design all equipment mountings to resist forces of 0.5 times the equipment weight in any direction and 1.5 times the equipment weight in the downward direction. This standard does not preclude the need to design equipment mountings for forces required by other criteria such as seismic standards.

B-4.6 STANDARD 22. UNDER BUILDING ACCESS

To limit opportunities for aggressors placing explosives underneath buildings, ensure that access to crawl spaces, utility tunnels, and other means of under building access is controlled.

B-4.7 STANDARD 23. MASS NOTIFICATION

All inhabited buildings must have a timely means to notify occupants of threats and instruct them what to do in response to those threats.

B-4.7.1 New Buildings

All new inhabited buildings must have a capability to provide real-time information to building occupants or personnel in the immediate vicinity of the building during emergency situations. The information relayed must be specific enough to determine the appropriate response actions. Any system, procedure, or combination thereof that provides this capability will be acceptable under this standard.

B-4.7.2 Existing Buildings

For existing buildings, the above requirement is mandatory for primary-gathering buildings and billeting, but recommended for all inhabited building.

C-1 SITE PLANNING

The following additional measures, if implemented, will significantly enhance site security with little increase in cost and should be considered for all new and existing inhabited buildings.

C-1.1 RECOMMENDATION 1. VEHICLE ACCESS POINTS

The first line of defense in limiting opportunities for aggressors to get vehicles close to DOD buildings is at vehicle access points at the controlled perimeter, in parking areas, and at drive-up/drop-offs points. Keep the number of access points to the minimum necessary for operational or life safety purposes. This will limit the number of points at which access may have to be controlled with barriers and/or personnel in increased threat environments or if the threat increases in the future.

C-1.2   Recommendation 2. High-Speed Vehicle Approaches

The energy of a moving vehicle increases with the square of its velocity; therefore, minimizing a vehicle's speed allows vehicle barriers to be lighter and less expensive should vehicle barriers ever become necessary. To facilitate reductions in vehicle speeds in the future, ensure there are no unobstructed vehicles approaches perpendicular to inhabited buildings at the required parking and roadway standoff distances.

C-1.3   Recommendation 3. Vantage Points

Vantage points are natural or man-made positions from which potential aggressors can observe and target people or other assets in and around a building. Identify vantage points outside the control of personnel in the targeted building and either eliminate them or provide means to avoid exposure to them. Means to avoid exposure may include actions such as reorienting the building or shielding people or assets in and around the building using such measures as reflective glazing, walls, privacy fencing, or vegetation.

C-1.4   Recommendation 4. Drive-Up/Drop Off

Locate these points away from large glazed areas of the building to minimize the potential for hazardous flying glass fragments in the event of an explosion. For example, locate the lane at an outside corner of the building or otherwise away from the main entrance. Coordinate the drive-up/drop-off point with the building geometry to minimize the possibility that explosive blast forces could be increased due to being trapped or otherwise concentrated. For further discussion of this issue, refer to the DOD Security Engineering Manual.

C-1.5   Recommendation 5. Building Location

Activities with large visitor populations provide opportunities for potential aggressors to get near buildings with minimal controls, and therefore, limit opportunities for early detection. Maximize separation distance between inhabited buildings and areas with large visitor populations.

C-1.6   Recommendation 6. Railroad Location

Avoid sites for inhabited buildings that are close to railroads. Where railroads are in the vicinity of existing buildings, provide standoff distances between the railroad and any inhabited buildings based on the standoff distances and explosive weight associated with controlled perimeters in Table B.1. Where those standoff distances are not available, and since moving existing railroads may be difficult and prohibitively expensive, ensure that there are procedures in place to prohibit trains from stopping in the vicinity of inhabited structures.

C-1.7   Recommendation 7. Access Control for Family Housing

For new family housing areas, provide space for controlling access at the perimeter of the housing area so that a controlled perimeter can be established there if the need arises in the future.

C-1.8   Recommendation 8. Standoff for Family Housing

For new family housing construction, maintain a minimum standoff distance of 25 meters (82 feet) from installation perimeters and roads, streets, or highways external to housing areas.

C-1.9   RECOMMENDATION 9. MINIMIZE SECONDARY DEBRIS

To reduce the hazard of flying debris in the event of an explosion, eliminate unsecured barriers and site furnishings in the vicinity of inhabited structures that are accessible to vehicle traffic. Anchor exposed barriers and site furnishings near inhabited buildings with a minimum of 1 meter (3 feet) of soil or equivalent alternative techniques to prevent fragmentation hazards in the event of an explosion.

C-2   STRUCTURAL AND ARCHITECTURAL DESIGN

The following additional measures, if implemented, will significantly enhance building occupants' safety and security with little increase in cost. Consider these measures for all new and existing inhabited buildings.

C-2.1   RECOMMENDATION 10. STRUCTURAL REDUNDANCY

Unexpected terrorist acts can result in local collapse of building structural components. To limit the extent of collapse of adjacent components, utilize highly redundant structural systems such as moment resisting frames, detail connections to provide continuity across joints equal to the full structural capacity of connected members, and detail members to accommodate large displacements without complete loss of strength. This recommendation is consistent with paragraph B-2.1 (Standard 7) for preventing progressive collapse, but recommends selection of certain structural systems and greater attention to structural details.

C-2.2   RECOMMENDATION 11. INTERNAL CIRCULATION

Design circulation within buildings to provide visual detection and monitoring of unauthorized personnel approaching controlled areas or occupied spaces.

C-2.3   RECOMMENDATION 12. VISITOR CONTROL

Controlling visitor access maximizes the possibility of detecting potential threatening activities. Keep locations in buildings where visitor access is controlled away from sensitive or critical areas, areas where high-risk or mission-critical personnel are located, or other areas with large population densities of DOD personnel.

C-2.4   RECOMMENDATION 13. ASSET LOCATION

To minimize exposure to direct blast effects and potential impacts from hazardous glass fragments and other potential debris, locate critical assets and mission-critical or high-risk personnel away from the building exterior.

C-2.5   RECOMMENDATION 14. ROOM LAYOUT

In rooms adjacent to the exterior of the building, position personnel and critical equipment to minimize exposure to direct blast effects and potential impacts from hazardous glass fragments and other potential debris.

C-2.6   RECOMMENDATION 15. EXTERNAL HALLWAYS

Since doors can become hazardous debris during explosive blast events, doors designed to resist blast effects are expensive, and external hallways have large numbers of doors leading into inhabited areas, avoid exterior hallway configurations for inhabited structures.

C-2.7   RECOMMENDATION 16. WINDOWS

To minimize the potential for glazing hazards, minimize the size and number of windows for new construction.

APPENDIX C

CPTED CODES AND STANDARDS

The next section is an example the recommendations that might be that of a typical CPTED ordinance or resolution. The recommendations are modeled after the Tempe, Arizona CPTED Code that was adopted there in the mid 1990's and the Sarasota and Broward County Florida CPTED Ordinances and a proposed CPTED code for City of Miami developed by Atlas Safety & Security Design Inc., as part of a neighborhood grant program.

CPTED SITE DESIGN STANDARDS

1.1   STREET AND BUILDING IDENTIFICATION REQUIREMENTS

The purpose of the addressing standards is to provide for uniformity in street names and addresses and to facilitate emergency vehicle response by establishing a uniform system for street names and address numbers, street name standards, display standards, and addresses. Street numbers and other identifying data for buildings shall be displayed in accordance with Local Building Codes, Local Zoning Codes, and the applicable CPTED Resolution.

A.   RESIDENTIAL

1. Buildings less than fifty (50) feet from the curb require a minimum of three (3) inch high numbers displayed on the structure.
2. Buildings more than fifty (50) feet from the curb require a minimum of three (3) inch high numbers displayed a minimum of thirty-six (36) inches above ground at the primary access point.

B.   APARTMENTS (SEE FIGURE 16.1 AND FIGURE 16.3)

1. Entrance numbers shall be a minimum of twelve (12) inches high.
2. Building numbers shall be a minimum of twelve (12) inches high.
3. Apartment number ranges displayed below building numbers shall be a minimum of eight (8) inches high.

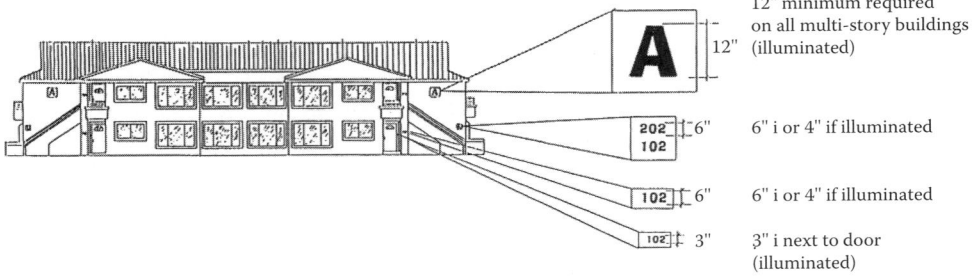

FIGURE 16.1   Residential signage for apartment buildings. (Image ©1997 City of Tempe, Arizona. Reprinted with permission.)

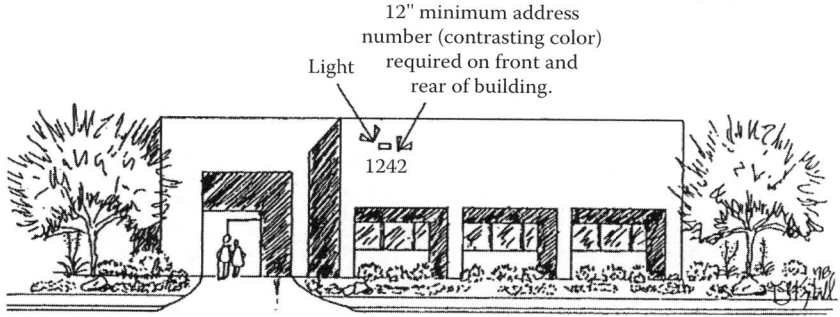

FIGURE 16.2 Signage requirements. (Image ©1997 City of Tempe, Arizona. Reprinted with permission.)

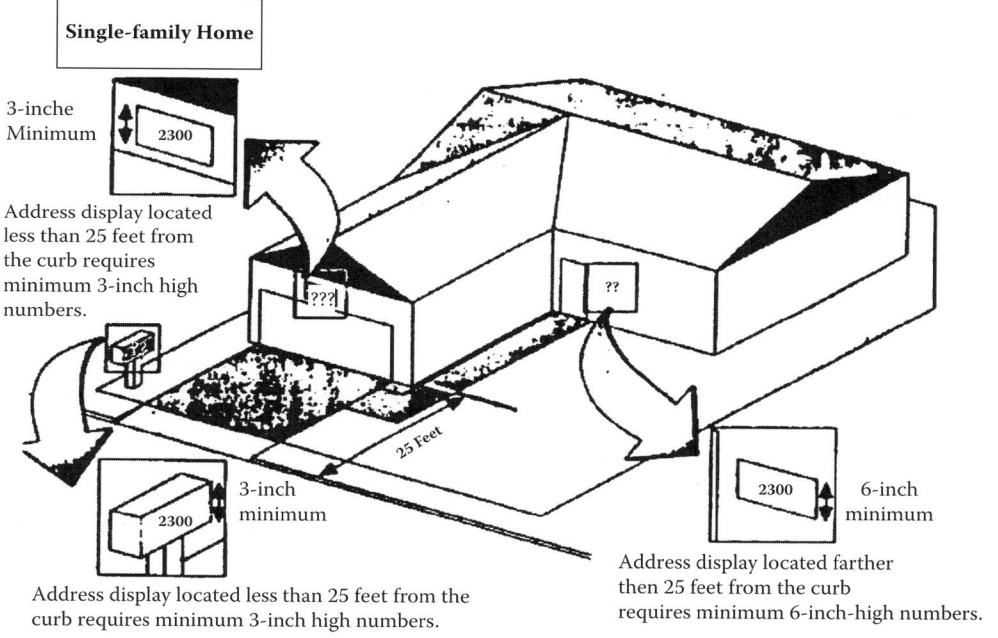

FIGURE 16.3 Residential signage requirements. (*Source: Las Vegas Sun* 1995.)

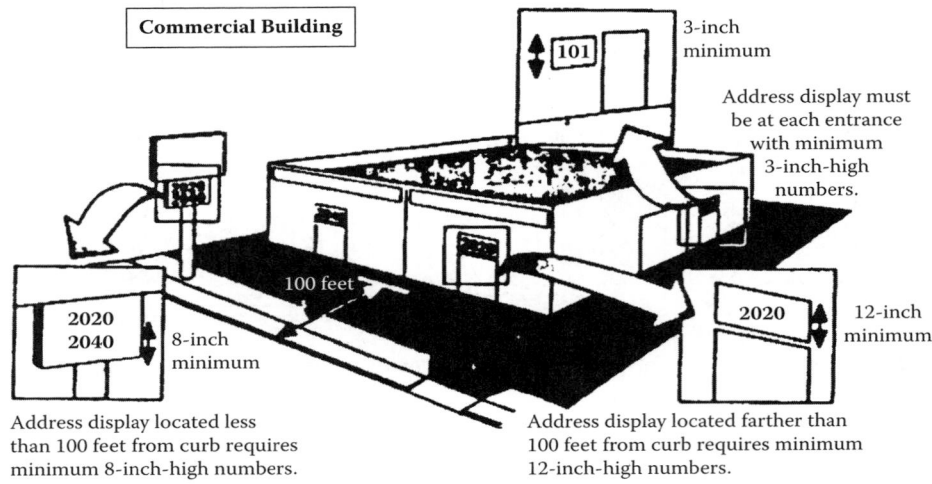

FIGURE 16.4   Signage requirements. (*Source*: *Las Vegas Sun* ©1995.)

4. Apartment number ranges displayed on signage near the building shall be a minimum of two (2) inches high.

C.   COMMERCIAL

1. Buildings less than fifty (50) feet from the curb require a minimum of eight (8) inch high numbers displayed on the building.
2. Buildings more than fifty (50) feet from the curb require a minimum of twelve (12) inch high numbers displayed a minimum of thirty-six (36) inches above ground at the primary access point.
3. Tenant space numbers shall be a minimum of three (3) inches high.

D.   RV AND MOBILE HOME PARKS

1. Entrance numbers shall be twelve (12) inches high.
2. Building numbers shall be six (6) inches high.
3. Space numbers shall be three (3) inches high.

E.   ADDITIONAL REQUIREMENTS

1. There shall be positioned at each entrance of a multi-family dwelling complex an illuminated diagrammatic representation (map) of the complex that shows the location of the viewer and the unit designations within the complex (see Figure 16.5).
2. No other number may be affixed to a structure that might be mistaken for or confused with, the number assigned to the structure.
3. The assigned address, including the suite number, shall be displayed on all electric meters in accordance with utility company standards.
4. The number for each building shall be placed on both the front and rear of the structure. In a commercial development, the numbers assigned shall be displayed at both the front and rear entrances.
5. If the building is adjacent to an alley, the number shall also be placed on or adjacent to the rear gate accessing the alley.

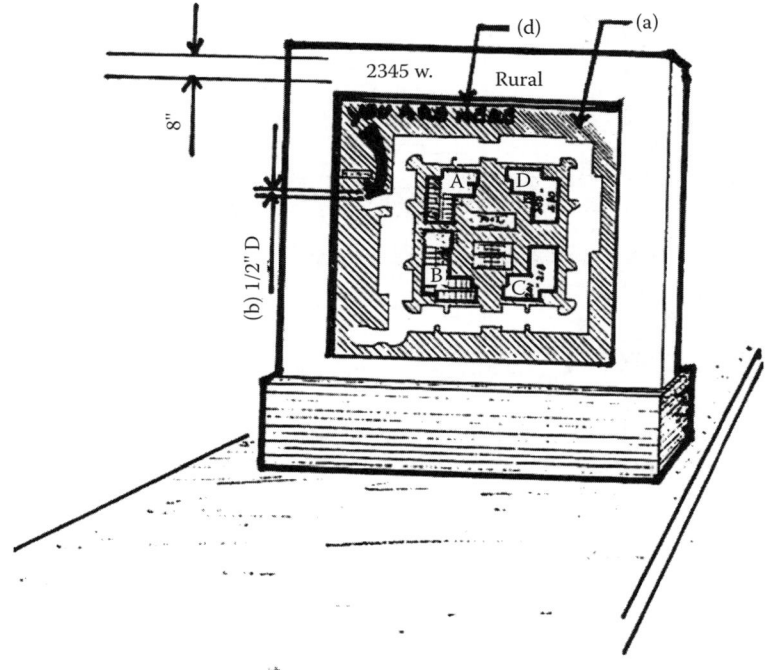

FIGURE 16.5   Design features of a wayfinding map. (Image ©1997 City of Tempe, Arizona. Reprinted with permission.)

6. For commercial structures, the name of the occupant shall be displayed on the rear entrance of the building.
7. Properties occupied by more than one dwelling unit shall have an illuminated diagrammatic representation (map) of the complex that shows the location of the viewer and the unit designations within the complex. The enforcing authority based on the site layout must approve the number and location of maps.
8. For buildings with recessed entryways of over two (2) feet in depth, an additional lighted address must be placed at the entryway to the recessed area. If the recessed area provides access to more than one dwelling unit, each unit number shall be displayed.

Each principal building shall display the number or letter assigned to that building on each corner of the building. Additional display of numbers/letters shall be required at the midpoint of the building, if the structure is between 120 and 200 feet in length. For structures over two hundred feet (200) in length, additional numbers/letters shall be placed every one hundred (100) feet. Any modification of this criterion must be approved by the enforcing agency.

2.1   LANDSCAPING, PLANTINGS, WALLS, FENCES, AND SCREENING

The positioning, location, and type of planting material, screening, and other landscape elements should allow for natural surveillance of the outdoor areas from within buildings, from outdoor locations on site, and from adjacent buildings, sites, and rights-of-way. Landscaping and screening should complement efforts to define public, semi-public, and private spaces. Security is enhanced when entrances and exits to buildings or open spaces around buildings, including pedestrian walkways, are open and in view of the surrounding neighboring or adjacent sites. The more open

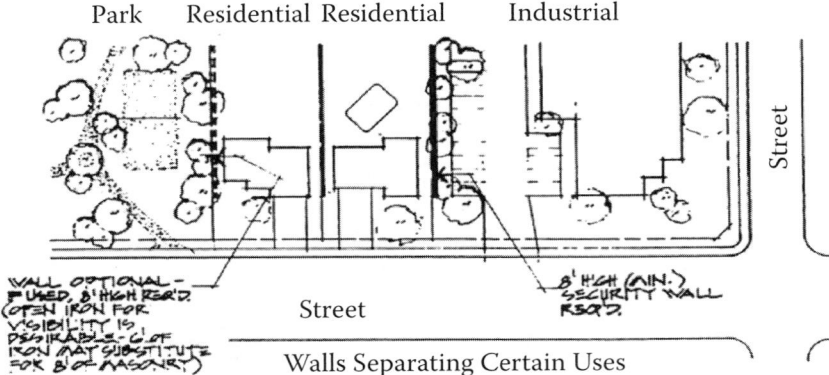

FIGURE 16.6 Choices for barriers separating different uses. (Image ©1997 City of Tempe, Arizona. Reprinted with permission.)

the view of a space is, the less likely that space will be used with visual obstructions for the commission of offenses (see Figure 16.6).

A. Shrubs and ground cover located within six (6) feet of a walkway shall not exceed two (2) feet in height. Shrubs and ground cover located more than six (6) feet but less than twelve (12) feet from the edge of a walkway shall not exceed three (3) feet in height. Trees located less than twelve (12) feet from the edge of a walkway shall be trimmed to a minimum of six (6) foot canopy height. Use of barrier plants in these areas adjacent is recommended.

B. Mature trees shall be trimmed to create a minimum six (6) foot clear area from the ground.

C. River rock is not recommended for use near parking lots or buildings. River rock (stone) and other masonry materials such as brick and riprap that are normally used for landscaping accents, borders, or scuppers frequently lend themselves for use as weapons and/or tools for the commission of crimes. When river rock and other masonry materials are used, they should be grouted to prevent removal by hand. River rock should be grouted so that only one-third (1/3) of the rock is exposed above ground.

D. Barrier plants (a plant with a dense vegetation structure that is thorny or has needles) shall be planted below and extending at least twelve (12) inches to each side of windows. Plant materials in this area shall be no higher than the sill height of the window. Vegetation shall not hinder the egress requirements for emergency escape from sleeping areas.

If gates are provided between residential back yards and reverse frontage, retention areas, parks, commercial or industrial areas, or similar features, they must be approved by the CPTED reviewer. Back yard gates shall otherwise be the full height of the wall or fencing and capable of being locked. The entrance shall be lighted and visible from neighboring properties.

E. Front yards or public spaces should be arranged to afford visibility and opportunity for surveillance by on-site users and passerby.

F. Barriers, both real and symbolic, should be designed to afford opportunities through the barrier.

G. Access control for gated communities.

H. For residential development, walls or fences with vertical pickets, shall be a minimum of eight (8) feet in height when adjacent to any of the following:
1. Reverse frontage
2. Retention areas
3. Parks

4. Commercial areas
5. Industrial areas
6. Bike paths

The walls shall have no vehicular access points to or from the alley. Within the first twenty five (25) feet from the street property line, the height of the wall may be reduced, gradually, to three (3) feet in height if there is potential of obstructed vision for pedestrian and vehicular traffic. All required walls should be located on-site and be of masonry or concrete construction. All walls shall have an architectural texture, color, and material compatible with the primary building on-site (or on respective sides). Where walls are along alleys, only the alley side painting is required. Alternate wall finishes must receive written approval by Development Services Director.

Walls may have ornamental decorative wrought iron fence panels or stainless steel picket fence panels, with vertical pickets placed a maximum of four (4) inches on center, as an integral part of the design of the wall. Six (6) of wrought iron or galvanized steel picket may substitute for masonry.

I. Blank walls should be limited and public and commercial courtyards should require at least six feet of opening to provide emergency egress, and natural surveillance for security and visual interest. Private courtyards would not require openings onto public spaces.

3.1 LIGHTING

The intent of this section is to establish lighting levels for various typical uses to promote visual surveillance, reduce the potential for criminal activity, and meet energy constraints. This standard is to be used in conjunction with the most current Illuminating Engineering Society of North America (IESNA) Standards, and the applicable Building Codes. If there is any conflict between any of these codes or standards, then the most restrictive shall apply.

Lighting should be sufficient to provide for security and to allow for natural observation of both enclosed and semi-enclosed structures (example: Parking structures) and outdoor spaces. Lighting is necessary in enclosed and semi-enclosed structures during both the day and night hours. More lighting must be provided in enclosed and semi-enclosed structures during day hours to compensate for eyes that are habituated to natural outdoor lighting conditions. A well-lighted space is less likely to be used for commission of a crime because of increased opportunities for natural surveillance.

A. Open parking lots, carports, and refuse areas shall be illuminated to a medium level of activity, as specified by the IESNA, which requires a minimum level of footcandles between sunset and sunrise.

B. Aisles, passageways, pedestrian walkways, and recessed areas related to and within a building, structure, or providing access to a building or buildings from a parking lot or right-of-way shall be illuminated with uniformly maintained minimum levels between sunset and sunrise. The primary lighting reading should be at ground level. A supplemental reading may take between three and five feet.

C. All exterior entrances shall be illuminated with a uniformly maintained minimum level of five (5) footcandles of light at ground level within a minimum radius of fifteen (15) feet from the center of the exterior entrance and/or exit between sunset and sunrise.

D. Parking structures and covered parking lots or covered portions of parking lots shall be illuminated with a uniformly maintained level of five (5) footcandles of light at ground level between sunset and sunrise. Entrances and exits into garages should facilitate light adaptation and be higher during the day and lower at night to allow your eyes to adjust.

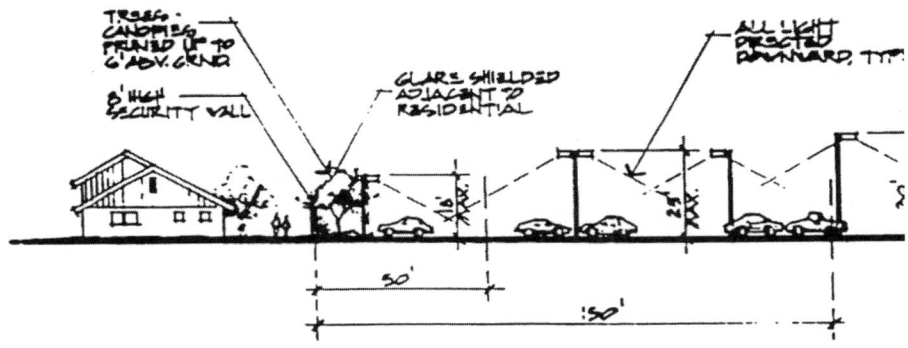

Pole-Mounted Exterior Lighting Adjacent to Residential

FIGURE 16.7   Pole-mounted exterior lighting. (Image ©1997 City of Tempe, Arizona. Reprinted with permission.)

E. To facilitate light adaptation at parking entrances and exits during daylight hours shall be illuminated with a uniformly maintained minimum level of ten (10) footcandles of light at ground level between sunrise and sunset (daylight hours).

F. Postal service "gang mail boxes" shall be located within twenty (20) feet of public street lighting or shall be illuminated with a uniformly maintained level of five (5) footcandles of light at ground level between sunset and sunrise.

G. Weather and vandal resistant covers shall protect all exterior lighting devices.

H. Lighting of all exterior areas shall be designed to maximize surveillance and reduce conflicts with building design and mature landscaping and to minimize glare (see Figure 16.7). Consideration shall be given to the mature size and canopy height of all plant materials. Trees and shrubs should not interfere with the distribution of lighting required by the CPTED resolution.

I. All light switches in public restrooms or identified for general public use shall be of the style that cannot be turned off or on by users, other than staff/employees.

J. All exterior light shall be directed downward and away from adjoining property and shall be shielded to prevent unnecessary glare.

K. Transitional lighting should be incorporated into exterior areas going to and from the buildings or uses within the site. Transitional lighting should be provided for: recreation/ office buildings, swimming pools, laundry and mail rooms, ramadas, covered breezeways, and similar areas.

L. Details of exterior lighting should be provided on a landscape site plan prepared to scale. Photometric calculations should be detailed on an exterior lighting plan unless waived by the CPTED review team. Photometric calculations should be based on the "mean" light output per the manufacturer's values of the specified lamp and luminaire photometry data formatted on Illumination Engineering Society of North America (IESNA) file compiled by an approved testing agency. The details provided for exterior lighting should include point-to-point photometric calculations at intervals of not more than ten (10) feet, at ground level, depending upon the applicable risk factors.

M. Minimum Illumination Guidelines: All minimum illumination guidelines listed in this section should be maintained from ground level. The minimum to average maintained uniformity ratio should not exceed 4:1 in an acceptable layout.

In some circumstances, customer convenience, closed circuit surveillance, and customer attraction may require a higher level of lighting. In addition, demographics, the crime index, and other factors particular to a certain geographic areas may require a higher level. A physical security site survey and an analysis of area crime should be conducted.

4.1 PARKING STRUCTURES

Parking structures can be challenging from a crime prevention standpoint. The scale of a parking structure is that of an automobile, not the pedestrian, creating the potential for long walking distances and large unobservable areas. The users of parking structures are frequently predictable in their behavior, especially those using parking garages that serve large employment centers. The following measures are intended to mitigate the inherent hazards of these conditions:

A. All parking structures will have open sides for any portion of the structure that is above design grade to allow unobstructed views through the structure from the outside. Opening within twenty (20) feet of design grade shall be secured with a steel picket or wrought iron type of fencing, or other type of material that allows for visual permeability while maintaining security from intrusion and trespassing. Landscaping shall be maintained to preserve visibility of the interior of the structure.

B. All parking structures will have a minimum of two (2) pedestrian ingress/egress points, such as stairs, elevators, or ramps on each level.

C. Outside stairwells shall be open and not obstructed from view. Access to spaces beneath stairwells shall be prevented with walls, screening, or fencing.

D. Security communication devices/telephones with monitoring capability shall be located on every level adjacent to pedestrian ingress/egress points. If pedestrian ingress points are more than two hundred (200) feet but less than three hundred (300) feet apart, additional security telephones shall be located at the midpoint between pedestrian access points. If pedestrian access points are more than three hundred (300) feet apart, security telephones will be located at one hundred (100) foot intervals. Security telephones shall be visible from all vehicular and pedestrian ingress/egress points, ADA accessible, and identified with appropriate signage and graphics.

E. Wherever possible, elevators will be observable from the outside, using a transparent glazing enclosure for maximum visibility.

F. Blind corners will be provided with shatterproof convex mirrors to improve visibility for both operators of vehicles and pedestrians.

G. It is recommended that the ceilings and vertical elements of parking garage levels, where poured in place concrete is the structural material, be painted white to reflect the interior and exterior lighting of the garage.

5.1 AUTOMATIC TELLER MACHINES (ATM) AND NIGHT DEPOSITORIES (ND)

The principle concerns for security for ATM & ND are: location, lighting, and landscaping (3Ls).

A. It is the intent of these guidelines to enhance the safety of consumers using automated teller machines without discouraging the placing of automatic teller machines and night depositories in locations convenient to consumers and workplaces.

B. The placement, installation, and maintenance of automatic teller machines and night depository shall consider the extent to which lighting for the ATM and ND complies with the lighting standards of the American Banking Association (ABA) and this resolution. There shall be a minimum of twenty (20) footcandles at the face of the ATM /ND and extending in an unobstructed direction outward ten (10) feet. There shall be a minimum of ten (10) footcandles from ten (10) feet to twenty (20), and two (2) footcandles from twenty (20) feet to fifty (50) feet from all unobstructed directions from the face of the ATM/ ND.

C. ATMs and NDs shall have an external closed circuit television installed with recording capability.

D. The presence of landscaping, plantings, or other obstructions in the area of the ATM/ND, the access area, and the defined parking area (that portion of any parking areas which is contiguous to an access area with respect to an ATM/ND, and principally used for parking by users of the ATM/ND while conducting transactions during hours of darkness) shall be minimized and provide maximum unobstructed visibility.

6.1 SECURITY REQUIREMENTS FOR RESIDENTIAL MULTI-FAMILY PROPERTIES

A. All individual dwelling units and rooming units other than owner occupied dwelling units shall be equipped with the following minimum security devices:

1. All windows and doors to the exterior of a dwelling unit shall be equipped with locking devices. A lock shall have a one-inch minimum throw. A lock shall be constructed so that the bolt shall be retracted by the action of a single inside knob, thumb turn or lever. A lock must be capable of being deadlocked, not spring loaded, from the interior and by an exterior key. One exception is that fire escape doors do not require an exterior key.

2. The strike plate shall be securely attached to the frame of the doorway. Strike plates shall be installed, replaced, or attached by woodscrews a minimum of two (2) inches in length, if the frame is made of wood.

3. Exterior doors and dwelling unit doors which are required by Code as a means of egress, shall not be equipped with locks that require a key for operation from the side of the structure which egress is to be made.

4. All double hung windows must be equipped with sash locks securely attached to the inner window frame by screws a minimum of 3/4 inch in length. Double hung windows, which are ground level, or otherwise reasonably accessible from the exterior shall also be equipped with steel pin locks or other metal window ventilation locks. These window-securing devices must be of sufficient strength and quality to require the window to be broken to permit entry. The pins (one per window) for such locks shall be secured to the window by a chain.

   The pins shall be inserted into holes drilled at a slight downward angle through the inner frame and halfway into the outer frame. There shall be a second hole drilled approximately five (5) inches high to permit the window to be secured in an open position to allow natural ventilation. If metal window vent locks are used, they shall be capable of locking the window closed or that it may not be opened more than five (5) inches to allow ventilation. The pins or locks shall not require the use of a tool or key for locking or unlocking, so its parts cannot be lost or misplaced. Locks shall be capable of being released from the interior to allow full ventilation and emergency fire egress.

5. Sliding doors and windows at ground level or otherwise reasonable accessible from the exterior must be equipped with a securing device in width and length to prevent the window or door from being opened when desired. Where the sliding portion of the window or door is on the outside, there shall be a pin or other locking device installed that the door or window may not be opened or removed (or lifted from the track) when on closed and locked position. Aluminum frame windows and doors for which pins or metal locks cannot be used may have another type of lock device as permitted by regulations adopted by the CPTED review team.

6. Casement type windows at grade or otherwise reasonably accessible from the exterior shall have a hardened steel slide bolt installed. If the window is over four (4) feet high, it shall be provided with a bolt at the top and bottom.

7. If the principal entrance door has a window or sidelight, the sidelight shall be located on the opposite side from where the door handle and lock is. Door window larger than 8 inches by 8 inches shall use a break resistant glazing material. Entrance doors with no sidelight or window shall be equipped with a wide-angle peephole viewer.

8. Exterior wood doors shall be of solid core construction such as high-density particle-board, solid wood, or wood block core with a minimum thickness of one and three-fourths (1 3/4) inches. No panel inserts should exist on the doors.

9. Exterior installed steel doors shall be a minimum thickness of 24 gauge. If exterior doorframe is metal, the frame shall be constructed of eighteen (18) gauge or heavier steel and reinforced at the hinges and strikes. All steel frames shall be anchored to the wall in accordance with manufacturers' specifications. Frames shall be installed to eliminate tolerances inside the rough opening.

10. The inactive leaf of an exterior double door shall be provided with flush bolts having an engagement of not less than one inch into the head and threshold of the doorframe. All double doors shall be equipped with a vertical drop rim-mounted deadbolt with a one-inch (1) throw.

11. Hinges for exterior swinging doors shall comply with the following:
    a. At least two (2) screws, three and one-half (3 1/2) inches in length, penetrating at least one (1) inch into wall structure shall be used. Solid wood fillers shall be used to eliminate any space between the wall structure and doorframe behind each hinge.
    b. Hinges for out-swinging doors shall be equipped with a mechanical interlock to preclude the removal of the door from the exterior.

12. Exterior door strike plates shall be a minimum of 18-gauge metal with four (4) offset screw holes. Strike plates shall be attached to wood with not less than three and one-half (3 1/2) inch screws, which have a minimum one-inch penetration into the nearest stud.

13. All exterior doors shall have escutcheon plates with back plates or wrap around door channels installed around any locking device. Plates are to be secured from the inside with three-quarter (3/4) inch carriage bolts or wood screws that cannot be removed from the exterior.

7.1 RESIDENTIAL DESIGN GUIDELINES

A. SITE PLANNING

1. Cluster units into comprehensible groups within the framework of the development so that residents can easily recognize and identify their neighbors.
2. Develop a road network that permits multiple access points but deters cut-throughs.
3. Orient building fronts to the street so as to facilitate observation and movements of people and traffic.
4. Avoid backing structures onto arterial and collector roads.
5. Limit the length of cul-de-sacs to encourage increased intra-neighborhood observation and interaction.
6. Cul-de-sacs should border on a central open neighborhood park as opposed to a thoroughfare or another cul-de-sac.
7. Provide sidewalks along streets to encourage pedestrian traffic.
8. Provide physical barriers between commercial areas and residential areas with fences or walls.

9. Provide for uniform street lighting that meets IESNA standards for residential communities.
10. Layout parking areas in small pods immediately adjacent to their corresponding residences.
11. Avoid remote parking areas that are not observable from the buildings they serve. Orient the spaces so they are easily visible from the building windows, doorways, and walkways.

B. OPEN SPACES

1. Community parks, recreational facilities, play lots, and local open spaces should be made a focus for the new development. Centrally locate the major open space or park within the development to make them convenient attractions or magnets for legitimate activity support.
2. Locate open spaces and recreational facilities to maximize views or surveillance from residences and public roads.
3. Provide lighting to enable users to easily detect hazards where night use is anticipated.
4. Differentiate between public and private spaces through grading, path locators, landscaping and fences, and natural boundaries.
5. Avoid designing spaces that are unassigned. All space should become the clear responsibility of someone.

C. WALKS AND PATHS

1. Provide well defined pedestrian routes to and within the open space areas. Route paths past areas where the public is likely to congregate or frequent. Take advantage of natural opportunities to bring people into contact and increase interaction, such as trash collection sites, mailboxes, and laundry rooms.
2. Clear site lines reduce opportunities for crime to occur undetected. Keep walks and recreational paths in view of as many residents as practical including public roads. Avoid jogs that create concealed areas. Anticipate natural pedestrian routes and locate walks and recreational paths so the two will coincide and generate enough pedestrian traffic to deter crime.
3. Keep underbrush and other vegetation clear of paths to provide comfortable site distances, which offer persons ample time to perceive any hazards. Avoid plantings that create hiding spaces near paths and walkways.
4. When paths lead into wooded or landscaped areas provide an alternate route in clear view of roads or houses.
5. Provide access points along pathways for emergency and security vehicles.
6. Provide adequate lighting on walks and pathways when night use as anticipated.

D. BUILDINGS

1. Entry doors, frames, and windows should be of quality construction material and have security hardware meeting minimum standards, i.e., deadbolt locks with minimum one inch throw, metal strike plates secured with three (3") inch screws, security bars on sliding doors, ventilation locks on windows.
2. Provide uniform lighting meeting minimum standards (IESNA).
3. Provide enclosed garages rather than carports when feasible.
4. Locate laundry rooms, storage lockers, and other convenience facilities such that visibility from the outside is enhanced. Users and passers-by should be able to easily observe potential dangers and avoid them.
5. Make certain addresses are visible from the street.

E. Landscape

Landscape: Plantings

1. Provide for adequate visibility of public areas with low plantings of shrubs and high-branched deciduous trees.
2. Arrange planting areas to allow surveillance of public areas such as parks, playgrounds, parking lots, building entrances, and walks.
3. Select planting that will maintain an appropriate height that will not overly obscure sight lines (3 feet for motorists, 5 feet six inches for pedestrians).
4. Landscape parking lots so that users may be seen from appropriate vantage points such as building entrances, windows, streets, and sidewalks.
5. Provide breaks in landscape screening of storm water retention ponds to facilitate observation and reduce opportunities for these areas to be used for dumping of trash and other crimes.
6. Provide low plantings at building entrances, corners, and below first floor windows.
7. Coordinate landscaping with site lighting to avoid creation of shadows or difficult to see locations.
8. Use landscaping, walls, and fences to define the boundaries or the development and encourage a sense of community. The continuity of landscape elements identifies an area that is associated with a particular neighborhood.
9. Provide neighborhood identification, signage, and landscaping at major access points.
10. Plant material should not be severely pruned such that the natural growth pattern or characteristic form is significantly altered.
11. All ground covers in parking landscape should be of a species that will not grow to interfere with natural surveillance.

Landscape: Site Grading

1. Set building grades higher than street and parking areas to facilitate visibility and define public from private areas.
2. Vary the height of landscape planting to accommodate sight lines and lighting.
3. Provide site lines through landscape and planting elements.

Landscape: Walls and Fences

1. Place walls and fences sufficiently back from walks to avoid blind spots or ambush opportunities.
2. Maintain pedestrians' visibility around corners of fences and walls.
3. Avoid placing retaining walls where the downhill side is not visible or cannot be secured.
4. Fences and walls should be sufficiently high to discourage cut-through.
5. Use fences to buffer residential properties from commercial areas to discourage trespassing. Define vacant or open land with rail fences, three strand low barbed wire fencing, or gully and berm to prevent cut-through and illegal dumping.
6. Walls for security and access gates are intended to minimize unauthorized access and reduce the risk of crime. In many locations, such as between residential and certain other uses, or at the rear of "reverse frontage" residential lots, walls may also provide additional privacy and buffering from unwanted noise.
7. Walls and access gates are to be designed and built in such a way as to provide the necessary security, compliment their surroundings, and maintain their function and appearance over time. A consistent standard of design, materials, and height of walls in an area or along a particular street frontage should be maintained.

8. Walls and fences in front yards of residential areas should not exceed four (4) feet. Walls or fences in side and rear yards should not exceed eight (8) feet. A steel or metal picket fence that is six (6) feet is equivalent to an eight (8) masonry or brick wall.

9. Access control gates that are used for pedestrian and vehicular access control to a commercial, industrial, or residential site should seek Fire Department plan check and approval prior to installation. In addition to Fire Department approval, the CPTED team for properties requiring CPTED approval must also review the location of gates. Submitted plans must indicate where the gate(s) will be located. Details on the type of gate and access control through the gate must also be submitted. All access control gates must provide access to the Police and Fire Departments at all control points.

Part III

Applications of CPTED in
the Built Environment

17 Designing Safe Communities and Neighborhoods*

SAFE NEIGHBORHOODS?

Except for recent statistical increases in the last few years, for over a decade crime in the United States has decreased (see Figure 17.1). Yet my personal experience is that people do not feel safer. When people do not feel safe, they act in different ways to protect their property and themselves. Whether the threat is from the workplace violence, threats of terrorism, or street crime, crime impacts how and where we work and play. Crime analysis for 2006 is projecting an increase in crimes of violence, and this will most likely continue in 2007.

Florida State Crime Rates for 2002

	Murder	Rape	Robbery	Aggravated Assault	Burglary	Crime Rate per 100,000	Percent Rate Change from 2001
FLORIDA	906	6,704	32,413	81,776	176,058	5,398.4	– 3.3%
MIAMI-DADE							
Miami-Dade Police Department	94	494	3,198	8,115	11,448	6,407.8	– 5.2%
Coral Gables	1	11	55	117	485	6,698.2	0.9%
Hialeah	9	48	431	1,012	1,609	5,282.6	– 0.8%
Miami	65	96	2,706	4,361	5,962	9,263.9	4.4%
Miami Beach	7	51	507	512	1464	11,677.8	– 8.2%
Miami-Dade Public Schools	0	5	127	215	608	–	–

FIGURE 17.1 In metropolitan Miami in 2002 the crime rate is the lowest in 30 years according to data gathered by the Florida Department of Law Enforcement, which reports crime to the FBI for their annual reports. (Crime statistics reported by The Florida Department of Law Enforcement, 2002.)

---

* Portions of the text in this chapter consist of articles and other publications previously written by the author including possible portions found in the following Wiley publications: *Planning and Urban Design Standards*, Steiner et al., American Planning Association, John Wiley & Sons, ISBN: 0471475815, ©2007. We offer special thanks to the American Planning Association and John Wiley & Sons for permission to reproduce common content in this work.

Every workday, nearly 8,000 Americans are violently attacked or threatened with a violent attack at work or while working outside the office. The growth of the private security industry suggests that Americans increasingly believe that public law enforcement cannot protect them against the threat of crime. There are three times as many private security officers as public police (Benson, 1998).

Crime rates in communities have often been thought to be associated with a wide variety of social problems, including a degree of community alienation, fear of crime, lowered housing values, and the associated erosion of the community's tax base. One study by Steven Stack from Wayne State University indicates that property values are one of the most measurable factors (Stack, 1997). In that study, crime had an independent effect of property values. An increase in 1000 crimes per 100,000 in population was associated with a decline in house values of $9,000 per house. For a community with 10,000 homes, this would amount to a $90,000,000 reduction in the tax base. As crime erodes the tax base of a community, there can be significant reductions in funds for education and other public services and infrastructure.

In contrast, according to Stack, people who reside in safe communities where crime is under control enjoy greater appreciation in the values of their homes, better schools, and other public services.

How do you promote an individual's sense of dignity and self-sufficiency while at the same time establish a sense of community? The answer may be a mixture of New Urbanism idealism and down to earth Crime Prevention Through Environmental Design (CPTED) pragmatism.

New Urbanism concepts—and the associated concept of Traditional Neighborhood Design (TND) principles—were established in the 1980s. New Urbanism is an architectural and planning movement aimed at creating new towns and neighborhoods based on traditional town design principles. Seeking to solve the problems of sprawl and modern suburbia, New Urbanism focuses on creating communities on a more human scale (see Figure 17.2). This scale is achieved through the use of codes, which control density, vehicular traffic, zoning, and other key elements to creating a neotraditional town. "Neo-traditional towns look and work like back streets of a comfortable pre-World War II city, with a rich mix of housing types, cultural centers, and shopping districts within walking distance and a vibrant public personality" (*Consumer Reports,* May 1996).

The structuring of New Urbanist towns begins with the aspirations and scale of its user. The creation of stable communities depends on a socially, economically, and physically diverse mix of residents intent on participating within the community. The life of the city or town is a result of the activity that takes place within it. It is this activity that is not only intended to create the city network, but also to develop a more socially responsible attitude toward the protection and growth of the community. "From helping to maintain it, to initiating security, education or employment programs, to willingly committing resources to ensure the health of it, active, engaged residents can become the neighborhood's biggest asset" (*Consumer Reports,* May 1996).

The needs of the user are emphasized, as the intent of the created environment is to build communities, not just houses. New Urbanism encourages a pedestrian nature of the block, building, and street. It also details guidelines for zoning and design to ensure that the built forms are interrelated with the consideration of the surrounding, walking environment (see Figure 17.3). In many ways, these New Urbanism strategies were a direct response to the suburban trends toward sprawl (see Figure 17.4) and fortressing, the most dramatic version of which is the *gated community.*

GATED COMMUNITY CRIME STUDY

A study was undertaken by this author (Atlas, 2000) to evaluate the changing crime patterns of four gated communities in one city that extensively uses street closures in South Florida.

The gatehouses or guard gates screen all nonresidents entering the neighborhood by having the car stop at a stop sign, and then writing the license plate of the car and entering the information on a daily time log. The guard then allows entry of the car by lifting up a gate.

Keystone Point, located in North Miami, is a residential area comprised of six islands, and has three land entrances. The Keystone Point Community is east of Biscayne Boulevard and surrounded

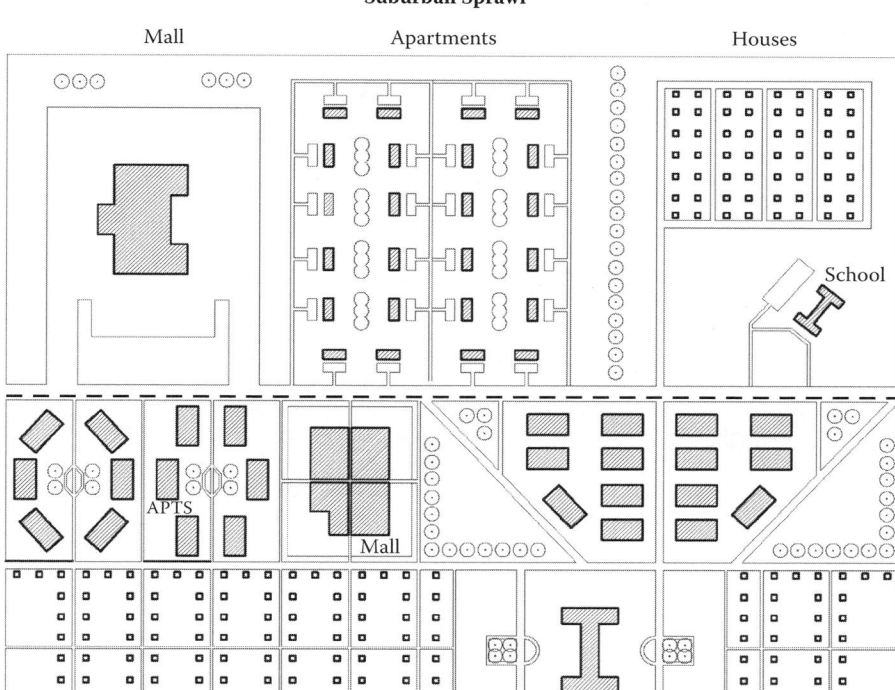

FIGURE 17.2 A diagram showing the differences between a traditional neighborhood and suburban sprawl.

FIGURE 17.3 An example of a New Urbanist home in Celebration, Florida; also uses a lot of CPTED in the design of the fencing, porches, window orientation, and landscaping.

FIGURE 17.4   Urban sprawl is overtaking inexpensive lands, and this development goes right to the edge of the foothills. This housing community is totally dependent on the car for services.

by Biscayne Bay. The residents are professionals in the middle to upper income class. The guard gate for Keystone Point was installed in May 1991. Crime data was analyzed from 1990 to 1997. Burglary and theft decreased dramatically over the study period. There was a 14% decrease in theft and a 54% decrease for burglary crimes. However, during the 8 years of the study, there were spikes of crime increases, and then a subsequent decrease. The pattern of the crime was a wave, ebbing and flowing.

The Belle Meade community, located within the city of Miami, is predominately white middle-class, single-family homeowners. The community is comprised of almost 400 homes that are east of Biscayne Boulevard and surrounded by Biscayne Bay. The residents started lobbying for increased security measures in 1982 and received five street barricades in 1987. The residents petitioned the Dade County Commissioners for approval to set up a special taxing district to pay for guards and a guardhouse. In 1991, a guardhouse was installed on Belle Meade Island, which supports 52 homes. A second guardhouse was added to the primary entrance to the entire Belle Meade areas in 1992. All vehicular traffic into Belle Meade passes through the gates. The barricades or guardhouse does not affect pedestrian traffic or those approaching by water. Crime data was gathered and analyzed from 1985 to 1996. The residents of Belle Meade have the perception that crime has gone down in their area, while crime reports show that the rate of crime has remained relatively constant. Robbery has decreased, burglary has decreased, and larceny has stayed relatively constant, as has aggravated assault. Since the barricades were put in in 1987, homes have doubled in value.

Do Gates Matter?

By the number of incidents reported for each crime in the Keystone Point area, it is clear that the gates do not make a significant difference in the increase or decrease of crime or deterrence to criminals. They do make the residents feel safer, and correspondingly increases the real estate value of the property and surrounding area.

In the city of Miami Shores, Florida, there appears to be a positive real estate value relationship with street closures (Table 17.1). The assessed value of the real estate was depreciating during the late 1980s (*Miami Vice* years), and after the street closure program went into effect in 1989, the assessed value of real estate has been steadily climbing. In the four years following the installation

TABLE 17.1
City of Miami Shores Crime Chart

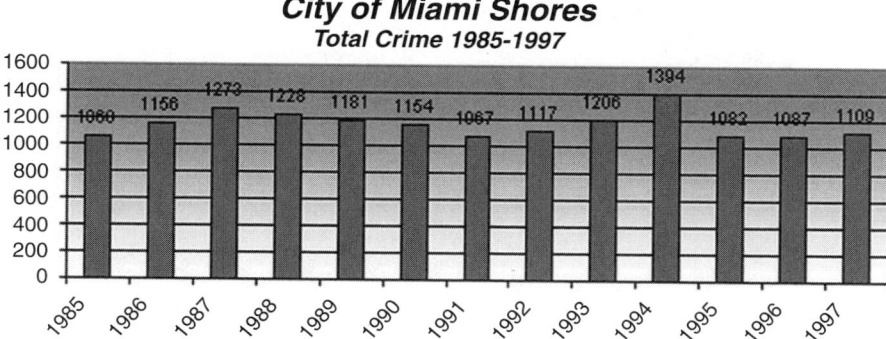

Source: Miami Shores Police Department .
Note: barricades installed in 1990.

of street closures, there was a 6.12% increase from 1994 to 1995, a 0.86 % increase from 1995 to 1996, a 0.03% increase from 1996 to 1997, and a 3.72 % increase from 1997 to 1998.

Although some residents opposed the barricade, mostly because of the inconvenience of not having immediate access to their homes, the majority of the residents (as revealed by several voter referendums) support the traffic calming and closures measures as a means of improving the sense of community and neighborhood. Although not as exclusive as a gated community, street barriers do deter crime, reduce unwanted cross traffic, and increase the difficulty for the criminal to commit crime in the neighborhood and easily escape to the interstate highway to flee quickly (see Figure 17.5 and Figure 17.6).

FIGURE 17.5 Miami Shores, Florida, used many tools of the traffic-calming pallet. Street closures along with traffic calming kept cars in residential neighborhoods to only those people who belonged there or had business there.

FIGURE 17.6 An example of a residential road cut off and barricaded from entering the major arterial street in Miami Shores, Florida. The restricted access changed how people use the neighborhood. Pedestrian activity increased dramatically as residents felt safe to come back onto the streets.

WHAT IS A NEIGHBORHOOD?

Neighborhoods are a mixture of people and uses. The delicate balance of traffic between pedestrian and vehicular activity can make a neighborhood thrive or die.

Conventional traffic engineers abhor road congestion, viewing it as the blight of modern cities. Yet in recent years, a school of unconventional traffic engineers has emerged that views congestion as good for pedestrians and businesses. According to City Routes, City Rights (Conservation Law Foundation, January, 1998), "streets should serve everyone who uses them, not just drivers." The concept of livable or walkable communities is consistent with the precepts of New Urbanism and CPTED. Walkable communities do pose a paradox, however. Congested streets with shoppers and residents are good for local business, but generate so much traffic that they worsen gridlock. Examples of successful walkable communities are South Beach (Miami Beach), Main Street in Miami Lakes, Mizner Place in Boca Raton, and the Beaches area of Toronto.

Building or widening roads has been the traditional strategy to deal with traffic congestion, even in dense urban areas where houses and shops are bulldozed if they stand in the way. That is how Overtown, Miami's historic African-American district, vanished as a livable or walkable community in the 1960s. Construction of Interstate 95 sliced the community in half, destroying hundreds of homes and businesses and displacing thousands of families. Some communities are burying their expressways, so they can free up large amounts of valuable real estate and not provide the visual eyesore and physical obtrusions of traffic barriers.

Do the New Urbanism strategies of mixed use, mixed income, and 5-minute walking radius through focused congestion of pedestrian and vehicular activity conflict with the CPTED goal of avoiding conflicting use of non-residents trespassing and having unauthorized access into a neighborhood? This conflict has brought the debate about gated and barricaded communities to a head. No, these concepts are not in conflict with the idea of land use diversity originally introduced by Jane Jacobs at the beginning of the CPTED movement. Jacobs often promoted just this kind of neighborhood as a way to minimize opportunities for many types of urban crime. Nevertheless, many CPTED practitioners take access control to an unwanted extreme. As a result, this conflict has brought the debate about gated and barricaded communities to a head.

New Urbanism takes form through the use of the following outlined planning and design guidelines, which in many ways are in direct accordance with some of the principles of Second-Generation

CPTED described in earlier chapters. In fact, the New Urbanism principles illustrate one practical way to put those principles into practice, especially social cohesion and neighborhood threshold. The key New Urbanism principles are:

1. The Neighborhood Has a Discernable Center and an Edge

The creation of a focus and limit forms boundaries to define a social identity and sense of community—a "circling of the wagons," if you will, through the use of infrastructure and natural barriers to form the boundary. The center is often a square or green, and sometimes a busy or memorable street intersection. A transit stop would be located at this center. The incorporation of public transportation becomes an integral factor in the success of the planned community as it hopes to disengage itself from the use of the automobile. "Public transportation is made possible by clustering pedestrian neighborhoods and offices along lines that can be readily serviced by buses, trolleys or light rail lines" (Neighborhoods Reborn," *Consumer Reports,* May 1996).

This transit center becomes even more important in the social order of the community as it moves away from the personal automobile use, and transportation outside of the neighborhood is dependant upon public transit. The transition toward public transit creates a greater need for a recognized center and station point for commuting and social interaction.

2. Certain Prominent Sites are Reserved for Civic Buildings

Buildings for meeting, education, religion, or culture are located at the termination of streets or vistas at the Neighborhood Center. Civic buildings, planned in coordination with public open spaces, are prominently sited, ideally terminating vistas and enclosing streets to serve as landmarks. These "landmarks" serve dual roles of supporting the public infrastructure necessary for the community and fostering a sense of civic pride (see Figure 17.7). The use of public infrastructure such as post offices, meeting halls, police departments, fire departments, courthouses, and so on, gives form and hierarchy to the neighborhood core. The neighborhood core is the "downtown," and must support the basic needs of the family.

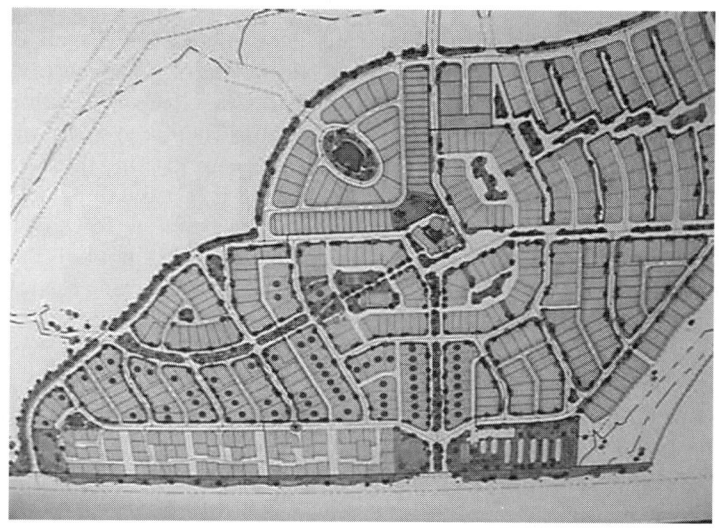

FIGURE 17.7 Civano, Arizona—a New Urbanist town. Their site plan shows the mixed-use zoning and the radial nature of the community.

FIGURE 17.8   Mizner Park in Boca Raton, Florida, is a good working example of mixed-use residential and commercial property that is thriving.

3. Buildings at the Neighborhood Center are Placed Close to the Street

This creates a strong sense of place. The placement of buildings in a uniform facade close to the street defines the space of an intimate street. It is possible to achieve a difference in scale by compacting the street. The feel of the urban city form is created for the core downtown, making the space "feel" different to the user, both the pedestrian and the driver. The streets are made "skinny." The recognized change in scale, form, and texture brings a different life to the space and through detailing, the street is relinquished to the pedestrian (see Figure 17.8). "Narrow streets—as thin as 26 feet wide—and tight, right-angled corners are a lot easier for walkers, and probably safer as well, because they force drivers to slow down" (Malone, 1995, p. 47).

4. Most of the Dwellings are within a 5-Minute Walk of the Center

This distance averages one-quarter of a mile. Herein lies the crux of the issue of the walkability of the town design. The 5-minute walk is not only to the center of town, but to what is necessary to allow the residents to access the necessities of life without the use of the automobile. This also strengthens the argument for the incorporation of civic infrastructure at a central location or town center for ease of access and meeting. The concepts and codes restricting the use of the car within the structure of the community upon which the development is based will be defeated without the presence of a strong physical and economic town center. If residents are forced outside of the community to fulfill common household needs, then the community will not only stop being a viable walking community, but it also will become dependant upon a neighboring metropolis or city.

"The well-structured neighborhood is the springboard for our relationship to a larger world. It is particularly important to two age groups: adolescents and the elderly" (Plater-Zyberk, 1996, p. 58). Reorienting the neighborhood to a pedestrian nature allows both the elderly and young to be active participants in the community through a more viable mode of transportation. The modern city is planned around the use of an automobile for all facets of life, leaving those without an automobile at a disadvantage (see Figure 17.9 and Figure 17.10).

5. There are a Variety of Dwelling Types Within the Neighborhood

These usually take the form of houses, row-houses, apartments, and mixed-use, such that younger and older people, singles and families, the poor and the wealthy may find places to live. Housing types are varied in size, type, and price to differentiate the kind of mix found in the city (see Figure 17.11). Diversity within the community allows for growth and learning, for all social and economic strata, for all those who participate. This is contrary to modern developments.

> So the new subdivisions go up behind ocher-colored stucco walls, six feet high, with guards and gates between the public roads and the inner sanctum of the residential streets. Other kinds of barriers defend something nearly as dear to suburbanites as their own skins, property values. Homeowners are isolated by design from apartments, shops, public squares, or anything else that might attract people with less money or of a different Race. Deed restrictions and community associations see to it that no one will ever bring down the tone of the neighborhood by turning his living room into a beauty parlor. Success for a development lies in freezing for eternity the social and economic class of the original purchaser. (Alder, 1995, p. 44).

FIGURE 17.9 A mixed-use facility with ground floor business, and residential apartments above. The mixed use provides users over a greater time span for eyes on the street.

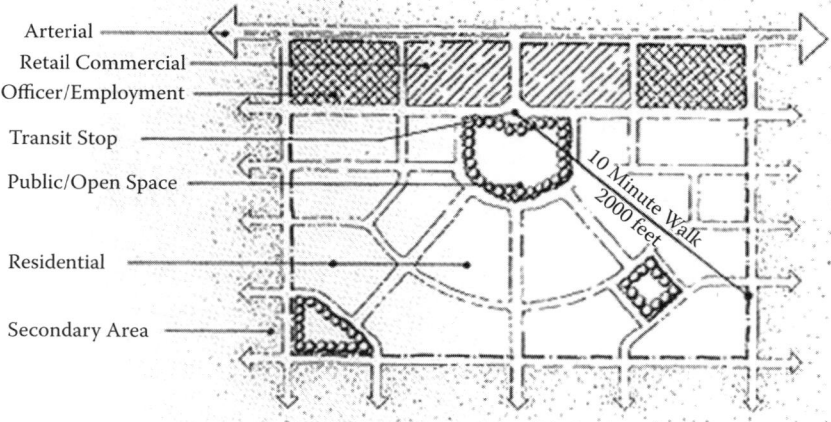

FIGURE 17.10 This diagram illustrates the concept of the New Urbanism ten-minute walking radius for a mixed-use town.

6. A Small Ancillary Building is Permitted Within the Back Yard of Each House

It may be used as one rental unit, or as a place of work. This perhaps takes on the greater role of displacing the conventional two-car garage allowing for the reinvention of the porch. "The porch becomes a symbolic element of neighborliness," says Richard Wagner of Goucher College in Baltimore. (Cosco, 1995) The porch provides a safe place for social interaction with the community through the proximity of the house to the street and the incorporation of sidewalks to encourage walking. A stronger relationship is formed with the casual passerby, as well as, neighbors (see Figure 17.12).

FIGURE 17.11   The diversity of a neighborhood is what gives it uniqueness and richness of character.

7. There are Small Playgrounds Quite Near Every Dwelling

This distance should not be more than one-eighth of a mile. Squares and parks are distributed throughout the neighborhoods, designed as settings for informal social activity and recreation as well as larger civic gatherings. The importance of these gathering spaces in the urban fabric must not be overlooked, as their role in creating a sense of togetherness is to serve as a watch points for the neighborhood (see Figure 17.13).

The use of designated play areas provides space for children and adults to meet in the absence of large lots. The distance of one-eighth mile also keeps children within a discernable neighborhood boundary. The intensified awareness of the pedestrian and the bicycle allows children to safely commute within the area.

FIGURE 17.12   The capable guardians of the house use the porch as their perch to view the local neighborhood activities.

FIGURE 17.13   The community play area is within earshot and eyesight of the homes in the neighborhood.

8. There is an Elementary School Close Enough so that Most Children Can Walk from Their Dwelling

This distance should not be more than one mile. "The research shows that the optimum size for elementary schools is less than 500 students. The small elementary school is best located in a greenbelt serving at most two to three neighborhoods" (Plater-Zyberk, 1996, p. 58).

In the age of both parents having full-time occupations, the ability of the child to take on a more independent role in the family and society is created in the small school system. This system provides the children with better teacher to student ratios encouraging a higher degree of learning and independence.

9. The Streets Within the Neighborhood Act as a Connected Grid Network

This provides a variety of itineraries and disperses traffic congestion. Traffic congestion is looked at in two fashions, through that of the driver and through that of the pedestrian. The incorporation of a grid network provides alternate routes and "shortcuts" but also further encourages walking within the community by the breakdown of long blocks. By car, getting to the other side of the block may take only a few seconds however; on the long, winding block of the suburbs, this may seem insurmountable. The breakup of the block through new streets and alleyways permits the resident to walk, not drive, to the corner store. The goal of the successful walking community is to make driving more of a hassle than to walk for the same task even if at the same distance.

10. The Streets are Relatively Narrow and Shaded by Rows of Trees

This slows traffic, creating an environment for the pedestrian and the bicycle. Walking is encouraged by addition of sidewalks, shade trees, front porches, narrow streets, and the inclusion of commercial, recreational, occupational, and worship areas located a short walk away from the houses. Creating pleasant walking paths promotes residential foot traffic to the normal daily-life activities (see Figure 17.14). The perception of risk in walking is reduced when there is less traffic, and barriers are provided between the pedestrian and danger. The use of trees, lighting, and parked cars defines the areas of this protection (see Figure 17.15).

FIGURE 17.14 At CitiPlace in West Palm Beach, Florida, the city razed a drug-infested, abandoned neighborhood and out of the ashes came a mixed-use New Urbanism community with retail, commercial, and residential facilities. It now is an end destination for people to live, work, and play.

FIGURE 17.15 Designing homes to have functional front porches is important for the health and welfare of a community. The porch provides the opportunity to relax and watch evenets unfold in the neighborhood and facilitates natural surveillance by the local guardians.

11. Parking Lots and Garage Doors Rarely Face the Streets

Parking is relegated to the rear of buildings, usually access by alleys. The moving of the garage to an ancillary building at the back or side of the house removes the car, and replaces the porch. Parking in commercial areas follow suit with moving the buildings forward to face the street, forming the outdoor mall, and placing parking spaces in the inner block, or designated landscaped areas. The car is relegated to the back seat, pardon the pun, and the design is geared toward the experience of the pedestrian.

12. There are Shops and Offices at the Core and Edge of the Neighborhood

The shops should be sufficiently varied to supply the weekly needs of a household. A convenience store is the most important among them, as it allows for residents to meet their essential needs

FIGURE 17.16 Main Street USA is a concept expanding that brings commercial and retail stability to otherwise decaying downtowns. Making the old or historic downtowns attractive for business and recreation provides economic stability from the draw of suburban sprawl.

without needing to travel a distance that might require a car. The variety of stores and businesses are important to the economic base of the community, providing necessary goods and services, as well as jobs and production, for a sustainable community (see Figure 17.16).

13. The Neighborhood is Organized to be Self-Governing

A formal association debates and decides on matters of maintenance, security, and physical change. Although this has the makings of a super-charged condominium association, the residents are able to assume a more responsible role in the growth of their community. A sense of ownership and communal partnership fosters continued maintenance, growth, and collective security.

In 1998, the Department of Housing Urban Development (HUD) granted a total of $507 million to 22 cities in 16 states across the country for HOPE VI Revitalization Programs for Severely Distressed Public Housing. The money was to be given to local public housing authorities to overcome crowding, poverty, and crime to create low-rise, private, single-family and duplex structures integrated into the surrounding community (AIArchitect, Dec. 1998).

By the year 2000, HUD had awarded almost $3 billion for 104 HOPE VI grants. The HOPE VI program strives to revitalize communities with physical improvements to public housing, management improvements, and social and community services to address residents' needs by replacing the most severely depressed public-housing units in the Countrycountry, and giving residents the chance to rebuild their lives, with offering a clean, safe, decent place to live. (see Figure 17.17). The philosophy of the HOPE VI developments is to build communities, rather than institutions—to build neighborhoods, not projects.

Architects of the grant projects developed residential designs that combine New Urbanism concepts with a rigorously practical CPTED

FIGURE 17.17 Safe neighborhoods encourage and invite residents to use the streets. This picture shows local nannies taking the kids out for a stroll.

FIGURE 17.18 Many gated communities try to recreate the strong symbolic entrance of a fort or castle. It is mostly symbolic as more often than not the gates are not manned and the gate arms are not working or placed in an open position.

approach. The designers and planners have created neighborhoods that foster a sense of community and connect to surrounding neighborhoods by defining public versus private spaces, establishing definable and defensible spaces, and addressing the needs for commercial and pedestrian activity. The goal was to create urban in-fill residential communities that blend into surrounding neighborhoods, while removing the stigma of public housing by creating mixed-income, mixed-use neighborhoods.

In recent years, the designing of traditional towns and communities has been embraced by developers, homebuilders, civic officials, and HUD, but has not been widely accepted in some academia, where modernism rules (*Architectural Record*, Nov. 1998: 48). Critics suggest that New Urbanism hasn't developed a sophisticated vocabulary, and suffers from lack of clarity in its use of forms, often manifesting in the form of "gated communities"—the new fortress of modern sprawl (see Figure 17.18).

In 1997, it was estimated that there were in excess of 20,000-gated communities, housing over 3 million housing units (Blakely and Schneider.1997:7). Approximately 16 million Americans live in gated communities (Benson, 1998). In some areas, citizens have moved from organizing neighborhood watches to prevent crime, to orchestrating campaigns to force undesirable neighbors to move out. Clearly, we need better alternatives for 21st century urban development. (see Figure 17.19).

THE NEW URBANISM/SPRAWL CONTROVERSY

Not all policy makers and academics agree that New Urbanism is a move forward. Some believe that modern, sprawling suburbs—with their focus on confusing, curvilinear street, random cul-de -sacs, and single use zoning with single-family residences—produce safer communities than New Urbanism. Some claim that crime rates are higher in sprawl cities versus smart growth cities. However, on closer inspection those studies tend to confuse smart growth, CPTED, and sprawl. For example, Burnett and Villarreal (2004) studied crime rates in a number of American cities and concluded sprawl cities are safer than smart growth cities. However that study compares apples to oranges. It glosses over the reality that since smart growth and New Urbanism are so new, no cities in America can truly be considered smart growth. There may be small neighborhoods that are smart

FIGURE 17.19   The gatehouse serves as a point to check visitors and vendors as to their legitimate purpose for being on-site. The residents can effortlessly pass through the right. The purpose of the gatehouse is for access control, but at what cost, and how many communities and neighborhoods can really afford this service?

growth/New Urbanism, but it is highly dubious to study crime at the level of a whole city and claim one theory works over another.

Even within neighborhoods, critical New Urbanism research is questionable. For example, one study by the English Association of Police Chief Officers examined two neighborhoods of similar size: one neighborhood that employed New Urbanism and the other a more traditional neighborhood that employed CPTED (in the UK CPTED is called Secure By Design). They discovered higher crime rates in the New Urbanism neighborhood compared to the Secured by Design neighborhood (http://www.operationscorpion.org.uk/design_out_crime/policing_urbanism.htm).

The English report concluded that New Urbanism differs from CPTED in some fundamentally important ways:

- Secure by Design maximizes the quantity of private property, since people are more likely to express ownership over their own property, whereas New Urbanism maximizes public areas.
- New Urbanism promotes walkable streets, not cul cul-de de-sacs. This makes pedestrians more vulnerable at night.
- New Urbanism places cars in areas that are difficult to watch, like rear alleyways. Secure by Design places them in areas that are easy to watch. In the UK this is frequently achieved by extensive use of CCTV in public areas. (www.operationscorpion.org.uk/design_out_crime/policing_urbanism.htm).

This critique is important for a number of reasons. First is it reveals that, regardless of the urban design style, the devil is in the details. There is no particular reason why rear alleyways in New Urbanism need to be designed so that surveillance is so difficult. That is only the case if designers pay no attention to CPTED concepts. In principle, the two concepts are very compatible.

Second, the English report glosses over the distinction of private versus public property. New Urbanism theory, as with all smart growth concepts (see chapter on CPTED Implementation) does not discourage private space. Poorly designed New Urbanism might, but that relates to the quality of design detail, not the theory of design. Instead, New Urbanism echoes the original formulation of

Jane Jacobs by breaking urban locations down into a hierarchy of space, from public, semi-public, semi-private, and private. If designers are properly training in CPTED and understand the basic territorial concepts of hierarchy of space, there is no reason that CPTED and New Urbanism cannot work together.

Finally, traditional CPTED (and Secure by Design for that matter) and New Urbanism do not deal with the social structure of neighborhoods. That is why Second Generation CPTED was developed (see chapter on Second Generation CPTED). Second Generation CPTED returns to the original formulations of early CPTED theory and addresses the reasons why people exhibit territoriality over their neighborhood. It is no wonder people living inside a fortress vehemently protect their own property—they can more easily keep outsiders away when they can see where the walls begin and end.

English researchers have compared New Urbanist neighborhoods with Defensible Space neighborhoods, which maximize private areas, limit densities, and mixed land uses, and close or eliminate alleys. They found that the New Urbanist neighborhoods had five times the crime rate and three times the policing cost of Defensible Space neighborhoods. (Town and O'Toole, 2005). New Urbanist neighborhoods typically discourage closed off streets or cul-de-sacs, but a British crime survey found that houses along grid streets were more likely to be burglarized than those in a cul-de-sac. New Urban Designs prefer more footpaths and areas that restrict cars, but this often prevents emergency vehicles from accessing an area in the event of a crime or emergency. New Urban neighborhoods urge use of common space for gathering, instilling in people a sense of protecting their communities from crime, but evidence suggests that people are more likely to protect private property from crime than public areas. New Urbanist planning advocates high-density housing and mixed land to provide more community interaction, but neighborhoods in England that contained only single-family, detached homes had the fewest crime problems. (Town and O'Toole, 2005).

As stated earlier, the devil is in the details. What is defensible space to one designer, can easily be New Urbanism to another. The English British research attempted to clarify these design elements, however some of the defensible space concepts are confirmed with gated communities and excessive use of access control. Unfortunately, as shown in the Miami research above, gated communities are not necessarily safer. Further, the reality of urban life is that fortress dwellers must eventually leave their fort and interact with the rest of society. When they do, there is a whole set of social, conflict resolution, and cultural skills they will need, including cultural values of diversity and inclusion, that are very difficult to express within the confines of an urban fortress. A New Urbanism that incorporates both basic CPTED and Second Generation CPTED is precisely the kind of urban development that can provide safe opportunities to achieve a better balance in urban society.

Criminologist Tim Crowe has proposed some basic CPTED strategies that are New Urbanist friendly (Crowe, 2000). They include the following.

1. Provide Clear Border Definition of Controlled Space

Through boundary or border definition, the user and the observer must be able to recognize space as public or private. The recognition of ownership allows for those illegitimate users to be spotted. The intention of the potential offender is to commit an act without detection or risk of being recognized. The defining of boundaries declares an ownership of space and thus creates a sense of territoriality. The declared space, when projected at a human scale, may then reach a point of then becoming defensible.

2. Provide Clearly Marked Transitional Zones

Transitional zones are a form of boundary definition and access control. A space where the user is made more clearly aware, through the design of the environment, that a change of ownership is taking place. The effort made to mark the entrance into the space reduces the range of excuses for improper behavior.

FIGURE 17.20   This mini-park is located in between a group of homes that can watch the activities from their second stories. Site plantings permit good natural surveillance from the street and surrounding homes.

3. Relocation of Gathering Areas

The relocation of gathering spaces to areas of good natural surveillance and access control enables those spaces to become more active and likely to support the activity, encouraging public participation. (see Figure 17.20).

This becomes important in the public sector with the selection of sites for civic buildings and gathering spaces. The feeling of safety and pride in the designed space fosters the encouragement of participation within the community.

4. Place Safe Activities in Unsafe Locations

The premise of safety in numbers is used as safe activities bring normal or safe users as magnets to control behavior. The unsafe location must be within reason with respect to the activity pursued. A critical density of users must be reached to change the acceptability of behavior patterns.

5. Place Unsafe Activities in Safe Locations

Vulnerable activities placed in areas of good natural surveillance and controlled space allows for the owners of the space to increase the perception of risk to offenders. The controlled atmosphere maintains a level of accountability for the offender and provides security to those attempting to act in accordance.

6. Redesignate the Use of Space to Provide Natural Barriers

Defining the boundaries of ownership through the use of distance, natural terrain, and landscape barriers. This may be accomplished by proper land planning and landscape design. This process in effect results in a lower general cost to the owner, and may create spaces more conducive to the natural environment. (see Figure 17.21).

7. Improve Scheduling of Space

The effective use of space lowers risk, as the density of space may be regulated for optimum physical and social attributes. The activities create a sense of place, and controls behavior through

FIGURE 17.21 Street furniture is magnet for activity. What kind of activity depends on the mix of people and the level of supervision.

recognition of the intended user. Proper scheduling legitimizes various users to achieve their individual goals in accordance with the structure of the community. (see Figure 17.22).

8. Redesign or Revamp Space to Increase the Perception of Natural Surveillance

Natural surveillance is simply the presence of eyes. The offender only perceives risk when able to be observed, thus through the removal of hiding places and the incorporation of improved sitelines, both natural and mechanical, increases the risk of detection, deterring the presence of offenders.

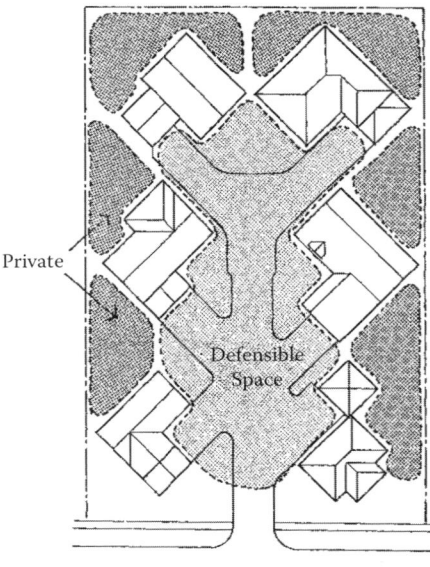

FIGURE 17.22 A suburban housing development in Mississauga, Ontario, Canada sited the homes in this development at 45 degrees to allow every front door and porch to have a line of site with the entrance of their street. The front yards and garages are part of defensible space of their neightbors, and neightbors can watch what is going on in their street easier by the site placement. The back yards are fenced to make them off limits to unauthorized users. This site plan was approved in the 1980s by the local police and has proven to be very successful in reducing residential burglaries.

The redesign of space must also pertain to the nature of the user, to increase the ability of the space to support more legitimate users.

9. OVERCOME DISTANCE AND ISOLATION

More is not always better as objects in the environment may create distance and isolation. The use of walls and objects to provide protection must be used properly. Communication and observance of the user increases the perception of natural surveillance. The opaque wall defines ownership, but it may also serve as a hiding place or barrier from protection on the outside. The walls also become obstacles for the legitimate users, i.e. police and rescue personnel. Open space lowers the cost of construction and improves natural surveillance of the environment in allowing for visual connection.

A SHEEP IN WOLF'S CLOTHING

By now it should be apparent that New Urbanism and CPTED are compatible. Much of the dissimilarity between New Urbanism and CPTED results from the perception of the respective goals. New Urbanism is viewed as a planning principle, mainly of new towns and developments. Crime Prevention Through Environmental Design (CPTED) is seen as a special security tactic to be employed to fix public housing or urban in-fill design. But is that an accurate view? Are we up to our necks in alligators in the swamp of residential infill? (See Figure 17.23.)

In previous chapters on the history of CPTED, we see another reality. The early neighborhood studies about community control and social disorganization at the University of Chicago School showed a CPTED legacy quite different than a security tactic. The pioneering planning work of Jane Jacobs also did not envision safe neighborhoods (and by extension the CPTED emerging from those ideas) as a security tactic. There may be crime opportunity reduction strategies in CPTED, like access control, however that is done in the service of enhancing a sense of neighborhood territorial control. In fact, New Urbanism and CPTED share similar neighborhood development goals.

The ownership, and sense of ownership, of space is the key to the two strategies. Developing a sense of territoriality is a main CPTED principle and has done much to shape the ideals of New Urbanism. "In order to nurture a feeling of pride and sense of belonging and ownership, it is important to design buildings or developments that are a collection of individual spaces. People need and want to have space they consider theirs and where they can express themselves." (Hope VI Developments. Aug/Sept 1996, p. 4.) Perhaps, now more than ever is the design of the neighborhood and home environment important. The advance of technology is allowing for more home offices and less need for travel. (see Figure 17.24). This is a goal of New Urbanism, to incorporate all the responsibilities of everyday life into a smaller distance making a walkable community neighborhood. A defined space where one can feel safe in both home and work raises the current level of the quality of life. Many designers and others overlook this basic point: CPTED serves to raise the quality of life through the creation of a sense of safety and the promotion of a healthier community.

The challenge for CPTED and New Urbanism is in the details. For many designers, urban

FIGURE 17.23 Sometimes we feel like we are in a swamp and up to our neck in alligators. There is a careful balance between social density and being overcrowded. Most people want to have a thriving neighborhood, but not sacrifice every shred of privacy.

FIGURE 17.24 Parking turf wars in shopping centers and aparment complexes is a reflection on the value and scarcity of real estate.

planners, and architects, CPTED is perceived as a security precept first, and is thus relegated to barbed wire and bars on windows. This lack of understanding emerges in the difference between symbolic and the real barriers. The real barrier is that which will directly deny one's ability to occupy a space, whereas a symbolic barrier is a definer of space that may be overcome and is primarily for visual clarity. White picket fences are more than creating a traditional town look; it is enforcing a definition of a hierarchy of territorial space, from private to public space. (see Figure 17.25). The three-foot wood picket will not stop the hardened thief, but it makes clear definition that unwanted users intending to victimize others, are at risk. That is the essence of territoriality.

New Urbanism proposes a fine network of interconnecting streets. In contrast, Crime Prevention Through Environmental Design (CPTED) may elect the closing of streets to form "mini-neighborhoods" where traffic flow is restricted to arterial roads within the community. The restriction of street entrances to these main points helps residents create their own sense of community. It also helps residents identify and challenge illegitimate users intent on victimizing residents. The street will have a lower vehicular activity level and will be able to become inhabited with pedestrian traffic, such as children and adults playing. (see Figure 17.26). "An interconnecting pattern of streets provides multiple routes that diffuse traffic congestion," states Peter Katz (1994).

Does design, such as this, provide too many routes of departure by unwanted users and offenders? "Limiting access and egress to one opening would mean that criminals and their clients would have to enter a small mini-neighborhood to transact their business, and they would have to leave the same way they had come in. There would no longer be a multitude of escape routes. A call to the police by residents would mean that criminals would meet the police on their way out." (Nasar and Brown, (1996.) The community awareness brings a sense of responsibility and encourages an active participation of the residents to police their own environment. The perceived territoriality

FIGURE 17.25 Picket fences and porches are the look that New Urbanists want to recreate a time and era of small towns, main streets, and a sense of community. The fencing creates a subtle form of territoriality and access control. The property looks like it is well maintained and that trespassers would be challenged.

and natural surveillance, and the limitation of escape routes deter offenders as criminal activities become too risky. The goal is not to create a series of fortressed, walled communities cut-off from the rest of society, but to empower residents and their role in the community.

The inherent nature to build safer towns based on human response is seen in the reversion of planning and design principles to the traditional neighborhood design. The use of the porch in New Urbanist towns is a particular example of this reversion, as it has both the role of an outside room supporting a response to the climatic environment and a media for social interaction. The presence of the social interaction allows for another CPTED principle to be employed, natural surveillance. Natural surveillance is implemented through a mix of activities and social interaction.

The encouragement of the walking community brings about the natural community Crime Watch, with concerned citizens to create natural surveillance and access control through territoriality (see Figure 17.27). The presence of legitimate users serves notice to the potential offender that a space has defined ownership through the physical design detailing and the social aspects of

FIGURE 17.26 Many new shopping plazas invite retail, commercial, and recreational activities with a main street feel and scale.

FIGURE 17.27 This picture demonstrates a courtyard concept. These walkup apartments are built above their garages and have good natural surveillance of their common area spaces. CPTED lighting and landscaping facilitate good surveillance.

user interaction. The interaction of residents within the neighborhood also strengthens the sense of togetherness and community identity (see Figure 17.28 and Figure 17.29).

The incorporation of town commercial centers and the local stores into the fabric of the community supports the importance of a social identity.

The old concept of the neighborhood store, with loyal repeat customers who protected their local businesses, ended after World War II. People used to live in apartments above retail businesses, thus providing the perception of surveillance at night and on weekends. However, stores and shopping centers now stand as islands within mixed land use areas that are constantly changing and often volatile, both financially and socially. These new development activities also changed the social environment. People no longer recognized each other when they went shopping. Territorial identity and proprietary concerns for the old neighborhood store vanished (Fennelly, and Lombardi, 1997).

FIGURE 17.28 Many of our New Urbanist communities are founded on Old World principles and experiences and scale. This picture demonstrates the typical European downtown scale with a strong sense of ground-level retail connection, and upper-level housing with balconies from which to watch the streets.

FIGURE 17.29 Many previously abandoned downtowns are being restored as safe and fun business magnets.

Knowledge of such subtleties allows for the recognition of shared concepts in the design and guidelines of New Urbanist and CPTED communities. Both philosophies are hybrids of each other. Thus, where one may say that CPTED is for "inner-city housing projects" and New Urbanism is for the design of "cute, neo-traditional towns," in reality the strengths lie in their cooperation. New Urbanist towns and developments are safer with the incorporation of CPTED concepts of territoriality, natural surveillance, and access control. The scope of work that now must be done is a collaboration of philosophies to create a more unified effort of design. We must move beyond, creative design versus security debates. The effects of design go beyond simply making attractive spaces. In architectural terms, the social responsibility of design will now enable the form and detail of the space to allow its function to take place effectively and safely.

The future of planning and design lies in the awareness and use of CPTED and New Urbanism principles to provide safe structures and communities for a society in which many urban cores are in decline. As we can see by successful walkable neighborhoods, results will prove to be physically successful as well as contributing to a positive change in the social structure and relationships within city neighborhoods.

CONCLUSIONS

New Urbanism is becoming a new source of fixing today's urban scale problems with projects in many cities around the United States. Henry G. Cisneros, former Secretary of HUD, has called for the implementation of New Urbanism and CPTED in urban revitalization grants that were recently issued. Stressing the use of small-scale communities, Cisneros states, "Residents have a better idea about who belongs there and who is intruding . . . involved residents can quickly spot and report suspicious activity. Use of the concept of defensible space has been successful in Washington, D.C., the South Bronx, Dayton, and in other areas where it can work" (Cisneros, 1995, p. 361).

Attitudes are changing toward the design and development of safe neighborhoods. Both New Urbanism and CPTED strategies need to become common in future development. The U.S. Department of Housing and Urban Development (HUD) is one agency at the forefront as it has the ability to bring the two together in many new development/redevelopment public sites. More than 75% of the new HUD sites will use New Urbanism and CPTED principles to create what seem to be well-designed developments that reflect, and are sensitive to neighboring communities; they will likely set a new standard for public housing. Although the perception remains that CPTED is a fix to current development, it is important to note that it is most effective when used in the initial planning stages. If we are to make a difference in the quality of life, designers must learn, apply, and teach advanced and up-to-date CPTED strategies of the 21st century. That is how we will best move forward.

REFERENCES

Adler, J. (1995) Bye-bye suburban dream. *Newsweek,* May 15, 41–45.

Atlas, R. (2004) Designing safe communities. *Strategies for Safe and Sustainable Communities.* Landscape Architectural Registrations Boards Foundation, Vienna, Virginia.

Atlas, R. (2002) The sustainability of CPTED: Less magic more science! *CPTED Journal,* 1(1).

Atlas, R. (1994) Environmental barriers to crime. *Ergonomics in Design.* 9–16.

Atlas, R. (1994) The impact on crime of street closures and barricades: A Florida case study. *Security Journal,* 5(3).

Blakely, E. J. and Schneider, M. G. (1997) *Fortress America: Gated Communities in the United States.* Washington, DC: Brookings Institute Press.

Benson, B. (1998) *To Serve and Protect: Privatization and Community in Criminal Justice.* New York: New York University Press.

Burnett, S. H. and Villarreal, P. (2004) *Smart Growth = Crime, Congestion and Poverty: Brief Analysis #473.* Dallas, Texas National Center for Policy Analysis.

Cisneros, H. (1995, October 23) Cisneros calls for "New Urbanism" stressing small-scale communities. *MDR Current Development,* 361.

Clarke, R. V. (1992) *Situational Crime Prevention: Successful Case Studies.* Albany, NY: Harrow and Heston.

Consumer Reports (1996) Neighborhoods Reborn. May.

Conservation Law Foundation (1998) Take Back Your Streets. January.

Crowe, T. D. (1991) *Crime Prevention Through Environmental Design.* Boston: Butterworth-Heinemann.

Duany, A. S. and Plater-Zyberk, E. (1996, January) The thirteen points of traditional neighborhood development. *FFF Newsletter,* 2–3.

Fennelly, L. J. and Lombardi, J. H. (1997) *Spotlight on Security for Real Estate Managers.* Chicago: IREM Institute of Real Estate Management.

Hope IV Developments (1996, November) U.S. Hud, Washington, DC, p. 2–4.

Katz, P. (1994) *The New Urbanism: Toward an Architecture of Community.* New York: McGraw-Hill.

Malone, M., et al. (1995, May 15) 15 Ways to fix the suburbs. *Newsweek,* May 15. 47–53.

Mills, K. M. (1996, July) Crime prevention through environmental design: Public facilities and applications and strategies. *Security Journal.* New York: Elsevier, 109–115.

Nasar, J. L. and Brown, B. B. (1996) *Public and Private Places.* The Environmental Design Research Association: Oklahoma.

Newman, O. (1973) *Defensible Space: Crime Prevention Through Environmental Design.* New York: Macmillan.

O'Toole, R. (2005) New Urbanism Promotes Crime. Reason Public Policy Institute. Los Angeles: Available at: www.operationscorpion.org.uk/design_out_crime/policing_urbanism.htm. Accessed 10 September 2006.

Plater-Zyberk, E. (1996) It takes a village to raise a child. *Consumer Reports*, May, 59–67.

Richards, S. J. (1994) *Crime Prevention through Environmental Design: Training Course Overview.* Texas: Churchill International.

Stack, S. (1997) Crime and housing values in Detroit 1980–1990. *Journal of Crime and Justice,* 20(1).

Town, S. and O'Toole, R. (2005) Crime-friendly neighborhoods: How New Urbanist planners sacrifice safety in the name of openness and accessibility. *Reason*, February.

Miami Herald. (April 17, 2003) State's crime rate in 2002 was the lowest in 30 years. 4B.

18 Creating Safe and Secure Environments for Schools and Colleges

Randy Atlas and Richard H. Schneider

Creating safe schools (elementary through college) is the responsibility of the entire community where a school or school system resides. Yet the day-to-day operation is primarily the responsibility of the teachers, administrators, and security or law enforcement officers at the school. But, before the first student walks the halls, an architect creates the design of the school and what will be the subsequent relationships between people and their buildings. The success or failure of that school is predisposed to the quality of design and the limitations of budgets. A good administrator could run a great school in an "old red barn," but it is sure going to take a lot more effort and supervision than in a well-designed and functional academic space. The basic CPTED premise is that through the effective use and design and management of the built environment, there can be a reduction in the opportunity and fear of crime, and result in the improvement in the quality of life. If we can build effective spaces using CPTED in the next generation of schools, we will substantially reduce the opportunity and fear of crime in them.

Many schools have been becoming fortresses over the last two decades because of the fear of crime and the vulnerability of young people engaging in violent crime or becoming a victim of violent crime. In 1998, over 2000 juveniles were murdered nationwide. (OJJDP, 1999). Juveniles as a demographic were involved in 12% of murder arrests, 35% of burglary, 27% of robberies, and 24% of weapons arrests. (OJJDP, 1999). Thirty-seven percent of schools (U.S. DOE, 1998) had one to five serious crimes at their schools, and 20% reported six or more crimes. Forty-five percent of elementary schools reported one or more violent crimes occurred within the school property, and 74% of middle school, and 77% of high schools (US DOE, 1998, p. v). Fear exists in our schools for good reason (see Figure 18.1).

Some of the most notorious events in recent history include:

- 8/1/66—Charles Whitman barricades himself on the observation deck of the tower at the University of Texas, Austin and shoots 45 people, killing 14.
- 1/15/78—Ted Bundy enters Chi Omega sorority house and kills two women and assaults three others.
- 8/20/90—Danny Rollins murders five University of Florida students.
- 12/1/97—3 students killed, 5 wounded at Padukah, KY High School.
- 3/24/98—4 girls and teacher killed, 10 wounded in Jonesboro, AR Middle School.
- 5/21/98—2 teens killed, 20 injured in Springfield, OR High School.
- 4/20/99—15 teens killed, 23 injured in Columbine, CO High School.
- 4/26/02—13 teachers, 2 students, 1 policeman killed, 10 wounded in secondary School in Enfurt, Germany.
- 3/21/05—5 students, 1 teacher, 1 security guard, and family members for a total of ten people killed at this Red Lake, MN High School.
- 9/13/06—1 student killed, 19 injured in a Montreal, Canada, College.

FIGURE 18.1 Workplace violence and school violence—close cousins. (©1999 *The Miami Herald*. Reprinted with permission from *The Miami Herald*.)

- 10/3/06—A deranged adult goes into an Amish one-room schoolhouse in Pennsylvania and shoots 10 girls; 5 die.
- 01/04/07—The son of Cambodian immigrants was shot to death in a Tacoma, WA, High School hallway by a fellow student.
- 04/16/07—A South Korean Student at Virginia Tech University shoots and kills 32 students and faculty in a dorm and mechanical engineering building and then kills himself.
- 02/14/08—The gunman, a former school graduate, shot and killed five students at Northern Illinois University before committing suicide.

A 1996/1997 survey of public schools by U.S. Dept. of Education (1998) found that:

- 96% required visitors to sign in before entering the school building
- 80% had a closed campus policy prohibiting students leaving for lunch
- 53% controlled access to buildings
- 24% controlled access to grounds
- 19% conducted drug sweeps
- 84% had police or security reps inside school during the school day
- 4% performed random metal detection checks on students
- 1% used metal detectors daily

There is a connection between the design and management of the schools and the relationship to crime. Some examples of potential environmental design problems for schools are:

- Campus borders are often poorly defined
- Informal gathering areas are out of sight
- Building layout produces isolated spots
- Bus loading areas are often in conflict with cars
- Student parking lots are often on outermost areas
- Periphery parking creates conflict with the neighborhood
- Parking areas are often obscured by plantings
- Locker areas often create conflict and confusion and hiding of contraband

- The overuse of corridors creates blind spots
- Rest rooms are located away from supervision

The design and management of schools has broadened in focus to create environments where people can learn, and also be safe refuges from the crime and violence of the streets and homes. Schools must address the conflicting goals of being an accessible facility to its students and faculty, yet be secured and controlled environments. The architectural and security communities have been reexamining the traditional approaches to school design to include the increased awareness of security issues being

FIGURE 18.2   Schools behind bars?

integrated into the overall design and management without making the experience akin to being in a detention facility (see Figure 18.2).

The design of elementary schools through college campuses needs to address the functional integration of CPTED and security features to control access onto the site and in the buildings, reduce vandalism, document activity on the property, control movement in areas of the building that are restricted, and provide communication between faculty and administration and emergency assistance.

It is critical to predict and determine the *Type of User* and ask the questions: What is the intended purpose of the user? Are the people using the spaces legitimate or illegitimate users?

School administrators and architects cannot select appropriate countermeasures without clear objectives. Integrated school security measures include prevention, control, detection, and intervention in order to be comprehensive and effective. The threats to a school are either going to be external (threats from outside influences and persons), or internal (threats from students, faculty, staff, workplace violence). CPTED can make a direct impact on reducing the *outside* external threat through use of natural access control, surveillance, territoriality boundary definition, management, and maintenance strategies. The *internal* threats can be deterred through policy and procedure strategies and management techniques, and not as much on physical design. When a school has multiple entrances and many ground floor windows, the threat and vulnerability levels are increased greatly and make the facility infinitely more difficult to protect. Traditional campus designs found in many community colleges and universities make it extremely challenging to seal off exits and entrances against threats, whether these are external or internal in origin.

UNDERSTANDING THE UNIQUE SCHOOL ENVIRONMENT

While school builders and designers implement security innovations into the latest generation of schools, the vast majority of schools were designed and built in less stressful and dangerous times. As a result, the typical school or university's appearance depended on when it was designed. Schools of the 1940s had a look and feel of civic authority, typically a two-story façade with classical columns and arches and had a sense of presence (see Figure 18.3).

In the 1950s, a new era of school design centered on practicality, as compared to grandeur. Air conditioning was uncommon so schools had low-profile "fingers" that divided the school into several long skinny buildings. This configuration provided classroom windows on opposing walls to allow for natural cross-ventilation.

The 1960s ushered in the era of open classrooms and open campuses. Educational experts of the time thought that traditional classrooms were too confining and they envisioned big rooms that could hold several classes at once. The reality was that the open rooms were loud and difficult to manage. The open classrooms did not have enough wall space for blackboards and display. In

FIGURE 18.3 The classical elegance of architectural design. The building looks like a school with a well-defined entrance and good natural surveillance.

addition to the open classroom, school designers began to design windowless schools in order to improve the students' attention inside the building (not daydreaming!). Schools started taking on an industrial and detention-like look and feel. As a result of removing the windows, utilities costs dropped, and vandalism decreased, but school builders had decided to install air conditioning. The windowless schools turned out to be a faulty design philosophy and schools were required to have windows in classrooms.

The 1970s and 1980s returned to the windowless school era and state laws required natural light and ventilation for every classroom. Architects favored one-story buildings and laid out the schools in an open campus plan, using courtyards surrounded by classrooms. As school crime and violence started to escalate the 1990s, schools started to rein in the open campus plan, to something more like "circling the wagons," tightly controlling access through a well-defined main entrance. Schools of this era more commonly look like a large rectangle with an interior courtyard. School designers dropped the use of glass mirrors in bathrooms for detention grade polished stainless steel, and removed the double doors from bathrooms and use an open lazy S design so teachers can hear and smell trouble. Metal louvers are added over windows for vandalism and burglary protection (see Figure 18.4).

FIGURE 18.4 School architecture can have a fortress mentality.

Twenty-first-century schools have learned from the past decades' styles by incorporating design elements that are based on control and accountability. But the architects and administrators are struggling with tight budgets and often severe overcrowding. Schools that were considered large decades ago accommodating 600 to 700 students, are being replaced with schools that can accommodate 3000 to 5000 students. Smart schools are the trend today with technology being totally accessible to students and faculty. Protecting the assets of the students, faculty, buildings, equipment, and information is more critical than ever.

Many school buildings in the United States have been constructed to achieve an inviting and open campus style with multiple buildings, multiple entrances and exits, big windows, and many opportunities for privacy. These design configurations are not inherently conducive to many current requirements that need to encompass security needs. Unless there is an intensive program of safe management practices and a school culture of cohesive and collaborative students/faculty focused on safety, it will be difficult to deter opportunities and fears of crime. Even with these necessary social and management programs, attention to basic CPTED is always advisable.

Consider, for example, the 1970s fortressing in schools and the windowless and sterile physical structures that emerged. That fortressing sent a message of paranoia and fear.

Despite the best design strategies, involvement by parents, faculty, students, and the community at large is critical in maintaining a safe environment. School officials hope to boost safety by encouraging parental involvement by keeping facilities open longer than normal school hours for theatre groups, community meetings, adult education, sports programs, and after-school programs. This puts more adults on school campuses, during after school hours, which deters loitering and vandalism and instills a sense of community ownership in the schools. At the same time this can also increasse security risks based on the local context.

One of the major challenges to school security is the lack or inconsistency of funding. It is not lack of interest but the inability to implement the recommendations of the threat risk assessment. Many school and school districts have very limited budgets and cannot afford the fencing, lighting, cameras, access control, bulletproof glass, and so much more that is recommended by the CPTED or security consultants. If schools and universities conduct their annual or periodic assessments that identify the vulnerabilities of crime and disorder, it is possible that they can prioritize the specific issues and needs for systematic improvement. The local schools, administrators, and school resource officers know where the problems are taking place and can help make small changes that are part of a bigger picture (see Figure 18.5). Moreover, schools need to take advantage of local

METRO&STATE

TUESDAY, AUGUST 16, 2005 | EDITOR: MANNY GARCIA magarcia@herald.com 305-376-3638 or 954-538-7150 | THE HERALD

EDUCATION

Tighter school security will cost a bundl

■ Some school district leaders fear that strict new security regulations department will cost an exorbitant amount of time and money.

BY MATTHEW L PINZUR
mpinzur@herald.com

State officials are broadly interpreting a new law that requires background checks for thousands of school dis-

trict contractors who have access to campuses, according to guidelines released Monday by the Florida Department of Education.

District leaders in Miami-Dade and Broward counties said the new guidelines will require a massive mobilization to fingerprint construction workers building additions, and sports officials and vendors selling yearbooks and

class rings at school — all before the law goes into effect Sept. 1.

Across the state, thousands of those workers will be required to submit fingerprints to the FBI and Florida Department of Law Enforcement, costing hundreds of thousands of dollars.

"I do think the law is very clear on that issue," said Pamela Stewart, a deputy

chancellor with the Department of Education, who said she "couldn't even begin to try to estimate" the number of workers who will be affected.

Spokesmen in Miami-Dade and Broward were also unable to provide estimates, but both districts said it would be a major undertaking.

"We're talking about thousands of people who interact with our schools," said Miami-

Dade spokesman Joseph Garcia. "That number will increase as we have more and more construction sites."

The background checks were required by the Jessica Lunsford Act, a law signed this year by Gov. Jeb Bush to tighten monitoring and punishment of sexual offenders. It was named for the the 9-year-old Homosassa girl who was kidnapped, raped and mur-

dered this year, allegedl convicted sex offende did construction work school.

"It seems extreme,

• TURN TO SECURITY, 4B

■ RECESS DELAYED: PLANS F MANDATORY RECESS ON HOI

■ HERALD.COM: TO READ THI GUIDELINES, CLICK ON TODA EXTRAS

FIGURE 18.5 A newspaper article touting the high cost for school safety. (©2005 *The Miami Herald.* Reprinted with permission from *The Miami Herald.*)

community knowledge, because neighbors, local police, courts, news agencies, mental health professionals and crisis prevention groups often have significant insights into problems and issues that are school related, but that take place off school grounds. Although some personal information may be protected by law, other data is publicly available and worrisome behavioral patterns may be discernable. In these cases, it is important to "connect the dots" based on coordination among institutions that may not normally communicate with each other. This is one threat assessment lesson, among many, made clear by the Virginia Tech massacre.

A review of the national crime data and reports on school security yield important clues on which schools need the greatest security resources. For instance, the Florida Safe Schools Project Update, conducted by Michael Kunstle, Nancy Clark, and Richard Schneider from the University of Florida, found that in 2002–2003 there were fewer fighting and disorder problems at elementary and high schools compared to middle schools. Colleges and universities have their own unique sets of problems and challenges because of large sites, the knowing use of residential housing, and big team sports. When the architect or CPTED practitioner is applying the methodology, the type of school environment is important to understand the unique risks, threats, and vulnerabilities.

Kunstle, Clark, and Schneider's research (2003) uncovered these important findings on security and design. Principals reported that fighting, disorderly conduct, and vandalism are the top three crimes on their campuses in terms of number of incidents, while community college respondents say that larceny, theft, vandalism, and breaking and entering are the crimes they perceive to be the most serious based on event frequency. These findings suggest that the architect and CPTED practitioner needs to address these issues through design and management strategies. Their research also reports that school design, corridor design, and surveillance are the most important concerns among the schools surveyed. Following close behind were concerns on perimeter enclosure issues and removing niches or hiding spaces. Community college risk managers reported that their most critical areas of school design related to security are exterior lighting, alarm systems, and interior lighting.

The Florida Safe Schools Guidelines research also found that schools surveyed identified parking lots, off-grounds adjacent buildings, locker rooms, and restrooms as the *top* four places for crime, with rooftops of covered walkways, building rooftops, lobby and reception areas, and main entrances as the *lowest* reported criminal activity. The crimes typically reported in parking lots were trespassing and vandalism. Adjacent buildings typically reported offenses in the use of alcohol, tobacco, drugs, and fighting. Locker rooms reported the most crimes being larceny, theft and fighting. Restrooms reported acts of vandalism, alcohol, tobacco, and drugs. Knowing that specific areas create unique stressors and vulnerabilities is helpful to the design professional, police, and faculty to develop effective countermeasures.

Another universal lesson from the research: Students prop open doors so they can skip class, or skip class and return later (see Figure 18.6). Better door control and management is imperative to reduce this vulnerability. In a new school design, door alarms and door position switches are easily accommodated, but retrofitting an older school is expensive and painful. A key suggestion that emerged from the research was that students themselves were the best likely sources of information about school crime and design issues and that they ought to be consulted by designers along with resource officers, teachers, and school administrators, facility managers and neighbors. At the individual level it is clear, for example, that many students were aware of the aberrant behavior of the deranged Virginia Tech gunman, Seung-Hui Cho, well before the massacre took place. Although it is certainly arguable that such knowledge could have prevented the murders, there is little doubt that students generally have better insights than outsiders into the idiosyncrasies of their peers and that of their physical learning environments. In short, they need to be listened to as part of the design process and subsequent management practices.

Unwanted and illegal roof access, though a low priority problem, was compounded by existing natural features such as trees or low roof canopies that students can use to access the rooftops (see Figure 18.7). Care should be taken in the design of structural elements such as columns and poles, so that they cannot be scaled (see Figure 18.8). An easy CPTED solution is to use slippery paints. Signage is

FIGURE 18.6 An exterior fire exit door to a school opens into the path of view of the CCTV camera, thus blocking the camera from seeing who is opening the door and persons entering.

needed at the main entrance to direct visitors to sign in at the main office. Many schools did not have adequate ground-rule signage even though they all had policies for visitor sign in.

THE SCHNEIDER SCALE: LOCATING THE OFFICE

An additional source of practical information on school safety is contained in Schneider, Walker, and Sprague's handbook "Safe School Design: A Handbook for Educational Leaders" (2000). They describe a broad range of useful safety measures including administration, security, and CPTED. For example, they describe the role of the front office location and then provide a scale—the Schneider Scale—with levels of security for different office designs. Office designs and locations are then rated on a 7-point scale (Schneider et al., 2000, pp. 62–63.)

At the lowest security level (Level 1), the school office is not located at a place to provide access control or natural surveillance of those entering the school. It may be too far within the building and not within site of the main entranceways or hallways. At the highest security level (Level 7), both natural surveillance and access control are at their maximum potential. There will be an entry vestibule, requirements for office check-in (see Figure 18.10), clear sightlines to the

FIGURE 18.7 Catwalks provide an illegal secondary travel path around many schools by encouraging or allowing students to be able to climb on top and gain access to second story windows and roofs.

FIGURE 18.8 An exterior courtyard is covered with protective screening, but the screening acts as a ladder to the roof.

main doors and nearby hallways, and possibly metal detectors in the entry vestibule. Visitors will be monitored on entry and school staff can easily be alerted to intruders (see Figure 18.9).

Each school administrator must ultimately determine which level of design for the main office best applies to that school environment. However "although it may not have always been the case, the role of the office as school guardian is now of primary importance" (Schneider et al., 2000, p. 60).

SAFE AND SECURE SCHOOL DESIGN PRINCIPLES

Beyond office design and other specific designs that may vary from school to school, there are some general principles for success in security. They are defined here as Safe and Secure School Design Principles. They are:

- Effectiveness of security design modifications and security programs
- Affordability of security programs and features
- Acceptability of security technology and practices
- Define assets that are worthy of being protected
- Define threats of what is vulnerable to attack and loss
- Characterize the environment and balance the needs to the threats

FIGURE 18.9 Visibility of the office staff to the school entrance and administrative offices.

FIGURE 18.10 The front desk should have a view of the doorways and key offices.

Safe and Secure School Principles involve five key areas, and each area should include security layering planning practices:

1. SITE DESIGN

Site design includes features of: Landscaping, Exterior Pedestrian Routes, Vehicular Routes and Parking, Recreational Areas.

2. BUILDING DESIGN

Building design includes features of: Building Organization, Exterior Covered Corridors, Points of Entry, Enclosed Exterior Spaces, Ancillary Buildings, Walls, Windows, Doors, Roofs, and Lighting.

3. INTERIOR SPACES

Interior spaces include features of: Lobby and Reception Areas; Corridors; Toilets and Bathrooms; Stairs and Stairwells; Cafeterias, Auditoriums, Gyms; Libraries and Media Centers; Classrooms; Locker rooms; Labs, Shops, Music, Computer Rooms; and Administrative Areas.

4. SYSTEMS AND EQUIPMENT

Systems and equipment includes features of: Alarms and Surveillance Systems; Fire Control; HVAC (Heating Ventilation and Air-conditioning Equipment); Vending Machines; Water Fountains; Elevators; Telephone and Info Systems.

5. COMMUNITY CONTEXT

Schools need to be functionally integrated into the community. Impacts of schools to surrounding neighborhoods include traffic, parking, pedestrian flows, crime and disorder.

A school's relationship to its immediate surroundings is communicated through the edge connections. Landscaping denotes school boundaries. Restrict accessibility through edge conditions. Establish natural observation areas by clearly defining use. Territorial boundaries include perimeter fencing. Landscaping barriers include gates and fences that restrict unwanted entrance and access. The goal is to use gates and fences that permit observation of surrounding areas. Appropriate landscape, trees, and flowers can improve the aesthetics of these barriers. Be sure that the solution does not turn into the problem by providing hiding areas within barriers. Moreover, while physical boundaries are important features in creating territorial integrity, it is important that these be balanced by connections to adjacent landowners and to the community at large. After all, neighbors have first-hand knowledge of the day-to-day operations of schools, including traffic and pedestrian flows and the activities of students on or near their properties. They, like the students themselves (as noted earlier) have insights into crime and disorder issues that occur in places adjacent to but off school grounds. Schools need to be functionally integrated into the community and not seen as fortified islands by the community at large. This is an example of an area in which management, local politics, and design converge.

Access to the school buildings should be restricted to those individuals who are directly related to the school and will facilitate quick evacuation if ever deemed necessary. The site planning of a school should take advantage of any physical or natural barriers that are present. Develop a clear sense of boundary definition by using fencing, plantings, signage, and level changes. School property needs to be distinctive and appear to be private property (see Figure 18.11, Figure 18.12, and Figure 18.13).

Access to the site should be limited to where students, faculty, and visitors can park. Improve access control by separating public parking from student and faculty parking. School bus drop-off

FIGURE 18.11   Perimeter fencing around a school defines its boundaries and reduces trespassing and unauthorized access.

FIGURE 18.12   Fencing directs people to desired and monitored entrances.

areas should be separate from public drop-off areas. Public transportation access routes should be carefully designed to facilitate use by students, but they also can be loitering spots for criminals and vagrants. Sidewalks should encourage pedestrian traffic where it is desired, and funnel it to the main administration entrance of the building for maximum surveillance and supervision. Students might be routed past a security office when using a school's main entrance (see Figure 18.14) Security design relative to vehicular access should be coordinated with life safety and health management planning, as embodied in the *Safe Ways to School* programs that have been implemented in a number of states such as Maine and Florida (see, for example, Maine FDOT 2003 and the Florida Traffic and Bicycle Safety Education Program).

Administrative offices should have clear lines of sight of the play, gathering, and parking areas. Accountable management has direct view of critical areas. Perpetrators are discouraged from trespassing and illegal behavior because of the increased risk of identification and intervention. Legitimate users feel safer. Design features can allow visual access of courtyards, classrooms, and high-risk areas (see Figure 18.15 and Figure 18.16).

FIGURE 18.13 School boundaries are important but must not be intended to make the property look and feel like a prison. The intermediate support railing on the fence pretty much renders the security fence worthless. A juvenile could scale the fence in seconds.

FIGURE 18.14 Main entry under natural and mechanical surveillance.

Safe school design can make circulation choices of how the school will limit the number of students to specific areas at one time and restricting access to others. Courtyards might only be used during school breaks for example, or the cafeteria might be accessible during specific times only. Library space might have a much longer time range of availability. As with any CPTED design, the goal of a safe school is to have transitional zones going from public space, to semipublic space, semiprivate space, to private space. Public spaces might be the site perimeter, or exterior play areas, whereas semipublic areas could be gymnasiums or large group instructional spaces. Private spaces might be administrative offices, or computer labs, or equipment areas.

Having sufficient capable guardianship of the large public areas such as gyms and cafeterias is often a challenge. Many fights break out in these areas and the courtyards that are adjacent. But the fights are not always because of bad design. One troubled school experienced fights in the cafeteria on days they ran out of pizza. The shortage caused frustration and conflict: smaller kids were bullied for pizza slices and other kids left the school entirely to get food. Clearly good design cannot

FIGURE 18.15 Interior courtyards allow supervision by staff but semi-private areas for students to congregate.

replace proper planning and effective management. Rather management and design must complement each other.

SPECIFIC DESIGN STRATEGIES

OBSERVATION FROM CLASSROOMS

Parking and circulation areas should be placed in view of the classrooms. A high volume of students in classes means more chance for casual observation.

FIGURE 18.16 Interior courtyard at this school allows personal space for the students but can be supervised by staff without obstructions.

FIGURE 18.17 Fencing and gates around the basketball courts is needed for more than stray balls.

OBSERVATION OF VEHICULAR TRAFFIC

Adequate observation of vehicular traffic is as important as observation of pedestrians. Administrative spaces should have clear lines of sight to entry roads and parking lots. Anyone entering a school area should never go undetected, and any vulnerable entry should be secured. An example of the conflict between good design and poor management discovered by field research for the Florida Safe School Design Guidelines was a middle school whose windows were purposely oriented to overlook student parking lots and drop off areas. But the principal allowed staff to cover them with posters and signs, thereby defeating any but the most determined surveillance opportunities.

OBSERVATION OF RECREATION AREAS

The school recreation resources serve a needed function for the students during school hours when activities are supervised. However, many schools do not have their ball fields fenced, the basketball courts screened, and equipment protected (see Figure 18.17). After hours, the school's recreational spaces and equipment become open invitations for the neighborhood kids to use them without supervision. Although this might seem desirable, the premises liability of the school is wide open because the school resources entice outsiders. If someone is hurt and assaulted, the liability is directed toward the property owner. Thus, litigation has driven the need to secure exterior sports activity spaces such as basketball courts.

Decisions have to be made whether to allow neighborhood kids to play on the school grounds.

SURVEILLANCE POINTS

Providing surveillance points can increase safety. Providing views to potential problem areas from publicly used spaces, such as a common use stairwell, ensures that many people will be observing at any given time. Designers must be sure that the surveillance advantage goes to legitimate users of the space, not the possible perpetrators. If cameras are to be used, they would be used typically to monitor parking lots, main entrances, playground areas, courtyards, loading docks, and special equipment areas such as computer labs. Landscaping and plantings should be carefully placed and considered so that they do not pose maintenance problems for upkeep and trimming, and provide blind spots for hiding, placing of contraband, or ambush (see Figure 18.18).

FIGURE 18.18 Walkways near walls, empty windows and overgrown bushes create dangerous hiding places.

EXTERIOR CIRCULATION

Exterior circulation paths are as important as interior paths. Paths should be large enough to accommodate large numbers of students, yet comply with the Americans With Disabilities Act of 1990. Students should be prevented from using exterior paths as informal gathering places. Bicycle racks should be placed in high visibility areas near the main entry and separated from vehicular traffic. Landscaping should screen bicycles but not restrict view of the area (see Figure 18.19 and Figure 18.20).

TRAFFIC CALMING AND SIGNAGE

School traffic can become a source of deadly problems. Design parking lots with few or no long runs to prevent speeding. Install and maintain speed and stop signs. Bus pick-up/drop-off areas should not conflict with other traffic. Signage and Notice: Signage should announce intended and prohibited uses. Signage should be clear, reasonably sized, and placed in a way that is easily viewed. Signage must be complete and up to standard. Signage also must be mounted correctly not just taped on (see Figure 18.21).

SPATIAL/TEMPORAL SEPARATION

Place "safe" activities in "unsafe" locations, such as placing Driver's Ed lessons in parking areas where hangout activities happen after school hours. Place "unsafe" activities in "safe" locations such as potential bicycle theft storage areas near the main office windows. Separating the cafeteria entrance and exit by space can help define movement and avoid conflicts. Temporal separation could also be used separating the school's gym and theatre from the classrooms, so that the classrooms can be locked during concerts or basketball games.

Covered circulation ways must be designed with care. Blind spots and entrapment points must be minimized. Potential "door in the face" incidents must be eliminated. Covered corridors should be designed so access to the upper floors of a structure is not possible (see Figure 18.22).

FIGURE 18.19 Bike racks close to building are filled with bikes by students who can observe their bikes.

FIGURE 18.20 View of bike racks from school windows provides good visual connection.

FIGURE 18.21   Critical security signage is only scotch taped on the wall. Is this secure?

ACCESSIBILITY

Main entry into the school is required to be handicapped accessible (see Figure 18.23). Ramps with proper slopes and handrails are required. Nonslip materials should be used. All travel ways must be wide enough to permit wheel chairs without disrupting pedestrian traffic. ADA standards must be followed for all access control and security systems equipment. Proper ramps and handrails must be used. Any safety hazards must be clearly identified. Desks, telephones, water fountains, and other features need to conform to ADA standards.

MAIN ENTRY SECURITY

Many techniques and devices can be used to increase security. Although they are costly, weapon detectors can be integrated within an entryway. Access to other areas from main entryways should be carefully planned and not obscured. Main entryways should be obvious. Entryways can be very dangerous if not designed with CPTED in mind. Potential for getting confused and lost should be limited. Too many entryways can create confusion and often provide ambush points. Treatment of secondary entries is just as important as

FIGURE 18.22   Catwalks access into second-floor window.

FIGURE 18.23   Recessed doors provide hiding spaces and piggybacking opportunities for unauthorized access.

primary entries. ADA, signage, and hardware requirements also must be met at all secondary entrances. It is important not to create entrapment points at secondary entries.

RECESSED ENTRIES—BLIND SPOTS

These should be avoided whenever possible. When the configuration of a building demands a blind spot, corners can be tapered at 45 degrees to allow a view around a corner to avoid an ambush situation (see Figure 18.24). Bathrooms are required to have recessed entries or blocked line of sight of the toilet areas, however, having an opening that allows sound and smell (of smoke) to be transmitted to the hallway deters many illegal or inappropriate behaviors.

FIGURE 18.24 Noncompliant, nonaccessible entrance to a classroom building.

Doorway and corridor design should coexist safely, not create hazards. Poorly designed, recessed doorways can create dangerous blind spots. It is important to consider safety and security when designing entries and corridors. Using the lazy S or maze design allows for improved surveillance and yet supports the privacy required in a bathroom without having to use doors that lock or block (see Figure 18.25 and Figure 18.26).

COURTYARDS AND GATHERING PLACES

Formal gathering places should be well defined. There should be no doubt where people are intended to gather within the school grounds. Observation, lighting, accessibility, and safety are

FIGURE 18.25 A lazy S design bathroom door entry.

FIGURE 18.26 A lazy S design bathroom door entry.

FIGURE 18.27 Skateboard-proof notches remove the opportunity and excuse for using the wall to skate on.

FIGURE 18.28 Incisions or notches are designed into the retaining wall prevent the surface being used by skateboarders.

all design and management considerations. The architecture for schools is for legitimate uses such as walking, sitting, and learning. However, the basic hardware and furnishings of construction are merely the stage props for young people to engage in extreme sports (see Figure 18.29 and Figure 18.30). Skateboard, rollerblade, and razor scooters and dirt bikes use curbs, planters, railings, stairs, and more as their stage to practice. But with minor architectural design innovations the builder can remove the opportunity and ease to engage in such activities (see Figure 18.27 and Figure 18.28).

INTERIOR CIRCULATION

Certain functions and spaces require access control by definition, such as the library (see Figure 18.31). However, the same strategies are being used now in some schools for screening of persons coming into the main entrance comparable to courthouses and airports. If screening is

FIGURE 18.29 Legitimate spaces need to be provided for extreme sports so kids don't use the public architecture as their playground.

FIGURE 18.30   This skateboard park recreates the surfaces on which kids practice edging.

FIGURE 18.31   Screening devices are commonly found in libraries and retail stores to prevent theft and pilferage.

required by function or need, special considerations are needed for queing, staffing, equipment, and requirements of package and person screening.

WALLS

The characteristics of a wall directly influence the potential for crime. Walls should not be placed in a way that will provide hiding areas. Landscaping along walls should reduce hiding areas, not produce them. Walls located in high vandalism areas should be constructed of durable material resistant to graffiti and vandalism. Using plant material on the wall can deny the artist a good surface. This strategy is referred to as a living wall (see Figure 18.32). The

FIGURE 18.32   Living wall removes painting surface.

FIGURE 18.33 Fence closing the gap between two buildings and thus creating a unified security perimeter using the architectural skin and minimal fencing.

FIGURE 18.34 Graffiti and climb resistant wall is accomplished by the terracing of the of the top edge and the rough texture surface of the block.

architectural choices for finishes of the school must reduce the potential for acts of vandalism. Conscious choices must be made for durable and long lasting materials, fixtures, furniture, and finishes. If exterior windows of the school face a road, bullet resistant glass may need to be considered. Though it is expensive, properly framed glass will resist burglary, wind damage, and the threats of drive-by shootings. Another alternative might be polycarbonate and security laminated glass for high-risk areas, although these glazing materials are costly compared to regular insulated tempered glass.

When the buildings themselves become the exterior perimeter, as compared to a fence around the property, then openings between the buildings must be connected and secured (see Figure 18.33). Careful selection of fencing to reduce climbing and cutting is critical (see Figure 18.34).

Interior and exterior walls of schools can use a finished concrete masonry block that is fired or glazed on one side, or painted with grafitti- and scratch-resistant epoxy paint. Another alternative is to centralize graffitti on an approved wall, which becomes the focus of artistic expression (see Figure 18.35). Another choice is to have blocks with texture and colors that remove the palette on which the person would write or vandalize (see Figure 18.36).

Screen Walls

Screens provide physical access barriers to windows and walls, and provide privacy where needed. Make sure the barriers do not negatively effect ventilation. Decorative materials should be used for aesthetic value, but the walls must be designed in a way that makes climbing impossible.

Building Exterior Shape

The form that the school buildings take should be designed to create open spaces, yet eliminate blind corners and increase natural surveillance by students and staff (see Figure 18.37). Adequate exterior lighting and the correct type of building material choices will reduce the opportunity for vandalism.

FIGURE 18.35 Sanctioned graffiti wall encourages artistic expression.

FIGURE 18.36 Textured wall painted with graffiti resistant paint removes the attractive surface to vandalize.

FIGURE 18.37 The alcoves in the building architecture create hiding spots and can attract persons to loiter and use as a refuge area.

WINDOWS DESIGN

Groupings of smaller windows function as a large window but increase security, while still providing ventilation and natural lighting. The smaller size makes it difficult to crawl through or remove property. Clerestory windows, which are windows constructed high on a building wall to admit natural daylight, and provide multiple functions with high security benefits. The goal for the school architect in designing some classrooms and spaces is to provide natural light, natural ventilation, and shield occupant privacy, yet does not permit easy entry. Glass block combined with clerestory windows will minimize wall penetrations and provide good security and natural lighting. Ventilation and natural lighting are not compromised. This configuration provides greater privacy at the cost of functional observation, depending on whether or not the blocks are clear. If the windows have steel or metal jalousies that close, the jalousies must engage in the window frame so they may not be pried open to expose the glass to breakage and the interior spaces to vandalism and theft. Exterior windows on classroom buildings, labs, or libraries must be secure from outside intrusion (see Figure 18.38).

FIGURE 18.38 Vulnerable classroom equipment needs protection: the author is able to reach through an open ground floor window and grab a computer.

DOOR SECURITY

Any door is a critical point of access. Lighting, signage, hardware, and observation are all key elements. Doors should be checked to ensure their security. Management should be held accountable for maintenance and inspection. If doors are not designed for security in the architectural stage, the retrofitting of walls, door frames, and conduits is expensive and ugly (see Figure 18.39).

Special access areas require careful attention to detail. Roof access needs to be secure, but also in an area that permits quick and effortless entry for maintenance staff. Other access

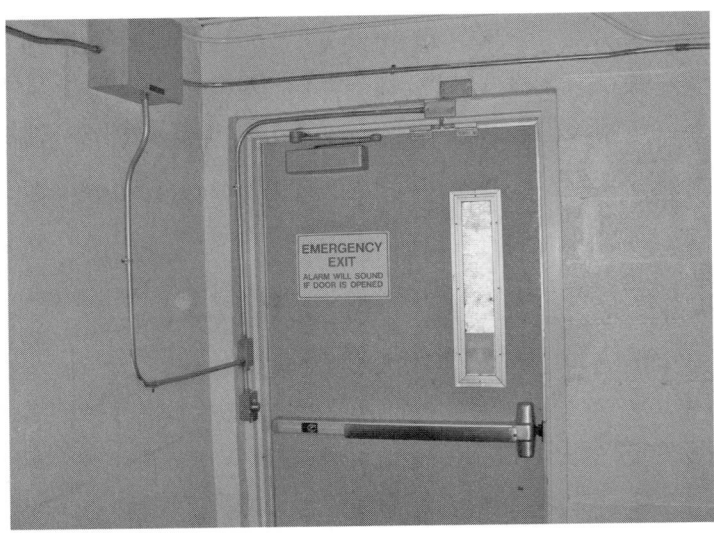

FIGURE 18.39 Retrofitted door for security with exposed conduit and wires. This is expensive, unsightly, and invites tampering.

areas such as electrical or mechanical rooms need to be placed so they are not in danger of being compromised (see Figure 18.40).

Signage on doors is important to let people know whether the doors are exit-only or an entrance (see Figure 18.41, Figure 18.42, and Figure 18.43).

FIGURE 18.40 Secured roof access requires a special stairway and access control.

CCTV can be placed strategically at entrances, exits, hallways, stairwells, and exterior doors. Cameras should operate continuously and videotapes analyzed and archived. There is an over reliance on technology. Many of the kids committing school crime are trying to have their moment of fame on video. CCTV gives the kids their chance to be famous and be on videotape, which is what they want. Thus cameras should be low profile or hidden from view. Broadcasting which areas are under surveillance will not have the desired effect of reduced criminal behavior, but could actually increase the number of incidents with kids showing off for the camera.

FIGURE 18.41 Signage stating the ground rules.

FIGURE 18.42 Signage on doors.

FIGURE 18.43 Signage on doors.

FIGURE 18.44   Duress and panic alarms.

There is no doubt that the use of surveillance technology of all forms will continue to grow as prices drop and as the sophistication and miniaturization of the devices increase. Fundamental questions that designers and school administrators must grapple with are whether and to what extent retrofitted technology can ameliorate bad design, incompetent management and the failure to understand what may seem to adults to be the counterintuitive behavior of students, as noted earlier. The danger is the substitution of technology for good security planning, design, and management.

DURESS ALARMS

Duress alarms provide security in isolated areas. Duress alarms should be located in isolated areas, such as rest rooms and locker areas. Duress alarm system should be integrated with other security systems (see Figure 18.44). Several types of devices can be used to improve security. Electronic sensors can detect anything ranging from weapons to stolen library books. Security mirrors can be used in areas containing blind spots.

COMMUNICATION SYSTEMS

Communication systems must be integrated within the design of the facility and with other systems such as fire and duress alarms, and CCTV systems. Periphery observation and security checkpoints should have a clear and secure line of communication to main administrative areas. Many schools now incorporate expensive hardware and technology. It is important to secure and regularly check high-end items, such as computers. Besides security emergencies, there will be medical emergencies in schools. A comprehensive communications system is essential in schools and universities to account for emergency situations. Some schools have incorporated monitoring and locator systems (Figure 8.45), others have used intercoms and man-down alarms in the phone systems, and panic buttons in administrative offices (see Figure 18.44 and Figure 18.46). In the wake of Virginia Tech, more schools are devoting resources to incorporating systems that provide instant emergency text and e-mail messages to students through cell phones, computers, and other devices. There is no doubt that such systems will become standard features on many university campuses. They will be limited in K–12 schools for the foreseeable future because of general bans on the possession or use of cell phones.

FIGURE 18.45 Signage posting notice.

FIGURE 18.46 Communications redundancy, phones, radios, and panic alarms.

MANAGEMENT

Management plays a key role in CPTED. It is the designer's responsibility to ensure that an area or space can be properly and sensibly managed. Once an efficient design is constructed, it is up to management to maintain a secure atmosphere. One way for the effective management and integration of security into school design is the codification of Safe Schools. For example, CPTED guidelines and security features in the architectural planning process are under the Florida Building Code Chapter 423.8.8, Safe School Design requirements. The code says that school boards should design educational facilities and sites "to enhance security and reduce vandalism through the use of safe school design principles including but not limited to: natural access control; natural surveillance; school and campus territorial integrity; audio and motion detection systems; designs which promote prevention of school crime and violence; open exterior stairs, balconies, ramps and upper level perimeter walkways; and open areas visible to workers inside buildings."

In addition to legal requirements, CPTED-trained architects should be involved in the following aspects of new capital construction and renovation of existing buildings including building and site selection, and reviewing plans and specs during new construction.

GENERAL GUIDELINES

The following suggestions are some design and management tips for a safer school:

- Conduct a security needs assessment for each school with a uniform survey instrument, such as the various assessment tools provided throughout this book.
- Consider the views of students, faculty, administrators, school resource officers, neighbors and community groups in school crime prevention planning and design decision making.

- Have a district-wide crisis response plan, and review practices annually.
- Integrate the school security systems, and have them remotely monitored.
- Natural and mechanical access control is a must.
- Selective use of CCTV. CCTV can attract nuisance behavior, so low profile cameras are preferred. Time-lapse digital recording is essential for evidence of any criminal mischief.
- Eliminate design features that provide access to roofs or upper levels.
- Develop a Safe Corridor program so that students can safely walk to and from school without being solicited for drug or gang activity.
- Communicate your security policy to faculty and students, and have them acknowledge their understanding of the ground rules; for example, no propping open the exit doors.
- Have lighting on grounds from dusk to dawn. Use motion sensors on exterior areas and common use areas after hours to notify staff and police of inappropriate use.
- Operate schools after hours as adult education facilities to expand hours of use. However, care should be used in the design of school facilities that co-locate community recreational facilities, such that proper access control prevents school grounds from trespass and damage coincident to after hour adjacent uses.
- Have self-engaging locking mechanisms on all windows.
- Provide landscape buffers to reduce access to vulnerable graffiti walls.
- Provide piano hinges on vulnerable external doors to reduce access for vandalism.
- Rooftop air conditioning units require secure access, and any pull down ladders should be secured and locked, or placed inside of a building to restrict access.
- Be careful of placement of utility boxes along side of building walls that could provide climbing access to the roofs or balconies.
- If basketball courts are exposed, provide an external water fountain to reduce need to climb over fences to get water.
- If basketball, volleyball, or tennis courts are attracting nuisance behavior after hours, remove the nets and hoops and end of day diminish any opportunity for use. Consider relocating the courts and lights in areas where there can be natural surveillance and supervision of responsible adults or capable guardians.
- Be sensitive to placements of internal space protection devices near air conditioning vents or exhaust grills, as the vibrations of the compressor kicking on can trigger false alarms.
- Doors and frames must be institutional grade to withstand heavy use and abuse. Faceplates should be used over locks to prevent jimmying.
- Reconsider the use of student lockers. The trend is for no lockers and to encourage the use of clear or transparent backpacks. Athletic lockers would only be used during the class and overnight storage prohibited.
- School boundaries and exercise areas should be fenced with vandal-resistant picket type fencing.
- All fire exits should be exit only with no handles for reentry. Doors should be alarmed and have door position switches to notify staff if the door is opened.
- Limit the number of buildings to as few as possible, preferably one, to restrict access to outsiders and illegitimate users.
- Minimize the entrances to as few as possible, preferably one for student and faculty, so as to restrict access to legitimate building users.
- Allow for a security person to be positioned at a single entrance onto the school campus to challenge each vehicle for identification of all occupants, if needed. Buses and school employees would have their own separate and controlled entrance.
- Minimize the number of driveways or parking lots that students use to walk across to gain entry to the school.
- Allow for the ability to lock off the rest of the campus from the gym during after-hours activities.

- Provide a conduit for present and future communication and security systems in the classrooms and common areas.

CLOSING THOUGHTS ON SCHOOL SAFETY

Incorporating the principles and practices of CPTED in the design and remodeling of schools can contribute to the safety of the school while reducing the target hardening and fortressing effects of a bunker mentality. Technologies of security, such as cameras, sensors, weapons screening, and so on, can contribute to the overall security of a school, but they are no solution. They also do not work in all situations. Schools must not undervalue the importance of good maintenance, good construction, good design, and Second-Generation CPTED principles with a school administration that supports a cohesive and collaborative school culture focused on safety.

REFERENCES

Atlas, R. (2002) Designing safe campuses, *Campus Security and Safety Journal*. Dec, 16–42.

Atlas, R. (2002) The ABCs of CPTED. A Florida case study of Barry University. *Campus Safety Journal*. Aug.

Atlas, R. (2002) Barry University: A CPTED Case Study. *Campus Law Enforcement Journal*. June.

Atlas, R. (1997) Designing security in school environments, *Library Administration and Management*, Spring, 11(2).

Florida Center for Community Design and Research (1993) *Florida Safe School Design Guidelines*. Florida Department of Education. Tallahassee, FL. July.

Florida Traffic and Bicycle Safety Education Program (ND), University of Florida, Florida DOT Safety Office, available at http://www.dcp.ufl.edu/centers/trafficsafetyed/html_safe-ways.html

Green, M. W. (1999) *The Appropriate and Effective Use of Security Technologies in U.S. Schools, A Guide for Practical School Security Applications*. Washington, DC: National Institute of Justice, U.S. Department of Justice.

Hill, M. S. and Hill, F. W. (1994) *Creating Safe Schools: What Principals Can Do*. Thousand Oaks, CA: Corwin Press.

Kunstle, M., Clark, N., Schneider, R. H. (2003) *Florida Safe School Design Guidelines*. Tallahassee, FL: Florida Department of Education. Available at: http://www.firn.edu/doe/edfacil/safe_schools.htm

Maine DOT (2003) Safe Ways to School Report. Available at: http://www.maine.gov/mdot/opt/safe-ways-to-school.php

Schneider, R. H. and Kitchen, T. (2007). *Crime Prevention and the Built Environment*. London: Routledge.

Schneider, T., Hill, W., and Sprague, J. (2000) *Safe School Design: A Handbook for Educational Leaders*. ERIC Clearinghouse on Educational Management, University of Oregon.

Stover, D. (1994) High schools or high-tech prisons? *Education Digest*, 60.

OJJDP Office of Juvenile Justice Delinquency Prevention (1999) Juvenile Justice Bulletin. *Juvenile Arrests 1998*, Dec.

The Miami Herald (2005) Tighter school security will cost a bundle. August 16, 2A.

Moran, J. (cartoonist) (1/1/1999) *The Miami Herald*.

U.S. Department of Education and U.S. Department of Justice (1996) *Creating Safe and Drug Free Schools: An Action Guide*. Washington DC. www.ed.gov

U.S. Department of Education and U.S. Department of Justice (1998) National Center for Education Statistics. Violence and Discipline Problems in U.S. Public Schools. 1996–1997. NCES 98–030. March.

U.S. Department of Education. National Center for Education Statistics (2001) *Indicators of School Crime and Safety 2001*. NCES 2002–113. October.

19 Designing Safe ATMs*

Michael Scott and Randy Atlas

There is a scene in the movie *LA Story* with Steve Martin and Sarah Jessica Parker that shows them going to an ATM on the outside of a bank in Los Angeles late one night. A line of yuppies is withdrawing cash for late-night dining and clubbing, and adjacent to them, a line of robbers in typical robber garb . . . masks, shotguns, knives, handgun, and so on. A robber waits for Steve Martin to make his withdrawal, and then introduces himself: "Hi, I'm Bob. I'll be your robber tonight!" The robber takes the money and walks away (see Figure 19.1). A very funny scene, but in real life people get hurt and killed. Both Atlas and Scott have been hired as a premises security negligence expert on a dozen cases involving robbery and assault at ATMs or drive-thru deposits.

The U.S. Department of Justice Problem Oriented Policing Program published a booklet, "Robbery at Automated Teller Machines" (Michael Scott, 2002). We are referencing some major portions of that report in this chapter, as it so effectively captures the essence of the problem and contains directly applicable CPTED recommendations.

The DOJ guide addresses the problem of robbery of people using automated teller machines (ATMs) and night cash depositories. It notes that robberies at night cash depositories, at which cash can only be deposited, not withdrawn, are sufficiently similar to ATM robberies to make most of the proposed security responses apply. Although reference will be made only to ATMs, all information applies equally to night cash depositories (Scott, DOJ, 2002, p. 1).

FIGURE 19.1 A typical line of people waiting for an ATM withdrawal. At night, it can be a life-threatening experience.

---

* Portions of the text in this chapter consist of content found in the following publication: *Robbery at Automated Teller Machines*, Guide No. 8, Michael S. Scott, Center for Problem Oriented Policing, ISBN: 0471475815, ©2001 (www.popcenter.org). We offer special thanks to the Center for Problem-Oriented Policing, Inc., and the U.S. Department of Justice, Office of Community Oriented Policing Services for permission to reproduce common content in this work.

ATMs were first introduced in the mid-1960s in the United Kingdom, and in the late 1960s in the United States. The number of ATMs has increased dramatically since that time. ATM users now annually conduct billions of financial transactions, mostly cash withdrawals. Where once one would find ATMs only on bank premises, today one finds them almost everywhere along sidewalks and in airports, grocery stores, gas stations, shopping malls, nightclubs, and casinos. There are even mobile ATMs that can be set up at disaster sites or temporary entertainment venues such as fairgrounds. Bank customers have come to expect that they can access their funds virtually any time and any place. To some extent, they have traded safety for convenience (Scott, DOJ, 2002, p. 1).

ATM services are highly profitable for banks, and banks aggressively market the use of ATM cards. ATMs that are off the bank premises are usually more profitable for banks because they attract a higher volume of nonbank customers, who must pay service fees. Unfortunately, customers using off-premise ATMs are more vulnerable to robbery.

Rosemary Erickson (1996) made these observations in a 1995 study of armed robbers:

- One-third of the robbers had robbed five or more times;
- 41% had robbed convenience stores, 46% had committed street robberies;
- One-third had injured someone in the course of the robbery;
- Robbers' big concern is not getting caught at the time, nor do they want to be shot by an armed guard;
- 83% of robbers don't think they will be caught;
- Having an escape route is the most important factor for a robber, which feeds into their desire not to get caught.

Chris McGoey (2004) has written many articles on ATM and bank security, and has published these findings:

- Most bank ATM robberies occur at night between 7 p.m. and 4 a.m. and accounts for 60% of ATM crime time frame.
- Bank ATM robberies usually position themselves nearby (50 feet) waiting for a victim to approach and withdraw cash.
- Half of the ATM robberies occur after the cash withdrawal.
- Many ATM robbery victims are women and were alone when robbed.
- Although most robberies are committed by a lone offender, robbers will use some type of weapon against a lone victim.
- Robberies are somewhat more likely to occur at walk-up ATMs than at drive-thru ATMs.

The American Bankers Association, Bank Administration Institute, conducted a survey in the early 1990s and found that 96% of ATM crime involved a single customer. About 50% of the ATM crimes occur between 7 p.m. and midnight. Customers are injured in about 14% of the crimes.

High rates of all types of street robbery, including ATM robbery, are likely to coincide with crack cocaine drug markets, as street robbery is a quick way for addicts to get the cash they need to buy crack, and it does not require a lot of planning or skill.

What can be done to design ATMs so that they are safer and not an attractive target for crime (see Figure 19.2)? Scott (2002, pp. 13–25) developed 17 recommendations. These crime prevention strategies are drawn from a variety of research studies and police reports and incorporate most of the principles of CPTED and Situational Crime Prevention and warrant repeating in this publication as an industry standard.

FIGURE 19.2 Does everyone really need to know your business? Can people see over your shoulder for your PIN and private information?

General Security Considerations for Effective ATM Robbery Prevention include the following:

1. Imposing Mandatory Minimum-Security Standards

Banks and other institutions that operate ATMs must comply with applicable U.S. federal laws, principally the Federal Electronic Funds Transfer Act (Regulation E) and the Bank Protection Act (Regulation P) (12 CFR § 216.1). These federal laws, however, primarily address matters related to the security of the ATMs themselves and to fraudulent transactions, rather than matters related to ATM users' safety.

No federal law has set forth any minimum-security standards to protect ATM users. Rather, several states and a few cities have passed their own laws mandating minimum-security standards for ATMs. Most of these laws set minimum standards for lighting, landscaping, visibility, security reviews, and customer safety tips. The State of New York's law requires, in addition, surveillance cameras and locked vestibule doors that require an ATM card to access. Some laws provide for fines against ATM operators for violations of the standards. Some require annual compliance certifications for each ATM. If security standard laws are enacted, adequate resources must be dedicated to inspection and compliance enforcement. Under some state laws, ATM operators who comply with the security standards are statutorily protected from civil liability. Some laws apply retroactively to all ATMs, others only to new ATMs.

There are both positive and negative implications for specific security standards. Highly specific standards leave little room for debate about compliance, but they also inhibit technological innovations that could provide more security than mandated by the minimum standards.

Florida legislators have no plans to regulate ATM security especially because statistics on ATM related crimes are typically not available or are otherwise difficult to distinguish from general robbery data (coded as robberies and not specified as an ATM robbery!). Florida's banks and ATM vendors want to avoid the New York style ATM security legislation that can be costly and result in more defined liability for the banks for security negligence. In 1992, New York passed the toughest ATM requirements to date, following a murder of an off-duty police officer at an ATM robbery gone bad. The law requires the banks to provide surveillance cameras and around-the-clock security guards or a security vestibule with magnetic door locks. In 1990, California and Nevada set standards for lighting and landscaping around ATMs. The ordinance was originally drafted to require guards and

CCTV coverage of high-risk ATMs, but was later watered down to address lighting requirements, and directs the ATM operators to evaluate the safety of their machines, and give customers notice of basic safety precautions. The safety evaluation must take into account the level of compliance with the lighting standards, the presence of landscaping and plantings that can obstruct the visibility around the ATM, and the incidence of violent crimes in the immediate neighborhood (Lewis, 1992, p. 87).

Chicago approved security enhancements after a 1989 murder near an ATM. But unless banks take proactive measures with facilities, more people will get hurt and lawsuits will be expensive. A Florida man was awarded $1 million after he was shot in the face while making a night deposit next to an ATM in 1986.

2. Using Civil Liability

Although police do not play a direct role in civil lawsuits resulting from ATM robberies, it is important to understand that ATM operators and premise owners carefully consider their civil liability when deciding where to place ATMs and what security measures to adopt. Much of the published literature addresses ATM security from a legal liability premises negligence perspective. Statutory and case law on liability for injuries sustained during ATM transactions varies across jurisdictions. The courts take into account the knowledge that ATM operators had, or should have had, about the risk of robbery at particular ATMs when determining their liability for victims' injuries. Consequently, ATM operators are advised to consult frequently with local police about reports of crime around ATMs. Courts will usually hold ATM operators to the industry standards for basic crime prevention measures, although establishing liability also depends on other legal issues. Among the legal issues concerning ATM operators' civil liability are the issues of foreseeability that the crime would occur; the standard for determining foreseeability; the victim's expectation of protection; and the various liability of the institution operating the ATM, any ATM network involved, the owner of the premise where the ATM is located, and the victim.

Certain types of businesses are at higher risk for the temptation and opportunity for criminal behavior. Having a cash machine on the side of a building with the customer's back to the street or alley necessarily places the customer in a vulnerable position. Thus, the business of providing cash or making night deposits at a facility, should make the owner of such an establishment anticipate careless or criminal acts on the part of third parties to their customers and take special precautions to protect and patrol their properties. Until such precautions become the accepted standard of care, or implemented by standards and codes, criminal acts at ATMs can be expected to continue. Civil suits for injuries and deaths resulting from the lack of security, along with emerging standards and regulations for ATM safety will eventually force banks to make the necessary changes.

The State of California (Cal. Fin. Code § 13000–070) and the City of New York (N.Y. Admin. Code § 10–160) pioneered minimum-security standards for ATMs. Among the other states that have enacted similar laws are Nevada (Nev. Rev. Stat. Ann. §§ 660.115–.235), Washington (Wash. Rev. Code Ann. § 19.174), Oregon (Or. Rev. Stat. § 714.280–.315), Georgia (Ga. Code. Ann. § 7–8-1 to 8–8), Louisiana, Maryland (Md. Code Ann., Fin. Inst. § 1-207), Florida (Fla. Stat. Ann. §655.960–965), Illinois, New York, and New Jersey. New York City documented poor security conditions through a careful survey of ATM sites before enacting its legislation (City Council of New York, 1991). City legislators have expressed concern that when the State assumed responsibility for enforcing the minimum ATM security standards in 1996, it failed to adequately fund the monitoring and enforcement function (City Council of New York, 1998).

Current case law defining the circumstances under which banks may be held liable for ATM crime remains limited. Courts are beginning to expand the elements of premises liability (Deitch, 1994, p. 34). Courts are moving toward the standard of care that owners are liable for the foreseeable acts of others if they fail to take reasonable precautions. ATM crime is foreseeable because banks

FIGURE 19.3 This ATM is shielded by structural columns at this bank, making visibility almost impossible.

have long known about the specific deterrents to ATM crime, with articles from industry trade magazines dating back to the 1980s, which have recommended a variety of precautions. (Deitch, 1994, p. 35). Many of the prescribed precautions include fencing, controlled access, lighting, landscaping, alarms, guards, and remote monitoring.

SPECIFIC RESPONSES TO REDUCE ATM ROBBERY

ATM operators should consider security, as well as marketing, in deciding where to install ATMs. The most commonly mentioned ATM robbery prevention measures in the literature are those that will be familiar to crime prevention through environmental design (CPTED) practitioners the 3 "Ls": lighting, landscaping, and location. ATM sites should be inspected regularly to ensure that safety features have not become compromised. ATM operators, police, and bank regulators all should share responsibility for monitoring compliance.

Architects responsible for designing banks and the adjoining ATMs should be cognizant of the security issues and concerns, and the liabilities if their designs are inviting to robbers (see Figure 19.3).

The structural column in front of the bank in Figure 19.3 largely blocks the view of the ATM and provides great hiding spaces, and prevents drive by surveillance by police or passersby. What was the architect thinking?? This two-story building does not require a six-foot-wide structural column. This was a design element intended to give the bank a more monumental look. The result is an almost hidden ATM and night deposit box.

FIGURE 19.4   The ATM is brightly lit, but the adjoining brush and blind spot around the corner is an invitation for a robber to hide and ambush an unsuspecting ATM user.

ALTERING LIGHTING, LANDSCAPING, AND LOCATION

3. Ensuring Adequate Lighting at and Around ATMs

Adequate lighting at and around ATMs allows users to see any suspicious people near the ATM, and allows potential witnesses, including police, to see a crime in progress and get a good look at the offender. Good lighting can deter people from robbing ATM users in the first place. There should be adequate light around all building corners adjacent to the ATM (see Figure 19.4), as well as for nearby parking places (see Figure 19.6).

There are no national guidelines or standards for bank facility lighting that exist in the United States. However, some cities and states have begun to set lighting standards. The New York City ordinance outlines lighting requirements for ATMs in that city (Goetzke, 1994, p. 57). Most ATM lighting standards, including some mandated by law, call for minimum light levels at and around ATMs. Typical minimums are 25 footcandles at the face of the ATM, 10 footcandles within 5 feet of the face of the ATM, and 2 footcandles 50 to 60 feet away from the ATM, measured at 3 feet above the ground (Goetzke, 1994, p. 59; Ellis, 1996; CUNA Service Group, 1999; Illinois Office of Banks and Real Estate, 1999)) (see Figure 19.5).

According to lighting designers, however, most minimum lighting standards do not address all the factors that affect visibility. Shadows, light types, light colors, light-source direction, light uniformity, glare, and obstructions all affect visibility for the observer. A qualified lighting designer should plan ATM lighting to not have shadows or glare. Excessive illumination at the face of the ATM or night depository, and very low light in the areas surrounding the devices can hinder the user's ability to see out and perceive danger that is approaching or hiding. People's eyes require time to adjust to the light change from bright to dark, otherwise known as *retinal eye adaptation*. The light source that is designed should not only light the face of the ATM but also provide light for the surrounding walking paths, parking areas, and approaches to the ATM. The design goal is to provide evenly distributed ambient lighting and avoid shadow and glare affects (Goetzke, 1994, p. 58) (see Figure 19.6).

Lights should turn on automatically with photo sensors rather than by manual or timer switches that are subject to human error. Light levels, once set properly, should be monitored regularly to ensure they do not fall below acceptable levels. Long-lasting light bulbs should be used. Automated light-detection monitors can alert the ATM operator if light levels drop. Light fixtures must be

FIGURE 19.5   There are several large lights shining into the parking lot, but the planter will be in shadow and provide a hiding spot. Note the signage on the column next to the ATM for no parking, stopping, or standing at any time.

adequately protected so that offenders cannot disable them. Illumination requirements should be approached as a three-phase task, the amount of light at the face of the ATM, the amount in the immediate area (10 to 20 feet from the face of the machine), and the amount outward from that point to the parking lot or drop off area. Each step away requires less light, but designed in a way that provides an even distribution of light and minimizing of deep shadows (Fared, 1991, p. 62) (see Figure 19.7).

FIGURE 19.6   Lighting at a drive-thru ATM needs to be bright and consistent and avoid any hiding spaces or ambush opportunities.

FIGURE 19.7   Plantings must be trimmed low to prevent hiding spaces for ambush of customers.

4. Ensuring that the Landscaping Around ATMs Allows for Good Visibility

Trees and shrubbery should be trimmed routinely to remove potential hiding places for offenders and ensure the ATM is visible to passersby. Slow-growing shrubbery that does not need trimming as often is preferable. Obstacles such as dumpsters, benches, or walls that obstruct clear views of the ATM should be removed.

This bank shown in Figure 19.8 had a remote corner location for its "special" commercial customers, which was a robbery ambush waiting to happen. Night deposits and cash drops by local businesses were allowed at this dangerous intersection.

FIGURE 19.8   A remote teller window and deposit is a perfect location for a robbery. Notice the blind spots and ambush areas created by the high bushes. This would be an especially high risk at night with the cover of darkness and the element of surprise.

5. Installing Mirrors on ATMs

Rearview mirrors on ATMs and adjacent building corners allow ATM users to detect suspicious people and behavior.

6. Installing ATMs Where There is a Lot of Natural Surveillance and Potential for Visibility by Others

ATMs should be placed in areas where there is a lot of routine vehicle and pedestrian traffic. The potential for witnesses deters offenders, and heavy traffic increases the probability of victim assistance when a robbery occurs. ATMs are increasingly being placed inside businesses such as grocery and convenience stores, where there is a lot of natural surveillance; this should help prevent ATM robberies. Some security experts recommend that ATMs have high visibility and activity on all three adjacent sides—ideally, with high-speed traffic on one side, slow-speed traffic on another, and relatively permanent observers (e.g., residents) on the third side. Indoor ATMs should be free of sight obstructions like plants and blinds, and should be visible from the street through transparent windows and doors. Reflective or tinted glass should not be used.

The ATM itself is sometimes a target and must be built in the architecture to rigid standards set by the requirements of the Bank Protection Act of 1968 and Underwriters Laboratory. The ATM must have alarm system components, shock and seismic sensors, sufficient weight and tensile strength, heat detectors, door contacts, and locking mechanisms, to deter attacks to the machine itself. Thieves have attached the ATM to a chain and pulled it out of the building wall. Devices are needed to provide early warning of an impending attack. People who service ATMs are vulnerable to robbery and should be considered in the security design by having duress alarms and secure closets to service the machines (Fahed, 1991, p. 63).

7. Installing ATMs in Police Stations

Some jurisdictions have installed publicly accessible ATMs in police stations to attract ATM users to a safe place to conduct their business. Although the idea has merit, many police stations might not be able to accommodate the added vehicle and pedestrian traffic generated by an ATM. Where this is a problem, ATM use might be limited to nighttime hours when the risk of robbery is greatest, and when the police business being conducted at the station is at a minimum. ATMs also might be installed in or near other government buildings such as post offices or fire stations, where there is at least some natural surveillance.

8. Relocating, Closing, or Limiting the Hours of Operation of ATMs at High-Risk Sites

ATM operators should assess crime rates from local police crime grids and other measures that suggest the overall risk level of the area in which they are considering installing an ATM. ATMs should not be placed in areas known for drug trafficking and sites near abandoned property or crime-prone liquor establishments. While ATM operators should not avoid placing ATMs in all low-income areas with higher crime rates, it might be reasonable to restrict ATM operation to daylight hours in such areas (see Figure 19.9).

FIGURE 19.9 This ATM is placed well, using good CPTED features, and has unobstructed visibility from the street and patrolling police.

FIGURE 19.10   The bank drive-thru had an ATM aisle. Visibility is good around most of the lanes.

ATM operators should consult with local police when choosing sites and notify police of all ATM locations (see Figure 19.10). Local laws should require such consultation as part of the routine site planning and business licensing processes.

The Bank ATM shown in Figure 19.11 is well-lit and has good visibility. However, the location is in a high crime area and is high risk, and several people have been robbed at this location. When design solutions can't work, then administrative remedies should be considered, such as limiting the hours of operation or hiring of security guards.

IMPLEMENTING PUBLIC AWARENESS AND EDUCATION INITIATIVES

9. PROVIDING ATM USERS WITH SAFETY TIPS

ATM users should be advised about what steps they can take to reduce their risk of getting robbed. Although it is unlikely that providing safety tips will prevent any particular robbery, the larger purpose is to change ATM users' habits. Safety tips can be provided through mailings to cardholders, signs posted at ATMs, messages printed on ATM receipts, messages displayed on ATM screens, safety presentations, and public awareness campaigns. Listed here are some standard safety tips for ATM users:

- Be aware of your surroundings, especially between dusk and dawn. If you notice anything suspicious—a security light out, someone loitering nearby—consider coming back later or using a supermarket or convenience store ATM.
- If using the ATM at night, take someone with you.
- Park in a well-lit area as close as possible to the ATM.
- At a drive-thru ATM, be sure the doors are locked and the passenger windows are rolled up.

FIGURE 19.11   This bank's ATM had good lighting but was located in a high-crime area with a history of robbery.

- If you withdraw cash put it away promptly; count it later, in private.
- Put your ATM card and receipt away promptly; never leave your receipt at the ATM.
- Keep your PIN secret—don't write it down, and don't share it with anyone you don't trust absolutely. Your PIN provides access to your account.
- Shield the keypad when entering your PIN to keep it from being observed.
- Avoid being too regular in your ATM use—don't repeatedly visit the same machine at the same time, the same day of the week, for instance.

Chris McGoey (2004, p. 2) suggests some of the following tips:

- Only use ATM machines in a well-lighted, open, high-traffic area.
- Use ATMs at inside busy supermarkets when possible.
- If lights around the ATM are not working, don't use the machine.
- Avoid bank ATM machines adjacent to obvious hiding spaces.
- When you approach an ATM, scan the area first for loiterers.
- Have your card ready and leave quickly, not counting your cash in public.
- Walk, run, or drive away immediately if your instincts tell you so.
- Beware of offers for help from strangers during an ATM transaction.
- Don't argue with a robber; if confronted, give up the cash.
- Don't attempt to fight with or to follow a robber.
- If you are robbed, drive or walk to a safe place and immediately call the police.

ATM users should further be advised to close any vestibule doors securely and not to open doors for others. In addition, signs at ATMs should state that the site is being observed by cameras, and mean it.

Some victims resist during robberies either to protect their valuables or because they believe the offender is about to get violent. Some succeed in preventing the robbery through resistance, whereas others get injured or killed. Offenders want to get the crime over with quickly so they can escape. Any delay increases their nervousness and, therefore, the likelihood they will become violent. Robbers are usually highly agitated and easily perceive the victim's actions as threatening. Drug and alcohol use will obviously influence their emotional state. Some use violence immediately to preempt any resistance. In cases with multiple offenders, the risk of violence increases because each offender is also concerned about appearing tough and in control to the other(s).

As with other violent crimes, victims should assess the particular situation, taking account of nearby assistance, weapons they are threatened with, offenders' behavior and emotional state, their own defensive abilities, and their own psychological need to resist. Given an imperfect understanding of why robbers become violent, compliance is usually the safer course of action for victims, and the best advice for police to offer. Widespread victim compliance, however, undoubtedly leads some offenders to perceive lower risk and, therefore, increases their ATM robbery rates.

USING SURVEILLANCE

10. Installing and Monitoring Surveillance Cameras at and Around ATMs

Surveillance cameras at and around ATMs serve two main purposes—to deter robbery and fraud, and to facilitate offender identification. If the experience with surveillance cameras inside banks is any guide, they serve the latter purpose better. There are two basic types of surveillance cameras—those that capture live images (such as CCTV), and those that merely record images that can be viewed later. Surveillance cameras should record both close-up images of the ATM user and the view immediately behind the user. A camera placed on or inside the ATM that is activated when a transaction is initiated serves this purpose. Such cameras should have wide-angle lenses not exposed to direct sunlight and should be mounted high off the ground to prevent vandalism (see Figure 19.13 and Figure 19.14).

Plainly visible cameras are more effective deterrents to robbers, but are more vulnerable to vandalism. Older technology uses videocassette recording; newer technology, which costs less to maintain, provides digital color images that are transmitted via Internet networks to remote sites, where they can be viewed online or stored and retrieved later. Dummy surveillance cameras should not be used unless there are also working cameras at the site, because they create a false sense of security among ATM users, and creates conditions for security negligence know as "Illusion of Security." At least one ATM operator has installed heat sensors around the ATM that detect the presence of people out of

FIGURE 19.12 A well-planned ATM with lighting and CCTV coverage.

FIGURE 19.13 An ATM placed in an office lobby foyer under camera surveillance.

FIGURE 19.14 This ATM had alarms and CCTV and good lighting, but the blind spot around the corner provided cover for someone hiding and waiting in the dark.

view of surveillance cameras. The sensors can activate either a recorded voice message warning the person to move away from the ATM, or a silent alarm.

11. Installing Devices to Allow Victims to Summon Police during a Robbery

There are several mechanisms by which ATM users can summon police quickly:

- Panic buttons installed on the ATM. Some security consultants and police, however, worry that panic buttons will just exacerbate the false-alarm problem that is already burdening police resources.
- Telephones next to the ATM.
- Live microphones in the ATM. A security company can monitor such microphones.
- Door alarms. Door alarms can be set so that they are automatically activated if a door to an enclosed vestibule is left open too long.
- Reverse PIN technology. An ATM user can activate a silent alarm by entering his or her PIN in reverse order or by entering an additional digit after the PIN. This so-called reverse PIN technology has been patented, and acts as a duress code. A study of its feasibility conducted for the State of Illinois concluded it was cost-prohibitive and unlikely to be effective because robbery victims are under such extreme stress to think clearly to enter their PIN backward.

12. Deploying Private Security Guards at ATMs

Security guards can either be assigned just to high-risk ATMs or be assigned to randomly patrol many ATMs. This response is considered the least attractive to ATM operators because of the high cost.

TARGETING OFFENDERS

13. Controlling Street Drug Markets to Reduce the Need for Robbery

High rates of street robbery usually coincide with high levels of street drug trafficking, particularly in crack cocaine. Crack addicts have frequent and immediate cravings for the drug; street robbery, especially around ATMs, is one of the fastest ways for them to get cash to buy the drug. Therefore, whatever you can do to control the volume of street-level drug trafficking will also likely reduce the street robbery rate, including ATM robbery.

14. Targeting Repeat Offenders

Where it can be established that a few offenders are likely responsible for many local ATM robberies, the offenders should be targeted by repeat offender programs. Detectives and patrol officers should cultivate informants to identify and apprehend active offenders. Offering rewards for information is also good practice. Interviewing offenders after they have been convicted is useful both for clearing other cases and for improving intelligence about the rate of ATM robbery committed by a few repeat offenders.

There are limits, however, to what arresting, prosecuting, and incarcerating ATM robbers can do to prevent ATM robbery. Most street robbers are so highly motivated to get quick cash that they discount the likelihood of getting caught and sent to jail as the cost of doing business.

15. Prohibiting Loitering and Panhandling Near ATMs

Some ATM robbers loiter around ATMs waiting for a suitable victim, and some ATM robberies are extreme cases of aggressive panhandling. Laws that prohibit loitering and panhandling near ATMs give police authority to keep opportunistic offenders away from potential victims.

FIGURE 19.15   This ATM is clearly visible through the glass door and reduces the opportunity for ambush or surprises.

HARDENING TARGETS AND DENYING BENEFITS

16. Requiring that ATMs be Located in Enclosed Vestibules with Doors that Lock

The State of New York requires that ATMs be in enclosed vestibules with doors that lock. Door locks can be programmed to admit only bank customers, but given the profits to be earned from noncustomer service fees, most banks dislike this added security measure (see Figure 19.15). Some security consultants believe that enclosed vestibules create more problems than they prevent. Door locks are frequently vandalized. Moreover, ATM users habitually open locked doors as a courtesy to others, or allow others to follow them into the vestibule. An offender who gets into an enclosed vestibule with a victim can more easily trap the victim. Enclosed vestibules also attract homeless people looking for a warm, dry place to sleep.

17. Setting Daily Cash-Withdrawal Limits

Bank regulations that limit the amount of cash a customer may withdraw each day from an ATM reduce the potential financial loss from a robbery, and potentially discourage some robbers who decide that the benefits of the robbery are not worth the risk of apprehension. However, most street robbers do not expect much cash from a robbery, while concluding it is worth the risk. It is not known what effect raising, or lowering cash withdrawal limits would have on ATM robbery rates, but in general, cash withdrawal limits make sound crime prevention sense, but many drug crazed robbers will kill for $20. The customers of ATMs need to be in a more secure environment in order to give them the advantage and lower the risk.

SUMMARY

ATMs are where the "easy" money is. Criminals know that ATMs are typically located in isolated locations and that people are going there to withdraw cash, or make a night deposit. Good security design and use of CPTED features can deny the opportunity for robbers and reduce the risk of assault, murder, and robbery of bank customers. ATMs by their very mission are high-risk facilities. They are essentially the convenience stores for cash (Lewis, 1992, p. 87), and as such are an attractive magnet for opportunistic criminal activity.

To date, many banking facilities have still not implemented the basic security features needed to protect their ATM and night depositor customers. As a result of litigation and many injured or killed customers, extra efforts are needed to make these facilities a safe experience. Lighting should be provided that is ample to illuminate the ATM but also the surrounding areas so there are not hiding spaces and shadows.

Landscaping and location are important elements in deterring crime at these locations. In order to be effective, there needs to be careful consideration of design features and structural elements to provide great natural surveillance. Architects are in a position to recommend placing of exterior ATMs in locations that are clearly visible to people walking or driving by and within the view of police patrols and camera surveillance. Opportunistic criminals will typically avoid open, unobstructed locations because crime there is more likely to be observed and reported to police or private security.

Where ATMs are placed in enclosures or vestibules, there should be large vision panels, which are free of obstructions, and allow the customer to conduct transactions, but not be ambushed from adjoining hidden spots. Vestibules should have panic or duress alarms in case a customer feels threatened, and there must be a real response capability.

Customers need to be educated as well to contribute their part to preventing crime. Customers need to put money away discretely before they leave, look around to see if they are being observed, take a companion when they visit ATMs at night, look inside the vestibule before entering, don't let persons in line look over their shoulder to observe their PIN, and be observant of the parking area for persons loitering or hiding spaces like dumpsters or parked cars.

Crime prevention is a joint effort between the behavior of the person and the environment. Both have responsibilities to do their fair share to act safely and reduce criminal opportunity. Preventing robbery at ATMs calls for both sensible behavior by potential victims and smart environmental design.

REFERENCES

ABA Banking Journal (1987) How Safe Are ATMs? 79:44–45.

ATM Crime Survey Report (1987) Washington DC: American Bankers Association.

ATM Crimes Bulletin Number 2 (1987) Rolling Meadows, IL: Bank Administration Institute.

Second National Survey on ATM Security (1989) Rolling Meadows, IL: Bank Administration Institute.

ATM Security in the 1990s: The Final Report of the Electronic Funds Transfer Association's ATM Security Task Force. Alexandria, VA: Electronic Funds Transfer Association, 1997.

Boyle, W. (1983) ATM Security. Rolling Meadows, IL: Bank Administration Institute.

Cross, R. (1994) *Bank Security Desk Reference*. Warren, Gorham & Lamont, Boston, MA.

California Bankers Association (1996) ATM Crime Survey Report. Available at: www.calbankers.com/legal/atmsurv.html

City Council of New York (1998) "ATM Insecurity." Press release, Aug. 6.

City Council of New York, Office of Oversight and Investigation (1991) Report on ATM Security. New York: City of New York.

Courter, E. (2000) ATM Trends: Networking and Security. *Credit Union Management,* 23(5), 42–44.

CUNA Service Group (1999) ATM Security Devices Protect Cash and Members. *Credit Union Magazine,* 65(6), 25–26.

Deitch, G. (1994) ATM Liability: Fast Cash, Fast Crime, Uncertain Law. *Trial,* 30(10), 34–39.

DeYoung, J. (1995) ATM Crime: Expanding the Judicial Approach to a Bank's Liability for Third-Party Crimes against ATM Patrons. *Valparaiso University Law Review*, 30, 99–159.

Eck, J. (1983) *Solving Crimes: The Investigation of Burglary and Robbery*. Washington, DC: Police Executive Research Forum.

Ellis, H. (1996) ATM Safety and Security: Do You Know Where Your Customer Is Tonight? *Bankers Magazine*, 179, 31–34.

Erickson, R. (1996) Armed Robbers and Their Crimes. Athena Research Corporation, Seattle, WA.

Fahed, J. (1991) Armoring ATMs Against Attack. *Security Management*, June, 63–64.

Goetzke, R. (1994) Shedding New Light on ATM Security. *Security Management*, September, 57–60.

Hall, D. (1989) ATM Security Under Scrutiny. *ABA Banking Journal*, 81(11), 70, 72.

Hawthorne, W. (1991) How To Increase Customer Safety at ATMs. *ABA Banking Journal*, 83(1), 34, 37.

Hoskins, G. (1994) Violent Crimes at ATMs: Analysis of the Liability of Banks and the Regulation of Protective Measures. *Northern Illinois University Law Review*, 14, 829–860.

Hudak, R. (1988) How Safe Is Your ATM (Automated Teller Machine)? *Security Management*, 32(6), 41–46.

Illinois Office of Banks and Real Estate (1999) ATM Safety and Security: Report to the 91st General Assembly, Senate Resolution No.134. Springfield: State of Illinois.

Indermaur, D. (1996) Reducing the Opportunities for Violence in Robbery and Property Crime: The Perspectives of Offenders and Victims. In R. Homel (Ed.), *The Politics and Practice of Situational Crime Prevention. Crime Prevention Studies, Vol. 5*. Monsey, NY: Criminal Justice Press.

Kaplan, H. (1992) Technics Focus: ATM Security Lighting. *Progressive Architecture*, 73(8), 101–103.

Kennish, J. (1984) ATMs A New Breed of Security Problems. *Security Management*, 28(5), 33–36.

Knapp, R., III (1996) Words in Collision: Preemption of the New York ATM Safety Act after *Barnett Bank v. Nelson. New York State Bar Journal*, 68, 30–36.

Lewis, J. (1992) ATMs: Magnets for Crime. *Trial*, 28, 87–89.

Matthews, R. (1996) *Armed Robbery: Two Police Responses. Crime Detection and Prevention Series, Paper 78*. London: Home Office.

McGoey, C. (2004) Bank ATM Security. Available at: Crimedoctor.com

Morgan, K. (1997) Banking Under the Watchful Eye of the Law. *American City and County*, 112, 16.

Morrison, S. and I. O'Donnell. (1996) An Analysis of the Decision-Making Practices of Armed Robbers. In R. Homel (Ed.), *The Politics and Practice of Situational Crime Prevention. Crime Prevention Studies, Vol. 5*. Monsey, NY: Criminal Justice Press.

Painter, K. and N. Tilley. (1999) Surveillance of Public Space: CCTV, Street Lighting and Crime Prevention. *Crime Prevention Studies*, Vol. 10. Monsey, NY: Criminal Justice Press.

Peterson, A. (1998) ATM Security. *Credit Union Magazine*, 64(2), 42–45.

Schreiber, F. B. (1994) The Future of ATM Security. *Security Management*, 38(3)(Suppl.), 18A–20A. (1994).

Schreiber, F. B. (1992) Tough Trends for ATMs. *Security Management*, April, 27–31.

Scott, M. S. (2002) Robbery at Automated Teller Machines. Problem Oriented Guides for Police Services. Series #8. 2002 U.S. Department of Justice. Washington, DC: Office of Community Oriented Policing Services.

Spelman, W. (1990) Repeat Offender Programs for Law Enforcement. Washington, DC: Police Executive Research Forum.

Stockdale, J. and P. Gresham. (1998) *Tackling Street Robbery: A Comparative Evaluation of Operation Eagle Eye*. Crime Detection and Prevention Series, Paper 87. London: Home Office.

Tough Trends for ATMs. (1990) *Security Management*, 36(4), 27, 29–31.

Wipprecht, W. (1991) Strike Back at ATM Crime. *Journal of California Law Enforcement*, 25(3), 53–58.

Wright, J. (1996) Automatic Teller Machines (ATMs). In L. Fennelly (Ed.), *Handbook of Loss Prevention and Crime Prevention*, 3rd ed. Newton, MA: Butterworth-Heinemann.

Wright, R. and S. Decker. (1997) *Armed Robbers in Action: Stickups and Street Culture*. Boston: Northeastern University Press.

20 Landscape and Site Design*

The first contact any building user has with a particular project is accessing the property, and gaining entry to the building through the site. The first and most important line of defense of a building is the accessibility of the site, its relationship with placement of the building, and the landscape design. Landscaping helps identify borders between public and private space and helps reinforce desired behaviors by defining movement areas and patterns (Crowe, 2000, p. 124). This chapter begins by presenting natural methods of CPTED with landscape architecture. It ends with a presentation of mechanical techniques for high security environments using landscape CPTED strategies.

Landscape architects design public and private spaces and environments that serve a particular function hopefully, in a pleasing aesthetic manner. Also important in fulfilling this task, the site and landscape design should protect users, ensuring their safety and security (see Figure 20.1).

FIGURE 20.1 A well-maintained and well-defined front yard.

The main guardians of health and safety for building designs are building codes, but these typically address architectural features such as egress design, fire safety, and structural integrity while ignoring the considerations of crime or terrorism. As safety is a prime consideration of building codes, security of the site and land around the building must also be one of the highest priorities.

Landscaping can establish one of the most important action steps against trespassing by establishing a property line. Marking the property boundary is the first step in crime prevention and antiterrorism design because it actually deters illegitimate users who might otherwise walk in unnoticed and unchallenged (see Figure 20.2).

There is typically a dilemma in priorities when it comes to establishing privacy versus security in most architectural project developments. The balance can be difficult and varies from application to application. A low hedge or fence establishes a psychological and physical barrier between public and private property. A picket fence establishes an edge without obscuring the view or limiting surveillance (see Figure 20.4). If trees are added above the fence, there can be a sense of enclosure, but trespassers still have the ability to see into the property between the fence and tree canopy (see Figure 20.3).

Block or brick walls offer protection to hiding the thief as well as securing the property owner. Bare walls are easy to maintain but invite graffiti. Supplement walls with landscaping to provide protection, and a more effective barrier to unwanted intrusion. Thorny bougainvillea, carissa, wild lime, or rather toothy brushes planted in combination with a wall can combine the best of planting resources (see Figure 20.5 and Figure 20.6).

* Portions of the text in this chapter consist of articles and other publications previously written by the author including possible portions found in the following Wiley publications: *Landscape Architectural Graphic Standards*, Hopper (Ed.), John Wiley & Sons, ISBN: 0471477559, ©2007. We offer special thanks to the American Institute of Architects and John Wiley & Sons for permission to reproduce common content in this work.

FIGURE 20.2 A good application of landscaping and fencing behind homes with good territoriality and border definition, natural surveillance, and restricted access.

FIGURE 20.3 This photo shows a pedestrian walking path burned into the grass between the fence and shrubbery. The CPTED practitioner should evaluate whether the mobility path is desired or needs to be blocked with stronger physical security measures.

Strategically place individual plants to discourage trespassers. Thorny shrubs could be a safety problem if small children are abundant, and poses a challenge for maintenance crews. Many of the thorny plants come in different sizes to fit the different landscaping needs. Carissa comes in three sizes: emerald blanket, which is a dwarf variety, boxwood blanket, which is an intermediate variety growing up to 6 feet, and *Carissa Grandiflora*, which grows 7 or 8 feet.

FIGURE 20.4 The experience we are looking for is low ground cover, high canopies and unobstructed views of patrol. (From *Safe Schools Design Guide*, (Moore/Powers, 1993). Used with permission from the Florida Center for Community Design + Research (www.fccdr.usf.edu).)

FIGURE 20.5 This thorny plant will deter casual climbing and cause trespassers to rethink their approach.

In a residential application the landscaper should provide shrub masses or low ground coverage and setback from the building wall or glazing systems. This may discourage the breaking and entering of windows. It is best to avoid tall large-leaved plants that could visually protect the intruder (see Figure 20.7). Pygmy date palms in front of windows will not block breezes, but their needle-sharp thorns at the base of the palm fronds will slow down anyone climbing through them. Other plants that provide similar coverage are the Jerusalem thorn and Cinnecord.

FIGURE 20.6   This thorny plant is good for low bushes and deterring access to the building façade.

FIGURE 20.7   Overgrown shrubs and lack of maintenance make this an inviting opportunity for a car burglary or personal assault.

LANDSCAPING CPTED TIPS

A well-maintained hedge by the building perimeter can discourage people from reaching or crawling through to access a window. Even if a burglar enters through a door and leaves through a window it will be much more difficult to carry out stolen assets like a television or computer through bushes, hedges, ferns, and other landscaping barriers. The fencing combined with carefully considered plantings will divide the public and private areas (see Figure 20.8)

Earth berms are common in landscaping, but if not carefully used can create visual obstructions. One example, in Figure 20.9, is a public park where berms broke up the monotony of the flat site. The result was a near-total visual obstruction of play areas, an obstruction used by local gangs to avoid supervision by local police. The berms were lowered to a height two and a half feet so police could patrol and supervise the property (see Figure 20.10 and Figure 20.11).

Landscaping can be used appropriately to create effective crime prevention measures, or it can create criminal opportunities. The following landscaping and planting considerations are critical for safety and security design:

- Avoid planting that obscures extensive parts of a main path or recreation area
- Planting should take into account growth rates and any maintenance requirements and expectations (see Figure 20.12)
- Low-growing plants should be set back one yard from the edge of paths or walkways (see Figure 20.13)
- Maintain low growing shrubs not to exceed 32 to 36 inches in height.
- Use spiny or thorny shrubs in places that could be hiding places, or areas of illegitimate activity, or close to walls where it is desired to keep people away from windows. Thorny plantings may attract garbage and litter and may need a low perimeter fence to prevent foot traffic or wind blown debris.
- Hard landscaping should be vandal resistant and not provide potential throwing objects, such as loose gravel, stones, or cobbles.
- Landscape features and furniture should not provide the means to gain access to the property, or to see over walls or hedges into rooms or gardens. Street furniture should be designed for short-term use and should not allow use as a bed or sleeping surface.
- Tree canopies should be trimmed up to 8 feet in height where appropriate to provide a clear unobstructed line of site, and reduce hiding spots and ambush opportunities (see Figure 20.14, Figure 20.15, Figure 20.16, and Figure 20.17).

FIGURE 20.8   A good example of ground cover and plantings that support the fencing and mobility paths.

FIGURE 20.9   This berm is separating a park from the road, and with the trees not pruned there is little possibility of natural surveillance by patrol cars or passersby.

FIGURE 20.10   This berm provides separation between road and walkway, but does not block observation and surveillance.

FIGURE 20.11   The berm is almost four feet high and screens the cars from street, but makes natural surveillance from the street by police or passersby almost impossible.

FIGURE 20.12 Not all regions have tropical growth, and in drought environments, xeriscaping, and low water plants must be considered.

FIGURE 20.13 A good example of natural surveillance and boundary definition with well maintained low level landscaping and fencing. (Used with permission from David Wright, urban design planner and former president of Action Assessment Group, Inc. [AAG Inc.].)

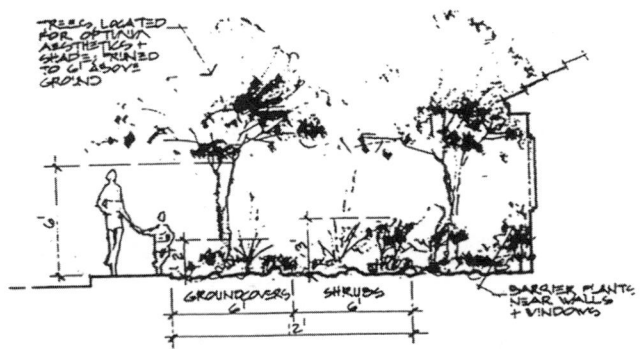

Planting Adjacent to Walks and Walls

FIGURE 20.14 Design guidelines can give design professionals some guidance on the experience that is desired. (Image© 1997 City of Tempe, Arizona. Reprinted with permission.)

FIGURE 20.15 Low fencing deters pedestrian cross throughs and guides people to the sidewalks with access control.

FIGURE 20.16   The tree canopies of this house were pruned to allow good natural surveillance around the property.

FIGURE 20.17   Street furniture can be integrated into the landscape design to create interesting and intimate settings without being dangerous. In troublesome areas where the bench becomes a sleeping surface, it is possible to specify the bench with intermittent railings to prevent that.

PLANTINGS AND SECURITY

The kinds of shrubs you include in your landscape—and where you plant them—can add to your home's security as well as beautify your property. This will also increase resale value (see Figure 20.18).

GROUND COVERS

Ground covers are surface-growing plants that rarely grow taller than 12 inches. Ground covers include ivy, pachysandra, vinca, and myrtle. These low-to-the-ground plants can be used to designate site areas as well as establishing the site boundaries (see Figure 20.19). When planted in a

FIGURE 20.18 This residence has some contours and low ground cover along with well-pruned tree canopies. It is attractive but does not support hiding.

FIGURE 20.19 This office building has a monkey grass ground cover that blended nicely with the vehicle barriers. The bollards and low screening are painted green and does not draw attention to them.

bed or panel these plants create an attractive symbolic barrier or buffer area. When planted in mass these selections can fill in large, vacant, and anonymous areas with no designated use. Appropriated in this manner, ground covers neutralize space, lending aesthetic sensibilities while clearly indicating that a space is not to be walked upon (see Figure 20.20).

Low Shrubs

Low shrubs are bushy plants that do not grow beyond 3 feet in height, consisting of several woody stems rather than a single trunk. Low shrubs will form a tight-knit symbolic barrier when planted 2.5 to 3 feet apart. Because of their limited height, these shrubs are an excellent way to define site areas over which visual surveillance is required. Low shrubs are also used to define a project perimeter as well as buffer on-site use areas. (Figure 20.21).

FIGURE 20.20 This photo is a good example of low ground cover and fencing and walls to create a lush boundary to the facility. The living walls reduce the opportunity for graffiti.

FIGURE 20.21 A thick thorny bush goes a long way to reduce trespassing and wandering into areas you don't belong.

Shrubs such as hawthorn that have tough, thorny branches can present a formidable obstacle when planted under first-floor windows. Dense, spiny shrubs such as barberry make an effective barrier hedge along property lines.

- A particularly hardy and attractive evergreen shrub, *Three-Spine Barbary*, has 5/8-inch long spines that appear in groups of three at regular intervals on stems and branches.
- *Japanese Holly* is a rugged, easy to cultivate broad-leafed evergreen shrub with dark green foliage. The holly makes a good protective hedge at 2.5 to 3 feet in height.
- The *Andorra Jupiter* is a hardy and reliable shrub compact and horizontal in growth. This plant has needle-like evergreen foliage, featherlike in texture, and medium green color. The Andorra Jupiter is excellent for holding soil on slopes and banks.
- Although somewhat difficult to grow, *rose bushes* are an especially elegant deterrent to intruders when planted in mass. Under windows and around sheds, intersperse your plantings with gravel or pebbles. They are noisy underfoot and will announce the arrival of anyone who comes too close.
- Other recommended low shrubs include the *Dwarf-winged Euonymus* and the *Spreading English Yew.*

Cost Benefit Analysis

The principal advantage of plant materials compared to equivalent architectural features, such as low walls or fences are relatively low cost. This is especially true if in-house staff, versus outside landscaping companies, installs the plants and handles the installation and maintenance.

Although plants require more frequent maintenance and care than constructed elements, and are more easily vandalized, they present a more aesthetically pleasing environment. It is possible to minimize vandalism through landscape layout, for example careful planting around individual residential buildings. Plantings will also contribute to a positive and attractive environment, softening the frigidity and raw elements of urban projects and enriching the texture, color, and spatial qualities of the project site.

Mid-Sized Shrubs

Mid-sized shrubs present substantial symbolic barriers while reducing site penetrability and forming a screen or buffer separating adjacent areas. These plants must be arranged appropriately so as not to block natural surveillance into key areas. Reaching a possible height of 6 to 10 feet within 5 to 10 years, mid-sized shrubs can be either deciduous or evergreen. A few of these shrubs have thorns or spines, which aid the plants in their own defense while establishing a convincing barrier. Due to these elements, shrubs with thorns or spines should be planted at least 3 to 4 feet from walkways and other locations, which are heavily used by residents.

Mid-sized shrubs may grow tall enough to block visual surveillance of a site and must be pruned lower if they present a security hazard. Shrubs of this height may also be used to form screens defining semi-private to private front and rear yard areas. They are also effective in small groupings to landscape lawn, garden, and yard areas.

Examples include the Burford Holly, which has large, bright red berries in autumn and winter. The Ibolian Privet is vigorous, quick growing, and hardy, with evergreen foliage. Small black berries grow in the autumn and winter. Finally, the Firethorn, which can be planted against walls or to form a barrier hedge, has numerous clusters of orange berries in autumn and winter.

Trees

Large trees can form effective symbolic barriers when planted 20 to 25 feet apart. Because of their heavy trunks and large canopies of foliage, large trees can define a project perimeter, or indicate the limits of an on-site active playfield or other use area. Large trees often enhance sitting areas since their shade during the warm months of the year encourages the use of outdoor seating and thus promotes informal surveillance on a site. Because large trees' foliage canopy is above eye level, they do not hinder the surveillance of site areas.

Small trees are usually 10 to 15 feet tall and are often shrub-like; they are best utilized as a barrier or screen. For perimeter protection, small trees are most effective at separating potential conflicts between adjacent use areas. These trees must not block site surveillance areas.

Examples of recommended large trees are:

- Bradford Pear
- Japanese Pagoda Tree
- Sweet Gum
- Norway Maple
- Northern Red Oak
- Little-Leaf Linden

Examples of recommended small trees are:

- Crabapple
- Lavalle Hawthorn
- Purpleleaf Plum
- Saucer Magnolia
- Star Magnolia
- Washington Hawthorn

LIGHTING AND LANDSCAPING

The earlier chapters on lighting describe general security lighting practices. Some specific lighting methods related to landscaping must be kept in mind. For example, lighting for security should be from the tops of trees downward, keeping in mind not to obstruct lighting with tree foliage. A security director should be involved in the landscaping and lighting plan coordination. It is important to consider whether trees are deciduous and shed their leaves, or remain full all year round like pine trees. The type and placement of trees can drastically affect the exterior lighting for full security coverage (Figure 20.22).

A security light that is too bright may reduce the observer's ability to see into the site. Low-level, well-distributed lighting helps reduce night blindness. Also keep in mind that the type and placement of trees also affects the ability of CCTV to function properly by blocking the lines of sight (Figure 20.23 and Figure 20.24).

FIGURE 20.22 Landscaping and lighting are appropriately spaced along the sidewalk of this office building.

FIGURE 20.23   Lighting too close to trees only affords expensive tree lighting!

FIGURE 20.24   The lighting is under the tree canopy and can create a nice environment and still provide good visibility for pedestrians.

On a blueprint of a site plan the camera placement may appear to have clear lines of vision. However, when the CCTV plan is overlaid with the landscaping design there may be numerous blind spots. The height and fullness of the trees must be considered for camera placement. The geography of the building will play a role in the transparency of a tree. In South Florida, the trees don't lose their leaves in winter, like northern climates. Deciduous trees, those that shed their leaves, have to be a consideration when planning lighting and CCTV coverage of the site.

SECURITY ZONES

The "Urban Design Guidelines for Physical Perimeter Entrance Security: An Overlay to the Master Plan for the Federal Triangle," prepared by GSA, presented the concept of security zones. *National Capital Planning Commission* (NCPC) also has used and developed the same guidelines for identifying security zones located between a particular building and the street. These zones are the same as the hierarchy of space concept in CPTED that transitions space from public to semipublic to semiprivate to private spaces. Each of these zones, ranging from the building's interior to the public streets around the building, has different security risks and responses. These can be translated into different architectural, landscape, and streetscape responses to meet these security needs.

GSA's security zones include:

Zone 1: Building Interior
Zone 2: Building Perimeter
Zone 3: Building Yard
Zone 4: Sidewalk
Zone 5: Curb or Parking Lane
Zone 6: Street

Zones 1 and 2 are related exclusively to the architecture of the building (see Figure 20.25). They are not the subjects of these guidelines for physical perimeter security. Zone 6, the street itself, is not subject to these guidelines. Zones 3, 4, and 5 are related to both the public right-of-way and the surrounding landscape design context of the building and site. Design guidelines are recommended for these zones.

ZONE PROTOTYPES

Extending GSA's concept of security zones, the NCPC Task Force developed prototypes for the exterior zones of buildings.

BUILDING YARD (ZONE 3)

The building yard is that portion of the site located between the building wall or façade and the sidewalk or public right-of-way. The building yard is the exterior space between a building and the sidewalk, usually the grassy area bordering the building. This space can be planted with raised flowerbeds beside the sidewalk to create a barrier from a building to the public domain. Pedestrian entries and loading docks are typically in this category making it necessary to integrate security seamlessly to compliment the buildings architecture and remain effective at monitoring entries and exits. When the security barrier is provided in this location, for example, through the use of a raised plinth or wall, the sidewalk can remain free from intrusive security elements.

A sidewalk that incorporates security measures should not look like a sidewalk to which security has been added; instead, security measures should be incorporated into the overall design of the streetscape. GSA security criteria take a balanced approach to security, considering cost effectiveness, acknowledging acceptance of some risk, and recognizing that federal buildings should be not bunker or fortress-like, but open, accessible, attractive, and representative of the democratic spirit of the country (see Figure 20.26). Prudent, rather than excessive security measures are appropriate in facilities owned by and serving the public.

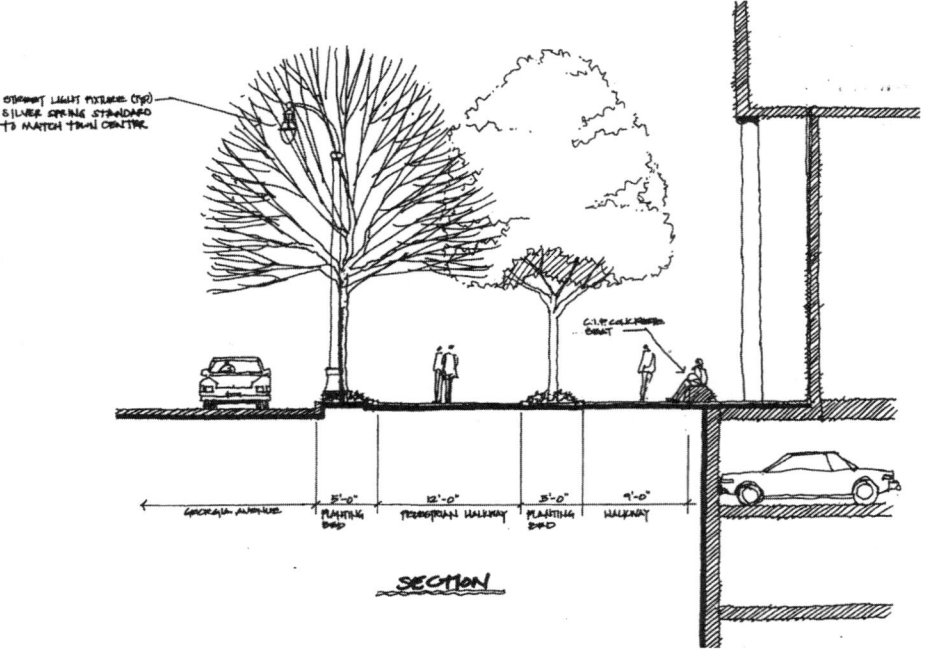

FIGURE 20.25   Zones for setbacks. (Reproduced courtesy of the National Capital Planning Commission (www.ncpc.gov/).)

FIGURE 20.26   Street furniture that is CPTED friendly.

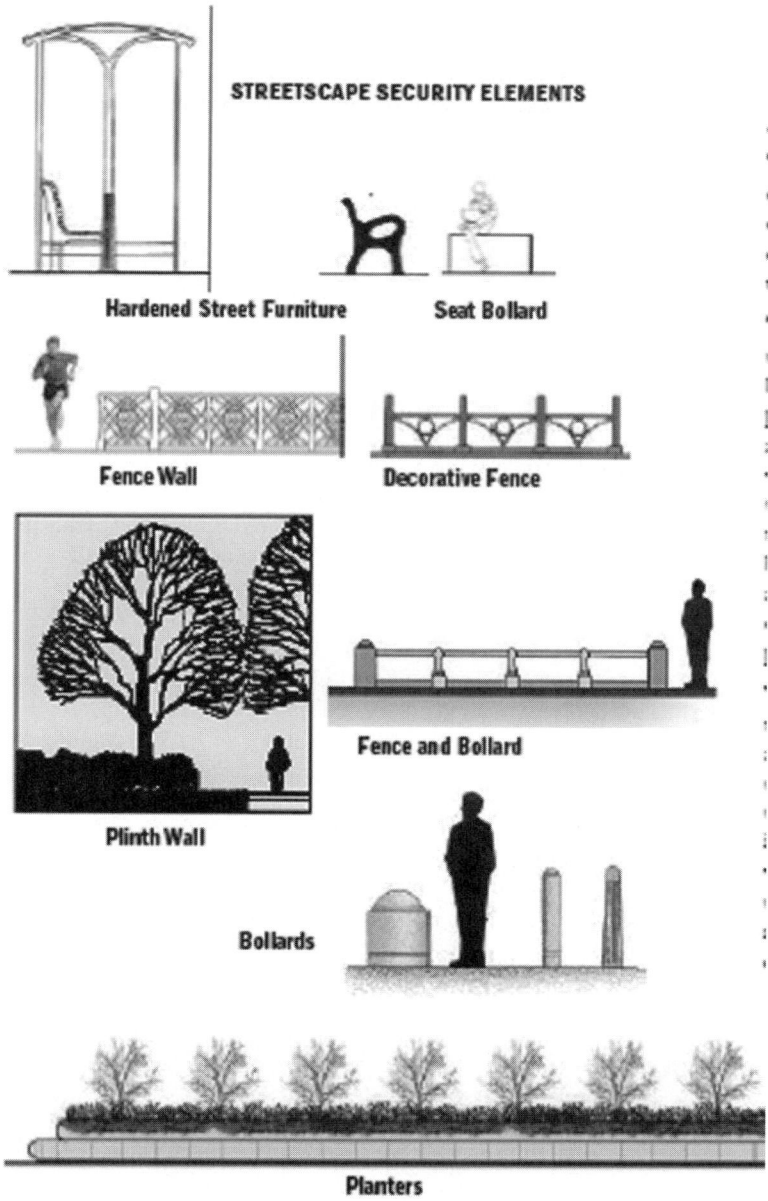

FIGURE 20.27 National Capital Planning Commission (NCPC) diagram of street furniture that can be vehicle resistant. (Reproduced courtesy of the National Capital Planning Commission (www.ncpc.gov/).)

Many of these new designs need to be engineered and "crash-tested" to verify their effectiveness. Individual assessments will determine the feasibility and cost of these solutions for the private and commercial sector (Figure 20.27).

The following are recommended guidelines for security measures in the building yard security zone:

- Design security measures, such as gatehouses and other entry facilities, to relate primarily to the access control of the building.
- Design other security measures to relate to the character of the surrounding area.
- Do not impede pedestrian access to building entries or pedestrian circulation on adjacent sidewalks.
- Use a raised planter or building terrace as a vehicular barrier, and integrate landscaping and seating.
- Use bollards, light standards, planters, or other furnishings to secure gaps and limit vehicular access through pedestrian access points.
- Plant trees in the yard adjacent to the sidewalk to create a double row of trees flanking the sidewalk.
- Incorporate furnishings and amenities into the building yard.

Sidewalk (Zone 4)

The sidewalk zone is located between the building yard and the curb or parking lane. This zone is located between the curb or parking lane and the aforementioned building yard. In the urban context it serves as a common space for pedestrian activity and interaction. Thus, it is important to allow for and promote active public use of the sidewalk allowing the sidewalk to be left open and accessible to pedestrian movement (see Figure 20.28).

Generally, streetscape security components should be excluded from Zone 4. Sidewalks should not be too wide or narrow. Urban planner Alan Jacobs describes some effective widths for different sidewalk contexts in his book, *Great Streets* (1995). Adjustment to the width of the sidewalk zone may occur to make it appropriately scaled for pedestrian use. Streetscape security components should be placed at least 18" from the edge of the curb to allow for the opening of car doors and pedestrian movements from car to sidewalk. This is the best location for streetscape elements and offers the most compatible location for security barriers. There is no need to remove curbside parking and traffic lanes when security requirements can be met at the curb.

Parking meters, streetlights, benches, planters, and trash receptacles are familiar curb items. Streetscape designs incorporating hardened versions of these elements should be designed to reinforce the pedestrian realm (see Figure 20.29).

FIGURE 20.28   CPTED friendly bench with low ground cover and retaining wall that can act as a vehicle barrier.

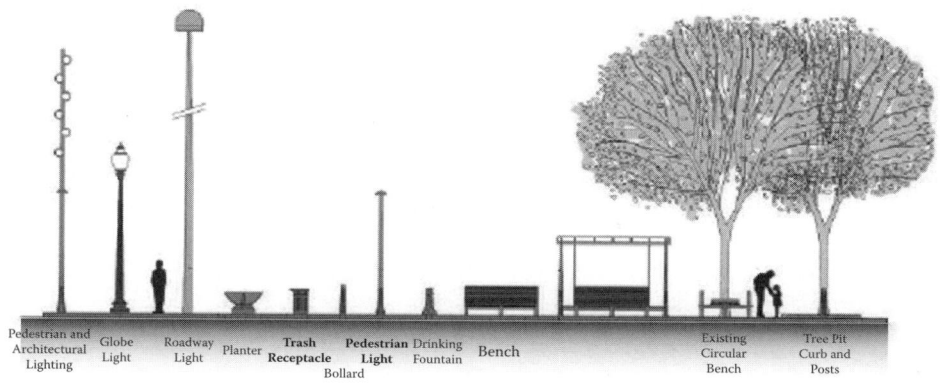

HARDENED STREETSCAPE ELEMENTS

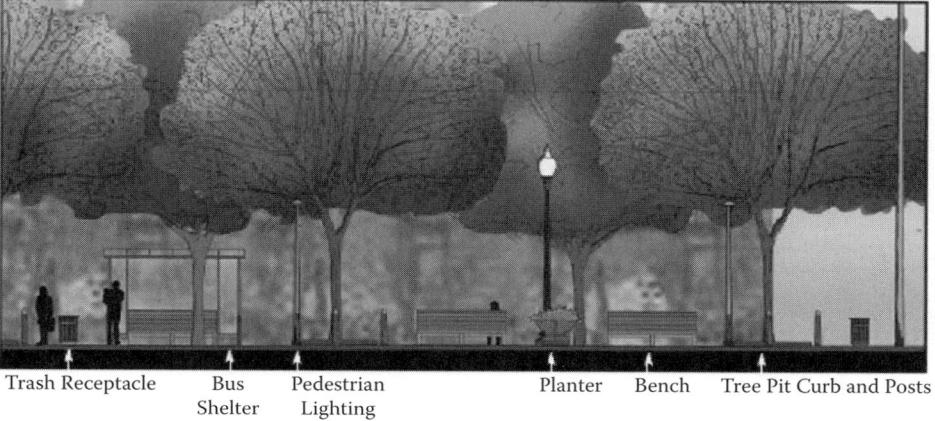

Trash Receptacle   Bus   Pedestrian   Planter   Bench   Tree Pit Curb and Posts
                    Shelter   Lighting

STREETSCAPE ELEVATION

FIGURE 20.29   Streetscape elements as suggested by NCPC. (Reproduced courtesy of the National Capital Planning Commission (www.ncpc.gov/).)

The following are recommended guidelines for security measures to be implemented in this zone:

- Design security measures to relate primarily to the character of the adjacent designated street or contextual zone.
- Incorporate security design within the design of street lighting, planters, bollards, streetscape amenities (seating, trash receptacles, flagpoles, kiosks, signage, drinking fountains, water features, etc.) and landscaping.
- Do not impede pedestrian access to entries or pedestrian circulation on the sidewalk;
- Integrate planters and bollards into the overall streetscape design.

CURB LANE (ZONE 5)

The curb or parking lane is that portion of the street adjacent to the curb. The curb lane is the lane of the street closest to the sidewalk. Curbside parking, passenger drop-off, loading, and service vehicles most often use this lane. Curbside parking should only be removed in areas where the need for additional standoff distance is absolutely essential and only for buildings with the highest security threat. The parking needs of the adjacent owners of a property should be assessed and parking replaced prior to any changes in the access of existing curbside lanes.

FIGURE 20.30   Planter bollards, acting as a vehicle barrier in front of a Federal Building.

The following are recommended guidelines for security measures to be implemented in the curb or parking lane security zone:

- Eliminate parking in this lane where warranted by the security risk assessment.
- Eliminate curbside loading zones and service access.
- Incorporate the curbside lane into a widened sidewalk zone.
- Reserve sections of the curb lane for exclusive agency use where such use can be controlled and monitored.

Vehicular Barrier Design

The goal for landscape architects and design professionals is to minimize target hardening and fortress design whenever possible, except where required after thorough analysis and study. The design professional must address the issue of how architectural design features and approaches may be enhanced security without intruding objectionably on the aesthetics and functionality of the building (see Figure 20.30).

BOLLARDS AND BARRIERS

Landscape architects are already familiar with the most common ways to control access to a site using physical barriers such as bollards, planters, security gates, turnstiles to control traffic and parking. Deciding on the type of physical barrier necessary for a specific project is based on what level of protection is needed, how important aesthetics are, and how large a budget is available (Figure 20.31, Figure 20.32, Figure 20.33, Figure 20.34, and Figure 20.35).

FIGURE 20.31 Crash-resistant fencing and bollards.

Plain barriers such as jersey barriers are mass-produced. These barriers are strong and crash-worthy, made of steel-reinforced concrete, and relatively cheap. Jersey barriers are easy to install and move but remain aesthetically unappealing. One solution to this problem is the Jersey Bib System, a decorated planter produced by Stonewear that is a decorative apron that fits over the top of a standard jersey barrier. One reason landscape architects have made extensive use of the Jersey barrier is the range of options which range from a standard premanufactured model or custom designed alternative model (Figure 20.36).

Bollards are an ideal way to separate pedestrians from vehicular traffic and for limiting vehicular access. Available as fixed models or as removable or retractable, models are constructed of steel, cast iron, precast concrete, ductile iron, aluminum high-density polyurethane, or recycled plastic. Fixed bollards are typically set in concrete or welded onto a base plate or bolted down (Figure 20.36, Figure 20.37, and Figure 20.38).

Bollard systems consist of one or more bollards operating independently or in groups of two or more units. Rising bollards are below ground and raised into the guard position by a remotely located precision hydraulic or pneumatic power unit. The beam barrier can be used with fiber optic net barrier.

Planter barriers are frequently constructed of glass-fiber reinforced concrete, with a steel cage built of reinforcing bars. As security structures, these barriers have a strength and resistance comparable to highway barriers, although they are designed to divert trucks into the air rather than simply stopping them. Planter security barricades are aesthetically pleasing while improving security at the same time. Stonewear produces a product line called Terra Cotta, which has the look and feel of sun-baked clay. Although nice to look at, these planters carry a hefty price tag (see Figure 20.39).

FIGURE 20.32   Vehicle barriers around the Washington Monument

Barriers and gates have been around for centuries and are still being used due to their effectiveness, reasonable price, and ease of operation. These gates are available to landscape architects in a variety of styles including those that slide, raise and lower, swing, or pop up from the ground. Most gates are manufactured from rectangular hollow sections to provide the necessary strength while keeping weight down (Figure 20.40).

It is designed to roll backward on impact and impale the vehicle from the underside. The result is that the gate acts as a massive friction anchor that will slow or stop most vehicles in their tracks. Road blockers fundamentally consist of a box section welded with reinforcement struts that are submerged in the ground, with a wedge shape that can be raised or lowered to control vehicular traffic (see Figure 20.42 and Figure 20.43).

With the increased sophistication of modern technology, many of the newest barrier arms feature hydraulic power packs, photocells, and programmable controllers to raise and lower the barrier. These help ensure that gates will open and close smoothly and will act efficiently, once activated. Most barrier gates include standard features such as a manual operation override in case of a power failure, and a safety system that prevents the gate from closing on pedestrians or vehicles (see Figure 20.41).

FIGURE 20.33   Washington Monument HaHa or barrier wall.

FIGURE 20.34 Street planters and bollards around the Federal Reserve Building in Memphis uses CPTED landscaping and plantings.

FIGURE 20.35 Groundcover and plantings camouflaging bollards.

FIGURE 20.36   Ugly comes in all colors. Jersey barriers used at an airport offer no security value as they are not secured into the ground and can be easily moved by a car or pushed by several people.

FIGURE 20.37   Jersey barriers used as an ugly and temporary solution for site protection. The barriers offer little to no site protection from a car/truck bomber.

FIGURE 20.38 Security planters offer protection and a sense of territoriality around the perimeter of the property.

FIGURE 20.39 A good view of how the bollards are actually installed.

FIGURE 20.40 A view of the mechanics and pneumatics of a retractable bollard. The bollard is dropped into the steel casing and submerged below the ground. The bollard is shown in an extended position.

FIGURE 20.41   A combination of barriers, architectural and mechanical at the service and employee entrance of a federal office building.

FIGURE 20.42   Mechanical barriers protect the service entrance to the FBI building in Washington DC.

FIGURE 20.43   Guards watch a van go by as the barriers are lowered.

PHYSICAL BARRIERS FOR LANDSCAPE SECURITY

Physical barriers may be two general types—natural and structural. Natural barriers include mountains, cliffs, canyons, rivers, or other terrain that is difficult to traverse. Structural barriers are man-made devices such as fences, walls, floors, roofs, grills, bars, or other structures that deter penetration. If a natural barrier forms one side or any part of the perimeter, it should not automatically be considered an adequate perimeter barrier. Provide structural barriers for that portion of the perimeter where a determined intruder may overcome the natural barrier.

FENCING

Fences are the most common perimeter barrier or control. Two standard types are chain link and picket fencing. Although chain links are typically unsightly, they are sometimes necessary and appropriate for certain contexts; the choice is dependent primarily upon the degree of facility permanence and local ordinances. A good perimeter fence is continuous, kept free of unwanted plant growth, and maintained in good condition (see Figure 20.44, Figure 20.45, Figure 20.46, and Figure 20.47).

FIGURE 20.44   A perimeter fence with CPTED friendly landscaping makes for an attractive and secure border.

FIGURE 20.45 The U.S. Border fence between Mexico and Texas is intended to be daunting and serve as a real barrier to prevent trespassing.

FIGURE 20.46 A perimeter fence was added around a university to create a safe boundary and control access of pedestrians and vehicles to the property.

FIGURE 20.47   Good intentions for this perimeter fencing, but it has serious design flaws. The edifice on the support column only acts as a ladder, easily compromising the value of the steel picket fence.

SUMMARY

It may sound obvious, but the architect, landscape architect, and security designer, need to keep records of the decision making process. This is why it is so important to conduct a proper risk assessment, with all the data recorded in hard copy. This not only helps designers choose appropriate CPTED strategies, but it helps later on if a reassessment becomes necessary during a postoccupancy evaluation or during litigation resulting from a security breach.

Finally, it is important to involve the landscape architect in a collaborative process with the architect, and the electrical engineer to integrate the security and crime prevention features into the site design. The health, safety, and welfare of building users depend on good security site planning and design.

REFERENCES

Atlas, R. (2006a) Is There a Difference Designing for Crime or Terrorism Interagency Cooperation. *Law Enforcement Executive Forum.* 6(6) November.
Atlas, R. (2006b) Architect as Nexus: Cost Effective Security Begins with Design. *ArchiTech*, May–June, 30–34.
Atlas, R. (2006c) Designing for Security. *The Construction Specifier*, April, 83–92.
Atlas, R. (2006d) Security Site Design and Landscaping. *Planning and Urban Design Standards.* Graphic Standards, Wiley.
Atlas, R. (2005) The Security Audit and Premises Liability. *Spotlight on Security for Real Estate Managers*, 2nd ed. IREM, Elsevier.
Atlas, R. (2004) Security Design Concepts. *Security Planning and Design: A Guide for Architecture and Building Design Professionals.* Washington, DC: American Institute of Architects, Wiley.
Atlas, R. I. (2000) Crime Prevention through Environmental Design. In J. R. Hoke Jr. (Ed.), *Architectural Graphic Standards.* New York: John Wiley & Sons.
Atlas, R. (2002) Planting and Shaping Security Success. *Security Management.* August, 46–51.
City of Los Angeles (1997) Crime Prevention through Environmental Design: Design Out Crime Guidelines. Los Angeles, CA: Author.

Florida Center for Community Design + Research (1993) *Florida Safe Schools Guidelines*. Tampa: University of South Florida.

Hopper, L. (2005) *Security and Site Design: A Landscape Architectural Approach To Analysis Assessment and Design Implementation*. New York: John Wiley & Sons.

Jacobs, A. (1995) *Great Streets*. Cambridge, MA: MIT Press.

Sipes, J. et al., *Landscape Architecture Magazine*. (2002) Designing For Security. September. 58–88.

NCPC National Capital Planning Commission (2002) *The National Capital Urban Design and Security Plan*. Washington, DC: Author. Available at: http://www.ncpc.gov

U.S. Department of Housing and Urban Development (1979) *Planning for Housing Security: Site Elements Manual*. Annapolis, MD: William Brill Associates.

Wekerle, G. and Whitzman, C. (1995) *Safe Cities*. New York: Van Nostrand Reinhold.

Russell, J., Kennedy, E., Kelly, M., and Bershad, E. (Eds.) (2002) *Designing for Security: Using Art and Design to Improve Security*. New York: Art Commission of the City of New York and the Design Trust for Public Space. Available at: http://Nyc.gov/artcommission.com

ORGANIZATIONAL RESOURCES

Atlas Safety & Security Design: www.cpted-security.com
The Infrastructure Security Partnership: www.tisp.com
American Society for Industrial Security: www.asisonline.org
Defensible Space, nonprofit organization created by Oscar Newman: www.defensiblespace.com/start.htm
General Services Administration, Office of Federal Protective Service: www.gsa.gov/Portal/content/orgs_content.jsp?contentOID=117945&contentType=1005
International CPTED Association: www.cpted.net
National Capital Planning Commission: www.ncpc.gov
National Crime Prevention Council: www.ncpc.org
CPTED page: www.ncpc.org/2add4dc.htm
National Crime Prevention Institute: www.louisville.edu/a-s/ja/ncpi
Security Industry Association: www.siaonline.org
Terrorism Research Center: www.terrorism.com/index.shtml
U.S. Department of State, Counterterrorism Office: www.state.gov/s/ct
White House Office on Homeland Security: www.whitehouse.gov/homeland

21 Designing Safe Green Spaces and Parks

The planning and design of parks and recreational spaces are those special areas that communities use to relax and play. Many park designs encourage a wide range of activities and attract a wide range of users. Urban designers and landscape architects create green spaces and parks with varied purposes and therefore parks are a study of scale. They range from New York's Central Park, to neighborhood parks, to children's play areas in an apartment building.

When designed well and widely used, parks help create a sense of community. Parks bring people together and add cultural richness to the community. Parks are a source of recreation, which can create great spaces for people to use. As cities undergo renovation and growth there is a direction to add open spaces, river walk trails, bike trails, skateboard parks, and simple green spaces (see Figure 21.1).

When is a park viewed as safe, fun, and successful? As a CPTED practitioner, I often have to evaluate the green spaces and parks that are included in and around multifamily housing developments and commercial properties. I am often left with many unanswered questions about park design. For example, many parks experience crime, vandalism, graffiti, drug use, and drug dealing. These types of activities are a conflict of use and of users. Playgrounds for infants or small children are often placed in leftover spaces at the end of a site or an apartment building. Locating swings and sandboxes in an area that has little or no natural surveillance can invite older kids who may use the play areas inappropriately. One common result I see is play areas or parks being abandoned or used by undesired persons. When I see parks, green spaces, and play areas in isolated areas, I wonder: What was the developer or architect thinking? Was that design decision because parks are a non-income-producing real estate and go in the "leftover" spaces? Was there any consideration of how the parks were going to be used and by whom? (see Figure 21.2 and Figure 21.3).

Another example of incongruent use and users is the park that has a swing set and sandbox adjacent to a basketball court. Park planners and designers include mixed uses like this very often.

FIGURE 21.1 Kids enjoying the Extreme Park in Louisville, KY.

FIGURE 21.2 A neighborhood park in Albuquerque, New Mexico.

FIGURE 21.3 A family enjoying a picnic in a park in Chicago.

What is wrong with having these two activities next to each other? The legitimate users of the swings and sandbox areas are small children within specific age ranges and some likely capable guardians such as a parent, grandparent, nanny, or baby sitter. Most likely the guardian is a young mom or elderly grandmother (see Figure 21.4). Generally, the parent wants a quiet and unobstructed area with good natural surveillance. The swing and sandbox area needs to be clean and without contraband (needles, bottles, prophylactics, etc.). The guardian uses the area to observe the children play and have some brief reprieve outside to enjoy the fresh air.

However, right next to the swings or sandbox is a basketball court with a pick-up game in full play (see Figure 21.5). The normal behavior on a basketball court is jumping, yelling, cursing, spitting, scratching, and banging into each other. It's all common, legal, acceptable behavior for teenagers or adult males during a boisterous game (see Figure 21.6). This behavior may not physically threaten children or their typically female guardians, but it is disturbing and can be frightening to small children. In fact, too often I witness such incongruent recreational activities linked together in leftover spaces on a site.

FIGURE 21.4   Moms enjoying some quiet time in a swing set and sandbox.

FIGURE 21.5   User conflict between adults playing basketball and swings in immediate proximity.

We must learn to better design parks, green spaces, trails, and outdoor recreational spaces with CPTED principles. Most parks in urban locations need to incorporate territoriality to clearly define what is considered public property and what is the park. Too often, I observe behavior reflecting a public misunderstanding that parks and green spaces are "no-mans land" (see Figure 21.7, Figure 21.8, and Figure 21.9). Some think park space is fair game for all kinds of inappropriate or illegal behavior. In fact, parks are owned property by the federal, state, or local government entity, or the private sector. Because those groups control, and then assign someone to maintain the park, ground rules can be set regarding usage.

FIGURE 21.6 User conflicts between small children and their guardians and the basketball court adults and teenagers.

FIGURE 21.7 A small child play area with abundant natural surveillance.

FIGURE 21.8 The small children's play area was not being utilized because it was too far away from the mothers' supervision in the housing in the background.

FIGURE 21.9 Where the play area is in close proximity to the capable guardians the children come and play.

PARK SIZE

Large parks with many acres of land and an infinite number of entrance opportunities bring special challenges for access control. Here are several CPTED considerations:

- Have a well-defined and clear entranceway to the park. This also applies if there is more than one entranceway.
- Green spaces typically do not have an entrance, as they are buffer zones between other commercial or residential spaces. Green spaces require clearly defined edge boundaries both physically and operationally. Without clear design definition, there is room for "misunderstanding" who should legitimately use the space.

Smaller neighborhood parks are more common and generally receive CPTED recommendations best. Small parks can be, and often are, fenced for boundary definition and have clearly defined entry points to control access into their grounds (see Figure 21.10). The choice of where to place sidewalks and where to direct people and cars is a result of the access control decisions by designers.

CPTED access control decisions will impact where the most desired, observed, and desired use areas are located. Entrances should be well defined and celebrated with signage, ground rules, and lighting. Fencing should be used along the perimeter of the property where it is reasonable and appropriate as determined by the risk threat assessment.

Parks are generally areas that combine green spaces with defined areas for recreation, seating, or special use. Where natural foliage and plantings are dense, it is unreasonable and impractical to prune them for natural surveillance. In fact, the dense undercover can act as a natural barrier and does not invite normal pedestrian use. Sidewalks and trails invite use by intended and unintended users; therefore, wherever possible, natural surveillance and unobstructed sightlines is desired adjacent to the paths of mobility (see Figure 21.11).

Seating areas should also have good surveillance and sightlines. Seating areas should be designed with personal space separation. Intermittent rails define seating, and, in some cases, can be used to prevent sleeping on the benches when required (see Figure 21.12, Figure 21.13, Figure 21.14, and Figure 21.15).

FIGURE 21.10 A well defined pathway supports good access control, natural surveillance, and territoriality.

FIGURE 21.11   Pedestrian paths provide direction for people using the park and the ability of police to patrol.

FIGURE 21.12   Not many legitimate users in this park for all the benches there. Homeless people were enjoying the park.

Where appropriate in urban parks, ground cover and plantings should be pruned to be less than 32 inches, and tree canopies to be over 8 feet. This will ensure an unobstructed field of sight between the ground cover and the tree canopies (see Figure 21.16 and Figure 21.17).

Not all parks are flat, as in Florida, and must take into consideration the natural terrain. Even in Colorado, many of the trails are well-defined paths with good lines of sight and natural surveillance (see Figure 21.18 and Figure 21.19).

In order to get the desired outcome of legitimate activities in the parks, it is important to have basic rules of behavior posted in easy to observe locations. The situational CPTED matrix uses the principle of inducement of shame and removing the excuses for inappropriate behavior. Posted ground rules are essential to accomplish that goal. As earlier chapters regarding situational crime prevention discussed, signage rules can make transgressors think twice by inducing shame and

FIGURE 21.13   Almost good enough, but still room to lie down on the bench and prop up legs. The squirrel likes it, though.

FIGURE 21.14   Good design allows conversation but prevents sleeping with individual railings.

removing excuses for inappropriate behavior. The signage should state the hours of usage, what types of activities are allowed and not allowed, and who enforces the rules and the consequences (see Figure 21.20, Figure 21.21, Figure 21.22, and Figure 21.23).

FIGURE 21.15 A picture worth a thousand words. This is a park bench with legitimate and non-legitimate users. Had there been intermediate railings, the homeless persons could not have used the bench for sleeping.

FIGURE 21.16 CPTED guidelines for trails. (From *Safe Schools Design Guide*, (Moore/Powers, 1993). Used with permission from the Florida Center for Community Design + Research (www.fccdr.usf.edu).)

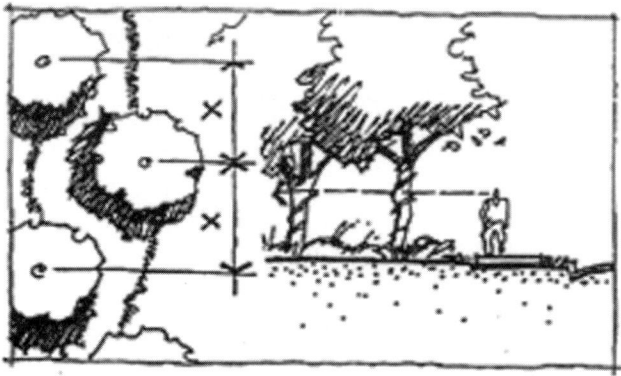

FIGURE 21.17 CPTED trail guidelines. From *Safe Schools Design Guide*, (Moore/Powers, 1993). Used with permission from the Florida Center for Community Design + Research (www.fccdr.usf.edu).)

FIGURE 21.18 CPTED implemented.

FIGURE 21.19 Safe trails in parks and recreational spaces.

FIGURE 21.20 Park signage specifying the user age and supervision.

FIGURE 21.21 This park signage was telling a story of no supervision.

FIGURE 21.22 Park signage stating ground rules for dogs, people, and most importantly about restricting access late at night.

FIGURE 21.23 Parks can be declared drug-free zones as per ordinance, which carries enhanced penalties for drug use or dealing.

PUBLIC ACCESS RIGHTS AND STALLONE-GATE

An example of park access and conflict of users and uses was the famous case in Miami called "Stallone-Gate." Sylvester Stallone and Madonna both lived in an exclusive area facing Biscayne Bay next to a small public park. During the day, the park was relatively problem-free, with typical users walking their dogs and enjoying the water vistas. However, at night, the park was used by drug dealers/users, and men engaged in illegal sexual behavior in the public restrooms. The entrance to the fenced park was through a gate that was left open because of disrepair.

The City of Miami Police seldom if ever patrolled the park, and local residents were left to fend for themselves against the unwanted park users. Walking one's dog at night in the park was a high-risk activity. After complaining to the City of Miami repeatedly and getting no resolution to the problem, Mr. Stallone fixed the gate at his own expense and made sure the gate was locked according to park regulations after sunset. Crime ceased in the park, although there was some political fallout about private persons restricting access.

Then the City of Miami received "civil rights" complaints that the gate was locked in the evenings and the public was being denied unencumbered access to public property. The political escapade escalated into a high-profile fight about access to the park by the common people and not for use by the wealthy residents. Eventually a compromise was worked out, and the police department enforced the hours of the park.

Not all parks have to be closed after sunset. One example that I observed was in Reno, Nevada, across from some downtown casinos. The casinos operated 24 hours a day and, with staff working all three shifts, it was a common sight to see persons exercising, jogging, and walking their dogs at 3 or 4 a.m.

Many parks have restrooms on their grounds. Restrooms often attract illegal behavior and there is much debate on whether the bathrooms should be open day and night or locked up after park hours.

FIGURE 21.24 The idea of having a *passive park* for quiet activities and meditation; no group sports.

As you have seen throughout this book, proper CPTED begins with a diagnosis of the risks. In Chapter 29, you will find the CPTED Risk Assessment Guide that will help you determine precisely how to analyze what CPTED strategies might work. The CPTED perspective examines the specific problems before quickly answering the problem with restrictive behaviors. For example, factors determining the appropriate response might include the size of the restroom, the number of stalls, and the size of the common area space. When the bathrooms are single stalls, it is easy to have them locked after hours. When the bathrooms are large and do not have doors—"lazy S" openings—the control of access is very difficult after hours. If the park is used in the evening hours the need for random patrol becomes more important. Lighting will be an important consideration and personal alarms in the bathrooms might be a design consideration. The activity level in the park is going to drive the need for support spaces to be available (see Figure 21.25).

FIGURE 21.25 Park restrooms were designed to be small and very observable. The parks maintenance locked the doors after the sun went down to prevent "tearoom" activity or illicit sexual behavior.

LANDSCAPE DESIGN

In many green spaces, the plantings and flora are determined by the geography of local plants and trees. Unless the green space is in the southwest United States and the plants are cactus, one challenge is from overgrown bushes and trees creating hiding spaces. Convicted Florida mass murderer Danny Rolling used the adjacent wooded area next to an apartment building to reconnoiter when persons were leaving their apartments in order to select good targets for burglary.

When woods or green spaces adjoin multifamily residential and commercial spaces, there should be fencing between the green spaces and the grounds of the functional space.

The choice of landscaping design and plantings in ground floor multifamily residential housing should take into consideration thorny ground brushes and tree canopies pruned according to the 3 × 8-foot principle (see Figure 21.26) This CPTED landscaping rule of thumb also applies to commercial establishments including office parks and office buildings.

FIGURE 21.26 Tree canopies were pruned sufficiently to provide unobstructed natural surveillance of the park.

FIGURE 21.27 Homeless people encamped on the edge of the parks where staff could not monitor activity easily, and where fencing and bushes obscured activity.

When landscaping parks, there is an infinite variety of plantings that are available to use by the landscape architect or park planner. There is no perfect solution that is applicable for all parks, but the correct solutions go back to the risk assessment on what are the desired activities and users in the park space. Some parks discourage nighttime use; some parks encourage it. One example of risk-based problem solving is the challenge of homeless persons sleeping in the park space and/or loitering in shaped areas at night after the park is closed (see Figure 21.27 and Figure 21.28). Most urban parks plan for water sprinklers in the design stage to keep the grass green and watering the grass and trees at night serves as an effective tool to keep the homeless from making encampments in the park.

Another common challenge with parks is the inappropriate use of earth berms. Many municipalities have zoning regulations that dictate parking lots must be shielded from public view, because cars and parking lots are an ugly blight. As a result, zoning regulations require landscape architects to use berms or plants to shield the parking lots. Unfortunately this means that passers-by, security,

FIGURE 21.28 The play areas are best when bordered by fencing and have enough clear area to prevent any visual obstructions.

FIGURE 21.29 Woman walking on sidewalk disappears behind earth berm. The berms block surveillance by police on patrol.

FIGURE 21.30 Lighting and street furniture at Fort Lauderdale's Riverwalk.

or police officers no longer have direct natural surveillance in the parking areas, which are inviting targets for car thieves and burglars. In one case, the Sarasota Florida Police Department petitioned the zoning board for a waiver to this rule on their busy Highway 41 for a new local college parking lot. The architect developed an attractive picket fence along the highway with low ground cover and the crime in the parking lot significantly decreased because of the increased patrol by the sheriff's deputies and police officers. This Sarasota experiment was a good application of CPTED by police. It enlightened the zoning and code officials to look for alternatives in shielding and screening to accomplish their design goals but not compromise security.

Berms have a place in park design; however, very careful thought must be given to their placement and function. If there is a need for natural surveillance from one side of a berm to another, the berm serves as an impermeable barrier and should be reconsidered. Criminals can use the berms to hide from police and screen themselves from casual observance by pedestrians or security personnel (see Figure 21.29 and Figure 21.30).

LIGHTING DESIGN

Lighting in parks is often a hotly contested issue. The appropriate use of light is based on the risk threat assessment and the types of activities that will be happening at night in the park or green spaces. If there are organized activities in the park in the evenings, such as softball or basketball, then the park will need specialized lighting sufficient to play those games. The walkways, pathways, or sidewalks should be lit sufficiently to identify facial features from 25 to 30 feet away. Toronto research during the development of the safety audit method suggests that distance should be 75 feet (Wekerle and Whitzman, 1995). Knee-high pedestrian lighting pedestals are good for lighting the ground surface to prevent slip and fall accidents, but are insufficient to identify faces of people approaching. The CPTED goal is to have enough light to identify potential attackers from 30 feet away so that a pedestrian has time to make the choice to walk forward, retreat and back away, or stop and take no action and observe the activity ahead to determine if it poses a threat.

For specific design standards that are applicable to outdoor spaces, please reference the Illumination Engineering Society of North America publication "Guidelines for Security Lighting for People, Property and Public Spaces" (IESNA G-1–03 2003).

Many municipalities have rivers and by adding riverwalks to take advantage of this attractive water feature, The CPTED challenge becomes attracting enough legitimate activity by pedestrians to overcome the territorial encroachments of the homeless, drug dealers and users, and street criminals. The movie *Field of Dreams* had the famous tag line, "If you build it, they will come!" This is an accurate observation. If you build a trail, riverwalk, or mobility path, users—both legitimate and not legitimate—will use them. Therefore, if paths of travel are present and are advertised for legitimate use, they can also be used in the evening hours (unless posted or gated otherwise). If the paths are open in the evening hours, there is an implicit expectation that they are going to be patrolled and lit (see Figure 21.31).

An example of this is in Albuquerque, New Mexico. The city, like many others in the southwest United States, has an arroyo system that channels runoff water during downpours and rainstorms. Along the arroyos are gravel or paved paths that local residents use to walk, bike, or jog. Police do not officially patrol these pathways, and at night young people, drug users, and street criminals use these pathways to engage in illegal or mischief behavior. Residents have been forced to overcome the obstacles of the drug and criminal activity. They also have been assaulted, robbed, and even killed.

The CPTED perspective on this challenge is fairly straightforward: If you build it they will come. The park designer or police agency must diagnose the risks clearly. Accordingly, the pathways should either be lit and patrolled, or secured and closed off and posted as no trespassing areas. There is little room for compromise. The risks outweigh the benefits.

Dark skies and darkness also can be an effective strategy for park design. Not every part of the park has to be lit up like a nuclear flash. Pathways need to be illuminated sufficiently for facial recognition from about 30 feet. In addition, changes in grade need to be apparent and obvious. The remaining open spaces need only enough light to determine shape and movement. The police officer wants to have the ability to see persons moving around, and have the ability to challenge them, if necessary. Lighting the entire grounds to the level of a football field is impractical, intrusive, very expensive, and usually unnecessary.

FIGURE 21.31 Pictures of public housing lighting going into bedrooms.

Luminaries are often chosen by the architect or lighting designer to cast light all over

FIGURE 21.32 Globe-style luminaries cast light up and not just on the pathways of this park in Miami Beach, which is problematic for turtle nesting.

FIGURE 21.33 This street lighting fixture along a park shines light *upward* and produces light pollution and light trespass.

including upwards, instead of down and forward. The effect of poor luminary positioning is light pollution. Light pollution can cause people to close their blinds, thereby losing potential natural surveillance from nearby residents. Even to passersby, too much illumination, especially when inappropriately directed, can overpower the ability or desire to observe play areas and parks. Lighting can be a friend or foe, depending on how it is used and directed (see Figure 21.31, Figure 21.32, Figure 21.33, Figure 21.34, and Figure 21.35).

FIGURE 21.34   Lines of sight from balconies of apartments to streets and sidewalks below.

FIGURE 21.35   Good graphics and wayfinding signage is critical for legitimate users and legitimate uses.

WHAT IS THE ROLE OF PUBLIC ART AND CPTED?

Many cities around the world support art in public places (Patak and Atlas, 2004). Often, a percentage of funding from all capital improvement projects in a city is dedicated to having art in the public forum. The most typical location for public art is in parks. Placing art in public spaces is an extension of CPTED's use of generating legitimate activity support. By providing amenities, like art, the park will attract the type of users that are desired. CPTED practitioners have used public art as an activity generator or attractive magnet of desired legitimate activities. The legitimate users will displace the illegitimate users, and attract capable guardians (parents, teachers, supervisors, coaches, tourists, sightseers, etc.) and increase natural surveillance.

Public art can be interpreted in different ways such as fountains, sculptures, paths and gardens, stages and performance areas, and sitting and reflective areas (see Figure 21.36).

Art can help provide the transition between public space and private space with rock gardens and trails. The art, if done thoughtfully, can be inviting to observe. It is becoming common to see street furniture as pieces of art (see Figure 21.37, Figure 21.38, Figure 21.39, Figure 21.40, Figure 21.41, Figure 21.42, and Figure 21.43).

Public art is often subject to vandalism and graffiti, so it is important to design the art and sculpture so that it is resistant to tagging and breaking. The CPTED challenge is, how can we remove the canvas for the graffiti artist? If the texture of surface of the art is not suitable for tagging, then the tagger will move on and be deflected. Underpasses and large walls that have art on them can be designed to have fluted or textured forms, making them an undesirable surface to paint, and the surfaces can be pretreated with graffiti-resistant sealers so that if a surface is tagged, it can be easily and quickly washed off (see Figure 21.44, Figure 21.45, Figure 21.46, and Figure 21.47).

Art in public spaces occurs in parks, paths, greenways, trails, and roadways. There is an endless amount of opportunity on how we present those spaces as being blessed or blighted. In the most interesting cities around the world that I have visited, there was usually a large amount of public art where people gathered, celebrated, relaxed, or conducted commerce. Increasing legitimate activity is an achievable and powerful CPTED tool, and should not be underestimated.

FIGURE 21.36 This industrial area was run down and abandoned. Art, murals, and lighting brought legitimate commerce to this historic district and now it thrives as a tourist end destination for nightclubs, restaurants, and stores.

FIGURE 21.37   Street furniture can be funny and yet functional.

FIGURE 21.38   Public art can be cows, horses, or flamingos (Miami Beach!).

FIGURE 21.39   Public art in public places attract legitimate activity and a variety of users.

FIGURE 21.40   Fountains are an entertaining form of public art, especially in the summer.

FIGURE 21.41   The playgrounds in the park had monkey bar sets that mirrored the city bridges in the background.

FIGURE 21.42 Art can be used as security vehicle barriers for a courthouse.

FIGURE 21.43 Art can be used as gates for service alleyways.

FIGURE 21.44 Art in public spaces can be functional and resistant to graffiti.

FIGURE 21.45 A graffiti artist caught in action prepares his surface for his illegal artwork.

FIGURE 21.46 Art and murals can be an important part of the community, especially when the local school children are involved in its creation.

FIGURE 21.47 Even unattractive electrical substations and transformers can be made into public art.

TECHNOLOGICAL FIXES

Some suggest that high-tech solutions in parks, such as motion sensors and CCTV, are the only solution to park crime. There is a dangerous tendency to slip back into technological solutions without first diagnosing the specific context and considering better design options. As this chapter has shown, there are many other possible CPTED design solutions that can have positive impact.

For example, in the case of CCTV, there is growing evidence that lighting can have more positive results when properly deployed (Saville, 2004). This is especially the case in research showing that thousands of downtown CCTV cameras in the United Kingdom have not always had the desired impact (Welsh and Farrington, 2004).

However, in some situations, in certain park areas, there may indeed be effective application of technological solutions. One good example is security lighting that employs motion sensors connected to exterior lights. This can be useful if there is undesired movement through the park after hours—the darkened lights are activated acting as an alarm system for police and neighboring residents. Obviously, a proper risk assessment will identify whether this is appropriate for the circumstances.

SUMMARY

The CPTED methodology is directly applicable to the planning, design, and use of parks, green spaces, and recreational areas. Proper park design requires an appreciation of who, why, what, where, when, and how the park will operate in order to deter crime and acts of incivility. Why is the park going to be needed, and by whom? What is the mission or purpose of the park and what are the activities that are allowed and encouraged? Who are the legitimate users of the park? Where is the park located so it can encourage maximum use and achieve maximum natural surveillance? When is the park available for use? How will the park achieve the design goals according to the mission statement and risk assessment? These simple questions launch the CPTED risk assessment process and help developers, designers, and government entities understand how to better design parks. They provide the direction and tone that a safe park design should take.

REFERENCES

Atlas, R. (2002) Creating Safety. *Landscape Architect.*
Atlas, R. (2004) Security Design Concepts. *Security Planning and Design: A Guide for Architecture and Building Design Professionals.* Washington, DC: American Institute of Architects, Wiley.
Atlas, R. (2004) Designing Safe Communities. *Strategies for Safe and Sustainable Communities.* Vienna, VA: Landscape Architectural Registrations Boards Foundation.
IESNA G-1–03 (2003) Guidelines for Security Lighting for People, Property and Public Spaces. IESNA.
Leslie, R. and Rogers, P. (2001) *The Outdoor Lighting Pattern Book.* Lighting Research Center. McGraw Hill, Washington DC.
Lighting for Security and Safety (1990) National Lighting Bureau. Washington DC.
Patak, G. and Atlas, R. (2004) Public Art and CPTED. Presentation at the American Society of Industrial Security (ASIS) Congress, September.
Saville, G. (2004) Surveillance and Crime Prevention. *Criminology and Public Policy,* 3(4), 493–496.
Welsh, B. C. and Farrington, D. P. (2004) Surveillance for Crime Prevention in Public Space: Results and Policy Choices in Britain and America. *Criminology and Public Policy,* 3(4), 497–525.
Wekerle, G. and Whitzman, C. (1995) *Safe Cities: Guidelines for Planning Design, and Management.* New York: Van Nostrand.

22 Lighting Provides Choice

Lighting for reducing crime and improving security is a logical and natural evolution of the CPTED principles of natural surveillance and good visibility. The goal of safe lighting design is to make our architectural, urban, and suburban projects as safe and secure in the nighttime as they are in the daytime hours of the day, using proper lighting design.

The role of lighting in crime prevention and security has been a close-knit relationship. There have been some excellent books and documents published on lighting and security, most notably by the Illumination Engineering Society of North America and the Guideline on Security Lighting for People, Property, and Public Spaces (IESNA G-1–03 March 2003), and the National Crime Prevention Institute handout on Security Lighting and The Outdoor Lighting Pattern Book (1996). I have conducted lighting analysis on numerous properties, especially residential and commercial properties. Most all of the publications to date take a deterministic view that lighting prevents or stops crime. It is my opinion and experience that this is incorrect. Lighting is neutral regarding changing or preventing behavior (see Figure 22.1). It is similar to CCTV. CCTV does not stop crime but can be effective if applied in the proper way to altering how persons perceive their space. Lighting does not stop you from obtaining entry, as a door or gate would prevent intrusion. Lighting does not call the police or scream for assistance. *Lighting provides choice.*

Lighting provides the users of the built environment the choice to move forward, retreat back, or stay put. Lighting provides the information to decide if the people walking towards you are friends or foe. Lighting provides the choice to walk, run, or gather in a familiar area. Lighting also provides information for the predator to see his next victim. Lighting provides the potential victim information about where the predators may lay-in-wait, and how to steer clear of them.

If lighting does not conclusively stop crime, why have there been 35 years of marketing saying that everyone should light his or her porch and street? Recall that the definition of CPTED was about reducing the fear and opportunity for crime. Lighting helps people *feel* safer and reduces the opportunity for being a victim of ambush. This draws on Jacob's pivotal work decades ago about safe streets and placing legitimate "eyes on the street."

Lighting is a subjective and interpretive art form. There has to be just the right kind and level of light. Too much light is not good, as it causes glare and light pollution. Too much contrast between light and dark areas make it difficult for the eye to adapt, and people are blinded and may trip and fall. Too little light does not provide enough clarity. Sometimes, darkness or lack of light is a CPTED strategy as well. Light attracts activity. The CPTED question is what kind of activities do you want to attract or detract?

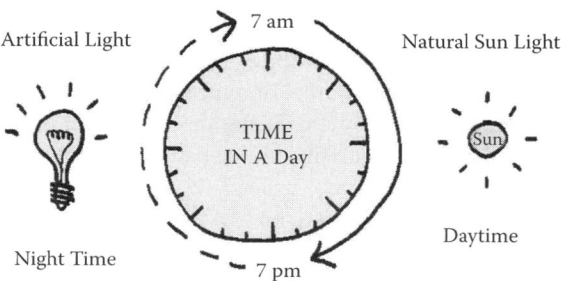

FIGURE 22.1 Lighting paridigm.

The CPTED goal of lighting is to make a place unattractive to offenders or illegitimate users. Making spaces uncomfortable for criminals can be accomplished through the proper placement of windows, adequate and appropriate light, and removing obstructions or enhance sightlines.

CPTED practitioners should recognize that during the hours of darkness most buildings are not as busy or populated as during the daytime. During nighttime then, is typically when most properties are more silent, isolated, and vulnerable. A well-lit site is not only easier to observe; the lighting acts as a psychological deterrent. It is not by lighting alone that places are rendered safer, but it helps when combined with other security measures such as guards, fencing, alarms, and so on. Adequate lighting design should be used for both the interior and exterior of the site.

Security lighting has good justifications because it improves the marketability of the buildings, improves their perception of safety of users and their performance, reduces trip and fall accidents and assaults, and other types of incidents that result in premises security lawsuits.

From a security CPTED point of view, there are two primary areas of focus for lighting that provide good choices to legitimate users in an effort to deter crime and victimization:

1. Lighting can create a psychological deterrent to criminals and terrorists engaging in crimes of stealth and unwanted intrusion.
2. Lighting can enable and improve detection and capture of the potential intruder or criminal.

When the built environment and infrastructure are provided with appropriate lighting systems, the level of crime and terror may be diminished because of increased natural surveillance and because of the increased perception of security. The lighting provides the legitimate users and capable guardians the ability to distinguish between friends or foes and identification of persons coming onto the properties and into the buildings.

THE LIGHTING CHALLENGE

The good deal of street crime isn't carefully planned, but happens spontaneously. Some circumstances and places create, promote, or allow the opportunity for crime. In order to feel safe and enjoy our cities and places at night, we must implement good lighting design as part of the basic infrastructure and architecture.

Before the first lighting luminaire is specified, the architect or security consultant should consider the proverbial CPTED question: What is the experience you are looking for? The experience that we should be looking for from a CPTED perspective is:

- To deter illegal behavior and criminal activity and encourage law-abiding behavior that promotes feelings of safety
- To maximize the probability of visual identifications of intruders and trespassers
- To support and enhance the CCTV operation of a facility
- To deny criminals and terrorists camouflage and places to hide
- To provide sufficient light in an area to allow an object or person to be easily seen and allow surveillance by guards, normal users of a facility, police patrols, and passersby
- To deter possible criminal activity by increasing the likelihood of detection with surveillance by guards, normal users of a facility, police patrols, and passersby

LIGHTING FACTS AND TERMINOLOGY

- Footcandle—a measure of light striking the surface one square foot in area on which one unit of light (lumen) is uniformly distributed
- Lux—a metric measure of illumination approximately 1/10 of a footcandle
- Lumen—a measure of light at its source and the amount of light output

- Luminaires—the complete light fixture with the light source and ballast
- Light Trespass—light pollution in unintended areas
- LPW—lumens per watt, a measure of efficiency
- HID—high-intensity discharge lamp
- Ballast—a device used with an electric discharge lamp to obtain the necessary voltage and current to start and operate the lamp

WHAT ARE THE APPROPRIATE USES OF LIGHTING?

Lighting has many different applications in the architecture of buildings, but there are only a few that really impact life safety and security. They are:

- Exterior surface lighting
- Building entrance service areas
- Exterior pedestrian and vehicular traffic
- Perimeter area lighting
- Spotlighting

Exterior surface lighting is used by architects to wash a building's façade or wall surface. It glorifies the building but does not do a lot to promote security.

Lighting of building entrances and service areas is a primary security lighting function. Celebrating the entrance focuses people on where they should be going, and, more importantly, where you want them to go (see Figure 22.2)

Most lighting engineers illuminate the streets well beyond the actual needs. Uniform minimum standards for the design, construction, and maintenance for streets and highways require the lighting for roadways, and are typically better illuminated than the sidewalks and pathways. After all, cars have headlights, people don't! Yet, the focus of most exterior lighting is about vehicular traffic not pedestrian traffic (see Figure 22.3). This is because there are more obvious liability issues for car crashes because of insufficient streetlights than from sidewalk muggings. Traffic engineers tend to be the persons who designate the streetlights, not landscape architects. Obviously traffic engineers are concerned about traffic, and their concern with pedestrians is related to how they intersect or cross the streets (crosswalks, curb cuts). There may be more people driving than walking at night, but my guess is that if the streets felt safer and were better lighted, there would be more people walking at night (see Figure 22.4). There seems to be an unspoken rule to rank cars first, and people second. Nighttime lighting reflects that bias (see Figure 22.5).

FIGURE 22.2   Lighting on a public plaza draws people to the entrances.

FIGURE 22.3   Parking lot and entrance lighting interact with each other to draw customers to the entrance.

FIGURE 22.4   This picture demonstrates the interface of streetlights and sidewalks.

When the real estate shifts from public sector (the roads and streets) to private sector (the property line of the school, shopping center, hospital, apartment complex, etc.) the responsibility of lighting becomes that of the property owners. The appropriate lighting level for perimeter area lighting varies between the different types of properties and their uses. The risk threat assessment will determine what the appropriate lighting levels should be on the exterior perimeter and grounds on the property being studied (see Figure 22.6).

When specific items or places need increased observation, the lighting designer will use spotlighting (see Figure 22.7). Many homeowners use spotlighting around their house, sometimes integrating it with motion sensors. This dual technology conserves energy by only using the lighting when someone has come into the detection field (see Figure 22.8).

Spotlights also can be used as ballpark lighting, car lot lighting, recreational lighting, and for other specific needs.

FIGURE 22.5   A relationship between the sidewalk lighting, street lighting, and landscaping.

FIGURE 22.6   Perimeter lighting.

FIGURE 22.8   Dual technology.

FIGURE 22.7   Sidewalk and street lighting.

LIGHTING CHOICES
(SO MANY BULBS, SO LITTLE TIME)

The Institute of Community Security and Public Safety at the University of Louisville has a "wall of light" (see Figure 22.9) that demonstrates the various types of luminaries and the differences in colors and output. Because this book is in black and white (apparently color photos would triple the

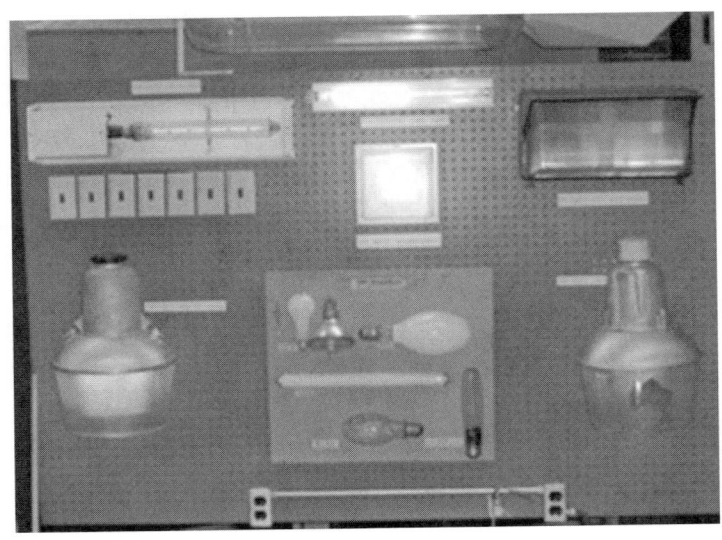

FIGURE 22.9   The "wall of light" demonstrates the menu of choices.

cost of the book!), we have to demonstrate the concept of lighting and color indexing without the benefit of color diagrams. Although somewhat limiting, the concepts can still be communicated to the reader and CPTED practitioner effectively to make good choices and smart decisions.

The primary types of lighting sources are:

- Incandescent
- Fluorescent
- Mercury Vapor (MV)
- Metal Halide (MH)
- Low Pressure Sodium Vapor (LPSV)
- High Pressure Sodium Vapor (HPSV)

INCANDESCENT LIGHTING

A lamp that produces light by using electric current to heat a filament.

- Advantages
    Instant response
    Low initial cost
    Good to excellent color rendition
    Can be dimmed
    Compact size
    Widely available

- Disadvantages
    Energy inefficient (LPW) 17–23
    Short lamp life (500–5000 hrs)
    Produces sizeable amounts of heat
    Inefficient conversion of energy to visible light
    High heat output

(see Figure 22.10 and Figure 22.11.)

FIGURE 22.10   An incandescent light on a typical front porch.

FIGURE 22.11 Interior light fixtures often use incandescent bulbs and are easy to change out, but can be subject to vandalism and produce heat gain.

Fluorescent Lighting

A fluorescent low-pressure mercury lamp is one in which a phosphor coating transforms UV energy into light. These phosphors maintain their light output through the life of the lamp. Excluding breakage or failure of electrical components, this lamp fails when there are no more phosphors present on the inside of the glass bulb. The chemical composition of the phosphors determines the color of light emitted by the lamp. Fluorescent lamps require a current regulator, called ballast (see Figure 22.12 and Figure 22.13).

- Advantages
    Low initial cost
    Relatively efficient energy use (LPW) 67–83
    Long life: 12–20,000 hrs.
    Good color rendition
    Almost instant response
    Can diffuse light source

- Disadvantages
    Poor optical control
    Adversely effected in cold temperatures
    Vulnerable to power fluctuations and surges

Mercury Vapor

High Intensity Discharge (HID) lamps produce light by excitation of mercury vapor. These lamps produce visible light by passing electricity through a gas rather than a filament. The type of gas in the bulb determines the color of light emitted. Current flowing between the two contacts ionizes the gas. The ionization of the gas completes the electric circuit. These ions (the arc discharge) collide with atoms of the gas present in the bulb; the atomic collisions generate visible light.

This process of generating light is the reason for the start-up and re-strike times required by HID sources. It takes time for the gas contained in the bulb to become vaporized and begin emitting light. If an interruption in the power supply occurs, the arc may extinguish. The lamp must then cool

FIGURE 22.12 Exterior florescent lights can be used effectively when they are not accessible to vandals and the temperature remains moderate.

FIGURE 22.13 This parking garage used florescent bulbs for lighting under the structural elements.

down before the arc will "restrike." Restrike time is dependent on the type of lamp, the ballast used, and the ambient temperature. Hotter conditions require longer restrike times (see Figure 22.14).

- Advantages
  Bluish white light
  Long lamp life (16–24,000 hrs)
  Low initial cost
  Color rendition can vary depending on the type of lamp

- Disadvantages
  Inefficient (LPW) 45–53
  Light output drops over life (2–3 years)
  Delayed hot restart

FIGURE 22.14 Mercury vapor lamps are often used in gyms and high-ceilinged department stores. Although apparently used in fewer situations across North America than before, mercury vapor is another bright industrial light source.

Metal Halide

HID arc tube in which light is produced by the excitation of metal halides.

- Advantages
  Sparkling white light
  Very energy efficient (LPW) 80–100
  100W bulb lasts 10,000 hrs.
  Good optical control
  Excellent color rendition

- Disadvantages
  Hot restart up to minutes
  High initial cost

(See Figure 22.15.)

High-Pressure Sodium

HID arc tube that produces light with sodium vapor under high pressure.

- Advantages
  Pink or golden illumination
  Efficient (LPW) 20–28,000 hrs.
  Lowest life cycle cost: 20–28,000 hrs
  Good optical control

- Disadvantages
  Fair color rendition
  High initial cost of fixtures
  Hot restart up to one minute

(see Figure 22.16 and Figure 22.17.)

FIGURE 22.15 Metal halide bulb producing sparkling white light.

FIGURE 22.16 High-pressure sodium vapor (HPSV) luminaires.

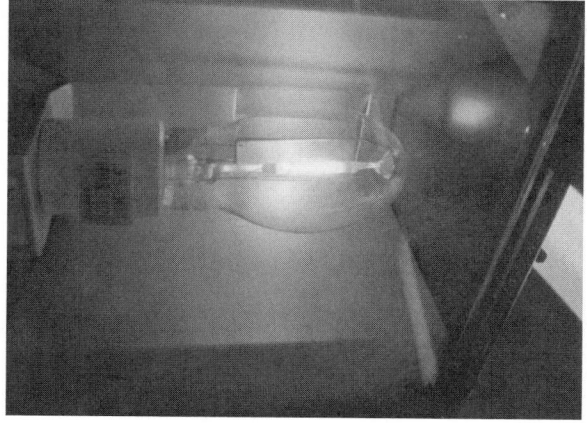

FIGURE 22.17 HPSV lighting used in a garage.

Low-Pressure Sodium

HID arc tube that produces light with sodium vapor under pressure.

- Advantages
  - Yellow illumination
  - Efficient (130–183)
  - 90-watt bulb lasts 16,000 hrs
  - Instant hot restart

- Disadvantages
  - Poorest color rendition
  - Monochromatic
  - Poor optical control

(See Figures 22.18, 22.19.)

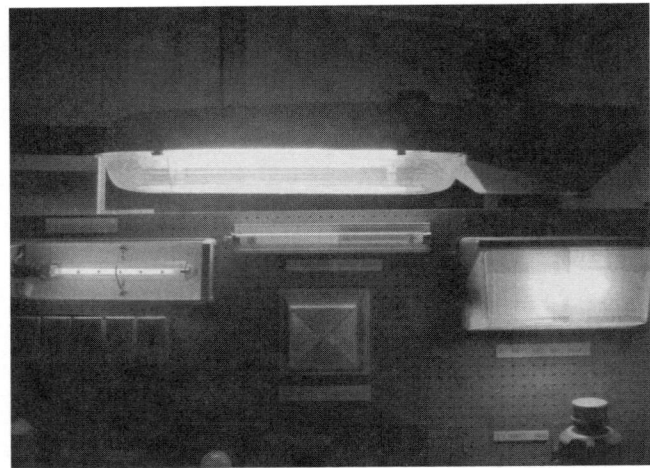

FIGURE 22.18   LPSV bulb giving off a bug light yellow glow.

FIGURE 22.19   LPSV have a variety of luminaries that are available.

LIGHTING CONTROLS

A major factor in the decision-making process of which type of lighting is appropriate for specific applications is how easily the light is controlled.

The choices for control are:

- Manual
- Photoelectric cell
- Timer
- Automatic—that is power failure, alarm
- Motion sensor
- Group lamping in series

A manual switch turns on many front porch lights in people's homes or apartments. In an application such as a large apartment complex, or shopping center, the lights are typically turned on and off by a timer, or photoelectric cell. Most exterior lighting systems in commercial and industrial applications have their power source connected with the emergency power back up system. It is important to access in the CPTED survey or risk assessment what kind, and where the emergency lighting is used. Motion sensors can be used to control how lights are used, and when they are used for people occupying the spaces. The clever use of motion detection and lighting is that the lighting can act as an alarm to the residents that persons are in areas they should not be at night, and create an alarm condition. An example of this technology is motion-activated spotlights in the back yards of people's homes, or in the back of school grounds, or parks (see Figure 22.20).

In public housing properties, one of the challenges has been to get the residents to turn on their porch lights. Because the residents pay their own utility bills, they feel the porch light costs are too expensive and compromise their financial well-being. As a result, a CPTED solution to this challenge is to have common area spaces wired in series so that there is group lamping and the ownership or management takes responsibility for turning on the lights, and now the front porches have become part of the common area space. While residents might not like the light on,

TABLE 22.1

Lighting Lamp Choices and Qualities

Lamp Type	Start-Up	Re-Strike	Average Life	Initial Lumen
Incandescent				
General use	Instant on	N/A	200–22,828	–
Traffic signal	Instant on	N/A	8,000	–
Halogenen	Instant on	N/A	2,000–6,000	–
Fluorescent				
Rapid start	Instant on	N/A	18,000–20,000	550–3,775
Preheat	Quick-on	N/A	7500–9,000	225–2,200
High/very high output	#	N/A	9,000–18,000	1,400–17,500
Outdoor	Exterior temperature dependent	N/A	10,000	7,000–14,900
HID				
High pressure sodium	2–5	1–20	10,000–24,000	2,150–140,000
Low pressure sodium	5–8	0–8	18,000	1,800–32,000
Induction	Instant on	Instant	100,000	3,500–12,000
Mercury vapor	5–8	10–20	24,000	1,580–63,000
Metal halide	5–8	10–20	3000—20,000	

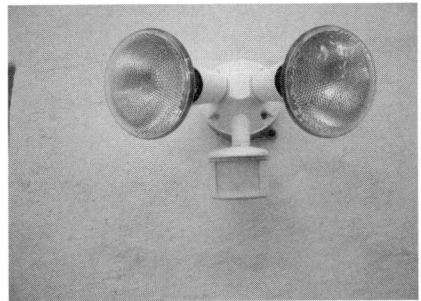

FIGURE 22.20 Flood lights are combined with a motion sensor to come on when movement is detected.

FIGURE 22.21 This porch light has a protective screen over it to reduce vandalism.

FIGURE 22.22 This picture illustrates the transition of spaces from dark to light and the deep shadow that happens from too drastic a transition.

it does accomplish some important CPTED goals: the uniform lighting level lights the entrances to everyone's unit and does not advertise who is home (and who is not) to a potential burglar (see Figure 22.21). The residual effect of the group lighting is to have an even and wide swath of light extend to the perimeter and surrounding spaces of the buildings to deny camouflage to intruders, drug dealers, vandals, and trespassers. Porch lights typically use incandescent bulbs, which consume more energy and produce residual heat. Consider replacing all incandescent bulbs with compact energy saving fluorescent bulbs.

A security guard leaving a normally lighted guard post and entering an area of darkness will require 20 minutes to become fully adapted to the dark. It is important to remember the human factor and ergonomics of going from bright spaces to dark spaces, and vice versa. Criminals will wait in the shadows close to a potential target, unseen by the victim because of the brightness and glare of strong lighting (see Figure 22.22). When a potential victim transitions into a dark area, he never sees the attacker coming. Many trip-and-fall accidents occur with similar conditions, especially with older persons who have weakened eyesight and slower retinal response because of aging (see Figure 22.23).

FIGURE 22.23 The lighted sidewalk goes into pitch darkness and provides a perfect opportunity for an ambush.

ALL LIGHT IS NOT CREATED EQUAL . . .

Many factors may be taken into consideration for security lighting. The primary factors for choices are:

- Light spectrum
- Strike/restrike times
- Lamp life hours
- Percentage of lumens maintained as rated lamp life
- Color discrimination
- Energy consumption
- Ease of replacement and servicing

Finally, it is important not to overlook the maintenance of luminaries and bulbs. This is a maintenance consideration, but it overlaps with the CPTED and security consideration because the ability to have an instant-on or strike is very important in certain applications. If the amount of heat generated from the bulbs impacts energy consumption and discoloration of the lens, there are consequences that may later affect the lighting effectiveness. For example, having a bulb with a short life span in a luminaire that requires a mechanical lift to change (such as in a shopping center parking lot, or a high foyer lobby) will be expensive and may be slow to be serviced. A poorly maintained and difficult to service light fixture can result in having no light at all.

These are the basic criteria that the security consultant and lighting engineer should use in determining the features that create the quantity and quality of lighting. The next chapter provides more specific guidelines on lighting security and how to employ effective CPTED lighting.

REFERENCES

Russell P. L. and Rodgers, P.A. (1996) *The Outdoor Lighting Pattern Book*, Lighting Research Center, RPI; New York: McGraw Hill.
Guideline for Security Lighting for People, Property and Public Spaces (2003) New York: Illuminating Engineering Society of North America.
Higgins, L. R., and Morrow, L. C. (1977) *Maintenance Engineering Handbook,* 3rd ed. New York: McGraw Hill.
Hopf, P. (Ed.) (1979) *Handbook of Building Security Planning and Design.* New York: McGraw-Hill.
Industrial Lighting Application Guide (2004) Somerset, NJ: Philips Lighting Company.
Lamp Specification and Application Guide (2004) Somerset, NJ: Philips Lighting Company.

Lighting for Safety and Security (1989) Washington, DC: National Lighting Bureau.

Rea, M.S. (Ed.) (1993) *Lighting Handbook: Reference and Application,* 8th ed. Illuminating Engineering Society of North America.

OTHER RESOURCES

National Lighting Bureau*: www.nlb.org.*
Illuminating Engineers Society of North America: *www.iesna.org.*
National Council on Qualifications for the Lighting Professional: *www.ncqlp.org.*
National Association of Lighting Designers: *www.iald.org.*
Philips Lighting Company: *www.lighting.philips.com*
GE Lighting: *www.gestpectrum.com*
Sylvania Lighting: *www.sylvania.com*
National Fire Protection Association (NFPA): *www.nfpa.org*
International Code Council: *www.iccsafe.org*
National Institute of Standards & Technology: *www.nist.gov*
American National Standards Institute: *www.ansi.org*

23 Security Lighting Part 2

Can the luminaries withstand the abuse given to them by the weather, children, drug dealers, bad drivers, lightning, rocks, and bullets (see Figure 23.1 and Figure 23.2)? What are the characteristics of good security lighting? Lighting that is going to be in high-risk areas should have the following characteristics:

- Unbreakable exterior—use polycarbonate
- Secure and vibration-free surface mounting
- Shock absorbing lamp socket bracket design
- Tamperproof hardware
- Noncorrosive design components
- Conduit acceptability—for retrofitting

Plan carefully for the type of lighting based on the risk and area where it will be placed. Anchor the poles well so they cannot be throttled causing breakage to the luminaries. The housing and the wire shield need tamperproof screws. In 1993, Miami street vagrants attacked the streetlights on a major interstate highway near the Miami International Airport (Figure 23.3 and Figure 23.4). The thieves were taking the copper wiring and selling it to the recycling centers. Meanwhile, the highways were dark and tourists were getting lost and sometimes robbed (or worse) when they drove off the dark highways seeking directions in the bad parts of town. The wire covers did not have tamperproof screws and could be removed with a dime. After several tourist robberies and deaths, the county and Department of Transportation wired the lights in series, with a wire along the top of the light poles. The situation could have been avoided by using tamperproof security screws on the wiring shields. So the threat of vandalism is real, and serious consequences can result. What is the expectation for providing lighting in our built environment?

FIGURE 23.1   Broken security light.

FIGURE 23.2   A polycarbonate lens over the bulb will protect it against thrown objects, and even gunfire in extreme circumstances.

FIGURE 23.3   Street lights along Interstate 95 in South Florida were vandalized by street criminals stealing the copper wiring and rendered unusable. The lights had to be wired on top like a Christmas tree because the wiring was not secured in the bases.

FIGURE 23.4   Open base of light poles vandalized for the copper and aluminum recycling. The lack of security screws on the face plate allowed access to the wiring.

MINIMUM LIGHTING GUIDELINES

1. If a space is for use at night, then a goal is to be able to identify a person's face from 40–75 feet away.
2. Pedestrian pathways, laneways, access routes in outdoor public spaces should be lit to the minimum standards of IESNA, including alleys, laneways and other inset spaces, access and signage routes, and signage.
3. Lighting has to be consistent with no areas of shadow or glare in order to reduce contrast between shadows and illuminated areas.
4. Sidewalk lighting should shine on pedestrian pathways and possible entrapment spaces rather than on the road where the streetlights are already illuminating.
5. Inset doorways, alcoves, and above or below grade entrances should be properly lit.
6. Lighting has to take into account vegetation, including mature trees, and other potential blockages.
7. Light fixtures must be protected from casual vandalism by such means as wired glass or a lantern-style holder.
8. Lighting should not illuminate guards or patrols. Where security patrols cannot be kept out of the zones of illumination, a judgment must be made between the advantage of the lighting and the reduction in patrol effectiveness by having glare and the disadvantage of not being able to see into the darker areas.
9. Lighting must be combined with surveillance. The deterrent effect of lighting depends on fear of detection and arrest. This requires surveillance by CCTV or guards on static and mobile patrols.
10. Lighting must not cause nuisances or hazards. Adverse effects may be caused to adjacent roads, railways, airports, harbors, and neighboring buildings.
11. Lighting must be cost-effective and compatible with site conditions. It may not be economical to light very large areas. Both existing lighting outside the perimeter (the district brightness) and the lighting installed within the site for operational or safety purposes must be considered.

RECOMMENDED CPTED LIGHTING STRATEGIES:

1. Demand lighting: In the right places, light fixtures connected to motion sensors are an excellent way of attracting attention to suspicious activity. This method is also very economical to operate because not all lights are running all the time. Areas that are not supposed to be used at night can be controlled with motion-sensor lighting.
2. Explore the use of new lighting sources currently under development, such as **sulfur lamps,** which are more energy efficient, generate similar light levels, and are cheaper to operate than metal-halide or mercury-vapor lamp installations.

Lumens per Watt (new lamp)	
Sulfur lamp	100
Mercury vapor lamp	40
Metal halide lamp	75
Full-sized fluorescent	85

At an air force lighting installation only two sulfur lamps are needed to illuminate two 104-foot-long-pipes (Figure 23.5). The prismatic film that wraps the light pipes ensures

FIGURE 23.5   Sulfur lamps in a warehouse.

even, high-efficiency distribution (Figure 23.6). Sulfur lamps provide more than twice what metal-halide lamps deliver at working surface (Figure 23.7).

3. Overlapping techniques: Figure 23.8, Figure 23.9, and Figure 23.10 show the aiming of parapet-paired fixtures for protective lighting.

4. Color rendition: If evenness of illumination is the most important concern, color rendition is the secondmost concern. Daylight sun lets the human eye see a determinate range of colors. To approximate this range of colors as much as possible at night, the quality of the lamp inside the fixture is important. The better the lamp, the better the color rendition. When there is a problem identifying colors, the whole lighting system could be counterproductive for promoting a safe environment. It is not a matter of technology but a matter of cost. Better lamps are more expensive. Figure 22.11 and Figure 22.12 show a good and a bad color rendition situation.

Color Rendition Index data assembled from *Lamp Specification & Application Guide,* 2004, Philips Lighting Company:

Type of lamp	CRI
Incandescent	100
Halogen	100
Fluorescent	51–90
Metal Halide	60–96
High Pressure Sodium	21–83
Low pressure Sodium	Monocolor; no color index
Mercury Vapor	20–45

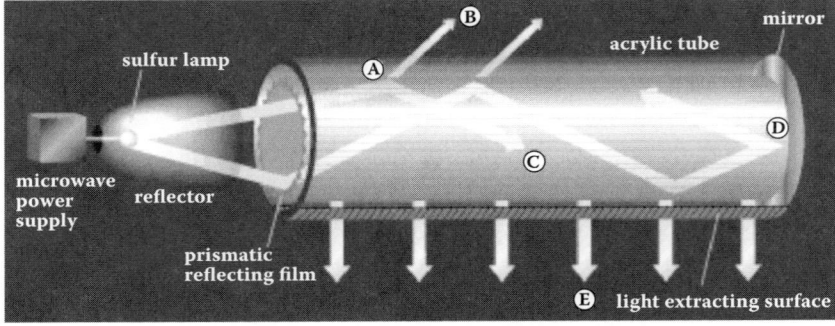

FIGURE 23.6   The workings of a sulfur bulb as used in the National Air and Space Museum and the Department of Energy in Washington DC. (CBS Newsletter, Spring 1995, p. 5).

FIGURE 23.7 Hangar using sulfur lamps.

FIGURE 23.8 The goal is to provide an even work of light on a building facade.

FIGURE 23.9 Cones of light showing overlapping coverage. (From *Safe Schools Design Guide*, Moore/Powers 1993. Used with permission from the Florida Center for Community Design + Research. (www.fccdr.usf.edu).)

FIGURE 23.10   Cones of light providing even coverage.

FIGURE 23.11   Metal halide luminaries come on many diverse pole types.

FIGURE 23.12   At a public housing authority, LPSV was used with an eerie science fiction-type effect. This is not the kind of lighting you would find in the "nice" parts of town, further creating isolation and stigmatization of low-income areas.

5. Coordination with street elements: There are a large number of objects that will always obstruct lighting systems, whether they are located before or after the lighting system is designed and installed—such as recently planted and mature trees, and present and future street furniture and objects (see Figure 23.13 and Figure 23.14).

6. Backup, invulnerable, and recovery systems: A comprehensive lighting system will serve reliably, and in the case of a terror attack or penetration, must be strong enough to continue lighting to withstand the challenge. Criminals and terrorists may try to dismantle the lighting system, so it must be set up in such a way that is difficult to dismantle, and must not be vulnerable to attack. In the event of fire, lightning, explosion, or power outage, the lighting system could fail; it is important that the backup power system continue to provide power to the emergency lighting until the situation is resolved.

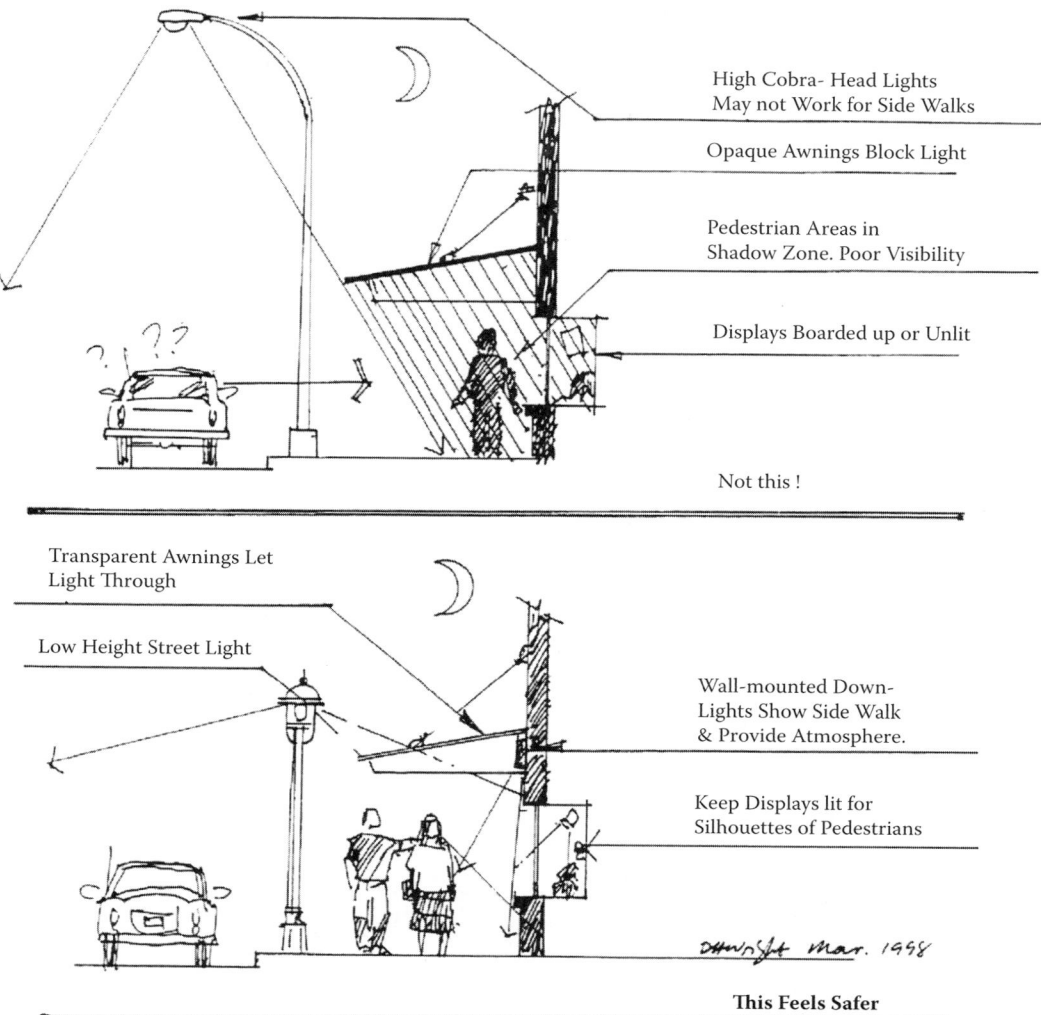

High Cobra- Head Lights
May not Work for Side Walks

Opaque Awnings Block Light

Pedestrian Areas in
Shadow Zone. Poor Visibility

Displays Boarded up or Unlit

Not this !

Transparent Awnings Let
Light Through

Low Height Street Light

Wall-mounted Down-
Lights Show Side Walk
& Provide Atmosphere.

Keep Displays lit for
Silhouettes of Pedestrians

Mar. 1998

This Feels Safer

Street lights are often not designed or installed with the pedestrian in mind.
Ambient lighting along building fronts and shop windows can provide security and
visibility with a more relaxed, urbane atmoshpere for pedestrian traffic.

Urban Street Lighting

FIGURE 23.13 Urban street lighting and the use of canopies. (Used with permission from David Wright, urban design planner and former president of Action Assessment Group, Inc. (AAG Inc.).)

7. Painting the surfaces around ceiling lighting light colors to reflect the light. Many garages have low ceilings and have the luminaries buried in the structural Tees, which result in limited lighting with shadows being cast. One way to get more lighting reflection from the luminaries is to paint the ceilings white. Many jurisdictions have ordinances requiring covered and underground parking facilities to be painted white for this purpose (see Figure 23.15, Figure 23.16, and Figure 23.17).

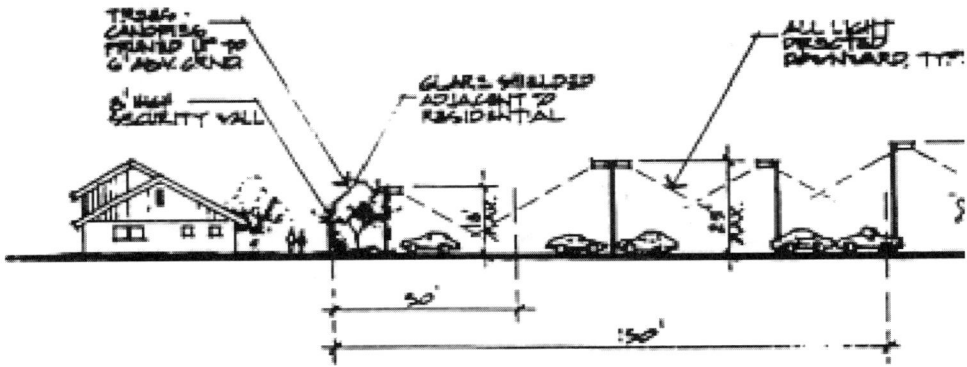

Pole-Mounted Exterior Lighting Adjacent to Residential

FIGURE 23.14 Sketch showing the relationship of pole height to housing. (Image© 1997, City of Tempe, Arizona. Reprinted with permission.)

FIGURE 23.15 Ceiling before painting.

FIGURE 23.16 Ceiling after painting it white. Light reflection has greatly increased.

FIGURE 23.17   Example of painting ceiling to reflect light in garage.

8. Darkness can be a legitimate CPTED lighting strategy. In certain circumstances, having no lighting is an effective crime prevention strategy. The entire environment does not need to be lit up brightly in order to provide safety and visibility. One example that was shared by CPTED founder Tim Crowe is having schools go dark after classes are over and the cleaning crews have finished. The only lights that need to be active, by building code, are the emergency exit signs. When the building is closed and locked at night, the school and grounds are dark. Lights are wired into the alarm system. Some burglars will turn lights on after entry, which triggers an alarm condition. The basketball courts will be dark because if there is light out there, the kids will shoot hoops. and the lights serve as an attractive magnet for activity. The parking lot is locked and off limits, and the pole lights are wired into motion sensors. If cars use the lots after the hours, the lights will come on, alarming police and neighbors that there has been a breach in security; this alerts neighbors to call police or pay attention.

9. The quality of lighting. Security lighting does not prevent crime, but it can help protect people and property. Good pedestrian lighting offers the natural surveillance people need to feel comfortable walking ahead or across a parking lot to their cars. Lighting can prevent surprises from jump-out criminals, or can give pedestrians the opportunity to request assistance, to turn and go another way, or to retreat.

Security lighting objectives should be to achieve a uniform, consistent level of light on both pedestrian and vehicular paths of travel. Lighting is critical for the illumination of street and building names and numbers for effective response by police, fire, and emergency personnel. Design lighting to avoid light intrusion into residential settings.

FIGURE 23.18   Gas station lighting typically far exceeds what is needed in order to attract customers to the light.

FIGURE 23.19   Pedestrian lighting. Good for preventing trip and falls but ineffective for facial recognition of persons walking toward you.

The quality of lighting may be an important security feature. True-color, full-spectrum light rendition can help with identification of vehicles and persons. Car lots and gas stations are examples of building types where metal halide luminaries are used for full spectrum light rendition (see Figure 23.18).

Proper beam control saves a system from glare, loss of light energy, and light intrusion. Fixtures should be installed to cast a light pattern over a broad horizontal area rather than a tall vertical area. Light surfaces reflect light more efficiently than dark surfaces. Keep in mind the line of sight between the location of a light fixture and objects that may cast a shadow. Careful placement will avoid dark corners behind doors, trash cans, and other features.

Protective lighting is a valuable and inexpensive deterrent to crime. It improves visibility for checking badges and people at entrances, inspecting vehicles, preventing illegal entry, and detecting intruders both outside and inside buildings and grounds (see Figure 23.19). Protective lighting must accomplish the following goals:

- Provide for proper illumination of all exterior areas in a facility, including pedestrian and vehicular entrances, the perimeter fence line, sensitive areas or structures within the perimeter, and parking areas.
- Discourage or deter attempts at entry by intruders by making detection certain. Proper illumination may lead a potential intruder to believe detection is inevitable.

Objectives of security lighting placement:

- Avoid glare that handicaps guards and annoys passing traffic and occupants of adjacent properties.

- Direct glare at intruders, where appropriate, as a means of handicapping them.
- Provide that guard posts and CCTV cameras are in low-light locations to render their positions harder for the intruder to pinpoint.
- Provide for redundancy, so that a single lamp outage does not result in a dark spot vulnerable to intrusion.
- Provide for complete reliability such that, in the event of a power failure, standby illumination is available.
- Provide for convenient control.
- Be covered under a maintenance agreement such that repairs are made in a timely fashion.
- Be resistant to vandalism and sabotage. Fixtures should be installed high, out of reach of potential intruders and be of the vandal-resistant type.

CONDUCT LIGHTING SURVEY (PHOTOMETRIC PLAN)

Evaluate lighting every 6 to 12 months or every time camera surveillance systems are improved, changed, or upgraded. Proper security lighting requires attention to a number of factors. The quantity of light is not the only aspect to consider in proper security lighting.

Distribution of light is important; for example, dark areas require the viewer to constantly adapt to varying light levels, increasing visual fatigue and recognition time. The visual tasks performed by security personnel also determine light levels. Camera systems may require specific light levels in order to perform at their best.

It is easy to monitor light meter readings. Obtain a light meter and adjust the settings to lux or footcandles (see Figure 23.20). Practice the difference between horizontal and vertical readings. Measuring existing light levels requires an accurate meter. This instrument should be sent to a laboratory specializing in this type of work to be checked for accuracy; it should be recalibrated if necessary and certified as accurate. Records of such certification should be retained for the length of time recommended by your legal counsel.

Obtain a scale site drawing that shows the locations of the existing luminaries. Plot light meter readings at corresponding locations on the drawing. Readings and notations should include:

- Description of lamp (mercury vapor, full-spectrum fluorescent, low pressure sodium, etc.)
- Type of luminary (mount, height above ground if applicable, etc.)
- Luminance at source, surface, and reflectance
- Vertical and horizontal illumination

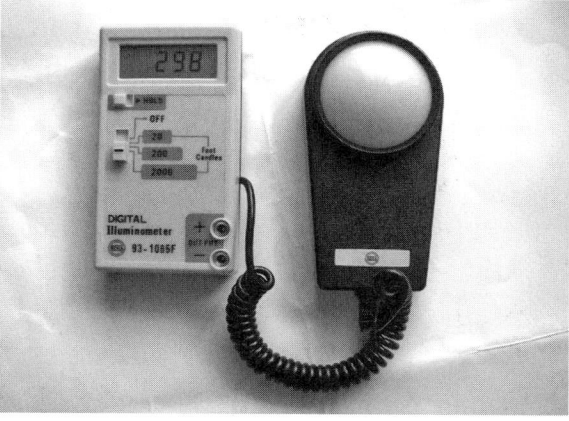

FIGURE 23.20   A typical light meter that is used for surveys.

- Areas of glare
- Areas of relative darkness

The major steps of a lighting survey are first to determine the function of light at given location. List the type of tasks the lighting performs—detection, recognition, and identification. Then measure the existing light levels at locations throughout the site. Research the illuminance levels recommended or required at specific places using the IESNA guidelines as a reference. Evaluate existing equipment for deficiencies. If there are outages or equipment that is inoperative, select and install equipment to supply required light levels.

Particular attention should be given to the approaches of a property, such as public roads and sidewalks, vehicle and pedestrian entrances to the property, perimeter areas, particularly fences, open areas outside and within the property, parking areas, roadways and sidewalks within the property, building entrances, particularly if recessed. Landscaping, walls, building facades, and other areas of potential concealment should be evaluated to lighting levels (Table 23.1).

TABLE 23.1
IESNA Guidelines for Minimum Lighting Levels*

Type of Space	Illuminance Horizontal Average—Footcandles (FC)
Unoccupied Spaces	
Storage yards	0.5–2 fc
Industrial equipment	1–2 fc
Building facades	0.5–2 fc
Facial identification	0.5–1 fc
Guarded facilities	10 fc
ATM exterior	10 fc within 10 ft. 2 fc from 10–40 ft.
ATM interior	15 fc within 10 ft. of ATM
Parking facilities garages, covered spaces	6 fc on pavement
Parking gathering areas, stairs, ramps, elevators	5 fc
Parking for elderly	50 fc
Walkways around senior facilities	5 fc
Parking for public parks	3 fc
Trails, walkways	0.5–1 fc
Supermarket—major retail parking	3 fc
Fast food restaurants	3 fc
Convenience stores/gas stations	
Pump areas	6 fc
Sidewalks and grounds	3 fc
Store interior	30 fc
Single family residence, exterior doorway	0.8 fc
Multifamily residences common areas	0.3 fc
Multifamily residence mailbox areas	1 fc
Senior housing entrances—active hours	30 fc
Senior housing entrances—sleeping hours	10 fc
Schools and Institutions (general parking)	3 fc
Schools sidewalks and footpaths	1 fc
Hotels and motels; general parking	3 fc

TABLE 23.1 (CONTINUED)
IESNA Guidelines for Minimum Lighting Levels*

Type of Space	Illuminance Horizontal Average—Footcandles (FC)
Hotels and motels; sidewalks and grounds	1 fc
Police, fire, EMS service facilities	8 fc
Police, fire, EMS service; general parking/walkways	3 fc
Perimeter fence	0.5 fc
Outer perimeter	0.5–2 fc
Open areas	2 fc
Open parking lot	0.2–0.9 fc
Covered parking structure	5 fc
Pedestrian walkways	0.2 fc
Pedestrian entrances	5 fc
Vehicle entrances	10 fc
Building facade	0.5–2 fc
Gate houses	30 fc
Loading dock exterior	0.2–5 fc
Loading bays	15 fc
Offices—general	30–50 fc
Offices—task	50–70 fc
Interior public areas	10–20 fc
Retail stores	50 fc
Bank—lobby	20 fc
Bank—teller	50.00 fc
Bank—ATM	15.00 fc

* Recommended Lighting Levels in footcandles by the IESNA G-1–03 By Building Type.
Source: Guidelines for Security Lighting for People, Property, and Public Spaces, IESNA, 2003.

COORDINATION BETWEEN THE TRADES

The number one reason why security lighting does not reach its full potential on most jobs is because there is no coordination between the architect, the landscape architect, the electrical engineer, and the security consultant. In most construction projects, the drawings are done using computer-aided design drafting (CADD). The drawings are on different layers. Typically, each of the different trades produces their drawings and specifications. The architect is supposed to coordinate between the different trades, but that does not always occur. The end result is that the landscape architect is scheduling trees and plants that conflict with the exterior lighting, and you may end up with very expensive tree lighting (see Figure 23.21).

The CPTED practitioner needs to review the plans of the landscape architect and the lighting plan and look at where the tree canopies impose the lighting arcs. He should ask the lighting or electrical engineer for the lighting level photometric plans and lay them over the landscape planting ground cover and tree canopy plans. Look for things that abut (see Figure 23.22).

FIGURE 23.21   A common sight on many projects is the merging of landscaping and site lighting, but not in a good way.

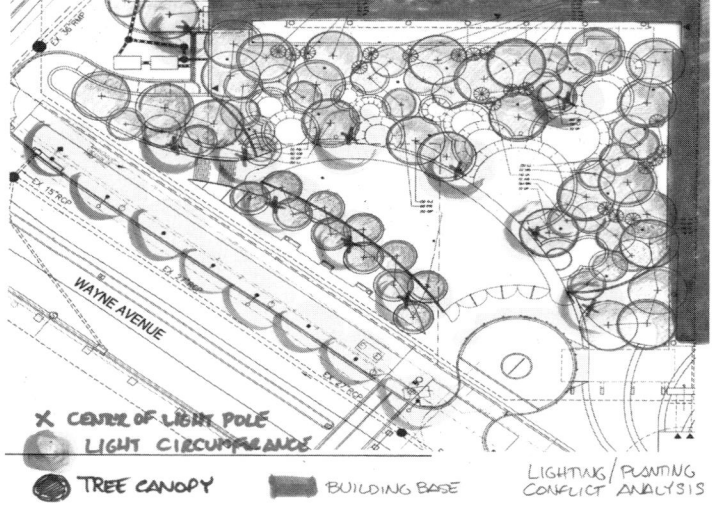

FIGURE 23.22   Example of landscaping overlayed with lighting patterns looking for conflicts.

SUMMARY

The Top 10 Tactics for Safe Lighting design should include:

1. Include lighting design into the project as early as possible.
2. Design with easy maintenance and invulnerable system in mind.
3. Evaluate potential risk areas.
4. Design lighting with both physical and psychological effects.
5. Light up your project by areas:
   a.   Light up your building façade
   b.   Light up your building perimeter
   c.   Light up your site perimeter
   d.   Light up your street frontage
   e.   Light up your pedestrian pathways
   f.   Light up your public areas
   g.   Light up your parking areas
   h.   Light up your landscaping.

FIGURE 23.23   Good lighting quantity and quality for a restaurant with drive thru.

6. Automatic light control and back-up systems are recommended.
7. Factors to avoid:
   a. Glare and blindness.
   b. Light pollution to the skies
   c. Light leakage.
   d. Shadows and blind spots.
   e. Future landscape growth to interfere with lights.
8. Inform project team on insurance and security systems savings.
9. Consult CPTED trained lighting engineer or security consultant on light bulb and fixture specifications and locations, fixture spacing and height.
10. Be clear on what you want the experience to be!

The benefits of having smart and efficient use of security lighting include less vandalism, fewer break-ins, improved perception of safety, legal savings from premises liability litigation, improved curbside appeal (see Figure 23.23). and building value, and increased utilization of areas. It makes good business sense to use lighting wisely and effectively.

REFERENCES

Crouch, S., Shaftoe, H., and Fleming, R. *Design for Secure Residential Environments*, 1999, pp. 24–43.
Fennelly, L. J. *Effective Physical Security*, 2004, Third Ed. Elsevier Butterworth–Heinemann, Burlington, MA, pp. 175–180.
Fundamentals of Light & Color Measurement, Mecom, 1994.
Guideline for Security Lighting for People, Property and Public Spaces, Illuminating Engineering Society of North America, 2003, New York, NY. (IESNA G-1-03 March 2003).
Healy, R. J. *Design for security* 1968. John Wiley & Sons. NY, NY, pp. 136–172.
Hopf, Peter S. *Handbook of Building Security, Planning and Design*, 1979, Ch. 14 by Weibel, William A. P.E., F.I.E.S. McGraw-Hill, New York, NY, pp. 14–1 to 14–21.
Illumination Engineering Society of North America. Lighting for Parking Facilities (IESNA RP-20-98 Dec. 1998).
Industrial Lighting Application Guide; 2004, Philips Lighting Company, Somerset, NJ.
Lamp Specification and Application Guide, 2004, Philips Lighting Company, Somerset, NJ.
Lighting Handbook, North American Philips Lighting Corporation, 1984.

Lighting for Safety and Security, 1989, National Lighting Bureau, Washington, DC.

Lighting Technology. *Architectural Record*, Nov. 1998, pp. 165–166.

Lyons, S. L. *Lighting for Industry and Security: A Handbook for Providers and Users of Lighting*, 1992; Butterworth-Heinemann, Newton MA.

Neidle, M. *Emergency and Security Lighting Handbook*, 1988. (A U.K. text distributed in the U.S. by Butterworth-Heinemann, Newton, MA.)

Physical Security, U.S. Army Field Manual 19–30; March 1979, U.S. Government Printing Office, S/N 0–635–034/1069.

Rubenstein, F. Center for Building Sciences. CBS Newsletter, Spring 1995. p. 5.

Russell, P. L. and P. A. Rodgers, *The Outdoor Lighting Pattern Book*, Lighting Research Center, RPI; McGraw Hill. NY NY. 1996 pp 3–150.

Wekerle, Gerda R., and Whitzman, C. *Safe Cities*, Van Nostrand Reinhold, NY NY, 1995, pp 28–30.

24 Parking Lots and Garages

Parking facilities, by their very nature, are challenging to make into secure environments. They are a land use with a single purpose, and they do not easily allow for mixed uses that might encourage territoriality. They contain large high-rise garage walls, structural columns, and multi-levels, which create poor visibility and make them vulnerable to crime. Subsurface or underground parking facilities are often part of a building's foundation, have little to no outside exposure for visibility, and can be an easy target for terrorism (World Trade Center 1993, Madrid airport parking lot 2006). It Is difficult to control access to large open parking lots, and they make an inviting environment for car thieves, purse snatching, and car burglary. Parking structures, whether they are surface lots, above or below ground, are perceived as dark, isolated, and dangerous environments.

The primary goal of designing safe garages and parking facilities is to create an atmosphere that makes potential criminals feel that they will be observed, and improve the chances they will be challenged. The eventual goal is for the criminal to realize that the gain is not worth the effort.

In order to accomplish these goals, careful application of CPTED principles and practices are necessary. In some jurisdictions, such as New South Wales, Australia, parking design guidelines include CPTED requirements (McCamley, 2002). But in most others, there are none. This chapter details some basic CPTED design considerations.

STANDARD OF CARE

Parking facilities are supposed to provide a safe area for auto storage and passage of users to and from their vehicle. Of all of the premises liability litigation occurring over the last decade in the United States, 18% of the lawsuits were related to parking lots or facilities (Bates, 1994). Forty four percent of the reported rapes and sexual assaults in the United States in 1994 occurred in parking facilities. Of 1994 reported violent crimes, 8.5% took place in parking facilities. In a 2004 update of previous research (Bates, 2004, p. 15), parking facilities are the most common location for an incident to occur for all business categories combined, especially for sexual assault and assault and battery.

Parking facilities have many factors that create opportunities of high risk of criminal behavior, because there is generally a low level of activity in parking facilities, with lots of hiding places and numerous areas of shade and dark shadows. Parking facilities usually have multiple means of entry and thus provide many easy means of escape after a crime.

The TOP TEN most commonly made errors in the design and operation of parking facilities include: (1) having unattended facilities, except for someone occasionally stationed at the entry or exit to collect revenue; (2) the parking facility is designed with numerous hiding spaces; (3) the lack of electronic security measures for surveillance and access control; (4) the observation by users between parking bays is obscured with structural or design elements; (5) foot or vehicle circulation signage is usually absent creating confusion and dementia with little sense of direction; (6) the facility is usually dirty and undermaintained; (7) the structure is exclusively designed as a stable for vehicles and serves no other purposes for people; (8) the perimeter access by persons walking or driving is usually unsupervised; (9) pedestrian access points fail to provide natural surveillance from the sidewalk through the garage door; (10) the same access protocol is allowed 24 hours a day, not taking into factor staffing patterns, late evening checkouts, or other use considerations.

This book has recommended throughout the use of a proper risk assessment prior to CPTED recommendations. Chapters 29 and 30 delve into risk assessment in more detail. For some time, the national standard of care for safe parking facilities was based on position that parking facilities should conduct a security assessment for the considerations that include: (1) criminal history of the site, (2) landscaping issues, (3) lighting issues, (4) attendant facilities for revenue collection and supervision, (5) restroom access, (6) stairwells and elevators for vertical access, (7) signage and graphics, (8) surveillance capabilities, (9) access control equipment, and (10) policies and procedures for the operation and staffing of the parking facility.

PERIMETER CONTROLS

The first and most important point to consider in planning a safe and secure parking area is the layout. Good design will allow for smooth traffic ingress and egress. The spacing of the parking slots and travel lanes can prevent or initiate accidents. Location of entrances and exits is a design factor that can assist in blocking or creating opportunities for outsiders to gain access to the parking area. The necessary movement of person or vehicles is known as the circulation patterns of the facility.

Access control and territoriality principles translate first and foremost into good perimeter control. Perimeter definition and access control deters unwanted pedestrian level access to the lot or garage. Perimeter control can be fencing, level changes, ground floor protection, and other architectural and environmental barriers that channel people to designated entry points onto the property and into the lot or garage, and discourage persons from hiding outside and inside the property or buildings. Fencing around the perimeter of the parking lot or garage will discourage trespassing and unauthorized access and deter any criminal looking for an opportunity. Fencing can be a symbolic barrier, such as and 3- to 4-foot picket fencing, or in remote areas it could be as high as 7 to 8 feet (depending on what building and zoning codes will allow in a given area).

Ground level protection of a garage should be designed to resist unauthorized access on the ground floor, but also not be designed in a way that serves as a ladder to climb up to a second floor. Screening that reaches from floor to ceiling is preferred to solid walls, as the screening allows natural surveillance and the ability to call out for assistance and be heard. The screening provides visibility into the structure from the street, and that can serve as a deterrent to criminal activity (see Figure 24.1 through Figure 24.7).

FIGURE 24.1 Ground-level protection; good intention but the screen webbing is too big and can facilitate easy climbing to the next story.

FIGURE 24.2   Subsurface parking under an apartment complex with ground level protection screens.

LANDSCAPING AND ACCESS POINTS

Landscaping decisions can impact access to the site and building. Low shrubs using CPTED criteria are important to deflect persons from the edge of the building. Trees and bushes should be properly maintained so as to provide a proper field of vision. Open-area parking lots should consider the parking surface and the impact that it has on maintenance, visibility, reflection of lighting, and drainage. Open parking areas often have landscaping that can provide hiding places and block visibility. Landscaping under CPTED criteria should be intermittent in size and texture. Instead of planting a solid hedge of bushes or trees, a more effective way to achieve environmental security is a combination of low hedges and high-canopy trees. This combination allows unobstructed vision and no hiding places for criminals, while providing the required greenery on the site. Plantings that are higher than 3 feet should not be placed within 10 to 15 feet to the entrances of building in order to deter hiding spots. If the bushes or ground cover are maintained below 3 feet, they can be

FIGURE 24.3   A Memphis parking lot with ground-level screening.

FIGURE 24.4   Ground-level screening of a garage showing defined pedestrian paths. Doors can be locked at night or after hours if needed.

placed close to the perimeter wall to discourage persons from climbing or cutting the ground level screening. Entrances should be relatively clear of obstructions and distractions so as to provide good natural surveillance for users, especially during evening hours. As recommended in Chapter 21, ground cover should be under 3 feet and tree canopies pruned above 8 feet for mature trees. The result will be a clear zone for visibility between 3 and 8 feet (see Figure 24.8).

If the parking lots or garages have persons collecting tickets or monies, there is a need for careful placement of the parking attendant. The goal is for a well-defined vehicular entrance as well as providing good lines of sight, as much as is structurally feasible. Vehicular access points and toll takers can be very effective security measures. They advertise to potential criminals or terrorists that they probably will be observed by some form of guardian or by other patrons, and/or recorded.

FIGURE 24.5   Ground-level screening and railings have large openings, which create a ladder for someone to climb to the third floor.

FIGURE 24.6 Secondary exits are closed with screening, and other openings are screened, creating a secure perimeter.

Architects can design the pedestrian and vehicle paths to intersect or pass by the parking attendant station to create the opportunity for surveillance and monitoring.

One of the greatest security challenges with parking lots and garages is the number of entrances and exits. Traffic engineers will often encourage multiple access points to increase the circulation patterns and time of entry or leaving. However, from a security and control perspective, the more entrances there are, the less ability to control who comes and goes and to enforce a level of security

FIGURE 24.7 The ground floor screening was intended to provide security but merely provides a ladder to the second floor. The landscaping and plantings are maintained at a good height for visibility.

FIGURE 24.8 This garage has smart placement of trees and plantings that does not interfere with lines of sight or the ground level screening.

on the grounds (see Figure 24.9). The CPTED recommended method is to have one means of entry and exit for vehicles (see Figure 24.10). If the volume of traffic is so great as to require more, then at each subsequent access point an attendant should be placed in a booth, and access gate arms and roll-down shutters should be intstalled for after-hours closure and ground floor protection, along with CCTV and good lighting.

FIGURE 24.9 This garage has a well-defined entrance and a clear and aesthetically pleasing perimeter that directs cars and people to the designated points.

FIGURE 24.10 This underground entrance uses the architecture to direct cars in and out and, does it in a way that is very attractive.

CPTED Solution: closing designated points of entry or egress during periods of low activity. Examples are shopping malls, or theme parks such as Disney World (see Figure 24.11). When at all possible, persons entering a parking facility by foot should have little choice but to enter near a parking attendant booth or security check point. Just having a CCTV is not sufficient, but having a real person who can observe and respond is desired wherever possible.

FIGURE 24.11 Disney World parking lot and staff directing traffic to parking spaces.

CPTED Solution: The parking attendant station needs to have security issues addressed. In the summer of 2006 at the CityPlace mall in West Palm Beach, a parking attendant was robbed and assaulted in her booth by two men she observed loitering in the parking garage (see Figure 24.12). She locked herself in the booth, but she did not have a radio or telephone to call for assistance. She had a cash drawer of monies collected from patrons parking, and the men wanted it. They beat on the glass with a baseball bat and eventually broke in and took the money and beat the attendant.

FIGURE 24.12   Some garage cashiers are isolated from support by security staff because of lack of cameras and personal alarms.

If the "guardian" of the garage is going to be handling money, then the staff needs to be afforded security in the form of communications, CCTV, security glazing, and duress alarms.

CCTV AND SURVEILLANCE

The cashier booths are a high-risk target for robbery, especially with the use of vehicles for an easy escape. If a parking attendant were going to be collecting cash, the built-in feature of a drop safe would reduce the availability to the cash. Signage must clearly state that cash is drop-safe deposited and that the cashier does not have access to it. The cashier should also have duress or silent alarms to notify security or police of a robbery. If there is CCTV coverage of the garage, a camera should be focused on the attendant booth. The camera coverage should be recorded so that law enforcement can respond to accurate information. Cashier booths should be designed to allow 360-degree visibility. Drop-down gates and barrier arms can be designed to allow for orderly entry and exit by the attendant booth and deter piggybacking behind another car.

Cash collection in parking structures is an important security design consideration. Cash can be handled manually at kiosks or automatic systems. The cashier, however, can provide an important link in providing surveillance during operation hours. Automatic systems should be located where cashiers are visible to other employees in order to reduce the opportunity for vandalism or burglary.

All CCTV cameras should be strategically placed in areas that would be provided with constant light (by day light or by luminaries) to provide proper illumination for the lens. Low-light cameras can be used, but they are more expensive and acknowledge that lighting conditions might be poor. Camera placement in garages should be chosen where there is the highest percentage of unhindered view. Most cameras are not fixed lens but allow zoom, pan, and tilt for maximum flexibility of what is being watched. Camera placement on surface parking lots should be prioritized with good lines of sight and cover as much ground as possible. The cameras should be protected within polycarbonate domes to resist vandalism, and usually dark domes to prevent people from seeing where the cameras are watching. Camera systems need to be monitored in real time and digitally recorded for playback and enhancement. Cameras should be color rather than black and white, to make it easier to identify specific vehicles and persons, especially in the playback mode to recover important evidence.

FIGURE 24.13 CCTV is watching persons that might be using the exits stairs.

Panic-button callboxes should be integrated with the video surveillance system, allowing a camera to be activated when a callbox is pushed so that security can receive a call for assistance instantly. CCTV systems can also be integrated into the access control system so that license plate numbers can be entered into a log when vehicles enter or exit the parking facility.

If public restrooms are in a parking garage, they should be located near the attendant booth for casual supervision and located in areas of open, well-traveled areas for maximum surveillance opportunities. The doors may be locked during operating hours and the attendant may be able to give a key or remotely lock and unlock a door. The bathrooms should contain personal alarms in case of an attack. Restrooms available for public use should be avoided if at all possible. Bathrooms serve as a natural meeting place for victims and predators. If restroom access is unavoidable, then bathrooms should be placed where the doors are visible from the attendant's normal working position. Instead of providing a double-door system, which has been used to lock victims in, an open maze-type "lazy S" entrance that allows a person's cries for assistance to be heard unobstructed is a better choice. Alarms, panic devices, and motion-activated lighting can make public bathrooms safer places.

Communications equipment in the form of radios is necessary for staff as attendants, patrol rovers, or security staff. Communications are also important for patrons. Panic or assistance alarms are desired in stairwells, mid-floor locations, by elevator lobbies, in elevators, and even walkway paths leading to the garage or parking lot. The alarm call systems must also be designed with American With Disabilities Act (ADA) accessibility compliance in mind that would address persons with hearing and visibility disabilities. (see Figure 24.14 and Figure 24.15). Even though vision impaired persons might not be driving, it is very possible that they will meet someone for a ride in a lot or garage and are vulnerable to attack.

FIGURE 24.14 A personal alarm system should be obvious visually and responded to quickly. This requires preplanning and conduit.

FIGURE 24.15 An example of an intercom system in a university garage and the blue light system to help direct security staff where the problem is quickly.

If security guards are going to be used in the garage or open lots, it makes good sense and planning to design a guard tour system that accounts for the guard making patrol stops and punching in. The guard tour system creates a paper trail and accountability that the security guard is not sleeping or slacking on the job, and documents the patrol patterns. Having a guard tour system requires electrical conduits and systems planning and should be considered in the initial design stages so that the asphalt or concrete does not have to be damaged to place in conduit for the devices.

Parking lots by definition are typically open, with few visual obstructions. On the other hand, garages have structural elements and ramps that obstruct visibility. Parking lot obstructions typically come from landscaping and planting choices, and the vehicles will create hiding spaces between themselves. In the daytime, persons hiding would be pretty obvious, but in the evening the cover of darkness makes observation difficult. Thus in parking lot design, lighting becomes a critical design feature. Lighting should be a combination of high and pedestrian level lighting to reduce the shadows produced by the vehicles.

Stairwells and elevators should be located centrally, where they are visible from the attendant's position. If stairwells are located in blind spots, have them monitored with cameras (see Figure 24.13), panic alarms, and door position switches to alert the attendant that someone is in the stairwell. Stairwells can be constructed of clear glazing materials to allow visibility from the street into the stairwells in event of an incident (see Figure 24.16).

For parking garages, the fewer structural elements and ramps, the better surveillance is by the patrons and attendants of the facility. Interior walls in garages are often minimized because they are not load bearing, and it is common to see cabling or metal railings used to separate levels, which permit hearing and visibility to occur yet divide the floors as needed (see Figure 24.17). Where solid walls are needed, portholes and windows, or openings wherever possible, are desired to create porosity in the wall fabric that enables casual observance (see Figure 24.18, Figure 24.19, and Figure 24.20).

Enclosed parking structures should consider the location and visibility of the stairways and elevators. Many parking structures have the sides of the parking garage covered for aesthetic reasons. However, with a priority given to surveillance, the design would allow open building fronts with heavy cables as the wall system. The cables have been used to prevent cars from falling over the edge. Cable systems have been used extensively in parking garages for over a decade. The benefits of open facades for garage structures are visibility and surveillance from the ground to the cars, and increased audio capability for hearing calls for assistance.

Ramp design for driving from one level to another is one of the great challenges of parking garage design. Although many creative design solutions exist, having an exterior looping ramp allows for floors that are level and have unobstructed lines of sight. The real estate of many garages

FIGURE 24.16 Exterior stairwell has good lighting and visibility.

FIGURE 24.17 Open structural bays provide the best visibility. Wire cabling is used to prevent crossing through and as support against cars going though, yet allows air movement, visibility, and protection of the cars.

FIGURE 24.18   Exterior ramps allow the floors to remain level rather than sloping.

FIGURE 24.19   The famous Marina Towers in Chicago uses the lower one-third of the building as a parking garage and has a continuing sloping floor that acts as the ramp.

will not support this kind of design, but where possible the exterior placement of ramps provides a relatively unobstructed view of the parking level (see Figure 24.18).

The owners of parking structures also have a legal responsibility to provide a safe and secure environment for the users and invited guests. Pedestrian access is one of the most commonly overlooked design features of parking lots and structures. Parking garages and lots are commonly designed to provide a space that "works" for moving the cars in an orderly and efficient way, but in reality, the cars are providing a means for people to arrive at a destination. This priority is important to remember.

Pedestrian access involves safety and security design planning. For open parking lots a key design consideration is full handicap accessibility. Accessibility includes dedicated handicap spaces, ramps, stair design, elevator location and design, railings, floor surfaces, pedestrian crossovers, and dedicated pedestrian paths. A primary design rule for designing parking areas is to avoid whenever possible a pedestrian crossing the path of a car. With double-sided lots this may be unavoidable; however, the design can create a "safe" passageway for pedestrians and handicapped persons to move along a clear path until they come to a marked crosswalk, which serves as a caution for drivers.

Wheel stops are a security and safety consideration in most parking facilities. The wheel stop is supposed to give you feedback when you have pulled into your parking space fully. But wheel stops can also slow down some one who accidentally puts their foot on the gas and jumps forward and could run through a wall or onto the curb or sidewalk and strike someone. One wheel stop is intended for each car, yet some contractors have tried to save money by using wheel stops between two parking spaces. The problem with this is that there is an expectation that when you step out of your car the travel path is clear. The wheel stop between the cars may be a tripping hazard, and many persons have been seriously injured (see Figure 24.21).

FIGURE 24.20   The use of a curved ramp system allows for the garage levels to be flat and not sloped.

FIGURE 24.21   Wheel stops between cars may be a tripping hazard for persons not expecting an obstruction.

In many office and apartment buildings, parking is placed underneath the structure. In the Northeast United States, parking levels may be below ground. In Florida, parking levels are ground level and may occupy the first few floors, with the building located above the parking. The structural elements must be carefully considered with regard to parking alignment but also the lines of sight. When garages must make do, with parking taking second place to structural issues, CPTED design practices are even more critical. For these types of garages, having one way in and out it essential. Having a parking attendant at the entry and exit points controls parking and revenue considerations, and the attendant booth and its location serve as the security border for that building. Another simple recommendation is use round rather than rectangular structural elements. A round column allows for` much greater visibility around the corners than a rectangular or square column. Structurally, there is no difference between using the two shapes. It is usually a design decision (see Figure 24.22).

In addition to wheel stops, other tripping hazards common in open parking lots are speed bumps. Speed bumps must be painted to visually stand out, and have warning signs to provide enough notice to slow down so drivers do not lose control of their cars. Speed bumps must be carefully designed, as they can be severe tripping hazards to pedestrians walking, and to motorcycles and bicycles. Speed bumps and humps provide a means of slowing cars and trucks down. They also provide a means to damage cars, provide tripping hazards to pedestrians, and have been the source of numerous personal injury lawsuits (see Figure 24.23).

Underground parking also brings the consideration of what else is located in the basement. For example, the 1993 attack on the World Trade Center was through a van that carried explosives and detonated in the lower levels of the garage. The building survived, but located in the basement were the security office, mechanical spaces, backup generators, smoke evacuation systems, fire stand-pipes, and fire protection systems and pumps; virtually every backup system the building had was located in the basement. When the bomb went off, if brought down all of the emergency and safety equipment features of the building. The lesson learned from this was to have the distribution of

FIGURE 24.22 The huge structural columns of this garage are troubling for security concerns because they are difficult to negotiate with a car, can hide people, and make lighting difficult to accomplish.

FIGURE 24.23 The speed bump is well identified, but the designer forgot to provide a curb cut in this hospital parking lot, and the patient in the wheelchair is facing a tough choice.

mechanical and safety features of the building in multiple locations, not all located in the out-of-sight, out-of-mind proverbial basement location. Another lesson was to plan for redundancy, and space the stairwells to opposite parts of a building plan, and have redundancy in mechanical and fire safety systems.

When parking garages are multilevel, the national and state building codes require emergency exits from the building levels. The number of exits is determined by the square footage of the floor plans, and the building footprint or shape of the building. Fire exit stairwells can be used for going from level to level, and must be accessible for persons leaving the building. However, there is no requirement that fire stairwell exits must be used to get into a building.

Stairwells are often security risks because they are typically enclosed, or opaque, and become potential entrapment areas for criminal activity because of their lack of natural surveillance. Garages that use CPTED features will design stairwells that use fire-resistant glazing and provide full natural surveillance. Stairwells should be visible from grade level, and located where visibility into the stairwell is on a high traffic area or where police or security staff can casually observe. Some garage stairwells have personal alarm buttons for calling assistance. Stairwell doors can be made from glass, or have glass vision panels in the frames and still comply with building and fire codes (see Figure 24.24).

At the lowest level of stairwells, care should be taken to secure the area under the landing to prevent persons from hiding there, or materials from being stored there against code regulations. Stairways that exit to the roof or elevator closet should be secured from unauthorized entry and to prevent access to the roof or mechanical spaces. If there is rooftop parking, mechanical spaces should be secured, monitored, and alarmed. Doors exiting to basement or rooftop mechanical spaces should be predrilled and wired for door position switches, intercoms, and alarmed with screech alarms and

FIGURE 24.24 The lobby foyers and elevator landings should be easily identifiable from the far end of the garage; this can be facilitated by signage and lighting.

a signal sent to security staff or police. Garage rooftops have been used for criminal and terrorist activity and should be carefully considered if included as part of your project.

Stairs and elevators of high-rise or subsurface parking garages that have offices, residences, or other mixed uses should have the elevators empty into a lobby level and not go directly into the business or resident floors. Anyone can enter off the street and park their car without being screened for legitimate use. If the office building has street-level security, one can park in the garage and take an elevator up to an office floor, totally circumnavigating the security function. The parking floor and elevators should empty to a floor level that requires exiting and then lead to another dedicated bank of elevators, stairs, or escalators that can facilitate screening, access control, and surveillance by security staff if desired (see Figure 24.25).

Although stairs are required for fire egress, elevators are the primary means of moving into and up through the garage. Elevators are required because of accessibility requirements, and have become the primary means of vertical transportation in multilevel parking garages. Elevators, like stairwells, should use as much glass and open visibility as is structurally possible. Glass-walled elevators placed along the exterior of the building can provide for good natural visibility by persons on the street and other persons within the garage. Cameras can also be used to watch how people use the elevators, and many elevators have intercom capability and phones to comply with the ADA Accessibility Guidelines. Many elevators have alarms in them as well in the event that an elevator gets stuck and the rider needs assistance.

GRAPHICS AND WAYFINDING

Signage of the parking facility should be located in full street view for ease of identification by users and police. The building signage should be a minimum of eight inches high and well lit at night. Wall signage for pedestrian and vehicular traffic should be graphic whenever possible to ensure universal understanding. Symbols and colors should be used to reduce confusion and dementia and provide a sense of clear direction. Disney World is the best example of how graphics, signage, and one-way traffic flow allows easy parking for several hundred thousand people a day without incident.

Parking areas should be well marked with graphics and color coding so patrons can easily remember where they parked their cars (see Figure 24.26). Mechanical systems have been developed

FIGURE 24.25 People want to see and be seen to feel safe and avoid confrontations.

that can sense where spaces are available and help direct persons looking for spaces. Many accidents and fights in parking lots are related to finding those last few spaces. The technology is available to easily direct persons to a floor or specific space because a green light is illuminated in the driveway to be seen by drivers hunting for spaces.

FIGURE 24.26 Color-coding of floors and elevators is helpful for wayfinding.

FIGURE 24.27 Advertising that this is secure parking creates a false illusion that the lot is patrolled, well lit, and has a secure perimeter.

Signage in parking lots and garages need to accurately reflect the level of safety. Creating an "illusion of security" is worse than having no security at all. So when there are signs advertising "secure" parking, it better be (see Figure 24.27).

Graffiti in parking environments has become another form of illegitimate signage that can be designed for, and addressed by, the architect. Graffiti management is an important consideration, as this represents a territorial ritual-type marking of gangs or vandals. Graffiti is a form of vandalism and should not be ignored. If a wall surface is a frequent target, the surface should be painted with graffiti-resistant epoxy paint for easy removal, or lighting and surveillance should be increased to catch perpetrators. Graffiti should be covered as soon as possible, to prevent further vandalism and creation of "territorial" messages.

LIGHTING

Lighting in parking garages and open-surface lots is a critical design feature that can support all of the other security features. Without good lighting, CCTV systems become relatively useless and natural surveillance impaired. The quantity and quality of the lighting are the design goals for lighting up parking environments. To accomplish the goal for uniform levels of lighting, illumination standards are written with average to minimum lighting levels.

Lighting in garages is addressed in detail in the IESNA G-1–03 Guidelines for Security Lighting publication. They recommend lighting levels of 5 to 6 footcandles in gathering areas such as stairs, elevators, and ramps. Walkways around garages should have a 5-footcandle range. Open parking lots should have a minimum of 3 footcandles, as would open parking lots in retail shopping areas, and parking lots for hotels and motels and apartment buildings. Entrances should have 10 footcandles of lighting or twice the level of lighting in the surrounding area to make them stand out and increase visibility. Perimeter fencing should have at least a half a footcandle of average horizontal illumination on both sides of the fencing to reduce hiding spots.

The height of the light fixtures makes a difference in the ability for pedestrians to see past the shadows caused by cars and other obstructions naturally occurring in parking lots. Typical light poles that are 30 to 45 feet high cast a wide swath of lighting, but create deep shadows between cars. Pedestrian-level lighting in the 12- to 14-foot range casts light that will go through the glass of cars and reflect off the cars to dramatically reduce shadows and dark spots. Ideally, an open parking lot should have a combination of high and low lighting to provide maximum coverage, and maximum visibility with minimum shadows and hiding opportunities (see Figure 24.28 and Figure 24.29).

The interior of parking garages should be painted in light colors to increase the reflectiveness of the lighting luminaries. Luminaries should use polycarbonate lenses for vandal- and break-resistance. Maintenance protocol should be established that repairs and replaces damaged lights or burned out bulbs in a timely manor, and replaces existing bulbs based on their known life expectancy (see Figure 24.30).

Guard houses and cashier stations must have adequate levels of security lighting, and considerations of lighting placement to support CCTV coverage and dimmable to allow a guard to see outside. The paths to garages must be illuminated to provide clear and unobstructed mobility paths (see Figures 24.30 through Figure 24.35). Lighting should be approximately 3 footcandles to

FIGURE 24.28   Tall parking lot lights that cast deep shadows. (Used with permission from David Wright, urban design planner and former president of Action Assessment Group, Inc (AAG Inc.).)

FIGURE 24.29   Lower lights give better visibility and less shadow. (Used with permission from David Wright, urban design planner and former president of Action Assessment Group, Inc (AAG Inc.).)

allow visibility of persons at least 30 feet away, with an average to minimum uniformity ratio not to exceed 4:1.

Does color of light matter? Sometimes. Different bulbs can achieve different types of lighting levels and their ability to accurately reflect the colors of the area being lit up. The CRI, or Color-Rendering Index, is used as the measure for the light source to accurately reproduce the true color of an object. The current lighting source of choice by most CPTED practitioners is metal halide because they have a lamp life of approximately 20,000 hours and have a CRI index of 90 out of 100. Their bright white sparkling light accurately portrays the color of cars and clothes and people. However, there have been successful applications of low-pressure sodium vapor (LSPV) lamps, which have the longest lamp life of all (around 50,000 hours), and are the most energy efficient of lamps, but the CRI index is 0, so everything looks yellow or brown. LSPV have been used extensively in Canada and some cities in the United States on highways and bridges, and airport parking lots. LPSV are also used in industrial applications for night parking. But these are not parking applications that expect an accountability of what is happening, and they have low traffic volume. Garages and parking lots have commonly used high-pressure sodium vapor lamps and mercury vapor lamps, but their lamp life and color rendition are factors in selection for parking environments where the continuous comings and goings of people and cars require accurate accounting by security personnel, CCTV, and the property users.

Where it is important to be able to recognize potential threats and identify suspects and witnesses, metal halide is the lighting of choice. The CPTED approach allows for diversity in lighting, based upon the risk and threat assessment and clear understanding on what is the experience that the designer and user is looking for. Having a parking lot of parked trailers is different than an urban parking garage with a continuous flow of traffic, such as in an entertainment district,

FIGURE 24.30 Lower-height ceilings should still be painted white to get as much reflection as possible. However, the structural elements will block the lighting from going sideways.

FIGURE 24.31 This garage is well lit and also has a well-designed stairwell using metal halide luminaries.

FIGURE 24.32 This garage uses all of the CPTED principles effectively, ground-level fencing for protection and access control, well-distributed metal halide fixtures, and a visible stairwell.

where it is desirable to provide a bulb with full-spectrum lighting. Lighting fixtures that are subject to vandalism should use polycarbonate break resistant covers. Wiring should be in conduit underground to prevent tampering. The height of the fixtures should be carefully thought out to prevent glare to users and security personnel. Lighting is an important link in a parking building's security design.

FIGURE 24.33 This garage uses high-pressure sodium vapor as its bulb choice and good ground floor protection with screening.

MIXED AND MULTIPLE USES

New trends in parking include making parking part of a mixed-use development. By having legitimate users in and around the parking facility, the number of users and casual walk-by "eyes on the street" is increased. The increased pedestrian activity acts as a way of increasing the number of

FIGURE 24.34 This garage uses fluorescent bulbs, which are typically not recommended. These bulbs are problematic in cold environments and are easily vandalized. The ground floor protection is a mesh that could easily be used as a ladder.

FIGURE 24.35   The garage may be lit up brightly now because this is a new building, but the openness to outside elements make the fluorescent luminaries a poor choice, considering the likelihood of severe weather and salt air in Miami.

potential witnesses of criminal or inappropriate activity. Many garages are adding retail storefronts such as Kinko's or Starbucks, pizza places, or car washing to have complementary safe activities that draw people to their business. Another trend is to have multiple uses for parking, as compared to mixed use (see Figure 24.36, Figure 24.37, and Figure 24.38). Multiple use might have the loading to a restaurant on the edge of a garage take place in the garage, or having car washing vendors, coffee or snack food vendors, or having reserved parking during the day for businesses, but at night a flat fee parking for the nightclub and restaurant district. Whether the uses are mixed, or multiple, the goal is to attract as much legitimate activity and increased natural surveillance (see Figure 24.39 and Figure 24.40). The experience that most people would like to have is a fast, inexpensive, and safe place to park their car and go on about their business. Whether the parking is open lot, subsurface, or a garage, the experience is desired to be the same.

FIGURE 24.36   This garage has combined mixed uses and users, to create a facility used much of the time and by many different user groups including food court, retail, and shopping.

FIGURE 24.37   The garage entrance does not have to look like a garage; this one has more of a movie theater feel.

FIGURE 24.38   This garage camouflaged the garage with landscaping and plantings and celebrated its ground-floor businesses, which are open around 18 hours a day.

FIGURE 24.39 This garage has shops on the ground floor, but because this is an office building, the garage and most of the shops are closed on the evenings and weekends.

FIGURE 24.40 The placement of activities in the parking garage can create the opportunities for natural surveillance and activity support, key CPTED elements.

SECURITY MANAGEMENT

These suggestions are aimed at the design of parking facilities. However, they should not be separate from sound security management practices. Security management principles are varied and there are many examples of texts that cover these topics.

Security management can also play an important role in the upkeep and maintenance of parking lots and garages because of their consideration for security and safety concerns. A building may be designed to operate very efficiently and look good. However, if the building is not given the necessary maintenance, it will deteriorate quickly. Maintenance is the commitment by the owner, for example, to replace light bulbs, fix damaged fencing, fix potholes and cracks, and paint over graffiti.

If quality materials are specified in the design stage, the products will have a long life. If products and materials are abused, the facility will fall into disrepair quickly. Maintenance is one of the first budget items to get cut in tough times, and has the greatest impact in keeping operating/capital costs low for the future.

SUMMARY

Typically, parking lot and garage operators respond to security challenges with technological security equipment, such as cameras, alarms, and access control devices, gates, and barriers. While the equipment does create notice to the patrons and the criminals that security is being addressed, it ultimately does not serve as an absolute deterrent. Many architectural and design decisions impact the attractiveness of the facility as a target for crime, terrorism, or vandalism. The architect can make smarter decisions on the type and placement of lighting. He can reduce the number of access points and have them attended, make exit stairwells for exit only and not street level entrance, design visible stairwells and elevators. He can provide for reduction or elimination of hiding spaces, good lines of sight throughout the parking levels, controlled access to sensitive areas such as roofs, basements, and mechanical areas, and ground floor protection and screening to reduce trespassing and unauthorized access. The architect can also limit the use of solid walls where not needed structurally and provide a well-defined perimeter protection.

The designer can reduce concealment opportunities with the landscaping suggestions made in this chapter. Ground floor doors should be securely locked from the outside and comply with building, fire, and safety codes. Pedestrian entrances should be positioned next to vehicle entrances. Elevators should be placed close to the designated main entrance. Elevator doors should reveal the entire interior when open. If more than one entrance, that all entrances should be monitored. Transparent materials should be used for elevator cab surfaces and stair enclosures. Metal halide lamps are preferred over other types of bulbs for best color rendition. Garage surfaces should be kept clean and painted with light colors. Parking areas should be patrolled by designated staff or assigned security personnel. Hours of use should be established to reflect the local businesses or services, unless it is a service industry such as hotels, restaurants, and convenience stores.

Crime prevention through environmental design provides the designer with many choices and solutions to the challenges presented by surface parking lots and garages. Parking facilities do not have to pose a security liability, but with proper forethought can be attractive and safe environments. Garages can be secure facilities if visibility is a priority, the number of entrances is limited, and the ground floor perimeter is secure. Surface parking lots are able to provide the best natural surveillance because of the lack of structural obstructions. The technology and design is available to provide good access control into parking facilities. Surveillance can be improved with good lighting and open walls to allow natural light. With good management and random patrols, the predatory activities of criminals can be reduced. Parking lots and garages do not have to be attractive targets for crime and terror.

Parking lots and garages appear on the outside as simple structures. However, a look inside reveals that car parking areas are a careful compromise between man and machine. Criminals know that parking areas have a history of being dark, abandoned, and that they can provide a wealth of criminal opportunities. Parking areas and garages can use CPTED features to increase environmental security with surveillance, access control, and territorial reinforcement. The interface of design, security patrol, and technology provides the means to achieve these CPTED goals.

Checklists for Parking Security

Conduct the security vulnerability assessment. Ask the who, why, what, when, where, how questions. Here are a few:

What are the number of cars, number of turnovers, hours of operation and the need behind the parking, or who will be the users?

Are there clear lines of sight?

Are there obstructions of walls, columns, ramps?

What is the quality of lighting? (natural and manmade, ceiling height, color of ceilings, placement)

What about the CCTV? (placement and types, recording)

Is there ground floor protection, gates and barriers?

What is the quality of vehicle entrances and pedestrian entrances?

Are there the required paths of mobility for ADA compliance?

Are there signage and wayfinding concerns?

What is the state of the elevators, stairwells placement and visibility issues?

Is there staging and stacking parking, selective closing of lightly used areas, after-hours usage?

REFERENCES

Bates, N. (1999) *Major Developments in Premises Security Liability II, 1999 Study.* Sudbury, MA: Liability Consultants.

Bates, N. (2004) *Major Developments in Premises Security Liability III Study.* Sudbury, MA: Liability Consultants.

IESNA G-1–03 Guidelines for Security Lighting (2003) New York: Illumination Engineering Society of North America.

IESNA RP-20–98 Lighting for Parking Facilities (1998) New York: Illumination Engineering Society of North America.

McCamley, P. (2002) A new risk assessment mode for CPTED: Minimizing subjectivity. *CPTED Journal,* 1(1).

NFPA 730 (2006) Parking Facilities. National Fire Protection Association. Braintree, MA. Ch 21.

Shoemaker, E. (1995) The multi-level parking garage as an asset to security. *Parking,* February.

Smith, M. S. (1989). Security and life safety. *Parking Structures: Planning, Design, Construction.* New York: Van Nostrand Reinhold. Ch 4.

Smith, M. S. (1996). Crime Prevention through Environmental Design in Parking Facilities. Research in Brief. National Institute of Justice. U.S. Department of Justice.

25 Designing Safe Gas Stations and Convenience Stores

IN THE BEGINNING

The convenience store evolved from a variety of sources early in the 20th century. Convenience stores drew on characteristics of many types of retail establishments in existence during that time. Some of these were the classic mom-and-pop general store, dairy stores, supermarkets, delicatessens and, most important, the "ice house" of pre-refrigerator days.

In 1927, on the corner of 12th and Edgefield Streets in the Oak Cliff section of Dallas, Texas, "Uncle Johnny" (Jefferson Green) of the Southland Ice Company realized that customers sometimes need to buy things other than ice. He offered his patrons milk, cheese, and bread, in addition to 25-pound blocks of ice. Unlike the grocery stores, which closed by late afternoon, his store stayed open 16 hours a day, 7 days a week, so consequentially he began stocking more and more items. This idea turned out to be very convenient for customers. Seventy-five years later, the Southland Ice Company, which owned Uncle Johnny's store, had evolved into the 7–11 store that we know today. The Uncle Johnny store in Dallas is now recognized as the site of the world's first convenience store.

The pattern of emerging "convenience" type stores grew modestly until World War II, but they were still mom-and-pop general stores. The biggest factor in these operations was convenience and fast service. By the end of World War II, the increase in automobile ownership sparked the rapid growth to the industry in the 1950s. Stores were conveniently located between the suburbs and the supermarkets, and continued to serve the commuting patrons. Customers could park in front of the stores, and could even leave children in the car and still keep an eye on them (windows rolled down). With a complete variety of items it was virtually one-stop shopping without waiting in line. When self-service fueling became popular in the 1970s, convenience stores began offering gasoline. Now the number of gasoline stations declined, while the number of convenience stores selling gasoline increased. By the early 1980s over 80% of the stores constructed were built with the ability to sell gasoline.

ATTRACTIVE FOR SHOPPERS/ATTRACTIVE FOR ROBBERS

The convenience stores of today are unique commercial-based properties that are usually open 24 hours, are largely a cash-based business, can be operated by one clerk, and are conveniently located for quick in-and-out shopping. These sophisticated corporate designs hardly resemble the mom-and-pop general stores from which they evolved. Although the nature of this business makes it very attractive for its customers, it also makes it an attractive target for robbers and criminals. In the 1970s, this late-night business became targets for robberies, basically because they were the only game in town. Typical stores were located mid-block in high-density residential neighborhoods. Security then consisted of a small floor safe, a manual cash register, and a cigar box under the counter for the change bank. At first, most of the crime was petty, and typically shoplifting. As the stores remained open during longer hours with only one clerk, criminals realized they were able to net at least $300 to $500 per robbery job. Store robbery was no longer just a police problem, whose only preventative tactics were typically stake-outs, undercover graveyard clerks, and even backroom shotgun squads. Unfortunately, the police tactics were not successful in preventing this emerging problem.

FIGURE 25.1 This station had a fatal shooting of a customer during a robbery at the pumps. The shooter parked his vehicle behind the back of the store in the blind spot of surveillance and in the shadow and darkness cast by the bright lights under the pump canopy (where the truck is parked). The clerk did not have CCTV coverage of the back of the site behind the building. The customer never saw his attacker coming. The getaway was quick and flawless. The victim's survivors sued the station and corporate for damages from premises security negligence.

In 1975, the Western Behavioral Sciences Institute (WBSI) published a study on robbery deterrence. This groundbreaking study put together the basis for today's robbery prevention program. It set out to prove the theory that robbers used a selection process before choosing targets, and therefore could be deterred by making convenience stores less attractive to them. The study found that the typical robber considered escape routes, how many people on duty, amount of money available, and amount of witnesses that might see them. As a result of these findings, an entire robbery prevention program was developed by the Southerland Corporation (7–11 Stores) and was implemented in over 6,500 stores nationwide, starting in 1976. Since then, the convenience store industry has made major strides toward the prevention of robberies (see Figure 25.1).

THE INTEGRATION OF CPTED IN CONVENIENCE STORE DESIGN

The dramatic increase in convenience store robberies has been of major concern to the convenience store industry, customers, and public officials, not only because of the financial losses incurred but also to the physical and mental harm to employees and customers. These robberies are the result of the industry's inability to protect itself and its employees and customers. Ronald Clarke (1997) defined robbery as "the taking or attempted taking of anything of value from the care, custody, or control of a person or persons by force or threat of force or violence and putting the victim in fear."

Although the average value of property stolen from convenience stores is approximately $300 to $400, which may seem minimal but is often under life-threatening circumstances. The actual loss in dollars as a result of customers who are now afraid to shop in those stores; the loss of personnel who are also afraid to work in them; and the successful litigation by individuals who were harmed by the robberies, far exceed the original monetary value of a few hundred dollars. In addition to those costs are costs incurred by local police departments. Police activities now include upgraded preventative patrols, surveillance, emergency responses, investigations, apprehension, and judicial proceedings and incarceration of offenders as part of the industry of gas stations and convenience stores.

Numerous studies have been conducted on convenience store robberies. One of the first, by Crow and Bull, conducted in 1975, has had the most impact on subsequent attempts to prevent convenience store robberies. Their recommendations for prevention included cash handling procedures that limit the amount of cash on hand, signs indicating limited cash, enhanced visibility inside and

FIGURE 25.2   A well-sited and designed facility with good lines of sight and building placement.

out, eliminating escape routes, use of security and monitoring devices, encouraging visits from local police departments, enhancing employee alertness, and keeping the stores clean. After implementation of these recommendations on a group of experimental stores they concluded that "The results support the concept that robbers select their targets," and that "physical and behavioral changes at the site can significantly reduce robberies."

Although there are many applications of CPTED design in convenience store environments, some of the greatest lessons are that good store design and merchandising are key to achieving a safe and a potentially crime-free environment. Both of those objectives can be enhanced through thorough space planning and understanding behavioral concepts of both the customers and the would-be offenders.

The convenience store industry is using new building shapes to attract customers. Gondolas, shelves, racks, and displays are being dropped to enhance visibility into and through the store. Parking is being relocated to the front of the stores, with good landscaping to screen the autos from view and to provide safe access to the patrons. Illumination is being increased inside and outside the stores at night for a safer and more welcoming atmosphere for the customers driving or walking by (see Figure 25.2). In addition, the cash registers are being strategically placed to increase the perception of surveillance, improve customer convenience, and enhance employee productivity. The revised register and service counter orientation can also help to increase the feeling of proprietary concern and cut employee theft. Although the list of CPTED applications to the convenience store may seem endless, CPTED can provide positive effects on employee and customer behavior. Therefore, productivity and profit will be enhanced, while the would-be offenders will be more visible and aware that they will be at greater risk.

MORE THAN ONE CLERK

As a result of several Florida studies (Hunter,1987; Jeffrey et al.,1987; Erikson, 2000) on convenience store robberies, and the implementation of the 1999 Florida convenience store statute, all convenience stores must employ at least two employees at all times from 11:00 p.m. through 5:00 a.m. The purpose of this strategy is that there is safety in numbers, where the addition of a clerk would increase the perception of surveillance, deny the offenders access control, and increase the area of territoriality. In addition, the presence of more individuals usually attracts more customers.

This is generally a primary concern for businesses trying to attract more customers during the off hours.

Unfortunately, multiple clerks may only create a perception of safety to employees, and these feelings can cause conflicting effects, which could be detrimental to their safety. The presence of two clerks can also increase the presence of resistance during a robbery, if the clerks feel that they can overpower the robber, or if one clerk startles the robber by emerging from a back room during the event. Whenever resistance is offered during a robbery the likelihood of violence increases by more than 80%.

A 1997 study by NIOSH (National Institute of Occupational Safety and Health), designed to estimate the risk of injury in a robbery situation for various risk factors, found that employee risk of injury was not significantly different with one employee rather than two. Because the risk of injury is no different whether there is one clerk or two, according to the Erikson study, when there are two clerks in the store and there is an injury-producing event, the risk for injury is doubled because the potential number of people who might get hurt is doubled. Erikson's study states that Florida's statewide statistics are consistent with these findings. Where robberies were reduced by 45% in convenience stores, homicides had increased by 50% in the same period, and the rate of death per robbery had doubled.

The data suggests (Wellford, 1997) that the number of clerks on duty is not a significant factor in whether convenience store robberies are likely to result in injuries to those clerks. Far more important seems to be the interaction between victim and offender. Offenders report that the behavior of the clerk or clerks is more important than the number of clerks in determining whether they use force in the robbery. Clerks appear to believe there is little they can do to prevent the occurrence of robberies and whether they are injured during the robbery. While Wellford found some factors that appear to influence offenders in the selection of stores for robbery, the data suggest a very simple selection process that is guided mostly by the offenders' perception of the existence of "place guardians" in the location. For many years the effort to prevent convenience store robberies and clerk injury has focused on the environmental characteristics of the store and the number of clerks. Whether or not the number of clerks is a factor in robbers' selection of stores, Wellford's data indicate that the presence of more than one clerk may not have the desired impact on injuries that result once a robbery occurs. Clerk training may be far more important at this point. The data suggest that the behavior of clerks may be the most significant factor in determining the extent of injury that results during these robberies. Offenders may not be attuned to these "target hardening" efforts. Rather, the existence of "place (capable) guardians," those perceived to be assigned the function of protecting the potential victim, is more important to the offenders. This is not to say that design factors are not important. It may be that the benefit from the improvement of design characteristics has reached its peak and that design characteristics may be more important in determining the monetary loss associated with the crime than they are in affecting the likelihood of injury during these crimes.

CASH HANDLING TECHNIQUES

Most studies and experts say that one of the best ways to deter robberies in a store is to keep as little cash in a register as possible; this can be done through the use of safe drops. Training the convenience store employee is essential to this strategy. Clerks are trained to drop larger bills such as twenties and fifties in safes as soon as they receive them. Implementing a policy of not accepting bills larger than $20 will reduce the amount of money in the cash register and quickly reduce the temptation of a robbery. An architectural solution is to place signs throughout the store clearly stating that clerks keep no more than $50 in the cash drawer, and bills larger than $20 will not be accepted. This method will inform the offender of lack of a worthwhile robbery at that particular store.

In addition, the Florida 1999 Convenience Store Statute states that stores have:

1. A drop safe or cash management device for restricted access to cash receipts.
2. A conspicuous notice at the entrance which states the cash register contains $50 or less.
3. A cash management policy to limit the cash on hand at all times after 11 p.m.

Proper etiquette in these techniques is important. When a customer is asked politely for a small bill, or is asked to wait until the clerk gets more change in the register, the customer will usually not complain. This also shows any would-be offender that there is little money in the cash register to steal.

Another safety strategy to cash handling techniques is to practice safe banking. The store operator's number one priority is to deposit money and avoid the accumulation of large sums in the establishment. Therefore regular drops to the bank are needed. Unfortunately, this method alone does not stop an assailant from robbing a depositor on the way to the bank. Some things to consider are to avoid establishing a pattern when banking and try to make deposits during different hours using different delivery methods, such as a different vehicle or person. Always go directly to the bank without making any stops. The banking bag should be placed in another bag, and that bag should be kept under the driver's seat, out of sight. Use of armored car pickups is another option. The use of armored car pickups makes cash inaccessible and is probably one of the best robbery deterrent techniques. Note, though, that although this method is very safe, it is also very expensive and therefore is only feasible for high-volume stores.

Erikson (*Miami Herald,* 2007, p. 5A) noted that she has gained insight about store robberies by interviewing more than 400 adult and teen robbers in the Texas prison system. Among her findings was that $50 in cash motivated far more robbers than $40 did. Erikson reaffirmed that employees should be instructed to cooperate when robbers confront them. Stores can also discourage robbers with perimeter fencing that makes it harder to escape, and stores should have drop boxes for cash, and large signs noting that the register holds $40 cash or less (*Miami Herald,* 2007, p. 5A).

STORE LAYOUT AND DESIGN

The Back Door

One of the best ways to deter a robbery is to limit access to any potential robber; therefore elimination of access to the back door of the store is essential to preventing use of this as an escape route. What purpose does a back door in a convenience store have over the primary entrance? Aside from any safety evacuation issues, there is none. All vendors and service people should enter through the front door; this enables the proprietor to see exactly who is coming in and out of the store. Not only does this discourage outside robberies but it greatly reduces theft by vendors and employees.

Considering that there is usually only one clerk working during the graveyard shift (except in Florida, where statute may require two clerks), it is essential that the employees have a complete view of everything within the store. In a situation where it is not possible to exactly see the entire store, then some sort of electronic device could be used to sound an alarm if the back of the store is breached. In addition to a sound device, a locking mechanism on the back door that can only function with a key is also important. This will prevent an offender from unlocking the back door and returning at a later time to commit his robbery. Back doors may never be eliminated, but their vulnerability can. The use of peepholes, door closers, contact door alarms, door position switches, and good lighting can reduce the risk of a clerk being surprised, ambushed, or robbed when he needs to accept deliveries or take out the trash.

CASHIER AND SALES AREA

Considerable debate has taken place on the placement of the cashiering area. Studies, such as the Tallahassee Studies (1987), found that if the cashier is located in the center of the store and more than one clerk is on duty, and there is clear visibility within the store, it is less likely to be a potential target for a robbery. On the other hand, the financial burden of having two employees during the late evening hours makes this difficult. Therefore, placement of the cashier's area is recommended to be in the front corner of the store. With this arrangement, it is not possible for anyone to be out of the cashier's field of view inside the store. The cashier will also have a better view of the parking, and customers will have a better view of the cashier.

Another method to protect the cashier and prevent crime is to create a security enclosure around the cashier. Many methods have been developed to achieve this. The most common is to surround the sales area with bullet-resistant glass or Lexan polycarbonate glazing. In addition, a pass-through window can be placed between the outside wall and the inside cashier's area in order to conduct simple transactions such as sales of gasoline, cigarettes, and beverages. This simple method has been found by most of the leading studies (Athena [1981], Wilson, Rivero, and Demmings [1990], Butterworth in 1991), to be most successful in preventing crime, according to Ronald Clark.

According to the 1999 Florida Convenience Store Statute section 812.73 (4a), if two or more employees cannot be on the premises between the hours of 11 p.m. and 5 a.m., the establishment shall install for the use of the employees at all times after 11 p.m. and before 5 a.m. a secured safety enclosure of transparent polycarbonate or other material that meets at least one of the following minimum standards:

1. Provide ASTM standard D3935 that has a thickness of at least .0375 inches and has an impact strength of at least 200 lbs, or UL standard 752 for medium-powered small arms (level one, bullet resisting materials).
2. Provide a security guard on the premises, lock the business, and conduct transactions through a pass-through drawer, or close during those hours (see Figure 25.3).

The Americans With Disabilities Act of 1990 (ADA) has developed guidelines on how sales counters should be designed. The ADA Accessibility Guidelines state that in new construction, where the selling place is under 5,000 square feet, only one checkout aisle is required to be handicap-

FIGURE 25.3   Bullet-resistant glazing offering protection to the employees.

accessible. Clear aisle width for accessible checkout aisles shall comply with Section 11–4.2.1, whereby maximum adjoining counter height shall not exceed 38 inches (965 mm) above the finish floor. The top of the lip shall not exceed 40 inches (1015 mm) above the finish floor. Signage identifying accessible checkout aisles shall comply with Section 11–4.30.7 and shall be mounted above the checkout aisle in the same location where the checkout number or type of checkout is displayed. All customer checkout isles not required by the ADA to be accessible shall have at least 32 inches of clear passage.

Bathrooms

Location of bathrooms is an important consideration during the design of the facility. Placing these facilities within plain view of the personnel will discourage hiding or staging of a robbery in the convenience store. The use of a simple lock and key will eliminate someone from entering the restrooms without the knowledge of the person on duty. With the bathroom doors out of view by the clerk, it is difficult to observe men going into ladies bathrooms. Numerous assaults and robberies occur where a man will enter into the ladies bathroom, drop and roll under the partition, assault the woman and/or steal her purse, all in the blink of an eye. Having direct line of sight for bathroom entry is not foolproof; the assailant will be aware that he can be observed and challenged. When it is not possible to place the restrooms in plain sight of the cashier, the placement of motion-detecting sensors that operate both the lights and a central security warning system can be installed. With this device, the cashier can easily see whether the restrooms are occupied or not (see Figure 25.4).

Interior/Exterior Visibility

The placement of the gondolas and sales displays is extremely important to the safety and security of both the employees working in the store and the customers shopping. Orienting the shelves in a diagonal manner gives a complete view between the fixtures to the cashier, and is essential to the reduction of shoplifting and the use of the shelves as a hiding and staging area for a potential robbery. It is also important to consider the requirements of persons with disabilities. The ADA states that the aisle space between the gondolas shall be at least 36 inches clear, with the heights to be no more than 42 inches, with some exceptions. A sales desk can be higher than 42 inches as long as there is an employee present to assist the disabled person. This is where it might conflict with convenient store design. Considering that there may be only one person, locked within a security enclosure, working during the graveyard shift. The best solution is to keep shelf heights down to a maximum of 42 inches.

FIGURE 25.4 The bathroom in this store was located so as to provide good visibility and not be hidden. Persons entering the wrong room could be seen by the clerk.

Another thing to consider is the use of auxiliary counters within the store. These counters are most commonly used for express beverage and deli food isles. The ADA states that these counters shall be no more than 36 inches tall; when the position of a soda fountain or other self-serve item exceeds 42 inches the counter needs to be lowered in order to comply.

ATMs

The location and placement of ATMs should be considered in any convenience store design.

Placing the ATM in a location that would be easy for an assailant to snatch and grab from a victim with an easy escape route should be avoided. Ideally, the machine should be placed inside the store in plain sight of the cashier. A good strategy is to limit the amount of money that is available to be dispersed to a customer per transaction. A small withdrawal from the ATM is not a lucrative target for a thief.

The installation of the ATM should also be considered. The best way to secure the ATM is to physically attach it to the ground by drilling 5/8-inch holes into the floor and bolting redheads (self-expanding bolts) through the inside of the machine. Placing the machine next to the front door should also be avoided. The placement should be in such a way that it would be difficult for someone to break through the front door, attach a chain around the machine, and quickly pull it out with the use of an automobile.

PHONES

Phones and convenience stores and gas stations are almost synonymous. In fact, as pay phones are rapidly becoming extinct, one of the few places that you can find one is at a convenience store. Pay phones are a big moneymaker for convenience stores, and thus the reluctance to make them disappear entirely. Pay phones are often placed too close to the store entrance, and attract loitering by young people or undesirables. Robbers like to stand at a pay phone as a cover for casing a store, or drug dealers may use the phone to conduct their illegal business (see Figure 25.5).

There is an active debate in police circles whether it is better to have the phones inside the store or outside. Good arguments can be waged for both possibilities. Regardless of the decision, the CPTED considerations should be that the phone is observable by the clerk inside the store, or within the line of sight through the store to the phone. The phone should be programmed as a collect call-only phone to reduce or eliminate the drug activity where buyers call in to the pay phone. The pay phone should be well illuminated and have no visual obstructions or blind spots (see Figure 25.6).

When phones are placed on the outside of the property, it is very easy for an assailant to orchestrate a robbery and cue to the arrival of police and rescue. In addition, it is common for narcotic dealers and prostitutes to conduct their business from outside telephones. Therefore, as stated above, the best location is inside the store within plain view of the cashier. This strategy is dependent on the natural surveillance by employees and customers shopping in the store.

FIGURE 25.5   This pay phone is located in a blind spot of the building's architecture and offers no surveillance or supervision.

CCTV COVERAGE

CCTV is widely used in the convenience store industry today (see Figure 25.7). The technology has changed dramatically, and the equipment has become much smaller and less obtrusive. Robbers sometimes try to sabotage the camera lens with spray paint, or will demand the tape of the recorder. Stations may have a dummy recorder with a tape in it, when the incident is really being recorded on a DVR (digital video recorder) in a remote location, or elsewhere on site. The clerk then gives the fake tape to the robber while the incident is still being recorded.

FIGURE 25.6 An exterior pay phone is located within clear view of the clerk, well lighted, and not hidden by any obstructions.

Many family-owned stores do not have a professional installation and resort to overlapping and unprofessional applications such as that shown in Figure 25.8. CCTV should be installed to observe the pump transactions, record drive-offs, record activities and transactions of the clerk, and observe hard-to-see areas around the property such as the car wash, bathrooms, tire air/water pumps, telephones, and ATMs.

SITE DESIGN

BUILDING PLACEMENT

Some of the best CPTED strategies are with the positioning of the building within the site. One of the best layouts is placement of the building in the corner of the site. By doing this, the site naturally eliminates any way of getting behind the building. When the placement of the building is in the corner, Crowe (2000) states: "A fenced line that takes the corner of the building diagonally to the property line will reduce or eliminate the robberies that come from behind the store. The fence increases the offender's perception of exposure, even though the fence does not provide a continuous enclosure of the property." Corner siting of the store also facilitates surveillance on the bathrooms,

FIGURE 25.7 Cameras and their placement can be used to put customers and criminals on notice that they are under surveillance and that their activities will not go unnoticed.

FIGURE 25.8   How many cameras do you really need to get the job done?

if located on the exterior of the property. Car washes are problematic as well. Figure 25.9 shows the car wash behind the store and vulnerable to robbery and undesired activity. With a corner siting of the store, the car wash can be placed on a side of the property, where the traffic patterns are directly observable by the clerk and other customers (see Figure 25.10).

Traffic patterns for vehicles and pedestrians are also important for safety and security considerations. Careful consideration should be given to how cars enter and leave the site (see Figure 25.11). On small sites, many gas stations allow entrance to the pumps from both directions, and this can cause chaos, with cars competing for pump access and pedestrians crossing car paths. Figure 25.12 demonstrates the conflicting circulation patterns of such station. One-way in and out is preferred and permits more controlled and orderly movement. Stores also discourage robbers by having perimeter fencing, as shown in Figure 25.13, because the fencing makes the path of escape more difficult.

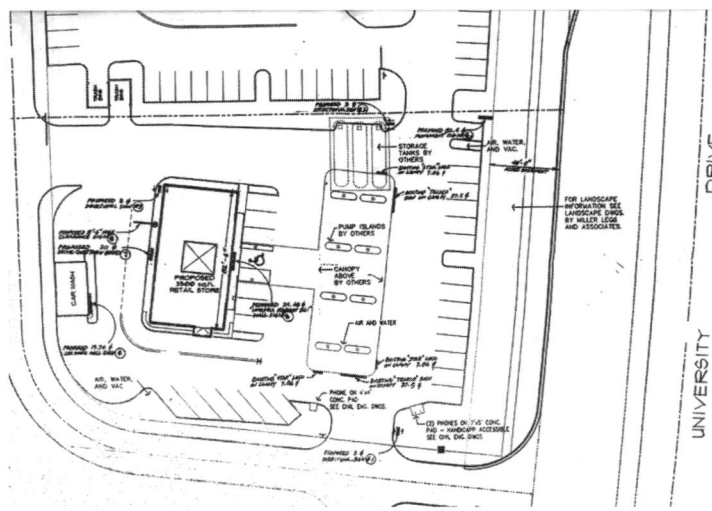

FIGURE 25.9   This site plan has the gas station/convenience store sitting in the middle of the site, and as a result activities can occur on the sides and in the back that are out of view of the clerks, who are watching the pumps in front.

FIGURE 25.10 This car wash is using punchouts of the side wall to allow for visibility into and out of the building, promoting better natural surveillance.

FIGURE 25.11 This gas station and store uses many CPTED design features successfully. The store is located in the corner of the site, the traffic flow is one way in and out. There is site fencing and borders to direct pedestrian traffic on the property. Bathrooms and carwash are located to the sides, in direct line of sight of the clerk.

FIGURE 25.12 This gas station has conflicting travel paths for cars going to and from the pumps, and during busy times there are chaos and fights.

FIGURE 25.13 Good property definition, with fencing behind the gas station and site lighting remove any hiding or loitering places.

EXTERIOR VISIBILITY AND LIGHTING

According to the NACS (National Association of Convenience Stores), well-lit places scare off would-be robbers. They take the position that the would-be robbers don't want to be seen, and would rather operate in shadows and in darkness. Taking an active role in designing the site for appropriate lighting will make the site unattractive for robbers, while making it more attractive for customers. Proper lighting makes customers feel safe, and, like moths, there is human tendency to gravitate toward well-lit areas. According to studies performed by Crow and Bull (1975) for the Southerland Corp. (7–11 Stores), and Swanson (Gainesville studies), enhancing exterior visibility within parking lots by removing obstacles and increasing available lighting will reduce the chances that the site will be chosen for a robbery.

The main strategy behind exterior lighting is to make the site visibly more unattractive to the would-be robber. The 1999 Florida Convenience Store Statute states that a lighted parking lot will be illuminated at an intensity of at least 2 footcandles per square foot and 18 inches above the surface. Some strategies outlined in the General CPTED Guidelines by the Development Services Department of the Gainesville City Code are as follows:

1. Trees and shrubs should not interfere with the distribution of lighting required by CPTED.
2. Transitional lighting should be incorporated in exterior areas going to and from the building or uses within the site.
3. All exterior lighting should be directed downward and away from adjoining property, with luminaries shielded to prevent unnecessary glare.
4. All exterior fixtures should be illuminated from dusk to dawn unless otherwise designated.

Any exterior lighting luminaries designed for security applications should be protected with weather- and vandal-resistant coverings, and have a managed light source that is directed down to minimize glare and intrusiveness.

FIGURE 25.14 Windows allow visibility and surveillance of both sides and front of station and site.

FIGURE 25.15 This convenience store has totally blocked visibility by overuse of window posters.

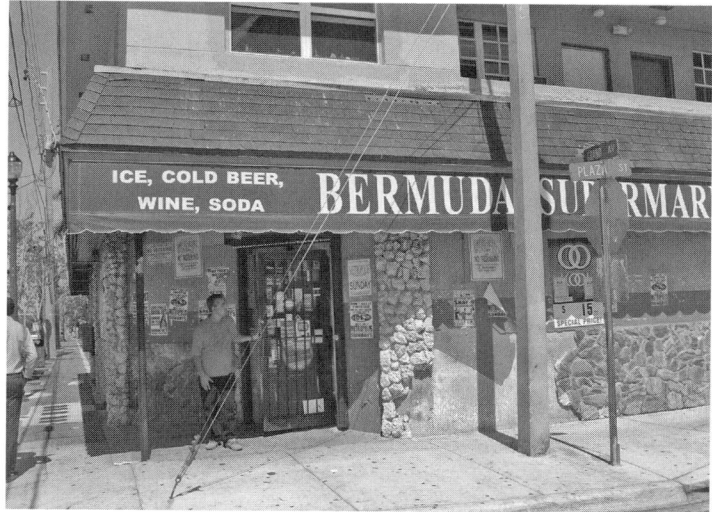

FIGURE 25.16 Storefront is blocked by signs and security bars.

Exterior Visibility

One strategy to consider to increase outside visibility is to position the fuel pump islands directly in front of the store. By taking advantage of this arrangement, the employees inside will be able to see the majority of the site, and the customers fueling will be able to see inside the store. Hence the natural surveillance created by this association is increased (see Figure 25.14).

Another factor to consider for this strategy to work correctly is the exterior windows. They should be large and free of signs and advertisement; this keeps the visibility clear of obstruction for people passing by, and most important, clear for routine police surveillance. According to the 1999 Florida Convenience Store Statute Section 812.73 (2): "A convenience store business shall not have window tinting that reduces exterior and interior view in a normal line of sight" (see Figure 25.15 and Figure 25.16).

SUMMARY

Crime at convenience stores and gas stations is no accident. Sites are chosen based on a number of design and operational characteristics. Convenience stores are not high on the architectural pecking order, but they are part of our American culture and cannot be ignored. The convenience store serves a valuable and needed function in our local and national commerce, and for the delivery of services needed to support our dependence on the automobile. As a result, there is a duty to design and manage these types of facilities in a safe and secure manor. Site placement is critical for utilizing the small number of staff employed to be effective as capable guardians of their facilities. For convenience store and gas station workers, one key to reducing robbery and workplace violence is better lighting and visibility. With good sightlines and visibility, the standard functions of the convenience stores, pumping gas, shopping, buying lottery tickets, freshening up, and buying food and drink, can be done quickly and safely.

REFERENCES

1999 Florida Convenience Store Statute Section 812.73 (4a).

Amandus, H. E. et al. (1997) Employee injury in convenience store robberies. *Journal of Occupational and Environmental Medicine* 39:5 May.

Amandus, H. E., Zahm, D., Friedmann, R., Ruback, R. B., Block, C., Weiss, J., Rogan, D., Holmes, W., Bynum, T., Hoffman, D., McManus, R., Malcan, R., Wellford, C., & Kessler, D. (1996) The estimated number of convenience store robberies and robbery-related injuries in selected eastern metropolitan areas. *Journal of Occupational and Environmental Medicine* 38(7), 714–720.

Butterworth, R. A. (1991) Study of Safety and Security Requirements for At-Risk Business. Tallahassee, FL: Florida Department of Legal Affairs.

Calder, J. D. & Bauer, J. R. (1992) Convenience store robberies: Security measures and store robbery incidents. *Journal of Criminal Justice*, 20, 553–566.

Chambers, C. P. P. (1988) Gainesville Convenience Store Ordinance: A Review and Analysis. Gainesville, FL: Assets Protection Systems Associates, Inc.

Clifton, W. J. and Callahan, P. T. (1987) Convenience Store Robberies: An Intervention Strategy by the City of Gainesville. Florida. Gainesville, FL: Gainesville Police Department.

Crow, W. J. and Bull, J. L. (1975) *Robbery Deterrence: An Applied Behavioral Science Demonstration-Final Report*. La Jolla, CA: Western Behavioral Sciences Institute.

Crow, W. J. and Erickson, R. J. (1984) *Cameras and Silent Alarms: A Study of Their Effectiveness as a Robbery Deterrent*. Winslow, WY: Athena Research Corporation.

Crowe, T. D. (2000) *Crime Prevention Through Environmental Design*, 2nd ed., National Crime Prevention Institute. Boston, MA: Butterworth-Heinemann pp. 161–163.

Clarke, R. V. (1997) *Situational Crime Prevention: Successful Case Studies*, Albany, NY: Harrow and Heston, p. 192.

Erikson, R. J. (1998) Convenience Store Security at the Millennium, National Association of Convenience Stores, Alexandria, VA. February.

Erikson, R. J. (1990) Convenience Store Homicide and Rape, National Association of Convenience Stores, Alexandria, VA. March.

D'Alessio, S. and Stolzenberg, L. (1990) A crime of convenience: The environment and convenience store robbery. *Environment and Behavior* 22(2), 255–271.

Duffala, D. C. (1976) Convenience stores, armed robbery and physical environmental features. *American Behavioral Scientist* 20, 227–246.

Hendricks, S. et al. (1999) A matched case-control study of convenience store robbery risk factors. *Journal of Occupational and Environmental Medicine* 41:11.

Hunter, R. (1987) The Relationship of Selected Environmental Characteristics to the Incidence of Convenience Store Robbery within the State of Florida, unpublished paper presented at the 39th Annual Meeting of the American Society of Criminology.

Hunter, R. and Ray, J. C. (1991) Environmental crime prevention: An analysis of convenience store robberies. *Security Journal*, 2(April), 78–83.

Hunter, R. D. and Jeffery, C. R. (1992) Preventing convenience store robbery through environmental design. In R. V. Clark (Ed.), *Situational Crime Prevention-Successful Case Studies*. New York: Harrow and Heston.

Jeffrey, C. R., Gibson, M., Hunter, R., Tayloe, D., Poulos, M., and Hendrix, G. (1987) Spatial Computer Analysis of Commercial Crime Sites in Atlanta and Tallahassee, unpublished paper presented at the 39th Annual Meeting of the American Society of Criminology. Montreal.

Florida Building Code (2004) Chapter 11 Handicap Accessibility Guidelines, Section 11–7.3.

Figlio, R. (1990) An Assessment of Robbery Deterrence Measures at Convenience Stores: Multiple Clerk Staffing, Central Station-Based Interactive Television and Bullet Resistant Barriers, National Association of Convenience Stores, Alexandria, VA. March.

The Miami Herald (2007) The workplace getting less deadly. January 2, 5A.

McGoey, C. E. Convenience Store Security: C-Store Robbery Prevention History, www.crimedoctor.com/convenience1.htm.

NACS, A Short History of the Convenience Store industry, 2005. www.nacsonline.com/NACS/Resource/IndustryResearch/cstore_history.htm.

NACS, National Association of Convenience Stores. (2005) Robbery Awareness/Deterrence, www.nacsonline.com/NACS/resource/StoreOperations/robbery_awareness_072700.htm.

Reiss, A. J. and Roth, J. A. (1993) *Understanding and Preventing Violence*. Washington, DC: National Academy Press.

Schreiber, B. (1991) National Survey of Convenience Store Crime and Security. St. Cloud University, Minnesota, National Association of Convenience Stores, Alexandria, VA. February, 1992.

Sherman, L. W. et al., (February, 1997) Preventing Crime: What Works, What Doesn't, What's Promising? University of Maryland. U. S. Department of Justice, Office of Justice Programs. NCJ 165366.

Swanson, R. (1986) Convenience store robbery analysis: A research study of robbers, victims, and environment. Gainesville, FL. In W. J. Clifton (Ed.), *Convenience Robberies: An Intervention Strategy by the Gainesville Police Department*. Gainesville, FL: Gainesville Police Department.

Wellford, C., MacDonald, J., and Weiss, J. (1997) Multistate study of convenience store robberies. Justice Research and Statistics Association. Washington, DC, October.

Wilson, D. J., Rivero, R., and Demings, J. (1990) Convenience Store Robbery Analysis, unpublished report to the Gainesville Police Department.

Wilson, J. V. (1990) Gainesville convenience store ordinance: Findings of fact. Conclusions and recommendations. Unpublished report on file at the Crime Control Research Corporation: Washington, DC.

26 Design Considerations for Office Buildings

The renovation, addition, or new construction of office buildings may require the security professional and owner to collaborate with the design professional in new and challenging ways. The security professional may be an employee of the business responsible for many sectors of security and safety within that business. The architect or design professional will need many aspects of information from the owner/client and security professional to develop the architectural program (see Figure 26.1). The person who can provide critical information to the architect on security is typically the security director. If no security director exists, then a trained security professional should be hired to provide assistance.

Even though most of the private sector corporate world provides only the minimal amount of security required for common area spaces in office buildings (parking and garage controls, lobby guard, intermittent access control, spotty CCTV), it has traditionally been the responsibility of the tenants to protect their own assets. What many developers fail to understand is what market value

FIGURE 26.1 Skyline of Chicago and the downtown core of office buildings.

having great security can bring, even though there are costs associated with these extra features. The single largest tenant in the United States is the federal government. The federal government currently operates 3.2 billion square feet a year in different structures, with approximately 610 million square feet of office space. The U.S. Government leases approximately 380 million square feet, of which 195 million square feet is office space. What does this mean to the developer and architect? All federal-owned and leased space must comply with the GSA Security Standards as discussed in earlier chapters. The federal government adopted the ISC Security Standards in final form in October 2005, and it applies to all federally owned or leased properties. All new construction and leases must now comply with the security standards, and leases cannot be renewed unless the standards are met. Whether the space being rented is for a post office, Social Security office, or ATF, INS, or DHS, the space and adjoining common area spaces must be surveyed for security and have the appropriate corresponding security features for the assessed risk level. Leased spaces might be required to have building setbacks for blast protection, window protection, magnetometers and secured lobbies, security guards, identification stations, parking control, mail screening, dedicated HVAC systems, CCTV, and access control capabilities. Therefore if there is any intention to lease or rent space to a government agency in the building, the marketability of that space will hinge on having basic security features as part of the structure or added on.

In order to provide the information in a format that the architect can work with effectively, the security professional should identify the corporate assets vital to protect. The three most common assets to businesses are:

People
Information
Property

ASSET: PEOPLE

The resource of people is the first and most valuable asset to be protected and elaborated on for developing security criteria for the architect. With any of the three assets, the critical questions in a needs assessment are:

Who are the users? (Visitors, staff, service crew, sales?)
What can the users do in the building? (Tasks, recreation, work?)
Why are the particular users there? (Official business, guests?)
When do the users get there and leave? (Time, shift, patterns?)
Where can users go in the building? (Horizontal, vertical?)
How can the users get there? (Access methods, circulation?)

The security professional will need to be clear on the implications of each of the answers to these questions (Table 26.1). It is recommended that a task summary be prepared to give to the architect. An example of the end product might be:

TABLE 26.1
Asset to be Protected: PEOPLE

Who	Why	What	When	Where	How
Vice President	Company business	Administration manage	8 am–6 pm M-F	All areas total access	Staff elevator
Janitor	Clean offices	Clean/garbage vacuum	1 am–4 am M-F Pick-up	Lobby Floors	Guard lets in, has keys to special service offices

It might be helpful to develop a scenario for asking the six key questions in the same fashion to a vice president of a company through to the janitorial cleaning service. The security professional will then determine the security implications and design implications.

Using the example of the janitor service, the **SECURITY IMPLICATIONS** might be:

Control of after-hour access
Verification of cleaning employee status
Security manpower to sign in and supervise entry and exit
Key control

These security concerns could then translate into **DESIGN IMPLICATIONS** such as:

A sign-in desk for the service trades
Design of access control system to allow staff to control entry and log-in movement
Placement of garbage dumpsters
Location of service elevator
Location of service doors
Alarm systems for offices and control room ties in and deactivation.

These examples are just a small sample of the kinds of issues and concerns that need to be addressed by the architect based on information that the security professional has developed.

Without professional assistance or specially designed CPTED risk assessment software, the security professional must learn to ask the right questions to develop security criteria. At a minimum, the architectural program or problem-seeking stage should incorporate the information developed from answering the above six questions. Later, the information will be passed on to the problem solution stage of architecture: the schematic drawings, design development drawings, and construction documents.

ASSET: INFORMATION

In protecting the asset of information, the critical questions that can be asked as part of the need assessment are:

- Who has access to the information (staff, management, and mailroom)?
- What is the information being protected (data, trade secrets, personnel records, blueprints, computer programs)?
- Why is the information worth protecting (What is the physical, operational, and dollar cost you are willing to incur)?
- When is the information accessible or vulnerable?
- Where is the information available or vulnerable?
- How can the information legitimately and illegitimately be acquired or compromised?

When the security professional is clear on the answers to these questions, a description of the threats and proposed solutions is presented to the architect. An example of what a security professional might present the architect is shown here (see Figure 26.2).

- **WHO**: The president of the company and top management has unrestricted access to all records. Personnel record supervisor only has access to job reviews and drug tests results. Mail clerks screen mail and make copies of memos. Operation managers are responsible for control of shipping and receiving. Stock persons have access to storerooms, computer disks, and archives.

FIGURE 26.2   The Sears Tower has a comprehensive security system in effect to deter terrorism and criminal acts.

- **WHAT:** Assets of information might include personnel files, sensitive memos, trade secrets, computer software, financial records, quarterly statements, formulas, documents, marketing plans, client information, and so on.
- **WHY:** Personnel and financial records must be protected from outside intrusion and used for promotion or discharge. Computer software, records, data, contains all of the programs and information that is proprietary, classified, or sensitive. Data are protected from competitor espionage, for audits, and decision making. Owner must be prepared to provide physical protection of records, fire protection, backup protection, with strict access and accountability.
- **WHEN:** Personnel records are available for review upon request Monday through Friday, 8 a.m. to 5 p.m. Storage rooms are available during working hours. Shipping and receiving 7 a.m.–noon, Monday through Friday. Mail and copying normal working hours. Computer rooms operating 24 hours a day. Service delivery Saturdays and Mondays. Most vulnerable times are during shifts, after hours from threat of burglary, and cleaning crews at night.
- **WHERE:** Information is stored typically on most management personnel desks within their computers. Data storage on computer disks located within computer room. Classified and sensitive archival documents stored in a vault. Vulnerable areas are computer room, loading docks, storage rooms, vaults, file cabinets, top management offices, personal computers, and desktops.
- **HOW:** Office information is most vulnerable to compromise by internal threats by employees stealing memos, computer info, through their unobserved availability and absence of

screening and access control. Outside threats are from burglars breaking in for equipment, and collusion from staff with service people and night cleaning staff.

Once the security professional has discussed the threats and vulnerabilities with the owner/client, then counterstrategies can be developed. Architectural, technological, and organizational (security manpower) responses can now be examined for practicality and cost.

Architectural design changes that could reflect the security professional's concern for protection of information could be as follows:

- Limit the number of exterior penetration to a minimum and easily observable. Doors should be controlled and monitored for accountability. Architecturally define location of main entrance for visitors and staff. Design a service entrance that is under supervision and secure. Storage rooms can be monitored and placed where a supervisor can oversee movement.
- Design a reception desk or counter that screens visitors, vendors, and outsiders. The counter or reception desk should be designed to view all entry doors, and elevators if provided (see Figure 26.3). The reception area establishes the layering of public versus private entry into the building.
- Provide clear demarcation of VIP areas with layering of access to these zones.
- Design the computer room for strict access control, protected utility lines, high security glazing for easy supervision and visibility, centered building location.

FIGURE 26.3 This office building has a security vestibule or sallyport that permits screening yet allows good surveillance and blends into the architecture.

- Computers can be secured and protected in workstations with anchor pads.
- The access and egress of employees must be controlled. Controlled and supervised employee egress will permit screening of packages, briefcases, and purses. Staff locker area should be well lighted and located in an area supervised to prevent theft and pilferage.
- Elevators should be designed to open up to the supervised core area. Special floors or VIP offices may require special elevator access control programming or dedicated elevators.
- Service delivery areas should have a separate or clear roadway system that does not conflict with employee or visitor travel. The loading dock should be designed with ground loops and intercom to notify security staff when a truck is in the loading area during hours when personnel are not directly supervising it.
- The mailroom should be located within a clear and unobstructed line of travel from loading or mail delivery area. The mailroom should be a secure room with monitoring of the door to provide controlled access and accountability. If security of interoffice mail is critical, pneumatic tubes can be used for delivery of letters without human intervention.
- Placement of the vault, fire safes, and record files will depend on the frequency of use. The placement and location of these functions can be as layered or open as defined by the client. Supermarkets place the vault in the front of the store for visibility, and other stores place the vault in a hidden undisclosed area.

ASSET: PROPERTY

To examine the asset of property, the same process of asking the six questions, determining the security criteria, the architectural criteria, and scenario development would apply. No asset is too small to take through this process. Those companies that go the extra yard in asset identification and scenario development will realize more profits and gain **MARKET ADVANTAGE**. Market advantage of designing out shoplifting, pilferage, espionage, assaults, terrorism, and employee theft will result in a better bottom line for the company, lower prices to the consumer, and greater profits for the owner/client.

Crime Prevention Through Environmental Design (CPTED) uses a number of architectural, technological, and operational innovations to enhance security. The possibilities are limitless, only subject to your creativity.

The greatest temptation is to jump to a shopping list of technology and design solutions. Competent CPTED experts will always emphasize that, in practice, the answers are not as important as the questions. Each building has a unique function, operation, and combination of materials and methods of construction. If the security professional uses the threat/asset vulnerability analysis to develop a needs assessment for the architect, a much more robust and reliable design will emerge. The architect can best respond to the security professional when they participate fully, together, in the early stages.

To achieve environmental security, the designers and users must have a balanced development, adequate support systems, predominant land use, and territoriality. This is true in spite of the reality that, on any individual building, the owners may not have control over: the neighborhood streets, surrounding activities such as stadiums, bars, parks, and waste dumps, control over land use conflicts, competition for use of roads, public services, or police protection. That is why risk assessment and a diagnosis are necessary for good CPTED design in office buildings.

There is seldom just one element out of scale, so a building can have many environmental conflicts, which provide opportunities for would-be offenders. Each conflict can precipitate a pattern of crime. Therefore, CPTED principles are the key to success that planners, designers, and architects can use to prevent or reduce crime opportunities.

ADDITIONAL SECURITY TIPS FOR DESIGNING OFFICES AND OFFICE BUILDINGS

Because offices and office buildings are vulnerable to such a large range of crimes, there is a number of additional tips given in this chapter for safe and secure design. The many vulnerabilities include walk-in thefts, burglary, theft by deception and fraud, vandalism, loss of information, and employee theft. With these kinds of risks the owner and security director should identify the major areas to be considered for security design that include site security, building security, and internal security needs. These include the following.

- Location of the site: What are the zoning and building code limitations and restrictions for the site and surrounding area? Existing and proposed landscaping should be examined for security application.
- External areas need to be considered for security design. Car parks, garages, and parking lots need to be carefully designed. Entrances and exits, paths, and roads need to be carefully thought out for circulation conflicts and security issues. Fences, gates, and site lighting should be identified and prioritized. CCTV should be thought out once the circulation patterns are planned. Decisions must be made for the delivery areas and waste disposal services. Scenario development, or role-playing, should be made for all service delivery situations to the building.
- Primary and secondary access points must be considered. Scenarios must be developed as to how the owner or client wants the employees, visitors, and service personnel to gain entry. Fire exits and life safety code requirements need to be considered in the early phases, so as not to undermine the security features. Loading bays should be identified and designed for secure shipping and receiving. Security needs for basement areas, mechanical plant rooms need to be considered. Careful planning should go into the planning of external stairways, roof access, doors, and windows.
- Internal points of security to be considered are the lobby entrances, secondary entrances, reception area, cash office areas, computer areas, electrical/telephone service areas, executive areas, canteens, location of staff restrooms, security central control, and point protection of vault rooms or special equipment (see Figure 26.4).

FIGURE 26.4 A typical open office plan has special security considerations to protect employee computers, equipment, data, and company property.

- The lobby entrance is the point where most visitors and public enter a building. The architect uses a lobby entrance of a building to create a landmark point for establishing that you have arrived and that this is the entry point. Usually richer, higher-grade materials are used in the lobby to create an image and ambiance of success, stability, and power.
- A checkpoint, usually known as the reception desk, complements this atmosphere. Many people who gain entry to the building pass through this reception desk. CEOs to janitorial staff all pass through this checkpoint.
- To create a secure working environment, the lobby entrance and reception desk create the first layer in the building perimeter security system. The receptionist serves an important function of identifying everyone who enters the building or office, and establishing a legitimate purpose for being there. Having a person checking identity and purpose of visitors is often preferred to having an automatic credential reading system. Many visitors do not have automated credentials and must be screened personally.
- The reception desk must be positioned with good surveillance of entranceways and persons entering the building or office. The desk can be located in a way to prevent access to all areas into an office or restricted areas. The reception desk should be positioned to be able to intercept persons before reaching elevators or stairs.
- The design of most reception desks is semicircular or oval to give maximum working surface and visual flexibility. Because the receptionist will usually be seated, it is common for the seating platform to be raised twelve to eighteen inches to permit unobstructed visibility by the receptionist. Human factor considerations are important in the design of counters. Most reception counters are forty-two to forty-eight inches high to allow placing of your elbow on the desktop. The normal height of a desk is thirty to thirty-two inches from the floor. However, at this height the receptionist is looked down on rather than at an equal height.
- Psychologically, a receptionist is more likely to successfully challenge a visitor if eye contact is parallel and the receptionist does not have to raise her voice. Therefore, visitors should be funneled to the desk and not access the restricted areas without having to pass close to the desk. It is common for a locked door or gate entry system to control passage of visitors.
- Reception desks may serve other distracting functions in addition to the security function of screening people. Receptionists also may be answering phones, controlling door entry, screening mail, and serving as a drop-off counter for packages and deliveries. Protection of company assets depends on the receptionist being able to conduct her screening function in as unimpeded a manner as possible.
- If a reception desk contains CCTV equipment, switchers, VCRs, and other electronic equipment, the counter must be designed to allow concealment of equipment. It must also allow tilting of monitors for proper viewing angles, and allow ventilation for equipment. Conduit considerations must be planned for in the design of the building to avoid expensive after-the-fact renovations.
- Emergency assistance call buttons are a feature often overlooked at reception desks. With this duress device, the receptionist can summon help if a visitor or employee becomes a problem. Backup from security is important to reduce the opportunity of a physical attack on the receptionist. The design of the counter can slow an attack. Bank teller counters are designed wide to prevent the quick reaching over and grabbing of money or papers. The desk is designed high to prevent easy jumping over.
- Design of receptionist desks may serve high-rise, low-rise buildings, single- or multitenant operations. The receptionist serves as the point person for a layered security system. The lobby and reception point can be designed for aesthetics and restrictive movement. As always, the first step is the threat analysis to determine what goals, directives, and threats need to be considered. Input from the management, employees, and security consultant

FIGURE 26.5 Receptionist or security position greets people in the lobby and screens visitors and employees.

need to be expressed to the architect. Through this clear communication the function of access control can be natural, flowing, and unobtrusive (see Figure 26.5).

- Access control and surveillance systems should be designed as part of the building design and architectural programming phase, not after the fact. Stairs, elevators, and corridors should be examined for security requirements. Key systems should be carefully addressed to accommodate growth, change, and flexibility.
- Pedestrian access should be direct from the road to the front of the building.
- Buildings should be oriented to allow views into the site.
- Doors and windows may need extra security considerations, especially on the ground floor.
- Limit the entrances into the building to as few as possible. There may be additional exit only doors, but they should not allow ground level entrance.
- Finally, one of the most important design features to be considered for internal security is planning for conduits. If dedicated security conduit is planned for in the beginning, it will be very little inconvenience and expense. Conduit should be run horizontally and vertically in mechanical chases and sized to accommodate future growth and servicing of wires. Lines may need to be shielded depending on the communication systems being used.

In providing for the security of office buildings against crime, the security professional can identify the risks and plan for the security and welfare of the people, information, and property. When a building has just one tenant, the security features become infinitely simpler, because employees can be directed on specific security procedures and have a uniform level of compliance. Lobby and parking screening are straightforward credential checks for a single tenant building. The number of visitors and outsiders in a single tenant building is usually small and controllable. However, many office buildings have multiple tenants with diversified client needs, assets, and risks. Multitenant buildings need to be divided into two major groups of users. The first are the users who are engaging in common area spaces, businesses and equipment in the base of the building, and secondly, the tenant spaces are the other major area. Persons going into the tenant spaces should be screened and access controlled before they can get into the elevators or stairwells. Tenants going to their office spaces should be issued credentials so that their entry to the lobby or parking areas is fast and

FIGURE 26.6   Example of optical turnstile.

minimally inconvenient. Visitors will need to be signed in for temporary credentials, and parking designated to certain areas with certain charges.

The control of grade entrances and below grade entrances such as loading docks represents the primary line of defense in most office buildings (Ahrens, 2006). Most office buildings are directly adjacent to public streets and do not have any site perimeter to defend other than the skin of the building's architecture. Therefore, security at the main entrances, and loading docks are the primary security control points for this building type. Security features should unobtrusively allow access to legitimate users, prevent unauthorized access, and segregate visitor traffic to a concierge or security desk to validate a visitor's need to access the building (Ahrens, 2006).

A mechanical CPTED solution for accomplishing the diverse security goals in a multi-tenant office building is using turnstiles in the lobby. An optical turnstile is a good device to use in large open atriums to accommodate a large number of persons entering and exiting a common space. Optical turnstiles provide a quick and convenient way for persons with proper credentials to pass through unobstructed. These turnstiles can be equipped with clear barriers and have photoelectric sensors to detect unauthorized access (see Figure 26.6, Figure 26.7, Figure 26.8, and Figure 26.9).

Unfortunately, screening of visitors for verification is still slow and painful. There is no easy way to ask people to sign in, show an ID, and be issued a temporary time limited pass. These tasks must be conducted using trained security guards, and are expensive and labor intensive. Complaining is pretending you have a choice! There aren't many choices to allow non-authorized persons into the building. A good example of how annoying and inconvenient screening of visitors is going through airport security. The TSA (Taking Stuff Away) officers are so focused on taking scissors

FIGURE 26.7   Optical turnstile.

FIGURE 26.8   This office building uses optical turnstiles to allow people to exit, and there is also a mechanical gate on the far side for persons with disabilities.

FIGURE 26.9 Full body height optical turnstiles with clear panels.

and cuticle cutters and bottles of shampoo away, rather than focusing on the likely profiles of who the offenders are likely to be, the experience of traveling is joyless and obtrusive and no safer. A well-designed security counter that is ADA compliant and has good cueing areas is the best one can hope for.

Unlike the user-friendly screening of main entry lobbies, back-of-the-house or loading docks and service areas require a more stringent level of physical security. High occupancy commercial or institutional grade doors and hardware are required because of the physical demands and abuse on the fixtures, furnishings, and finishes (see Figure 26.10).

Vertical movement is one of the more difficult things to control in office buildings. Stairwells can be locked, but elevators by design carry multiple people to different floors. It is preferable for persons to be screened before they get to the elevators, but if this is not possible, it becomes the responsibility of the capable guardian, the receptionist, to screen people in individual tenant offices. One way of improving security in both the base building and the tenant spaces is to subcompartmentalize elevator and floor access (Ahren, 2006). A visitor may be required to use an access credential to enter a building, and have to use that credential for elevator access to a specific floor that was cleared upon entry to the building at the security desk. Stairwells are controlled because they are typically fire exit only corridors and not used for floor-to-floor traffic. Once in the stairwell, a user would have to walk all the way down to the ground level and exit the building. Door monitoring, intercoms, and exit alarm devices can be used to deter unwanted traffic in the stairwells (see Figure 26.11).

FIGURE 26.10   Lobby receptionist separates persons entering and leaving.

Security vestibules can be used to access the building or the bank of elevators in an office building. The security vestibules are easy and quick if you are a legitimate user, but require a backup plan on how to screen visitors who do not have credentials (see Figure 26.12, Figure 26.13, and Figure 26.14).

FIGURE 26.11   Signage indicating floor-to-floor traffic.

LOCATION OF THE SECURITY OFFICE AND SECURITY EQUIPMENT

In most mid- and high-rise office buildings, there is a space requirement that needs to be planned for placement of the security systems technology and conduits, and the security office and/or control room. Architects and space planners need to program the space and systems need in the early stages of the design process, so that all of the electronics are not stuffed into a closet later. Without adequate space, the effectiveness of the security system and staff may be compromised, and it will absolutely be more expensive to retrofit once the building is completed and operational. Typically a space of 1000 to 1500 square feet will be required for an area that will support the access control, CCTV, and monitoring equipment. The security control room will have more functions than strictly access control and CCTV, but also will house the head end system, intercoms, fire safety systems, elevator control monitoring, key boards, forms, records, and report writing areas. The amount of the space depends on the type and complexity of equipment and operations.

FIGURE 26.12 Security vestibule for lobby entrance.

NOT IN THE BASEMENT, PLEASE!

It is a common joke in the security industry that security directors' offices, and often the control rooms are out of sight and out of mind, or, more typically, in the basement or dungeon (see Figure 26.16). Although security and crime prevention offices are often located in remote and windowless locations, it is not necessarily the best placement. In many industries, the risk manager's

FIGURE 26.13 Security vestibule for elevator lobby.

FIGURE 26.14 Security vestibule for access to an elevator lobby.

office is typically on the same floor or close to a vice president's, CEO's, or president's office. Yet security and crime prevention offices are typically in the most remote location. Security operations have a big financial and operational impact on many business and property management of buildings. Placing the security operations in areas of high traffic can advertise that the building takes it protection of assets seriously (see Figure 26.15 and Figure 26.17).

Like water mains and fire safety equipment, security systems and their conduits should be stacked in a riser so that the security spaces are located on the same space on every floor. This is beneficial in maintenance and also can keep the cost of conduit to a minimum (Aherns, 2006).

The riser closet does not need to be large; typically, it is 24 square feet, but it should have dedicated power and communications, and it should be large enough conduits to allow for future expansion, or equipment change outs as the technology changes. Security systems may share closets with communication closets, but it is not preferred because of the different missions and the lack of control of persons working on the telephone lines on a weekly basis for new or old tenants.

The security department for a large building might have the need for a remote badging area or station. When staff or employees get badged for the building, where it is desired for people to do this. Providing sufficient space to support the badging equipment is often an afterthought, and often the equipment gets piled onto someone's desk. Understanding the role of access control is critical to the design, operation, and function of the building. The badging station on the main floor is busy issuing temporary badges for visitors and vendors. Making a conscious choice of where the building occupants get badged will assist in good circulation flow.

The integration of security features into the architecture requires consideration of compliance with the Americans With Disabilities Act of 1990. Turnstiles and security vestibules need to be wide enough to accept someone in a wheelchair. Access control readers need to be mounted 42 inches above the finished floor height on the same side as the door handle, and mounted for a front and side approach by someone in a wheelchair. Fire pull stations, light switches, thermostats,

FIGURE 26.15 The risk manager's office is right down the hall from the manager's office.

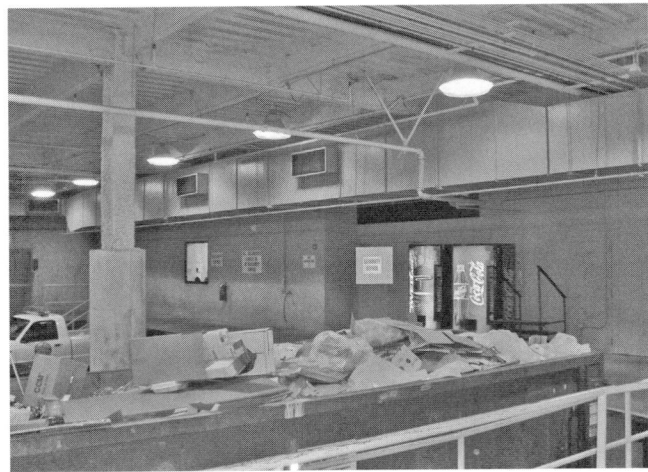

FIGURE 26.16 The security office of this urban downtown high-rise office building is in the sub-basement loading dock area next to the trash bins.

FIGURE 26.17 This security office is located in the lobby in a prominent location and has observation of the staff entrance.

biometric readers, and alarm panel stations must be mounted in compliance with the ADA. Not only will building occupants have to be accommodated, it is also feasible that staff may have disabilities requiring reasonable accommodations.

SUMMARY

The top ten things to remember for good office security are, (1) Secure the loading and receiving dock, garbage, and service delivery areas. The back of the house is usually the most vulnerable and easiest to compromise. (2) Protect any ground floor air intake vents and have them relocated to nonaccessible heights to prevent introduction of outside contaminants. (3) Protect the perimeter of the property to prevent accidental or intentional compromises of the base of the building to car or truck bombs, or crashes in the lobby. The street furniture can act as barriers to prevent unauthorized access to the perimeter of the building's architecture. (4) Change the exterior perimeter garbage cans to transparent or screen materials to reduce the opportunity for introducing contraband and explosives close to the building shell. (5) Use cameras sparingly but wisely to observe areas of extraordinary use, not ordinary use. Use CCTV for accountability and records of activity if needed, but CCTV has limits on how much activity it will prevent. (6) Have a well-defined entrance that looks, acts, and feels like the entrance to the building. Secondary entrances and fire exits should be clearly defined on their use and users. (7) Access control and screening by security staff should occur at well-defined areas near the front or primary entrance. Use mechanical solutions to permit unencumbered access for building occupants, but there is no short cut for screening visitors and vendors for badging and credentials. (8) Protect the window and glazing systems from burglary, blasts, natural disasters, and outside air contamination. Based on the risk assessment, the level of protection for the glazing can be determined and designed accordingly. (9) Design for security and access control of the elevators, stairwells, and other forms of vertical circulation paths. Stairwells must have ADA compliant safe refuge areas, and now be designed with lessons learned from 9/11 on placement, width, communication systems, positive pressurization, and fire protection. (10) The office building should have a secured rooftop, and protected infrastructure, mechanical spaces, and equipment. Many office buildings have chillers, elevator equipment, communications towers, air conditioning units, vents, and more located on the roof. These critical infrastructure items must be protected from unauthorized access.

There are many ways in which early planning makes it possible for architectural design to improve building safety and security. The CPTED process provides a comprehensive approach to plan for, and address the mechanical, organized, and natural strategies of good security features.

REFERENCES

Access Control & Security Systems Integration Magazine, April 2006.

Ahrens, S. (2006) High rise security from the ground up. *Building Operating Management*. Milwaukee, WI. October.

Atlas, R. (1991) Security as afterthought ensures long-term costs. *South Florida Business Journal*. Focus on Maintenance and Security. March, p. 18.

Atlas, R. (1999) Secure Facility Design, Environmental Design that Prevents Crime! *The Construction Specifier*, April.

Atlas, R. (1999) Security Design: Access Control Technology. *Door and Hardware*, April, p. 49.

Atlas, R. (1999) Stairwell Security. *Door and Hardware*, May, p. 55.

Atlas, R. (2004) Security Design Concepts. *Security Planning and Design: A Guide for Architecture and Building Design Professionals*. American Institute of Architects. Washington DC: Wiley.

Atlas, R. (2005) The security audit and premises liability. *Spotlight on Security for Real Estate Managers*, 2nd ed. Chicago: IREM.

Atlas, R. (2006) Designing for Security. *The Construction Specifier*, April, 83–92.

Atlas, R. (1991) Architect input among first steps in design. *Access Control*, June, pp. 25–26.

BOMA, Building Office Managers Association. Available at: http://www,.boma.org

Building Security Council. Available at: http://www.buildingsecuritycouncil.org

Demkin, J. (2003) *Security Planning and Design: A Guidebook for Architects and Building Design Professionals*. American Institute of Architects. NY: John Wiley & Sons.

Nadel, B. (2004) *Building Security: Handbook for Architectural Planning and Design*. Hoboken, NJ: McGraw Hill.

San Luis, E. (1973) *Office and Office Building Security*. Boston, MA: Butterworth Heinemann, 1st ed.

Witherspoon, R. *Office Building Security*. www.security-expert.org/officebuildings.com

27 Designing against Workplace Violence

Workplace violence is the most important security threat to America's largest corporations, according to a Fortune 1000 survey conducted by Pinkerton's Inc. in Westlake, California (*Security Management,* 1999, p. 9; Pinkerton, 2001, p. 5). The threat of criminal assault during the course of employment has always been a recognized hazard for certain workers, but now we see that threat expanding to potentially all work environments. Almost every day, there is an article in the paper about a fired employee coming back and killing a supervisor, and usually a few innocent bystanders.

THE EXTENT OF THE PROBLEM

Workplace violence is like an act of terrorism, except it is inside of a business organization. Workplace violence is when people problems go very wrong. Internal violence has always been present in the work environment but the scale of it today exceeds the threats of street crime or acts of terror. After September 11, 2001, concern for workplace security peaked as people feared a foreign terror threat to corporate America, but the greater threat was from violence of the workers within. From 1992 to 1996, there were over 2 million violent victimizations of workers on duty. The most common type of workplace violent crime was simple assault, with an estimated annual average of 1.5 million in 1996, and as of 2001 some 2 million American workers were victims of workplace violence each year (Bureau of Labor Statistics, 2006). In addition, there were 396,000 annual aggravated assaults, 51,000 rapes, 84,000 robberies, and 1,000 homicides in 1996. Current employees were 43.6% of the killers, and another 22.5% were former employees. Domestic violence accounted for 21.4% of the workplace fatalities, while violence from the business clients accounted for the remaining balance of 12.5%. In a typical year, 723 workers are attacked, 16,400 workers are threatened, and 43,800 workers are harassed. About 70% of the victims were between ages 25 and 49 years old. Fifty-six percent of the employers of workplace violence were private sector, and 34% were state and local government workers. Annually, 330,000 retail workers became victims of workplace violence, of which 61,000 were workers in convenience and liquor stores. More than 160,000 workers annually were victims in the medical occupations. In 2005, there were 564 workplace homicides, down from a high of 1080 in 1994, and 177 self-inflicted deaths (which is typical in that the perpetrator will kill themselves after killing the fellow employees) (Bureau of Justice Reports, 1998; Chavez, 2004; Bureau of Labor Statistics, 2006) (see Figure 27.1 and Figure 27.2).

In 1992, the Centers for Disease Control (CDC) declared workplace violence a serious public health problem, according to the U.S. Department of Labor OSHA Guidelines for Workplace Violence in 1996. Death and injury from workplace assaults can be cited under the OSHA Act of 1970, which cites under Section 5 (a)(1) that each employer shall furnish to each of its employees a place of employment which is free from recognized hazards that are likely to cause death or serious physical harm to its employees (29 U.S.C. 654 [a][1]) (Smith, Professional Safety, 2002). As a result of legally imposed duty to provide a safe and secure work environment, court decisions regarding foreseeability, and the actions of workplace safety regulatory agencies, safe and secure work environments are fast becoming the industry standard. Security administrators must realize these issues and plan to enforce the most efficient means to secure their workplace. Nearly all fatal workplace violence incidents have been followed by premises security negligence lawsuits brought on by the surviving

32A The Herald THURSDAY, APRIL 25, 2002 **NATIONAL NEWS**

Engineer is found guilty of slaying seven coworkers

BY DENISE LAVOIE
Associated Press Writer

CAMBRIDGE, Mass. — A man who gunned down seven co-workers at a software company in what he called a divine mission to prevent the Holocaust was convicted of murder Wednesday by a jury that rejected his insanity defense.

Michael McDermott, a hulking 43-year-old with long, shaggy hair and a bushy black beard, stood impassively as the verdict was delivered.

The convictions on seven counts of first-degree murder meant an automatic sentence of life in prison without parole. Massachusetts does not have a death penalty.

Prosecutors said McDermott went on his rampage because he was angry about the company's plan to comply with an IRS order to withhold a large portion of his salary to pay back taxes. They said he concocted the Holocaust story after boning up on how to fake mental illness.

The defense claimed the software engineer was insane, suffering from depression and schizophrenia, and didn't know what he was doing at Edgewater Technology Inc. in suburban Wakefield on Dec. 26, 2000.

The trial featured chilling testimony from workers who hid under their desks or ran out of the building after McDermott began shooting. Some said they heard coworkers begging for their lives before McDermott blasted them with an AK-47 and a pump-action shotgun.

The jury deliberated for

JOHN BLANDING/POOL PHOTO

CONVICTED OF MURDER: Michael McDermott, 43, listens as the verdict is delivered Wednesday in a Cambridge, Mass., court.

nearly 16 hours over three days.

McDermott spent two days on the witness stand testifying in his own defense. He matter-of-factly told the jury he was given a mission by St. Michael the Archangel, who told him he could earn a soul and prevent the Holocaust if he killed Adolf Hitler and six German generals.

In vivid detail, McDermott described being transported back in time to 1940 and entering a bunker where he heard Hitler's thoughts and saw men and women wearing swastika armbands. He described killing Nazis, one by one, as horrified family members of the real victims wept and eventually left the courtroom.

McDermott's defense presented medical experts who said he had a long history of depression, obsessive-compulsive disorder and schizophrenia. He testified that he was raped repeatedly by a neighbor as a child and that he tried to commit suicide at least three

times.

He also said he heard voices in his head and even "clustered" them into different groups.

"The major one I call the chorus," he testified. "The chorus continuously tells me what a bad person I am, what a waste of space and skin and air I am."

The day of the killings, McDermott was suffering from hallucinations and delusions and did not know right from wrong, a defense psychologist testified.

Prosecutors, however, said McDermott cooked up the story. McDermott even acknowledged buying a textbook for psychiatrists attempting to detect when criminal defendants are lying or faking mental illness.

McDermott said he researched the subject in order to make himself appear sane and to make sure his doctors prescribed Prozac, the anti-depressant he preferred.

FIGURE 27.1 Typical article on workplace violence. (Article ©2003 *The Associated Press.* Reprinted with permission from *The Associated Press.* Image by John Blanding/Pool Photo. ©2002 Landov.)

families of the victims. When the businesses are forced to disclose information under subpoena that there were prior threats of violence and the company's failure to prevent the accident, this action amounts to negligence and results in huge monetary awards to the victim's families. The cost of a single fatal incident of workplace violence would have far exceeded any costs to physical improvements, training, and staffing needed to prevent the problem.

Traditionally, internal and/or external theft of funds, product, or property has been the major threats faced by businesses. The new age of technology has included the aspect of information security. Information can be stolen or compromised, leading to devastating time and financial loss. When that loss, or theft, results in layoffs of employees and dissolution of lifetime pensions, the propensity for retribution and violence is high by employees on management and others viewed as responsible. Instances of domestic violence have been increasing in the workplace. Former employees who have

THURSDAY, AUGUST 28, 2003 **www.herald.com The Herald 3A**

Fired worker kills 6 at Chicago job site

CHICAGO — (AP) — A man who had been fired from an auto parts warehouse six months ago came back with a gun Wednesday and killed six people in a rampage through a maze of engine blocks and 55-gallon drums before being shot to death by police.

The dead included two brothers who were part owners of the business, and the son of one of them.

Salvador Tapia died in a gun battle with police inside and outside of the building, hiding behind a container as he fired off rounds from his semiautomatic pistol, authorities said.

"He got up, he had the gun, they ordered him to drop the gun, he refused to drop the gun. That's when the officer shot him," acting Police Superintendent Phil Cline said.

Tapia, 36, lost his job at Windy City Core Supply about six months ago for causing trouble at work and frequently showing up late or not at all, Cline said. He said Tapia had made threatening calls to the owners since being fired.

Tapia had at least one previous conviction for unlawful use of a weapon, officials said.

Cline said when police arrived shortly after 8:30 a.m., they tried to get in the building but were driven back by gunfire.

He said when an assault team entered the building they had trouble maneuvering through all the auto parts.

Cline said four people died

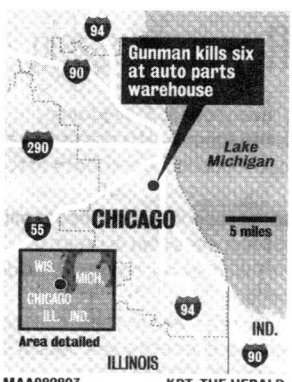

at the scene.

Tapia and two others were taken to hospitals and died there.

Authorities identified the dead as part-owners Alan Weiner, 50, of Wilmette, and his brother Howard Weiner, 59, of Northbrook. Howard's son Daniel Weiner, 30, also was killed.

The other victims were Calvin Ramsey, 44; Robert Taylor, 53, and Juan Valles, 34, all of Chicago.

"From the scene it appears that he went throughout the supply warehouse shooting them," Cline said.

Tapia also tied one man's hands behind his back, but the employee escaped unharmed, Cline said.

He was the only person inside the warehouse who survived the shooting, police said.

FIGURE 27.2 Article on workplace violence in a factory. (Article ©2003 *The Associated Press*. Reprinted with permission from *The Associated Press*. Image ©2003 *The Miami Herald*. Reprinted with permission from *The Miami Herald*.)

been the victims of downsizing or company reorganization have the potential to commit retaliatory violent acts on those who they deem responsible.

The greatest workplace risks include rape, murder, armed robbery, burglary, theft of company products, theft of company supplies, theft of company equipment, employee-to-employee theft, sabotage of machinery or production, falsifying records or claims, disgruntled employees, disgruntled customer, aggravated assaults, sale and consumption of drugs in the workplace, drug dealing, and violent crimes by employees and nonemployees, and disclosure of trade secrets, proprietary data, and financial information.

Risk factors that equate to the greatest risk for workplace violence are when employees are required to exchange money with the public; work alone or in small numbers; work late night or early morning; work in high crime areas; guard valuable property or possessions; work in a community setting such as taxi, security, or police. Workplace violence has many sources, and understanding who commits it is the first step in prevention. There are four types of perpetrators of workplace violence. Perpetrators may have no relationship with the business or employee and are just committing a crime such as robbery, shoplifting, or trespassing, in which violence occurs. A majority of workplace homicides fall into this category (85%) (Report to the Nation, 2001).

Other perpetrators have a legitimate relationship with the business, and become violent while being served by the business. Some perpetrators are an employee or ex-employee of the business who attacks or threatens another employee or past employee in the workplace. Worker-on-worker violence accounts for 7% of violent workplace homicides. The last type of perpetrator usually does not have a relationship with the business but has a personal relationship with the intended victim. This includes victims of domestic violence assaulted or threatened while at work (Report to the Nation, 2001).

The business community, and their management need to understand the actual dynamics of crime, so that crime prevention measures will be based on informed assumptions and decisions. The standard of care in most industries is to conduct a risk analysis to understand what risks, threats, vulnerabilities, and assets are being protected. By understanding the threats and risks, the businesses should have identified and determined the probable location of potential or actual crimes, the probable offender source, the nature of the crime, and the motivation behind the crimes (revenge, greed, sabotage, personal), and how crimes are committed. When management and business owners understand these patterns, then a comprehensive approach of multiple strategies for detection, intervention, prevention, and control can be developed to reduce or remove the opportunity for crime and loss to occur.

WHAT CAN YOU DO?

There are three approaches to preventing workplace violence according to the literature review: *organizational and administrative, behavioral and interpersonal, and environmental design* (Report to the Nation, 2001).

Organizational approaches are involved in developing awareness programs, policies, and procedures and practices that maintain a safe working environment. Conducting background checks of employees and hiring, firing, and supervision practices are examples. Management can reduce the risk to workplace violence from perpetrators that are not fellow employees by increasing the number of staff at vulnerable times, providing training in conflict resolution and nonviolent response, teaching employees to avoid resistance during a robbery; having police check on workers routinely, and, if necessary, closing the establishments during high-risk hours (see Figure 27.3).

Behavioral and interpersonal approaches reinforce training the staff and supervisors and fellow workers to anticipate, recognize, and respond to the signs and symptoms of conflict resolution and reducing the potential for conflict and violence.

FIGURE 27.3 Sending a clear message of guarding personal property.

Environmental design approach looks at how the physical environment can be improved to reduce the opportunity for workplace violence. CPTED Strategies that can be employed to reduce the risk and opportunity of workplace violence that include:

- Limit the access to your facility to those who have legitimate use and purpose to be there.
- Where possible, secure the reception area and screen clients and visitors.
- Compartmentalize and electronically control access to sensitive areas, such as, computer rooms and communications rooms.
- Provide access control into lobby and foyers areas, especially at high-risk locations and times.
- Adjust lighting levels to increase visibility of staff to the outside street and to reduce hiding spots outside. Provide adequate lighting and surveillance of employee and visitor parking.
- Enhance entrance and parking lot lighting to provide maximum visibility and ability to identify persons and vehicles.
- Have unobstructed view of the street from a retail store environment, clear of shrubbery or clutter that a criminal could use to hide or block view by patrolling police.
- Clearly sign and alarm entrances and exits.
- Provide planned escape routes for employees should violence break out in their work environment. Make sure that escape route is not through an area where violence is erupting, and thus compromise more people as hostages or victims.
- Provide duress or panic alarms for human resource offices, women's restrooms, reception desks, and other sensitive areas. Provide reception personnel with a means to covertly signal duress situations.
- Provide a peephole viewer in rear doors to restaurants to allow surveillance outside before opening the rear door and being ambushed by an awaiting perpetrator.
- Designate employee and visitor entrances, as they need not necessarily be the same.
- Use employee and guest or visitor badging; badging should be worn by all persons, especially management. Clearly delineate employee, visitor, vendor, and contractor status on badges along with the location and times they are allowed access.
- Eliminate designated executive parking, especially do not place the name of the person on the wheel stop or place signage identifying it as the "president's" spot.
- Keep plantings on perimeter of parking areas and buildings to less than three feet to minimize hiding and maximize natural surveillance.

- Establish physical control over loading docks, equipment sheds, boiler rooms, and trash bins and other ancillary buildings.
- Provide tenants with the means to control their own office area.
- Establish a uniform means of identification and access for multitenant sites.
- Utilize primary and secondary authentication methods for access to highly sensitive areas.
- Design factory and floor layout plans with security in mind.
- Enable employees to see surroundings and not have blind spots that could provide entrapment opportunities. Hiding points such as trees, shrubs, and excessive clutter must be removed.
- Control pedestrian access to the store and deter easy escape routes with strategically placed fences.
- Use drop safes to limit the amount of cash on site. Install signage indicating that cash on hand is minimal.
- Use door alarm and door position switches to alert employees when someone enters the facility.
- Control access to the facility with door buzzers.
- Require all visitors and vendors to register before entering the worksite.
- Make sure that the employee that is assigned to register visitors has ready access to a panic button that is monitored and can be responded to.
- Evaluate the use of locks that unlock automatically from the inside (which is required by fire and life safety codes), but are secured from the outside. Fire exit doors should have crash bars or handles in the inside, but should not have a door opening mechanism from the outside to prevent piggybacking and unauthorized access.
- Put height markers on exit doors to help witnesses provide better descriptions of assailants.
- Use silent and personal duress alarms where appropriate.
- Equip field staff with cellular phones and hold up alarms or noise devices, and require them to prepare a daily work plan and keep a contact person informed of their location throughout the day.
- Keep employer-provided vehicles maintained, even using GPS to track vehicles and provide accountability and follow-up if someone goes missing or does not report in.
- Instruct employees not to enter any location that they feel unsafe, and consider using a buddy or escort system in potentially dangerous situations or at night.
- Install physical barriers such as bullet resistant enclosures with pass-through between customer and employee (see Figure 27.6).
- Have building managers assess business threats, identify vulnerabilities, assets, and above all coordinate efforts to update policy and procedures and training updates annually.
- Train and motivate staff; this is more important than any technological fix to prevent workplace violence.
- Tightly control access to shipping and receiving areas. Monitoring deliveries is important to prevent unauthorized persons from entering in the loading dock to the facility and to reduce pilferage and loss. All deliveries should be registered, screened, and logged in before being accepted.
- Move or seal ground floor vents. Street level air intakes should be sealed and moved to higher floors to prevent sabotage from below.
- Provide security cameras to spot trouble, offer deterrence and detection, and increase chances of identification. But cameras are only as good as the human backup; a lone guard watching 24 monitors is pointless (see Figure 27.5).
- Train security guards appropriately. Three guards checking the same ID are not likely to make a difference, but security personnel trained to spot and react to real threats will make a difference (see Figure 27.6)
- A single entrance allows for greater control, but delayed check-in procedures can increase security risks, and be impractical. Better screening should include weapon screening,

FIGURE 27.4 Weapons policy must be clearly delineated.

FIGURE 27.5 Guard is protecting entrance from unscreened visitors.

FIGURE 27.6   Bullet proofing the lobby to protect against robbery in a high crime area retail store.

FIGURE 27.7   Cameras and monitors greeting you in an entrance lets the employees and visitors know you are being watched to prevent pilferage and theft.

FIGURE 27.8 TSA-trained people screening carryon items for weapons and explosives.

baggage and package scanners, and optical turnstiles that check ID cards of employees and visitors and vendors.

- This way out! Clear evacuation plans are critical. Occupants must know what to do and what not to do and when to do them. Drills and practice are essential. Over 20,000 people were saved from WTC in the second attack in 2001 by improved and practiced evacuation procedures and equipment from the first attack in 1994.
- Strategically locate blueprints for police and SWAT team but keep secure from Web users or persons trying to plan an attack on your building.

Many of the CPTED strategies mentioned here clearly are applicable to perpetrators with criminal intent, but they may not be effective if the perpetrators are current or past employees. Little research has been done to measure the effectiveness of environmental strategies to protect employees from fellow employees. Behavioral and organizational approaches make common sense, but very little research has been conducted to see if the programs work and on what level of effectiveness.

So, what is the experience that we are looking for in a safe and secure work environment? The workplace should provide a sense of security. People want to come to work in a building that is useable and accessible, a building that is open, yet controlled. People want to work in a building that avoids circulation conflicts and responds to the many user needs. People do not want to be harassed, threatened, abused, or assaulted verbally or physically.

SUMMARY

There is no national legislation, or regulations, specifically addressing the prevention of workplace violence (Report to the Nation, 2001, p. 8), but OSHA has published voluntary guidelines for workers in late-night retail environments. Some states have enacted regulations requiring comprehensive safety programs in all workplaces, including addressing the prevention of "reasonably foreseeable" assaults on employees.

Combining CPTED approaches of reducing crime opportunity, along with complementary management approaches can combine to have effective strategies that create a safe and secure work environment. The range of strategies can be natural type of CPTED approaches to take advantage of the design and architecture, such as the materials and methods of construction, setbacks and site planning, layouts and circulation patterns of people and vehicles. Prevention strategies can also include mechanical CPTED strategies of security hardware, electronics, cameras, access control, barriers, and lighting. And the organizational aspect of CPTED can be used for security personnel and management, such as policies and procedures, badging systems, guard tours, and training.

Prevention strategies should be based on a thorough analysis of the crime risks and threats so that the strategies of technology and architecture integrate into a complete workplace security and safety prevention program. The development of strategies needs to be responsive to the specific types of crimes and risks that are around and inside the workplace environment. Management and owners need to be prepared to think comprehensively and not just have quick-fix solutions. Workplace violence is especially challenging because the perpetrators and victims are usually employees, and know the "drill." They have access to the keys, codes, data, merchandise, and people. Special measures are needed to provide safety from inside threats, not just the stranger from the street. Safe and secure work environments can be created through the implementation of a comprehensive CPTED approach that uses the key elements by the staff and management in a meaningful way.

REFERENCES

Atlas, R. (1992) Internal Employee Theft Prevention Workshop presented by the Greater Miami Chamber of Commerce, 12 March.

Atlas, R. (1998) Risky Business Security Workshop, ALFA International, American law Firm Association. Dallas, Texas, 29 January.

Atlas, R. (2002a) Neocon World Trade Fair on Designing against the Threats of Workplace Violence and Crime, Atlanta, Georgia, 11 April.

Atlas, R. (2002b) The University of Wisconsin-Madison seminar on Planning against Today Threats of Crime, Workplace Violence, and Terrorism, 17–19 April.

Atlas, R. (2003) Florida Association American Institute of Architects, "Designing against today's threats of crime, workplace violence and terrorism." Miami, Florida, 2–3 October.

National Institute of Occupational Safety & Health (NIOSH) (1993) *CDC Alert: Preventing Homicide in the Workplace.* U.S. Department of Health and Human Services, Centers for Disease Control and Prevention.

Guidelines for Preventing Workplace Violence for Health Care and Social Service Workers, OSHA (1998).

Biles, P. (1996) Guidelines for Workplace Violence Prevention Programs for Night Retail Establishments. Washington, DC.

Pinkerton Study on Greatest Threats to Businesses (1999) *Security Management* May, 9.

Report to the Nation (2001) Workplace Violence, University of Iowa Injury Prevention Research Center. Iowa City, Iowa, February.

Preventing Workplace Violence (2004) Handbook of the American Federation of State, County and Municipal Employees.

Chavez, L. (2004) Workplace violence and can we do more to prevent it? *Human Resource Executive.* October.

Workplace Violence, 1992–1996. (1998) Bureau of Justice Statistics Special Report. National Crime Victimization Survey. July.

Workplace Violence: Issues in Response. (2004) U.S. Department of Justice, FBI. Critical Incident Response group. Quantico, Virginia, 1–100.

National Census of Fatal Occupational Injuries in 2005. (2006) Bureau of Labor Statistics: News. U.S. Department of Labor. Washington, DC. August 10.

Top Security Threats (2001) Survey of Fortune 1000 Companies Eighth Annual Report. Westlake, CA: Pinkerton.

Smith, S.(2002) Workplace Violence. *Professional Safety,* November, 33–43.

OSH Act of 1970, Section 5(a)(1) P.L. 91–596. 29 U.S.C. 654(a)(1)

WEB SITES

National Institute for Occupational Safety and Health: www.osha.gov/workplace_violence/wrkplaceViolence. table.html

Bureau of Labor Statistics: stats.bls.gov

National Center for Injury Prevention and Control: www.sdc.gov/ncipc

California OSHA website on workplace security: www.dir.ca.gov/dosh_publications/index.html

Workplace Violence Checklist: www.afscme.org/health/violaa.htm
General Services Administration: www.gsa.gov/pbs/fps/fps.htm
Office of Personnel Management:www.opm.gov/workplac/index.html-ssi
Minnesota Center Against Violence and Abuse:www.mincava.umn.edu/workviol.asp
Workplace Solutions: www.wps.org

28 Graphics, Signage, and Wayfinding for Security

"Signs, signs, everywhere are signs" are the lyrics from a popular song in the 1960s by the Five Man Electrical Band. When users of an environment or building occupy a space, messages are given by the environment to indicate the appropriate use of the space, for which it was designed. The use of graphics and signage is one way of giving the intended messages to the user. Signage and wayfinding are part of the Situational CPTED matrix (Clarke), under the section on "removing of excuses and inducement of shame and guilt." Stating the ground rules for proper or legitimate usage of a space is critical for achieving compliance and reducing the facilitators of crime and terror. Having a clear sense of direction creates safe mobility paths for people and vehicles.

Signs can convey a message—good or bad—depending on what the information is, and how it is perceived. For example, the sign in an elevator pictured in Figure 28.1 lets the users know that they are being watched and recorded, especially if they engage in inappropriate activities.

Graphics are referred to as the symbols that pictorially portray an image or convey a message. An example is the symbol of a person in a wheelchair, or a man or woman (see Figure 28.2).

Signage refers to conveying a message with letters, words, or graphics/symbols. One of the major purposes of security signage is to put the user of that space on notice; that is, shifting the load of responsibility to the user. The expression "Let the buyer beware" is becoming translated by the courts to be "Let the user beware" (see Figure 28.3).

The warning sign has good intention, but the owners of a facility cannot legally relieve themselves of the responsibility for providing security by just denying that they have no responsibility. In order for the building and/or the owner/manager to partially shift the load of responsibility, the building must clearly state what the expectations or ground rules are (see Figure 28.4).

Figure 28.5 demonstrates a sign asking hotel guests to present their keys the to security officer before getting into the elevators that take guests to their rooms. Guests are expected to carry their room keys with them or they must go to the front desk to ask for a duplicate key. The symbolic barrier of the sign puts guests and potential trespassers on notice that they will be challenged

FIGURE 28.1 Signage that puts the user on notice for inappropriate activity.

FIGURE 28.2 Bathroom graphics on who are the desired users.

FIGURE 28.4 Signage stating ground rules.

FIGURE 28.5 Signage for hotel security.

FIGURE 28.3 Sign of warning notice that the garage users are on their own.

FIGURE 28.6 Just painting a curb red and labeling it a fire lane is usually sufficient to get drivers attention not to park there. Just saying "no parking" probably would not have the same effect.

and blocked from unencumbered access. The real barrier is the security guard, who will ask for the keys and prevent persons from entering the elevators. With hotels being a very public domain, it is imperative to control access to guest areas in order to prevent trespassing, robbery, prostitution, and other crime typical of hotels, dorms, housing, and residences.

The red-painted curb and the signage of "fire lane" and "no parking" is a threat that car owners understand and fear. Most drivers will think twice about parking their car in a fire lane. The expectation is that a car in a fire lane will be ticketed and towed. The implied threat is usually sufficient to prevent inappropriate parking (see Figure 28.6).

FIGURE 28.7 Ground rules for a university dorm entrance. This could be too much for parents visiting, but does put the students and their local visitors on notice.

Signs can state the ground rules for what are allowed or forbidden behaviors. Most of the time signage is taking on the parental role of stating what is not allowed, as seen in Figure 28.7. But it is as important to state what is allowed. For example, if picnics are allowed at a certain area, then be clear on where that activity is encouraged, and where that behavior is forbidden or discouraged. If bottles are forbidden, then this rule must be enforced so that broken glass is not introduced onto the grounds of the park.

Some ground rules that we are used to seeing are (see Figure 28.8 and Figure 28.9):

Do not walk on the grass
Enter at own risk
Lock your valuables
No trespassing
Don't even think of speeding
Don't litter
No weapons

FIGURE 28.8 Signage graphics at a shopping mall entrance.

Signs can be monumental entrance signs or informational signs. It is desirable to have the main entrance of a facility open, obvious, and readily apparent. Monumental signage helps define the sense of arrival, and where you desire people or vehicles to arrive at (see Figure 28.10 and Figure 28.11).

Just putting up a sign does not relieve the building owner of liability or guarantee compliance (see Figure 28.12). However, the building or property can put the users on notice of what to expect and how to behave and what the consequences will be for violations. The fencing around the sign helps ensure compliance.

FIGURE 28.9   No-weapons signage at an office building.

FIGURE 28.10   Entrance signage at an apartment complex.

FIGURE 28.11 University entrance that has wording inscribed into wall, and serves as the main monumental entrance.

FIGURE 28.12 Warning signage on a dock to keep an eye on children.

FIGURE 28.13 "Don't invite a thief" signage at a parking lot.

FIGURE 28.14   Signage at a university gym warning to not leave one's belongings unattended.

FIGURE 28.15   Warning signage about trespassing and citing what laws the behavior violates and who enforces it.

A common example of signage in action is the building type of parking garages. Good signage and graphics can give garage users the following information (see Figure 28.16):

Where the entrance and exits are located
Location of speed bumps; posted speed limits
Direction of traffic
To lock all valuables
Head-in parking only
Management not responsible for losses
This parking lot is under CCTV surveillance
Location of fire exits and alarms
Location of panic buttons and intercoms for assistance
Cars parked incorrectly will be towed and fined
Persons violating rules will be arrested for trespassing and prosecuted

FIGURE 28.16 Signage in garages is critical, and among the many pieces of information is letting customers know what the limits of liability and responsibility are.

Security signage and graphics have architectural design criteria. The architectural design criteria starts with the architect or graphics consultant. Some considerations are:

- What is the size of the letters?
- What is the type style of the letters?
- At what distance is graphics to be read?
- What is the color contrast between letters and the background?
- Does the signage comply with the Americans With Disabilities Act?
- What kind of illumination is needed to support signage visibility at night?
- Where is location of signage?
- Who is sign intended for?
- Is there a reference point showing the "you are here" on wayfinding map?
- Is the north arrow shown for reference on wayfinding maps?

For a sign to be clearly read by a person with 20/20 vision at a distance of 50 feet, the letters would need to be 6 inches in height. If the signage uses graphics or symbols, it should be at least 15 inches in height. The type style or font is an important consideration for clarity in reading. Letter styles with fancy serifs, such as Gothic, are difficult to read at distances. Font styles popular with architects are Helvetica and Times Roman. Lighting levels at the signage should be at least 20-foot-candles and positioned to avoid glare on the signage.

The City of Las Vegas passed a signage ordinance in the 1990s that provided some guidelines for building numbering to assist police and first responders (see Figure 28.17, Figure 28.18, and Figure 28.19).

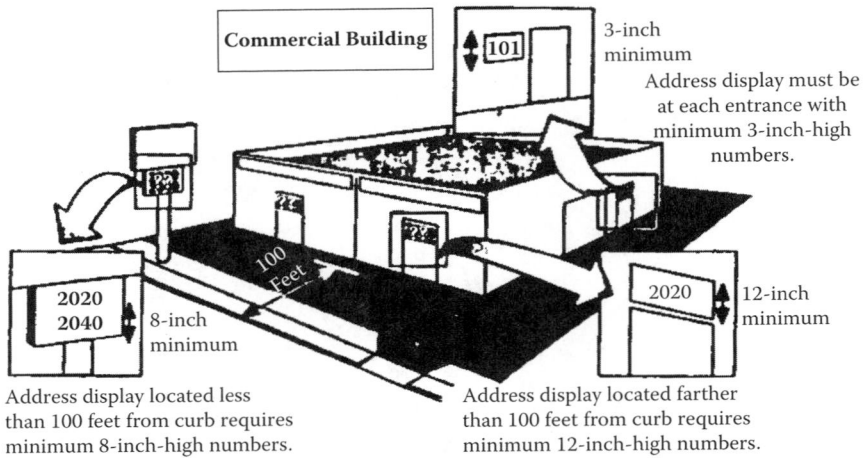

Commercial Building

101

3-inch minimum

Address display must be at each entrance with minimum 3-inch-high numbers.

100 Feet

2020
2040

8-inch minimum

2020

12-inch minimum

Address display located less than 100 feet from curb requires minimum 8-inch-high numbers.

Address display located farther than 100 feet from curb requires minimum 12-inch-high numbers.

FIGURE 28.17 Example of clear building signage that gives the building number, the unit numbers, and the street on which the building is located.

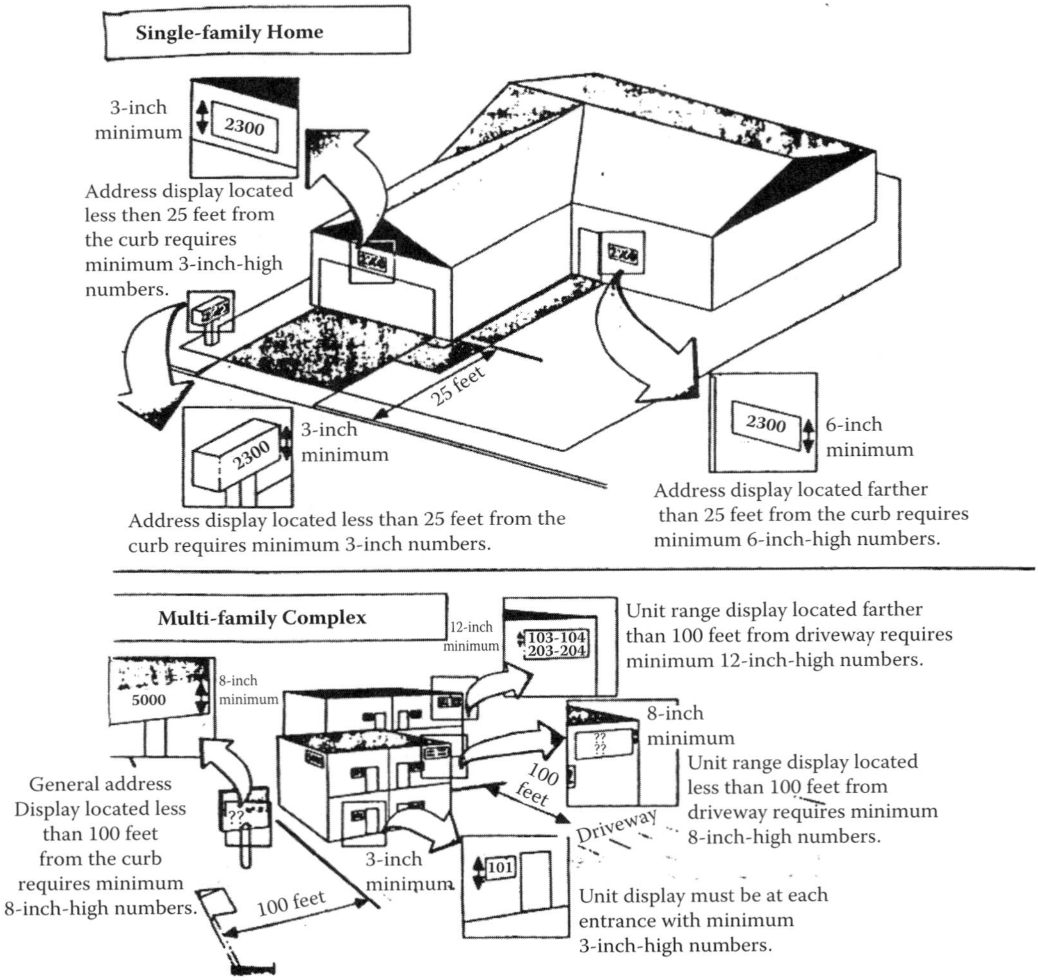

Single-family Home

3-inch minimum

2300

Address display located less then 25 feet from the curb requires minimum 3-inch-high numbers.

25 feet

2300

3-inch minimum

Address display located less than 25 feet from the curb requires minimum 3-inch numbers.

2300

6-inch minimum

Address display located farther than 25 feet from the curb requires minimum 6-inch-high numbers.

Multi-family Complex

12-inch minimum

103-104
203-204

Unit range display located farther than 100 feet from driveway requires minimum 12-inch-high numbers.

8-inch minimum

5000

8-inch minimum

??
??

Unit range display located less than 100 feet from driveway requires minimum 8-inch-high numbers.

General address Display located less than 100 feet from the curb requires minimum 8-inch-high numbers.

100 feet

3-inch minimum

101

100 feet

Driveway

Unit display must be at each entrance with minimum 3-inch-high numbers.

FIGURE 28.18 Residential signage and numbering guidelines.

FIGURE 28.19 Example of clear building signage that describes the building number, the unit numbers, and the street the building is located on.

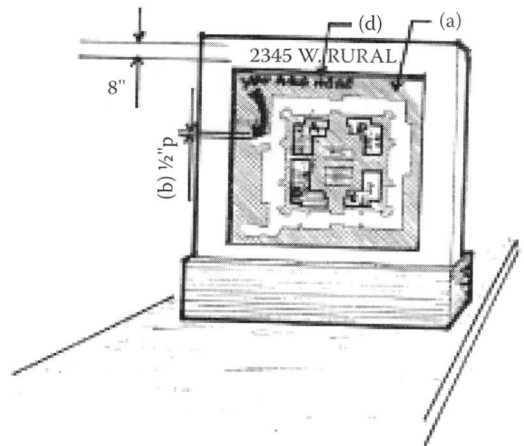

FIGURE 28.20 Building wayfinding graphics specifications. (Image© 1997 City of Tempe Arizona. Reprinted with permission.)

The following is an example of design recommendations for a directory graphic (see Figure 28.20 and Figure 28.21).

The CPTED considerations for graphics and signage are to establish a consistent, uniform, and well-distributed graphics package. Just as fire exits must be illuminated and displayed at all stairways, security signage should be systematically displayed at all critical areas. Signs may need to be in multiple languages to communicate clearly to mixed audiences and remove the excuse that a certain group of persons did not have to comply because they could not understand the sign, as demonstrated in Figure 28.22.

Procedural considerations develop the process on what the signage is to say, whom the signage is directed for, and where it should be located. Examples of signage clarifying procedures are having employees wear ID badges for clearance, letting guests of a restaurant know of a level change, or putting shoppers on notice of shoplifting surveillance. It is important not to give mixed messages (see Figure 28.23).

Signs need to accurately reflect the ability to deliver or perform. For instance, if a sign says that the parking lot is secure, there is an expectation of security. If the signage creates "an illusion of security," then the landowner is in the vulnerable position of having premises liability and negligent security (see Figures 28.24 through Figure 28.27).

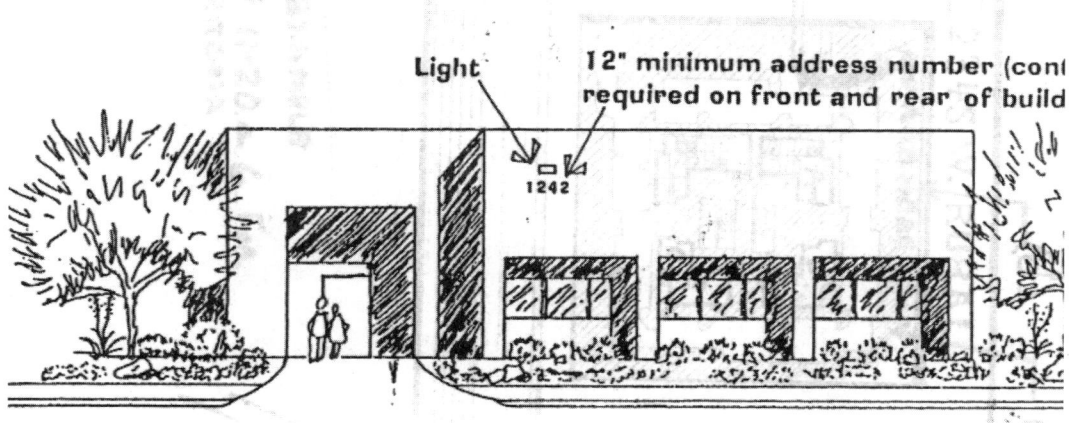

FIGURE 28.21 Example of building number placement for maximum visibility. (Image© 1997 City of Tempe Arizona. Reprinted with permission.)

FIGURE 28.22   Bilingual sign prohibiting trespassing.

FIGURE 28.23   Mixed messages in signage should be avoided.

Pedestrian paths of travel or movement predictors are good examples of the merging of signage and graphics/wayfinding and CPTED. The use of speed bumps is common before a crosswalk to slow people driving and to redirect their attention from the usual distractions of driving (cell phones, children, radio, makeup, eating, text mailing, daydreaming, etc.). The speed bump or speed hump should be signed and painted, so persons are not caught unprepared and slow down, and the texture and color change in the crosswalk is intended to further alert drivers of pedestrians (see Figure 28.28 and Figure 28.29).

FIGURE 28.24   Signage of alleged security in parking lot.

FIGURE 28.25   So many no's, so little time.

FIGURE 28.26   Advertising that there is no cash on the premises and that there is surveillance.

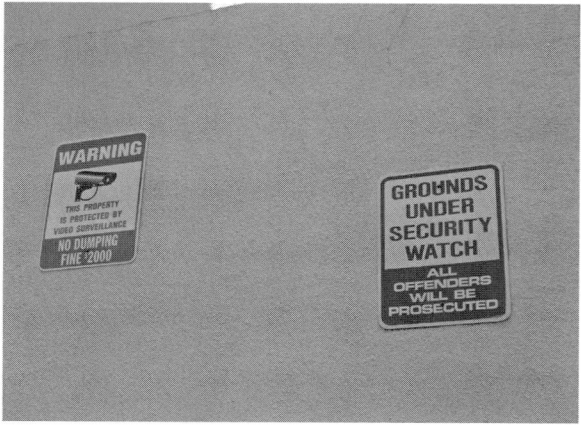

FIGURE 28.27   Putting the criminals and customers on notice.

FIGURE 28.28   Crosswalk signage warns drivers to be aware of pedestrians.

FIGURE 28.29   Speed bump and warning signage

SUMMARY

The role of graphics and signage in the security and the crime prevention arena is to make the users clearly aware of the permitted and allowed uses in an environment. If the users or invitees of the property do not follow the ground rules, then the burden of responsibility shifts, and they can be challenged as to their intent and face the appropriate consequences.

Without the notice given by signage, people's actions are subject to personal interpretation and are difficult to challenge (see Figure 28.30). When there is lack of clarity, the potential violator will create excuses for loitering, littering, trespassing, and otherwise use the lack of rules and confusion to the advantage of the violator. Early involvement of the architect with the security manager is the best step for creating a secure environment with the clear and concise use of signage and graphics.

FIGURE 28.30 Signage can be used on monitors to put users on notice.

REFERENCES

Brantingham, P. L. and Brantingham, P. J. (1991) *Environmental Criminology*. Beverly Hills, CA: Sage.

Clarke, R. V. (Ed.) (1992). *Situational Crime Prevention: Successful Case Studies*. New York: Harrow and Heston.

Clarke, R. V. (1993) Fare evasion and automatic ticket collection in the London underground. In R. V. Clarke (Ed.), *Crime Prevention Studies*, Vol. 1. Monsey, NY: Criminal Justice Press.

Clarke, R. V. (1995) Situational crime prevention. In M. Tonry and D. P. Farrington (Eds.), *Building a Safer Society: Strategic Approaches to Crime Prevention, Crime and Justice*, Vol. 19. Chicago, IL: University of Chicago Press.

Clarke, R. V. (Ed.) (1997) *Situational Crime Prevention: Successful Case Studies*, 2nd ed. New York: Harrow and Heston.

Crowe, T. (2000) *Crime Prevention through Environmental Design: Applications of Architectural Design and Space Management Concepts*, 2nd ed. Oxford: Butterworth-Heinemann.

City of Tempe Arizona CPTED Ordinance.

City of Las Vegas Signage Ordinance.

Part IV

How Do You Know You Are Making A Difference?

29 Measuring Success

Randy Atlas and Gregory Saville

There are two tactics for measuring success in crime prevention—the academic and the practical. The first is geared to the researcher who studies which CPTED strategies work, on what kind of problems, and then suggests how those strategies might prevent crime. It is generally what criminological researchers have done for decades. There are a number of bibliographic reviews of CPTED effectiveness (Cozens, Saville, and Hillier, 2005).

The other tactic is geared to the practitioner and designer. They conduct research to collect baseline information before suggesting CPTED strategies. That baseline information, also known as a CPTED Risk Assessment, helps the practitioner conduct a thorough analysis and indicates which CPTED strategies will work best. After implementation, the CPTED practitioner can then measure the success and, if necessary, fine-tune responses. Unfortunately, that is not generally what practitioners do. It is what we advocate in this chapter; in fact, we are certain it must happen if CPTED is to move forward as a science and not just an art form.

Security and CPTED are geared to prevent a possible future outcome. How do you measure what has not yet happened? Stock investments are measured on their rate of return. Doctors measure success on the time of recovery for a patient from treatment or surgery. Architects are measured and praised on their success if their buildings are being built on time and budget, and also if they don't leak or fall down.

Fire departments have a peculiar position of being measured not only how quickly they respond to a fire, and how many fires they put out, but more importantly on how many fires they prevent. The absence of fires in buildings is an accepted indicator that the fire department and design/construction professionals are doing a good job. Many workplaces have signs on the employee board showing the number of accident-free days. Why is it acceptable for fire departments to consider success the "lack of" fire incidents and loss of life, but security and police departments struggle in getting the same recognition and funding for doing the same? Are we more interested in preventing a stairwell fire than preventing an assault in a parking garage?

THE MEASUREMENT PARADOX

There are some major distinctions between fire and crime prevention. The factors that cause fire are fairly straightforward: a combustible substance, oxygen, and enough heat. Preventing fire means controlling one of those basic ingredients, or getting the help of residents and building owners to do it themselves.

In contrast, ingredients that cause crime are not straightforward. After decades of research they are still in debate. Poverty, substance abuse, conflicts between cultures, family dysfunction, social alienation, unequal distribution of resources, to mention a few, are all considered crime-causing—criminogenic—in one way or another. But academic studies that measure the effectiveness of CPTED rarely look at the underlying criminogenic causes of particular crimes. In fact, CPTED evaluations tend not to deal with criminogenic causes at all; they deal with whether opportunities for crime exist and whether minimizing those opportunities reduce crime. That may sound very reasonable, but it is a paradox. It means that in CPTED, unlike fire prevention, we never know whether the underlying conditions that lead to crime are ever addressed.

Does this paradox really matter if crimes go down? It probably doesn't matter to the potential victim. But to the CPTED practitioner, designer, or place manager, it means we can never know which particular CPTED strategy will work best in different circumstances. This is a dilemma for evaluators. Fire preventers know with certainty that removing combustible materials means there will be no fire. Not so with crime prevention. As Schneider and Kitchen report, it is "as difficult as untangling a spider's web to evaluate the effectiveness of specific place-based crime prevention measures" (2002, p. 158).

Academic CPTED evaluators respond by ignoring this measurement paradox. Some researchers claim that reducing crime opportunities, and crime, is good enough to determine whether CPTED works. They conclude there is enough academic evidence that CPTED works in a variety of places. But it is at level of the practical CPTED evaluator where, as they say, the rubber meets the road. That is where we focus our attention in this chapter.

BUILDING CODES

Another major difference between fire prevention and crime prevention is the "building code." Codes such as the Life Safety Code and local and state building codes require the fire department to conduct annual inspections, and review and approve preconstruction drawings. In those codes, there are standards for fire-resistant construction materials, methods, and the required application of technology systems (e.g., alarms, signs, strobes, horns). This degree of attention is rare in crime prevention. Other than the handful of communities that have passed CPTED ordinances, bylaws, and a small number of other regulations such as the federal government's GSA Security Standards, CPTED and security is an option. It is subject to personal choice. It is a case of let the buyer beware.

The new climate of fear of crime and risks from terrorism suggest that the practical side of CPTED evaluation is where we need to refocus our efforts. It is time for change. Civic officials, municipal leaders, and political representatives must lead that change.

HOW TO MOVE CPTED INTO THE 21ST CENTURY

In order for fire departments to receive their annual funding, their success is measured on the decrease of fires and the amount of property damage prevented. Colleges and universities are required to publish the amount of crime on their campuses because of the Clery Act. The universities fully understand and appreciate that parents look at the crime on campus as selection criteria for placing their children and investing hundreds of thousands of dollars in their education.

How can antiterrorism and crime prevention programs be measured? As argued throughout this book, crime and terrorism have similarities in prevention, but they are certainly not the same.

With terrorism, it is apparent that strategies of Homeland Security, law enforcement, and intelligence services have all had a role in preventing a serious major attack in North America since 9/11. Several attacks or threats have been prevented in both the United States and Canada, and it can be argued that one measure of success of our security improvements is the absence of major attacks. This is no reason to ignore the threat; attacks have occurred elsewhere in the world during the same time periods, including the Madrid train attacks, the London subway attacks, the Bali discotheque, and elsewhere in Indonesia.

Especially with antiterrorism initiatives, it is important to look at all these cases not only from an intelligence and law enforcement perspective but also from the perspective of protecting critical infrastructure. To measure success in practical CPTED evaluations, the critical factor in all these cases is to keep good data of before and after security changes. In architecture, this is known as the Post Occupancy Evaluation (POE), and few architects have the time, inclination, or funding resources to conduct them with any regularity. POE are a valuable tool to understand how our built environment works, and should be conducted whenever possible.

Ideally, crime analysis is conducted as part of the risk vulnerability assessment. We have presented risk assessment strategies throughout this book. We have also presented a CPTED Risk Assessment guide in other places (Saville and Wright, 1998; Atlas, 2002; Gamman and Pascoe, 2004). We have updated and revised that guide and present it later in this chapter. But unlike the vulnerability and threat assessment methods in previous chapters, such as the computerized ATRiM risk assessment program, there are still very few cases where practical evaluation research is part of development. There are still too few cases where our research directly guides our action (Cozens et al, 2005).

Compare this with the code requirements for annual fire inspection of any property. Consider the requirements for review of architectural plans for fire and life safety compliance for proposed and future buildings. Can security and crime be prevented and evaluated without the same standard of care?

As we discussed previously in the CPTED implementation chapter, without the requirements of code and regulation compliance, making appropriate and reasonable security improvements based on risk assessments becomes wishful thinking in the private sector. True, attention is greater with large corporations that have bigger commitments and greater liability. But the likelihood of evaluation-based design elsewhere is absent, such as mom-and-pop stores or apartment buildings. In truth, it is never too late to measure the security features of your actual, or proposed, building and then design accordingly. It is the only way that we will develop a coherent body of best practice knowledge to determine what is successful, and what is not.

WHERE DO YOU START?

Success can be measured by both an increase and decrease in crime statistics. Keep in mind that many people use statistics like a drunk uses a lamppost—for support, not illumination! In fact statistics, especially officially recorded crime statistics, are not terribly reliable. In order for a crime to become a statistic, a victim must report it (for a variety of reasons, many do not) and police must record it (with minor disorder incidents they might not). Unreported crimes—the so-called dark figure—are a major problem with crime statistics. That does not mean you should ignore official crime statistics, it just means you must use other methods such as interviews, surveys, site visits, and safety audits to back up your evaluation. We present the CPTED Risk Assessment Guide here as a way to determine which method best applies.

It is also useful to remember that, if a crime prevention program is successfully implemented and gets full participation from residents, employees, and building users, reported criminal incidents could increase. The increased calls for service can look like a crime wave, but in reality it is only the closing of a gap between unreported crimes and actual levels of crime. Once the level of reporting becomes a more accurate reflection of what is happening, then CPTED strategies can be more accurately targeted.

The CPTED Risk Assessment Guide helps practitioners and designers determine the type of data and research they will require on each project. The guide is classified into six Risk Assessment Categories:

Category 1: Small Scale before construction
Category 2: Small Scale on existing developments
Category 3: Medium Scale before construction
Category 4: Medium Scale on existing developments
Category 5: Large Scale before construction
Category 6: Large Scale on existing developments

In describing how to use this guide, Gamman and Pascoe note that because "context is key; methods can be picked and mixed for each individual location. Evaluation afterwards is also necessary to model building and judging success." (2004, p. 44).

Each category contains a series of suggested research steps and data that are suggested for that level of development. The data and research allow the CPTED practitioner not only to determine which CPTED strategy best applies but also to revisit the project afterwards to evaluate results. That is how to measure success.

CATEGORY 1 AND 2 METHODS

CPTED practitioners, designers, and architects are often called upon to assess the potential impact of crime on a relatively small-scale project. New walkways, redesigned building foyers, and ATM machine placements are a few examples.

This level of CPTED is typically fairly straightforward; however, there is often a tendency for the CPTED practitioner to walk onto the site and begin making recommendations without conducting any analysis whatsoever. Many practitioners bring a simple CPTED checklist that they fill out on site. That is insufficient. That approach cannot possibly capture the information needed for formulate sensible CPTED recommendations. At a minimum, there is a series of analytical steps and data that must precede any recommendations.

Category 1 and 2 methods include:

1. Plan Review: Review proposed design plans or the concept drawings if the project is in conceptual stages, such as landscaping plans.
2. Site Visits: Conduct site visits (both daytime and nighttime) to examine the area for lighting patterns, mobility patterns of site users, entrapment areas, adjacent land uses that might cause conflicts, territoriality, access control, and natural surveillance.
3. Demographics: Collect local demographic data to identify population characteristics that impact crime. Data should be gathered on the gender, socioeconomic status, age, population density, ethnicity, mobility, and other relevant information on the potential users, victims, and predators of an environment.
4. Crime Stats: Examine the existing crime data to look at the types of crime (property crime, crimes to person, drug related) and sort by date, location, and time.
5. Site Interviews: Interview local residents and employees to determine the travel routines, how the site is typically used, and whether the design fits the actual designated use. Interview the designers and property owners to determine the intended use, and future plans, for the site.

CATEGORY 3 AND 4

At the Category 3 and 4 levels, the time and resources spent on analysis should increase. That is because the size and scale of the project is larger. Projects at this level include a townhouse complex, a new urban park, or a large parking lot.

The analytical sophistication also increases in this category. This can be achieved by enlisting the support of police crime analysts, local university or college researchers, or professional consultants. There are now semiprofessional, nonprofit associations of crime analysts who provide advice, and skills that a qualified crime analyst brings to the table, for example the International Association of Crime Analysts.

One useful method for looking at the geography of crime is GIS (geographic information system) mapping. Several software companies make GIS mapping software that can plot crime spots. Part of the crime analysis looks at the site during many different times and conditions. The site analysis will evaluate and track activity pathways and nodes of activities (legitimate and illegitimate).

The site analysis will also look at maintenance features, lighting, upkeep, graffiti patterns, and levels of decay or renovation. Use analysis looks at what activities create, promote, or allow crime to take place. Data would be gathered on the number of available housing units, liquor stores, schools, abandoned storefronts, code violations, fast food outlets, strip shopping centers, auto repair shops, adult entertainment stores, parks, bus stations, and so on (Rondeau, 2005). This is a fairly basic level of crime mapping, and it should accompany Category 3 and 4 analyses.

Another data collection method in these categories is taking pictures or video, and keeping good logs of the data over time. If the facility is going on undeveloped land, then the process of visioning is needed to imagine what can and will be the possible futures in one year, five years, or twenty years from now.

Category 3 and 4 methods include:

1. Surveys: Mail-out questionnaires, including victimization surveys and perception data about the community.
2. GIS: GIS crime mapping and pattern analysis, such as examining crime hot spot trends.
3. Time Series: Crime trends over various timeframes and historical patterns.
4. Social Analysis: Demographic trends and social patterns, such as speaking to difficult-to-reach groups like the homeless. Marketing studies also help analyze shopping patterns in malls and the potential targets that may be on site.

CATEGORY 5 AND 6

The most advanced level of analysis is applied to large-scale developments, or to very high-risk developments. Projects included at this level include the construction of new towns, rebuilding downtown areas, large infill housing redevelopments, and development of new suburbs. They may also include highly vulnerable developments, such as new buildings in a skid row area or in an area with open air, illegal drug markets.

Data collection and analytical techniques in these categories build upon those of previous categories, but some are new. For example, the basic crime mapping conducted for early analysis of medium scale development analyze where there are any hotspots or geographic concentrations of a high level of crime. At this more advanced level, sophisticated GIS mapping analysis allows more in depth analysis of the nuances of crime patterns. Density mapping may be needed to address the problem of stacked overlaid points and crowding, and provide smooth and regular transitions over a study area (Iseki, 2006). Issues of crime displacement can be observed and addressed since crime is not a constant but ever-evolving.

In addition, advanced analytical methods capitalize on collaborative research and planning. Planning meetings, design charrettes, and safety audits are also part of the analyst's toolbox.

Category 5 and 6 methods include:

1. Co-planning meetings: Numerous stakeholders, with the various data from the analysis steps, working alongside designers to interpret the data and co-design the site plan.
2. Search conferences: Community planning and visioning workshops facilitated with small groups over a few days. Facilitators help local residents, property owners, city council members, police, CPTED specialists, and designers to create a vision, and a set of design guidelines, for new developments.
3. Safety audits: Property owners, residents, local police, and CPTED practitioners conduct nighttime audits and collect perception data about problems and solutions at a specific site, including fear of crime areas. The safety audit is the most effective method to collect fear of crime information and it may be done for categories 1 through 4 if time permits.

4. Crime forecasts: Crime data should be gathered for time series analysis. This includes at least three years prior to the existing start of the analysis in order to see if the trends are changing in the present. Future projections can be made with different statistical models.
5. Design charrettes: In a design charrette architects, property owners, CPTED practitioners, and other key stakeholders conduct a desktop exercise together on a site plan and brainstorm CPTED design ideas with the actual drawings.

This CPTED Risk Assessment Guide provides a comprehensive CPTED process for any given site. It also provides the baseline data that will allow measurements afterward to determine the effectiveness of CPTED strategies. It will help determine whether crime has been displaced, or whether crime has increased, or still persists. Table 29.1 shows various research tasks that correspond with different types of CPTED projects.

Regardless of the category, crime analysis and evaluation give property owners, community leaders, and corporate bosses the data to justify funding security staffing, equipment, and design

TABLE 29.1
CPTED Risk Assessment Guide

	Category 1	Category 2	Category 3	Category 4	Category 5	Category 6
Plan Review: Concept drawings, site plans, architectural renderings, territoriality, access control, surveillance, space hierarchy, boundary definition, movement predictors, entrapment areas, lighting, landscaping						
Site Visit: Daytime, nighttime, photo surveys, territoriality, access control, surveillance, maintenance, crime generators, space hierarchy, boundary definition, movement predictors, entrapment areas, lighting, landscaping						
Demographics: Density, age, mobility, movement patterns, ethnicity						
Crime Stats: Property/personal crime, drug crime, rates increasing/decreasing?						
Site Interviews/Data: Travel routes, public transit routes, perceptions/experiences of crime, use of space in the project area, property owners and designers' perceptions, designated use and design fit						
Surveys: Mail-out, telephone questionnaires, victimization surveys, perception data						
GIS: Crime mapping and pattern analysis, hot spot trends, density analysis, traffic counts and patterns						
Time Series: Crime trends over time, historical patterns						
Social Analysis: Housing tenure, speaking to difficult to reach groups, marketing studies, potential targets on site, ethnicity, gang issues, focus groups						

TABLE 29.1 (CONTINUED)
CPTED Risk Assessment Guide

	Category 1	Category 2	Category 3	Category 4	Category 5	Category 6
Co-Planning: Meetings with stakeholders to analyze data, codesigning site plan, advisory design panels, crime commissions, facilitated community groups						
Search Conference: Facilitated visioning workshops searching for "ideal" plans, multiple stakeholders						
Safety Audits: Multiple stakeholders conduct night-time audit to collect perception and fear data and suggested solutions to perceived problems						
Crime Forecasts: Time-series analysis, trend projection of crime patterns, computer simulations						
Design Charrettes: Multiple stakeholders collaborate on tabletop design exercise with site drawings						

improvements. The ability to process and analyze the crime data can contribute substantially to visualizing and understanding the depth and frequency of crime and terror as a risk or threat factor in making design and operational decisions.

SUMMARY

CEOs want to show a return on investment and unless the security director, or for that matter the Director of Homeland Security, can show effectiveness, funding and support will diminish or cease. Return on investment can be showing a loss in pilferage in a department store, increase in SAT scores in a high school, increased attendance at recreational events, or fewer car break ins in the parking garage. Measuring practical CPTED success, and evaluating strategies during project development, is no different. Measuring the success of CPTED is the way of the future and the CPTED Risk Assessment process is the best way to move forward.

REFERENCES

Atlas, R. I. (2002) The sustainability of CPTED. *The CPTED Journal,* 1(1), 3–16.
Cozens, P., G. Saville and D. Hillier (2005) Crime prevention through environmental design: A review and modern bibliography. *Property Management,* 23(5), 328–356.
Cozens, P., T. Pascoe, and D. Hillier (2004) The policy and practice of secured by design (SBD). *Crime Prevention and Community Safety: An International Journal,* 6(1), 13–29.
Cozens, P., D. Hillier, and G. Prescott (2003) Safety is in the upkeep. *Regeneration and Renewal,* 7. 4.
Cozens, P., D. Adamson, and D. Hillier (2003) Community CPTED: A case study of a housing estate in South Wales (UK). *The CPTED Journal,* 2(1), 2–15.
Cozens, P. (2002) Sustainable urban development and crime prevention through environmental design for the British City: Towards an effective urban environmentalism for the 21st century cities. *The International Journal of Urban Policy and Planning,* 19(2), 219–237.
Gamman, L. and T. Pascoe (2004) Seeing is believing: Notes toward a visual methodology and manifesto for crime prevention through environmental design. *Crime Prevention and Community Safety: An International Journal,* 6(4), 9–18.

Gamman, L., A. Thorpe, and M. Willcocks (2004) Bike off! Tracking the design terrains of cycle parking: reviewing use, misuse and abuse. *Crime Prevention and Community Safety: An International Journal,* 6(4), 19–36.

Gamman, L. and T. Pascoe (2004) Design out crime? Using practice-based models of the design process. *Crime Prevention and Community Safety: An International Journal,* 6(4), 37–56.

Hillier, B. (1973) In defence of space. *RIBA Journal,* 11, 539–544.

Hillier, B. and S. Shu (2000a) Crime and urban layout: the need for evidence. In S. Ballintyne, K. Pease, and V. McLaren (Eds.), *Secure Foundations: Key Issues in Crime Prevention, Crime Reduction and Community Safety.* London: Institute of Public Policy Research.

Hillier, B. and S. Shu (2000b) Do burglars understand defensible space? *Space Syntax.* Available at: http://www.bartlett.ucl.ac.uk/spacesyntax/housing/BillCrimePaper/BillCrimePaper.html

Iseki, H. (2006) Examining the relationship between built environments and crime incidents using GIS. *The CPTED Journal,* 2(1), 17–24.

Saville, G. and G. Cleveland (2006) CPTED and the social city: The future of capacity building. *The CPTED Journal,* 2(1), 43–51.

Saville, G. and G. Cleveland (2003) An introduction to 2nd generation CPTED—Part 1. *CPTED Perspective,* 6(1), 7–8.

Saville, G. and T. Clear (2000) Community renaissance with community justice. *The Neighborworks Journal,* 18(2), 19–24.

Schneider, T., H. Walker, and J. Sprague (2000) *Safe School Design.* Eugene, OR: ERIC Clearinghouse on Educational Management, University of Oregon.

Schneider, R. H., and T. Kitchen (2002) *Planning for Crime Prevention: A Transatlantic Perspective.* London: Routledge.

30 Conducting a CPTED Survey

Randy Atlas

Without fail, the first step in improving security on a property is conducting a security survey. The security survey includes the elements described in earlier chapters: risk, threat, and vulnerability analysis. There are more versions of security surveys and checklists than there are alligators in the Everglades. The challenge is to determine which methodology to use. Several accepted methodologies for risk analysis and vulnerability assessments exist. The Sandia Labs Risk Assessment Methodology (RAM) is available for several different types of environments: water and dams, infrastructure, cities, and more. The Homeland Security Critical Assessment methodology of HLS-Cam is another. The GSA security methodology has been available for federal buildings. The Department of Defense has their survey form and methodology, and the recent FEMA 426 publication, *Mitigating the Impact on Terrorism,* has survey forms. Our book proposes the ATRIM risk model for assessments. Companies now sell security survey software for use on laptops and palm pilots. But the questions remain as to how user-friendly they are, and will you really use the survey?

I conduct CPTED surveys on many buildings and facilities, and sometimes use a checklist. But no matter how user-friendly the checklist, it always seems cumbersome and does not reflect the subtleties of the existing conditions. Additionally, writing legible, worthwhile comments in little square boxes is next to impossible. The survey checklist and prepackaged software does not capture the real essence of the conditions being surveyed.

So how does a layperson or an experienced practitioner survey a property and organize his thoughts to be logical, thorough, and coherent? This is where the art of CPTED meets the science. The CPTED ***data assessment process*** is what typical CPTED survey uses as a methodology. Let's review what those basic steps are:

Crime Analysis
Gathering Demographic Data
Gathering Land Use Information
Conducting Site Inspections
Observing and Noting User Behavior Patterns
Organizing the Security Report or Audit

The crime analysis is one of the first background steps taken to research the history of the property. One of the key elements in establishing security negligence is the history of prior crime on and around the property. This factor is known as **foreseeability**. Should the commission of prior crime on and around the property give actual and constructive notice to the owners, property mangers, building users, and visitors? The crime analysis is the data gathering process of several years' worth of calls to law enforcement and analyzing the types of local threats. However, this kind of analysis is slow and expensive. Many police departments have computer-generated crime mapping using GIS or Geographical Information Systems. Ideally, the local law enforcement agency will produce a crime analysis for the area and may even be able to give a map of the area indicating the types of crime. Another group that does crime analysis professionally is the CAP Risk Index. They research the location and the surrounding area to within a one-mile up to a five-mile radius, and then they analyze the UCR part I and II crime, and compare the data to the local, state, and national levels of

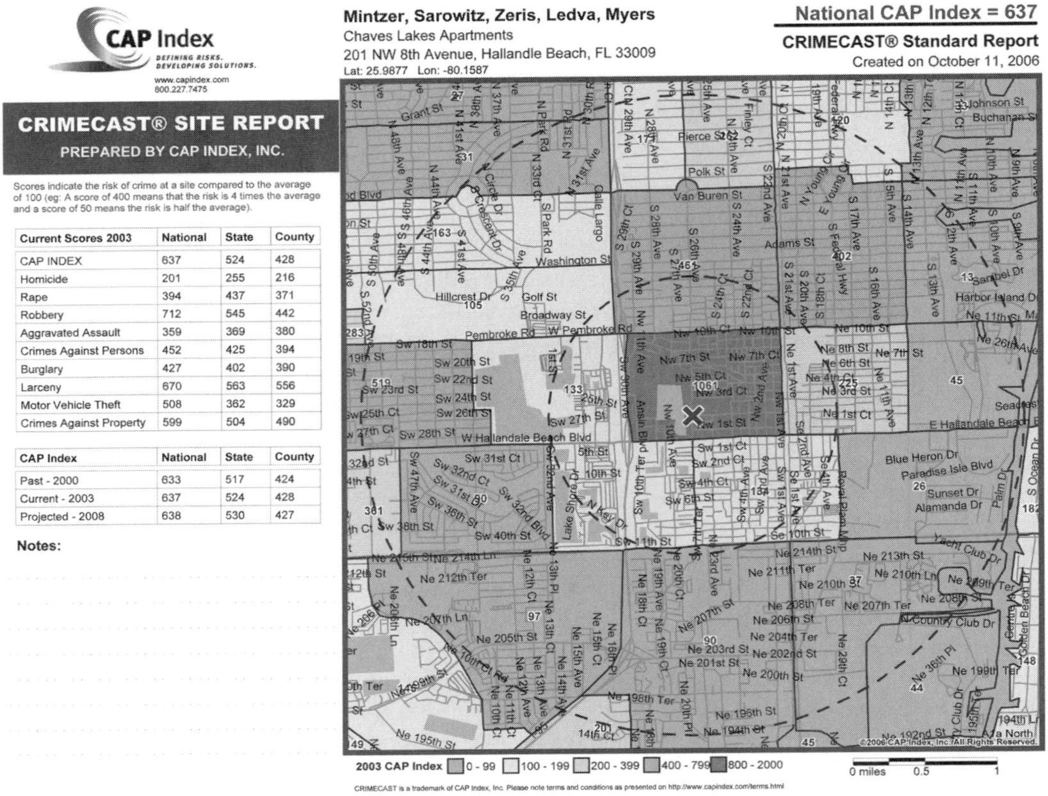

CAP Index
DEFINING RISKS. DEVELOPING SOLUTIONS.
www.capindex.com
800.227.7475

CRIMECAST® SITE REPORT
PREPARED BY CAP INDEX, INC.

Scores indicate the risk of crime at a site compared to the average of 100 (eg: A score of 400 means that the risk is 4 times the average and a score of 50 means the risk is half the average).

Current Scores 2003	National	State	County
CAP INDEX	637	524	428
Homicide	201	255	216
Rape	394	437	371
Robbery	712	545	442
Aggravated Assault	359	369	380
Crimes Against Persons	452	425	394
Burglary	427	402	390
Larceny	670	563	556
Motor Vehicle Theft	508	362	329
Crimes Against Property	599	504	490

CAP Index	National	State	County
Past - 2000	633	517	424
Current - 2003	637	524	428
Projected - 2008	638	530	427

Notes:

Mintzer, Sarowitz, Zeris, Ledva, Myers
Chaves Lakes Apartments
201 NW 8th Avenue, Hallandle Beach, FL 33009
Lat: 25.9877 Lon: -80.1587

National CAP Index = 637
CRIMECAST® Standard Report
Created on October 11, 2006

2003 CAP Index 0 - 99 100 - 199 200 - 399 400 - 799 800 - 2000
0 miles 0.5 1
©2006 CAP Index, Inc. All Rights Reserved.
CRIMECAST is a trademark of CAP Index, Inc. Please note terms and conditions as presented on http://www.capindex.com/terms.html

FIGURE 30.1 Example of CAP risk analysis. (Image reprinted courtesy of CAP Index, Inc. (www.capindex.com).)

same type of crime. CAP Index then color codes the area to be less than or greater than the local or state averages (see Figure 30.1).

The end result is a map of the area that tells the survey professional and the client if they are in a high crime area or a low crime area, or if the area falls within an average range. The crime analysis should be evaluated with regards to the type of crime, and whether it is crime committed against persons or property. The location and time of day are most critical in determining patterns or trends of crime as it relates to other factors in the analysis process. An example of this is if a downward trend could be related to a reduced population of young people, or work layoffs, or men in service near an army base.

In developing the level of risk from acts of terror or workplace violence, the criterion is different and evaluated on a case-by-case basis. If there is a history of workplace violence, or in an area that that has experienced acts of terror, or the facility is a landmark or identified target, then the survey will need to consider terrorism as a survey criteria.

Beyond the challenge of gathering crime data, collecting the demographic data of the facility or area and user group is next in importance (see Figure 30.2). What is the available information on housing patterns, and the average price for rental or owned home; that is, is housing affordable? Are there many homeless people? What are the income levels of the area, city, and facility users? Who is the target audience? It makes little difference if you are surveying a hospital, school, office building, bar, or Wal-Mart Super Center. Who are the expected and actual clients or users? Are they seniors, youth, adults, or families? The demographic data is gathered from the Census Bureau reports, and other local studies that might be available from the Chamber of Commerce, or regional planning

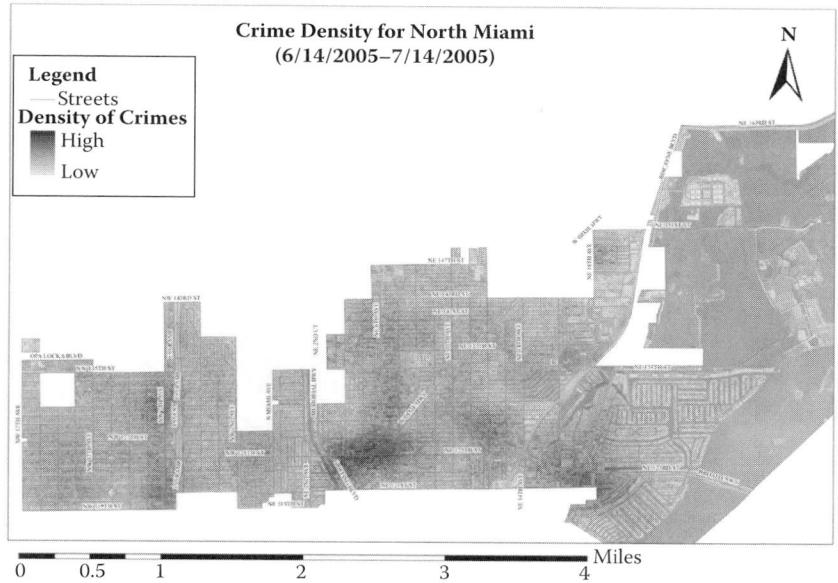

FIGURE 30.2 Crime density GIS map city of North Miami. (Image reprinted with thanks and courtesy of the City of North Miami.)

councils. Data may be available from newspaper reports, or from real estate studies. The information is usually available at the library or the Internet (see Figure 30.3).

Closely related to demographic data is Land Use information. The land use information tells the story of the land or building zoning purposes (see Figure 30.4).

Land use data may include zoning code maps, building codes or ordinances, regional master plans, highest and best use real estate reports, traffic studies, transportation reports, and other types of master planning or urban studies reports. Most of the private and public reports will be available under the government in the Sunshine Laws around the United States. Zoning maps are available at most city and county government planning departments. The different land uses are highlighted in different colors to differentiate residential low density from high density, commercial, industrial, parks, and natural boundaries (see Figure 30.5).

After gathering the background data on crime, land use (see Figure 30.6), and demographics, then the observation of the site become paramount. If the CPTED survey is on an existing site, then the approach is to do a front and back door site visit. The back door visit is to visit the site unannounced and at normal, as well as after-hours operations. Putting on some casual clothes and just blending in with the local environment is the approach. If it is safe, then talk to the people in the area. If not, then just observe and make notes of lighting conditions, movement patterns of vehicles and pedestrians, legitimate versus illegitimate users and behavior. Get a feel for what really happens on the site or property.

Then conduct a front door site visit. Meet the property manager, owners, clients, staff, and building users. Observe how the people use the property differently during the day or while being supervised. For example, observing a school in the late afternoon or on a weekend is going to be dramatically different than on a Monday morning at 9 a.m. Observing a loading dock in the early hours at an office building, hospital, or industrial/commercial warehouse will be different than during normal working hours or on weekends. How are trucks coming and going? How close is the trash dumpster to the loading docks and are they locked or sealed?

If the CPTED survey is for a property yet to be built or developed, it requires the surveyor to have some skills in "visioning." Do you have the ability to project what that property will be like

City of North Miami Zoning MAP

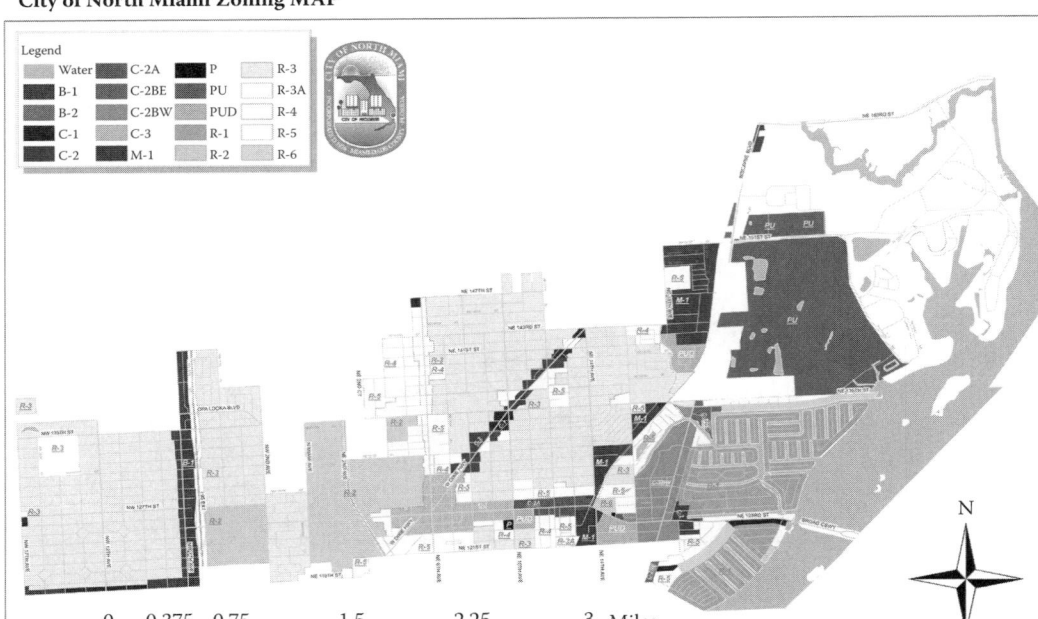

FIGURE 30.3 An example of a zoning map, distinguishing the commercial from the residential areas. (Image reprinted with thanks and courtesy of the City of North Miami.)

when constructed, and how people will be using the site? Can you visualize how design features might help or hinder safety and security? If, for example, Wal-Mart is building a new Super Center across from a low-income housing area, because that may be their target audience, the crime data will show nothing at that address because the location at present is an empty field. But, with a new bustling shopping center within walking distance of a high-crime area, can it be anticipated that

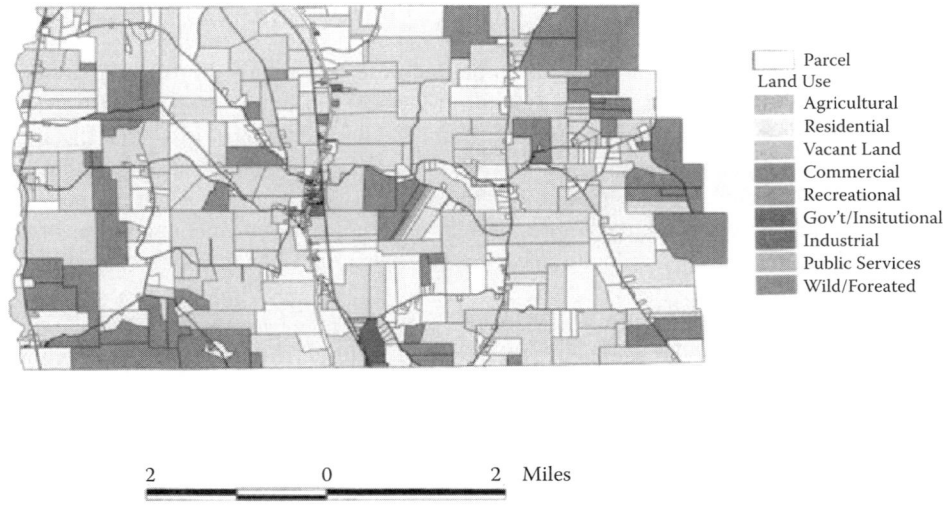

FIGURE 30.4 Zoning land use map example.

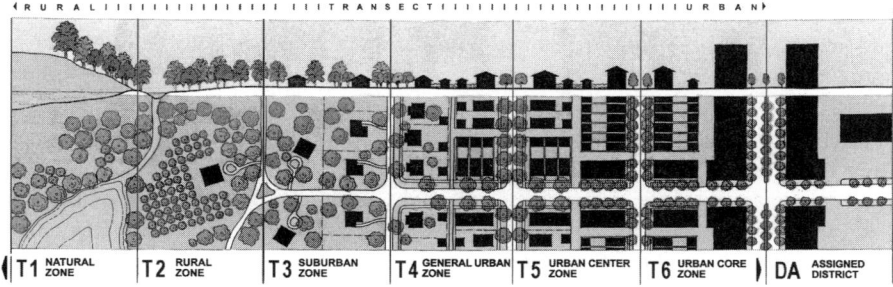

FIGURE 30.5 Zoning boundaries for a Miami master plan. (Image ©2007 Duany Plater-Zyberk & Co. Image reprinted courtesy of Miami 21 and Duany Plater-Zyberk & Co.)

crime in the parking lot will be likely, and that the dumpster and loading dock areas will be easy targets? Therefore, a visioning of what could be is required to design the store with perimeter fencing or boundary definition, site lighting, security patrols, signage, careful window placement, careful landscaping and planting decisions, and so on.

Making a record of your observations is critical. In addition to just observing the site and neighborhood, it may be necessary to conduct user surveys and interview persons living, working, and playing in the area. The surveyor needs to ask questions and understand how legitimate and illegitimate users use the space and the kinds of activities in which they are engaging. The interviews and surveys should ask about the user's perception of crime and terror versus the actuality or statistics in the area. The questions should ask about transportation issues, public and private. Questions should

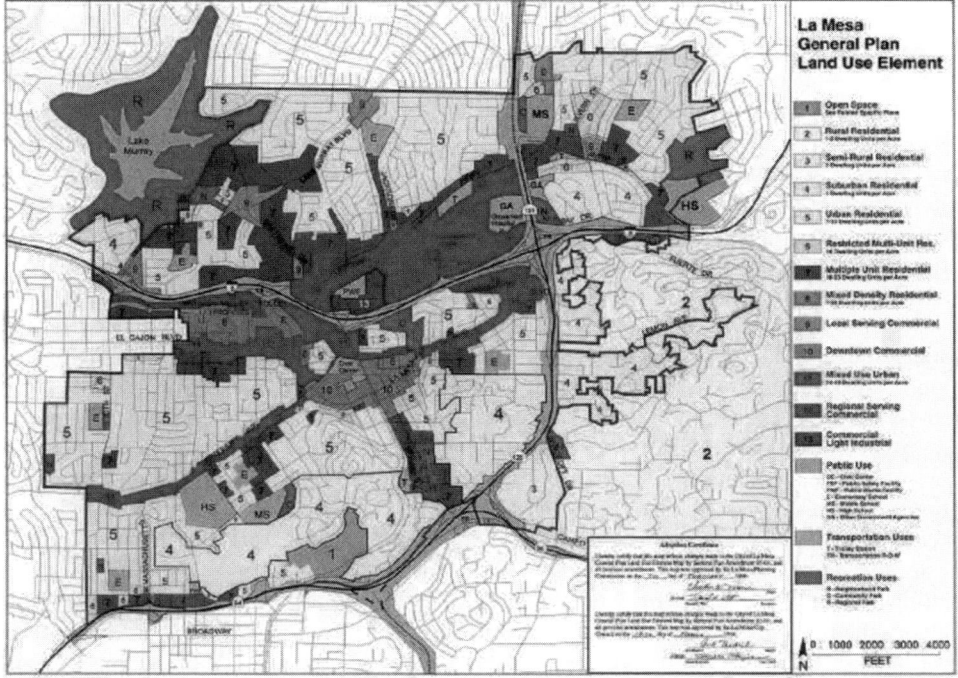

FIGURE 30.6 An example of a land use map. (Image reprinted with thanks and courtesy of the City of La Mesa, Arizona.)

be asked about garbage pickup and access to fire department, law enforcement, and private security. From the data, observations, and interviews, the surveyor can start to get a "feel" of how things can and should operate. The surveyor will need to know if there are any standards of care applicable to that particular environment under study.

When it is time to put the report together, the surveyor should organize the report by first presenting a lasered and concise executive summary. The bulk of the report should be the background information and summary of what lead to the need of this report. The next section should be the background information that is relevant for the study. The findings and observations should follow and be presented in a concise and lasered way. Any complete documentation and survey findings, survey instruments, and reference documents should be included as appendices. Having now presented your observations, or envisioning of what is or what could be, then it is time to present recommendations. Recommendations should be presented on a rank-ordering based on importance, priority, or threat/risk level. Each recommendation should have some discussion of time and money constraints as it applies to the practicality of implementation.

The different methodologies have slightly different approaches as to which observations should be done first, and the sequencing of the survey. Generally, the site information should be gathered that includes boundaries, landmarks, infrastructure commodities, and site and facility diagrams. As classic CPTED teaches, use the layers of the onion approach: we start with the site, then go to the building perimeter, then the interior space, and finally with policy and procedures.

When surveying the outer perimeter of an existing property or facility, be sure to note the adjoining streets, buildings, and landmarks. What are the standoff distances between the buildings, cars and surrounding streets? What are the circulation patterns of cars, people, and the location of parking facilities? Where are there dumpsters or outbuildings? What are the types, locations, and effectiveness of freestanding exterior lighting? What are the types and placement of CCTV cameras? Do the landscaping and planting conceal potential criminal activity, terrorist activity, or contraband (bombs)? Is the signage and wayfinding clear? Are the natural, organizational, and mechanical surveillance systems working well? Are the natural, organizational, and mechanical access controls working well? Are the natural, organizational, and mechanical territorialities working well?

When surveying the building exterior of an existing property, it is best to start at the basement or sublevel spaces and work your way up to the roof. Is there access to the building by adjoining buildings, rooftops, walkways, manholes, or trees? Where are the doors and windows, and are they secured? Are there hiding spots? Where are the utility connections into the property and building for water, sewage, electricity, and gas? Where are the emergency generator and backup systems? Where are the loading and shipping areas and docks? Where and what kind of exterior wall lighting is available? Where are the ventilation intake vents? Is the roof secured? Are the mechanical rooms secured? Where do the public and employees enter and leave?

When surveying the building interior, look at floor plans to understand the security layering of public versus private spaces. Who are the different users or tenants in the building? Are there user conflicts? What and where are spaces off-limits to the public or even staff? How are doors secured—with access controls or keying? Are there adequate and maintained fire safety detection and suppression systems? Are there fire hydrant connections? Where are the mechanical closets and are they secured and accountable for who enters them? Is there a reception area, capable guardian, door guard, or access control of how and who gets into the building? Where and what kind of CCTV cameras and monitoring are being used? Are there interior space protection alarms, and where? Where are the areas of greatest use and activity? Are there user conflicts? What kind of signage and wayfinding are being used? Where is mail handled? Are there separate ventilation systems and blow out walls in the mail sorting area? Are the mechanical HVAC rooms secured? Are elevators under observation and service areas secured? What are the ceiling materials and are they secure? Are the walls between sensitive areas secured all the way to the roof? Are the fire exits and routes clear and working? Are stairwells locked or open and observable? Are there intercoms and CCTV at critical areas for crowd control and accountability?

Many buildings have secure or private data that must be protected. Schools, hospitals, office buildings, and commercial plants often have computer rooms. When surveying the security for computer rooms, the key elements for security and crime prevention goes back to the 3D's: definition, designation, and design. What is the space defined to do and used for? Who is designated to use the space with proper authorization? How is the space designed to support screening, access control, surveillance, and protection of the equipment? The surveyor will need to understand the type and level of computer technology utilized in the facility, and if there are remote facilities that have external connectivity. Ventilation systems, power backup systems, and fire-extinguishing systems are also critical design and operational considerations that impact security. Securing the data is very important, and access to desktop machines and computer rooms are a major vulnerability in any facility. Considerations should undertaken to protect the hardware or machines on worker desks from theft by anchoring devices, but the software is just as critical, suggesting that passwords and logins should be protected and updated regularly.

An important security consideration of today's buildings is whether there are hazardous materials stored on site that could be used to contaminate the building or area and whether it may be an asset worthy of taking to be used by a terrorist as a weapon elsewhere. Not every building has chemical, biological, or radiological materials that could be hazardous, but many buildings do have substances that could be used by persons with bad intentions for harm's sake. While nuclear power plants have the strictest security design available, there are other facilities that have nuclear waste that are not so secure. Almost every hospital has radioactive waste from the X-ray and screening machinery that is stored in closets on site. Many large universities have power plants and some are nuclear, like the University of Michigan in Ann Arbor, which is next to the Detroit Metro airport and near Detroit. Can you imagine the consequences of a mishap or attack on the generator at the university and its impact the entire Detroit metropolitan areas?

The author has observed that these sites do not have the same level of security as a nuclear power plant. Many industrial plants have fire-extinguishing systems using special argon or gases that are hazardous to humans, but spare the computer rooms of damaging water. Battery storage areas have large quantities of acids. Hospitals have biological contaminants. A Sony manufacturing plant uses many flammable and toxic chemicals to make the TV and plasma screens that we have in our homes and businesses. There are many more examples of common things that can are stored or used in today's business environment. The CPTED surveyor needs to know if there are chemical, biological, or nuclear hazardous substances on the site or in the building, the description of them, the quantity on hand, the storage location, and the security measures taken to protect those assets (see Figure 30.7).

The existing security measures used on a facility or a building are infinite in variety, from minimal (door locks and windows) to maximum security as in a prison or military facility. Whatever building type it might be, the surveyor will need to document the physical security and the systems security. The physical security typically ranges from fences, gates, doors, windows, locks, and hardware. Security systems can be access control systems, surveillance systems, space protection, motion sensors, biometrics, audio and intercom systems, panic alarms, silent alarms, monitoring and recording, central station alarm control and monitoring, and so on.

The surveyor should always question what the purpose or function is of a piece of equipment,

FIGURE 30.7 Liquid nitrogen container next to hospital building.

and what is it about the architecture or circulation pattern that would require a physical or psychological barrier, or actual security equipment. The utilization of security manpower is also part of your security systems assessment. Many facilities have an unreal expectation of what one person can do sitting in a dark control room watching half a dozen monitors with dozens of cameras and hundreds or thousands of access control points. The CPTED surveyor must analyze the effectiveness and highest and best use on the utilization of capable guardians or security people resources.

Any facility can throw money shamelessly at the problems of crime and terror and hope that they go away. The U.S. Department of Homeland Security is a good example of that. Millions of dollars have been given to cities, states, ports, and water treatment facilities that have been documented as having been used on CCTV, radio systems, and other technologies without even requiring a complete independent need (threat, risk, vulnerability) assessment. Regardless of how much technology or manpower is available, if the operational policies and procedures are not thought out and followed, the rest of the security is for naught. Therefore, the CPTED surveyor needs to determine if the facility has a security plan in place. Are employees and visitors required to wear badges or identification? Does upper management wear badges? Are there consequences for not wearing them? Who controls the issuance of the badges and are the badges part of an integrated smart card system that allows the badges to be used for access control as well? How are individuals deactivated from the system? How are visitors and public screened and badged for your property? How are keys issued, controlled, and duplicated? What are the procedures in place for evacuation, bomb threats, or hostage situations (workplace violence)? What are the procedures for screening vendors and contractors? What are the building opening and closing procedures? What are the procedures for mail handling, contaminants and letter bombs, and cyberattacks?

SUMMARY

There are some subtle and some obvious differences between the CPTED practitioner and security systems designer. A good example would be how to go about securing the doors and hallways in a generic high school. Typically, my experience has been that the security consultant will quickly and competently determine the best way to secure the door with cameras and locks, a guard, pressure mats, and biometrics. The CPTED practitioner asks the question: Why is the door there? What are you keeping out? What are you keeping in? Maybe the best security is not to have a door there at all. The doors in most school hallways are fire doors, not security barriers, and are held open by magnetic locks that are released in a fire alarm condition. Not having the doors closed adds to the needed natural surveillance of teachers being able to monitor the hallways. Having the doors closed and secured would not support the highest and best use of allowing undeterred and supervised student movement during school hours. The fire doors do not have to be closed except in an alarm condition. Therefore, the key to good security and CPTED surveying is remembering the affirmation: problem seeking before problem solving!

REFERENCES

Aherns, S. and Atlas, R.Y. (2006). CPTED Security Survey for the American Society of Industrial Security Standards Development Committee.

CAP Index CrimeCast Exton, PA. Available at: http://www.capindex.com/

FEMA 426, Risk Management Series (2003) *Reference Manual: Providing Protection to People and Buildings*. Washington, DC: Federal Emergency Management Agency.

ATRiM (use reference in bibliography)

HLSCAM Homeland Security Comprehensive Assessment Model, National Domestic Prepardness Coalition. Orlando, FL. http://www.ndpci.us/

Sandia National Laboratories Risk Assessment Methodology. Available at: http://www.sandia.gov/ram/

City of North Miami, FL. (2005) Zoning Map, Crime Density Map.

La Mesa, CA. (2001) General Use Land Map.

APPENDIX: SAMPLE SURVEY
CPTED Survey from ASIS Standards Development 2006

	Yes	No	Not Applicable	Comments
General and Site Questions				
What type of facility or property is it?	–	–	–	
Who needs to have access to the property?	–	–	–	
When should user groups have access to the property?	–	–	–	
What are the borders of the facility or property?	–	–	–	
Are there continuous fences or walls?	–	–	–	
Is there a sense of ownership? (No trespassing/private property warning) signs and property upkeep?	–	–	–	
Are there areas that could be described as areas without ownership or no mans land?	–	–	–	
Where are the paths for pedestrian and vehicular traffic?	–	–	–	
What type of site lighting is used and where is it located?	–	–	–	
What and where are there any natural barriers?	–	–	–	
What are the kinds, types, and placements of plantings and landscaping?	–	–	–	
Building Questions				
Are the materials to be utilized in the building of substantial construction to mitigate break-ins or an explosive device?	–	–	–	
What is the setback (distance from the façade of the building to the street)?	–	–	–	
Are all building entrances controlled?	–	–	–	
What is the primary entrance(s) to the building and where are they located?	–	–	–	
Are building windows and doors accessible or locked?	–	–	–	
Is there access to the roof or upper floors by trees, fences, adjoining buildings, etc?	–	–	–	
Are the mechanical spaces accessible?	–	–	–	
Are the loading docks accessible?	–	–	–	
How and where is trash and waste stored and disposed of?	–	–	–	
Is there natural surveillance from building to the perimeter and vice-versa?	–	–	–	
Interior Space Questions				
What are the expected and peak periods of vehicle or pedestrian traffic?	–	–	–	
Where are the public restrooms and lockers located?	–	–	–	
Are there security barriers between public and private spaces?	–	–	–	
Where are the capable guardians (security officers, receptionist, etc.)?	–	–	–	
Are the mechanical spaces locked and secured?	–	–	–	
Where are the valuable assets located?	–	–	–	
Is there any use of CCTV?	–	–	–	
Is there access control natural mechanical or organized?	–	–	–	

APPENDIX: SAMPLE SURVEY (CONTINUED)
CPTED Survey from ASIS Standards Development 2006

	Yes	No	Not Applicable	Comments
Is there interior space protection?	–	–	–	
Are there conflicts between the use of the building and its occupants? (i.e., a secure building that has public transportation (train station) beneath it.)	–	–	–	

Point Protection Questions

	Yes	No	Not Applicable	Comments
What is the asset being protected?	–	–	–	
Where is it located?	–	–	–	
Is it replaceable?	–	–	–	
How critical is its protection?	–	–	–	
Who has access to the asset?	–	–	–	
When is the asset accessible?	–	–	–	
Does the asset move or is it subject to restocking?	–	–	–	
Does the asset require constant monitoring or time specific monitoring?	–	–	–	
Is there a security system that is being used already?	–	–	–	
Is the security system sufficient?	–	–	–	
Is the asset more valuable to certain groups or people?	–	–	–	
Is the asset a person, product, or proprietary information?	–	–	–	

Designation

	Yes	No	Not Applicable	Comments
What is the designated purpose of this space?	–	–	–	
For what purpose was it originally intended?	–	–	–	
How well does the space support its current use or its intended use?	–	–	–	
Is there any conflict of uses or users? If so, how and where?	–	–	–	

Definition

	Yes	No	Not Applicable	Comments
How is the space defined (i.e., what are the borders of public and private space, are they clear)?	–	–	–	
Is the ownership of the space clear?	–	–	–	
Where are the borders of the space?	–	–	–	
Are there social or cultural definitions that affect how the space is being, or will be used (i.e., do all persons follow the rule that access control needs to be enforced in a high-security building, or does existing office culture override these principles)?	–	–	–	
Are the legal/administrative rules clearly established in the security policy and effectively enforced?	–	–	–	
Are signs present indicating the proper use of the space or defining limits of access?	–	–	–	
Are there any conflicts or confusion between purpose and definition of the space? (A business unit that is defined as high-security cannot operate with a customers service function, which is public.)	–	–	–	

Design

	Yes	No	Not Applicable	Comments
How well does the physical design support the intended function?	–	–	–	
How well does the physical design support the desired or accepted behaviors for the site?	–	–	–	

APPENDIX: SAMPLE SURVEY (CONTINUED)
CPTED Survey from ASIS Standards Development 2006

	Yes	No	Not Applicable	Comments
Does the physical design conflict with or impede the productive use of the space or proper functioning of the intended human activity?	_	_	_	
Is there any confusion or conflict in which physical design is intended to control or modify behaviors (i.e., is it not clear where the main entrance of the building is? As a result do people enter in the building through non-approved entrances)?	_	_	_	

Deter

	Yes	No	Not Applicable	Comments
Does the presence of security personnel deter illegitimate activity and promote intended behavior?	_	_	_	
Does the physical design and layout permit good surveillance and control of access to and from the property?	_	_	_	
Do legitimate activities deter or discourage illegal or unintended activities?	_	_	_	

Detect

	Yes	No	Not Applicable	Comments
Is there the ability to control entry onto the property or building?	_	_	_	
Is there an assessment process of when an intrusion is legitimate or illegitimate?	_	_	_	
Is the detection of an intrusion accomplished by physical design, technology, or personnel systems?	_	_	_	
Is the intrusion communicated to some person or agency responsible for responding?	_	_	_	

Delay

	Yes	No	Not Applicable	Comments
Are there passive barriers (i.e., small hedges, which define expected path of pedestrian traffic)?	_	_	_	
Are there active barriers (i.e., vehicle arresting devices or doors that delay entry)?	_	_	_	
Are there security personnel or designated responders?	_	_	_	
How much delay time is needed in delay for the personnel to detect and respond?	_	_	_	

Respond

	Yes	No	Not Applicable	Comments
What are the roles and the post orders of the responding security personnel?	_	_	_	
What equipment is needed to support a complete response?	_	_	_	
What are the tactics used to respond quickly and clearly?	_	_	_	
What training is provided and is it commensurate with the threat?	_	_	_	

Report

	Yes	No	Not Applicable	Comments
What communications are used to call for further assistance?	_	_	_	
What is the written protocol for incident reports?	_	_	_	
Is the information clear and detailed?	_	_	_	
How is the documentation organized and stored?	_	_	_	

Discriminate

	Yes	No	Not Applicable	Comments
Is there training for staff to recognize legitimate threats?	_	_	_	

APPENDIX: SAMPLE SURVEY (CONTINUED)
CPTED Survey from ASIS Standards Development 2006

	Yes	No	Not Applicable	Comments
Is the technology sufficiently sensitive to distinguish false from real threats?	_	_	_	
Neutralize				
Has the threat been sufficiently deterred?	_	_	_	
Has the detection system been reset and tested to prevent complacency or false alarms?	_	_	_	

Source: Used with permission from American Society of Industrial Security, Standards Development Committee, June 2006.

31 Implementing CPTED

Randy Atlas and Gregory Saville

The big question is, why hasn't security been designed into our infrastructure and building environment to any significant degree? One possible answer is quite simple: no one had to. It is not possible to design and construct a building without fire prevention features, but most buildings are designed without crime prevention and security features. Building codes and standards require that all structures comply with fire and life safety codes. Until 9/11, security was typically considered only in high-risk buildings like embassies, banks, nuclear power plants, and 7-11s! Now that the soft underbelly of our infrastructure and buildings has been exposed, sometimes in a tragic way, the consciousness of security is permeating the design community. Yet some communities have been considering security and crime prevention for several years and seeing positive changes in the built environment by increased use and lower crime. What is the status today of security being integrated into architecture and infrastructure? There are some international jurisdictions that have had significant success with CPTED implementation, such as New South Wales in Australia, the Design Out Crime program in the United Kingdom, and the Safe Label program in The Netherlands. Unfortunately, the situation in North America has not progressed that far in the past few decades.

ATTEMPTS TO REGULATE

THE CANADIAN CONNECTION

In the late 1990s, the Canadian government's Canada Mortgage and Housing Corporation sponsored research into the feasibility of implementing national CPTED standards with compliance regulations and measurement strategies (Saville and Wright, 1998). The intent was to review a successful Dutch CPTED program called "Safe Labeling" and determine how to implement such a system in Canada. Although the program appeared initially feasible, there were complaints from some sectors of the building industry about increased costs. Lacking political leadership, no national program emerged.

Today, only a small number of individual municipalities across Canada have taken progressive steps to implement some form of CPTED compliance, such as Vancouver and Victoria in British Columbia, and the region of Peel in Ontario. Most have nonbinding CPTED guidelines in the form of brochures or committee meetings that they provide to developers and architects during the permit process. Unfortunately, when push comes to shove, there is no way to compel those recommendations upon the developer. City politicians, mindful of the property tax dollars that accompany new developments, have been hesitant to make binding laws that slow the process.

Calgary, Alberta, with a population of one million residents, has embarked on an ambitious plan to bring both First-Generation CPTED (physical opportunity reduction) and Second-Generation CPTED (crime motive reduction) into their citywide planning and development process. A large international conference was conducted in 2006 that brought international safety and CPTED experts from around the world to examine Calgary's major redevelopment plans (Lyons and Arber, 2006). The police department conducts basic First-Generation CPTED surveys. Most recently, CPTED specialists have begun to apply crime analysis and CPTED to a few local neighborhoods under development. They have begun by training local urban designers and city planning staff in

Second-Generation CPTED and Safe Growth planning techniques. Additionally, the University of Calgary's faculty of environmental design is teaching a new course, the first in the country, in more advanced Second-Generation CPTED to the next generation of designers.

Perhaps the shape of the future is in places like Saskatoon, a city of 250,000 in Saskatchewan. There a city safety and planning program is moving to become among the most advanced in the country by training the majority of planning and urban design staff in CPTED and Safe Growth planning techniques, collecting regular and extensive crime mapping and safety audit data on city neighborhoods, and reviewing new developments for CPTED compliance. Their approach is a combination of education and suggestion. It is not yet binding, but it is the closest Canada has come to regulation. Unfortunately, the majority of cities across Canada have done little or nothing to regulate or measure CPTED success.

THE AMERICAN SITUATION

The situation is virtually identical in the United States. Some states, such as Florida and Virginia, have brought a limited number of CPTED ideas into legislation, but only a small number of municipalities have followed suit. Here are a few:

- Since 1997, Tempe, Arizona, has used a CPTED ordinance to guide architects, planners, and developers to minimize the risks and opportunities of crime. The Tempe ordinance is considered the strictest of the CPTED codes, and has the Tempe police and urban planners conducting inspections, plan reviews, and enforcement. The Tempe CPTED ordinance addresses design elements of minimum lighting levels, landscaping elements, walls and gates, address specifications to ensure identification and location of buildings, directories for building complexes, and parking structures.
- In Sarasota, Florida, a CPTED resolution was adopted in 1992 that addressed issues of compatible and conflicting land use, along with minimum lighting recommendations, maintenance and upkeep of properties, maximum density and minimum yard requirements, signage requirements, parking security considerations, landscaping buffering and separation requirements, and CPTED plan review requirements. What made the Sarasota CPTED resolution special was the fact that the recommendations were not mandatory, but it was felt that the liability of having an official police and planner CPTED experts Stan Carter and Sherry Plaster-Carter review the architectural drawings pressured the developers to make changes where possible, and would absolutely consider those issues on the next project. The gentle coercion was an alternate way of making changes rather than through a mandate of ordinance or code.
- Broward County, Florida, passed a CPTED resolution in 1996 that requires a site plan review by two trained CPTED practitioners, including one from The Strategic Planning Department, a CPTED trained law enforcement officer. Their resolution called for firms applying for new county facilities should have a CPTED trained person on their staff to include CPTED as part of the design process and would be looked upon favorably in the selection process. While compliance with the staff comments was voluntary, the implied threat of premises liability litigation for being on notice and not taking recommended actions was a sufficient enough threat to result in most changes needed.

Other municipalities that have CPTED ordinances or resolutions include Tampa, Orlando, and St. Petersburg, Florida; Durham, North Carolina; Tucson, Arizona; Dallas, Texas; Irvine, California; Ann Arbor, Michigan; and several cities in Virginia. Stan and Sherry Carter were instrumental in implementing the CPTED resolution in Sarasota and identify four ways of implementing CPTED in the local planning process:

- First, CPTED should be included into the planning documents that regulate land.
- Second, trained CPTED staff should be included in reviewing project development plans incorporating CPTED principles and practices.
- Third, trained CPTED staff should participate in local community planning activities such as neighborhood revitalization efforts, masterplans, and community studies.
- Fourth, CPTED design criteria should be included in any planning and design contract awarded through a local government.

Seizing on the Saskatoon example, a fifth step also might be added: a crime analysis and risk assessment vetting process to highlight which CPTED strategies make most sense in each new development. These five steps are intended to ensure that new infrastructure development to our communities include basic security considerations. By local and state governments adopting CPTED and security features into codes, ordinances, bylaws, and resolutions, it can demonstrate that public health and safety will be addressed in future planning and construction.

DESIGN GUIDELINES—USING THE BACK DOOR

Formal CPTED regulations have proven difficult to implement without political will. In the years to come, that may change. Now that the social and political world is responding to fear of crime and infrastructure vulnerabilities to terrorism, there may be renewed effort to consider the safety and crime implications of urban design and community building. But in the meantime, if the front door doesn't work, how about the back door? This refers to the tools known as the *design guideline*. Although not as comprehensive as an overall CPTED compliance process, the design guideline has had more implementation success.

Although many municipalities are reluctant to mandate security requirements, sometimes other code requirements have a residual security impact. The Florida Building Code adopted new stringent requirements for hurricane resistance that included new hurricane rated glazing for windows. The laminated glazing will deflect debris and winds of 120 miles per hour, but also deter breakage from burglars. Although special codes for impact-resistant glazing started in Miami–Dade County, Florida, following Hurricane Andrew in 1992, they have spread throughout Florida. The South Florida Building Code was the country's first building code to mandate windborne debris protection for all new construction. The Miami–Dade County Building Code and the Southern Building Code Congress also adopted the impact resistant glazing requirements, which is the code for much of the Southeast United States. The insurance industry is making it a financial necessity for building owners to participate, on a voluntary basis, if they want insurance. After Hurricane Katrina in 2005, many additional states are looking to adopt more stringent flood and wind protection requirements, which will positively affect crime and terror resistance.

THE STORE SECURITY ACT

Another example of implementing CPTED is a statewide security act that combines both design guidelines and management procedures. The State of Florida adopted the Convenience Store Security Act of 1990 and amended it in 1992, which required security measures for convenience stores be applied to reduce robberies. Measures included having two or more employees on the premise between 11 p.m. and 5 a.m., bullet-resistant safety enclosures, silent alarms, security cameras, drop safes and cash management devices, meeting minimum specific lighting standards, height markers, signage of limited cash availability, having a security guard on premise or only conducting business through a pass-through window between 11 p.m. and 5 a.m. The camera system had to be capable of recording and retrieving an image to assist in offender identification and apprehension. The lighting levels in the parking lot must be at least 2 footcandles per square foot at 18 inches above the ground. Window signage could not block the inside of the store in order to provide an unobstructed view from outside to help in natural surveillance and police patrol. Window tinting that would reduce the exterior or interior view in a normal line of sight could not be used. Studies evaluating the success of the security measure generally show a small improvement in deterring robberies.

The problem with the Convenience Store Security Act on the state level is enforcement of the act. As with the obstacles mentioned above with implementing a CPTED process, the law had good intention but did not include how local law enforcement agencies enforce it, and what the consequences are for not complying with the state law. In 2006, there was an attempt to have the state law overturned, and then redrawn as county ordinances for the sheriff and police departments to enforce. Several counties in Florida already have local ordinances for convenience store security, are aggressively enforcing it and fining violators.

SAFE SCHOOL DESIGN GUIDELINES

Designing safe schools is another opportunity for CPTED implementation. The State of Florida adopted the Florida Safe School Design Guidelines of 1993 and updated them again in 2003. The Safe School Design principles were incorporated into the 2001 Florida Building Code and promoted through the Florida Department of Education. The Act included design guidelines that are primarily based on CPTED principles and applicable to elementary school all the way through to the community colleges. The guidelines address site design issues that include parking, pedestrian routes, signage, landscaping, and utilities. Building design issues included entry points, covered walkways, doors, windows, walls, roofs, and lighting. Interior spaces were addressed and included lobbies, administrative areas, classrooms, stairways, bathrooms, auditoriums, gyms, locker areas, and more. The final section addressed security concerns regarding equipment and systems like mechanical and ventilating systems, fire control and alarm systems, camera systems, and security systems.

THE GSA SECURITY STANDARDS

On a national level, security standards for the public sector have been the GSA Security Standards adopted after the Murrah Federal Courthouse bombing. State and local governments were left without a mandate, and left to figure it out for themselves. The private sector has been slow to evolve security and CPTED standards. Since the early 1990s, several different national organizations have tried to establish standards or the voluntary version known as "guidelines." In 2005, the National Fire Protection Association Technical Committee on Premises Security proposed the NFPA 730 Guide for Premises Security and NFPA 731 Standard for the Installation of Electronic Premises Security Systems. They were adopted as an American National Standard. Compliance with NFPA 730 is voluntary, but is being used as a reference point in newer generations of building codes. NFPA 730 makes many direct references to CPTED and infrastructure protection in its contents.

Security starts with a security vulnerability assessment. Throughout the guidelines, all the occupancies first address the need to assess the risks and conduct a vulnerability assessment. The book addresses exterior security, interior security, physical security, security personnel, security planning, and then specific security needs for educational facilities, health care facilities, one and two family dwellings, lodging facilities, apartment buildings, restaurants, shopping centers, retail establishments, office buildings, industrial buildings, parking facilities, and special events.

Communities throughout the United States are developing design guidelines for new development. These guidelines often address the philosophy that communities want changes in the way their community grows. One example is Smart Growth.

THE SMART GROWTH CONNECTION

Perhaps one of places where CPTED has the greatest potential to reshape the 21st century metropolis is in the Smart Growth movement. Smart Growth represents one of the most notable planning trends sweeping our urban fabric. Smart growth is a catchall phrase representing a constellation of

New Urban development and design approaches based on new attitudes of ecological stewardship, livability, and social sustainability. Some of the ideas are theoretical, such as bioregionalism, others fall into a range of specific design approaches including:

- New Urbanism, an architectural response to sprawling suburbs and car-oriented cities. New Urbanist designs feel like a return to the "Mayberry" towns of the past, including front yard porches, smaller and more walkable streets, gazebos in street parkettes, and alleyways to remove garages from front yards (Langdon, 1994). The intention of New Urbanism residential neighborhoods is to increase walkability and the social interaction of people in public places, which is also a central tenet of CPTED. New Urbanist towns now exist in every region of North America, and various styles of New Urbanist architecture is showing up in virtually every plan.
- Transit-oriented development. A transit engineering response to the 1950s style pedestrian unfriendly, curvilinear street designs and auto dependent suburb. The concept emphasizes public transit expansion, constructing neighborhoods around transit nodes, rail stations and rapid transit platforms, all within a walkable distance to residences (Calthorpe, 1993). As with New Urbanism, a premium is placed on walkability and eyes on the street.
- Cohousing. Differing from condominiums or cooperatives, co-housing started in Europe in the late 1960s. It comprises equity housing and includes developing an entire neighborhood. It is codeveloped and codesigned by groups of people who want more control over their environment and more interaction with their neighbors. Cohousing is characterized by single family or duplex/fourplex housing clustered along a common walkway, near a common house, landscaped courtyards, and other common facilities such as community gardens and workshops. Because of the importance placed on creating semipublic and semiprivate places within cohousing, there is careful attention paid to the hierarchy of space and territoriality. There are now hundreds of co-housing projects across North America (McCamant and Durrett, 1988).

As with all urban design forms, smart growth has both positive and negative features from a CPTED perspective. But the overall philosophy of these forms encourages social interaction, natural surveillance, and neighborhood territoriality of public spaces—all of which are linchpins of successful CPTED implementation. If civic officials and CPTED specialists spend time thinking about safety and security, smart growth may become the best place to successfully implement CPTED in years to come.

NEW URBANISM'S CHALLENGE

New Urbanism guidelines are used in new towns such as Celebration and Tradition in Florida and elsewhere around the country. New Urbanism has many CPTED principles integrated within its goals for mixed-use and functional pedestrian friendly communities. Many once-vibrant downtowns are now empty and blighted, deserted by the shoppers that have gone to large shopping malls and discount box stores with free parking, and affordable housing in the suburban landmasses. With suburban land now rapidly filling up, and real estate costs skyrocketing for that dream house in the country, many developers are looking back downtown for the depressed land values and proximity to the business centrals of most towns (see Figure 31.1 and Figure 31.2).

There is now a resurgence that is sweeping America's outer perimeter known as the *suburban village* (Kotkin, 2005). The new suburbanism is creating brand new downtowns as people are building and moving back to the excitement and location of the central city. Boston, Chicago, Miami, Fort Lauderdale, and hundreds of other cities around the country are experiencing a revival. New Urbanism tries to work within urban sprawl rather than fight it. The local suburban towns are moving towards becoming self-contained towns or villages, and are more than residential communities for downtowns. Massive new developments are under construction or planned to include housing,

FIGURE 31.1 Celebration's downtown view, showing mixed-use development, balconies, patios, and safe streetscapes.

shopping, transportation, and the necessary infrastructure of power, water, gas, roads, and support systems. CPTED and infrastructure protection is an important design criteria, as new construction design against natural risks of wind, floods, fire, and earthquakes. Now crime and terrorism are becoming an expansion of the list of criteria for consideration.

FIGURE 31.2 Main Street in Louisville, Kentucky.

Are design professionals ready for these new challenges in the 21st century? A study conducted in 2004 of several thousand architects in the southeastern United States found that few, if any, architects knew about CPTED. Although many of the architects surveyed heard of Defensible Space Concepts, none were familiar with CPTED (EDRA, 2004). And this is after 9/11! It is hard to imagine why architects designing schools, medical facilities, and multifamily housing are still not familiar with CPTED principles—principles with a thirty-year history. Many architects agree that the built environment can impact or influence behavior, but they have not been mandated to include security in the design and architecture process. CPTED and security is not taught in architecture schools, and is only occasionally brought up in the state and national conventions of the American Institute of Architects.

The reality of the architectural practice may make it extremely difficult to incorporate nonmandated initiatives such as security and CPTED into professional practice. Courts now, more than ever before, recognize the relationship between design and crime. Cases of premises liability litigation increasingly find the architect responsible for injuries as a result of attacks. Isn't it time to change how we teach architects? Isn't it now time for design professionals to update their education regarding contemporary CPTED in all of its most advanced forms? There were lawsuits filed after 9/11 suing negligence for structural collapse of the towers, even though the architects in the early 1970s did design the towers to resist plane crashes as large as Boeing 707s. Many police departments teach officers about CPTED and security in police academies. There are only a handful of CPTED classes being taught in college around the United States (Florida Atlantic University School of Architecture, Virginia Tech, Rutgers.) What is the price for security? How much are we as a society willing to sacrifice in civil liberties, outrageous costs, and inconvenience to have our next generation of architecture built to resist and deter emerging or exiting threats? Design professionals may not fully understand the relationship between the built environment and personal safety, but court litigation and emerging standards of care, building codes, resolutions, and design guidelines are the carrot and stick that are changing how we design and build buildings.

REFERENCES

Architects and Defensible Space. (November 2004) Unpublished paper submitted to the *Environmental Design Research Organization Journal.*

Calthorpe, P. (1993) *The Next American Metropolis: Ecology, Community, and the American Dream.* New York: Princeton Architectural Press.

Florida Convenience Business Security Act of 1990. 812.170—812.175, Florida Statutes, State of Florida.

Florida Safe School Design Guidelines of 1993. The Florida Center for Community Design + Research, Florida Department of Education, Tallahassee, FL. 28 July 1993.

Florida Safe School Design Guidelines of 2003 Florida Department of Education, School Of Architecture University of Florida. Tallahassee, FL. 2003.

Kotkin, J. (2005) The New Suburbanism. *Architectural Magazine,* June, 21–76.

Langdon, P. (1994) *A Better Place to Live: Reshaping the American Suburb.* Amherst: University of Massachusetts Press.

Lyons, G. F. and M. Arber. (2006) Safe streets—safe city: A community-based crime prevention project. *The CPTED Journal,* 2(1), 33–38.

McCamant, K. and C. Durrett (1988) *Cohousing: A Contemporary Approach to Housing Ourselves.* Berkeley, CA: Habitat Press.

NFPA 730 Guide for Premises Security 2006 Edition, National Fire Protection Association, Quincy, MA. 2005.

NFPA 731 Standard for the Installation of Electronic Premises Security Systems 2006 Edition, National Fire Protection Association, Quincy, MA. 2005.

Saville, G. and D. Wright (1998) Exploring the Feasibility of a Canadian Home and Community Security Labeling Program. A report to Canada Mortgage and Housing Corporation. CMHC: Ottawa.

32 Epilog

The future of infrastructure protection and CPTED depends on how events unfold over the next few years. The reorganization of many government agencies under the umbrella of the Department of Homeland Security (DHS) is one of the most significant changes in government structure in decades. The mission of DHS is the protection of people and the critical infrastructure of the built environment. The United States and the countries of the free world are all struggling with the same problems: terrorism, workplace violence, and crime.

This book is intended to provide guidance to the professionals who are responsible for designing, constructing, and securing our built environment: architects, engineers, security directors, law enforcement, and urban planners. The goal is to provide a clear and comprehensive approach to protect our built environment from the wide range of possible threats.

When attacks occur against our buildings and structures in the future, will we be prepared to adapt, and to adjust our way of life to respond to the ever-increasing restrictions of movement and freedom? Since the events of September 11, 2001, terrorism has become a dominant theme in government policy decisions, and that has filtered down to the built environment. Security can no longer be viewed as an after-the-fact add-on feature of a facility (guards, CCTV, access card systems, etc.). Rather, the real value is to have security and life safety decisions made from the beginning of site analysis and the design process.

What will be the tolerance for the inconvenience of personal and baggage search for every public activity? Are corporate America and government agencies prepared to incur the expense needed to design the protection needed to reduce the opportunities for threats that face us in the 21st century?

It is my hope that this book will be a valuable reference guide to design, security, and law enforcement professionals and students, and will help them to understand the theory and practical applications of CPTED and how the methodologies suggested here can make a positive difference.

I have seen the positive difference that CPTED and community-oriented policing have made to public housing in the last 10 years. I have seen the difference made in designing safer schools and convenience stores. I have seen transportation centers designed to be safe and well organized. Our built environment can be built strong and safe, yet aesthetically pleasing, with unobtrusive and transparent security. This book is designed to assist relevant decision makers in making smart decisions for the next generation of buildings. Will they evaluate the performance of their buildings in light of current and future threats of terrorism and crime? Will the decision makers be willing to put the resources in to undertake the risk threat assessment for their properties and operations? Will the political structures be willing to require security and CPTED in all new infrastructures for our cities under the mandate of code or resolution? There is so much untapped potential to make a difference. It is my hope that in the next generation of architects and urban planners and their fulfillment of new buildings and communities we can see successful implementation of security and CPTED to reduce the vulnerability of our buildings and infrastructure to terrorist threats and subsequently reduce the vulnerability of people and property to crime and workplace violence.

Index

A

ABA, *see* American Banking Association
Access control, building, 30
Activity theory, 56
ADA, *see* Americans With Disabilities Act
ADAAG, *see* Americans With Disabilities Act
    Accessibility Guidelines
AIA, *see* American Institute of Architects
American Banking Association (ABA), 247
American Institute of Architects (AIA), 22, 529
Americans With Disabilities Act, 200, 204, 292, 423, 446,
    471
Americans With Disabilities Act Accessibility Guidelines
    (ADAAG), 200, 205
American Society of Industrial Security (ASIS), 91
American Society of Testing Materials (ASTM), 176
Anti-Terror Risk Infrastructure protection (ATRiM)
    model, 161–171
    anthrax attacks, 165
    asset appraisal, 162
    audit process, 165–169
        applying matrix cells, 169
        audit activities for assessing bomb risks, 167
        audit process, 168
        beyond checklists, 165–166
        documenting data within each cell, 166–167
        primary and secondary audit teams, 168
        risk assessment matrix, 166
    CCTV placement, 168
    CPTED risk audit, 162
    critical infrastructure protection plan, 162
    critical infrastructure and terrorism, 163–165
    cyber-terrorism, 163
    dirty bombs, 164
    introduction to problem, 163
    lessons learned, 161–162
    National Strategy for The Physical Protection of
        Critical Infrastructure and Key Assets, 163
    nonmilitary infrastructure, 161
    Patriot's Council, 165
    planning process, 169–170
        asset identification and vulnerabilities, 169
        audit, 169
        implementation, 169–170
    prevention of terror events, 161
    risk assessment, 162
    risk assessment matrix, 166
    threat assessment, 162
    vulnerability analysis, 162
    vulnerability challenges, 161
    weapons of mass destruction, 164, 165
Architect(s)
    bubble diagrams developed by, 29
    critical information provided to, 6

    inattention to security details by, 135
    job interviews, 23
    security design challenges for, 7
Architects, interface between engineers and, 39–52
    access control screening, 47
    aesthetically pleasing barriers, 40
    architectural process programming phase, 40
    command center design, 40–44
    command center signage, 43
    construction documents, 39
    control center design, 42
    electronics specialist, 51
    ergonomically incorrect design, 41
    Force Protection and Antiterrorism, 50
    integrated design, 40
    involving other in design, 39–40
    ISC Security Design Criteria, 50
    loading dock design, 47–51
    lobby design, 44–47
    lobby equipment backup, 49
    lobby layout, 46
    lobby screening at federal courthouse, 48
    millwork design, 46
    out-of-control control room, 42
    retrofitted lobby, 45
    risk assessment, 49
    security design criteria, 44
    slab depressions, 49
    squint-a-vision, 41
    turnstiles, 45, 46
    USACE Protective Design Center, 50
    video camera images, 41
    well thought-out security system, 51
    x-ray package inspection, 45
Architecture, challenge of in free society, 17–28
    architect job interviews, 23
    architectural program, 22–24
    congestion in critical areas, 20
    CPTED, 24–27
    defensible space, 18
    financial resources required, 18
    form vs. function, 18
    fortress mentality, 17
    glass exteriors, 19
    goals, 26–27
    GSA General Services Administration Security Design
        Standards, 22
    job training, 25–26
    key players of building process, 21
    keys in building design, 20–22
    modernism, 19
    natural surveillance, 24
    New Urbanism, 25
    Oklahoma City bombing, 22
    police security review, 24

S